# MARKETING RESEARCH

# *The Wiley Marketing Series*

WILLIAM LAZER, Advisory Editor, *Michigan State University*

MARTIN ZOBER, *Marketing Management*

ROBERT J. HOLLOWAY AND
ROBERT S. HANCOCK
*The Environment of Marketing Behavior—Selections from the Literature*

GEORGE SCHWARTZ, Editor
*Science in Marketing*

EDGAR CRANE
*Marketing Communications—A Behavioral Approach to Men, Messages, and Media*

JOSEPH W. NEWMAN, Editor
*On Knowing the Consumer*

STEUART HENDERSON BRITT, Editor
*Consumer Behavior and the Behavioral Sciences—Theories and Applications*

DONALD F. MULVIHILL AND
STEPHEN PARANKA
*Price Policies and Practices*

DAVID CARSON
*International Marketing: A Comparative Systems Approach*

BRUCE E. MALLEN
*The Marketing Channel: A Conceptual Viewpoint*

RONALD R. GIST
*Management Perspectives in Retailing*

JOHN K. RYANS AND JAMES C. BAKER
*World Marketing: A Multinational Approach*

JOHN M. BRION
*Corporate Marketing Planning*

NORTON E. MARKS AND
ROBERT M. TAYLOR
*Marketing Logistics: Perspectives and Viewpoints*

JAMES BEARDEN
*Personal Selling: Behavioral Science Readings and Cases*

FRANK M. BASS, CHARLES W. KING, AND
EDGAR A. PESSEMIER, Editors
*Applications of the Sciences in Marketing Management*

ROBERT J. HOLLOWAY AND
ROBERT S. HANCOCK
*Marketing in a Changing Environment*

RONALD E. GIST
*Retailing: Concepts and Decisions*

KENNETH P. UHL AND BERTRAM SCHONER
*Marketing Research: Information Systems and Decision Making*

# MARKETING RESEARCH

## *Information Systems and Decision Making*

KENNETH P. UHL AND BERTRAM SCHONER

COLLEGE OF BUSINESS ADMINISTRATION
UNIVERSITY OF IOWA

*John Wiley and Sons, Inc.*

NEW YORK · LONDON · SYDNEY · TORONTO

Library of Congress Catalog Card Number: 68-8109
SBN 471 89550 4
Printed in the United States of America

# *Preface*

Marketing research courses traditionally have been oriented toward obtaining information for nonrecurring problems only. This, we believe, ignores a significant, if not major, problem—how to supply information that is required on a periodic basis for setting marketing strategies and identifying problem areas. Our major reason for writing this book was to provide a text that deals with obtaining information for both recurring and nonrecurring marketing problems.

Since 1965, when the name of the Marketing Research course at the University of Iowa was changed to Marketing Information, we have been developing and using text and case materials that focus on managements' total marketing information needs. This has meant the incorporation into the course of such topics as marketing information systems, ways of organizing for marketing information, methods of discerning information needs, content of continuing data bases, models and model building, "balancing" information costs against their benefits, and managing unanticipated information. In addition, newer tools such as Bayesian analysis had to be integrated into the course. Attitude measurement required more detailed and careful attention than it traditionally had received, and other changes as well were needed.

The inclusion of the new material made virtually mandatory the absence of some traditional material. The chapters that never got into the book included ones on advertising research, product research, and field data collection. Most of these topics, we believe, can be taught through the use of the various cases or class projects, if the instructor has sufficient time. In addition, we feel that the first two topics more appropriately should be dealt with in courses on advertising and product management. It should be pointed out, however, that most of the concepts and tools employed in advertising research and product research (such as attitude measurement and sampling) *are* covered in this book.

The book is neither a statistical nor a research methods text, although review material is provided in both areas. We have attempted to exercise restraint so as not to bury readers under mathematical formulas. The emphasis is on developing an intuitive understanding of the theory and its application.

Part I of the book (Chapters 1 through 3) is designed to provide background and an overview of marketing information. The primary concern in Chapter 1 is the establishment of the relationships among marketing decisions, information systems, and models. Marketing information systems are discussed in Chapter 2 and models and model building are the topics of Chapter 3.

Part II of the book (Chapters 4 through 7) develops the statistical design and analysis of marketing research. Chapters 4 and 5 are concerned with sampling and estimating population parameters. Decision making under uncertainty is the topic of Chapter 6, where classical and Bayesian approaches (using sample information) are contrasted. Chapter 7 is devoted to the design of marketing experiments and to their role in the decision process.

Part III of the book (Chapters 8 through 13) is concerned with securing information for use in marketing decision-making. Chapter 8 provides an overview of information needs, as well as several classification systems for viewing information. The differences between *continually collected information* and *special-problem information* are discusssd in this chapter. Chapter 9 examines ways in which to secure useful *internal* information on sales and marketing costs. Securing information from respondents is discussed in Chapters 10 and 11, with the latter chapter devoted to measurement of attitudes and other psychological information. Chapter 12 focuses on securing unanticipated information and commercial information. The final chapter in Part III is devoted to a discussion of securing *external* secondary information.

Part IV focuses attention on two major market measurements used by decision makers: potentials and forecasts. The chapter on potentials examines their use and their construction. The forecasting chapter discusses various techniques for preparing forecasts of marketing variables.

The final part of the book, Part V, discusses organizing for marketing information. It is limited to one chapter that explores alternative ways in which to organize marketing systems and information programs in response to various problems.

We have used most of the material in the book since 1966. Undergraduate and M.B.A. students who have had prior exposure to Bayesian analysis can be expected to cover all of the material in the book within a semester. If students have a very inadequate background in statistics, the instructor may choose to omit the sections on Bayesian analysis.

We have elected to have the discussion of Bayesian statistics follow the discussion of classical techniques in Chapters 6 and 7. This was done because (1) classical techniques are still much more widely used in industry than are Bayesian techniques and (2) a flow of topics from probability theory to classical statistics to modern decision theory is to a substantial degree the way these subjects build upon one another and, as a result, in this sequence facilitate student learning.

Although we have never used the material on a quarter basis, several alternatives seem feasible. Probably the best approach is to devote less class time to the discussion of cases. However, if necessary, Chapters 12 and 13 can virtually stand alone without classroom discussion.

Kenneth P. Uhl
Bertram Schoner

*Iowa City, Iowa*
*August 1968*

# *Acknowledgements*

Numerous companies and persons have released case material to us. We specifically thank William Applebaum and Andrew R. Towl, Director of Case Development, both of the Harvard University Graduate School of Business, for use of the case Superior Markets, Inc., and Stanley A. Tractenberg for the use of his case, Gem Frocks, Inc. To the various companies we can only say "thanks," for they wished to remain anonymous.

Our colleagues and students at the University of Iowa have been particularly helpful. The students, of course, were our subjects and classroom critics. Three graduate research assistants, Pat Gammon, Lance K. Poulsen, and Donald McManis, are no doubt delighted to see the work completed as are a host of skilled and patient secretaries. Our colleagues, particularly Professors Robert Miller and Jack Kennelly, provided numerous helpful suggestions.

We know that there are still errors present in the manuscript in spite of our efforts to ferret them out. They are certainly our errors, but as you find them, we would appreciate hearing about them.

We are also indebted to the Literary Executor of the late Sir Ronald A. Fisher, F.R.S., to Dr. Frank Yates, F.R.S., and to Oliver & Boyd Ltd., Edinburgh, for permission to reprint Appendix C from their book *Statistical Tables for Biological, Agricultural and Medical Research.*

K.P.U.
B.S.

# *Contents*

MARKETING RESEARCH

PART I

# *The Marketing Information System*

Part I is concerned with the concept of the marketing information system and its role in the decision process. Chapter 1 provides an overview of the information system, information valuation, and the importance of adequate decision models. Chapter 2 is concerned with the dimensions of marketing information systems and those characteristics that appear to be general to successful systems. Chapter 3 introduces the reader to models and model building.

*One*

# Decisions, Systems, and Information

Marketing activities account for an immense amount of expenditure in the economy. According to the United States Department of Agriculture (1967), for example, the total farm value of food products produced in the United States in 1966 was estimated at $28 billion. Marketing added $55 billion to this amount—thus the consumer spent $83 billion. The value added (calculated from the cost) of marketing was twice the farm cost of the food. In 1967, one consumer-oriented company (primarily in nonfood products), Proctor and Gamble, spent about $600 million in marketing activities out of total expenditures of about $2.2 billion.

It is evident that extremely large amounts of money depend on marketing managers' making correct decisions. These decisions, in turn, depend on the decision makers' being able to make intelligent appraisals of their alternatives and the consequences of their actions, a task that cannot be accomplished without the use of information about customers, competitors, and one's own activities. Obtaining this information and aiding decision makers in forming intelligent appraisals is the role of marketing research.

## A Case in Point—The Brewing Industry

A typical case in point is the brewing industry in the United States. A number of examples of the need for good information are provided by this industry.

In 1935 there were about 750 breweries, most of which were small (*Business Week*, March 9, 1957). Brew brands met only limited success in other than local markets—and success appeared to be more due to luck, complemented by haphazard trial and error, than to knowledge. In the local markets, the beer drinkers had grown accustomed to "their" brewmaster's brew and he to their beer preferences.

However, this marketing pattern proceeded to change as several breweries grew more sensitive to the market and particularly to outlying market opportunities. These breweries pushed into more distant markets with different brews and marketing programs. They used more market information to plan their products and their marketing efforts. And they increasingly used information to gain more control over their operations. These firms began tracing sales (and even some distribution costs) by type and size of container and by market (for competitors' activities, as well as for their own), they began testing advertising campaigns and other promotional activities through evaluations of costs and benefits and, in general, they relied more on marketing information.

During this time, many of the breweries that were oriented around brewmasters sold out and closed as more informed firms won away their markets. In fact, by 1963 there were fewer than 225 breweries left, and experts have estimated that 10 companies will produce 70% of the beer by 1970. And this activity has all occurred since repeal of the Eighteenth Amendment to the Constitution in 1933 (since the end of prohibition).

### *The Hamms Experience*

This marketing shakedown is still in process. The intelligent use of marketing information alone, obviously, will not guarantee success. However, it is one of the prime requisites that frequently has been neglected and has consequently led to marketing failures. For example, the Theo B. Hamms Brewing Company, formerly an independent, Minnesota-headquartered brewer, successfully (profitably) penetrated large sections of the Pacific Coast market in the 1950's with a nostalgic reminder to transplanted Midwesterners of the "beer from the land of sky blue water." In the 1960's this "tested and proven" campaign and market-penetration program was moved almost in total into New England. It was a colossal failure. The people, accustomed to Cape Cod Bay and Nantucket Sound, found the Minnesota appeal meaningless, if not insulting to their preferences.

There are numerous other specific cases in point. However, only two more will be offered at this time.

### *The Carling Lesson*

Carling Brewing Company purchased one of the Griesedieck Breweries of St. Louis and apparently tried to eliminate the very popular (in the Midwest) Stag brand beer and put in its place the favorite Carling brand, Black Label (*The Brewing World,* May 1963, p. 2). Untold dollars apparently were lost before key managers gathered and used marketing information. After consumer attitude information was obtained and used, the Stag brand was successfully reintroduced. The same mistake by the same company was apparently repeated in the Pacific Northwest. Carling bought Heidelberg Brewery in Tacoma in 1959 and attempted to replace the popular Heidelberg brand with Black Label (*Business Week,* June 20, 1959). The marketplace was ignored until the profit and loss statements demanded greater market sensitivity. Heidelberg beer was reintroduced into the product line and soon outdistanced the Black Label brand. The concluding chapter of this small Carling episode appears to have been written in 1964. Carling Brewing Company acquired the Arizona Brewing Company in Phoenix, Arizona, and immediately expanded the marketing program for the existing brand, A-1 (*Carling News,* April 1965).

*Anheuser-Busch versus Jos. Schlitz*

One of the clearer testimonies to the importance of marketing information is provided by the sales battle between Anheuser-Busch and the Joseph Schlitz Brewing Company. Since the early 1950's the two giants have both continued to expand their market shares and to battle for first place. Schlitz was first in sales in 1955 and 1956, but Anheuser-Busch developed a strong marketing team founded on a superb research and marketing information program. By 1957 Anheuser-Busch had gained the number one sales and profit position and by 1959 was leading the industry by more than three million barrels (*Business Week,* August 1964).

In the meantime, as stated by one writer:

> The old Schlitz was an efficient beermaker but a backward beermarketer . . . virtually no use was made of marketing research (*Fortune,* October 1964).

This picture started to change in the early 1960's when a new president was credited with building a "new scientific, capable management team" (*Business Week,* August 8, 1964). In the new group the emphasis was on marketing founded on relevant marketing information. Their Vice-President of Marketing said:

> We research and, out of research, develop specific things, develop the best programs we can, carry them out, and then do an evaluation. Our objective is to find out what makes the beer drinker tick and how to get to him—on his terms, rather than the brewer's.

Objectives of the Schlitz research group, according to its manager,

> . . . are mainly to supply information to management to enable them to make better decisions. The computer is our number 1 tool . . . because the mass of data which we have accumulated . . . is almost impossible to use unless you can reduce it to some form that management can look at and base decisions on (*Advertising Age,* March 15, 1965).

Schlitz apparently has developed a marketing information program equal to that of Anheuser-Busch. Schlitz sales and profits have increased considerably, but Anheuser-Busch appears assured of at least another few years of sales and profit leadership.

## THE ROLE OF THE COMPUTER

The computer has provided the mechanism by which vast quantities of data can be stored and analyzed in a small amount of time. The importance of the computer to the modern economy is highlighted by the fact that the International Business Machines Corporation, a medium-sized producer of accounting machines before World War II, in 1966 ranked ninth in size (by sales) in *Fortune* magazine's list of the 500 largest United States corporations and fifth in net income. Control Data Corporation, another manufacturer of computer equipment, did not even exist in 1956, but was on the *Fortune* list in 1966.

At first, the application of computers was confined to activities that had previously been performed in some other manner, such as keeping payroll records. Soon, however, the computer came to be widely employed in such diverse uses as controlling the operation of an oil refinery, planning the routing of salesmen, and determining the configuration of aircraft.

### The Computer in Marketing

Proper management of marketing, as already suggested, requires the gathering, analysis, storage, and dissemination of an immense amount of information. Management needs frequent, if not continuous, measures of potentials, sales, and costs by products (often by package size and type) and by markets. Often, on a less frequent reporting basis, this information must be available by customer, order size, channel of distribution, or other breakdowns.

The sources of data, the reporting parties, and the types of information are numerous—far more numerous than in the usual production cost accounting system, which focuses on the one major analysis by type of product. Furthermore, these sales and cost data must be taken apart and put together in numerous different shapes and forms for analysis and use by planning and operating managers at different levels and locations. Before widespread computer and transmitting facilities became available, the routinized task of sales and cost analysis, for example, for even a limited product line company, was overwhelming because of immense processing, analyzing, and feedback time requirements. Data were out of date before they could be used.

### Three Cases in Point

A large national brewery (which sells almost exclusively through independent wholesale distributors) requires that weekly distributor sales reports (itemized by product, by type and size of container, and by type of account) be in the headquarters office by each Saturday night. By Monday morning the information has been combined, synthesized, partially analyzed, and made available to marketing managers throughout the organization.

One of the largest department store chains requires each of its retail units to report daily activities by products to its information center. These daily reports, analyzed and compared with both past performances and planned performance, aid both top management and individual store managers to perceive the company's response to the market (*Business Week,* April 17, 1965).

A large manufacturer, which markets a line of women's clothes nationally, keeps track of both its marketing costs and its sales on a weekly basis. Such close contact with the market permits the company to make timely responses to market demands and to check production and distribution on slow-moving offerings (American Management Association, 1965).

These information programs, though somewhat atypical, certainly are not unique. In all three of these business organizations, programs of sales and distribution cost analysis account for only a part of a larger total marketing information program.

## THE SYSTEMS APPROACH TO MANAGEMENT

A recent development in management thinking, and one that probably would not have taken place without the informational storage and analysis capacity of the computer, has been the emergence of the concept of the firm as a system. Instead of treating the company as a conglomerate of activities that can be handled more or less independently, the systems approach is to treat the firm as a network of activities that are related.

Groups of activities, which for some decisions can be considered to be relatively independent of other activities, may be regarded as subsystems. Marketing activities can be considered as one such subsystem of the firm as a whole. Although it is obvious that marketing decisions will affect other activities in the firm, the relative homogeneity of the types of decisions to be made, the common data base required for many marketing decisions, and the specialization of personnel involved in making marketing decisions and carrying them into effect make it convenient to regard the marketing system as a subentity. Of course, the marketing system must at some stage be considered in its relation to other subsystems within the firm, particularly when fundamental decisions regarding goals, policies, and overall budgets are formulated.

## The Marketing Information System

The information function plays a role in the marketing system that in many ways is analogous to the role played by radar in artillery or by a temperature-sensing device in a heating system. Since the automatic heating system for a home is easily understood, this analogy shall be employed to give some perspective to the marketing system and the part played by marketing information.

### *Installation of a System*

Suppose that one were building a home in Iowa and had reached the stage where a heating system must be designed. The first step would be to establish what decisions are to be made within the system. If the answer were "decisions about heating the home," the set of choices would be confined to various furnace capacities and heating systems, such as forced air or water.

As frequently occurs in marketing situations, however, it may well be that the set of decisions has been stated too narrowly. In this case, it would be more appropriate to define the decision as follows:

1. Decisions about increasing the temperature.
2. Decisions about decreasing the temperature.
3. Decisions about increasing the humidity.
4. Decisions about decreasing the humidity.

Once the decisions have been defined, information must be obtained for each decision about the relevant environment, the objectives to be met, and the possible alternative courses of action. All these steps together are often referred to as "formulating the problem."

The objectives may be defined in terms of ranges of humidity and temperature that are regarded as comfortable. For humidity decisions, the alternative courses of action are the devices that increase or decrease humidity. For temperature decisions, the alternative courses of action are the devices that increase or decrease temperature. It should be noted that *these two decisions should not be regarded as independent,* since some devices (such as air-conditioners) affect both humidity and temperature. This lack of independence is also true of many marketing decisions (such as promotion and price), and in such cases decisions should not be made separately.

A decision is now required on the devices to be employed: an air-conditioner–furnace combination versus a heat pump; oil versus electricity or natural gas as the energy source; forced air versus water systems; and the associated requirements in humidifying and dehumidifying equipment. An information search of suppliers should now be undertaken to establish costs, dependability, and performance. Other informational sources, such as consumer reports, may be consulted for independent expert appraisals of the various alternatives.

### *The Ongoing System*

Once a "comfort" system has been installed, the problem is removed from that of the "special problem" category to that of making routine, recurrent decisions. For simplicity, only the heating aspects of the problem will be considered.

Figure 1-1 illustrates the system by which an ongoing heating system works in a house. The first necessary step here is to set the intermediate objective (temperature). (The fundamental objective, comfortable temperature, is not operational—i.e., one cannot make decisions to affect comfort without first defining comfort in terms of something controllable.) This objective depends primarily on the temperature that the members of the household find comfortable, but, when set, it is not static but is subject to environmental changes. For example, a temperature of 72° Fahrenheit feels cooler in the winter than in the summer because of body radiation. The walls of the house, being colder in the winter than in summer, absorb more radiated heat.

The firm sets many intermediate objectives (i.e., objectives that are met in order to attain some more fundamental objectives), such as market share, promotional budgets, and sales. It is obvious that a great deal of information is necessary in the establishment of these objectives. In particular, management is interested in the relationship between the attainment of intermediate objectives and the primary objectives such as profits and growth.

It is evident that the intermediate objectives of the firm are analogous to the temperature setting on the thermostat and that each requires information that may be termed *special problem information,* in that the setting of objectives is not a regularly recurring problem.

Once an objective is set, it is necessary to sample the pertinent environment to see if this objective is being attained. This is accomplished in a heating system by measuring the temperature of the air in the region of some sensing device. The answer obtained constitutes the relevant *continuing data base* or *continually collected information* for the heating system, in that such information is regularly or continuously gathered.

Once obtained, the data must be analyzed. In the heating system, when the information about actual temperature is acquired, it is compared with the goal and decisions made based on the results of the comparison. If all is well, the decision is to do nothing. If the temperature is below some preset figure, the decisions will be to turn on the furnace and leave it on until the temperature reaches some other present figure.[1] For example, the furnace may be turned on at 71° and turned off at 73°.

In the marketing system, one of the objectives of concern may be market share. If so, the informational system must yield information

[1] Note that this implies a continual sampling of the environment.

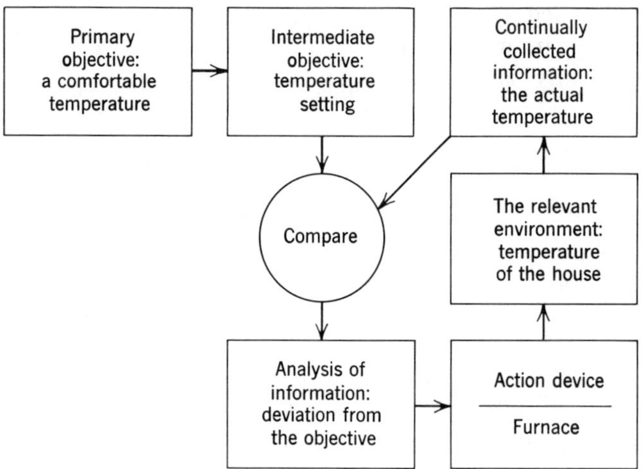


**Figure 1-1** A heating system. The decision—turn the furnace on or off.

| Decision type \ Information type | Special problem information | Continually collected information |
|---|---|---|
| Recurrent decisions | | X |
| Unique decisions | X | |

**Figure 1-2** Information classification.

on the market share being attained, most likely broken down by market segments. Based on this information it may be necessary to take action in terms of product, price, promotion, or channels of distribution if we see that the objective is not being attained. A similar analysis is pertinent for each objective.

### Categories of Information

The installation of the heating system (at least for the builder of his own home, if not for the contractor of many homes) may be regarded as a "special problem" inasmuch as it is nonrecurrent in nature. Hence the information collected for this type of problem is called *special problem information.* On the other hand, information regularly or continually collected is called *continually collected information* or the *continuing data base.*[2] The information provided by the temperature-sensing device, which continually samples air temperature, is information in the latter category. Figure 1-2 illustrates this dichotomy.

## THE DECISION IN TERMS OF INFORMATION, STRATEGIES, AND MODELS

The purpose of information is to reduce uncertainty with respect to the consequences of a decision. Clearly, if for every decision we knew in advance the resultant outcome of each alternative course of action and if each outcome could be ranked in terms of its contribution to meeting the established objectives, we would always make a correct

[2] The reader should note that these terms are peculiar to this book, and are not part of the usual systems vocabulary.

choice from the available courses of action. Unfortunately, in the real world we are seldom sure of the outcomes of an action. A decision to market a product may result in a profit or loss, or a promotional campaign may be successful or unsuccessful.

## The Elements Determining Information Value

Three basic elements determine the value of information to a business decision:

1. The degree of uncertainty regarding the outcome of the various possible courses of action.
2. The economic consequences of making an incorrect decision (i.e., not choosing that course of action which, unknown to the decision maker at the time of the decision, would lead to the "best" outcome).
3. The amount by which the information is expected to reduce the initial uncertainty, if obtained.

The greater the degree of uncertainty, the larger the economic consequences of making an incorrect decision, and/or the greater the amount by which the information is expected to reduce uncertainty, the more valuable the information becomes.

This implies, of course, that when the cost of information is greater than the value of that information, obtaining information is not worthwhile. It also suggests a scheme for choosing between various "packages" of information. For example, a firm may be considering obtaining information from a consumer panel maintained by some research firm or maintaining its own consumer panel.[3] Or a firm may be considering various different sample sizes in a survey. That particular information package which yields the greatest excess of value of information over the cost of the information should be selected.

The methods of determining the value of information are left until Chapter 6. Choosing between various information packages is part of the problem of selecting a strategy.

## The Selection of a Strategy

In the heating system described earlier, the thermostat may be "programmed" to do the following:

Measure air temperature. If the temperature is less than or equal to 70° Fahrenheit and the furnace is off, turn it on. If the temperature is greater than

[3] A consumer panel consists of a sample of consumers, who (generally) keep track of their purchases in a diary maintained for that purpose (see Chapter 12).

70° but less than 72°, leave the furnace in its current state (either on or off). If the temperature is greater than or equal to 72° and the furnace is on, turn it off.

Such a completely specified plan of action may be termed a strategy. The task of the decision maker is to select one strategy from the collection of strategies available to him. The strategy selected completely specifies both the information that is to be obtained, and a decision rule that dictates the action to be taken for each possible information return.

Consider the following example from marketing research. A soft-drink firm, having developed a new flavor, has to make a decision whether or not to market the new-flavored drink. Such a decision may involve a very large investment, particularly in promotional expenditures, hence the company would undoubtedly seek information before making a decision. The flow diagram in Figure 1-3 illustrates the sequence that might be followed.

The firm might begin with a consumer taste test. If acceptance were above some previously specified level, the firm might test-market the product. If results of the test-marketing were satisfactory, the firm might market the product.

The whole sequence is a particular strategy. If any part of the sequence was altered in some manner (perhaps by raising the level of sales for satisfactory results in the test market or by using some other test market), this would constitute a new strategy. As will be shown in Chapter 6, the strategy that yields the greatest "expected value" (a term to be defined in Chapter 6) is selected.

If testing new flavors is not a regular activity of the firm, the design of the research is likely to constitute a special-problem situation. The necessary research might even be designed and performed by a consulting

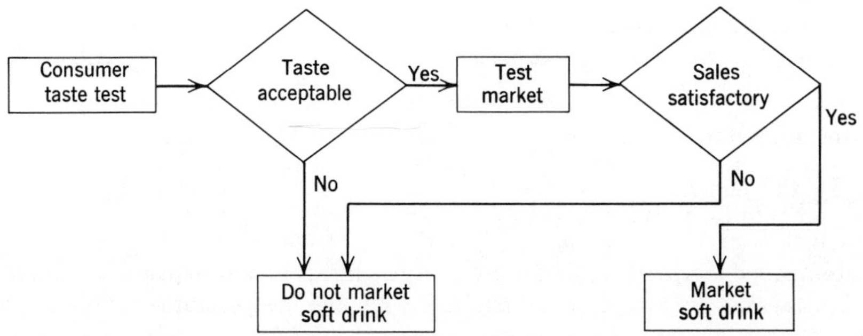


**Figure 1-3** A strategy for accepting or rejecting a new soft-drink flavor.

marketing research firm. It should be evident that the firm that regularly tests new flavors and has perfected a routinized decision process is likely to obtain better information with a lesser allocation of management resources. In general, it is to the advantage of a company to move information from the category of special-problem information to the continuing data base whenever it is feasible to do so. Such feasibility depends on the frequency with which the problem recurs, but the reader will appreciate the fact that managerial decision-making talent is most efficiently employed in the solution of new and unusual problems, not in the solution of recurring problems where clear decision rules may be formulated.

### The Role of the Model

We have so far assumed that the decision maker has a clear picture in mind of the problem he faces. That is, he knows his alternative courses of action, all the possible outcomes of his actions, the relationship between these outcomes and his objectives, the sources and kinds of information he may wish to obtain, and which outcomes are likely to result from which actions. In fact, the decision maker may possess only a vague idea of any of these elements basic to the decisions he must make.

At this point, we may loosely define what has been termed a "picture of the problem" as a *model*. Good models are basic to good decisions. No information system can be well designed without adequate models of the problems to be solved, since without an adequate model it is impossible even to specify the information that should be collected. Of course, adequate models are requisites to good decisions for special problems also. Chapter 3 is devoted to models and model building.

## SUMMARY

The purpose of this chapter has been to introduce the reader to the function of marketing research as an information-gathering activity in terms of information systems and decisions. The authors consider the distinction between continually collected information and special-problem information to be important. Continually collected information, which is best viewed from the framework of the marketing information system, has been all but ignored in most marketing research texts. Special-problem information, which, by definition, represents information specially gathered for unusual, nonrecurrent problems, has provided the focus of the field and literature of marketing research to date.

In the remainder of Part I important aspects of marketing information systems are discussed. Chapter 2 is devoted to a discussion of the dimensions of marketing information systems and Chapter 3 to models and model building.

## REFERENCES

American Management Association. *The Manager's Letter,* October 20, 1965.

"Carling Gears Marketing Plans to Growth," *The Brewing World,* May 1963, p. 2.

*Carling News,* April 1965, published by the Carling Brewing Company, Cleveland, Ohio, p. 6.

"Computer Helps Schlitz Brew Market Strategy," *Advertising Age,* March 15, 1965, pp. 3, 54.

"Computers Begin to Solve the Marketing Puzzle," *Business Week,* April 17, 1965, p. 115.

"How They Put Gusto into Schlitz," *Fortune,* October 1964, p. 106.

"New Ideas Shake Up Old Brewing Industry," *Business Week,* March 9, 1957, p. 90.

"Selling Suds Like Soap," *Business Week,* August 8, 1964, p. 60.

"U.S. Brewers Thirst for a Boom," *Business Week,* June 20, 1959, p. 47.

U.S. Department of Agriculture. *Agricultural Statistics, 1967.* Washington, D.C.: U.S. Government Printing Office.

*Two*

# Marketing Information Systems

Decision makers, to make good decisions, must have relevant information readily available for their use. In earlier years many firms attempted to meet this need by assigning persons, at least part-time, to collect special information and prepare marketing reports. This was followed in some firms by the establishment of formal marketing research departments. These departments have typically been responsible for securing, preparing, and disseminating only a part of the marketing information used within their firms. Today, many firms are investigating the possibilities of integrating their numerous particles of scattered and independent information programs into marketing information systems—and some firms have successfully completed the task. The fundamental purpose of the new information systems is to be able to discern and provide needed information to decision makers when they need it and in a form they can use.

This chapter examines marketing information systems. It is divided into four sections. The first section is concerned with defining the term "marketing information system." The second section describes the current state of their development and use. The third section looks at six general dimensions of marketing information systems that are helpful in examining various systems. The fourth and final section discusses the characteristics that appear to be associated with successful information systems.

## WHAT IS A MARKETING INFORMATION SYSTEM?

One definition states that a marketing information system is

> . . . a set of procedures and methods for the regular, planned collection, analysis, and presentation of information for use in making marketing decisions (Cox and Good, 1967).

Marketing information systems (MIS) are further divided into two major parts—support systems and operation systems. Support systems are made up of market research, data gathering, programming, data processing, and other activities used to generate and manipulate data. Operating systems, in contrast, are those that use the data in planning and controlling (decision making) marketing activities.

A second definition helps point up other features of an information system. Moravec has written:

> An information system may be defined as the procedures, methodologies, organization, software, and hardware elements needed to insert and retrieve selected data as required for operating and managing a company (Moravec, 1965).

All we need to do is change the last two words of his definition to *marketing activities* to have a definition of MIS.

These definitions do not quite capture the sense of what it is that differentiates an MIS from marketing research per se. The basic distinction is that a system is an integrated network or entity. It is not just a group of static, independent information activities placed in some nominal order relative to each other.[1]

Part of the difficulty of defining marketing information systems is that there are different levels of systems. Boulding, in *General Systems Theory* (Boulding, 1956), delineated nine different levels of systems, the last one being a system of systems. For example, the cells in the body of a man may be considered a system, man has a respiratory system, man himself is a system, and groups of interacting men may be considered a system.

The first definition in this chapter mentioned a *support* system and an *operating* system within an MIS. Within a support system, a data-processing system and other systems may be present. At a higher level, an MIS could be a system within a company-wide information system.

We shall focus on marketing information systems, that is, company-

[1] For additional description and models of information systems, see Head, (1967) and Johnson, Kast, and Rosenzweig (1967).

wide information systems that deal principally with marketing information.[2]

## CURRENT STATUS

Cox and Good (1967) indicate that since 1966 they have been studying the attempts of major United States firms to develop MIS. The firms include Chemstrand, Coca-Cola, General Electric, General Foods, IBM, Lever Brothers, Pillsbury, Schenley, and Westinghouse. Furthermore, they have screened more than 50 companies. From their study they make three summary statements about the current state of the art:

1. Very few companies have developed advanced systems, and not all of these are in operation. Some might even best be classified as subsystems, since they relate to only a portion of marketing decisions made.
2. Some companies, perhaps 15, are actively upgrading their systems to a high level. Of these about half seem to be progressing well; the others have been much less successful.
3. Many other companies are contemplating plans to develop sophisticated systems.

A 1964 study of 1000 large corporations conducted by Edward Brink[3] indicated that 80 companies had established some kind of formal marketing information system. Furthermore, a healthy number of companies had plans to activate such systems.[4]

Neither of these two studies attempts to measure accurately the incidence of marketing information systems. Instead, they report that marketing information systems are present in a minority of companies; they are receiving considerable attention, particularly by the larger United States firms; and it appears that many firms will be developing marketing information systems. Finally, the most meaningful aspect of the studies reporting on marketing information systems is that actual systems have been put under the microscope to see what they are made of and also to gain some insight as to why they do and do not function.[5]

[2] Dearden (1965) indicates that marketing information systems should be located within the marketing area and that they require little coordination with other systems. For a contrasting view see Spaulding (1964).

[3] Reported in *Marketing Intelligence* (1966).

[4] Cordiner indicated in 1956 that " . . . several corporations have attacked it [information problems] by creating full time management information departments" (Cordiner, 1956, p. 102).

[5] Additional studies include Albaum (1967), Amstutz (1966), and Head (1967).

## GENERAL MIS DIMENSIONS

There appears to be no generalized marketing information system. Each firm's management has unique information requirements, since each firm has a unique perspective on both the environment and their firm, a unique order of priorities, and a unique style of management based on the individual makeup and the interaction of the persons in the management group (Amstutz, 1966). Furthermore, successful systems are a matter of evolution (Amstutz, 1966; Cox and Good, 1967; Dearden, 1965).

Despite these differences, information systems do possess sets of general, identifiable dimensions that permit them to be described, compared, and contrasted. Six sets of dimension are examined—information recency, information aggregation, analytical sophistication, computer authority, transfer mechanisms, and information uses.[6]

### Recency

Information *recency* refers to the lapse of time between when an event occurs and when it is reported in the information system. The recency required of information depends on the use to which the information is put. An airline reservation clerk needs up-to-date or "on-line" information. The sales manager for a washing machine manufacturer, on the other hand, may find biweekly sales reports, for particular districts, sufficient.[7]

### Aggregation

Information aggregation indicates the detail in which information is maintained in system storage files. Data can vary from the relatively disaggregated individual item level to highly aggregate data like market share and industry sales statistics.

There is normally a relationship between the level of aggregation and the delay in getting information into the system. (See Figure 2-1.) In general, relatively disaggregated data are reported in the system sooner than highly aggregated data, because the highly aggregated information arises out of a longer batch process; that is, it must accumulate before being processed.

[6] The discussion of the first four dimensions is drawn principally from an excellent paper presented by Amstutz at the 1966 Fall Conference of the American Marketing Association (1966).

[7] For additional illustrations and comments, see Dearden (1966) and Diebold (1965).

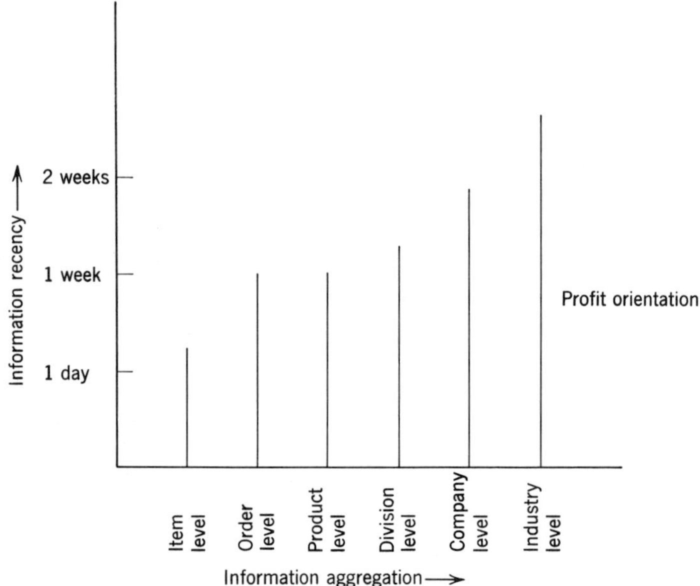


**Figure 2-1** Relationship between dimensions 1 and 2. *Source:* Amstutz, 1966.

## Analytical Sophistication

The third dimension refers to the complexity of the structures or models included in a system. At the *lowest* level, a computer only needs to identify a particular file and record, retrieve it, and display its information. At the *second* level of sophistication, the computer must be able to gather data from one or more records and produce a subtotal or total. At the *third* level the computer may be programmed to perform simple arithmetic operations, such as computing averages and differences. The *fourth* level involves logical analysis; in other words, the computer can aggregate data by various classification schemes. The *fifth* level of sophistication introduces analyses such as statistical best estimates, trend estimates, and analyses of variance. At the *sixth* level the computer is programmed to modify values of parameters or structures of models based on the data inputs it has received (this is called learning). The most *advanced* level of analytic sophistication occurs when simulation models are used in sufficient detail and magnitude to represent the real world through the information system, At this level, Amstutz indicates,

> . . . the system provides management with the capability of testing proposed policy and strategies in the simulated environment; choosing between alterna-

tives on the basis of resulting output; implementing the policies in the real world environment; and evaluating the effectiveness of implemented plans through the information system (Amstutz, 1966, p. 73).

## Computer Authority

The fourth dimension useful in describing and comparing information systems is the authority granted to the computer. Amstutz indicates that it is closely related to the system's analytic sophistication. The levels of computer authority and their general relationship to analytical sophistication are shown on Figure 2-2.

At the lowest level, decision makers may grant the computer authority only to *retrieve* certain information from designated locations. The next level is to have the computer *review* (check) the content of each record as to reasonableness.

The next level is to have the computer perform analyses on records and to *refer* exceptions (as defined by decision makers) for further review. At the fourth step, the further review noted at the prior level is programmed for the computer to do, and the computer reports a *recommendation* for action. When decision makers continually find these recommendations appropriate, they may give the computer authority to

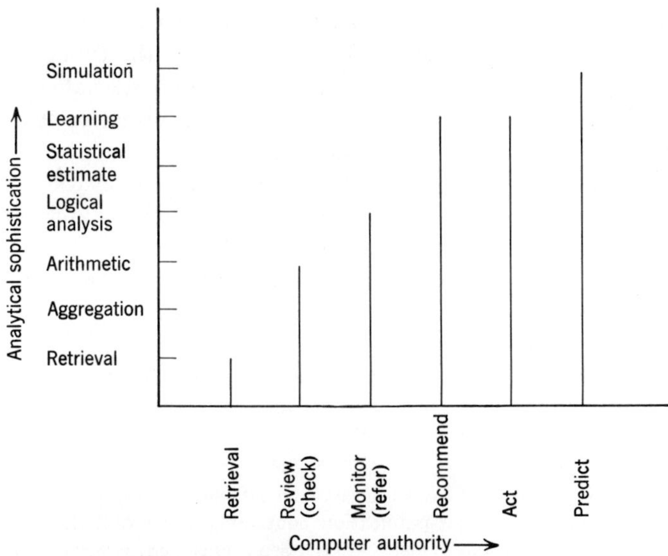


**Figure 2-2** Relationship between dimensions 3 and 4. *Source:* Amstutz, 1966.

take *action* on all but exceptional cases (as defined by the decision makers). The final level of authority occurs when the computer is permitted to *predict.* Computer involvement is greater here than at the prior level because predictions are used in planning affecting the future of the company whereas computer-directed action relates only to current operations.[8]

## Transfer Mechanisms

Dimension 5 refers to the transfer mechanisms for developing a close and harmonious linkage between the information base and the decision makers. Two factors that complicate this task are the continuing inflow of new information into the data base and the fact that *only information relevant to a decision maker should flow to him.* The objective is to construct a linkage through which relevant information can be selected and matched to decision makers.

The types of linkage vary from those where decision makers directly interrogate the computer to those where the decision makers never interrogate the computer, but always look to information specialists, who in turn provide the linkage to the information base (man-machine linkage). With the first type of linkage, the decision makers must have good knowledge of the content of the information system, the forms in which data outputs are available, and the language needed to communicate with the computer.[9] In the second type of situation, the decision maker needs only a very general understanding of the types and forms of information that are available. The information specialists, through their knowledge of the information base and the information-using activities of the decision maker, serve as matchmakers.

The man-machine linkage is very dependent on (1) decision makers' ability to provide adequate profiles of their decision-making situations and (2) information system specialists' knowledge of the available data base and its relationship to the decision makers' needs. One information center director using the man-machine linkage has written:

> Acknowledging the power of the computer, the heart of the system is the technical staff member. He provides the linkage between the . . . user and the base of information (Craven, p. 50).

[8] While numerous articles and books discuss the influence of computers on information and management, a single publication containing views of both academicians and businessmen is Shultz and Whisler (1960). See also current issues of *Datamation,* which is a monthly publication.

[9] For a prediction of things to come, see Diebold (1965).

## System Subsystems

The final dimension for describing and comparing marketing information systems is based on the type of decision for which the information is required. For example, a system may be made up of three subsystems: one to provide information for control decisions, one for planning decisions, and one for basic research decisions.[10]

The control system may provide continuous monitoring (sometimes employing exception reporting), rapid problem recognition, and trend development. Planning systems furnish the information that marketing decision makers need for planning, with such information generally required less frequently than is control information. For example, three companies are reported to be developing "data books" to bring together basic information needed by product managers for annual planning (Cox and Good, 1967). Simulation models are included in planning systems. They allow trial of alternative plans so that decision makers can make better decisions.

The basic research systems are designed to accumulate and analyze an immense amount of information on a specific problem or relationship at one particular time. Some companies, for example, are exploring the relationships between their advertising and sales through the use of basic research systems.

As a second illustration, a system could be composed of subsystems that are designated as selective dissemination systems (SDS), retrospective search systems, (RSS), and new opportunity systems (NOS) (Craven).[11] The SDS provides for a continuing flow of information as certain events occur. For example, this system could provide daily reports of company sales by products and territories, together with total annual sales to date, comparison sales figures for previous periods, and forecasted values for the present period. It could report changes in market share, competitive activity, and a host of other information about competition and the environment.

The RSS provides the mechanism for seeking information on special problems or areas of immediate, high-priority interest to the user (i.e., special-problem information). For example, the SDS may show deteriorating sales and profits for a key product, but not provide insight into the causes and corrections needed. Through the RSS, the decision maker could focus on this special problem. He could call for all past market studies on the product, more complete data on sales, market share, and special analyses of existing data, and have new research instigated.

[10] A two-subsystem output is discussed in Liston (1966).

[11] Liston (1966) divides subsystems into current-awareness and retrospective searching.

The NOS is directed toward communicating to users what could be called opportunity and unusual information. This, in general, is information that decision makers have not sought nor anticipated (and does not show up in SDS or RSS) but that seems to merit the attention of specific decision makers. This system (subsystem) represents the information specialists' avenue to keep the decision maker in contact with the unusual, but possibly relevant, information that enters the system. For example, a patent search initiated by a firm's legal counsel may contain information of possible value or a Congressional hearing may report on a marketing strategy used by competitive firms. Such information is discussed in Chapter 12 under the heading of Unanticipated Information.

## CHARACTERISTICS OF SUCCESSFUL SYSTEMS

Why are some marketing information systems succeeding while others are doing poorly or failing? Can the blame be placed on physical communication facilities, computers or computer programs, storage and retrieval systems, marketing research technology, or other technical problems? Information specialists say that difficulties are *not* due to the technical aspects (Lindsay, 1966; Spaulding, 1964).

Furthermore, these specialists agree that little explanation can be provided through examination of specific functions and outputs of successful systems, because there are almost as many variations as there are firms with successful systems. Instead, hypotheses for successful systems center in the characteristics of the systems and the environment in which they operate.

Amstutz has commented on four characteristics essential to successful systems (Amstutz, 1966):[12]

1. The system is founded on management's conception of the decision environment.
2. The user-manager understands and is involved in the construction of the system structure.
3. The system is based on disaggregated data files.
4. System development has proceeded to increasing levels of sophistication through a process of gradual evolution.

Cox and Good (1967) contribute a fifth characteristic:

5. A high-level information coordinator or "prime contractor," who reports to the user group, is used.

[12] The discussion of the first four characteristics is drawn largely from the Amstutz paper (1966) cited earlier.

Finally, we believe there is one other system characteristic that merits discussion.

6. Marketing information audits are used.

## Management's View of the Environment

To provide meaningful information to a group of decision makers, a system must reflect that group's priorities. Also, it must provide information of the type and in the amount and form that management wants and can use. Ackoff (1967), in fact, indicates that the overabundance of irrelevant information is a major cause of MIS failures.

An information system, therefore, must be based on a model that reflects management's conception of the environment. Management's initial statements must be examined, refined, made less ambiguous, and, in general, be transformed into more explicit statements before they are adequate to help shape the system to provide relevant information.

## Management Involvement and Understanding

Management must be involved in establishing the system. Managers must work at the detail level (e.g., they must spell out market boundaries and product groups and define the content of such measures as market share and net sales) as well as at higher levels. They must agree on the dimensions of their environment and must understand and accept the structuring of the system. Only then are they able to define the measures and the analytical activities they need as decision makers. Involvement helps them to reflect their views in the system and to understand the system. As Ackoff (1967) has put it: "No MIS should ever be installed unless the managers for whom it is intended are trained to evaluate and hence control it rather than be controlled by it." Also, the more involved they are, the more likely they are to support the system.

## Disaggregated Data Bank

A bank or file of "micro" or disaggregated data is very essential to the evolution of a system. It is the base that is added to over time. Data are recorded and stored in the lowest aggregation or detail level in which they are likely to be used in the future. For example, an individual sale may be recorded by product, location, price, and time of sale.

Amstutz has written:

> At the heart of every successful information system is a disaggregated data file . . . . As new inputs are received they are maintained along with existing

data . . . . The existence of a disaggregative file facilities system evolution . . . . In the first stages of system development it is simply impossible to anticipate the direction of later advancement . . . . The disaggregated data file provides the flexibility which is the prerequisite of intelligent system evolution (Amstutz, 1966, p. 76).

The more disaggregated the data bank is, the more costly it is. Therefore, management must consider the cost of the disaggregate data base against the likelihood that future decisions will require the detailed data.[13] Until more experience is gained, highly disaggregated data banks are generally recommended.

## Systems Designed for Evolution

There are three key elements that can preclude a system from evolving. One is a data bank whose least aggregated data are too aggregated for proposed new uses. For example, a company may want to analyze its sales by counties, but may find that its past information is disaggregated only to the state level. It can start accumulating information to the desired detail, but because of previous state data, the previous sales experience is lost.

Second, a data bank may be so designed that it is not expandable. A fixed-length record bank that initially appeared large enough may not hold sufficient data. An expandable data bank will permit an information system to evolve.

The third factor influencing evolution of a system is the ability of decision makers to understand and use it as rapidly as it can be developed. Cox and Good state that information quality can be upgraded much more rapidly than management quality. They recommend a master plan for system improvement[14] based on the managers' ability to use the improved information (Cox and Good, 1967).

## Organization and Leadership

Successful systems appear to require organization and leadership, both at the development stage and later. Cox and Good report four approaches they have observed with respect to the installation of a system: the fresh-start organization, or, as they call it, the "clean piece of paper"; committee; low-level leader; and information coordinator.[15] The organization and leadership of ongoing systems are discussed in Chapter 16.

[13] For more information regarding the degree of aggregation for data banks, see Chapter 9.

[14] For additional discussion of this topic, see Brown, (1962).

[15] The discussion of the four approaches is drawn largely from an article by Cox and Good (1967).

*Fresh Start*

This approach involves setting up an all-new organization for the handling of marketing information. This, of course, implies abolishing the traditional information-gathering and processing departments and in their place establishing a management information department. Proponents of this approach argue that much information produced by research and accounting departments does not fit the needs of decision makers. Furthermore, the information parts have *not* been sufficiently integrated to be ready for use by decision makers. Therefore, the argument goes, the "ideal" procedure is to abolish the old. This approach is not feasible in most companies. Cox and Good (1967), reporting on the firms they have studied, say:

> Traditions and positions are too well entrenched. Furthermore, it would not solve all the problems . . . it would not ensure the development of an MIS geared to management needs. For another, no management information department could supply all of the data the system needed . . . (Cox and Good, 1967, p. 150).

*Committee Approach*

Some firms have tried committees composed of members from key information-supplying and using areas to study and establish marketing information systems. Such an approach can gain involvement of many appropriate persons and serve to bring forth the unique information problems of various areas.

The typical committee, however, does not get the job done. Development and operation of an information system requires much time—far more than busy managers will spare for such committee work. Also, a committee usually lacks sufficient leadership and authority.

*Low-Level Approach*

Some firms have shown a lack of understanding of the difficulties of organizing marketing information systems—they have assigned a junior member of the marketing research department to the task. The key man needs perspective, knowledge, and power. A junior man, at best, may possess two of these.

*Coordinator Approach*

Some firms have used a top-level executive as a "coordinator" or director of marketing systems and retained traditional department boundaries. He works somewhat like a "prime contractor," in that he develops the information system plans and specifications and coordinates and inspects the work of various suppliers who contribute or subcontract to the program.

Cox and Good point out that such a coordinator must have cost control. That is, he is responsible for the overall budget and negotiates with decision makers to establish their marketing information needs and the funds that they must have to provide for their needs. On the supply side, he arranges with various departments to provide needed information and services and to compensate them.

Firms using this approach have located the coordinator within the marketing department, not in central or corporate systems departments. This placement results in the coordinator's representing the area that uses and pays for the information system. The major reasons for this placement are:

> Effective development of . . . systems requires a management, rather than a technical support systems, orientation. Furthermore, effective MIS can be developed only by people who understand users' problems and who can be responsive to users' needs (Cox and Good, 1967, p. 151).

This approach to leadership and organization has been the most successful of those studied. Its success is largely dependent on the "right" man filling the job. He should have the full support of top management and be a person who is capable of understanding decision makers' information needs and systems problems.

## Marketing Information Audits

A sixth characteristic of successful systems is marketing information audits. Ralph Cordiner (1956) while not specifically talking about MIS, sounds the need:

> What is required . . . is a . . . penetrating and orderly study of the business in its entirety to discover what specific information is needed at each particular position in view of the decisions to be made there (Cordiner, 1956, p. 102).

A marketing information audit is a systematic, critical, and impartial review and appraisal of the total marketing information program. It is concerned with the basic goals, policies, and assumptions underlying the information activity, as well as with the methods, procedures, personnel, and organizational structures used in the activity (Shuchman, 1962, p. 399). It is both diagnostic and prognostic in that it searches both for malfunctions and for new opportunities.

Specific objectives of audits are to pinpoint (1) users' information needs and supplies, (2) unnecessary duplications (including users' "needs"), (3) allocations of the various information activities within an organization, and (4) inefficient and efficient performance of information activities in an organization (from users through to information sources).[16]

A marketing information audit is made up of three major phases—a demand audit, a supply audit, and a management audit.

*Demand Audit*

The information needs of each decision maker depend on his tasks and role within the organization. An auditor cannot proceed by simply asking each decision maker to specify his information needs. It is our opinion that some demand far more information than they need while, at the other extreme, others simply do not realize they need information.[17] An auditor can *help* various managers see their needs in terms of type, form, and amounts of information. The individual manager contributes a detailed view of his situation, and the auditor contributes a view of divisional specializations, accompanying organization structures, and functional relationships in terms of the total performance of the firm.

Early reviews with decision makers are in terms of the information wanted and the estimated value of various information items. Later in the audit, when more meaningful information cost estimates become available, the earlier "ideal" wants are tempered by what decision makers can afford. (This problem of costing information supplies will be examined later.)

*Supply Audit*

The second audit phase is concerned with supplying marketing information. The auditor's starting point is a listing of his firm's information wants. Then he seeks possible sources of information and appraises the alternative processes and costs of transforming information into available, needed forms.

The auditor needs to be familiar with the activities and roles of each organizational unit within his firm in order to evaluate internal supply capabilities and capacities. Once again, he works with the managers of the various departments.

[16] For additional discussion of information audits, see Ackoff (1967) and Sessions (1950).

[17] Daniels (1961) discusses some of the difficulties of securing listings of decision makers' information needs. Ackoff (1967) is of the opinion that decision makers tend to request more information than they need or can use.

Supply audits are not limited to assessment of capabilities within a firm. Internal information is supplemented with knowledge of outside information supplies and of services and their costs.

### *Management Audit*

The third and final phase is the managing audit. This is an assessment, review, and evaluation of the information-managing activities. Put more specifically, such an audit is concerned with (1) the balance between needs and supplies, (2) duplications, (3) misallocation of information activities, (4) inefficiencies, and (5) the relationship between information benefits and their costs.

The demand and the supply audits provide the base for assessing the balance between information needs and supplies. Needs that are matched with appropriate information supplies provide one indication of adequate management. However, unmet information needs (that can and should be met) are indicative of difficulties.

Unneeded duplication of information activities is also indicative of weak information management. For example, an advertising manager may want market share information by media markets for a specific product and seek it through an advertising agency. The sales manager may need similar market share measures by sales territories and, in turn, have his sales force seek it. In addition, marketing research may want similar information and, accordingly, proceed to seek it from still other sources. Such a situation needs attention to see if one measure from one source is adequate.

Misallocation of various information supply activities is also an indication of difficulties. The concern is to see that the right specialists are performing each activity.[18] For example, large tabulation jobs should not be hand-tabulated within a department (because it lacks computer knowledge), but should be handled by the computer center.

Inefficient performance of information activities is a fourth identifiable sign of poor management. Such defects are difficult to identify because, normally, they do not stand out as do cases of poor balance, duplication, and misallocation. Instead, each supplying activity must be analyzed to ascertain the degree of efficiency being attained.

### *Information Benefits and Costs*

A part of the management audit is continuing review of the relationship between information benefits and their costs. Specifically, management would like to know (1) how much an item of marketing information

[18] Cyert and March (1965, pp. 106–107) discuss this matter in terms of securing information from the environment.

will cost and (2) the change in dollar profits (the benefits) that will result from the use of the information. These are also the two key questions asked about advertising proposals and numerous other proposed expenditures. What will they cost—what will they accomplish?

INFORMATION COSTS. There are four somewhat distinct costing situations facing information managers. In the first one, ready-to-use information is purchased in total from outside sources. Then, the paid price, for all practical purposes, becomes the cost. For example, a company may need an estimate of its current flow of products at the retail level and contract with a commercial audit and survey firm. When additional costs are directly associated with this information (e.g., transmitting, analyzing, or storing), they must also be charged against the information.

The second situation evolves around information secured and handled solely within the organization. For example, prices of competitive products may be needed from all outlets, and the information office handles the entire jobs. Then all of the direct and semidirect costs associated with the various tasks would be recorded and charged against the job. The costing procedures involved are very similar to cost analyses of other marketing activities (these matters are discussed in Chapter 9).

In a third type of situation, part of the information task may be handled outside the company and part inside. For example, a company may want to query a representative group about purchasing behavior. The specific questions are to be developed in the company, but the fieldwork and tabulations are to be handled by outside organizations. Then further analysis and communication are to be handled within the company. In this common type of situation, the prices paid to the outside groups are added to the incurred internal costs to arrive at a total cost.

Finally, the costs of not having the information facilities available for other activities (opportunity costs) must be considered.

INFORMATION BENEFITS. Information benefits have been briefly discussed in Chapter 1 and will be further discussed in Chapter 6, but some remarks are pertinent here. When information benefits exceed accompanying costs (and there are no better alternative uses for the funds), the information should be secured.[19] In some situations there is little need to undertake detailed evaluation of benefits, in that they clearly do or do not exceed costs. Often, however, information managers must attempt to assess information benefits.[20]

[19] Expressed in other terms, "Information . . . should be gathered up to the point where the incremental cost of additional information is equal to the incremental profit that can be earned by having it" (Simon, 1959).

[20] For a discussion of the value of information as viewed by an accountant, see Bedford and Onsi (1966).

Estimating the usefulness of marketing information presents problems similar to those found in attempts to evaluate the effectiveness of advertising and other marketing activities. Only in a few simple situations is the dollar contribution either easily discerned or obviously sufficient. In most situations, the dollar contribution must be inferred from some intermediate measure. In advertising, for example, Starch and other post-readership recall tests are used to help evaluate the "effectiveness" of advertising. They measure recall, which is not equivalent to measuring effectiveness in terms of contribution, but it provides a useful inferential base.

In Chapter 1 it was indicated that information benefits vary with the degree of uncertainty with regard to outcomes, the economic consequences of an incorrect decision, and the amount by which the information can reduce the uncertainty. Multiple-use information extends the benefits to a number of uses and, in turn, tends to raise the total benefit received. For example, detailed information on company and competitive sales would probably be used by at least the sales manager, the advertising manager, and the marketing manager in planning and controlling their activities. In contrast, a special-purpose piece of information would probably be used only by one manager, who then alone must pay out sufficient benefit to cover the cost. Multiple-use information normally includes estimates and measures of potential, product sales by markets (and other breakdowns), competitive product sales, distribution expenses by major categories, and channel and other promotional mix knowledge.

The use of Bayesian analysis in determining the precise value of information is discussed in Chapter 6.

## SUMMARY

The need for relevant marketing information has expanded rapidly as managers have needed to make more decisions about more products sold in more markets. Small market research units have grown into larger marketing research departments, and additional information units have been added in some firms. The continued need for better information has led some United States firms to develop marketing information systems.

There are no generalized marketing information systems. Instead each one is designed to fit the unique circumstances of individual firms. Despite the numerous differences, general identifiable system dimensions have been noted. The more prominent ones relate to recency of information, aggregation of information, analytical sophistication, computer authority and transfer mechanisms, and information use.

Marketing information systems have met with varying degrees of success in United States firms. In general, there is agreement that sufficient technical competence in such areas as computers, communication facilities, and marketing research is available. Therefore, hypotheses for successful systems have centered in the characteristics of the systems and the environments in which they operate. The principal hypotheses are:

1. The system must be founded on management's conception of the decision environment.
2. The user-manager must understand the system structure, so that he can control it.
3. The system must be based on disaggregated data files.
4. System development must proceed through increasing levels of sophistication and through a process of gradual evaluation.
5. A high-level information "coordinator" must be used.
6. Marketing information audits are essential to a marketing information system.

This chapter is concerned with the information system, rather than the nature of the information transmitted. It will be recalled from Chapter 1 that an adequate model of the decision is a prerequisite to specifying and obtaining information.

## REFERENCES

Ackoff, R. L. "Management Misinformation Systems," *Management Science,* December 1967, pp. B-147, B-156.

Albaum, G. "Information Flows and Decentralized Decision Making in Marketing," *California Management Review,* Summer 1967, pp. 59–70.

Alderson, W. "New Concepts of Information for Management Decisions in Marketing," *NAA Bulletin,* August 1959.

Amstutz, A. E. "The Marketing Executive and Management Information Systems." In Hass, R. (Ed.), *Science, Technology and Marketing.* Chicago: American Marketing Association, 1966, pp. 69–86.

Bedford, N. M., & Onsi, M. "Measuing the Value of Information—An Information Theory Approach," *Management Services,* January-February 1966, pp. 15–22.

Boulding, K. E. "General Systems Theory—The Skeleton of Science," *Management Review,* April 1956, pp. 197–208.

Brown, D. E. "Management Looks at Management Information Systems," *Advances in Management Information Systems Techniques,* Bulletin 16, New York: American Management Association, 1962, pp. 15–16.

Cordiner, R. J. *New Frontiers for Professional Managers.* New York: McGraw-Hill, 1965.

Cox, D. F., & Good, R. E. "How to Build a Marketing Information System," *Harvard Business Review,* May-June 1967, pp. 145–154.

Craven, D. W. "Information Systems for Technology Transfer." In Hass, R. (Ed.), *Science, Technology and Marketing.* Chicago: American Marketing Association, 1966, pp. 47–60.

Cyert, R. M., & March, J. G. *A Behavioral Theory of the Firm.* Englewood Cliffs, N.J.: Prentice-Hall, 1965.

Daniel, D. R. *"Management Information Crisis," Harvard Business Review,* September-October 1961, pp. 111–121.

Dearden, J. "How to Organize Information Systems," *Harvard Business Review,* March-April 1965, pp. 65–73.

Dearden, J. "Myth of Real-Time Management Information," *Harvard Business Review,* May-June 1966, pp. 123–132.

Diebold, J. "What's Ahead in Information Technology," *Harvard Business Review,* September-October 1965, pp. 76–82.

Head, R. V. "Management Information Systems: A Critical Appraisal," *Datamation,* May 1967, pp. 22–27.

Johnson, R., Kast, F., & Rosenzweig, J. *The Theory and Management of Systems,* (2nd ed.) New York: McGraw-Hill, 1967.

Lindsay, F. A. "Marshal Your Marketing Information," *Business Horizons,* Summer 1962, pp. 53–60.

Liston, D., Jr. "Information Systems: What They Do, How They Work," *Machine Design,* July 21, 1966, pp. 190–197.

"Marketing Intelligence Systems: A Dew Line for Marketing Men," *Business Management,* January 1966, pp. 32–34, 68.

Moravec, A. F. "Basic Concepts for Designing a Fundamental Information System," *Management Services,* July-August 1965, pp. 37–45.

Sessions, R. "A Management Audit of Marketing Research," *Journal of Marketing,* January 1950.

Shuchman, A. "The Marketing Audit: Its Nature, Purposes, and Problems." In Lazer, W., & Kelley, E. (Eds.), *Managerial Marketing: Perspectives and Viewpoints.* Homewood, Ill. Richard D. Irwin, 1962.

Schultz, G. P., & Whisler, T. L. (Eds.) *Management Organization and the Computer,* Chicago: The Free Press of Glencoe, Illinois, 1960.

Simon, H. A. "Theories of Decision-Making in Economics and Behavioral Science," *The American Economic Review,* June 1959, p. 270.

Spaulding, A. T., Jr. "Is the Total System Concept Practical?" *Systems and Procedures Journal,* January-February 1964, pp. 28–32.

*Three*

# Models and Model Building

Think of the complexities involved in turning on a light. Angular momentum is imparted to a contact mechanism, which allows electrons to flow through a conduit and into a device where the energy of the electrons is given up in the form of the energy of heat and light. But why worry about all that, when all we want to do is turn the light on? And that is precisely the point.

If man had to completely understand all the intricacies and details of every facet of an action before the action could be taken, no action could possibly be taken. From birth to death we learn to simplify, to abstract, *to model* the world around us by what is relevant and necessary. Every day of our lives we must be concerned with building models of reality merely in order to function.

It should not be surprising that marketing activities, even the simplest, must also be modeled to be "understood." As elsewhere, such models are most often implicit and seldom articulated. What do we mean when we say that a manager has good judgment or that experience is important? Perhaps we mean that the man with good judgment understands the implications of the situations he deals with because he has good models of them and that experience is a means of updating and reshaping models to better conform to the needs of decisions. If so, the study of models itself is a useful area of study.[1]

[1] An excellent general treatment of the application of models to marketing is given by Buzzell (1964). A general discussion may be found in Langhoff (1963). Specific applications are given in Bass Buzzel, and Others (1961), Day (1964), and Frank, Kuehn, and Massy (1962). The best overall treatment of the topic of models and model buildings is given by Ackoff (1962).

## MODELS

At this point, it seems appropriate to define more precisely what is meant by a model.

### Definitions of Models

Consider the following definitions:

1. A model is that which exactly represents something else, a copy.
2. A model is anything used to represent something else.
3. A model is something that comprises in itself the essential qualities of some other thing.

In judging these definitions we have a greater latitude than would be permitted if we were considering a definition of an elephant or some other tangible, concrete thing. A definition of an elephant can be tested against the specimen at the local zoo. If we have erred on some dimension, perhaps by underrating the dimensions of the proboscis, the definition has failed. The problem in defining an intangible thing such as a model is not that our definition can fail by omitting some vital detail, since there is nothing tangible to measure the definition against; the problem is that our definition may not prove useful.

If we examine the first definition, we see that it does not add very much to our conceptual tools—if a model is a copy, the word "copy" will do very well. The second definition is too broad to be useful. A social security number represents a person on a great many forms and I.B.M. cards, but there is very little, other than his identity, that can be ascertained about a person from his social security number. Thus in situations calling only for identification a social security number is an adequate model of a person, but if we wished to study, say, behavior, some other model would have to be used.

The third definition is the one to which the authors subscribe. The key phrase is "essential qualities." Depending on the circumstances under which the model will be employed, some qualities of the thing to be modeled may be superfluous and other qualities essential. Thus the purpose of the model is a major determinant of the model itself.

### Purposes of a Model—Prediction and Problem Solving

There are two basic purposes of building a model. One is to predict the future. In this context, analytical models of sales forecasting will be discussed in Chapter 15. Such models are descriptive. They may or may not include variables, such as price and promotion, under the control of the marketer. If such variables are included they become parameters, that is, they become fixed, in a given prediction.

## Problem Solving Models

A problem-solving or decision-making model includes some value function by which a choice can be made among the alternatives under the control of the marketer. For example, a decision-making model may be designed to set an optimal inventory level, where minimizing costs is the objective. That production schedule (and the resulting inventory) that minimizes total cost will be selected.

Where multiple objectives are held, the problem becomes more difficult. Yet this is the typical situation. The classical economic concept of the businessman as solely a profit maximizer is accepted by few students of business today. In addition to profits, a firm may be concerned with market share, the public image of the company, relations with the union, the price of their stock, and many other matters. It is extremely unlikely that a strategy that maximizes any one of these objectives also maximizes even one, let alone all, of the others.

Two alternatives exist for solving the dilemma. The first alternative is to weight the objectives so that a single summary variable is maximized. The second alternative is to maximize one objective, while ensuring that other objectives reach at least some minimum satisfactory level. These two approaches are discussed below.

### *A Weighting System for Objectives*

There is a growing body of literature on value theory—the theory by which multiple objectives may be combined.[2] We shall outline only one of these approaches. The method to be illustrated was formulated by Churchman and Ackoff[3] and is given here, since it is both easily understood and easily applied.

We first outline the method for a set of qualitative objectives and then show how quantitative objectives may be incorporated.

Suppose that we are faced with valuing the following objectives:

(*a*) Keeping family control of the company.
(*b*) Maintaining steady employment for our personnel.
(*c*) Producing quality merchandise.
(*d*) Having a favorable company image.

[2] A summary of much of this literature is found in Fishburn (1968).
[3] The method is outlined in Churchman, Ackoff, and Arnoff, (1957, 118–130) as well as in other publications.

The first step in the procedure is to obtain a ranking of these objectives. Suppose that the ranking is in the order *a, b, d, c.* We must then achieve a first approximation to the *relative* weights of the objectives. Arbitrarily, a weight of unity is assigned to the highest-ranking objective and weights relative to this are assigned to the other objectives. This may yield the following weights:

| | |
|---|---|
| (*a*) Family control | 1.0 |
| (*b*) Steady employment | 0.7 |
| (*d*) Company image | 0.5 |
| (*c*) Quality merchandise | 0.3 |

The reliability of these weights must now be checked. In the process, the assumption is made that weights are additive.

If the decision maker has the choice of *either* maintaining family control or maintaining steady employment, company image, and quality merchandise, which would he prefer? The sum of the latter three weights yields a value of 1.5 as contrasted with the value of 1.0 for the first objective. Thus, if the weights are correct, the answer should be to forgo family control in favor of maintaining the other objectives. If the answer elicited by the decision maker coincides with our prediction, no revision is necessary at this step. If not, the procedure is to raise the weight for family control above the sum of others, and a weight of 1.6 would be assigned to family control.

The next step is to compare the second-ranked objective with the remaining objectives (other than the first-ranked) in exactly the same manner. In the example shown in Table 3-1, a revision is necessary with respect to *b,* maintaining steady employment. The final step is to normalize the weights (i.e., maintain their relative position but have them sum to unity).

**Table 3-1** Ranking Objectives

| Rank | Objective | Initial Weight | Revised Weight | Normalized-Weight |
|---|---|---|---|---|
| 1 | *a* | 1.0 | 1.0 | 0.37 |
| 2 | *b* | 0.7 | 0.9 | 0.33 |
| 3 | *d* | 0.5 | 0.5 | 0.19 |
| 4 | *c* | 0.3 | 0.3 | 0.11 |
| | | | 2.7 | 1.00 |

### *Adding a Quantitative Objective*

Suppose that a further objective (as seems reasonable) is profitability.[4] Since profits may vary in a continuous fashion, a single objective of "profitability" is inadequate.

The procedure would be to translate all the above objectives into an equivalent profit measure. This is accomplished by asking the question, "How many dollars of profit is maintaining family control worth?" Once this is established, the remaining qualitative objectives are assigned a relative measure of profits.

### *Programming Approach*

Another approach to the problem is to take the most important quantitative objective and maximize it, subject to maintaining other objectives at satisfactory levels. For example, we may wish to

Maximize profits

Subject to:

Market share greater than or equal to 20%
Promotion less than or equal to $1,000,000

One difficulty here is that no trade-off is established between objectives. It may be possible to increase profits by relaxing one or more of the restraints.

If the mathematics is tractable, a technique known as parametric programming may be employed to investigate the problem of a trade-off. If not, the best approach is to reformulate the problem with the restraints adjusted and to solve anew. In any case, the decision maker must finally make a choice among the alternatives presented.

## Classification of Models

There are three basic ways to model the real thing—construct a scaled counterpart, replace some property of the original by something else, or use symbolic relationships. Each of these will be looked at in turn.

### *Iconic Models*

*Icon* is the Greek word for an image; thus iconic models are those that produce images of the original. A photograph, for example, is an

[4] The significant problem of establishing an appropriate period and discount rate for profits will not be treated here.

iconic model of a person and a road map is an iconic model of a road system.

Iconic models do not play a large role in marketing models. Perhaps the only significant application is with regard to scaled models used in store layout.

### *Analogue Models*

An analogue model substitutes one property for another. For example, a sales chart substitutes distance in the horizontal dimension for time and distance in the vertical dimension for sales.

Analogue models are extremely useful devices for representing a system and investigating changes in the system. A marketing information system, for example, can be represented by a flow chart showing where information is collected, the route it takes to analysis and storage, and the route it takes in dissemination. Such a program provides an invaluable tool in the analysis of the system.

### *Symbolic Models*

In a symbolic model the components of the thing being represented and their interrelationships are described by symbols. Mathematical and logical symbols form the basis of most symbolic models.

There are three types of mathematical equations: definitional, technical, and behavioral. It should be noted that all three provide interrelationships of mathematical symbols. We shall also introduce the concept of inequalities.

DEFINITIONAL EQUATIONS. A definitional equation defines a property mathematically on the basis of one or more previously defined properties. For example, if we use the symbols $P$, $R$, and $C$ to represent profit, revenue, and costs respectively, we may define profit by the equation

$$P \equiv R - C$$

A third bar is added to the symbol for equality to demonstrate that the left-hand side is *identically equal* to the right-hand side of the equation. That is, in any circumstance where the right-hand side may arise, we may always substitute the left-hand side. This is not surprising since the left-hand side is defined in terms of the right-hand side.

Definitional equations add nothing new to a model and explain nothing. Their sole purpose is to provide a concise notation for a more complex relationship. Instead of talking about profits, for example, a firm could equivalently talk about the excess of revenue over costs.

TECHNICAL EQUATIONS. A technical equation provides a relationship among previously defined symbols, the parameters of which do not depend on behavior. For example, a salesman may receive a base salary of $1000 per year plus 5 per cent of sales. If $C$ represents the salesman's income from the job and $S$ sales, we have

$$C = 1000 + 0.05S$$

Notice that, unlike in the definitional equation, we would not be redefining the quantity on the left-hand side by changing the quantity on the right-hand side. Thus if our salesman were put on a straight salary of $10,000 per year, we could have

$$C = \$10{,}000$$

as the equation representing the salesman's income. This is so because income is defined independently by something like "the amount of money received by the salesman from the firm in payment for his services" and is not defined by the equation. It is merely calculated by the equation.

BEHAVIORAL EQUATIONS. A behavioral equation is one that is empirically derived to describe behavior. A demand function, for example, is a behavioral equation describing the quantity of a good that will be sold at various prices. The parameters of this equation can only be ascertained by actually varying price and observing the quantity sold. This is in contrast to the technical equation where the parameters are generally known.

INEQUALITIES. An example of an inequality is given in the discussion of the programming approach to multiple goals. The statement that market share should be *at least* 20 per cent is a form of an inequality. The requirement that we keep the advertising allocation under some amount is another inequality in the other direction. The solution to a problem with inequalities will be discussed later in this chapter when we examine linear programming models.

A SIMPLE SYMBOLIC MODEL. A store owner decides that if pilferage in the past month has been as high as 3 per cent of sales in a department chosen at random, he will fire the store detective. The housewares department is selected. Let $S_{i,t}$ represent stock on hand of good $i$ as ascertained from a physical inventory check at the end of the $t$th period and let $\hat{S}_{i,t}$ represent the same quantity estimated from records. Let $R_{i,t}$ represent sales for the period of good $i$ and $P_{i,t}$ the amount received of good $i$ from suppliers in the period. Then stock on hand estimated from records is

$$\hat{S}_{i,t} = S_{i,t-1} + P_{i,t} - R_{i,t}$$

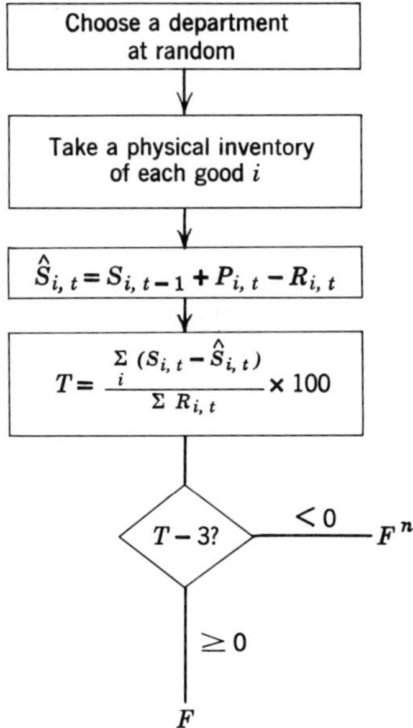


**Figure 3-1** A check on the store detective.

The amount missing is given by

$$\hat{S}_{i,t} - S_{i,t}$$

for good $i$. The per cent that pilferage is of sales is given by

$$T = \frac{\sum_i (\hat{S}_{i,t} - S_{i,t})}{\sum_i R_{i,t}} \times 100$$

If we let $F$ represent the decision to fire the store detective and $F^n$ the decision to keep him, a logical notation of the decision rule is:

If $T - 3 \geq 0$, then $F$.

If $T - 3 \leq 0$, then $F^n$.

The whole model can be represented by a flow chart, as in Figure 3-1. This model is a problem-solving model.

*Behavioral versus Black-Box Models*

Models may also be classified according to the degree to which the underlying process is understood. A *black-box* model is one in which the underlying process is poorly portrayed, while a *behavioral* model is one in which the underlying process is well understood. The word "behavioral" is here used in a different sense than previously when employed with reference to behavioral equations.

### *Black-Box Models*

Consider a simple table radio from the point of view of an average person. In order to operate the radio only three things need be known—the radio must be plugged in, there is one switch that controls the operation of turning on the radio and volume, and there is another switch that determines the station to be tuned in. Other than this, the radio is a magical "black-box."

Much marketing, if not most, is in the black-box category. Something is done because it seems to work and it will continue to be done in this manner until it stops working. The field of promotion is particularly in the black-box category—from the setting of budgets to the selection of appeals.

### *Behavioral Models*

The black-box model of a table radio is perfectly adequate for most circumstances. There are only two conditions when something more is needed. The first is when something goes wrong with the radio. The second is in designing a better radio.

Consider the trend-extrapolation approach to forecasting. As long as the conditions that contribute to the trend continue, extending the trend provides a reasonable forecast of the future. But trend analysis is a black-box prediction model. Should conditions change, the time series alone may give a very inaccurate prediction. Even more disturbing, *without a behavioral model it is often impossible to even ascertain whether conditions have changed or not, since one does not know what conditions to investigate*. Thus the time series itself is the only indicator of a change in the black-box prediction model, and it may reflect changes too late to be of use.

## MODEL BUILDING

In this section we follow the general outline of steps suggested by Churchman, Ackoff, and Arnoff (1957, p. 18):

1. Formulating the problem.
2. Constructing a mathematical model to represent the system under study.

3. Deriving a solution from the model.
4. Testing the model.
5. Establishing controls over the solution.
6. Putting the solution to work.

Each of these steps is discussed in turn.

## Formulating the Problem

The formulation of the problem is concerned with an analysis of the system under control (in a control or problem-solving model), objectives, and alternative courses of action.

### *The System under Control*

An excellent example of a marketing system analysis in a problem situation is provided by Applebaum (1965) in a case description. A supermarket chain is required to make a decision on whether to open a store within a discount house in a city where the chain already has a significant share of market.

One of the most important factors to consider in such a decision is the potential effect on the present stores of a discount store. Such questions as the following must be asked:

1. What are the trading areas of the present stores?
2. What would be the trading area of the discount operation?
3. Would the effect on the present stores be different if another firm went into the discount operation?
4. What is the general experience with discount supermarket operations?
5. What would be the shopping pattern in a discount operation with regard to such factors as number of weekly transactions, sales per transaction, and the type of merchandise (meat, produce, packaged groceries, etc.) bought?

At this stage, one is considering the questions that must be answered before a decision may be made. Of course, such questions cannot be divorced from the objectives of the firm.

### *Identifying Objectives*

The problem of dealing with multiple objectives has already been discussed. Here we discuss the problem of ascertaining these objectives.

As Churchman, Ackoff, and Arnoff (1957) point out, the first step in finding the objectives is to identify the decision maker or decision makers.

There may be a series of decision makers in an important decision. Rough screening of alternatives, for example, may be performed at one level on the basis of written policies, with the final decision made by some other groups or persons. One man may or may not have a veto. There may even be conflicting objectives by different people concerned with the decision.

Organization charts do not provide the necessary information about who makes what decisions, although they do provide a useful first cut at the problem. One of the great virtues of the information audit is that decision makers in the organization can be established through this means, provided that the right questions are asked.

One of the significant difficulties in establishing objectives is that decision makers, like consumers, often tend to give acceptable answers that may obscure real motivations. Answers tend to be couched in terms of return on investment, minimum costs, and other economic considerations. This is not to suggest that such considerations are unimportant—ultimately decisions must be justified on economic grounds. Other criteria, however, may play a critical role.

Churchman, Ackoff, and Arnoff (1957) suggest that the decision maker be asked what he would do if the research were to yield (one by one) each of the possible outcomes. If the decision maker were to indicate that he would not act on the basis of the recommendation in a particular outcome, exploration of his reason for refusal could lead to unstated objectives. One study, for example, is mentioned where research indicated a particular factory site, but the decision maker refused the recommendation because he did not want to have anything to do with a union leader in that region.

### *Alternative Courses of Action*

During the preliminary stage of problem formulation it is important not to restrict the list of alternatives, even though some may not seem possible. At this stage an active imagination is an asset. In the supermarket example, the obvious alternatives are to accept the offer to operate the supermarket in the discount house or not to accept it. A host of other alternatives, from opening our own discount house to clamoring for legislation against food discounters, also should at least be considered.

When the objectives are specified, the alternative courses of action are outlined, and some critical questions relating to the system are raised, the next step is to formulate a model of the system.

## Constructing the Model

The model may be thought of as a bridge between the objectives on the one hand and the alternatives on the other. What objectives may be satisfied by which alternatives and to what degree will they be satisfied? Associated with each possible outcome is a payoff. One model may be used to assess the payoffs associated with particular outcomes while another is used to construct and connect alternative actions to outcomes, or both steps may be taken in the same model.

For example, the Bayesian model begins with a payoff table and is a means of probabilistically connecting outcomes with actions. The payoff table itself is specified in some other manner.

What is the source of the model? Buzzell (1964, p. 47) suggests that the most common sources are analogies, implicit theories, historical data, and experimentation. We shall add one other source, surveys of behavior, to this list.

### *Analogy*

Perhaps the basic factor of any learning experience is to express what is new in terms of what is already understood. For example, it is common in teaching electricity in high school physics to draw the analogy between voltage and the height of a dam and between current and the amount of water flowing over the dam. Drawing analogies is both a weakness and a strength of man: it is a weakness in that it takes true creative genius to break the bonds of established thinking and to look at a problem in a completely new way, and it is a strength in that it allows man to comprehend a wide variety of phenomena on the basis of their similiarities.

The linear programming model is an example of a model that has had wide application in a variety of business problems, from production scheduling to media selection. Of course, there is often a tendency to "stretch" a model to fit a particular problem (where it does not really fit) because of much experience with that model. In this case, the answers generated by the model will be found to be at fault. Some of the essential features of reality are either left out or distorted. Many marketing experts, for example, feel that the linear programming model is not an adequate representation of the media selection problem because the relationships are essentially nonlinear.

### *Implicit Theories*

Executives familiar with the problem being modeled should have some notion of the underlying structure of the system. It is this implicit theory on which they would presumably act if a formal model were not being constructed. Why not ask them to formalize their theories, with the help of the researcher?

One would be foolish to construct a model of some system without interviewing those familiar with it. Nevertheless, Buzzell (1964) concludes that obtaining implicit theories may be both difficult and dangerous; difficult because managers "find it unnatural to develop systematic rationales for their decisions" and dangerous because there is evidence that managers' theories often tend to be internally inconsistent, as well as inconsistent between managers.

### *Analysis of Historical Data*

Historical data provide the most useful sources of models.[5] In particular, historical data become extremely useful if data are available for variables that could explain the underlying process via a behavioral model.

Although the literature is not replete with examples of great successes, marketing models have been built from historical data. The authors take the optimistic view that as marketing becomes better understood (particularly with regard to the incorporation of models from the behavioral sciences) models will become more useful.

One thing is certain. If a mathematical model cannot be built that adequately explains the past in a certain situation, no hope exists for predicting or controlling the future by the use of such a model.

### *Experimentation*

Of course, historical data suffer from the malaise common to all nonexperimental data—a lack of control of the administration of treatments. Quasi-experimental designs, as discussed in Chapter 7, are frequently possible. Otherwise, it may be necessary to experiment in order to resolve the question of causality with respect to some relationship.

As an illustration, consider the following problem currently facing one of the authors. All M.B.A. candidates at the University of Iowa are required to take a statistics course in which calculus is liberally employed. A prerequisite for the course is a quantitative methods course, which is waived if the student has completed two semesters of calculus.

It appears that students who achieved a grade of D in the second calculus course (even when followed by courses in higher mathematics in which grades were marginal) and who are waived out of the quantita-

[5] Buzzell (1964, p. 48) feels, however, that models based on historical data often degenerate to trend analysis.

tive methods course tend not to do well in the statistics course. Although this is fairly conclusively demonstrated from historical data, the causal factor and the solution to the problem do not naturally follow from the analysis.

Would students who have had calculus, but who have not done well in it, benefit by taking the quantitative methods course before proceeding to the statistics course? This depends on the reason for the poor performance in statistics. If the difficulty in the latter course is due to an inadequate background in calculus, and if a refresher course remedies this difficulty, requiring such students to take the quantitative methods course should help. But if the low grades in calculus can be interpreted as symptomatic of a general inability to cope with mathematics, there is less reason to be hopeful about any proposed action to require the quantitative methods course of students who have done poorly in calculus.

Historical data have provided the means here of problem identification, but not of solution. It is clear that the best way to ascertain the benefits to be achieved by requiring the quantitative methods course of all students who had not done well in calculus would be to assign such students at random to one of two treatments: to take the quantitative methods course or not to take the course. A comparison of the achievement of the two groups in the statistics course could then be made.

In general, any behavioral equation of aggregate behavior in a model is determined either from historical data or from experimentation.

### *Surveys of Behavior*

There is one further source of models that is very important in simulation studies—surveys of actual behavior. Such studies may or may not include motivation, but they must include a study of actual reactions to various situations. Typically, it becomes necessary to ascertain the rules, implicit or explicit, that guide decisions of a key person or persons in the model. For example, a number of studies have been directed to the question of how a physician becomes aware of and chooses to prescribe a particular drug.[6] These studies were not experiments but sample surveys.

## Deriving a Solution

A solution to a model should be found analytically, if possible; if not, it should be found by simulation. As models become more complex, the latter approach becomes more prevalent.

[6] A summary article on the topic is provided by Bauer and Wortzel (1966).

*Analytical Solutions*

Analytical solutions are achieved deductively and are perfectly general. For example, consider the following two equations:

$$v = 7x^2 \qquad \text{(A)}$$

$$y = 2v + 7x \qquad \text{(B)}$$

By substitution it is possible to reduce this system to one equation that yields $y$ as a function of $x$. We have

$$y = 2(7x^2) + 7x$$

or

$$y = 14x^2 + 7x$$

which is a general solution.

Given any value of $x$, we may now find values for both $v$ and $y$ directly.

*Simulated Solutions*

We shall consider simulated solutions under the classifications of numerical techniques and Monte Carlo techniques.

Numerical techniques. Numerical techniques consist essentially of trial and error, although efficient techniques, such as Newton's method, reduce the necessary computation. In the previous example, values of $v$, $x$, and $y$ could be substituted in the equations until they were satisfied. This would constitute numerical analysis.

Notice that the answer can be in numerical values only when such techniques are employed. For example, one solution is given by $x = 0$, $y = 0$, and $v = 0$. There are, however, an infinite number of possible solutions to the problem.

It is evident that numerical methods are inefficient and do not carry as much information as a general solution. Nevertheless, they are frequently necessary when analytical techniques are impossible.

Monte Carlo solutions. Frequently one or more relationships in a model are probabilistic. For example, we may build a model that includes a specification such that the consumer may respond in various ways to a particular stimulus, with specified probabilities of the possible responses. If the model cannot be solved uniquely, values are selected randomly from the probability distribution and then a solution is attained. The procedure is repeated a number of times, yielding a probability distribution on the outcomes.

Of course, such procedures require the use of a high-speed computer in about any realistic application. Thus years of time in the real world can be simulated in minutes or hours on the computer.

**TABLE 3-2** A Monte Carlo Simulation of Customer Processing

| Period | Customer Arrival | Backlog in Minutes | Period | Customer Arrival | Backlog in Minutes |
|---|---|---|---|---|---|
| 1 | | 0 | 16 | *L* | 5 |
| 2 | | 0 | 17 | *L* | 10 |
| 3 | | 0 | 18 | *S* | 15 |
| 4 | *L* | 0 | 19 | *S* | 15 |
| 5 | | 5 | 20 | *L* | 15 |
| 6 | | 0 | 21 | | 20 |
| 7 | *L* | 0 | 22 | *S* | 15 |
| 8 | | 5 | 23 | *S* | 15 |
| 9 | *S* | 0 | 24 | | 15 |
| 10 | *S* | 0 | 25 | | 10 |
| 11 | *L* | 0 | 26 | *S* | 5 |
| 12 | | 5 | 27 | *S* | 5 |
| 13 | *S* | 0 | 28 | | 5 |
| 14 | | 0 | 29 | | 0 |
| 15 | *L* | 0 | 30 | *S* | 0 |

We shall illustrate the procedure by a simple waiting-line problem (which could actually be solved analytically). Suppose that we have a check-out counter in a store. There is a 50 per cent probability that a customer will appear at the counter during any 5-minute interval. We shall assume that there is zero probability that two customers will arrive in any given 5-minute period. If a customer arrives with a large order, it takes 10 minutes to process the order. If the customer arrives with a small order, it takes only 5 minutes to process the order. Approximately half of the customers have large orders and half small orders.

It is evident that the average order takes 7½ minutes to process. Also, on the average, one order arrives every 10 minutes. Thus one check-out counter should be sufficient. But is it?

Table 3-2 represents a Monte-Carlo simulation of 2½ hours or thirty periods of operation of the store. A table of random numbers was used to generate a 50 per cent probability of a customer arriving in each 5-minute period.[7] If a customer arrives, the same procedure is used to determine whether the order is large or small. The first column of the table indicates the period number, with each period representing 5 minutes. A blank in the second column indicates no customer arrival, an

[7] Since it is impossible to truly find a "fair" coin, a table of random numbers is to be preferred to coin tossing.

$S$ indicates a small-order arrival, and an $L$ indicates a large-order arrival. All orders are assumed to arrive at the beginning of the period. If the order cannot be immediately processed, it is backlogged.

In the example, no orders arrive until the fourth period, when a large order arrives. Since it takes 10 minutes to process the order, a 5-minute backlog exists at the beginning of the next period.

It is not until the sixteenth period that a customer arrives with an order while another order is still being processed. Thereafter, eight other customers have to wait before their order can begin to be processed. Thus nine out of the seventeen customers who arrived have to wait for another customer's order to be processed. Five customers wait 15 minutes (in addition to the waiting time required for their own orders to be processed), one waits 10 minutes, and three wait 5 minutes.

Whether or not another check-out counter should be added would depend on the cost of another counter and clerk as compared to the cost of dissatisfied customers and lost sales because of the formation of waiting lines.

## Testing the Model

We have defined a model as containing within it the essential qualities of the thing being modeled. Although the solutions derived from a model may be perfectly consistent with the assumptions of the model, these solutions are invalid unless the assumptions themselves are realistic and sufficient. The validity of the model can be ascertained by examining the assumptions, the solutions, or both. The techniques employed are to look at face validity, to predict past results, to experiment, or to compare with alternate methods.

### *Face Validity*

Both assumptions and solutions may be examined from the point of view of face validity. That is, one raises the question of whether or not these assumptions and solutions make intuitive sense. Many marketing models, for example, have been constructed in which the level of promotional expenditures is omitted. Since promotional expenditures play a key role in most marketing strategies, any strategy derived from such a model is at best inadequate. In this case, the model has failed the test of face validity on its assumptions, since the assumption is that promotion is either constant or irrelevant.

If a model were to generate a solution suggesting that the firm put all its money into promotion and fire the sales force to a man, this too would make the model highly suspect. Although one can think of extreme instances where such a strategy might be optimal, the more likely explanation is that the model is invalid.

### *Predicting Past Results*

A commonly employed technique in testing a model is to see how well the model predicts the past. If the model cannot predict the past, for which data is available, it most likely will also do a poor job with respect to the future.

One unforgivable error is frequently made with respect to this technique. Sometimes researchers will use the same data in testing the model as were used to construct it. The model emerges from such a test with an absolutely undeserved aura of validity.

For example, suppose that a trend line of sales were established on the basis of two points. If the model were then employed to see if it could predict sales in those years, it would do so perfectly. Nevertheless, it is quite conceivable that the model would give grossly inaccurate results for any other year.

One way of guarding against this error is to employ the so-called "split-half" technique. This involves dividing the data into two parts, one of which is used as a base to construct the model and the other to test the model.

### *Experimentation*

Experiments may be performed to test both the relationships in the model and solutions from the model. For example, a behavioral equation of demand could be validated experimentally. A particular solution to the entire model could be tested by a field experiment involving the controllable inputs.

Generally speaking, most experimentation in modeling is confined to finding particular relationships during the stage of model construction. The more complex the model, the more difficult it is to perform an experiment that would test the entire model. Experimentation is discussed in Chapter 7.

### *Comparison with Other Methods*

Sales could be forecast industry-wide under a macro model, and company sales then derived by estimating market share. (Both macro and micro forecasting models will be examined in Chapter 15.) The solution to this model is thus aggregate company sales.

A test of the macro model may be accomplished by comparing the solution (predicted sales) with a solution to a micro model. The latter model could consist of individual predictions of customer sales, for example, which would be aggregated to yield company sales.

Such a comparison permits the researcher to have some confidence in his models when two approaches yield similar results. Of course, it still remains possible for both approaches to be incorrect. In addition, if the solutions of the two approaches diverge, one must look further in order to validate one or the other of the models.

### Establishing Controls over the Solution

A model describes a system at a particular point in time. Although the parameters and relationships in the system may be appropriate at that point in time, all systems undergo continual change. Eventually, this change is sufficient to make the original model inadequate.

Churchman, Ackoff, and Arnoff (1957, p. 597) list three steps in the design of a control system for a model:

1. A list is made of the variables, parameters, and relationships either in the model or in that which should enter the model under different conditions.
2. A procedure is developed for detecting significant changes in each of the parameters and relationships listed.
3. The adjustments to be made if a significant change occurs are specified.

In cases where a model is constructed for a special problem and then not used again, the control problem is not relevant. For models that are employed in the continual processing of information, such as real-time models, the control is mandatory.

Of course, elaborate procedures for a continual test of every parameter and relationship in a complex model are generally out of the question. For this reason, it is important to identify those parameters and relationships to which the model is most sensitive. These should be checked frequently, with the frequency determined by the economic consequences of errors due to unrecognized changes in these parameters and models, the cost of checking, and the probability of error.

## SUMMARY AND FINAL COMMENTS

It is difficult to separate the process of model building in marketing from the people involved, although we have attempted to do so. The advent of the computer signified an expanded vista for rational decision making. Nevertheless, the application of the computer in nonscientific work in business has been largely confined to data processing.

The potential applications of the computer are largely untapped when the role of the computer is confined to the processing of information, but this restricted role is the one that is least threatening to management. When routine decisions, such as initiating purchasing orders, are computerized, greater use is made of the capabilities of the system, and most large companies have gone this far. The next step is to use the computer to simulate the environment of the firm—where test-marketing is performed not in Milwaukee but in a magnetic core. This step is inevitable.

It is conceivable that at some future date (we hope far off) the computer will completely take over executive functions. Current research has produced computers that play chess and derive logical theories, completely debunking the once widely held notion that the computer is a fast-calculating idiot. As unpalatable as it may be to many of us, the eventual role of the *thinking* machine in business will undoubtedly be greater than we would like. The exact nature of this role, however, is now largely an unknown.

## REFERENCES

Applebaum, W. "Measuring Retail Market Penetration for a Discount Food Supermarket—A Case Study," *Journal of Retailing,* Summer 1965.

Ackoff, R. L. *Scientific Method: Optimizing Applied Research Decisions.* New York: Wiley, 1962.

Bass, F., Buzzel, R. D., & Others. *Mathematical Models and Methods in Marketing.* Homewood, Ill.: Richard D. Irwin, 1961.

Bauer, R. A., & Wortzel, L. H. "Doctor's Choice: The Physician and His Sources of Information About Drugs," *Journal of Marketing Research,* February 1966, pp. 40–47.

Buzzell, R. D. *Mathematical Models and Marketing Management.* Boston, Mass.: Division of Research, Graduate School of Business Administration, Harvard University, 1964.

Churchman, C. W., Ackoff, R. L., & Arnoff, E. L. *Introduction to Operations Research.* New York: Wiley, 1957.

Day, R. L. *Marketing Models—Quantitative and Behavioral.* Scranton, Pa.: International Textbook, 1964.

Fishburn, P. C. "Utility Theory," *Management Science,* January 1968, pp. 335–378.

Frank, R. E., Kuehn, A. A., & Massy, W. F. *Quantitative Techniques in Marketing Analysis.* Homewood, Ill.: Richard D. Irwin, 1962.

Langhoff, P. (Ed.) *Models, Measurement and Marketing.* Englewood Cliffs, N.J.: Prentice-Hall, 1963.

PART I

# CASES

1. Gem Frocks, Inc.
2. Superior Markets, Inc.
3. Wrigley Appliance Corporation

## GEM FROCKS, INC.*

### THE ROLE OF A MARKETING INFORMATION SYSTEM IN THE MANAGEMENT OF A SALES FORCE

In July 1965, Mr. Arthur Greenspan of Gem Frocks, Inc., which manufactured women's coordinated sportswear, was considering a proposal from Mr. Eugene Miller, the Boston office manager. This proposal advocated expansion of a recently installed marketing information system to encompass several new types of sales reports. According to Mr. Miller, the new reports would permit more effective management of the sales force, and would more than justify the time and expense of field and home office personnel in gathering the requisite information and preparing the reports. Ultimately Mr. Miller envisioned even further expansion of the marketing information system so that it would be a total "sales information system."

Mr. Miller, a 1963 graduate from a well-known eastern business school, was responsible for the budgeting and marketing reports of the company. In develop-

* This case was made possible by the cooperation of a company which remains anonymous. It was prepared by Stanley A. Tractenberg under the supervision of Associate Professor Robert D. Buzzell and Assistant Professor Scott M. Cunningham of the Harvard Business School. It is intended as a basis for class discussion rather than to indicate either effective or inffective handling of administrative situations.  This case has been made available through the courtesy of Stanley A. Tractenberg.

ing these reports, Mr. Miller utilized an IBM 1440 computer which Gem Frocks had rented in October 1964. This computer made it possible to carry out new kinds of analyses and to report more types of information, more accurately and frequently, than had previously been practical.

### *Apparel Industry Background*

The apparel industry was comprised of about 27,000 firms manufacturing clothing and related products from textile fabrics (knit and woven), and other materials, including leather, rubberized fabric, plastic, and fur.

Small profits, little capital equipment investment, and few employees per firm characterized much of the industry. The apparel industry had the lowest profit/sales ratio of all manufacturing categories. During the 1950's, annual investment in new capital equipment per concern had averaged $3,000, as compared to $30,000 for other firms in manufacturing. Companies employing less than 10 workers made up 40% of the firms in the industry, and companies that employed fewer than 50 workers encompassed 80% of the firms in the industry.

Trade association officials had predicted that the $15 billion retail sales of women's wear would increase at a rate of 8% to 12% annually between 1965 and 1970. The women's rate of growth was attributed by the officials to the move to suburbia, with its increased outdoor activities; to the higher proportion of women working which required office clothes; to the change from blue collar to white collar jobs, which made several outfits necessary in place of a uniform or outfit; to the increase in higher education, which stimulated the desire to be well-dressed; to the sale of 3.5 million fashion magazines monthly, that reached 10 million readers with the latest styles; and to continuing prosperity, with more money made available for purchases.

During the 1960's, industry publications had publicized several trends in the apparel business. The high growth rate in sales of the larger firms was attributed to both generated sales and acquisitions, as exemplified by Jonathan Logan (with annual sales of $135 million), Bobbie Brooks ($90 million), and Puritan Fashions ($50 million). Diversification from a single product to a full line, and from full line to lines for men *and* women were believed to lessen the traditional dependence for the success of a company on having a "hot number." In 1964, Russ Togs, a full-line manufacturer, led the industry in return on sales with 6.9% after tax. Garland Knitting had increased sales by $12 million in three years by changing to a full line from strictly sweater making. Vertical integration has also occurred as the larger of the concerns purchased or built textile plants, such as Bobbie Brooks and Jonathan Logan. Concurrent with the growth in larger firms, *Women's Wear Daily* reported an estimate emanating from a 1965 conference hosted by the investment banking firm of Lionel D. Edie and Company that since the mid-1950's, the number of firms in the industry had declined by 4,000. (See Exhibit 1.)

The publications also noted the trend for women's wear companies to go public, with over 100 firms doing so during 1961–1962 alone.

Part of the explanation for the growth of larger firms lay in the attitudes of store buyers. Most of the buyers, especially those representing the larger stores, stated their preferance for concentrating their purchases among fewer, larger manufacturers than they had in the past. Ease of viewing the new fashions, better quality control, competitive pricing, and faster refilling of orders were among the reasons given for placing orders with the larger, full-line apparel firms. In addition, they claimed that brand preferences among teenagers and young adults were developing because of full lines and advertising. A spokesman for Bobbie Brooks attributed sales of $1 million in a new skiwear line and $3 million in a new swimwear line to their known name and respected position in the industry.

In the decade 1953–1963, there had been a 36% increase in annual advertising expenditures for apparel; all other industries increased by 74% in the same period. The increase in advertising was credited by advertising agencies to the medium- and larger-sized firms in the industry.

### *The Sportswear Business*

Although there were many small firms in the coordinated sportswear market, there were approximately a dozen national firms that competed directly with Gem Frocks. Among them were: Russ Togs, Majestic, Evan Picone, Personal Rosecrest, Jack Winter, and Sportempos.

The phrase "coordinated sportswear" meant that the items within each group were compatible in terms of matching or harmonious colors, styles, and fabrics. The consumer was offered different sizes, e.g., a size 8 top and 10 bottom; different silhouettes, e.g., a jacket with a slim pleated or A-line skirt; and a selection of colors, e.g., a brown/blue sweater with either a brown or blue skirt.

Gem Frocks' management believed that coordinated sportswear would do better than the other categories of women's wear, because they felt coordinates offered the chance to "mix and match," and thus to create a variety of outfits, which especially appealed to young women. (Women between the ages of 15 and 24 purchased over 30% of all female clothes.)

### *The Retail Trade*

Retail outlets for women's sportswear included 43,000 women's clothing speciality stores, 27,000 women's ready-to-wear stores, 14,000 family clothing stores, and 3,000 department stores. Other outlets included mail order houses, discount department stores, general merchandise stores, and millinery stores.

BID RTW INDUSTRY AUTOMATE, CONSOLIDATE OR LIQUIDATE

*Focus Shake Off the Rust or Bite the Dust*

NEW YORK.—The apparel industry here is functioning inefficiently and with outdated tools.

The seventh largest among the nation's major industries, it is the least efficient in a list of 20.

Its manufacturers lack the spirit of real entrepreneurs and won't make meaningful capital investments for advanced machinery—like $100,000 machine units now becoming available—even as part of a concentrated effort to deal with foreign competition.

Soon the industry will also be deprived of tariff and quota protection.

The only way out of the dilemma for the apparel industry is automation and consolidation. In other words: Merge or be left behind!

This picture of the industry, painted during a panel discussion before a group of men's and women's apparel manufacturers by Lionel D. Edie & Co., management consultant, Wednesday, met with only meek protests from manufacturers.

"Where are those apparel making machines that machine makers have been talking about?" they asked. "All we are told is to be patient but the wonder machines are not forthcoming," they protested.

But the four Edie experts insisted they are available, are, in fact, being used by European apparel manufacturers right now.

The speakers were Jaromir Ledecky, John Enders, Dr. George Frey and Dr. Pierre Rinfret, with E. "Bud" Meredith as moderator.

These "four horsemen" drummed this message into the ears of the manufacturers:

- You must grow up, get big, become efficient.
- You are now where the automobile industry was 40 or 50 years ago when cars were made by small manufacturers in thousands of machine shops.
- "Frenzied" competition, such as was widespread in the 18th Century and still the practice on SA, must give way to consolidation and automation.
- Figure it out: Will you be around 10 years from now or will your customers patronize someone else, perhaps foreign makers? Will you be squeezed between giants?

Not only is "consolidation and automation" a matter of urgency from the efficiency point of view. It is also a prudent consideration given the way the industry's customers look at the manufacturer.

Thus, the manufacturers were told that the giant retail firms like Penney's, Macy's, Federated Department Stores and all the rest, prefer to deal with big people who can produce big. They demand quantities of merchandise, manu-

**Exhibit 1** Gem Frocks, Inc. *Women's Wear Daily* article on the future of the apparel industry. Reprinted by permission of *Women's Wear Daily,* May 13, 1965. Fairchild Publications, Inc.

factured to exact specifications for their growing number of units. Who else can supply them but big-time manufacturers?

Who else can deal with the retail giants but those makers who are financially strong to carry stocks, who can product fast and deliver with utmost speed?

Charts and tables were used to illustrate that the apparel industry is low man on the totem pole of American industry.

These statistics, shown on slides, made these points:

• The apparel industry has the lowest sales concentration in terms of per cent of total sales of the four largest companies in each industry.

• Among 20 industries operating plants with 20 or more employes, the apparel (and related) industries show the greatest number of plants—13,129—with the smallest sales volume per plant, only $1.29 million.

• The four largest companies in the apparel industry account for only 5 per cent of the industry's total output, compared with the textile industry where the four largest firms account for 22 per cent of total volume, and retailing where the four largest factors represent 10 per cent of the total.

THE INFERIORITY of the apparel industry, as shown by these statistics must be eliminated, the speakers insisted. Those who want to be important in dealings with the highly efficient and well concentrated customers must be in a position of "dealing with equals in order to survive and be profitable."

Yes, they said, bigness is the trend and "smallness" is fatal in our complex and rapidly growing economy.

The economists' concept of "economies of scale," as applied to the apparel industry, the speakers said, will have these effects on SA:

• It is more efficient for a salesman to sell a complete and diverse line.

• It is more economical to sell to a few large users than many small ones, scattered over a wide area. It saves time and money for seller and buyer.

• Our competitive economy forces industry to use modern tools such as new packaging. EDP and accounting machines, highly productive advertising and promotional material, all of which requires great capital outlay.

• In order to be competitive, individual concerns require expert services of outside designers, financial, legal and marketing talent as "no one person cannot wear so many different hats."

• Pricing problems become oppressive if one must buy from and sell to companies much larger than one's own. The price squeezes are likely to become unbearable.

• Transportation economies are *more* feasible in the framework of high-volume production.

THE AUDIENCE was invited to compare its production statistics with those of the rest of the nation's industries.

If a maker's investment per worker has not tripled since World War II, he is behind the average of American industry, the perplexed SA people were told.

If they cannot intensify their utilization of labor, either by cutting down

**Exhibit 1** (*Continued*)

on labor or by lowering the labor content of their product, they are in a bad way.

And if they cannot reduce the man hours needed to produce $1,000 worth of manufactured goods or increase the value added per man hour, they are in for trouble.

And what about automation? Will it put people out of work?

The opposite is the case, the speaker claimed: Automation requires capital expenditure. Industries using more capital, provide more jobs for more people, and vice versa.

THE CORRECTION of these shortcomings can only come through merging with or acquiring other companies. But in doing this, prospects for mergers or acquisitions must avoid stumbling blocks and pitfalls. There are material and psychological things to watch before one leaps, the listeners were told.

For instance, individuals who have been identified with their business all their lives, must know what they will be doing after the merger: Will they be part of the business or will they be sitting at a big desk with nothing to do?

Will their business be used for a "kiting" operation? Will they be compatible with their partners? What will the future of the business be? How will the management team that is being taken over function? And so on.

The speakers explained, after the meeting, that anti-trust considerations will not be involved for businesses in the $2 or $20 million bracket for some five years or so.

FRED EICHELBAUM

**Exhibit 1** (*Continued*)

The vice president for sales of Gem Frocks described the method by which the typical women's wear buyer for a department store or chain purchased clothes and the manner in which the function was being affected by the computer.

A buyer "shopped the market" before placing her initial orders. She examined the trade publications' articles and advertisements, discussed with other buyers the new styles, viewed visiting salesmen's lines, visited companies' showrooms in New York and/or other leading market cities, and reviewed her last year's sales to determine which companies' merchandise had and had not sold well.

When the buyer found items or lines she liked, she would place initial orders. She left a large proportion of her budget for later in the season, so that she had money left to add to her lines and to reorder out-of-stock items. The buyer typically purchased coordinated sportswear from more than one manufacturer to give a total "look" to her department.

Traditionally, buyers had also played the role of operating management. In this role, they were responsible for obtaining and/or reviewing information on what was and was not selling in their departments as well as expense and profit information. The department store buyer had traditionally obtained sales information by standing on the sales floor to watch what was being sold from manually maintained perpetual inventory records, and by physical stock counts of the merchandise after a selling period.

With the advent of computerized processing of sales slips and inventory data the buyer had less need to be on the selling floor. In addition, the increase in branch store operations of many large retailers made it difficult for the buyer to spend much time on the sales floor of each store. These two factors resulted in the buyer being increasingly separated from the selling function and more restricted to the purchasing function.

The computer made it possible for the buyers to determine sales and inventory in each price range by style, color, and size, and the manner in which sales of each of the categories varied by branch. Since additions to the line and reorders depended on quick, accurate determination of trends, the computer lessened the element of chance and permitted the buyer to reorder more quickly in more economic quantities than was previously possible. In addition, electronic data processing permitted the buyer to identify slow moving items and take markdowns quickly.

*The Company*

Gem Frocks was formed in 1944, but the family's experience in the clothing industry had started in the 1880's with the grandfather of the current owners-managers. Richard Greenspan was president and directed designing; Steven Greenspan was vice president; and Arthur Greenspan was treasurer and responsible for financial control and sales management. Each of the brothers had joined the firm after completion of college and military service. (See Exhibit 2 for an orgainzation chart and Exhibit 3 for comparative financial statements for 1963 and 1964.)

Gem Frocks produced Misses' sizes, for the average woman, as compared to Juniors',[1] for the short and petite girl or woman, and Womens', for the larger proportioned and heavier women. The prices were "upper-medium" for the sportswear market. For example, in the sportswear business the low-price range for skirts at retail centered around $5, the medium-price range centered around $10, and the higher-price range started from $18. Gem Frocks' skirts would sell for about $13 retail. (See Exhibit 4 for sample ordering form showing retail and manufacturer prices for the items comprising a group.)

Gem Frocks manufactured 30 groups over a 12-month period which comprised

[1] Within the women's apparel trade the "size" difference between Misses and Junior clothes had become somewhat obscure in recent years. Currently the word "Junior" in contrast with "Misses" was thought by some to emphasize a "young, slim look" rather than a real difference in sizes.

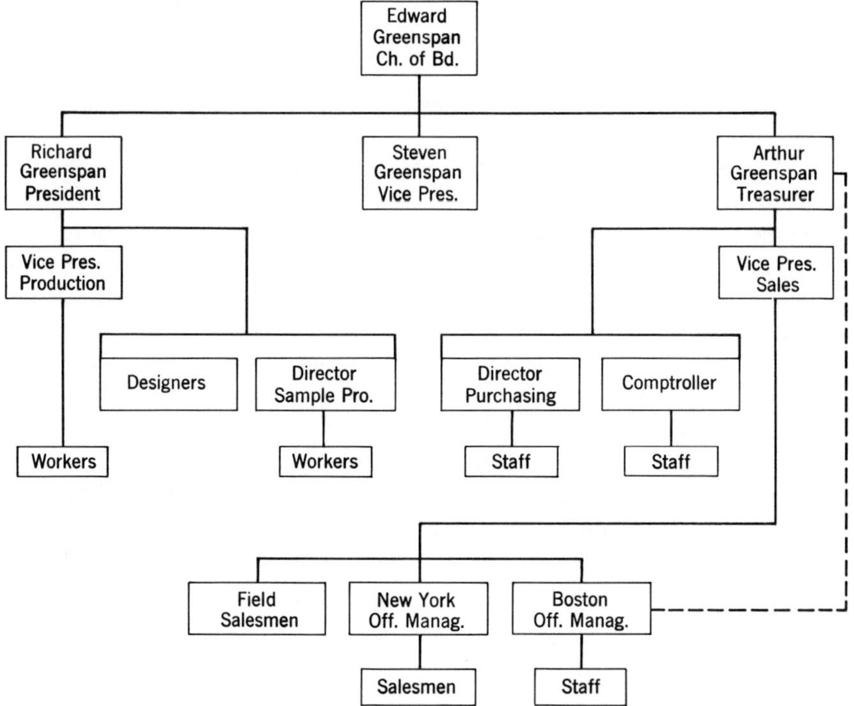


**Exhibit 2** Gem Frocks, Inc. Partial organization chart (as visualized by case writer—no formal chart existed).

seven seasonal lines. A line was a collection of groups which were designed to be sold during a specific time of the year or for a specific purpose. The seven lines were called: Early Spring, Late Spring, Summer, Transitional, Fall, Holiday, and mid-Winter. A group consisted of a number of items such as jackets, skirts, blouses, and shifts that were color coordinated and made of the same, similar, or coordinated fabrics in a series of styles. This coordination allowed the retailer to choose the items that she desired and yet present a full-range of clothes for the consumer. (See Exhibit 4 for the order form for the Irish Mist group.) The total number of items in a group ran into the hundreds because there were 9 to 100 styles, 1 to 5 colors, and 5 to 8 sizes. Some groups were: tweed group, boating group, shift group, and pants and tops group.

The groups were sold to 2,000 active accounts. The company had sold to 8,000 firms during its history. A sales executive said that if the company sold 7,500 accounts actively it would have essentially complete coverage of its poten-

| Balance sheet | Nov. 1, 1963 | Nov. 1, 1964 |
|---|---|---|
| Cash | $ 97,646 | $ 37,562 |
| Net accounts receivable | 1,398,722 | 1,695,620 |
| Inventory | 1,018,959 | 1,047,254 |
| Other current assets | — | 25,813 |
| Total current assets | $2,515,327 | $2,906,249 |
| Net fixed assets | 134,339 | 94,907 |
| Investments | 235,661 | 27,346 |
| Prepaid expenses | 18,798 | 85,444 |
| Other assets | 4,843 | — |
| Total assets | $2,908,968 | $3,013,946 |
| Due banks | $ 455,000 | $ 390,000 |
| Accounts payable | 830,540 | 784,345 |
| Other current liabilities | 202,415 | 434,881 |
| Total current liabilities | $1,487,955 | $1,700,239 |
| Common stock | 935,609 | 935,609 |
| Earned surplus | 485,404 | 378,098 |
| Total liabilities | $2,908,968 | $3,013,946 |
| Income statement for the year ended | Nov. 1, 1963 | Nov. 1, 1964 |
| Net sales | $8,929,133 | $9,754,325 |
| Cost of goods sold | 6,908,939 | 7,864,443 |
| Gross profit | $2,020,194 | $1,889,882 |
| Expenses | 1,646,990 | 1,739,664 |
| Net profit before taxes | $ 373,204 | $ 150,218 |

**Exhibit 3** Gem Frocks, Inc. Comparative financial statements for 1963 and 1964.

tial market. It made 65% of its sales to traditional department stores, 30% to specialty shops, and 5% to chain discount department stores.

*The Production Cycle*

In Gem Frocks' design department, three designers for style and one designer for color and fabric produced sketches, having used the sucessful items of the corresponding group of the past year, fashion magazines, styles of more

**IRISH MIST**

| Bill/To: Account No. | Ship To: Account No. | Mark For Account No. | ORDER DATE | |
|---|---|---|---|---|
| | | | CUST. ORDER NO. | DEPT. NO. |
| | | | SALESMAN | ORIGIN |

| BILL TO | SHIP TO | SHIP VIA P.P. ☐ EXPRESS ☐ |
|---|---|---|
| ADDRESS | ADDRESS | TERMS 8/10 EOM Net 30 Days FOB Factory |
| CITY / STATE | CITY / STATE | K.P. / K.V. |

| | STYLE | PRICE | PCS. | COST | DESCRIPTION | A.R.P. | SEAMIST — GREN 6 8 10 12 14 16 18 20 | ROSEMIST — RED 6 8 10 12 14 16 18 20 | LILACMIST — LILA 6 8 10 12 14 16 18 20 |
|---|---|---|---|---|---|---|---|---|---|
| TWO PART SUIT LOOK | 5400 | 11.75 | | | EMBROIDERED JACKET | 20.00 | | | |
| | 5401 | 10.75 | | | PORTRAIT COLLAR JACKET | 18.00 | | | |
| | 5410 | 6.75 | | | SLIM SKIRT | 12.00 | | | |
| | 5411 | 7.75 | | | A-LINE SKIMMER SKIRT | 13.00 | | | |
| | 5412 | 7.75 | | | A-LINE GORED POCKET SKIRT | 13.00 | | | |
| TWO PART DRESS LOOK | 5405 | 7.75 | | | EMBR. EMPIRE OVERBLOUSE | 13.00 | | | |
| | 5406 | 7.75 | | | EMBR. SCOOP NECK O'BLSE. | 13.00 | | | |
| | 5407 | 6.00 | | | COWL BOW OVERBLOUSE | 10.00 | | | |
| | 5408 | 6.75 | | | PETAL COLLAR OVERBLOUSE | 12.00 | | | |
| | 5410 | 6.75 | | | SLIM SKIRT | 12.00 | | | |
| | 5411 | 7.75 | | | A-LINE SKIMMER SKIRT | 13.00 | | | |
| | 5412 | 7.75 | | | A-LINE GORED POCKET SKIRT | 13.00 | | | |
| SHIFTS | 5415 | 11.75 | | | EMBROIDERED SHIFT | 20.00 | | | |
| | 5416 | 10.75 | | | SCALLOP COLLAR SHIFT | 18.00 | | | |
| FLORAL PRINT BLOUSE | 5420 | 4.75 | | | FLORAL PRINT BOW BLOUSE | 8.00 | | | |
| CREPE BLOUSES | 5425 | 4.75 | | | CREPE SHAWL COLLAR BLOUSE | 8.00 | | | |
| | 5426 | 4.75 | | | CREPE BOW BLOUSE | 8.00 | | | |

| TOTAL STYLE | TOTAL PCS. | TOTAL $ |
|---|---|---|
| | | |

**Exhibit 4** Gem Frocks, Inc. Order form showing retail and manufacturer prices for the items comprising a group.

expensive clothes, and their own experience and talent. The company's designers said that they did not originate fashion, but translated it into upper-medium price garments after the fashion had been established by the trend setters.

The sketches were used by the sample department to make garments. The finished garments were modeled for a top management committee. Those items that they judged had the best chance of selling were returned to the sample department. There, the department made samples for the sales force and for the cutting department. The cutting department used their samples to cut patterns. For each style, a master control and status report was made up on which the promised date of delivery was entered and on which there was space to enter unit sales by color and size. From the early orders, decisions were reached to produce quantities of some items in excess of orders on hand, to discontinue others, and on still others to await specific orders. Completed garments were either shipped immediately to customers or hung on racks in inventory to await the completion of some of the other garments included in an order before shipment. It took approximately 1 to 6 weeks for fabric delivery (depending on availability), and from 5 to 6 weeks for production. Over $1\frac{1}{2}$ million garments were produced every year, with an average wholesale price of $5.50 for cotton garments and $7.50 for wool garments.

*The Advertising Program*

A Gem Frocks official responsible for advertising stated that the large amount of funds needed to build a national image was the reason that the company did not have a national advertising campaign. Two forms of advertising were used on a regional or local basis. The company's fiber manufacturers sponsored Gem Frocks' advertisements, such as "du Pont presents Gem Frocks." The company also sponsored cooperative advertisements with retail stores in local newspapers.

Other forms of advertising used by Gem Frocks included enclosures which stores sent to their charge customers in the monthly bills, promotional pieces, and personal letters. Enclosures showed illustrations of several different outfits, provided the customers with an order form, and were imprinted with the name of the cooperating store. They were sold to the store to help defray Gem Frocks' printing costs.

Sales promotional pieces for the trade, such as "Gem Frocks Dining Recommendations in New York" were sent to out-of-town buyers. The company had also developed a "personal approach" to advertising its products to store buyers through the use of individually typewritten letters. Usually these letters were form letters in nature but personalized with the name and address of the store and buyer. These letters sometimes reached a peak of 400 a week and often new mailings were made every three or four weeks to the same account. The letters always contained a sales pitch about a service or product.

About 30% of the mail was individually dictated in order to encompass certain points that were of particular concern to a buyer. According to company officials, the effectiveness of the letters to the trade was hard to measure but that several accounts had remarked to the salesmen about them. The salesmen supplied the necessary information for the personalized aspects of this correspondence through his order forms, activity reports, and phone calls.

*Organizational Structure of the Selling Effort*

Gem Frocks employed a total of 28 salesmen. Of these, 21 were classified as field salesmen, and the remaining seven were assigned to the New York sales office. The field salesmen reported directly to the Vice President of Sales, who in turn reported to the Treasurer, Arthur Greenspan. The seven salesmen assigned to the New York office reported to the office manager for the New York office, who in turn reported to the Vice President for Sales. (See Exhibit 2 for an organization chart.)

The Boston office manager, Mr. Miller, supervised a number of the staff functions of the firm but did not have any salesmen reporting directly to him. He reported to the Vice President for Sales for most purposes, but reported directly to the Treasurer for a few assignments as indicated by the dotted line in Exhibit 2.

Mr. Greenspan was responsible for the over-all direction of sales and advertising, in addition to his duties as chief financial officer. He frequently consulted with the President, Mr. Richard Greenspan, who was an active participant in the marketing activities of the firm. The President served as a major contact with many of the more important customers.

*The Field Salesmen*

Of the 21 field salesmen, all but seven were exclusive salesmen for Gem Frocks. The seven non-exclusive salesmen were located in the Midwest where Gem's volume was not sufficient to support them on an exclusive basis. (See Exhibit 5 for a map of sales territories.)

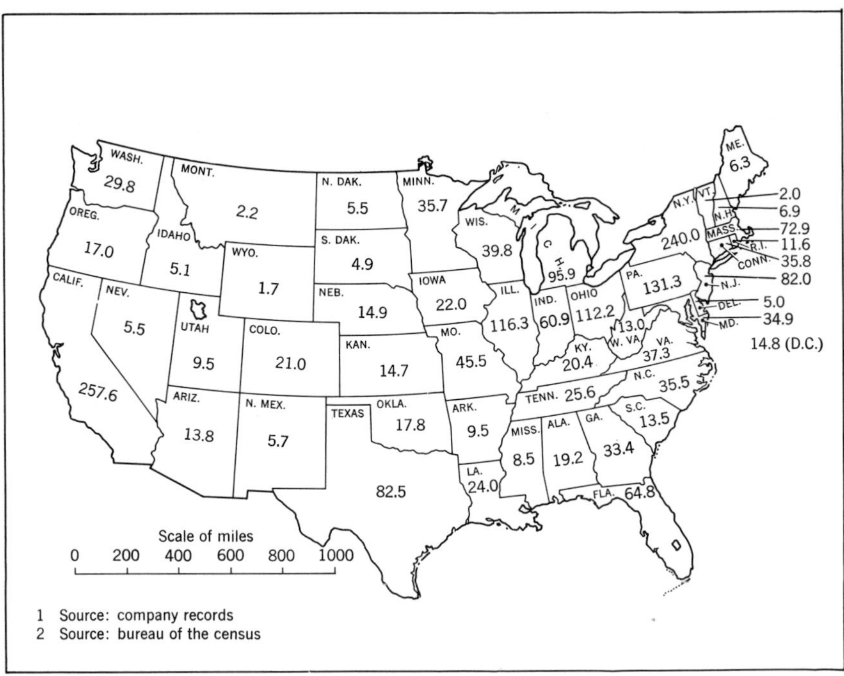


**Exhibit 5** Gem Frocks, Inc. Gem Frocks' salesmen's territories (*source:* company records) and retail sales of women's sportswear for all companies (*source:* Bureau of the Census) (in millions of dollars).

Although all of Gem's field salesman spent much of their time "on the road" four of them also maintained sales offices and showrooms at merchandise marts in either Los Angeles, Chicago, Dallas or Charlotte, N.C. A fifth sales office in New York City was maintained by the company for the convenience of out-of-town buyers on their periodic trips to New York.

All of the field salesmen spent some time each year in New York to visit with buyers from their own territories. Out-of-town buyers customarily visited New York during the two periods of heavy buying activity which preceded the traditional strong retail selling seasons of spring and fall by three to four months.

The two field salesmen in the New York area had office days in the New York sales office and showroom on Tuesday because it was the practice of the buyers in that area to visit showrooms (such as Gem Frocks') on that day. On other days the New York area field salesmen made calls on their existing accounts and prospects.

Nineteen of the 21 field salesmen were paid a commission of 6% of net sales. The remaining two field salesmen received a salary plus a commission for exceeding budget. These two salesmen were the most recently employed by the company.

One Boston sales executive noted that the company had three alternatives for controlling salesmen. The first two of these were adjustment of territory size and varying the amount of cooperation from the home office concerning mailings and publicity. Management felt that both of these methods had severe limitations, and thus neither had been used extensively. The third and most effective method of control consisted of the amount of service extended to customers of particular salesmen by the company. It was within the company's discretion to ascertain which salesmen's accounts obtained rapid delivery of reorders of fast-selling merchandise.

This same executive felt that the control problem was minimized with those salesmen who had confidence that the firm had their best interests at heart. Once this confidence was gained, the company was then in a position to influence the working habits of the salesmen. This executive hoped that an improved sales information system would be instrumental in this process. This executive described the salary plus commission for exceeding budget compensation plan under which the two newest salesmen worked as an experiment. Its purpose was to ascertain if more control could be exercised over the salesmen if their income depended not only on booking orders, but also on cooperating with the plans of the home office. The idea was to relate the base salary partly to cooperation with home office plans. Success to date was hard to determine.[2]

[2] Few experienced salesmen wished to work under such a compensation plan. Furthermore, management had been disappointed with the production of inexperienced salesmen in this field.

The company communicated with the salesmen through a weekly memo to salesmen which reviewed current articles from magazines about the trade or selling techniques and notices concerning the addition or the discontinuance of specific items in a group. Regional sales meetings were held before each major selling season (spring and fall) which provided an additional opportunity for the management of the company to communicate with the salesmen. Furthermore, a National Sales Meeting was held annually for primarily social and morale purposes. In addition, the President and Vice President traveled around the country before the beginning of each major selling season visiting salesmen and larger customers.

Salesmen were requested to file activity reports on their visit to each account. (See Exhibit 6 for a typical activity report.) These reports were intended to keep management up to date on the activities of the salesmen. Currently, only three field salesmen regularly file the reports. Two were the men on salary plus commission and one was a regular field salesman.

| DATE 4-1-65 | ACCOUNT ACTIVITY REPORT | SALESMAN MIKE ANDERSON 020 |
|---|---|---|
| ACCOUNT NAME THE HOUSE OF TEE | | BUYER MR. BERNARD TORTORICK |
| STREET ADDRESS 305 STATE ST. | | MDSE. MGR. |
| CITY AND STATE NEW LONDON, CONN. | | ADV. MGR. |

ORDER RECEIVED ☐ SUMMER ☐ MID-SUMMER ☐ TRANS-ITIONAL ☐ FALL ☐ HOLIDAY ☐ MID-WINTER ☐ TOTAL UNITS ______ $ ______

| WHERE SHOWED LINE | | STATUS OF ORDER | | TYPE OF STORE | | CLASSIFICATION | | SPECIAL INSTRUCTIONS |
|---|---|---|---|---|---|---|---|---|
| IN STORE | ✓ | MAILING ORDER | | DEPARTMENT | | EXCLUSIVE | | |
| SAMPLE ROOM | | PROMISED LATER | | SPECIALTY | ✓ | MEDIUM | | |
| N.Y. SHOW ROOM | | WON'T BUY NOW | ✓ | CHAIN OR BRANCH | ✓ | POPULAR | | |
| MARKET SHOW | | NO INTEREST | | DEPARTMENT | | ADVERTISING | | |
| PHONE | ✓ | BUYER OUT | | | | NO ADVERTISING | | |

MAILING LIST INFORMATION

PROSPECT ☐ NEW ACCOUNT ☐ OLD ACCOUNT ☑ PREVIOUSLY REPORTED ☐ CORRECT LIST ☐ NO MAIL ☐ REMOVE FROM LIST ☐

CUSTOMER REACTIONS AND COMMENTS

THIS ACCOUNT HAD TRIED THE LINE WITH FAIRLY GOOD DEPTH
AND WAS NOT TOO SUCCESSFUL WITH IT – CLAIMED WE'RE
TO MISSY – SUGGEST A LETTER EXPLAINING THE NEW CONCEPT
IN LOOK OF THE BIG 'R'

**Exhibit 6** Gem Frocks, Inc. Salesmen's account activity report requesting the Boston Office to write to an inactive account.

*The New York Sales Office*

There were seven salaried salesmen permanently attached to the New York sales office and showroom. This office was located in a building with 2,000 other manufacturers of sportswear and women's dresses. The salesmens' salaries ranged from $5,000 to $15,000 annually. The primary function of these salesmen was to service customers of field salesmen who frequently visited the New York office at times when field salesmen were traveling their territories. Full commissions were paid to the field salesmen on such sales even though they had been consummated by the New York office sales personnel.

In addition, these salesmen serviced a limited number of "house accounts." House accounts were large, retail organizations and chains with buying offices in New York or who periodically sent buying representatives to New York. The management of Gem Frocks believed these accounts to be too large to be assigned to any one commissioned salesman. House accounts were typified by organizations such as Macy's, Sterns, or J. L. Hudson. No commissions were paid on sales to house accounts.

The New York sales office booked about 40% of the annual sales of Gem Frocks. Of this amount, about 15% could be attributed to sales made to house accounts. The remainder were bookings made to nonhouse accounts and credited to specific field salesmen.

A company executive noted that plans were under consideration to place regional sales managers over all of the salesmen in the field. The managers would supervise and control the sales force to increase sales, to break into new markets, and to introduce new product lines. They would be responsible for the hiring and training of salesmen and in the opinion of management offered potential for better control over the sales force. While several of the salesmen had shown great managerial potential, the company had not committed itself to selecting managers from the sales force or any other single method of selecting managers.

*Sales Forecasting*

A sales forecast was used by the management for both production planning and in evaluating the salesmen. This forecast was developed by first deciding upon an expected or desired per cent increase over the previous year. Then individual lines and groups were apportioned a dollar amount in order to reach the total budget. Each salesman was then given a per cent of each group to book based upon his success or failure with the corresponding group the previous year. If a new group was introduced, a comparable group was used as a basis for the previous year. The forecasts, according to management, frequently had been inaccurate and usually were revised several times a season.

For example, the forecast for a particular group might be changed to make it more compatible with initial reactions from major retailers or with the actions of competitors. The forecast might also be modified for a specific salesman if management became aware of changes that had taken place in his territory. There were no separate forecasts, however, for specific accounts.

### *The Need for the Sales Information System*

In late spring of 1965 Mr. Miller proposed the systematic collection of sales information which, when processed on the computer acquired the previous October, would provide management with a better basis for controlling salesmen and making other marketing decisions. Mr. Miller explained why improved control of salesmen was of importance to many firms in the apparel field including Gem Frocks.

> Apparel salesmen have traditionally acted essentially as "agents" rather than as employees of the manufacturers. Since a majority of firms have not been able to generate sufficient volume to support their own sales force, salesmen in the industry have generally been encouraged to represent more than one manufacturer. The time savings involved in showing more than one line in a store also contributed to the salesmen's handling of several manufacturers.
>
> Feelings of independence are also fostered by the commission compensation system since the salesmen's incomes have been directly dependent upon their own efforts. The retail store buyer who has had success purchasing from a specific salesman has often developed a trust in the salesman's judgment and ability. These factors, coupled with the lack of much brand preference on the part of consumers, enable many salesmen to retain their accounts despite occasional changes in the manufacturer or manufacturers they represented.
>
> As apparel firms have become larger, the larger firms have tended to employ salesman on an exclusive basis in those territories where a salesman could potentially support himself on the offerings of one manufacturer. Even though these salesmen represent one firm exclusively, many of them still view themselves as relatively independent agents and tend to resent bookkeeping chores imposed by the manufacturer which do not obviously benefit the salesman. Indeed some manufacturers have been somewhat at the mercy of their exclusive salesmen. Many of the salesmen have taken great care to reveal as little information as possible about their customers and their relationship with the customers. Thus, if a good salesman decides to move to another manufacturer, he frequently takes the customers' loyalty with him and the manufacturer can not retain many of his accounts.
>
> Until we acquired the computer we were not able to compile enough information about a specific salesman to know in what direction we should try to move him. If we can get this system working, we should be able to

obtain quickly a reading of how well a salesman is doing relative to the potential of his territory. With this information we can then make some changes in his territory size or take other steps to bring him into line.

Mr. Miller went on to note that up until Gem Frocks acquired the computer, management had relatively little information with which to evaluate each salesman. At that time each of two reports were prepared on a seasonal basis (twice a year), and one on a weekly basis. One of these reports showed sales for each salesman listed by account. The second showed, for each salesman, sales of individual items within each group. The third showed total bookings per week for each salesman. This report was felt by management to be the most important of the three. These reports required the services of three clerks on a half-time basis for a year. These clerks were among eight who hand posted orders received from the salesmen to various billing and production forms. Clerks earned from $50 to $60 per week.

*The Sales Information System Proposal*

Mr. Miller's proposal (see below) suggested that a file be constructed for each salesman from which management could evaluate the salesman and decide what changes should be made. From a summary "recap" sheet prepared weekly for each salesman management would, according to Mr. Miller, be able to "evaluate each salesman without becoming burdened with excessive details. Each recap sheet would, however, be derived from several more detailed reports which management could use to evaluate any particular salesman in depth."

Memo to: Mr. Arthur Greenspan, Treasurer
From: Mr. Eugene Miller, Boston Staff
Subject: INTEGRATED USE OF MARKETING INFORMATION FOR BETTER SALES CONTROL

A file will be made up for each Salesman.

It will contain the latest copy of each Report.

It will be prefaced with a Weekly Recap Analysis of his Productivity (on a Standardized Form). (See Exhibit 7 for draft.)

All decisions regarding this man and his territory can be made on the basis of the information in his file.

RECAP ANALYSIS

A. From the Weekly Booking Report. (See Exhibit 8.)
   1. Compare Net Dollar Sales this year with last year and list percentage difference.
   2. Compare origin of sales—Road vs. N.Y. office in percentage.
   3. Compare Actual Sales this year with Budget and list percentage difference.
   4. Analyze which groups are strong or weak for him.

DRAFT OF PROPOSED RECAP SHEET

WK. ENDG.

| | LAST WEEK-ACTUAL | | | THIS WEEK-ACTUAL | | | ORIGIN | |
|---|---|---|---|---|---|---|---|---|
| | L.Y. | T.Y. | % DIFF. | L.Y. | T.Y. | % DIFF. | ROAD | NYO |
| SEASON-A | | | | | | | | |
| SEASON-B | | | | | | | | |
| A | | | | | | | | |
| B | | | | | | | | |
| | | | | | | | | |

| | LAST WEEK | | | THIS WEEK | | | LAST YEAR |
|---|---|---|---|---|---|---|---|
| | ACTUAL | BUDGET | % DIFF. | ACTUAL | BUDGET | % DIFF. | NEXT 2 WKS. |
| WEEK-A | | | | | | | |
| WEEK-B | | | | | | | |
| A | | | | | | | |
| B | | | | | | | |
| | | | | | | | |

| ACTIVITY THIS WEEK | TOTAL ACCTS. CALLED ON | CURRENT | PROPOSED | NO. TIMES SHOWED LINE | EFF. | NO. ACCTS. SOLD | EFF. | MAIL ORD. | TOOK ORD. | EFF. | TOTAL NO. ACCTS. SOLD STD. |
|---|---|---|---|---|---|---|---|---|---|---|---|
| | | | | | | | | | | | A / B |

| ACTIVITY THIS WEEK | NO CAPS COND. | EFF. | CUM. FIGS. | L.Y. SOLD T.Y. UNSOLD | NEW ACCTS. OPENED | OLD CURR. ACCTS. MAINT. | VOL. CATEGORIES 0–1000 | 1–5000 | 5–10,000 | OVER 10,000 |
|---|---|---|---|---|---|---|---|---|---|---|
| | | | | | | | | | | |

| SHIPPED | ORDERS CANC. NO. OF FIGS. | % SHIPPED | BACKLOG | | | |
|---|---|---|---|---|---|---|
| | | | | | | |

| GROUPS | CUM. ACTUAL SALES | CUM. BUDGET | % DIFF. | TRADING AREAS NAME | NO | NET SALES | | AREA POTENTIAL (GUIDE) | % OF POTENT |
|---|---|---|---|---|---|---|---|---|---|
| 1. | | | | | | | | | |
| 2. | | | | | | | | | |
| 3. | | | | | | | | | |
| 4. | | | | | | | | | |
| 5. | | | | | | | | | |
| 6. | | | | | | | | | |
| 7. | | | | | | | | | |
| 8. | | | | | | | | | |
| 9. | | | | | | | | | |

**Exhibit 7** Draft of proposed recap sheet.

WINSTON (0) WEEK ENDING 04/12/65

| T/YR GROUPS (1) | L/YR GROUPS (2) | T/YR GWB (3) | T/YR NWB (4) | T/YR NCC (5) | T/YR NET (6) | L/YR BOOKINGS (7) | PCT. DIFFERENCE (8) | DOL. DIFFERENCE (9) | L/YR N/T/W (10) | T/YR NUMB. (11) | L/YR OF ACCTS (12) | PCT. N/Y (13) | PCT. ROAD* (14) | BDGT (15) | DOL. DIFFERENCE (16) | PCT. DIFFERENCE* (17) |
|---|---|---|---|---|---|---|---|---|---|---|---|---|---|---|---|---|
| CACS | | | | | 1,2 | | | | | 6 | | 73 % | 26 %* | | | |
| CRET | MOHR | | | 7 | 20,0 | 102,8 | 80- % | 82,8- | 11,1 | 30 | | 23 % | 76 % | 44,7 | 24,7- | 55- %* |
| CRES | | | 2- | 1,1 | | | | | | | | | | | | |
| TWEE | | | | 5 | 1 | | | | | | | | | | | |
| TWES | | | | | | | | | | | | | | | | |
| HEAH | | | | | | | | | | | | | | | | |
| HEAS | | | | | | | | | | | | | | | | |
| DTOH | DTFT | 2 | 2 | 2,0 | 2 | | | | | | | | | | | |
| DTMS | | 3 | 3 | 9 | 2 | | | | | | | | | | | |
| P&PT | | 3 | 3 | | 1 | | | | | | | | | | | |
| P&TS | | 4 | 4 | | 1 | | | | | | | | | | | |
| CROC | | | | 1,5 | 3 | | | | | | | | | | | |
| PEAK | | | 2- | 2,9 | 1 | | | | | | | | | | | |
| LABR | | | | | | | | | | | | | | | | |
| | BLSE | | | | | | | | | | | | | | | |
| TFAL | | 1,4 | 1,0 | 11,6 | 19 | | | | | | | | | | | |
| SETS | | | | | | | | | | | | | | | | |
| VELV | VELV | 4,0 | 4,0 | | | | | | | | | | | | | |
| KNIT | LACE | 1,0 | 1,0 | | | | | | | | | | | | | |
| SHIFT | | | | | | | | | | | | | | | | |
| | BJER | | | | | | | | | | | | | | | |
| | GOLD | | | | | | | | | | | | | | | |

See Numbers ( ) Above

0. Name of Salesman
1. T/YR GRP: Name of this year's Group
2. L/YR GRP: Name of last year's Group
3. T/YR GWB: This year's Gross Weekly Bookings in 000's of $
4. T/YR NWB: This year's Net Weekly Bookings in 000's of $
5. T/YR NCC: This year's Net Cumulative Cancellations in 000's of $
6. T/TR NCB: This year's Net Cumulative Bookings in 000's of $
7. L/YR NCB: Last year's Net Cumulative Bookings in 000's of $
8. PCT.DIFF: Per cent difference between 6 and 7
9. DOL.DIFF: Dollar difference between 6 and 7 in 000's of $
10. L/YR NTW: Last year's Cumulative Business at the end of the next 2 weeks in 000's of $
11. T/YRNOAC: This year's number of accounts sold. (Total of accounts buying each group add to more than the total of accounts sold because store buying 4 groups will appear 4 times, but only once in the total season figure)
12. L/YRNOAC: Last year's number of accounts sold. (This information not available for last year yet)
13. PCT/ N/Y: Per cent of business booked in the New York Office
14. PCT/ROAD: Per cent of business booked on the road. (Total does not necessarily add to 100 % because of orders originating from store)
15. BDGT: Budget for Group in 000's of $
16. DOL.DIFF: Dollar difference between Budget and this year Net Cumulative Bookings in 000's of $ (Column 6)
17. PCT.DIFF: Per cent difference between Budget and this year Net Cumulative Bookings

**Exhibit 8** Gem Frocks, Inc. Salesman's weekly booking report.

| RODENBORN (0) CITY (1) | STATE ACCT. (2) | N A M E (3) | *GROUP (4) | LAST Y/T/D (5) | *GROUP (6) | CUR Y/T/D* (7) | DOL. DIFF (8) | PCT DIFF* (9) | LST.YR.NEXT 2 WKS (10) |
|---|---|---|---|---|---|---|---|---|---|
| | | | * BLAZ | 428 | * MEAN | 239 * | 189- | 45-% * | |
| | | | * | 918 | * TFAL | 931 * | 13 | 1 % * | |
| MUSCATINE | IOWA 26060 | GLASS SMART SHOP | * | | * TSPG | 1,996 * | | * | |
| | | | * | | * CACK | 348 * | | * | |
| | | | * NOHR | | * CRET | 633 * | | * | 444 |
| | | | * REGN | | * | * | | * | 346 |
| | | | * BLAZ | | * HEAH | 418 * | | * | 495 |
| | | | * | | * PEAK | 231 * | | * | |
| | | | * | | * TFAL | 1,638 * | 1,630 | % * | 1,385 |
| SIDNEY | IOWA 51600 | PAULYS | * | | * TSPG | 1,006 * | | * | |
| | | | * | | * TMIO | 186 * | | * | |
| | | | * | | * TTRN | 448 * | | * | |
| | | | * | | * BSIC | 88 * | | * | |
| | | | * | | * CACK | 224 * | | * | |
| | | | * | | * CRET | 408 * | | * | |
| | | | * | | * THEE | 118 * | | * | |
| | | | * | | * HEAH | 37 * | | * | |
| | | | * | | * PEAK | 124 * | | * | |
| | | | * | | * TFAL | 969 * | 969 | % * | |
| WASHINGTON | IOWA 45295 | A MCGANNON | * | | * TSPG | 891 * | | * | |
| | | | * | | | | | | |
| | | | * NOHR | | | | | | |
| | | | * REGN | | | | | | |
| | | | * BLAZ | | | | | | |
| | | | * | | | | | | |
| | | ***TOTALS TRADING AREA | * | | | | | | |
| | | | * | | See Numbers( ) Above | | | | |
| | | | * | 10,370 | | | | | |

**Exhibit 9** Gem Frocks, Inc. Salesman's weekly sales distribution report by city.

| | | | | | |
|---|---|---|---|---|---|
| AMES | IOWA 66100 | TOWN & CAMPUS | * | | |
| | | | * | | |
| | | | * PROP | 20R | |
| | | | * | | |
| | | | * | | |
| | | | * REGN | 380 | |
| | | | * BLAZ | 480 | |
| | | | * | 1,078 | |
| BLOOMFIELD | IOWA 12960 | CLARAS FASH SHOPPE | * | | |
| | | | * NOHR | 392 | |
| | | | * BEGN | 228 | |

0. Name of salesman
1. City/State: Location of store
2. Acct: Reference number of store
3. Name: Store
4. Group: Name of last year's group
5. Last Y/T/D: Last Year-to-Date Sales
6. Group: Name of current year's group
7. Current Y/T/D: Current Year-to-Date Sales
8. Dol.Diff: Dollar difference between 5 and 7
9. Pct.Diff: Per cent difference between 5 and 7
10. Lst. Yr. Next 2 Wks: Last year's sales for next two weeks

**Exhibit 9** (*Continued*)

5. Compare 1, 2, 3, and 4 against last week.
6. Comment on above: For example—
   Does Salesman know how to sell all groups?
   Is there a territory problem with specific groups?
   Is too much business written in the N.Y. office?
   How does he stand against company averages?
   Is next 2 weeks' sales last year reasonable for this year?

B. From the Sales Distribution Report (by trading area).[3] (See Exhibit 9.)
   1. Compare Net Sales against "Area Potential Guide."
      Is he obtaining volume where potential is?
      Is he travelling correct areas (Analyze Field Activity Reports)?
      Comment further.
   2. Check into specific trading areas.
      Compare this year with last year by account.
      Where does problem lie?
      Is executive help needed for specific accounts?
      Comment further.

C. From Field Activity Reports (filled out by salesmen after each call) (See Exhibit 5.)
   1. Total Number of accounts called on
      a. Current accounts (bought within the last year from Gem Frocks)
      b. Inactive accounts (formerly bought from Gem Frocks)
      c. Prospects (never bought from Gem Frocks)
   2. Number of times line showed
   3. Number of accounts sold
      a. Number mailing in orders
      b. Number took order-form from
   4. Number of groups sold to all accounts
      Analysis on above: For example—
      1. Is he covering enough accounts?
         If not—Why? Poor Planning? Lack of appointments?
      2. Is he adequately servicing Current and Inactive Accounts?
         Is he making sufficient number of calls on prospects?
      3. How effective is he in showing the line?
         (Number of times showed line divided by Number of calls made)
      4. How effective is he in closing the Sale?
         (Number of accounts Sold divided by Number of times showed line)
      5. How effective is he in taking orders with him?
         (Number of orders taken with him divided by Number of accounts sold)
      6. Is he placing enough groups with our accounts?
         (Number of groups Sold divided by Number of accounts Sold)

[3] A trading area was comprised of several cities.

*D. From Volume Distribution Report
   1. In what Volume categories are his accounts?
   2. Is there a trend in moving his accounts up into the next higher Volume category?
   3. How many accounts from last year are Unsold this year?
   4. How many new accounts has he opened?
   5. How many Old-Current Accounts has he maintained last year to this year?

*E. From the Weekly Shipping Report by Salesman
   1. Percentage unjustified cancellations to Gross Bookings.
   2. Percentage shipped to Gross Bookings—Less Unit Cancellations.
   3. Backlog this year.

F. From Linear Programming Study of Territories (Under discussions; not yet approved)
   1. Optimum Route Sheet for each territory
      a. Compare travel of Salesman with Optimum

*Components of System*

Although parts of Mr. Miller's system were still in the proposal stage, three reports which could contribute to the system had already been programmed for the computer and were available to management on a weekly basis. The first of these, the salesman's weekly booking report (see Exhibit 8), was a weekly tabulation of bookings (orders) by each salesman for each merchandise group presented on a "this-year" vs. "last-year" basis. The second report was a weekly sales distribution report by city (see Exhibit 9), which was a tabulation of sales to individual stores within a specific city for each salesman. It showed sales of each merchandise group for the year-to-date, last year's sales of the comparable group and last year's sales for the period corresponding to the forthcoming two weeks. The third report, the salesman's credit limit report (see Exhibit 10), was a listing of current credit limits for each store in a salesman's territory.

Each salesman was given access to each of these reports for his own territory. The reports were also distributed to the president, treasurer, sales VP, and office managers for the New York and Boston offices.

Much of the additional information needed for the proposed sales information system would be obtained from an analysis of the activity reports requested from each salesman after he called on an account. In addition, territory potentials would be developed by staff personnel in the Boston office from published, statistical sources and lists of stores in each town.

Mr. Miller indicated that, if the proposal were accepted by the management

* Not yet programmed for computer.

| ACCT. (1) | SLM (2) | T/A (3) | NAME (4) | STREET (5) | CITY (6) | STATE | CR. LIMIT (7) |
|---|---|---|---|---|---|---|---|
| 67520 | 365 | 589 | UHLMANS | | TROY | OHIO | 00250 |
| 67610 | 365 | 589 | UNION CO | HIGH & LONG ST | COLUMBUS | OHIO | 00200 |
| 67830 | 365 | 586 | V & V STORES INC | 3054 MADISON ROAD | CINCINNATI | OHIO | 00035 |
| 68391 | 365 | 586 | VICKIS | 342 LUDLOW AVENUE | CINCINNATI | OHIO | 00025 |
| 68450 | 365 | 607 | VICTORIA MODES | 6420 MARKET ST | YOUNGSTOWN | OHIO | |
| 68550 | 365 | 586 | VILLAGE SHOP | CHERRY GROVE PLAZA | CINCINNATI | OHIO | 00030 |
| 68390 | 365 | 581 | VIS FASHIONS | COLLEGE PLAZA | ALLIANCE | OHIO | 00025 |
| 27905 | 365 | 586 | W A GUENTHERS & CO | 910 E MC MILLAN | CINCINNATI | OHIO | 00060 |
| 69338 | 365 | 588 | WALKERS | 1621 NORTH | | | |
| 69540 | 365 | 589 | WALZS STYLE SHOP | 856 HAMILTON | | | |
| 70450 | 365 | 603 | WESTGATE LION STORE | SECOR & CEI | | | |
| 70931 | 365 | 586 | WILLENBRINGS | 5849 HAMILTON | | | |

See Numbers ( ) Above

1. Acct: Reference number of store
2. SLM: Salesman's number
3. T/A: Trading area
4. Name: Store
5. Street: Address of store
6. City/State: Location of store
7. Cr. Limit: Credit limit in tens of dollars

**Exhibit 10** Gem Frocks, Inc. Salesman's credit limit report.

of Gem Frocks, complete implementation of the system would take about one year. He indicated, however, that even if the complete system was not adopted. the present sales information reports would still be quite useful in making decisions concerning the sales force.

*Cost of the Proposed System*

The three reports that were currently being prepared (see Exhibits 8, 9, and 10) required intra-company charges of $6,000 in computer time charges each year which included the charge for the services of the computer operator. This figure, however, excluded the time needed to prepare the necessary input data in the form of punched cards or tapes. Mr. Miller believed these input charges were not appropriately chargeable to the sales information reports since the same data were also used for other purposes.

The programs used to prepare the three existing reports were constantly being modified to make them more efficient. Mr. Miller believed, however, that to date such increases in efficiency were offset by the charges allocated to the project for the time of the company's programmer in making the programs more efficient. The programmer was paid $7,500/year and Mr. Miller estimated that it would take 40% of the programmer's time over the period of a year to complete the programming of the as yet unprogrammed portions of the current proposal. Mr. Miller anticipated that the routine processing of the additional portions of the proposal would involve intra-company charges of $2,700 a year in computer and operator charges.

Even with these additional reports total usage of the computer would still be less than 40 hours per week. Under the present contract Gem Frocks was obligated to pay for a minimum of 40 hours of computer time per week. Within the next two or three years, however, use of the computer was expected to exceed 40 hours per week and at that time additional expense would be incurred both for machine time and operators.

Mr. Miller believed that the value of the additional data developed by the computer would more than offset the costs involved in processing the sales reports. He argued that the sales information reports could and should be used for many purposes beyond the evaluation and control of salesmen.

In evaluating the proposal Mr. Greenspan was concerned about the positive or negative effect the system would have on the salesmen; whether management could make effective use of the information developed; and whether the system adequately prepared the company for future changes in the apparel field. Specifically he wondered if all of the reports were necessary or if perhaps some other reports might be more useful to management.

Mr. Greenspan had completed his initial reading of the proposal just prior to attending the following sales meeting.

*The Sales Meeting*

In preparation for the Fall selling season in June, several of the salesmen had come to New York early to confer with the executives of the company. At one meeting, the participants in addition to Mr. Greenspan were Eugene Miller; Jerry Katz, the New York sales office manager; Jack Samet, a New England salesman on salary-plus-commission; and Arnold Barysh, a midwestern salesman on commission.

After discussing the best way to sell the new groups, the conversation drifted to the filing of reports by the salesmen:

Arnold Barysh: Gene, I keep receiving your request for all different types of forms to be filled out. I'm a busy man with a big territory to cover, so I don't have time to fill out additional paperwork. Between my records and the order blanks, I do enough pencil pushing. If I could see some constructive use for the reports, maybe I might feel differently but I just don't have the time.

Eugene Miller: Arnie, I know you're busy. But a couple of minutes after each account is all that is needed to fill in an activity report. It provides different information than the order blank. Under the present system, our information is about the successful order, not the reasons for firms not buying.

Arnold Barysh: I have all the useful information in my notebooks. As long as I know who to see and not to see, the company has nothing to worry about. Instead of worrying about my reports, why don't you help me get some additions to the line that would really sell in my territory.

Jerry Katz: Arnie, your problems are no different than anybody else's. If we listened to every one of you salesmen, we would be carrying twice the number of items and still have the same sales. It's like the budget, accept it—don't question it.

Arnold Barysh: The worst thing are those damn budgets. You boys keep sending me your figures on what you think I should sell. You sit back in your easy chairs, both you and Gene, having never had to travel hundreds of miles a week and never been on commission, and tell me that I'm not booking enough business. I get these figures with no explanation and every time I try to pin you down you hem and haw.

Jerry Katz: You can always protest if you think Boston is unfair. I noticed that you and Jack haven't picked up your weekly reports.

Arnold Barysh: Save yourself the money. My records are in shape. I don't know why I need a computer to tell me what I sold this year or last.

Jack Samet: I have been with the firm for four months so the report isn't worth anything to me. After all, the comparable figures were set by another salesman. Besides, I keep all my information on cards in black books, which I follow for a route.

Eugene Miller: Jack, how long do you spend each night bringing these cards up to date?

Jack Samet: To tell the truth, I have been getting a little lax. With my two youngsters running around, nothing gets done. After they're asleep, I do the reports in front of the t.v. That drags my report and the activity reports out to three instead of one hour.

Jerry Katz: I can sympathize with you. I spend anywhere up to three hours daily reviewing all the figures by territory and by line. In that way, I can spot trends to keep you men informed and tell you where to place your emphasis in selling. These reports may be an adjunct to the operations but they're the Bible as far as I'm concerned.

Arnold Barysh: If you didn't review each individual salesman, it wouldn't take that long. Why do you keep up with all of the statistics? That's our responsibility. Our personal records, like Jack's have all the information on one sheet that we need. There's no need to wade through the reports every week; instead you should allow the computer to do something more useful like bookkeeping.

Eugene Miller: The computer was purchased for both bookkeeping and marketing reports. The computer and the reports are here to stay.

At this point, two more salesmen joined the conversation, which turned back to the best way to sell the Fall line.

## SUPERIOR MARKETS, INC.*

### SUPERMARKET CHAIN—EVALUATION OF FOOD DISCOUNTING

In late May 1963, the executive committee of Superior Markets, Inc. met to review the effects of their one Joy discount supermarket on the company's three nearby conventional supermarkets. By now the Joy store had had a

* This case was prepared by William Applebaum of the Harvard University Graduate School of Business Administration as the basis for class discussion rather than to illustrate either effective or ineffective administration. 

full year's operating history. Mr. Robert Day, the treasurer, was troubled about what had happened to profits in the three nearby units since the opening of Joy.

Superior Markets was a very successful supermarket chain of 15 stores, all located in Metropolitan Waterville. Company sales in 1962 were $38 million and after-tax profit $640,000. Stockholders' equity at the end of the year was slightly under $4 million, and working capital $2 million. The company pursued a prudent policy on long-term borrowing, and the treasurer felt the firm was in a sound financial position.

Superior Markets, Inc. operated its own grocery and produce warehouse. It also owned a small but efficient bakery and kitchen which produced good Danish style pastry, specialty breads, some cakes, and a variety of salads and cooked foods for the stores. All stores had service delicatessen departments, and ten had service bakeries. Superior carried Choice grade beef and its other meat products were of high quality. Thanks to the skill and dedication of Tony Napoli, the produce merchandiser, the firm's fruit and vegetable departments were among the best in the country. In groceries, the stores sold a selection of over 5,000 items, which included the controlled labels Food Club, Elna, Top Frost, etc. of Topco Associates, Inc., a member-owned buying organization comprising a group of non-competing supermarket chains.

All Superior stores carried a variety of non-foods, such as health and beauty aids, housewares, toys, records, magazines, greeting cards, and some soft goods. These goods were secured from rack jobbers who serviced the stores directly. Eight stores had florist shops and all stores carried a limited variety of garden supplies. Superior sold beer and some wine, but no hard liquor. Three of the four newest stores had snack bars.

In general, Superior prices on groceries and non-foods were in line with those of its chief competitors, but on meats, fruits and vegetables, delicatessen and baked goods, its prices were a little higher. Superior executives felt, however, that they were actually offering better values to the customers than their competitors. Consumer surveys repeatedly showed that Superior had a quality image, but also one of "higher prices." Nonetheless, Superior stores were successful in all income areas of Waterville.

Unlike its competitors, all of whom essentially emphasized price only in their promotions and advertising, Superior employed timely institutional messages, in addition to price features, in its newspaper advertising. The president, Mr. David Goodman, personally wrote a message every week in a special "Customers' Corner" in the ad. Superior also used radio spots to emphasize special buys. Handbills were used for individual store promotion, where sales were thought to be unsatisfactory, or to combat serious competition in a store's primary trading area.

Superior was the first supermarket chain in Waterville to use trading stamps.

It gave S&H stamps, which were considered the strongest stamps in the area. The two competing chains, Blu-Bell Stores and Red Dot Foods, also gave stamps. Red Dot gave no trading stamps prior to 1960. Here again Superior differed from its chain competitors. It refrained from giving double and triple stamps in the early part of the week, as its competitors did with some regularity, and it rarely gave bonus (extra) stamps on a chainwide basis. Bonus stamps were used on special occasions to promote an individual store against the inroads of new or "tough" competition.

As of January 1963, Metropolitan Waterville was estimated to have a population of 825,000. This was 30,000 more than in 1960. Local authorities projected that by 1970 the population would be over 900,000 and by the 1975 fully one million. All the anticipated growth would be in the suburbs.

Metropolitan Waterville was a city of diversified economic activities. Its industries included chemicals, machines, machine tools, home appliances, food processing, and printing. It was a major distribution hub for a large agricultural hinterland. Waterville had a leading state university and a fine endowed college. Important research activities were carried on under contract by university scientists for the federal government. Waterville was also the home office of a major insurance company.

In 1955, the management of Superior Markets, Inc. decided that planned shopping centers were "the wave of the future" and that large supermarkets had the best chances for survival in the long run. At the suggestion of their banker, they engaged Professor J. Q. Thorp, a marketing specialist with a scientific interest in urban growth, to help them plan a long-range store location strategy. At that time, Superior had 27 stores, only three of which did over a $1,000,000 each annually.

With the help of Professor Thorp, a local shopping center developer (who in time became well known), and Mr. David Goodman's remarkable knowledge of Metropolitan Waterville and his uncanny intuitive ability "to size up" a location, Superior replaced almost completely its pre-1955 store facilities. Thus, by the middle of 1961, Superior had 13 large, modern supermarkets, all with ample parking. Seven of these stores were in planned shopping centers, three were in old but large business districts, and three were free-standing. A fourteenth store in a shopping center was scheduled to open before Thanksgiving. In addition, Superior was in the process of evaluating two other shopping center proposals in areas which were still rather thinly populated, but where future growth was quite promising.

In early July 1961, Superior was approached by Joy, Inc., a rapidly expanding discount house chain, which had received much publicity in trade and financial journals. Joy was coming to Waterville. A location had been acquired in the industrial area of Milltown, an older urban district mainly of blue collar and lower middle income population. Joy wanted a discount supermarket inside its store, which would have a total area of 85,000 square feet, of which 25,000 square feet would be occupied by the discount supermarket. Parking would be provided for 1,300 cars. Joy stated that Square Deal, a smaller but very aggressive local chain, had already indicated an interest in establishing a discount supermarket with Joy in Milltown, where Square Deal had no stores.

Superior engaged Professor Thorp to make a study on the effect which the Joy store would have on Superior's three highly successful supermarkets in Milltown. The report contained a number of "guestimates," as there was "little to go by." Nonetheless, it projected that the Joy discount supermarket would have sales of $75,000 to $90,000 a week and that $20,000 to $30,000 of these sales would be taken away from the three Superior stores in Milltown.

After visiting with supermarket friends who were already involved in discount supermarket operations, after studying Professor Thorp's report, and after much soul-searching and debate, Superior decided to join Joy in Milltown. Mr. Robert Day, the treasurer, was not happy about this decision, but "went along."

The Joy discount house opened the first week in May 1962. The discount supermarket had a selling area of 16,000 square feet. It carried 3,600 grocery items and essentially the same selection of perishable foods as the Superior conventional supermarkets. It did not carry any of the Topco controlled labels. By terms of the lease, it carried none of the items commonly called non-foods. These were carried in separate departments in the general merchandise part of the store.

The first four weeks of operation, the Joy discount supermarket averaged $104,000 a week, of which $42,000 came from the three Superior conventional supermarkets in Milltown. Competition in Milltown retaliated through extensive handbill advertising which featured deep-cut price specials, bonus stamps, free loaves of bread and other gimmicks, as well as long lists of price reductions on important national brand items. Superior joined the battle with its own handbills and price specials and reductions to "protect" its three conventional supermarkets in Milltown.

In time, the battle subsided and sales and profits became "normalized" again, but at a different level. A comparison of the sales and operating results of the Superior stores in Milltown for the 16 weeks just prior to the opening of the Joy discount supermarket compared with the same 16 weeks a year later is shown in Exhibit 1.

Total food sales in Metropolitan Waterville as of the beginning of May 1963 were estimated at $5.5 million per week. Supermarket sales (defined as food stores with two or more checkouts) were estimated at $3.5 million per week, as shown in Exhibit 2.

Superior had the most modern and largest markets, both in size and sales, of all competing firms in Waterville. Although it had only 15 of the 140 stores classified as supermarkets, its 21% share of this type of business was the largest

| | Store A | Store B | Store C | Stores A, B, C | Joy Store |
|---|---|---|---|---|---|
| *First 16 weeks 1962* | | | | | |
| Sales | 596,000 | 784,000 | 918,000 | 2,298,000 | |
| Gross profit* | 131,000 | 176,000 | 206,000 | 513,000 | |
| Store operating expense | 97,000 | 104,000 | 118,000 | 319,000 | |
| Administrative overhead | 18,000 | 23,000 | 27,000 | 68,000 | |
| Store profit B.T. | 16,000 | 49,000 | 61,000 | 126,000 | |
| Investment (annual)† | 123,000 | 155,000 | 139,000 | 417,000 | |
| *First 16 weeks 1963* | | | | | |
| Sales | 393,000 | 684,000 | 763,000 | 1,840,000 | 1,447,000 |
| Gross profit* | 80,000 | 143,000 | 168,000 | 390,000 | 251,000 |
| Store operating expense | 80,000 | 97,000 | 113,000 | 290,000 | 175,000 |
| Administrative overhead | 12,000 | 20,000 | 23,000 | 54,000 | 43,000 |
| Store profit B.T. | −12,000 | 26,000 | 32,000 | 46,000 | 33,000 |
| Investment (annual)† | 109,000 | 140,000 | 109,000 | 358,000 | 312,000 |

* Includes cash discounts and promotional allowances.

† Includes book value of equipment, unamortized leaseholds and supplies, and store inventory at cost. Does not include warehouse backup inventory and store cash; the last two items amount to about 50% of the investment shown.

**Exhibit 1** Superior Markets, Inc. Comparison of Sales and Operating Results of Company's Stores in Milltown for Same 16 Weeks 1962 and 1963 (in Dollars)

| Company | Stores | Sales Area (Square Feet) | Weekly Sales Estimated |
|---|---|---|---|
| Superior Markets, Inc. | 15 | 191,000 | $ 750,000* |
| Blu-Bell Stores, Inc. | 28 | 200,000 | 700,000 |
| Red Dot Foods, Inc. | 23 | 150,000 | 424,000 |
| Square Deal Supers | 11 | 139,000 | 470,000 |
| Independents | 63 | 387,000 | 1,126,000 |
| | 140 | 1,067,000 | 3,470,000 |

* Actual

**Exhibit 2** Superior Markets, Inc. Supermarket Competition in Metropolitan Waterville—May 1963

of all chains. Its largest single competitor, Blu-Bell Stores, Inc., was a regional chain with considerable strength in the Waterville market. Half of the Blu-Bell stores were, however, over ten years old and over a third had sales of under $20,000 per week each.

Until 1960, Red Dot Foods, Inc. was the price leader in food retailing in Waterville. When Red Dot started to give trading stamps in 1960, it increased its prices and lost its price leadership position. There was general agreement among food merchants in Waterville that trading stamps did not improve Red Dot's sales appreciably and sapped its profits. Of the present 23 Red Dot stores, 60% were more than ten years old and none of these was doing over $20,000 a week.

Square Deal Supers was a family business owned by the brothers-in-law, Wise and Black. Up to 1960, Square Deal had 5 large volume stores which gave no stamps but featured "bargain" prices. In January 1960, Square Deal acquired 3 more stores from the estate of Ben Gordon, who died suddenly. Square Deal's aggressive price merchandising immediately boosted the sales of the 3 newly-acquired stores.

When Red Dot announced that it was giving trading stamps, Square Deal made a major policy decision to go the way of food discounting, and adjusted prices drastically. Square Deal took a full page ad in both the morning and evening newspapers and proclaimed its full-fledged food discounting policy. Sales that week were reported to have "exceeded all expectations." Square Deal continued to advertise its food discounting, and the results were profitable.

In late 1961, Square Deal opened a free-standing food discount store with 15,000 square feet sales area. Store sales were reported to be well over $60,000 a week. Ten months later, another similar unit was opened inside an 80,000 square foot Big Dollar discount house, and this one was known to do between $60,000 and $70,000 a week. In March 1963, Square Deal opened a unit in the second Big Dollar discount house in Waterville. As of May 1963, sales in this store were "very slow," and food sales were less than $45,000 a week. It was known that Big Dollar was trying to "put together" several pieces of property in Milltown and, if successful, Square Deal would operate the supermarket.

The 63 independent supermarkets in Metropolitan Waterville, for the most part, were neighborhood stores. Sixteen belonged to the Arrow voluntary group, which had good leadership and was gaining strength in the market. Several of the independent supermarkets presented their stores as discount supermarkets, after sharply reducing 200 to 300 grocery prices and a few meat prices. In general, the independent supermarkets were located in the older areas of the city.

When the executive committee met in president Goodman's spacious office promptly at 10 A.M. on Monday in late May, all three members had with them the Thorp report on the Milltown situation. The report analyzed Superior's share of market in this area before the Joy store was opened, compared with the present share of market.

"Bob," began Mr. Goodman as he addressed Robert Day, the treasurer, and Tom Jacobs, the vice president in charge of sales, "you were particularly anxious that we should hold this special meeting, so maybe you should give us your thoughts first. I assume that we've all read Doc Thorp's report [see Appendix—it's an enlightening study. The old boy is retiring next year. Maybe we should bring him into Superior on a part-time basis."

Mr. Robert Day: "You all know that I was not for going into Joy. My reasons at the time were basically these. Superior has built a quality image. We give the customer a little something plus that even our competitors' big stores don't offer. The extra quality and service which we provide can't be retailed at a discount.

"Secondly, our three Milltown stores were among the most profitable in our chain. You all know how I sweat blood to put those pieces of land together so we could have three outstanding stores in superb locations. I was afraid of what we in Joy would do to the profits of these stores. I believe my fears were well founded.

"Thirdly, our store managers' pay is tied to store sales and profits. Our store managers earn very substantially more than those of our competitors, and we have the best store managers in town. I was afraid that the Joy move would undermine the high personnel morale that we built. Here, too, my fears were not altogether out of order.

"Finally, I felt that if Square Deal went with Joy, they wouldn't do the kind of business which we would do and therefore our stores in Milltown wouldn't be hurt as much.

"These were my reasons. I know that some of the folks at Superior are excited about the sales we have been able to do at Joy. There has also been some talk about going with Joy in their next ventures in Waterville, which they have on the planning board. I also know that there has been some talk about leap-frogging to new areas with Joy. Well, all this has me worried, so I asked for this special meeting."

Mr. Tom Jacobs: "Let me take it from here. I want to speak as a merchandiser. My responsibility is sales at a profit, and not profitless sales.

"There is much to what Bob says, and the points he makes must be examined carefully. Let me plead guilty from the start that I'm the one who is enthusiastic about expanding with Joy, both here in Waterville and by leap-frogging. I have been giving this a lot of thought, and my own views are jelled. Let me give them to you.

"At the time when we decide to go with Joy, I made two points, you will recall. I said that Superior had reached its own saturation point in Waterville. Sure, we had land for a couple more supermarkets at a future date. But our stores were modern, new, large and strategically located. In other words, we had arrived. Future expansion would be mighty slow. We needed to stretch to get more sales.

"The second point I made in August 1961 was that I felt discounting of general merchandise was here to stay, and that with this would come a wave of food discounting. The two go together like a pair of gloves. Joy was a well-managed discount store chain, and a comer. We at Superior had no experience in food discounting. Here was our chance; let's grab it. This is what I said, you will recall.

"Well, I believe Superior has demonstrated that we can merchandise and operate a food discount supermarket, in addition to conventional supermarkets. Square Deal, we must hand it to them, have done a very creditable job. The top brass at Blu-Bell is scared stiff and doesn't know what to do, because they have the most stores in Waterville and have been hurt the most.

"I consider the profit which we have shown at Joy for the first four periods of this year, as quite remarkable. We have corrected our product mix and have added about 500 more items to satisfy customers and get a little more gross profit. Store expenses are under control. I believe we stand a good chance to make 3% store profit before tax for 1963.

"Now the experience which we have gained at Joy in Milltown can serve us handsomely in other locations. Joy is planning to open two more stores in Waterville. They are lining up sites. They are pleased with us and want us to go with them in other locations. We should do it here and we should leap-frog.

"I've thought through very carefully the way we could leap-frog. We work out a deal with local grocery and other wholesalers to supply our store or stores. This is incremental sales for them so they will give us a favorable cost of goods basis. Transportation costs will be low. On advertising, we go along with Joy and should not be any higher than what it is now. The key is to get top-notch people to run the store. So we take managers and department heads from Waterville and transfer them to the new places. I see this as a real opportunity knocking on our door."

Mr. David Goodman: "Bob, you have done an outstanding job for Superior, and so has Tom. I know that you are both dedicated men, and totally sincere. In my job, I have to weigh carefully both your counsel. We have worked together remarkably well as a team.

"What we are discussing today has been on my mind for some time. I do not know the answers to all these problems. I'm reaching out for answers.

"Our sales this year should hit about $40 million. Considering that this will include a full year operation of Joy, which is going at the rate of $4.5 million for the year, our sales in the other 14 stores will actually be a little behind last year. Fortunately, so far, Square Deal has not nicked us much. If they open another two or three stores such as their last three we are going to feel it. Blu-Bell and Red Dot aren't going to stand still. They have been fighting back with bonus stamps and price cuts, but so far they have not gone discount in any of their stores. I expect they will soon, on an experimental basis at least.

"In a way, as I see it, so far we have been fighting skirmishes, brush fires. This has cost us gross profit. I estimate that we are going to show a drop in profit for the year of at least $50,000 and maybe more. If the battlefront spreads and becomes intensified we may not be able to show a net of $500,000 after tax.

"The situation in Milltown has cost us profit, even though I agree with Tom that we are doing a good job at Joy and have been gaining a lot of valuable experience. But if we look at the store profit plus the administrative overhead which we got during the four periods in 1963 in four stores compared to the same four periods in 1962 in three stores, the figures justify Bob's concern. And, as Bob has said to me recently, we have put a lot of new money into the bargain at Joy.

"The matter of leap-frogging is one thing. We must study this most carefully. Perhaps we should do it. I'm not sure, as yet. I am concerned about creating new opportunities for our able people. This may be a way. We also need opportunities to employ the cash flow which we generate. We certainly must do something about the cut in income of our managers in Milltown since the opening of Joy.

"The problem which troubles me most at present is what we should do about going with Joy in additional locations in Waterville, as these materialize. Doc Thorp's study shows what happened in Milltown to the primary trading areas of our Superior stores and to their share of market since the opening of Joy. The Doc in his characteristically cautious manner says in the report that we can expect similar results in other areas, and that the more successful the Joy discount food store is, the more will it take sales away from its sister Superior stores. He also makes the shrewd observation that Superior's merchandisers are faced with the dilemma of how to serve the three Superior supermarkets and the Joy store with equal loyalty and love."

Robert Day: "I hope you will not accuse me of wanting to kill any new idea. Somehow I can't help being uneasy about Tom's enthusiasm about discount houses and their future. The trade press has been reporting failures, mergers, unsatisfactory profits, and a fading interest in discount house securities. I don't question that the strong will survive. I've studied Joy's annual report; their expansion is all on borrowed money."

David Goodman: "Tom, what do you think about the future of trading stamps? No doubt a certain percentage of the public doesn't want them, and some supermarkets throughout the country are dropping them. But we have the strongest stamp."

Tom Jacobs: "I think Superior will be giving S&H stamps for a long time to come. What I would like to see is us capture the business that doesn't care for stamps. We now do about a fifth of the supermarket business in our area, but only a little better than one-seventh of the total retail food business."

David Goodman: "Bob, we have been enjoying a very healthy rate of return on our investment, far better than the supermarket industry as a whole. What sort of return on investment do you foresee for us in the future?"

Robert Day: "It will be less than now, and if we go deeper into the Joy operation, substantially less. So far, we have been in the food business only, plus some real estate. It need not be that way in the future."

David Goodman: "About 9:30 this morning, I had a call from Joy. They want to talk to us about a location which they are about to tie up. They are coming in this afternoon. I intend to listen. I believe we will not have too much time to make up our mind. Yet this is a major policy decision."

## APPENDIX

### EFFECT OF JOY STORE ON SUPERIOR SUPERMARKETS IN MILLTOWN

*by J. Q. Thorp*

#### *Objectives*

This study has two objectives:

1. It undertakes to measure the effect of the Joy discount supermarket on three Superior sister stores in Milltown.
2. It seeks guidelines for management in making decisions whether to open additional discount supermarkets.

#### *Scope and Limitations*

The study measures and compares the trading areas, market penetration, and customer shopping habits of the Superior stores in Milltown at two different points in time: in August 1961, *before* the opening of the Joy discount supermarket, and in April 1963, almost one full year *after* the opening.

The data on population, family income and per capita food expenditures are all derived from published U.S. Census and other government reports. These data have not been up-dated in this study, because there has been practically no change in total population in Milltown since 1950 and the changes in family income during the last two years are slight. Per capita food expenditures between August 1961 and April 1963 have increased by about 5%; for simplicity, we have not made any adjustments for this difference in our calculations of market share.

Competition was checked in the field both in August 1961 and again in April 1963, during the weeks when the Superior stores were customer spotted. A little over 1,400 customers were interviewed in the three stores in August 1961 and 2,000 customers in the four stores in April 1963. This represents one interviewed customer for each $100 weekly store sales.

The Superior management is keenly aware of the effect on profits since the opening of the Joy store. Therefore, this study does not deal with profits. We have examined various customer shopping habits for both periods, but did not explore the attitudes of people in Milltown toward trading stamps and food discount prices.

This study contains some innovations in our research techniques.

*Findings*

*Points of Reference.* In our 1961 study of Milltown, we prepared a map showing the distribution of population, major roads and the chief non-residential land areas. We described Milltown in some detail; it covers an area of 24 square miles, has 160,000 population, with a median family income of about $6,000 per annum. We also prepared a customer spotting map showing the distribution of the interviewed customers for each of the three Superior supermarkets, and described this map. Both of these maps are shown again, combined in Figure 1, as a point of reference.

*Competition in Milltown.* The Joy discount supermarket is the great change in the food retailing facilities in Milltown. It added 16,000 square feet of sales space. Blu-Bell renovated its large store in the northeastern section of Milltown just before the opening of the Joy store, and has gained strength there. Red Dot moved out of one location in the extreme northeast and the store was taken over by an independent who calls himself a food discounter, but does $18,000 to $20,000 a week. One independent supermarket changed ownership.

As of April 1963, the supermarkets listed in Exhibit 3 were in operation in Milltown.

In August 1961, we estimated that the 160,000 people in Milltown spent about $6.20 per capita per week for food consumed at home. Thus their weekly food sales potential was $1,000,000. From customer spotting of the three Superior stores, we determined that barely 3% of their $145,000 weekly sales came from customers living outside Milltown.

Since food prices increased by about 5% since August 1961, we estimate current weekly food sales potential in Milltown at about $1,050,000. The 1963

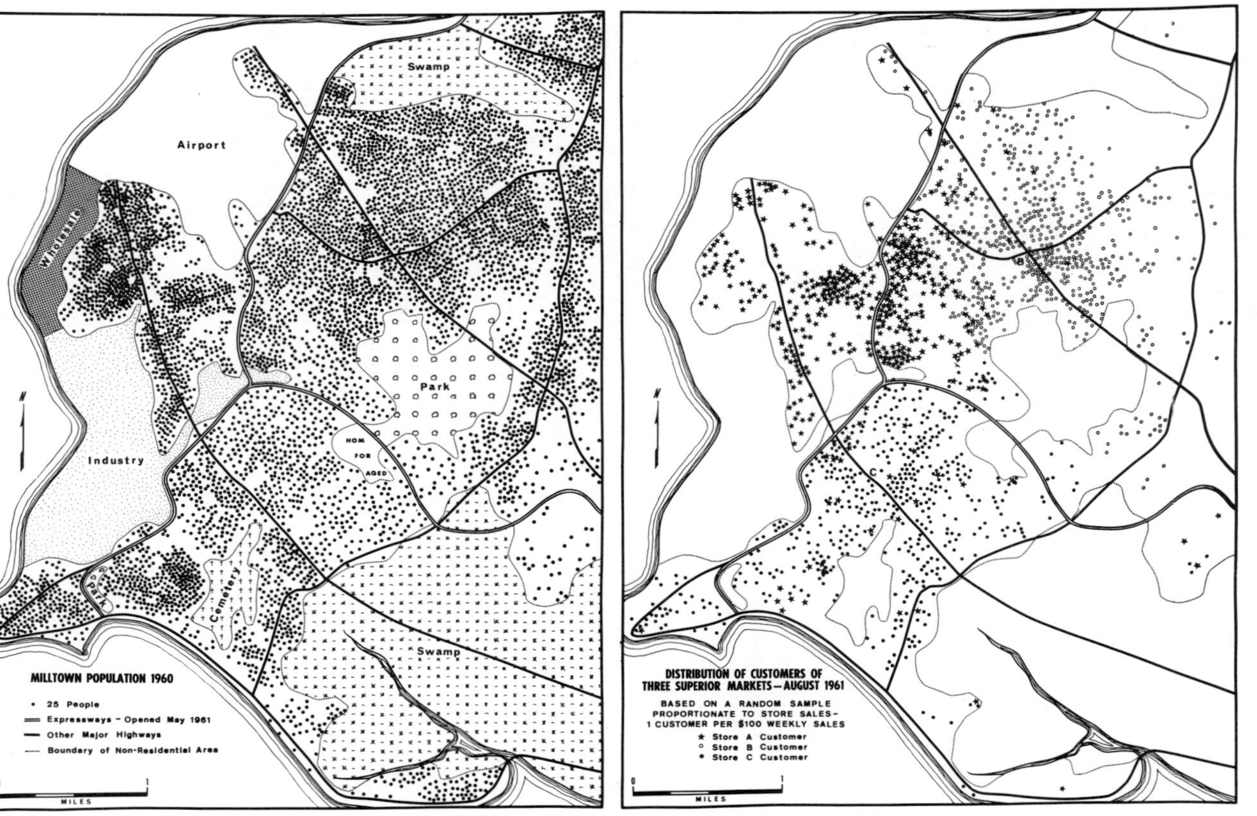

Airport
Wholesale
Industry
Swamp
Park
HOM FOR AGED
Cemetery
Park
Swamp
MILLTOWN POPULATION 1960
• 25 People
Expressways - Opened May 1961
Other Major Highways
Boundary of Non-Residential Area
0
1
MILES
DISTRIBUTION OF CUSTOMERS OF THREE SUPERIOR MARKETS—AUGUST 1961
BASED ON A RANDOM SAMPLE PROPORTIONATE TO STORE SALES- 1 CUSTOMER PER $100 WEEKLY SALES
★ Store A Customer
○ Store B Customer
• Store C Customer
A
B
C
0
1
MILES


Figure 1

| Company | Supermarkets | Sales Area (Square Feet) | Weekly Sales Estimated | Weekly Sales per Square Foot |
|---|---|---|---|---|
| Superior | 3 | 35,300 | $115,000 | $3.25 |
| Joy | 1 | 16,000 | 90,000 | 5.63 |
| Blu-Bell | 6 | 62,100 | 192,000 | 3.10 |
| Red Dot | 5 | 30,300 | 85,000 | 2.80 |
| Independents | 16 | 90,000 | 261,000 | 2.90 |
| | 31 | 233,700 | 743,000 | 3.14 |

**Exhibit 3**

customer spotting shows that the three Superior stores got less than 1% of their sales from customers living outside Milltown. The current sales of these three stores are around $115,000 weekly.

Customer spotting shows that 12% of the Joy store's customers live outside Milltown. Its current sales are around $90,000 weekly. Thus, this store gets only $79,000 sales weekly from Milltown, and of this amount, $30,000 in round figures (disregarding the changes in food prices and origin of customers) comes from the three Superior stores. In 1961, the Superior stores were getting about 14% of the Milltown food sales potential. Currently, they are getting around 11%. They lost about 20% of their 1961 sales to Joy.

If about $30,000 of Joy's sales come from the Superior stores, and $60,000 comes from the other food retailing establishments in Milltown (actually a little less because some of the 12% sales from outside Milltown is most likely new), then the other food retailers lost on the average only about 8% of their sales to Joy. The reason for this is not hard to find: the Superior stores are most vulnerable because of their close geographic proximity to the Joy store (see Figure 2) and because of their locations (in old, large business districts).

In August 1961, we calculated the food sales potential for each of the census tracts in Milltown. This was done on the basis of population within each census tract, times the per capita weekly food expenditures at home, based on the median family income. We have made a similar calculation for April 1963. The results are shown in Figure 3. In examining Figure 3, it should be noted that the Joy store does not secure trade from the northeast section of Milltown, and that Superior's store B has lost some sales in that the section to Blu-Bell's renovated and aggressively merchandised, large and very successful store.

*Changes in Primary Trading Areas.* In August 1961, we determined the pri-

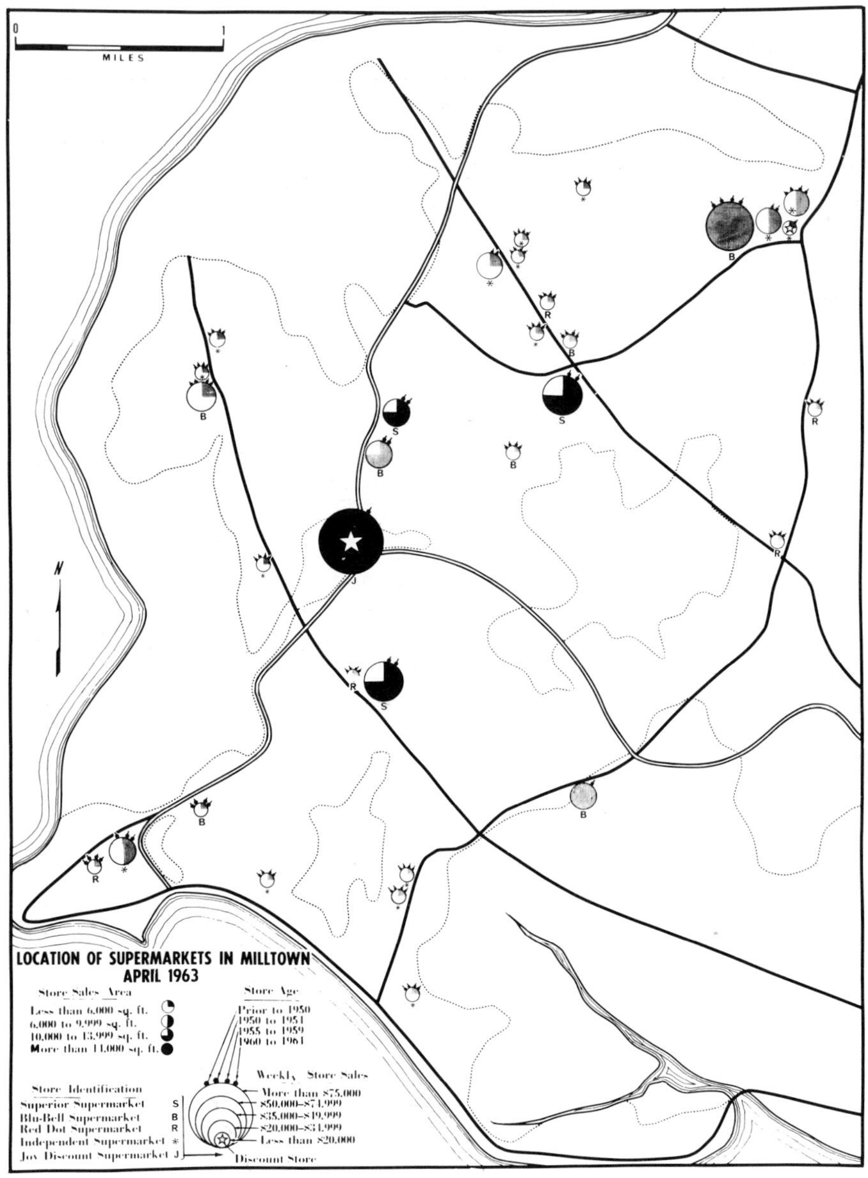
0
1
MILES
N
LOCATION OF SUPERMARKETS IN MILLTOWN
APRIL 1963
Store Sales Area
Less than 6,000 sq. ft.
6,000 to 9,999 sq. ft.
10,000 to 13,999 sq. ft.
More than 14,000 sq. ft.
Store Age
Prior to 1950
1950 to 1954
1955 to 1959
1960 to 1964
Weekly Store Sales
More than $75,000
$50,000–$74,999
$35,000–$49,999
$20,000–$34,999
Less than $20,000
Discount Store
Store Identification
Superior Supermarket S
Blu-Bell Supermarket B
Red Dot Supermarket R
Independent Supermarket *
Joy Discount Supermarket J

**Figure 2**

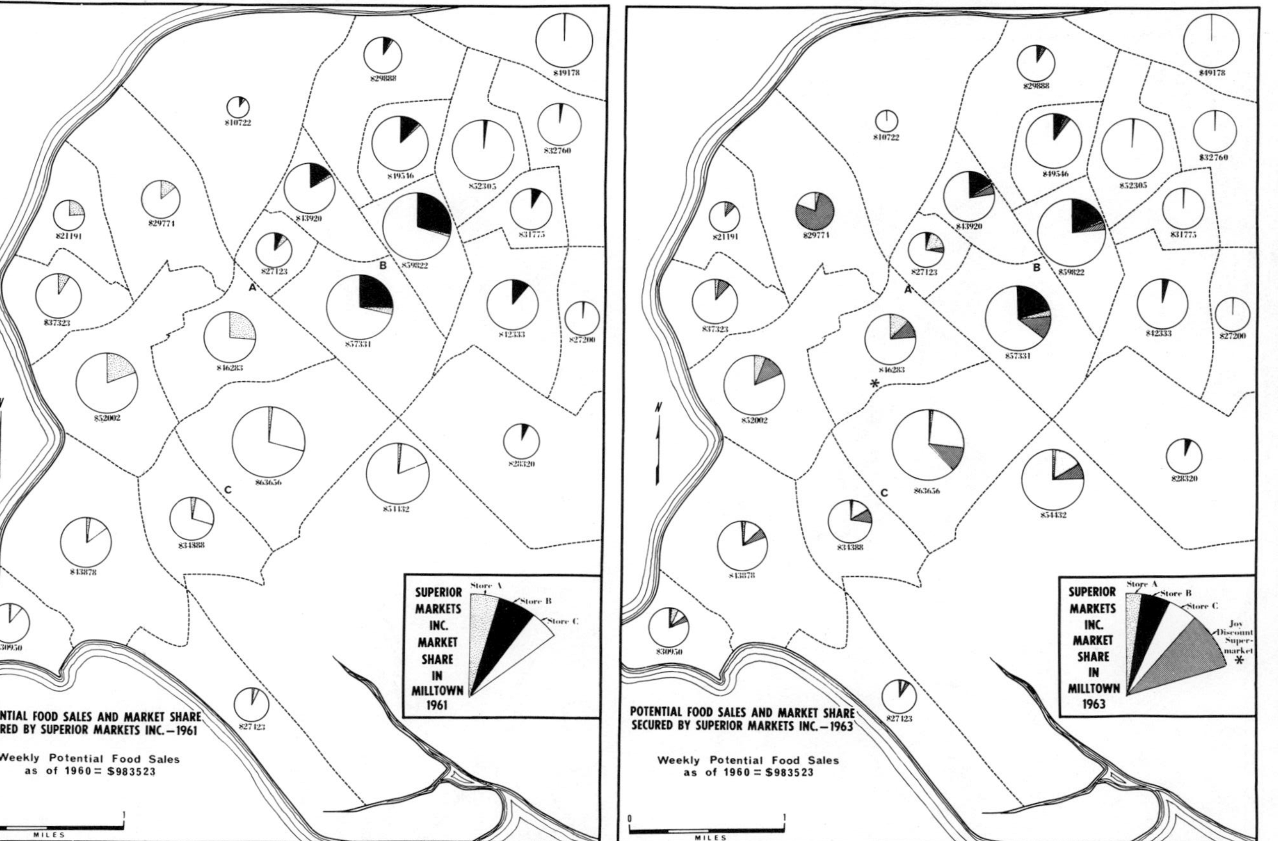
POTENTIAL FOOD SALES AND MARKET SHARE SECURED BY SUPERIOR MARKETS INC.—1961
Weekly Potential Food Sales as of 1960 = $983523
SUPERIOR MARKETS INC. MARKET SHARE IN MILLTOWN 1961
Store A
Store B
Store C
MILES
POTENTIAL FOOD SALES AND MARKET SHARE SECURED BY SUPERIOR MARKETS INC.—1963
Weekly Potential Food Sales as of 1960 = $983523
SUPERIOR MARKETS INC. MARKET SHARE IN MILLTOWN 1963
Store A
Store B
Store C
Joy Discount Supermarket
MILES

Figure 3

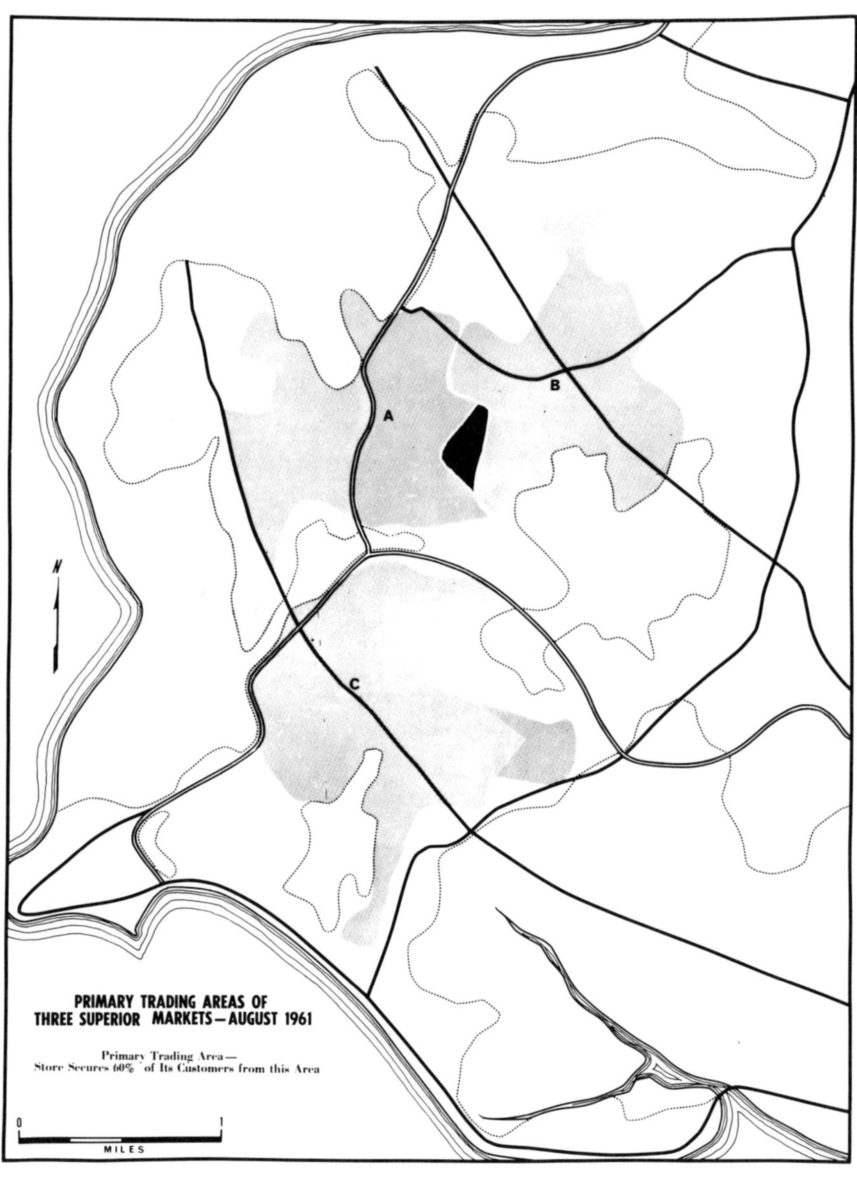
A
B
C
N
PRIMARY TRADING AREAS OF
THREE SUPERIOR MARKETS—AUGUST 1961
Primary Trading Area—
Store Secures 60% of Its Customers from this Area
0
1
MILES

Figure 4

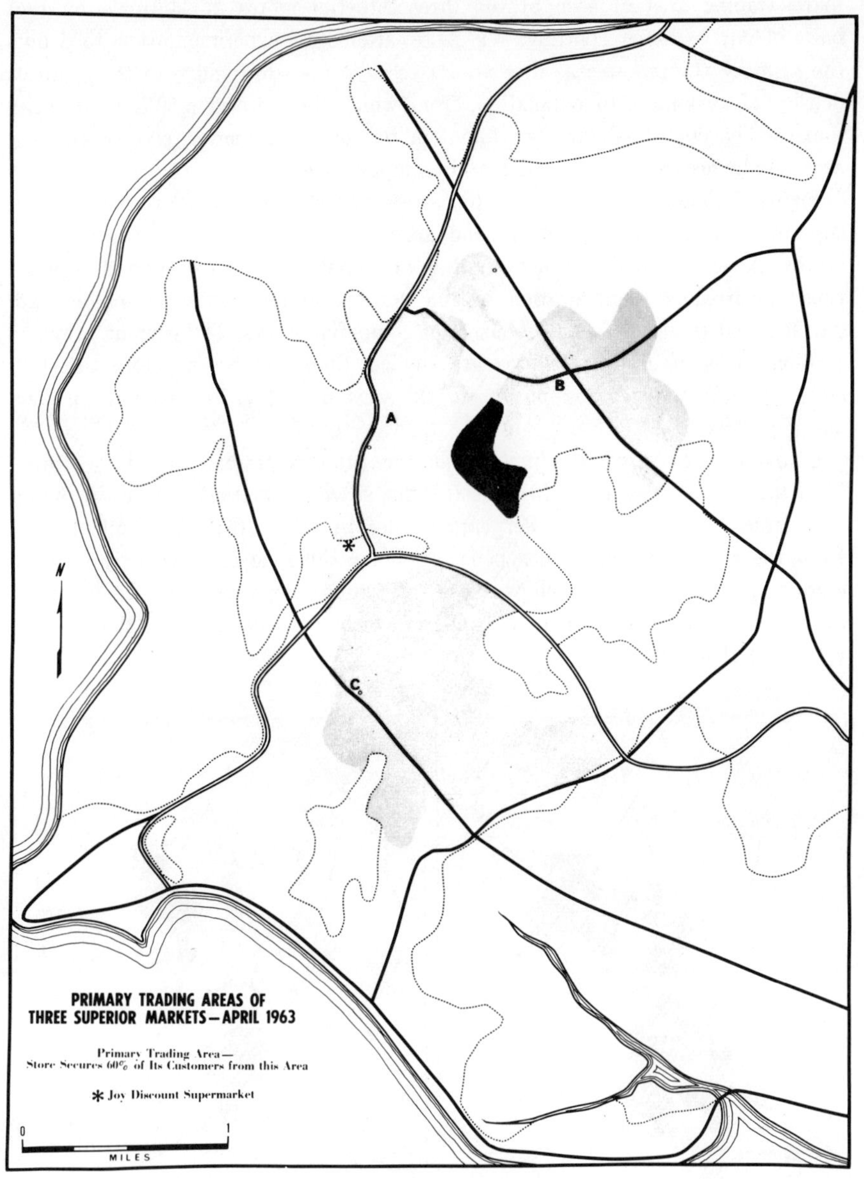


Figure 4 (*Continued*)

mary trading area of each of the three Superior stores in Milltown on the basis of our customer spotting. We chose, after some experimentation, to define the primary trading area as that area, closest to the store and with the greatest density of customers to population, from which the store gets 60% of its customers. The 60% boundary, we found in the case of Superior, showed trading area dominance of each store with a minimum of overlap.

Figure 4 shows the primary trading areas of the three Superior conventional supermarkets in Milltown before and after the opening of the Joy store. The ameba-like shapes of the primary trading areas reflect the distribution of population, the irregular configuration of the non-residential areas, the major road pattern, and the location and strength of competing stores. The current primary trading areas of all three stores are smaller than they were before the Joy store opened; they shrank mostly to the west of a N-S line passing through the Joy store.

*Changes in Sales Penetration.* While the primary trading area is a store's "heartland," we also need to measure the share of market which the store gets from its trading area. Per capita sales by zones (e.g., 0-½ mile radius from the store) measures sales penetration for the zone as a whole, but some sectors in it may have much weaker penetration than others. Hence we have measured market penetration by a different technique (described in the Technical Note) that overcomes this.

**Figure 5**

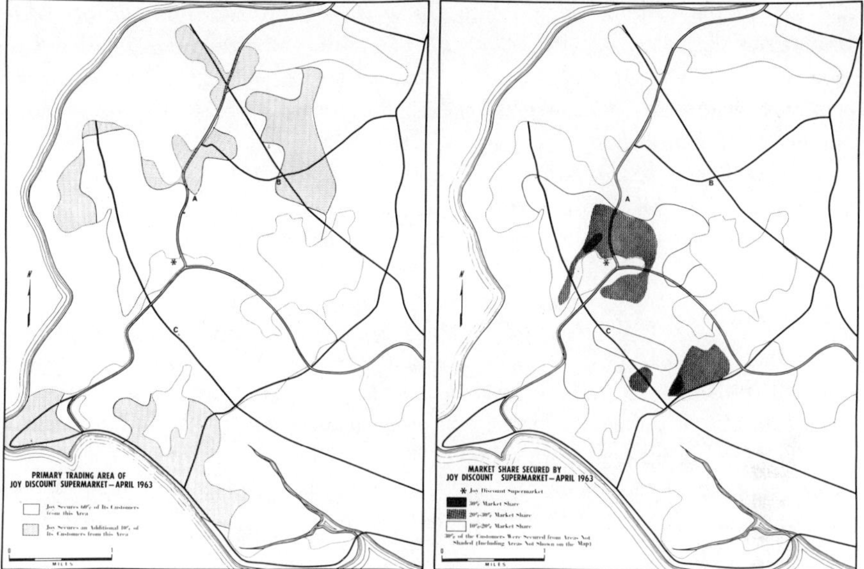


**Figure 6**

After some experimentation, we have chosen to measure two intensities of sales penetration: 30% or more, and 20% to 30% of the potential food sales. The results are shown in Figure 5. The changes after the Joy store was opened are quite dramatic. Store A's area of great sales penetration (20% or more) has almost shrivelled up, and the similar areas of stores B and C have been drastically reduced. Stores A and C no longer have great penetration west of a N-S line passing through the Joy store, where their primary trading areas have been lopped off (see Figure 4).

*The Joy Store: Primary Trading Area and Sales Penetration.* The primary trading area of the Joy store overlaps almost completely the August 1961 primary trading areas of the three Superior stores, and is substantially larger than the present primary trading areas of these stores (compare Figure 6 with Figure 4). When we include the contiguous areas from which Joy gets an additional 10% of its customers, then this 70% trading area embraces all of the population in Milltown, except a narrow strip in the northeast.

Joy's sales penetration reaches 30% or more in two tiny, widely separated "islands," one near the store, the other about 1.5 miles to the southeast, in the vicinity of Blu-Bell's new but unsuccessful free-standing store with 15,000 square feet of sales area. Joy has three separate areas of 20% to 30% market share. The largest of these loops around the store; the second largest is in the "front yard" of Blu-Bell's unsuccessful new store; the third is the smallest and lies to the east of the northern tip of the cemetery, within the primary trading area of store C. Its isoline of 10% sales penetration is blunted by each of the three Superior supermarkets. Joy's 10% market share isoline is contained within a 1-mile radius, except for a small lobe to the south and another to the southeast.

*Changes in Customer Shopping Habits—1963 versus 1961.* An analysis of the composition and shopping habits of the customers in the Superior stores in Milltown shows the following changes in April 1963 compared with August 1961:

1. The ratio of customers originating from beyond a 1-mile radius from the stores had declined.
2. The ratio of drive customers has declined.
3. The ratio of couple shoppers (man and woman together) has declined.
4. The ratio of customers who shop once or less than once a week has declined.
5. The ratio of customers who have been regular shoppers in these stores since opening has increased. (Proportionately more of the less loyal customers have been lost.)
6. The purchase of perishables to total product mix has remained unchanged.
7. Average sale per customer transaction has declined—much more at store A than stores B and C.
8. Number of customer weekly transactions has declined—more at store A than the other two.

The statistics supporting the above statements are given in Exhibit 4.

### *The Implications of the Findings*

This study of the Joy discount supermarket and its effect on the three Superior supermarkets in Milltown leads to several conclusions:

1. A discount supermarket in association with a general merchandise discount store exerts much greater drawing power than a similar conventional supermarket not so associated.
2. The discount supermarket does not achieve the high sales penetration that a conventional supermarket does, but because of its much larger trading area it can develop very large sales even with a relatively thin market share.
3. The opening of a strong discount store brings about changes in the shopping habits of segments of the consuming public. It also changes the network of trading areas.
4. Where the sales secured by a discount store represent business taken away from already existing stores, the latter will take measures to cope with the new competition. These measures may recapture some of the lost sales and profits, but will not restore the total dislocations caused by the discount store.

| | Store A | | Store B | | Store C | | Store J |
|---|---|---|---|---|---|---|---|
| | 1961 | 1963 | 1961 | 1963 | 1961 | 1963 | 1963 |
| Customers originating from beyond 1-mile radius from store | 29 | 19 | 26 | 21 | 16 | 13 | 62 |
| Drive customers | 88 | 74 | 90 | 72 | 83 | 67 | 97 |
| Couples shopping | 24 | 16 | 17 | 10 | 19 | 7 | 23 |
| Customers shopping once or less per week | 64 | 42 | 50 | 45 | 58 | 44 | 75 |
| Customers since store was opened | 65 | 77 | 64 | 74 | 70 | 63 | 75 |
| Meat and produce sales to total | 34 | 34 | 37 | 38 | 36 | 35 | 33 |
| Average sale per customer transaction | \$5.92 | \$4.59 | \$5.65 | \$5.27 | \$5.61 | \$5.18 | \$7.79 |
| Number of customer weekly transactions | 6,290 | 5,350 | 8,670 | 8,150 | 10,160 | 9,220 | 11,600 |

**Exhibit 4** Customer Shopping Habits—1961 and 1963 (Per Cent)

5. When a firm undertakes to operate both conventional and discount supermarkets in a metropolitan area, it may be faced with situations (as in Milltown) where as it increases its merchandising efforts to do more business at the discount unit it takes more sales away from its own conventional stores and vice versa. The merchandisers are therefore faced with a dilemma of how to serve the firm's two different types of stores with equal loyalty and love.

6. The Joy type of merchandising is carving out a place in our mass-production and mass-distribution economy. Therefore, we may expect that more such retailing facilities will be established. These will have disrupting effects, similar to the experience in Milltown, but not necessarily of equal magnitude.

7. Superior Markets' experience in Milltown is especially valuable because the Joy store here is most strategically located to take away business from its three sister stores. Therefore, it is not likely that there are more than one or two other areas in Metropolitan Waterville where a Joy store would affect equally as much Superior sister stores.

8. Should Superior Markets consider opening more discount supermarkets in Metropolitan Waterville, studies of what the effects are likely to be on existing company stores should be useful to management in making decisions.

*Technical Note: How to Measure a Store's Market Share*

Market share is the proportion of total potential sales which a store or company obtains from a given area. We can express market share as:

$$\text{MS} = \frac{s}{f} \quad \text{or} \quad \text{market share} = \frac{\text{store's sales per capita}}{\text{per capita food sales potential}}$$

The technique for determining a store's market share involves the following steps:

1. Place a grid of ¼-mile squares (or ⅛-mile squares for greater precision) along coordinate lines on a population spot map. Line up a point where four grid squares meet over the corresponding store site on the population map. Determine and record the population in each square.
2. Place the same grid over a customer spotting map, with each spotted customer equal to $100 weekly sales. If the scale of the customer spotting map is different from the population map, then use different scale grids, to correspond to the scales of these maps. Count the number of spotted customers in each square, multiply this by $100, and divide by the population in the square. The quotient is the store's per capita weekly sales.
3. Determine, from census tract data in the *U.S. Census of Population and Housing* (*a*) the median income in each square, and, from the Bureau of Labor Statistics' reports on *Consumer Expenditure and Income* (*b*) the per capita weekly home food expenditures for the corresponding income group.
4. Determine the store's market share in each square by the formula $\text{MS} = s/f$. The quotient in step 2 above is the $s$ and the figure in step 3 (*b*) is the $f$. The $s$ and $f$ can be adjusted for changes in the BLS index of food prices, for comparability of data over time.
5. Decide what isoline values are most meaningful for the analysis (30%, 20%, 10% of market share). Designate a range of values and shade each square in a manner to differentiate this.
6. Draw in pencil tentative isolines to delimit the squares which qualify. A square that fails to qualify, but is positioned between two squares which do, should be included if the average for all three squares qualifies. Segments of trading area that are isolated "islands" because of barriers should be included if they qualify.
7. Superimpose the grid with the tentative isolines over the population spot map. Modify the tentative isolines to correspond most realistically to the distribution of population on the map. Unpopulated areas may be included or excluded in drawing the final isolines.

Figure 7 partially illustrates the technique described above.

# TECHNIQUE FOR MEASURING MARKET SHARE

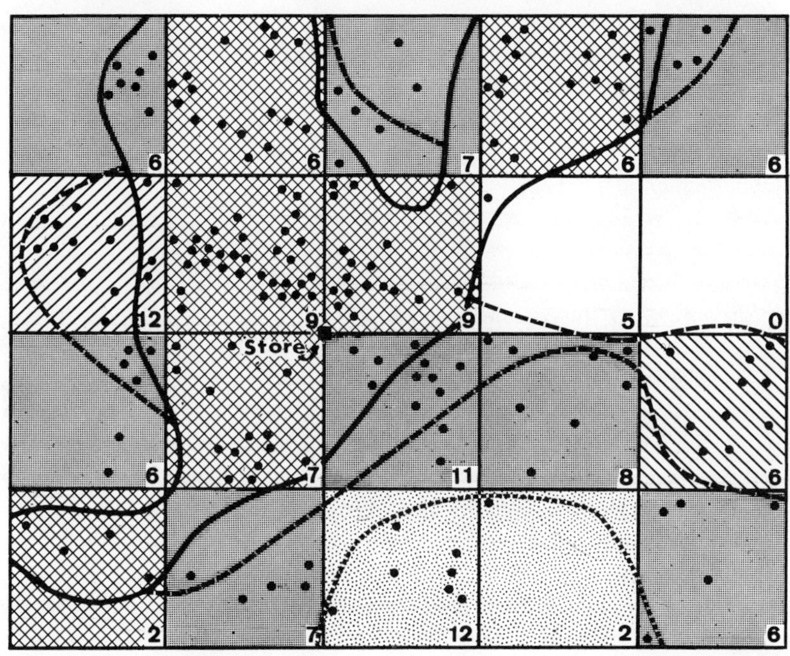


WEEKLY
PER CAPITA MARKET SHARE

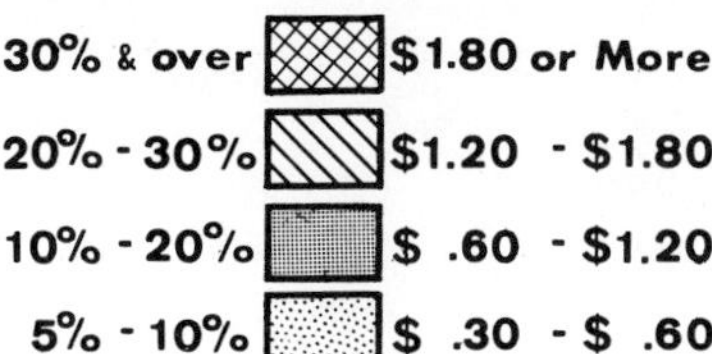


1/4 Mile Square Grids

• CUSTOMER
Each Symbol
Represents $100
in Weekly Sales

Number in Grid
is Approximate
100 Population

ISOLINES

30% & over
20% - 30%
10% - 20%

Figure 7

## WRIGLEY APPLIANCE CORPORATION*

The Wrigley Appliance Corporation was founded in 1939 by Joseph P. Wrigley. At first, the company manufactured only small electric cooking stoves, but after achieving market success in this area it began to expand its product lines to include other household appliances. Among the product additions were electric refrigerators, vacuum cleaners, automatic dishwashers, and, more recently, automatic laundry equipment.

By 1967 the Wrigley Corporation had been able to achieve market penetration with all of their product lines except the more recently added laundry equipment. Despite the disappointing initial sales volume of Wrigley's laundry equipment, all forecasts suggested future market success.

In less than thirty years Joseph P. Wrigley had built his company from a small single-product plant and warehouse to a large multiplant corporation that distributed all of its products nationally. Despite this incredible growth, Joseph P. Wrigley had been able to maintain financial control and remained the active president of the corporation. The company was a closed corporation, with the Wrigley family holding nearly 60 per cent of the outstanding shares.

Late in 1966 Wrigley formed an executive management board. The purpose of this board was to assist the president in long-range planning and in formulating broad company policies. The board had previously existed unofficially; however, because of the rapid growth of the company, the board was formalized to facilitate its function. The executive management board held regularly scheduled quarterly meetings; in addition, provision was made for meetings of an emergency type.

The board consisted of nine members:

1. Joseph P. Wrigley, President.
2. Frederick K. Arrow, Secretary-Treasurer.
3. George R. Davidson, Corporation General Controller.
4. Norman P. Dewitt, Assistant General Controller.
5. John R. Wrigley, Manager, New Product Development.
6. Robert B. Cornwell, Vice-President, Manager Eastern Division.
7. Albert P. Miller, Vice-President, Manager, Southwestern Division.
8. Paul C. Wrigley, Vice-President, Manager, North Control Division.
9. Raymond J. Wrigley, Executive Vice-President.

At the regularly scheduled first-quarter meeting of 1967, the executive management board began seriously considering its long-range plans. During the course of this meeting it became apparent that the various members of the board had widely divergent ideas about the future policies of the Wrigley Corporation.

* The name of the company and some of the figures are disguised.

There were a variety of suggested alternatives that the various board members felt should be incorporated into the firm's general policy. These alternatives can be summarized as follows:

1. Concentrate resources on improvement of existing products and on further penetration of the present marketing area.
2. Expand market to areas outside the United States. This would entail the organization of foreign sales offices and, if necessary, foreign production facilities.
3. Expand product lines. Some possible additions would be small household appliances, heating equipment, and air-conditioning equipment.
4. Expand both marketing area and product lines.
5. Maintain present products and marketing areas with emphasis on increased profits through more efficient operations. This alternative would entail minimizing expenses for product improvement as well as new product R & D.

Since the various alternatives were in obvious conflict, Mr. Wrigley felt that each of them should be rated in relation to how well they satisfied the firm's basic objectives. At that time, however, the basic corporate objectives had not been formally stated; hence the executive board began the task of proposing, discussing, and rating what they felt were their basic long-range objectives.

Mr. Wrigley had a strong belief in the democratic form of management. He felt, therefore, that the entire executive board should have a voice in formally setting and weighting the firm's objectives.

The generally agreed upon objectives were discussed fully and set down as follows:

1. Maintain family control of the business.
2. Maintain private ownership—that is, "closed corporation" status.
3. Maintain stable labor relations—as evidenced by the absence of strikes and slowdowns and by low employee turnover.
4. Attain market penetration for all of the firm's products.
5. Achieve a good public image and assume a position of leadership in the field of community service.
6. *Guarantee* the owners of the corporation a return on their original investment that is comparable to the bank rate of interest, such as 4 to 6 per cent.
7. Ensure that the company continually has available attractive investment alternatives such that the expected rate of return is in excess of 14 per cent.
8. Retain existing management personnel.

The president asked each member of the executive management board to rate the various objectives on a percentage scale so that the total sum for all the objectives would be 100 per cent (see Exhibit 1). He further instructed the board members to complete their ratings in time for the second quarter board meeting of 1967.

During the period between the two board meetings, Mr. Wrigley planned to meet with various members of the company in order to assess the effect of the alternative policies on each of the firm's objectives. The president reasoned that if one of the alternatives permitted absolute fulfillment of one of the objectives, it should be given a rating of 1.0 for that objective. If, on the other hand, one of the alternative policies was in absolute conflict with a company objective, the rating for that objective should be 0.0. Mr. Wrigley planned to rate each alternative action with respect to all eight of the company objectives; thus there were to be a total of forty ratings.

## QUESTIONS

1. Construct a table that reflects your ratings of objective satisfaction for each of the alternative policies.
2. You will note in Exhibit 1 that the objectives have not been weighted by Albert P. Miller (board member number 7). Using the background information on Mr. Miller that is contained in the Appendix, weight the objectives as you think he would.
3. Assuming that each member of the executive management board has an equal voice in determining the firm's policies, use the given information and the information that you have been asked to supply to choose that policy which best satisfies the firm's objectives.

## APPENDIX

| | Board Member Number | | | | | | | | |
|---|---|---|---|---|---|---|---|---|---|
| | 1 | 2 | 3 | 4 | 5 | 6 | 7 | 8 | 9 |
| Objective | JPW | FKA | GRD | NPD | JRW | RBC | APM | PCW | RJW |
| $\theta^1$ | 0.30 | 0.10 | 0.05 | 0.10 | 0.25 | 0.10 | | 0.25 | 0.25 |
| $\theta^2$ | 0.20 | 0.20 | 0.15 | 0.10 | 0.20 | 0.20 | | 0.25 | 0.30 |
| $\theta^3$ | 0.05 | 0.10 | 0.10 | 0.05 | 0.05 | 0.10 | | 0.05 | 0.05 |
| $\theta^4$ | 0.05 | 0.10 | 0.10 | 0.10 | 0.20 | 0.10 | | 0.10 | 0.10 |
| $\theta^5$ | 0.10 | 0.15 | 0.10 | 0.05 | 0.05 | 0.10 | | 0.05 | 0.05 |
| $\theta^6$ | 0.05 | 0.15 | 0.20 | 0.15 | 0.05 | 0.15 | | 0.10 | 0.05 |
| $\theta^7$ | 0.10 | 0.10 | 0.20 | 0.25 | 0.05 | 0.10 | | 0.15 | 0.15 |
| $\theta^8$ | 0.15 | 0.10 | 0.10 | 0.20 | 0.15 | 0.15 | | 0.05 | 0.05 |
| Total | 1.00 | 1.00 | 1.00 | 1.00 | 1.00 | 1.00 | | 1.00 | 1.00 |

**Exhibit 1** Weighting of Objectives

**Exhibit 2** Albert P. Miller

With the exception of John R. Wrigley, Albert P. Miller is the youngest member of the executive management board. Mr. Miller met the younger Wrigley while in the service during the Korean War. Following the war and their discharge, Mr. Miller was invited to join the Wrigley firm and to work with John Wrigley in New Product Development.

Albert Miller received his college training in Business Administration. After his graduation he worked as a sales representative for one of the country's leading appliance manufacturers. He had been granted a military leave of absence by his former employer when he was drafted into the service in 1950, but after his discharge he decided to take the Wrigley offer because the salary was higher and because he felt that the opportunities for advancement were better.

From the beginning, Mr. Miller's supervisors were very impressed with his work. He became familiar with some of the scientific and technical knowledge of his associates in the New Product Development section, while his knowledge of consumer needs and buying habits proved very valuable to the firm.

In 1957 the company decided to organize their marketing function into decentralized geographical divisions. Because of his success and definite orientation toward marketing, Albert Miller was appointed manager of one of the five marketing divisions, located in the Southwest area of the United States. Until the reorganization, Wrigley sales in this territory lagged far behind those in any of the other territories. In fact, except within a few of the larger cities, Wrigley products were nearly unknown.

Mr. Miller immediately began a sizable promotional program in his division and undertook a program to recruit the most capable sales representatives that could be found. As a result of his efforts, by 1960 the Southwestern division was in close contention with the other divisions for the top position in sales volume. In recognition of his efferts, Mr. Miller was granted a Vice-Presidency and a substantial salary raise in 1963.

In 1960 the Wrigley Corporation started the policy of giving their top executives a stock bonus at the end of the year. In addition, the company granted the members of the executive board stock options by which they could apply 20 per cent of their annual salary to the purchase of company stock at a cost that was considered to be well below fair market value. Mr. Miller had been given lucrative year-end bonuses, and he had exercised his stock options to the maximum allowable amount. By the end of 1966 he estimated that he held about 5 per cent of Wrigley's stock outstanding.

Mr. Miller had always enjoyed his work with the Wrigley Corporation, and he took great pride in his accomplishments. However, in the years after he had successfully opened the Southwestern marketing division he began to derive less satisfaction from his work. His marketing division had attained what was considered full sales potential; and, although he felt that maintenance of this position was a great responsibility that required dynamic leadership, Mr. Miller also felt that he wanted a greater challenge.

In recent corporate meetings Mr. Miller had been doing his best to arouse interest in forming an international division of Wrigley Appliances. It was his hope that if such a division were organized, he would be placed in charge of its operations.

PART II

# *Statistical Designs for Marketing Information and Decisions*

Part II provides a background in the statistical design of marketing research. Chapter 4 introduces the reader to simple random samples. Chapter 5 is concerned with more complex sample designs. Chapter 6 contrasts classical and Bayesian techniques for decision making, using sample information. Chapter 7 introduces the reader to experimental design and decision making, using information from field or laboratory experiments.

It is important for the reader to note that the material of Part II pertains both to the continuing data base and to special-problem information; hence no distinction between these two classifications is made here.

*Four*

# Sampling—Estimating Parameters

A cereal manufacturer wishes to know the proportion of teen-age Americans who have breakfast cereal four or more times a week. Another cereal manufacturer wishes to know the average number of ounces per week consumed by the same population segment. A third manufacturer has noticed that sales of one of his breakfast cereals are down and wishes to test the hypothesis that the average consumption by the teen-age group has not changed. These three problems are indeed very similar, and yet they are sufficiently different to illustrate the three principal concerns of sampling in the flow of market information.

In the first case, the manufacturer wants knowledge about the proportion of a particular *population* (see Figure 4-1 for definitions of terms most commonly used in sampling) or *universe* (the teen market) that possesses a particular *attribute* (i.e., the consumption of breakfast cereal four or more times a week). In the second case, the manufacturer wishes to know something about the *magnitude* of a *population parameter* (in this case, the average or mean) that summarizes information about a particular variable (ounces consumed). In the third case, the manufacturer is concerned with *testing an hypothesis* (that consumption has not changed from the previous period).

The first two problems involve the estimation of parameters that differ, insofar that the attribute is either held or not held, but that cannot otherwise be measured, whereas a variable has magnitude. Thus a person either does or does not possess the attribute of eating breakfast cereal four or more times a week,[1] and the parameter of interest is the propor-

[1] This question becomes operational if we define a person to possess the attribute if he had breakfast cereal four or more times *last* week.

The following definitions will prove useful in reading the chapter. Most other words peculiar to statistics will be defined in context.

1. The *population* or *universe* is the total domain under consideration; for example, all readers of *Life* magazine or all viewers of a certain television program.
2. A *parameter* represents a characteristic of the population; for example, the mean number or the total number of members of the population over eighty years of age.
3. A *sample* is that part of the population for which we have data and which will be analyzed.
4. A *statistic* represents a characteristic of a sample.
5. A *sampling unit* is a partition of the population such that every element of the population belongs to one and only one sampling unit and the aggregate of the sampling units includes the entire population; for example, in sampling the people in a city, the sampling unit may be an individual, the members of a family, or the persons living in a city block.
6. The *arithmetic mean* or *mean of* a finite population (sample) characteristic is the sum of the values of the characteristic for each unit in the population (sample) divided by the total number of units. Thus the mean is one measure of the central tendency of the population or sample. The mode and median, whose definitions follow, are other measures of the central tendency.
7. The *mode* of a population (sample) characteristic is the value that occurs most frequently.
8. The *median* of the population (sample) characteristic is the value of this unit such that half the remaining units have higher values and half have lower values.
9. The *variance* of a population (sample) characteristic is the mean of the squares of the deviations of the value of each unit from the population (sample) mean. Thus the variance is a measure of dispersion.
10. The *standard deviation* is the positive square root of the variance; hence it also is a measure of dispersion.

**Figure 4-1** Definitions.

tion of the population that possesses the attribute. The variable "ounces consumed," however, is directly measurable. The third problem requires a simple statement of belief predicated on the sample results—that is, that the *null* hypothesis of no change holds or that the alternative hypothesis (that consumption by teen-agers has changed) holds.

None of these problems would involve the use of statistics if a complete *census* of the population were posssible, that is, if one could contact every teen-ager in the United States and elicit the required information. The scope of such a project would ensure its failure. But even if every teen-ager could be contacted, the cost involved would be prohibitive. It is evident that where the population involved is large or widely dispersed, only a *sample* of the population can be looked at.

### The Bayesian View

Within the past few years some experts in the field of marketing information have come to the conclusion that analysis that merely yields estimates or beliefs about the truth of hypotheses is insufficient in that it divorces the problem from the consequences of actions taken. This so-called *Bayesian* view is that the economic payoffs of the alternative courses of action, the costs of sampling, and the probabilities of the various possible outcomes should be combined in one overall measure, the expected opportunity loss. That action which yields the minimum expected opportunity loss should be selected.

Thus Bayesians feel that the estimate of a parameter, or a test of hypothesis, ignores much of the economic information relevant to a decision. A related distinction between the Bayesian and the non-Bayesian lies in the reluctance of the latter to apply probabilities to facts, a reluctance that is the primary reason why the two groups attack the problem of decision making very differently.

Our discussion here is designed only to suggest that a controversy does exist in decision making under uncertainty and to give a very sketchy idea of what the controversy is about. A much more complete treatment is provided in Chapter 6. Thus the reader who is somewhat confused at this point should not be concerned.

## SAMPLING ATTRIBUTES

An attribute is some characteristic by which each sampling unit may be classified in two (or more) categories. Thus one may say that a car is or is not black or a pie is or is not sweet. Of course, such a simple dichotomous situation does not always occur. In some instances a classification scheme may indicate the degree to which an attribute is possessed. For example, one might say that a painting is excellent, good, or bad or that a color is very dark, dark, light, or very light. In most instances of interest in the sampling of attributes for market information, however, one is concerned with only two categories, that is, the sampling unit either does or does not possess the attribute.

## The Sample Frame

Suppose that one wishes to estimate the proportion of males in Chicago who use shampoo. In order to specify precisely the *target population* (i.e., the population in which we are interested), the first step is to define carefully the critical terms in this apparently simple statement of the objective. Does the term "males" mean all males, including infants? Do we mean all males in Chicago proper, or possibly in the Chicago trading area? What frequency of usage makes one a shampoo user? Finally, just what is a shampoo?

Typically, the actual population sampled will differ somewhat from the target population. This is because some people will be omitted from any list of sampling units from which the sample will be drawn (this list is called the sampling *frame*) either because the list is incomplete, because it would be too costly to include these people, or because they will not cooperate. The biases thus introduced are discussed in Chapter 10.

## The Binomial Distribution[2]

Now, suppose that all these points are satisfactorily resolved and a specific sampling frame is obtained. The actual proportion of male shampoo users in the frame is unknown and is designated as $p^*$. Each of the $n$ males in the sample may or may not use shampoo, but the *expected value* of the proportion $p$ of users, in any given sample, is $p^*$.[3] That is, if a large number of samples were taken, the average of the sample proportions would be very close to $p^*$. This is illustrated below.

If one were to draw a large number of samples of size $n$ and calculate the proportion of shampoo users $p$ in each sample, the distribution of $p$ would be given by probability distribution known as the *binomial distribution*. If the true proportion $p^*$ of the universe is 0.3 (meaning that 30 per cent of the male population in Chicago use shampoo), the distribution of $p$ for sample sizes of 5, 10, 20, and 50 is as shown in Figure 4-2.

Two very important inferences can be drawn from Figure 4-2. In fact, these inferences cast light on two basic theorems without which sampling would be useless.

[2] A concise review of probability including the binomial and normal distribution is given in Appendix A of this chapter.

[3] Note that $p^*$ is a parameter, while $p$ is a statistic.

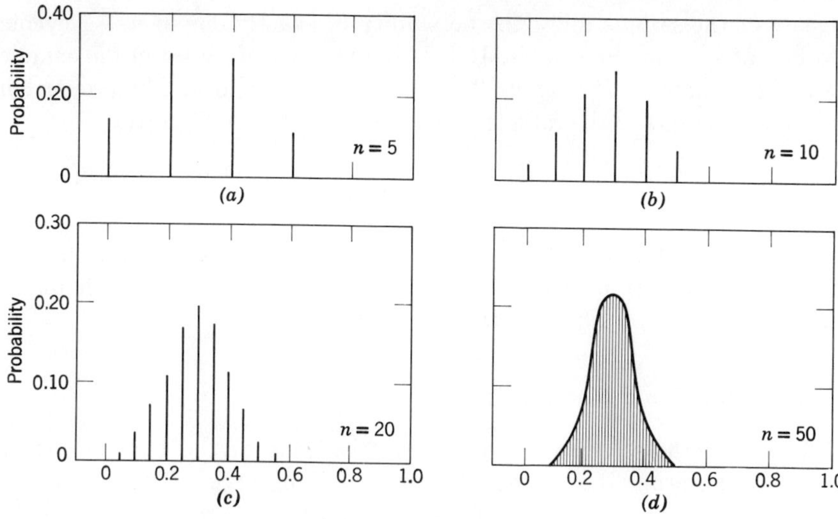


**Figure 4-2** $p^* = 0.3$.

The first thing to notice is that as the sample size $n$ increases, the distribution of $p$ tends to be concentrated closer to the expected value $p^* = 0.3$. This means that the probability of drawing an unusual sample where $p$ would be fairly different from $p^*$ decreases with increasing sample size. For example, when $p^* = 0.3$, the probability of drawing a sample showing that as many as *40 per cent or more* of the universe use shampoo would be 0.47 for $n = 5$, 0.23 for $n = 20$, and 0.08 for $n = 50$. The cumulative probabilities are represented by the sum of the probabilities from the proportion $p = 0.4$ to $p = 1.0$ in the respective distributions.

## The Law of Large Numbers

The fact that as the sample size increases the distribution of sample means concentrates closer to the mean of the universe is distinguished in statistics by being labeled a law, the *law of large numbers.* Without this law there would be little point in taking large samples rather than small samples. In fact, there would be little point in taking samples at all.

Figure 4-2 shows four *probability mass functions.* A probability mass function is distinguished from a *probability density function* by the fact that the former is discrete while the latter is continuous (as in the normal) distribution. In the case of attribute sampling, the $n$ elements of the sample allow the possibility of exactly one of $n + 1$ events to be noted from the sample. If $R$ is the number of males in the sample who use shampoo, $R$ may be 0, 1, or anything up to $n$. The proportion of shampoo users in the sample is thus calculated from the ratio

$$p = \frac{R}{n}, \qquad R = 0, 1, \ldots, n$$

For example, if a sample consisted of exactly 50 persons, we could observe anywhere from 0 to 50 persons in the sample who use shampoo, for a total of 51 possible observations.

## The Central Limit Theorem

If a smooth curve is drawn joining the ends of the bars in Figure **4-2** ($d$), a rather interesting phenomenon is observed. The continuous *density* function so constructed bears a remarkable resemblance to the well-known bell-shaped, normal distribution. This resemblance is, in fact, something more than coincidence. It brings the discussion to the second fundamental pillar of sampling alluded to earlier.

According to the *central limit theorem* of statistics, if we take a number of random samples each of size $n$ from a universe with mean $\mu$ and variance $\sigma^2$, the *sample means* tend to be normally distributed with mean $\mu$ and variance

$$\sigma_{\bar{X}}^2 = \frac{\sigma^2}{n}$$

as $n$ increases without bound. The $\bar{X}$ refers to the sample mean. In dealing with sample proportions $p$, the equation becomes

$$\sigma_p^2 = \frac{\sigma^2}{n}$$

and we say that the sample proportions $p$ tend to be normally distributed (i.e., have the normal distribution) with mean $p^*$ and variance $\sigma_p^2$ where $n$ is large. The square root of this variance, $\sigma_p$, is known as the *standard error of proportion.*

With a little thought, the reader should conclude that this is indeed a remarkable and powerful theorem. No matter what the form of the probability density distribution of the universe in question, provided only that the variance is finite, the sample means will have an approximate normal distribution for large samples. The point of particular practical significance to the market sampler is that he need only worry about the form of the distribution of sample means in the case of small samples—for large samples he may always assume it to be normal.

If our researcher wishes to estimate the population mean, it would seem that the sample mean would be a rather desirable estimate. It has the virtue of being *unbiased,* that is, the *expected value* of the sample mean equal the mean of the universe, $p^*$. It also has the virtue of tending to be distributed as close to $p^*$ as one would desire by taking a sufficiently large sample.[4] This latter property conveniently leads us into the topic of the confidence interval.

## Confidence Intervals for Attribute Proportions

Suppose that you, the reader, were hired to perform the research necessary to find the estimate of male shampoo users in Chicago. You decide to take a simple random sample of 100 males and it turns out that exactly 40 of them use shampoo. Naturally, you tell your employer that you estimate that 40 per cent of Chicago males are shampoo users. Unfortunately, the ungrateful wretch is unsatisfied with this answer and wants to know how sure he can be of your estimate. One approach that can be followed is to specify a *confidence interval* in addition to the estimate.

The meaning of a confidence interval is badly misunderstood by many researchers. Before discussing this point, let us construct a 90 per cent confidence interval for the sample proportions in our example. The standard error of proportion is given by

$$\sigma_p = \sqrt{\frac{p^*(1 - p^*)}{n}}$$

Our estimate of this quantity is obtained from the actual proportion $p$ observed as

$$\hat{\sigma}_p = \sqrt{\frac{p(1 - p)}{n - 1}} = \sqrt{\frac{0.4(1 - 0.4)}{100 - 1}} = 0.05$$

which measures the standard error of proportion. The caret over sigma in $\hat{\sigma}_p$ indicates an estimate.

Because $n$ is large, the sample proportion $p$ is approximately normally distributed. We seek an upper and lower bound for $p$, centered about $p = 0.4$, such that 90 per cent of the area under the probability distribution lies between these bounds. From the graph of the normal distribution

[4] There are other technical reasons why the sample mean actually turns out to have desirable qualities as an estimate of the population mean.

given in Appendix A it may be seen that 90 per cent of the area under the curve is contained between a lower bound that is 1.65 standard deviations below the mean and an upper bound that is 1.65 standard deviations above the mean. Thus these bounds are

$$\begin{aligned} 0.4 \pm 1.65\sigma_P &= 0.4 \pm 1.65 \cdot 0.05 \\ &= 0.4 \pm 0.08 \end{aligned}$$

We may then say with 90 per cent *confidence* that the true mean lies between 0.32 and 0.48.

### *Interpretation of a Confidence Interval*

The reader should note that we have said that the true mean lies between 0.32 and 0.48 with 90 per cent *confidence* and not with 90 per cent *probability*. This is not a play on words, but a crucial point.[5]

The "traditional" statistician[6] employs the term probability with a long-run frequency interpretation. Thus we may say that the probability of a head occuring in the toss of a fair coin is one half because in a long number of trials, $n$, the expected number of heads tossed is $n/2$. Similarly, *if we constructed a large number of confidence intervals (by taking a large number of samples) of the proportion of male shampoo users in Chicago in exactly the same manner as we constructed the interval above, we would expect approximately 90 per cent of these intervals to include the true proportion* $p^*$. Then we may say, *before* a confidence interval is constructed, that it will include the true mean with 90 per cent probability. *Once we have constructed a particular interval,* however, the interval either does or does not contain the true mean, and a (long-run frequency) 90 per cent probability figure is incorrect. The *probability* that the interval contains the true mean is either 0 or 1, although it contains the true mean with 90 per cent *confidence.*

The following example will illustrate the point. Suppose that a second sample of Chicago males is taken and it is found that the true percentage of shampoo users, as measured by that sample, lies between 50 and 60 per cent with 90 per cent confidence. Now, it would strike most people as unreasonable to say both that ($a$) the true mean lies between 0.32 and 0.48 with 90 per cent probability and ($b$) the true mean lies

[5] It is one of the reasons why Bayesian statisticians prefer not to employ the notion of confidence intervals.

[6] Bayesian statisticians usually refer to most other statisticians as "classical" or "traditional." This is a rather incongruous term when one considers that the forerunner of the Bayesian school, Thomas Bayes, was an eighteenth-century cleric whereas so-called "traditional" statistics was primarily developed in this century. Nevertheless, we shall follow the same practice for want of a better set of names.

between 0.50 and 0.60 with 90 per cent probability, considering that the two intervals do not even overlap. Yet it is conceivable that two such confidence intervals would occur.

To summarize the argument, a confidence interval is constructed by specifying the degree of confidence *before* a sample is drawn. Thus one may say that the interval will contain the true population mean, with 90 per cent probability, before seeing the sample results. A *particular* interval is then obtained, which contains the true mean with 90 per cent confidence, but not 90 per cent probability, since a frequency interpretation is no longer possible. Nevertheless, it is reassuring to note that if one assumes that the true mean lies somewhere in the 90 per cent confidence interval in each of a number of research projects, he will be right approximately 90 per cent of the time.

The Bayesian has one further objection to the confidence interval. Suppose that, in the example given, the researcher reports that the proportion of male shampoo users lies between 0.32 and 0.48 with 90 per cent confidence. The shampoo manufacturer, however, may be particularly interested in the interval 0.25 to 0.35 and would like to know what degree of confidence he can assign to this interval. Unfortunately, the theory does not permit you to assign any degree of confidence, good or bad, to any interval except the interval around the sample mean 0.40. Of course, you might have chosen some other degree of confidence before the sample was taken, but it would be fortuitous if it happened to generate the interval desired by the information user.

Where a particular interval is of concern, the confidence interval approach is unsuitable. What could be done within the realm of traditional statistics, however, would be to test the *hypothesis* that the true mean lies in the interval against the alternative hypothesis that the mean lies outside the interval. This approach will be demonstrated in the section of Chapter 6 devoted to hypothesis testing.

Before leaving the subject of confidence intervals for attribute sampling, we shall investigate the construction of an interval for a small sample, where one cannot assume that the sampling distribution is approximately normal.

### *Estimating Attributes for Small Samples*

Roughly speaking, the sample size should be at least 50 and both $np$ and $n(1-p)$ should be greater than 5 before the normal approximation for the binomial distribution is employed. When these conditions are *not* met, it is usually wiser to employ the binomial distribution directly.

The best estimate of $p^*$ is still given by $p = R/n$ where $R$ is the number of "successes" (shampoo users) in $n$ trials. The formulation of the confidence interval, however, is much more difficult than when the normal approximation is valid.

The confidence interval is constructed as follows. Suppose that we observe that exactly six males out of twenty are shampoo users ($p = 0.3$). If a confidence level of 95 per cent had been chosen, we must determine $p_1$ and $p_2$ such that (1) $p_1$ represents the largest value that $p$ can be and still have the probability of observing six or *less* successes in twenty trials less than or equal to 2½ per cent and (2) $p_2$ represents the smallest value that $p$ can be and still have the probability of observing six or *more* successes in twenty trials less than or equal to 2½ per cent. Appendix B contains a graph that has been constructed in precisely this manner.[7] From it, we may determine that the upper and lower bounds of the 95 per cent confidence intervals, where $n = 20$ and $p = 0.3$, are $p_1 = 0.11$ and $p_2 = 0.54$. It should be noted that this interval is not symmetrical with respect to the point estimate 0.3. This is not unexpected, since the binomial distribution is itself asymmetrical.

## SAMPLING VARIABLES

Most of the observations that have been made about sampling of attributes also hold in the sampling of other population parameters. Most important, the law of large numbers and the central limit theorem still hold.

Let us return to the problem of the cereal manufacturer who desires an estimate of the average number of ounces per week of breakfast cereal consumed by the teen-age population of Chicago. As in the shampoo example, certain definitional problems must be resolved before further analysis. Is cooked cereal a breakfast cereal? What are the geographical limits of Chicago?

A further problem is entailed by the timing of the sample. Does cereal consumption vary during the year? If so, a sample obtained in the summer will likely yield different results from one obtained in the winter. Do teen-agers who go to camp in the summer, hence are not available for inclusion in the survey, have a different consumption pattern from those who remain and are, presumably, in a lower income group?

[7] In probabilistic terms, if $1 - \alpha$ is the confidence level and $x$ is a random variable of the number of successes, $p_1$ is the largest value of $p$ such that $p(x \geq r) = \alpha/2$ and $p_2$ is the smallest value of $p$ such that $p(x \leq r) = \alpha/2$. Thus $p_1 < p^* < p^2$ is a $1 - \alpha$ per cent confidence interval.

## An Example—A Large-Sample Estimate

Suppose that the average cereal consumption of the population is given the symbol $\mu$. A simple random sample of size $n = 50$ yields the results shown in Figure 4-3. Our best estimate of the population mean $\mu$ is given by the sample mean, $\bar{X} = 10.7$.

| $i$ | $X_i$ | $X_i^2$ | $i$ | $X_i$ | $X_i^2$ | $i$ | $X_i$ | $X_i^2$ |
|---|---|---|---|---|---|---|---|---|
| 1 | 0 | 0 | 18 | 3 | 9 | 35 | 14 | 196 |
| 2 | 16 | 256 | 19 | 8 | 64 | 36 | 0 | 0 |
| 3 | 20 | 400 | 20 | 6 | 36 | 37 | 0 | 0 |
| 4 | 5 | 25 | 21 | 7 | 49 | 38 | 0 | 0 |
| 5 | 0 | 0 | 22 | 0 | 0 | 39 | 6 | 36 |
| 6 | 18 | 324 | 23 | 14 | 196 | 40 | 7 | 49 |
| 7 | 15 | 225 | 24 | 10 | 100 | 41 | 3 | 9 |
| 8 | 9 | 81 | 25 | 20 | 400 | 42 | 20 | 400 |
| 9 | 40 | 1600 | 26 | 6 | 36 | 43 | 8 | 64 |
| 10 | 27 | 729 | 27 | 3 | 9 | 44 | 6 | 36 |
| 11 | 10 | 100 | 28 | 9 | 81 | 45 | 15 | 225 |
| 12 | 13 | 169 | 29 | 15 | 225 | 46 | 0 | 0 |
| 13 | 0 | 0 | 30 | 10 | 100 | 47 | 10 | 100 |
| 14 | 0 | 0 | 31 | 24 | 576 | 48 | 4 | 16 |
| 15 | 8 | 64 | 32 | 13 | 169 | 49 | 11 | 121 |
| 16 | 32 | 1024 | 33 | 0 | 0 | 50 | 17 | 289 |
| 17 | 45 | 2025 | 34 | 8 | 64 | | | |
| $\Sigma$ | 258 | 7022 | $\Sigma$ | 156 | 2114 | $\Sigma$ | 121 | 1541 |

$\Sigma X_i = 258 + 156 + 121 = 535 \qquad \bar{X} = \Sigma X_i n = 10.7$

$\Sigma X_i^2 = 7022 + 2114 + 1541 = 10677$

$$s^2 = \frac{1}{n} \Sigma X_i^2 - \bar{X}^2 = 99.05$$

$$\hat{\sigma}^2 = \frac{n}{n-1} \cdot s^2 = 101.07 \qquad \hat{\sigma}_{\bar{X}}^2 = \frac{s^2}{n-1} = 2.02$$

**Figure 4-3** Cereal Consumption in Ounces per Week. The $i$ is the identifying number of the sample element (person), and $X_i$ is the amount of cereal consumed the previous week by the $i$th person in the sample. *Note:* Many texts reduce the computation in large samples by grouping the data in equal intervals and assigning the score of the mid-point of the interval to all the $X_i$ that fall in the interval. With the advent of the computer, this is no longer necessary or recommended.

The variance of the sample is given by

$$s^2 = \sum_{i=1}^{n} \frac{(X_i - \bar{X})^2}{n}$$

or, equivalently, by

$$s^2 = \frac{1}{n} \cdot \sum_{i=1}^{n} X_i^2 - \bar{X}^2$$

In the example, $s^2 = 99.05$. If the variance of the population is unknown, as is usually the case, it is estimated by the relationship

$$\hat{\sigma}^2 = \frac{n}{n-1} s^2$$

which equals 101.07 in the sample. By the central limit theorem, the distribution of $\bar{X}$ is approximately normal for large samples[8] with mean $\mu$ and variance $\sigma_{\bar{X}}^2$.[9]

$$\sigma_{\bar{X}}^2 = \frac{\sigma^2}{n} \doteq \frac{s^2}{n-1}$$

The value of $\sigma_{\bar{X}}$ is usually called the *standard error of the mean*. Here,

$$\hat{\sigma}_{\bar{X}} = \sqrt{2.02} = 1.42$$

Now, in order to construct a 95 per cent confidence interval for the average cereal consumption in ounces per week, we have the lower limit given by

$$\begin{aligned} \bar{X}_L &= \bar{X} - 1.96\sigma_{\bar{X}} \\ &= 10.7 - 1.96 \cdot 1.42 \\ &= 7.9 \end{aligned}$$

The upper limit is given by

$$\begin{aligned} \bar{X}_u &= 10.7 + 1.96 \cdot 1.42 \\ &= 13.5 \end{aligned}$$

Then we can say with 95 per cent confidence that $\mu$ lies between 7.9 and 13.5.

[8] The sample size of $n = 50$ in the current example is about the lower limit for the normal approximation of the sample means to hold.

[9] If the $N$ is not extremely large, a correction factor $(1 - n/N)$ is applied to the formula for the variance of $\bar{X}$.

## Small-Sample Estimates and Confidence Intervals of the Population Mean

If the researcher, for some reason, were only allowed to take a sample of size 15 in attempting to determine the mean number of ounces of cereal consumed per person in Chicago, his problem would be considerably more difficult. *One obvious implication is that the standard error of the mean would be greatly increased,* resulting in a wider confidence interval, unless the user of the research is willing to accept a relatively small level of confidence.

The other problem that may arise is more basic. It was previously assumed that $\bar{X}$ would be distributed normally, no matter what the distribution of $X$. With a sample size of only 15 this is no longer a very safe assumption, since the central limit theorem applies only to large samples. In this section we look at the procedures one should adopt if either (1) there is reason to believe that $X$ is normally distributed or (2) we have no idea of the distribution of $X$.

### *If The Sampled Population Is Normal*

If $X$ is normally distributed with mean $\mu$, the statistic $t = (\mu - \bar{X})/\hat{\sigma}_{\bar{X}}$ is distributed according to Student's $t$ distribution. As may be seen from Figure 4-4, the $t$ distribution is quite similar to the normal distribution and converges to the normal distribution as the sample size increases. For samples of size 30 or more, the normal distribution may be substituted for the $t$ distribution.[10]

[10] Earlier in the chapter the statement was made that the normal distribution is a good approximation for the distribution of sample means where $n$ is greater than about 50. The closeness of the $t$ distribution to the normal distribution for smaller sample sizes can be attributed to the assumption that the population is itself normally distributed.

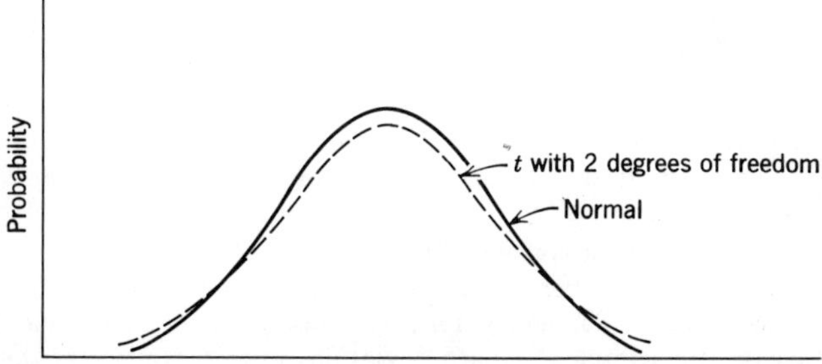


**Figure 4-4** Comparison of the $t$ distribution with 2 degrees of freedom with the normal distribution.

For a confidence level of 95 per cent, Appendix C indicates a value for $t_{0.95}$ of 2.145 for the $t$ distribution having 14 degrees of freedom.[11] If $\bar{X}$ were again found to be 10.7 and $\hat{\sigma}_{\bar{X}}$ to be 2.0, the confidence interval would be

$$\bar{X} \pm t_{0.95} \cdot \hat{\sigma}_{\bar{X}} = 10.7 \pm 2.145 \cdot 2.0$$
$$= 6.4,\ 15.0$$

Thus $\mu$ lies between 6.4 and 15.0 with 95 per cent confidence.

## Unknown Population Distribution

Suppose, however, that the population from which the sample is taken is not normally distributed (a not unusual occurrence, contrary to popular opinion). In fact, let us suppose that we have no idea at all what the distribution of male shampoo users in Chicago looks like. In this moment of apparent defeat, statistics, like the U.S. Cavalry, comes to the rescue. The rescuer, however, turns out to be a Russian by the name of Tchebycheff.[12]

One of the forms of Tchebycheff's inequality establishes the confidence interval as follows. If the lower bound of the interval is $\bar{X} - C \cdot \sigma_{\bar{X}}$ where $C$ is some positive number and the upper bound is $\bar{X} + C \cdot \sigma_{\bar{X}}$, then the probability that $\mu$ will lie in the interval is greater than or equal to $\alpha = 1 - 1/C^2$.

Now, if the level of confidence is chosen to be 95 per cent, then

$$0.95 = 1 - \frac{1}{(C_{0.95})^2}$$

or

$$C_{0.95} = 4.47$$

Looking at the sample of size 15 where $\bar{X} = 10.7$ and $\sigma_{\bar{X}} = 2.0$, the

[11] The degrees of freedom here are 1 less than the sample size. Intuitively, the reader can see that a sample size of 2 is the minimum necessary to obtain any idea of the dispersion of the population, and one "bit" of information is lost in calculating the statistic.

A rigorous treatment of the concept of degrees of freedom is beyond the scope of this text. In general, when a number of statistics are employed in estimating a population parameter, 1 degree of freedom is lost for each statistic. Since the above case employs only one statistic (the sample standard deviation) in the estimate of the population standard deviation from which the sampling error $\sigma_{\bar{X}}$ is derived, 1 degree of freedom is lost from the 15 bits of information provided by the sample.

[12] This name is spelled Chebyshev in older books on statistics.

95 per cent confidence interval becomes

$$\bar{X} \pm C_{0.95}\sigma_{\bar{X}} = 10.7 \pm 4.47 \cdot 2$$
$$= 1.8,\ 19.6$$

Thus $\mu$ lies between 1.8 and 19.6 with 95 per cent confidence. This is a considerably wider interval than was obtained using the $t$ distribution, which is not unexpected when we remember that Tchebycheff's inequality holds true no matter what the underlying population distribution. In other words, where the population distribution is known, we can make use of the extra information this gives.

## THE CHOICE OF SAMPLE SIZE

So far we have been concerned with estimating parameters given a preselected sample size. The question of how to select the sample size is discussed next.

We have seen that larger samples, for the same level of confidence, generate narrower confidence intervals and thus carry more information than do smaller samples. Unfortunately, larger samples also cost more than do smaller samples. Furthermore, as a consequence of the relationship between the standard deviation of the population, the sample size, and the sampling error, namely,

$$\sigma_{\bar{X}} = \frac{\sigma}{\sqrt{n}}$$

it is necessary to quadruple the sample size in order to cut the sampling error in half. Thus the sample size is a compromise between cost and precision.

### Attributes

Suppose, in the problem of estimating the proportion of shampoo users, that it was decided that the 95 per cent confidence interval desired should be no wider than 6 percentage points. If we assume the standard error of proportion $\sigma_p$ to be normally distributed, this implies that

$$1.96\sigma_p \leq 0.03$$

or

$$\sigma_p \leq 0.0153$$

Now, the size of standard error of proportion depends on the actual proportion of shampoo users (the quantity that we are trying to estimate) and thus cannot be known in advance. We do know, however, that $\sigma_p$ is largest when the true proportion is one half, and since the procedure is to limit the size of the interval no matter what the true proportion of shampoo users, we assume this proportion to be one half.

From the formula for the standard error of the proportion we have

$$\sigma_p^2 = \frac{p^*(1 - p^*)}{n}$$

or

$$n = \frac{p^*(1 - p^*)}{\sigma_p^2}$$

Here

$$n = \frac{0.5(1 - 0.5)}{(0.0153)^2}$$

$$= 1068$$

### Variables

If the problem were to estimate the average consumption of cereal, it would be complicated by the fact that there is no theoretical upper bound to the population variance. Thus it is necessary to have some idea of the population variance before determining the sample size. There are various ways in which this can be accomplished. First, from knowledge of similar problems one may be able to estimate the variance. Second, a pilot study may be undertaken to estimate the variance. Third, the first returns of the sample may be used to estimate the variance.

Given the population variance, the determination of sample size in this problem is not very different from the procedure used in estimating a proportion. Instead of specifying a maximum width of the confidence interval in terms of percentage points, it is specified in ounces of cereal. Again, it is typically assumed that the sample size will be sufficiently large for the sample mean to be normally distributed.

## SUMMARY

In this chapter, we have investigated how one might use a simple random sample to estimate a population mean. More complicated sample designs as well as practical discussions of the various types of sampling procedures are taken up in the following chapters.

APPENDIX A

# PROBABILITY

A brief and nonrigorous exposition on probability is presented here, followed by descriptions of two particularly important probability distributions—the binomial distribution and the normal distribution.

Suppose that various possible outcomes can occur if a random phenomenon takes place. For example, if a die is tossed, the possible outcomes of the trial are such that any one of the six sides may land face up. If a ball is thrown, the distance the ball lands from the thrower represents the outcome of this trial. In the latter case, the number of possible outcomes is infinite.

We may define an *event* as a collection of the possible outcomes. If any one of the possible outcomes comprising the event occurs, the event is said to have occurred. If $A$ and $B$ are two events, both of which cannot occur in one trial, the two events are said to be *mutually exclusive*.

## *Probability Defined*

Suppose that we assign weights to the possible outcomes. Weights that satisfy the following three axioms may be called probabilities:

1. Each weight is greater than or equal to zero and less than or equal to unity.
2. If an event $A$ is composed of[13] two mutually exclusive events, $B$ and $C$, the weight assigned to $A$ is the sum of the weights assigned to $B$ and $C$.
3. The sum of the weights assigned to a set of mutually exclusive events that together include all the possible outcomes is unity.

To illustrate, if a die is tossed, the following events may occur:

$$A = \{1, 2\} \qquad B = \{3, 4\} \qquad C = \{5, 6\} \qquad D = \{2, 4, 6\}$$

Thus if a 2 is thrown, both events $A$ and $D$ are said to have occurred.

If the die is fair, we may assign the following probabilities:

$$P(A) = P(B) = P(C) = 2/6$$

All the probabilities satisfy axiom 1. Events $A$, $B$, and $C$ are mutually exclusive. Since they have no possible happenings in common, if one occurs, neither of the others can occur. Now suppose that we examine the event $E$ composed of events $A$ and $B$.

Then $$E = \{1, 2, 3, 4\}$$

By axiom 2 $$P(E) = P(A) + P(B) = 2/6 + 2/6 = 4/6$$

[13] Those familiar with set theory will prefer the more rigorous term "union" for "composed of."

Since $D$ and $A$ are *not* mutually exclusive, axiom 2 does not hold for event $F$ where

$$F = \{1, 2, 4, 6\}$$

and event $F$ is composed of $A$ and $D$.

Since events $A$, $B$, and $C$, in addition to being mutually exclusive, exhaust all the possible outcomes, the sum of their probabilities is unity.

*Two Laws of Probability*

Axiom 2 describes the *addition rule* of probability. Whenever a set of events can be identified as mutually exclusive, the addition law holds.

Suppose, however, that two events $A$ and $B$ are independent, that is, the probability of $A$ given $B$ [notationally, $P(A|B)$] equals the probability of $A$. In other words, whether $B$ occurs or does not occur has no affect on the probability of $A$. An example is given by the toss of a coin. If the coin comes up heads on one toss, this has no effect in the next toss.

If two events are independent, the *multiplication rule* of probability holds. Thus the probability of a head occurring on the first toss of a coin and a tail on the second toss is given by

$$\begin{aligned} &P\text{ (head on first toss and tail on second toss)} \\ &\quad = P\text{ (head on first toss)} \cdot P\text{ (tail on second toss)} \\ &\quad = 1/2 \cdot 1/2 \\ &\quad = 1/4 \end{aligned}$$

The novice often has difficulty in deciding when the addition law applies and when the multiplication law applies. This should not be difficult if one notices that independent events are *not* mutually exclusive. In fact, the multiplication law is used to derive the probability of two or more events *jointly* occurring, a probability that is zero if the events are mutually exclusive.

*The Binomial Distribution*

A *Bernoulli process* is a set of independent trials characterized by {0, 1} or {failure, success} as the possible occurrences in a trial. The *binomial distribution* describes the probability of the number of successes in $n$ Bernoulli trials.

If $p^*$ is the probability of success on each trial, the probability of observing exactly $x$ successes is given as

$$P(x) = \binom{n}{x} (p^*)^x \cdot (1 - p^*)^{n-x}$$

where $\binom{n}{x}$ is the number of combinations of $x$ things from a total of $n$.

For example, the probability of observing three heads in five tosses of a fair coin is

$$P(X = 3|n = 5,\ \ p^* = 0.5) = \binom{5}{3}\binom{1}{2}^3 \cdot (1/2)^2$$

$$= \frac{5!}{2!3!} \cdot \frac{1}{2^5}$$

$$= \frac{5 \cdot 4 \cdot 3!}{2!3!} \cdot \frac{1}{2^5}$$

$$= \frac{20}{64}$$

Note that the notation 5! is read "five factorial" and means 5·4·3·2·1. The statement $P(X = 3|n = 5,\ p^* = 0.5)$ is read as the probability of observing exactly three success given that there are five trials where the probability of success on each trial is one half.

The expected proportion of successes $X/n$ is equal to the probability $p^*$. The standard error of the proportion of success is given by

$$\sigma_p = \sqrt{\frac{p^*(1 - p^*)}{n}}$$

where $p^*$ is known. If $p^*$ is estimated from the sample proportion $p$, this becomes

$$\hat{\sigma}_p = \sqrt{\frac{p(1 - p)}{n - 1}}$$

In our example, the standard error would be

$$\sigma_p = \sqrt{\frac{0.5(1 - 0.5)}{5}} = 0.112$$

since $p^* = 0.5$ and $n = 5$.

*The Normal Distribution*

The normal distribution is a continuous distribution that characteristically resembles the curve in Figure A4-1. It is symmetrical with very little area under the curve at the extremes and more and more as you move toward the middle. If one measures the width of an interval centered at the mean in terms of the number of standard deviations, it is found that an interval two standard deviations wide contains 68.26 per cent of the area under the curve, an interval four standard deviations wide contains 95.34 per cent of

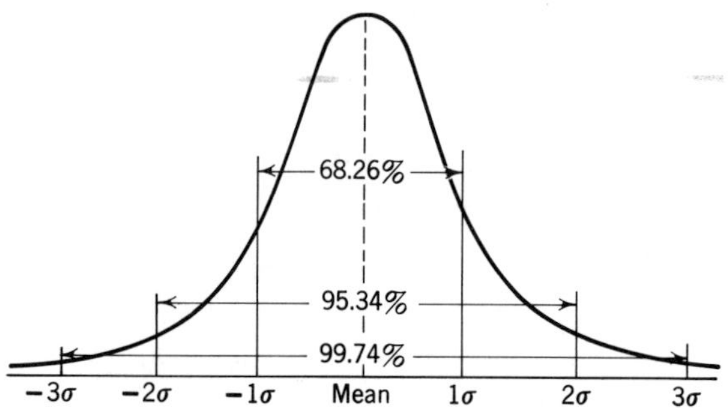


**Figure A4-1** The normal distribution.

the area, and an interval six standard deviations wide 99.74 per cent of the area.

The area under the curve between two points represents a probability. Thus the interpretation of the 68.26 per cent area in the interval from $-1$ to $+1$ is that a variable described by the normal distribution would have a 68.26 per cent probability of being selected within one standard deviation of the mean. For example, if income in a population were normally distributed with mean \$6000 and standard deviation \$1000, a person chosen at random from this distribution would have a 68.26 per cent probability of having an income between \$5000 and \$7000.

If $\mu$ is the mean of the distribution and $\sigma$ the standard deviation, any value $x$ would lie $(x - \mu)/\sigma$ standard deviations from the mean. In the previous example, a value of income of \$5500 would lie $(5500 - 6000)/1000 = -0.50$ standard deviations below the mean.

The probability interval most used is that interval, centered on the mean, which includes 95 per cent of the probability. This interval goes from a point 1.96 below the mean to a point 1.96 above the mean.

APPENDIX B

# BINOMIAL CONFIDENCE INTERVALS

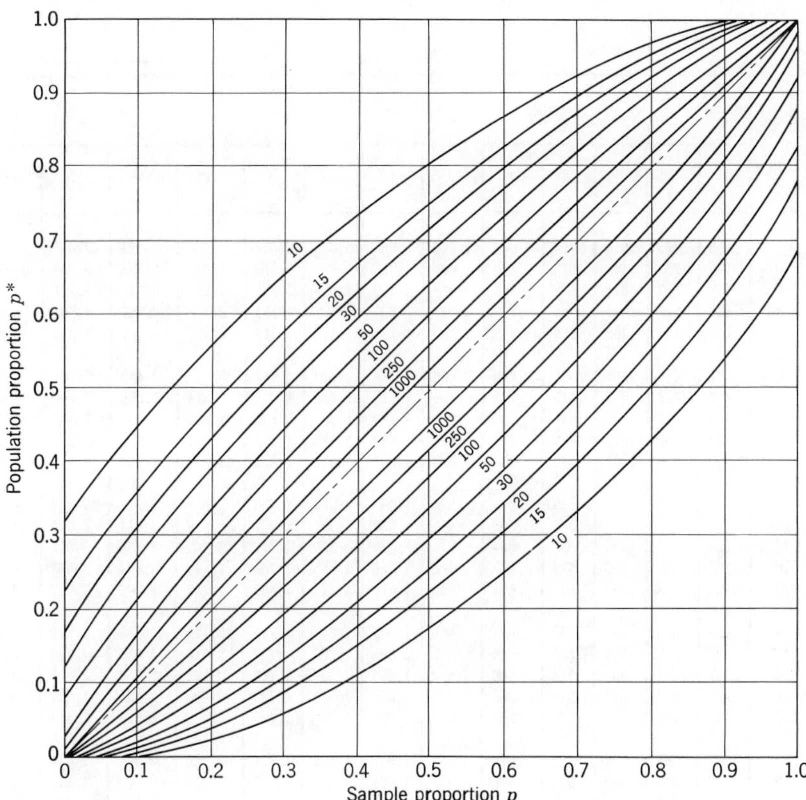


**Figure A4-2** Chart of the 95 per cent confidence limits for proportions or percentages. Confidence bands for $p^*$. (The numbers on the curves indicate sample size.) From C. J. Clopper and E. S. Pearson, "The Use of Confidence or Fiducial Limits Illustrated in the Case of the Binomial," *Biometrika,* **26** (1934). By permission of The Biometrika Office.

APPENDIX C

# STUDENT'S $t$ DISTRIBUTION

## Table of "Student's" Distribution*

This table shows: Values of $t$

| Degrees of Freedom | Level of Significance | | | | | | | | | | | | |
|---|---|---|---|---|---|---|---|---|---|---|---|---|---|
| | .9 | .8 | .7 | .6 | .5 | .4 | .3 | .2 | .1 | .05 | .02 | .01 | .001 |
| 1 | .158 | .325 | .510 | .727 | 1.000 | 1.376 | 1.963 | 3.078 | 6.314 | 12.706 | 31.821 | 63.657 | 636.610 |
| 2 | .142 | .289 | .446 | .617 | .816 | 1.061 | 1.386 | 1.886 | 2.010 | 4.303 | 6.965 | 9.925 | 31.596 |
| 3 | .137 | .277 | .424 | .584 | .765 | .978 | 1.350 | 1.638 | 2.353 | 3.182 | 4.541 | 5.841 | 12.941 |
| 4 | .134 | .271 | .414 | .560 | .741 | .941 | 1.190 | 1.533 | 2.132 | 2.776 | 3.747 | 4.604 | 8.610 |
| 5 | .132 | .267 | .408 | .569 | .727 | .920 | 1.156 | 1.476 | 2.015 | 2.571 | 3.365 | 4.032 | 6.850 |
| 6 | .131 | .266 | .404 | .663 | .718 | .906 | 1.134 | 1.440 | 1.943 | 2.447 | 3.143 | 3.707 | 5.959 |
| 7 | .130 | .263 | .402 | .649 | .711 | .896 | 1.119 | 1.415 | 1.896 | 2.365 | 2.998 | 3.499 | 5.405 |
| 8 | .130 | .262 | .399 | .646 | .706 | .889 | 1.128 | 1.397 | 1.860 | 2.306 | 2.806 | 3.355 | 5.041 |
| 9 | .129 | .261 | .398 | .643 | .703 | .883 | 1.100 | 1.383 | 1.833 | 2.262 | 2.821 | 3.250 | 4.761 |
| 10 | .120 | .260 | .397 | .642 | .700 | .879 | 1.093 | 1.372 | 1.812 | 2.228 | 2.764 | 3.169 | 4.587 |
| 11 | .129 | .260 | .396 | .540 | .697 | .876 | 1.088 | 1.363 | 1.796 | 2.201 | 2.718 | 3.106 | 4.437 |
| 12 | .128 | .259 | .395 | .539 | .695 | .873 | 1.083 | 1.356 | 1.782 | 2.179 | 2.681 | 3.055 | 4.318 |
| 13 | .128 | .259 | .394 | .538 | .694 | .870 | 1.079 | 1.350 | 1.771 | 2.160 | 2.650 | 3.012 | 4.221 |
| 14 | .123 | .268 | .393 | .537 | .692 | .868 | 1.076 | 1.345 | 1.761 | 2.145 | 2.624 | 2.977 | 4.140 |
| 15 | .128 | .258 | .393 | .536 | .691 | .866 | 1.074 | 1.341 | 1.753 | 2.131 | 2.602 | 2.947 | 4.073 |
| 16 | .128 | .258 | .392 | .535 | .690 | .865 | 1.071 | 1.337 | 1.746 | 2.120 | 2.583 | 2.921 | 4.015 |
| 17 | .128 | .257 | .392 | .534 | .689 | .863 | 1.069 | 1.333 | 1.740 | 2.110 | 2.667 | 2.898 | 3.965 |
| 18 | .127 | .257 | .392 | .534 | .688 | .862 | 1.067 | 1.330 | 1.734 | 2.101 | 2.552 | 2.878 | 3.922 |
| 19 | .127 | .257 | .391 | .533 | .688 | .861 | 1.066 | 1.328 | 1.720 | 2.003 | 2.530 | 2.861 | 3.883 |
| 20 | .127 | .257 | .391 | .533 | .687 | .860 | 1.064 | 1.325 | 1.726 | 2.086 | 2.528 | 2.845 | 3.860 |
| 21 | .127 | .267 | .391 | .532 | .686 | .859 | 1.063 | 1.323 | 1.721 | 2.080 | 2.518 | 2.831 | 3.819 |
| 22 | .127 | .266 | .390 | .532 | .686 | .858 | 1.061 | 1.321 | 1.717 | 2.074 | 2.608 | 2.819 | 3.702 |
| 23 | .127 | .256 | .390 | .532 | .685 | .858 | 1.060 | 1.319 | 1.714 | 2.069 | 2.500 | 2.807 | 3.767 |
| 24 | .127 | .256 | .390 | .531 | .685 | .857 | 1.059 | 1.318 | 1.711 | 2.664 | 2.492 | 2.797 | 3.745 |
| 25 | .127 | .256 | .390 | .531 | .684 | .856 | 1.058 | 1.316 | 1.708 | 2.060 | 2.485 | 2.787 | 3.725 |
| 26 | .127 | .256 | .390 | .531 | .684 | .856 | 1.058 | 1.315 | 1.706 | 2.056 | 2.479 | 2.779 | 3.707 |
| 27 | .127 | .256 | .389 | .531 | .684 | .855 | 1.057 | 1.314 | 1.703 | 2.052 | 2.473 | 2.771 | 3.680 |
| 28 | .127 | .256 | .389 | .530 | .683 | .855 | 1.056 | 1.313 | 1.701 | 2.048 | 2.467 | 2.763 | 3.674 |
| 29 | .127 | .256 | .389 | .530 | .683 | .854 | 1.055 | 1.311 | 1.699 | 2.045 | 2.462 | 2.766 | 3.659 |
| 30 | .127 | .256 | .389 | .530 | .683 | .854 | 1.055 | 1.310 | 1.697 | 2.042 | 2.457 | 2.760 | 3.646 |
| 40 | .126 | .255 | .388 | .529 | .681 | .851 | 1.050 | 1.303 | 1.684 | 2.021 | 2.423 | 2.704 | 3.551 |
| 60 | .126 | .254 | .387 | .527 | .679 | .848 | 1.046 | 1.296 | 1.671 | 2.000 | 2.390 | 2.660 | 3.460 |
| 120 | .126 | .254 | .386 | .526 | .677 | .845 | 1.041 | 1.289 | 1.658 | 1.980 | 2.358 | 2.617 | 3.373 |
| ∞ | .126 | .253 | .385 | .524 | .674 | .842 | 1.036 | 1.282 | 1.645 | 1.960 | 2.326 | 2.576 | 3.291 |

* This table is reprinted from Table III of Fisher and Yates, *Statistical Tables for Biological, Agricultural, and Medical Research*, published by Oliver and Boyd Ltd., Edinburgh, by permission of the authors and publishers.

*Five*

# Other Sample Designs and Sample Bias

So far we have looked at the problem of estimation employing a simple random sample. In the following pages we shall look at other probabilistic sample designs, that is, designs where each element has a known, but not necessarily equal, probability of being selected. A rigorous treatment of these designs is beyond the scope of this book.[1] We must necessarily impart the flavor and not the complete substance of the very rich literature on sample design. Following the discussion of probability sampling, a discussion of nonprobability or judgment sampling is presented.

The second half of this chapter is devoted to a discussion of nonresponse biases in samples. Sources of sample bias and methods of dealing with this source of bias are analyzed. Response bias is discussed in Chapter 10.

Before proceeding with the discussion of sample design, it will be necessary to define the meaning of the terms *bias, accuracy, validity, reliability,* and *precision.* These words have very restricted meanings in sampling theory (although all authors do not completely agree on precise definitions), and their rather imprecise use in everyday language may lead the unwary reader astray.

## Some Important Terms

The concept of bias is critical to an understanding of what is to follow. Suppose that we are interested in obtaining the average income of all families in the city of Chicago. Suppose, also, that our list of such families (the sampling *frame*) is derived from the Chicago telephone direc-

[1] More complete treatments may be found in Cochran (1963), Hansen, Hurwitz, and Madow (1953), or Deming (1961). Yamane (1967) has written a particularly lucid book on sampling for the nonstatistician.

tory. Now, all the families in Chicago are not in the telephone directory, since the very poor may not have telephones, the very rich may have unlisted ones, and the very mobile may have just moved into the area and not yet be in the directory. Thus even though our sample consisted of a census of the frame and every family in the frame responded accurately, we would be subject to what Mayer and Brown (1965) have called "frame error." The mean of the variable being measured (which here would be the expected value of the sample, since we have a census) would differ from the mean of the target population, and this difference would measure the bias introduced by frame error.

*Bias may be defined as the difference between the expected value of a sample statistic and the population parameter estimated by the statistic.* Notice that the sample mean, so long as all respondents answer accurately, is an unbiased estimator of the mean of the sampling frame. This is because the expected value of the sample mean is equal to the mean of the sampled population. If respondents do not give true responses, however, the sample mean is itself biased. This type of bias is produced by response error.

The *accuracy* of a sample measures the difference between the sample statistic and the actual population parameter. The error in this estimate is composed of the random error introduced by the fact that a sample, rather than a census, was taken and by the nonsampling errors created by biases. Thus both sources of inaccurate estimates are critical. A statistic is *valid* if it has no bias—that is, if it measures what it is supposed to measure. The *reliability* of the statistic is measured by the standard error. Thus a highly reliable statistic is one that would show small variance on repeated sampling. Note that a statistic can be highly reliable and yet not valid, and vice versa. Finally, there is a distinction between accuracy, already defined, and precision. If a statistic has high reliability, it may be stated with great precision to a number of significant places. As a rule of thumb, the statistic should be stated with precision up to the first significant digit of the standard deviation of that statistic. For example, if $\hat{\sigma}_{\bar{X}} = 0.00412$, it may be reasonable to state $\bar{X}$ as 3.007 but not as 3.00743. Yamane (1967) defines precision and reliability in terms of confidence intervals.

The accuracy of a statistic is thus determined both by its reliability (precision) and by its validity.

## SAMPLE DESIGN

One of the problems associated with a simple random sample is the necessity of obtaining a list of the population to be sampled. In the preceding chapter we discussed an example where the population of interest consisted of all males in Chicago. Obviously, before obtaining a simple random sample from this population it would be necessary to obtain a numbered list of the population so that the sample can be selected by some random device. Such a list is unavailable. In fact, such lists are generally unavailable for most problems of interest to marketers.

A second problem connected with the simple random sample is that of cost. It is conceivable, even likely, that a sample of 100 males in Chicago would yield persons scattered all over the city. One may envision a harried interviewer making three calls on some isolated prospective interviewee without response. If we were concerned with males all over the state of Illinois, this difficulty would become overwhelming. The picture of an interviewer traveling from Chicago to Carbondale for one interview would be sufficient to discourage most backers of the research.

## Cluster Samples

The method of *cluster* sampling may be employed to solve the problems of both the missing list and the scattered interviews. By enlarging the primary sampling unit from the individual to a cluster of individuals, a simple random sample of clusters may be formed. Once the particular clusters are drawn, various forms of sampling or a census may be employed on the cluster. For example, Green and Tull (1966) report a cluster sample design in a study of salesmen's attitudes toward management. Here the primary sampling unit or cluster was the sales district, with all salesmen in the selected districts interviewed.

*Area* sampling is a particular type of cluster sampling where the sampling units are geographical areas. A frequent form of area sampling is *block* sampling. As an example, consider the population of all families in Chicago. Rather than choosing families at random, blocks could be chosen at random (or in some other probabilistic manner), with all or part of the families living on those blocks being interviewed.

The statistical analysis of cluster sampling is frequently quite complex and will not be discussed here. Nevertheless, some general comments may be made.

### *Advantages and Disadvantages*

The advantage of the cluster sample relative to a simple random sample does not usually come through increased reliability for the same sample size. Nevertheless, a cluster sample may frequently be made much more reliable than a simple random sample of the same cost.

This is because clustering of interviews permits a much larger sample, at the same cost, than do dispersed interviews.

Another advantage of the cluster sample is that whereas a list of clusters may be available and a list of interviewees may be readily available for each of the clusters, such a list may not be available for the population as a whole. For example, one may not have a list of the families in Chicago but nevertheless have a list of blocks. Once a block is chosen, either each family may be interviewed, or house or apartment numbers may be chosen at random, or a list of families on the block may be compiled prior to further selection.[2]

A major disadvantage of cluster sampling is high intracluster homogeneity. In particular, when selecting geographical clusters, it may be necessary to choose a number of clusters because individual clusters are not typical of the population as a whole.

## Sequential Sampling

It is a common phenomenon during a national election that the election has barely begun before the television networks tell us who the winner is. Frequently the winner is predicted before all the ballots are in, let alone counted (a procedure that many people find disturbing). Furthermore, such predictions are seldom in error.[3]

Although the networks do not make their predictions on the basis of probability sampling, one basic principle remains the same: if we are concerned with making a decision (e.g., saying who will be elected) and not with making an estimate, the evidence may become overwhelming in favor of one decision rather early in the course of the sample. Thus one may keep a running tally and terminate the sampling at some point. This procedure is known as *sequential* sampling.

For example, consider the case of a firm whose decision on whether or not to market a new product depends on its ability to capture more than a 20 per cent market share within a year. Suppose that it is felt that if a 15 per cent market share is obtained in a number of test markets within four months, this will indicate that the goal of 20 per cent in a national market can be attained in the prescribed period.

[2] Of course, because more than one family may live at an address, selecting addresses at random is not exactly equivalent to selecting families at random.

[3] The classic blunder committed by the *Chicago Tribune* in announcing, in bold headlines, the election of Thomas Dewey in 1948 is not to be taken as evidence to the contrary. The *Tribune* did not and could not muster the computers and staff to the job that the networks do. In fact, the technology was not even available at that time.

If a 40 per cent market share is actually obtained in the test markets within two months, the firm can be quite sure that the product will prove successful. Even though it may be impossible to predict the test market share at the end of four months with any accuracy, it may nevertheless be fairly certain that this market share will be above 15 per cent.

Philosophically, sequential sampling fits in very well with the Bayesian framework. Each extra bit of sample information results in a new posterior probability set. At the point where the expected value of additional sampling becomes less than the expected cost, a decision should be made to stop sampling.

## Stratified Sampling

Suppose that we wish to sample the children in a particular grade school to determine the average height of students in that school. By chance alone, it is quite conceivable that the proportion of students selected from the higher grades would be greater than the proportion of higher-grade students in the school. This would be almost certain to result in the average height of students in the sample being greater than the average height of students in the school.

One could guard against this kind of error by insuring that the proportion of students chosen from each grade corresponds to the proportion that each grade is of the total number of students in the school. Thus if 10 per cent of the students in the school were in first grade, 10 students from the first grade would be selected for the sample if the sample size were 100. These students would be chosen at random from the population of all first-grade students in the school.

The principle involved is to select strata so as to make the intra-stratum population as homogeneous as possible while having the means of the populations of different strata as far apart as possible. In the example, the strata would be grades. Height would vary relatively little within grades compared to the variation in the school as a whole, while the mean height would be increased in higher grades. Of course, stratification on the basis of age would possibly produce even better results.

### *Minimum-Variance Stratification*

In some instances it may be preferable to choose a disproportionate number of sample elements for the various strata. If there is little variability in a particular stratum, there is also little reason to have many sample members chosen from that stratum. For example, suppose that we were sure that all first-graders in the school were within 2 inches of each other in height, whereas seventh-graders had a range of the order of 1 foot. It would not be very reasonable to take a larger sample from the first grade than from the seventh, even though the first grade may contain more students. With a minimum-variance sample, however, it becomes necessary to weight the mean of the stratum by the proportion of population members contained in the stratum, and not the proportion contained in the sample, in arriving at the estimate of the population mean. This procedure results in the smallest possible value of $\sigma_{\bar{X}}$ associated with a stratified sample.

*Statistical Analysis of Stratified Samples*

If $\sigma_i$ is the standard deviation of the $i$th stratum and $P_i$ is the proportion of the total population in the $i$th stratum, the optimal proportion $Q_i$ of the sample to allocate to the $i$th stratum is given by

$$Q_i = \frac{\sigma_i P_i}{\sum_{j=1}^{m} \sigma_j P_j}$$

where $m$ is the number of strata. Thus the sample size of each stratum is chosen by weighting the dispersion of the stratum and its importance in terms of size equally.

If $\bar{X}_i$ is the observed mean of the $i$th stratum, the population mean is estimated by

$$\bar{X} = \sum_{i=1}^{m} P_i \cdot \bar{X}_i$$

The standard error of the estimate is given by

$$\sigma_{\bar{X}} = \sqrt{\sum_{i=1}^{n} P_i^2 \left(1 - \frac{n_i}{N_i}\right) \frac{\sigma_i^2}{n_i}}$$

where $n_i$ is the number of population members drawn from the $i$th stratum, $N_i$ is the size of the $i$th stratum, and $n$ and $N$ are the sizes of the sample and population, respectively.

*An Example*

For example, consider a company that markets a certain good to specialty stores and departmental stores. Although the variance of sales of the product in each class of stores has remained fairly stable, average sales per store per year have varied considerably, and this is the quantity on which the sales manager would like information.

A sample of 100 stores is decided upon. Departmental stores have a standard deviation of \$10,000 in sales per store per year, while specialty stores have a standard deviation of \$5000. There are 900 specialty stores and 100 departmental stores in the regional market of interest.

SAMPLE SIZES. Let $Q_1$ be the proportion of the sample allocated to departmental stores and $Q_2$ the proportion allocated to specialty stores.

We have
$$\sigma_1 = 10{,}000 \qquad P_1 = \frac{100}{900 + 100} = 0.1$$

$$\sigma_2 = 5{,}000 \qquad P_2 = \frac{900}{900 + 100} = 0.9$$

$$Q_1 = \frac{\sigma_1 P_1}{\sigma_1 P_1 + \sigma_2 P_2}$$

Thus
$$Q_1 = \frac{0.1 \cdot 10{,}000}{0.9 \cdot 5000 + 0.1 \cdot 10{,}000} = 0.18$$

Similarly, $Q_2 = 0.82$

Thus 18 stores would be selected at random from departmental stores and 82 stores from specialty stores.

THE ESTIMATE. Suppose that average sales of the product in departmental stores, $\bar{X}_1$, were \$100,000 per year per store and that $\bar{X}_2$, the figure for specialty stores, were \$20,000. The overall estimated mean is

$$\begin{aligned}\bar{X} &= P_1\bar{X}_1 + P_2\bar{X}_2 \\ &= 0.1 \cdot 100{,}000 + 0.9 \cdot 20{,}000 \\ &= \$28{,}000 \text{ per store per year}\end{aligned}$$

The standard error of the mean is

$$\begin{aligned}\hat{\sigma}_{\bar{X}} &= \sqrt{P_1{}^2 \cdot \left(1 - \frac{n_1}{N_1}\right) \cdot \frac{\sigma_1{}^2}{n_1} + P_2{}^2 \cdot \left(1 - \frac{n_2}{N_2}\right) \cdot \frac{\sigma_2{}^2}{n^2}} \\ &= \sqrt{(0.1)^2 \cdot \left(1 - \frac{18}{100}\right) \cdot \frac{(10{,}000)^2}{18} + (0.2)^2 \cdot \left(1 - \frac{82}{900}\right) \cdot \frac{(5000)^2}{82}} \\ &= \$22\end{aligned}$$

It is left to the reader to calculate confidence intervals of average sales for each classification of store and for the overall average.

### *Advantages and Disadvantages*

Stratified sampling will often permit us to employ a much smaller sample than does simple random sampling of the same reliability. Suppose, however, that we did not know the relative sizes of the various strata. Then the variance of our estimate must be increased to account for the fact that we are estimating the strata sizes. This correction may increase the standard error to the point where it is as large as that of a simple random sample of the same size. Nevertheless, since we are provided with estimates for each stratum under the stratified sample design, this extra information may itself justify the design.

## Systematic Sampling

Systematic sampling has its greatest application in area sampling. It may frequently be difficult to compile a list of every block in the city or every household on the block. A much easier procedure would consist of choosing a starting point at random and then selecting, say, every tenth block or household for inclusion in the sample. Of course, systematic sampling is not necessarily confined to area samples; it may be applied to lists, such as names in a telephone book or salesmen in a firm.

As in a simple random sample, every element in the population has an equal probability of being chosen. Nevertheless, a systematic sample is *not* the same as a random sample. In fact, it is a form of cluster sampling.

This may be seen from the following illustration. If we were to sample 10 per cent of the blocks in a city, our procedure would be to start by taking a number from 1 to 10 at random. If this number were, say, 6, we would sample blocks numbered 6, 16, 26, and so on. These blocks form a cluster distinguished by the last digit identifying the block. There are 10 such clusters representing the entire population, and the procedure has been to choose one at random.

If the clusters themselves are randomly formed, say from a list of names ordered at random from which we choose every tenth name, the systematic sample would have the same sampling error as does a simple random sample. This may not be the case, however, when the list is ordered in some way, as most lists are.

For example, by choosing every tenth block in a city one may be fairly sure that the selected elements will present a fair representation of the socioeconomic strata in the city by block, but not by the percentage of families, since the population density on poor blocks may be expected to be higher than on affluent blocks. If a list were ordered by income, a systematic sample would be likely to be more representative of the income of the population under study than would a simple random sample.

If a list were periodic, such as would be the case in home building (which occurs primarily during the summer months), a systematic sample could conceivably lead us completely astray. Thus a systematic sample may have a higher or a lower sampling error than a simple random sample of the same size. Unfortunately, it is impossible to measure this error. Usually, it is assumed the standard error will be the same as for a simple random sample of the same size, an assumption that is most often conservative.

### Replicated Samples[4]

Instead of taking one simple random sample of size $n$, we may choose to take $r$ independent random samples of size $n/r$ from the same population. In fact, we may take a number of such *interpenetrating* samples from the same population using any sample design, but our discussion will be confined to the case of simple random samples.

The advantage of replicated sampling lies in the ability to check for bias in the subsamples. For example, if we were employing ten interviewers and each was assigned a tenth of the sample at random, we would expect the subsample means to differ only through chance. Given the ten subsample means and the subsample variances, we may test the hypothesis that the differences in the means arise by chance alone against the alternative hypothesis that one or more of the means differs as a result of interviewer bias. The disadvantage of this procedure lies in the costs involved in not assigning each interviewer to a geographically compact area within the area to be sampled.

One may also employ replicated sampling to test the hypothesis that geographical areas differ in the variable or attribute being investigated purely by chance. Again, in order not to confuse interviewer bias with geographical bias, it is necessary to have every interviewer interview in each of the geographical areas.

## NONPROBABILITY SAMPLES

Most discussions of sampling end with a brief discussion of nonprobability samples. The writer typically points out that no probability state-

[4] For a more complete treatment, see Deming (1961).

ments are possible, because the sample elements were not chosen according to a probabilistic design. Since this is taken to imply that no degree of certainty can be attached to the results of the sample, the conclusion is almost always that nonprobability samples are useful only in pilot studies or in studies of little importance.

The authors do not agree with this point of view. Much of our thinking has been shaped by an excellent paper by Mayer and Brown presented to the 1965 fall conference of the American Marketing Association (Mayer and Brown, 1965), and our discussion will follow their paper to a large extent.

## Sources of Error

Mayer and Brown (1965) classify the sources of the errors possible in drawing a sample into five categories: (1) measurement, (2) nonresponse, (3) process, (4) frame, and (5) randomness. It is only the last of these sources that is measured by sampling error through the standard error of the mean or the standard error of proportion. The other sources of error come under the general classification of nonsampling errors. These errors are explained below.

Frame errors occur because the sample population is often necessarily different from the population in which we are interested. This error creates a bias not measurable in the sample. The process error is zero in a true probability design, but may not be if the weights used in adjusting the estimated sample average are based on outdated or inaccurate data. Nonresponse errors, arising because of refusals or lack of returns (in questionnaires), are another type of errors that are not measured in the sampling error.[5] Finally, Mayer and Brown (1965) specify measurement errors, which arising out of respondents' unwillingness or inability to answer correctly, as a type of nonsampling error.

We alluded in Chapter 4 to the fact that in marketing problems our sampling frame may be *totally* different from the population in which we are really interested. Often the latter population does not yet exist or the circumstances surrounding the interview or questionnaire are totally different from the circumstances surrounding the actual consumer decision. Thus the test market of a new product in a confined geographical area at a particular time with no national promotion and with competitors possibly taking actions, such as "deals," to distort the results may give us a realistic picture of the product in the test market at that time under the peculiar circumstances described. But our results

[5] These errors and the refinements that help mitigate their effects are discussed in the next section of this chapter.

may not even be valid for the geographical area of the test market at some future date under different conditions, let alone for some larger area.

Inevitably, then, one can never arrive at a truly objective probability statement about the accuracy of an estimate from sampling, since the sampling error measures only one of the sources of error. Ferber, in a study of the reporting of financial holdings, found that 95 per cent confidence intervals contained the true mean less than 1 per cent of the time because of nonsampling errors (Ferber, 1965). In fact, it is quite conceivable that at times nonsampling and sampling errors may act in a way similar to $\alpha$ and $\beta$ errors, that is, one kind of error can be reduced only at the expense of the other, for a fixed sample size.

A quota sample is chosen by giving each interviewer a quota of persons having certain characteristics (e.g., income, age, sex, job) to interview. One study reports that a quota panel, selected to obtain the value of life insurance policies via mailed questionnaires, came within 1 per cent of the true value, on the average, whereas an interviewed probabilistically chosen panel came only within 12 per cent. Since both samples were quite large, the difference in the errors was attributed to nonsampling errors, apparently due to a bias introduced by the respondents' desire to impress the interviewer in the probabilistically selected sample with the amount of insurance carried (Nuckols, 1964).

## Conclusions with Regard to Nonprobability Samples

One major difficulty with the nonprobabilistic sample design lies in the paucity of theoretical work that has been done in the area. Mayer and Brown present a scheme for the construction of an "error index" that would allow the incorporation of subjective probabilities attached to all the sources of error, but much work remains to be done before this neglected area of sampling theory becomes as rich as probabilistic sampling theory.

Another drawback to nonprobability designs lies in the possibility of obtaining a nonrepresentative sample with respect to some important, but unrecognized, characteristic. To cite an unlikely example, if one were interested in obtaining an estimate of the proportion of families in the Chicago area who own outdoor barbecue equipment, quotas might be established on the basis of age, income, and other demographic characteristics. But if the sample included a disproportionate number of apartment dwellers, the result would undoubtedly be an understatement of the true proportion. On the other hand, if the important characteristics are many and well known, a quota sample might be bettered in accuracy only by a stratified random sample at considerably greater cost.

## SAMPLE BIAS

Pity the plight of the market researcher. Not only must he worry about error in his result introduced through those in his sample who do not respond, but also about error introduced by those who do. As has been pointed out in the discussion of nonprobability designs, nonsampling errors are frequently greater than the sampling error. The nonresponse error is one source of nonsampling error, while the response error [what Mayer and Brown (1965) call measurement error] is another source of nonsampling error. It should be noted that neither kind of nonsampling error can be measured from the sample itself, whereas the sampling error is measurable from the sample variance. Nonsampling errors thus create a *bias* in the sample.

### Nonresponse Errors

One of the greatest difficulties connected with sampling from human populations is that the sampling units frequently are unavailable or refuse to cooperate. If a person or family selected to be interviewed is unavailable or a questionnaire is not returned, it is dangerous to simply exclude such people from the sample. It is clear that they differ from the rest of the sample in at least one respect—accessibility. If people who are not easily accessible also happen to differ from the rest of the sample on the basis of some characteristic important to the variable being measured, the results of the sample will be biased by their exclusion.

Cochran (1963, p. 360) categorizes the nonresponse problem into noncoverage, not-at-homes, unable to answer, and the "hard core." Noncoverage may arise either from incomplete lists or from problems of transportation or weather that make it difficult to reach a dwelling. A list may be incomplete because it does not include the newest dwellings or streets or because people have moved. Respondents may be unable to answer because they do not know the answer or are unwilling to answer or because the answer does not exist. The hard core consists of those who absolutely refuse to respond or who cannot be reached despite a series of attempts to do so.

#### *Noncoverage*

Where the frame consists of a street directory, this sample may be supplemented by an area sample of new-built areas not included in the directory (Kish and Hess, 1968). But the problem of noncoverage is perhaps most significant in telephone surveys conducted via a telephone directory. New listings, not yet in the telephone directory, come from families more mobile than the population as a whole. Unlisted telephones are generally held by wealthier and more educated families. Thus these two population segments tend to be underrepresented in telephone interviews.

Cooper (1964) has suggested an alternative that solves the problem of incomplete lists in telephone directories. Instead of numbers being selected from the directory, he suggests that the numbers be generated at random from those numbers that have been assigned to the district. The difficulty here is that unassigned numbers and business numbers will be called in a greater frequency than are the numbers taken from a directory. Considering the bias introduced by leaving out unlisted subscribers [which Cooper (1964) found to be 18 per cent, in one survey, toward the end of the life of the directory], the extra calls made may be a small price to pay in many surveys.

*Not-at-Homes*

Surveys of personal interviewing indicate that only about one out of three first calls result in an interview, with not-at-homes accounting for the bulk of the noninterviews. Mayer (1964) reports a very comprehensive study on interview experience employing skilled interviewers by the Survey Research Center of the University of Michigan. Tables 5-1 and 5-2 are taken from this study.

It may be seen from Table 5-1 that the not-at-home rate decreases with the degree of ruralization, with a sharp drop in all areas after the third call. On the first call, approximately half of the cases *of those who are at home* result in nonterminal noninterview situations—that is, the interview is not completed but a future callback is scheduled. This proportion falls drastically after the first call.

From Table 5-2, it is evident that both the interview rate and the terminal noninterview rate rise for the second and third interviews. Thus previous contact seems to increase the proportion of terminal contacts on the next call, both interview and refusal. In large metropolitan areas previous contact seems to affect the interview rate adversely on the fourth and fifth interviews, but this does not hold in other urban and rural areas. It is interesting to use Tables 5-1 and 5-2 to demonstrate what would happen to a sample of size 1000 in a large metropolitan area if the proportions in the tables held. This information (not found in Mayer's paper) is presented in Table 5-3.

One rather disturbing fact emerging from Table 5-3 is that at the end of five calls, there still remain 27.5 per cent of the original sample

**TABLE 5-1** Result of Call by Degree of Urbanization (Percent Distribution)[a]

| | Not at Home on Previous Call | | | | | | | | | | | | | | |
|---|---|---|---|---|---|---|---|---|---|---|---|---|---|---|---|
| | Large Metro | | | | | Other Urban | | | | | Rural | | | | |
| Result of Call | First Call | Second Call[b] | Third Call | Fourth Call | Fifth Call | First Call | Second Call | Third Call | Fourth Call | Fifth Call | First Call | Second Call | Third Call[b] | Fourth Call | Fifth Call |
| Interview | 20.4 | 21.9 | 20.7 | 33.8 | 37.8 | 31.9 | 28.2 | 32.6 | 28.8 | 25.8 | 41.8 | 40.0 | 43.2 | 31.7 | |
| Terminal non-interview | 4.1 | 4.8 | 5.7 | 10.1 | 17.3 | 5.1 | 6.8 | 4.0 | 16.9 | 27.0 | 2.7 | 2.2 | 9.6 | 31.7 | Too few cases |
| Not at home | 46.5 | 51.9 | 53.3 | 36.5 | 36.7 | 35.1 | 44.8 | 44.9 | 36.2 | 31.5 | 30.7 | 42.8 | 39.6 | 29.3 | |
| Nonterminal noninterview | 29.0 | 22.4 | 20.3 | 19.6 | 8.2 | 27.9 | 20.2 | 18.5 | 18.1 | 15.7 | 24.8 | 15.0 | 17.6 | 7.3 | |
| Total | 100.0 | 100.0 | 100.0 | 100.0 | 100.0 | 100.0 | 100.0 | 100.0 | 100.0 | 100.0 | 100.0 | 100.0 | 100.0 | 100.0 | 100.0 |
| $n^c$ | 779 | 330 | 212 | 148 | 98 | 1609 | 530 | 319 | 177 | 89 | 749 | 227 | 125 | 41 | 19 |

[a] Reprinted by permission of the *Journal of Marketing Research*, American Marketing Association and the author.
[b] These percentages actually add to over 100. The error is somewhat greater than would be expected by rounding.
[c] Excludes cases where time, day, or result of call was not ascertained.

**Table 5-2** Result of Call within Degree of Urbanization, When Contact Is Made on the Previous Call (Percent Distribution)[a]

| | Nonterminal, Noninterview on Previous Call | | | | | | | | | | | |
|---|---|---|---|---|---|---|---|---|---|---|---|---|
| | Large Metro | | | | Other Urban | | | | Rural | | | |
| Result of Call | Second | Third | Fourth[b] | Fifth | Second | Third | Fourth | Fifth | Second | Third | Fourth | Fifth |
| Interview | 37.0 | 35.1 | 31.1 | 30.8 | 47.8 | 50.6 | 45.0 | 50.0 | 57.4 | 57.1 | 42.9 | |
| Terminal noninterview | 7.9 | 5.4 | 9.9 | 12.3 | 4.8 | 8.3 | 12.8 | 27.0 | 5.9 | 10.4 | 21.4 | Too |
| Not at home | 21.0 | 26.4 | 25.4 | 18.5 | 18.8 | 17.7 | 17.4 | 12.9 | 14.0 | 6.5 | 16.7 | few |
| Nonterminal noninterview | 34.1 | 33.1 | 35.6 | 38.4 | 28.6 | 23.4 | 24.8 | 16.1 | 22.7 | 26.0 | 19.1 | cases |
| Total | 100.0 | 100.0 | 100.0 | 100.0 | 100.0 | 100.0 | 100.0 | 100.0 | 100.0 | 100.0 | 100.0 | 100.0 |
| $n^c$ | 214 | 148 | 90 | 65 | 421 | 243 | 109 | 62 | 185 | 77 | 42 | 11 |

[a] Reprinted by permission of the *Journal of Marketing Research*, American Marketing Association and the author.
[b] These percentages actually add to 102. The error is somewhat greater than would be expected by rounding.
[c] Excludes cases where time, day, or result of call was not ascertained.

**TABLE 5-3** Large Metropolitan Area Sample

| Number of Persons \ Call Number | 1 | 2 | 3 | 4 | 5 | Final Net |
|---|---|---|---|---|---|---|
| Interviewed | 204 | 208 | 133 | 112 | 68 | 725 |
| Terminal noninterviews | 41 | 44 | 28 | 34 | 30 | 177 |
| Not at home | 465 | 301 | 214 | 110 | 56 | 56 |
| Nonterminal noninterview | 290 | 202 | 128 | 86 | 42 | 42 |
| Total | 1000 | 755 | 503 | 342 | 196 | 1000 |

who are either outright refusals (17.7 per cent) or have yet to be interviewed. In addition, 2796 calls were required in order to net 725 interviews. Can anything be done to remedy the situation?

The tables provide the clue that the major reason for the number of call-backs lies primarily in the large proportion of not-at-homes. The fact that the interview rate rises when previous contact has been made provides a further clue.

One remedy is to make the initial contact, at least in large metropolitan areas, by telephone. Since telephone directories are somewhat easier to use than other lists in sample design because they tend to be more up to date,[6] this provides another advantage in the use of the telephone to make appointments. Another remedy is to make the initial contact by mail, but this method has the disadvantage of not permitting a definite appointment to be made. One study of the effects of precontact indicated that greater cooperation in completed interviews was received when respondents were first contacted by telephone or mail, although precontact by telephone also increased (not statistically significant) the refusal rate (Dommermuth, 1963). Another study found that the percentage of completed interviews was higher where the initial contact was by telephone, with the average number of calls per completed interview reduced by one quarter to one third (Sudman, 1966).

The evidence, on balance, seems to indicate the efficacy of precontact in both reducing the number of calls required to complete personal interviews and in gaining greater cooperation in interviews. Since the casual or offhand reply may distort the findings of a survey with little opportunity to discover this distortion, the importance of respondent's cooperation cannot be overemphasized.

[6] As has been pointed out earlier, using random generation of telephone numbers may be superior to using a telephone book.

*Refusals*

Numerous studies have found that the refusal rate in interviews is far lower where trained interviewers are employed [e.g., Heneman and Paterson (1949) and Dalenius (1961)]. Another study indicates that it may be far easier to complete out-of-town interviews than in-town interviews (Robins, 1963). This suggests that initial letter mailed from some other city may be useful in in-town interviews.

It is not entirely clear what techniques generate high mail return rates, but some inferences may be drawn from the literature. In general, it seems advisable (1) to make questionnaires as short as possible; (2) to have a long and detailed typed covering letter stressing the importance of the study and the importance to the study of the group being canvassed; (3) to have stamps affixed (rather than using a postal machine) both to the outgoing envelope and the self-addressed return envelope; (4) to stress the confidential nature of all replies; (5) to offer a gift in return for the questionnaire; (6) to follow up with letter reminders, together with a new questionnaire copy in the case of unreturned questionnaires; and (7) to use special delivery postage on follow-up mailing.

The return rate in mail surveys seems to be higher when the sponsoring organization is reputable and has a history of maintaining confidentiality. Where the questions pertain to matters that one might expect the respondents to prefer not to divulge, such as questions about sexual habits or financial status, the reputation of the sponsoring agency is extremely important. In some cases it may even be necessary to allow respondents to remain anonymous, but this has the unfortunate restriction of not permitting follow-up surveys or mailings.

The literature reports mail-survey return rates that are as low as 15 per cent (far lower than in personal interviews or telephone surveys) and as high as 95 per cent. If adequate attention is given to the details that help to increase the return rate, few surveys yield return rates under 40 per cent. In any event, the return rate can be predicted with reasonable accuracy by a pilot study (Newman, 1962).

*The Treatment of Nonresponse Bias*

Given the unfortunate fact that, in any type of survey, a portion of the sample will not respond, what can be done? A number of techniques are available that *lessen* the impact of nonresponse bias, and some of these will be discussed. More extensive discussions are found in Cochran (1963), Dalenius (1961), and Hansen et al. (1953).

MAIL SURVEYS. A standard procedure in mail surveys is to sample the nonresponse population via personal interviews. This technique, while effective, has certain drawbacks, the most obvious being cost. In addition, the interview sample may itself not be perfectly representative because a portion of this sample will be refusals or not-at-homes and because respondents may not give exactly the same answers in personal interviews as in questionnaires.

Ferber (1948) suggests a very reasonable approach for detecting a source of bias in unreturned questionnaires. The assumption is made that later returns tend to look more like nonreturns than do early returns. If the variable of, say, attitude toward brand X were of interest, one would investigate whether there was an apparent trend in this attitude when measured against lateness of response. Empirical justification for the procedure, however, is lacking. Indeed, one study reports a lack of success in the procedure (Ford and Zeisel, 1949). Hendricks (1949) suggests predicting the nonresponse variable by fitting a quadratic to three waves of questionnaire response. This method also lacks empirical validation.

The Meredith Publishing Company, publisher of *Better Homes and Gardens,* has conducted experiments in which almost 100 per cent response was induced by such techniques as repeated mailings, telegrams, and telephone calls. The company concludes that a return rate of at least 75 per cent should be achieved, but that beyond this there is little gain in accuracy. Since 1960 no major study undertaken by the company has failed to better a return rate of 75 per cent.[7]

### *Politz and Simmons Technique*

Nonresponse in mail surveys is analogous to refusals in personal or telephone interviewing. In the latter two types of surveys, however, it is the not-at-homes who create a larger problem than do refusals. Hartley (1946) suggested a very useful technique, later amplified and refined by Politz and Simmons (1949), that lessens the bias in results created by the not-at-homes.

The Politz-Simmons technique will be illustrated by an example drawn from Simmons (1954). Suppose that interviews are to be made in the evening. The visits made by interviewers would then be scheduled at random within the interviewing period. Each respondent is asked if he would have been at home at that time on each of the six evenings including and preceding the interview. If a person were at home twice in the six periods, he would have had a probability of one third of being at home if one of those periods were drawn at random.

Suppose that no call-backs are scheduled. The procedure is then to

[7] Personal communication, Mr. J. T. Miller, Director of Research, Meredith Publishing Company.

weight each respondent in inverse proportion to his probability of being at home. Thus someone who was at home in each of the periods would get a weight of 1, someone at home in five of the six periods a weight of $6/5$, and so on. Simmons (1954) also shows how the technique may be extended to include call-backs.

This procedure diminishes considerably the bias introduced by not-at-homes. Of course, anyone who would not have been at home on *any* of the six evenings is still not represented in the survey, and the remaining nonresponse bias may be attributed to persons who fall into this category.

Unfortunately, while the technique reduces bias, it also increases the sampling error. Heavily weighting a response of someone who is usually not at home is *not* equivalent to obtaining interviews from the actual not-at-homes. Thus it may be necessary to increase the sample size when the Politz-Simmons technique is employed in order to compensate for the reliability loss. A good discussion of this point is given by Cochran (1963, pp. 371–374).

For surveys in which a telephone directory is employed as a frame for personal interviewing, Stock (1962) has suggested a technique similar to the Politz-Simmons method for reducing the bias created by persons not in the directory. If an area sample is taken with the first house in each cluster selected from the telephone book, Stock suggests weighting the cluster in inverse proportion to the number of households with telephones. The households without telephones thus generate a higher weight for their cluster to compensate for the bias introduced by such clusters' having a smaller probability of being selected than do clusters with more telephones.

## SUMMARY

In most studies, a simple random sample, as described in Chapter 4, is either undesirable or impossible. This chapter has been devoted to two areas of discussion. First, alternative sample designs (including systematic, cluster, stratified, replicated, and nonprobability samples) were discussed. The particular advantages and disadvantages of each type were briefly outlined.

The second section of the chapter discussed the various sources of nonresponse bias in sampling and what might be done to mitigate the effects of this bias. One must conclude, for any type of survey, that achieving a high response rate is first in priority. Methods of dealing with nonresponse exist, but these methods never fully eliminate the potential bias. With mail surveys, because the interviews costs associated with sampling nonresponses are so great, it is generally false economy to try to save money by not using such devices as gifts or airmail stamps in order to increase the response rate. The topic of nonsampling bias cannot be divorced from the content of chapters in which the problem of securing accurate, unambiguous information is treated in greater depth.

## REFERENCES

Cochran, W. G. *Sampling Techniques.* (2nd ed.) New York: Wiley, 1963.

Cooper, S. L. "Random Sampling by Telephone: A New and Improved Method," *Journal of Marketing Research,* November 1964, pp. 45–48.

Dalenius, T. "Treatment of the Non-Response Problem," *Journal of Advertising Research,* September 1961, pp. 1–8.

Deming, W. E. *Sample Design in Business Research,* New York: Wiley, 1961.

Dommermuth, W. P., & Cateora, P. R. "Can Refusals by Respondents be Decreased," *Journal of Marketing* July 1963, pp. 74–76.

Ferber, R. "The Problem of Bias in Mail Returns," *Public Opinion Quarterly,* Winter 1948, pp. 669–676.

Ferber, R. "The Reliability of Consumer Surveys of Financial Holdings: Time Deposits," *Journal of the American Statistical Association* March 1965.

Ford, R. N., & Zeisel, H. "Bias in Mail Surveys Cannot be Controlled in One Mailing," *Public Opinion Quarterly,* Fall 1949, pp. 495–501.

Francel, E. G. "Mail-Administered Questionnaires, A Success Story," *Journal of Marketing Research,* February 1966, pp. 89–92.

Gill, S. "How Do You Stand on Sin?" *Tide,* March 1947, p. 72.

Green, P. E., & Tull, D. S. *Research for Marketing Decisions.* Englewood Cliffs, N.J.: Prentice-Hall, 1966.

Hansen, M. H., Hurwitz, W. N., & Madow, W. G. *Sample Survey Methods and Theory,* Vol. 1, New York: Wiley, 1953.

Hartley, O. H. "Discussion of Paper by F. Yates," *Journal of the Royal Statistical Society,* 1946, p. 37.

Hendricks, W. A. "Adjustment for Bias by Non-Respondents in Mailed Surveys," *Agricultural Economic Research,* 1949, pp. 52–56.

Heneman, G. H., & Paterson, D. G. "Refusal Rates and Interviewer Quality," *International Journal of Opinion and Attitude Research,* 1949, pp. 9–31.

Kish, L., & Hess, I. "On Non-Coverage of Sample Dwellings," *Journal of the American Statistical Association,* June 1958, pp. 509–524.

Mayer, C. S. "The Interviewer and His Environment," *Journal of Marketing Research,* November 1964, p. 24–31.

Mayer, C. S., & Brown, R. V. "A Search for the Rationale of Non-Probability Sample Designs," *Proceedings of the 1965 Fall Conference,* American Marketing Association, pp. 295–308.

Newman, S. W. "Differences Between Early and Late Respondents to a Mailed Survey," *Journal of Advertising Research,* June 1962, pp. 37–39.

Nuckols, R. C. "The Validity and Comparability of Mail and Personal Interview Surveys," *Journal of Marketing Research,* February 1964, pp. 11–16.

Politz, A. N., & Simmons, W. R. "An Attempt to Get the 'Not-at-Homes' into the Sample Without Call-Backs," *Journal of the American Statistical Association,* March 1949, pp. 9–31, and March 1950, pp. 136–137.

Robins, L. N. "The Reluctant Respondent," *Public Opinion Quarterly,* Summer 1963, pp. 276–286.

Simmons, W. R. "A Plan to Account for 'Not-at-Homes' by Combining Weighting and Callbacks," *Journal of Marketing,* July 1954, pp. 42–53.

Stock, J. S. "On Methods: How to Improve Samples Based on Telephone Listings," *Journal of Advertising Research,* September 1962, pp. 50–51.

Sudman, S. "New Use of Telephone Methods in Survey Research," *Journal of Marketing Research,* May 1966, pp. 163–167.

Yamane, T. *Elementary Sampling Theory*. Englewood Cliffs, N.J.: Prentice-Hall, 1967.

*Six*

# Decision Making under Uncertainty: Classical and Bayesian Approaches

Appearances are to us in four ways: for either things appear as they are; or they are not, and do not even appear to be; or they are, and do not appear to be; or they are not, and yet appear to be. Further, in all these cases, to form a right judgment is the office of an educated man.

*Epictetus, Discourses, Book I, Chapter 27*

"For example" is no proof.

*Old Jewish Proverb*

Estimating procedures were discussed in Chapters 4 and 5. Estimates might be continually collected and processed in the flow of market information for ongoing problems or they might be required in a special-problem situation. Nevertheless, although useful to management, estimates of population parameters when divorced from economic considerations are not as useful as information that is specifically collected and *analyzed* with the purpose of affecting decisions. In this chapter, procedures specifically designed for decision making are discussed.

The first section of the chapter is devoted to hypothesis testing, where the decision to be made is to accept or to reject an hypothesis with the aid of the statistical information. The second section of the chapter shows how decisions are made employing a Bayesian approach.

Although neither section delves into the subject matter in great depth, the reader is forewarned that the material covered is by nature difficult. It is suggested that the examples be digested slowly and thoroughly.

## HYPOTHESIS TESTING—THE CLASSICAL APPROACH

Suppose that our company is in the process of making a decision whether or not to introduce a new product. Two types of errors can be made: we can introduce the product when we should not have or we can fail to introduce the product when we should have. We may gather sample or experimental information, and, based on the observed statistic or statistics, the hypothesis that the product has good profit potential may be accepted or rejected according to a predetermined decision rule. In Chapter 4 it was shown that the statistic will take on certain values with probabilities determined by the underlying population parameters; thus these probabilities determine the probabilities of making either kind of error.

We are concerned with two problems. The *statistical problem* is to determine the probability of rejecting the hypothesis of good profit potential when it should have been accepted and the probability of accepting the hypothesis when it should have been rejected, given the decision rule. The *economic problem* is the choice of a decision rule.

### Formulating the Hypothesis

The procedure of hypothesis testing is a fundamental tool of scientific research. For example, suppose that a new drug is to be tested. One half of a group of patients, randomly chosen, may receive the drug and the other half (called the *control* group) some innocuous substance like water or sugar. Typically, neither doctor nor patient knows whether or not the drug is being administered. Suppose that the recovery rate is higher in the treated group than in the control group. Can the researcher make the claim that he has discovered a useful drug? Not necessarily—he must consider the possibility that the difference in the two groups arose by chance alone.

In scientific research it is traditional to play the devil's advocate by assuming a *null hypothesis,* $H_0$, that the apparent discovery arose by chance alone. The *alternative hypothesis,* $H_a$, is that the researcher has indeed made a discovery.

A similar procedure is used in formulating marketing hypotheses. In marketing problems, however, it is often not clear, nor even very important, which hypothesis should be designated as the null hypothesis. Thus, in our new-product example, the null hypothesis might be that our market share would be large enough to profitably introduce the new product or it could be just the opposite.

From previous research, by estimation or from published figures, suppose that we assume the total market to consist of approximately five million units per year. At the projected price, we would have to sell half a million units per year in order to break even.[1] This implies that we make money if our market share is above 10 per cent and the product is marketed and lose money if our market share is below 10 per cent and the product is marketed.

We assume that if we knew that we would achieve a market share greater than 10 per cent, we would market the product. Conversely, the product would remain on the drawing board if we knew that market share would be below 10 per cent. The null hypothesis is taken to be the latter case, the alternative hypothesis the former case. Thus we state:

$H_0$—market share, if the product is marketed, will be at or below 10 per cent.

$H_a$—market share, if the product is marketed, will be above 10 per cent.

In a very real sense, it is often impossible to sample from the population of interest, since that population does not yet exist. It may take a year or more before the actual introduction of the product takes place. Or we may be asking potential customers what they would do *if* they were faced with the opportunity to buy the product, and they may be unwilling or unable to answer truthfully. One common phenomenon is that subjects will tell the interviewer what they think he wants to hear. Even if we are to test-market the product (i.e., to offer the product for sale in, say, a few selected or randomly chosen markets), competitor's actions, the newness of the product, changing conditions, and other factors tend to make the sampled population different from the "target" population.

These are the facts of life to a marketing man. His problems cannot be made so amenable to treatment as can the problem of the quality control man who has a batch of gadgets that must be accepted or re-

[1] The sophisticated reader, concerned with such things as the product life cycle, is doubtless aware of the fact that the market share varies over time, as does the size of the market and the product price. Market forecasting is treated in another chapter. The role of the produce life cycle in the decision is somewhat easier to handle under a Bayesian decision tree analysis than in the hypothesis-testing context.

jected. Nevertheless, the fact that much marketing information is less valid[2] than production information does not imply that it is less useful.

## A One-Tailed Test

Suppose that a sample survey of current users of competitive products is undertaken and 12 out of 100 repondents indicate that they would buy our product. Thus the expected share of market, from the indication of the sample, is 12 per cent. Does this mean that $H_a$ should be accepted? Not necessarily. It depends on how much risk we are willing to assume of rejecting the null ($H_0$) hypothesis when it is really true. This type of error is frequently called an alpha ($\alpha$) type error or error of the first kind. Accepting the null hypothesis when it is actually false is called a beta ($\beta$) type error or an error of the second kind.

One approach (but not the best approach) would be to assign a value to $\alpha$, the upper bound of the probability of an error of the first kind. This value is called the *level of significance*. For example, with a sample size of 100 we seek a decision rule such that the probability of making an error of the first kind is less than or equal to 5 per cent. This rule consists of choosing a value $c$ so that if the proportion of buyers in the sample is less than or equal to $c$, the null hypothesis is accepted; if it is greater than $c$, the null hypothesis is rejected.[3] The point $c$ is known as the *critical value*.

It is apparent that the error of rejecting the null hypothesis when it is true is more likely to occur in borderline cases, when the actual market share $p^*$ (expressed as a proportion) is close to 0.10 than when $p^*$ is close to zero, no matter what value of $c$ is chosen. In fact, the probability of making an error of the first kind is greatest when $p^*$ is exactly 0.10. Since $p^* = 0.10$ generates the highest probability of an $\alpha$-type error, we are faced with choosing a value of $c$ that gives us exactly a 0.05 probability of making an error of the first kind when $p^* = 0.10$. This probability will be lower when $p^*$ is less than 0.10.

[2] Recall that information is *valid* if it measures what it is designed to measure.

[3] Since the null hypothesis is rejected if a value of $p$ on the upper proportion of the distribution is obtained, this is known as a *one-tailed test*. A test where the null hypothesis is rejected if a value of $p$ is obtained at either end of the distribution (sufficiently far from the mean, under the null hypothesis) is known as a *two-tailed test*. This test is not as useful in marketing problems and will not be illustrated here. Descriptions of the two-tailed test may be found in almost any statistics text.

From Chapter 4 we know that the sample standard error of proportion is

$$
\begin{aligned}
\sigma_p &= \sqrt{\frac{p^*(1 - p^*)}{n}} \\
&= \sqrt{\frac{0.1 \cdot (1 - 0.1)}{100}} \\
&= 0.03
\end{aligned}
$$

The sample proportions, in the case where $p^* = 0.1$, are approximately normally distributed with mean 0.1 and standard deviation 0.03. This is illustrated in Figure 6-1. The shaded area under the tail of the distribution to the right of $c$ must contain 0.05 probability for $\alpha = 0.05$. The normal deviate (i.e., the distance from the mean in standard deviations) is equal to

$$z_{0.05} = \frac{c - 0.1}{0.03}$$

or $c = -0.1 + 0.03 \cdot z_{0.05}$. The value of $z_{0.05}$, obtained from tabled values of the normal distribution, equals 1.65. Thus

$$
\begin{aligned}
c &= 0.1 + 0.03 \cdot 1.65 \\
&= 0.15
\end{aligned}
$$

If the sample proportion turns out to be less than or equal to 0.15, the rule tells us, assume that the market share will be less than or equal to 10 per cent. If not, reject the null hypothesis and assume that the market share will be greater than 10 per cent. Thus, with a sample

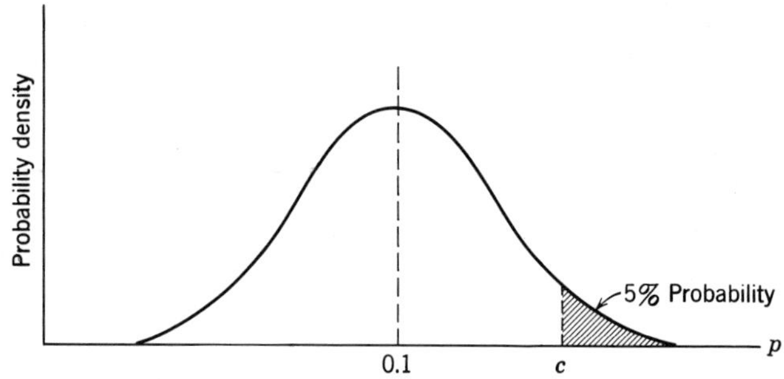


**Figure 6-1**

size of 100, the probability of rejecting the null hypothesis when it is right will be less than 5 per cent. In the example, since the proportion of buyers was seen to be 12 per cent, the null hypothesis would be accepted and the new product scrapped.

Let us recapitulate the procedure that has been followed in the one-sided test example. The null hypothesis is taken to be that the proportion $p^*$ is less than or equal to 10 per cent. The alternative hypothesis is that $p^*$ is greater than 10 per cent. A simple random sample of size $n = 100$ is selected.[4]

By choosing a critical value that is 1.65 standard deviations above the break-even value $p^* = 0.10$, 5 per cent of the probability remains under the upper tail beyond the critical point *if the actual population parameter $p^*$ happens to be equal to the break-even value.* Since the probability of making an $\alpha$ error is greatest when $p^* = 0.10$, the probability of this error is never greater than 5 per cent—the probability of observing a value of $p$ greater than the critical value.[5]

The standard error of proportion is calculated from the formula

$$\sigma_p = \sqrt{\frac{p^*(1 - p^*)}{n}}$$

which yields a value $\sigma_p = 0.03$. From this value, the critical value is calculated.

## The Power Curve

The course of action just examined would be undertaken by a great many (too many) practitioners. What is wrong with the procedure? The most glaring fault is that we have completely ignored $\beta$, the probability of making an error of the second kind. We may be entirely too cautious. In the interest of not introducing a product that will fail, we may be sacrificing too many products that would be commercial successes.

For a product with marginal success, where $p^*$ is minutely greater than 0.1, the probability of rejecting the product would be the area under the curve to the left of $c$, that is, 95 per cent. This is inevitable. The probability of making an error of the second kind must be unity minus the level of significance for borderline cases. But what about

[4] Note that we have given no justification for this particular sample size.

[5] If $p^*$ is less than 0.10, the probability under the upper tail above the critical value drops below 5 per cent.

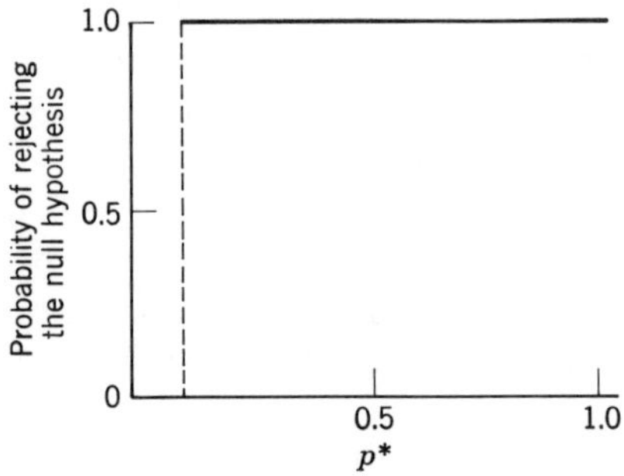


**Figure 6-2** Perfect information power curve.

the probability of making an error of rejection when it really counts, say when $p^*$ is 15 per cent and a good profit can be made?

Figure 6-2 gives us a curve, called the *power curve,* that could be achieved only with *perfect information.* This is the ideal power curve. It shows a probability of rejecting the null hypothesis of zero when the null hypothesis is in fact true and a probability of rejecting the null hypothesis of 1.0 when the null hypothesis is in fact false.

In our example, the probability of rejecting the null hypothesis may be calculated for each possible value of $p^*$ and $c = 0.15$. This yields the power curve shown in Figure 6-3. It shows that with our decision rule we have a 50 per cent probability of accepting the null hypothesis

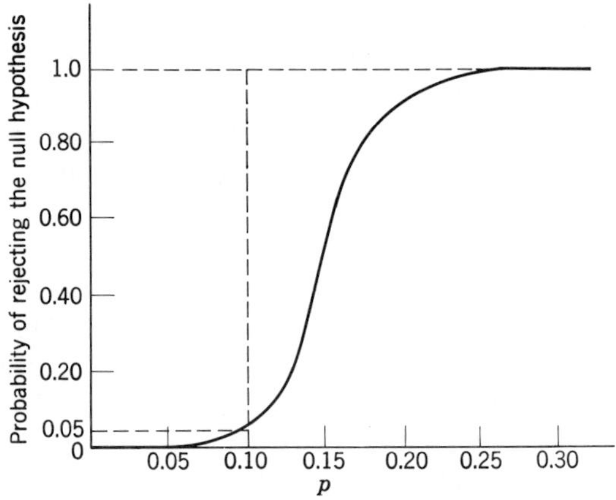


**Figure 6-3** Power curve; $c = 0.15$, $n = 100$.

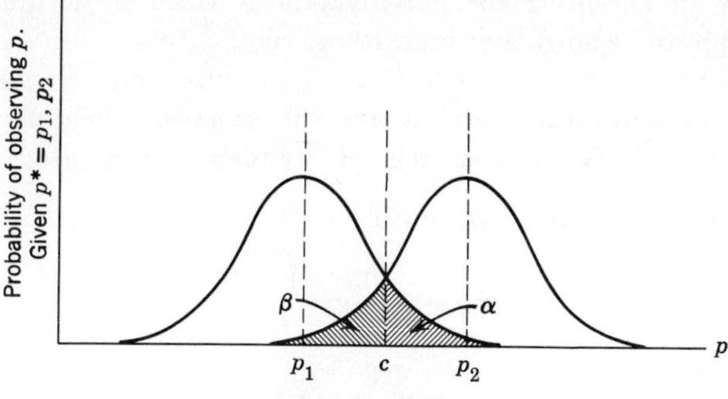


**Figure 6-4**

when it is in fact false and $p^* = 0.15$.[6] Clearly, it may be a false economy to protect stringently against one kind of error and, in the process, generate a high probability of incurring the other kind of error.

Figure 6-4 may serve to clarify the issue. Suppose that the break-even proportion is $p_1$ and that $p_2$ marks some greater proportion that would indeed signify a profitable product. The probability of observing a given sample proportion is shown for the two cases—the true mean $p^* = p_1$ and the true mean $p^* = p_2$. If a decision point $c$ is chosen at the intersection of the two probability distributions, the probability of a type 1 error equals the area to the right of $c$ under the $p^* = p_1$ distribution. Similarly, the probability of a type 2 error equals the area to the left of $c$ under the $p^* = p_2$ curve. Without changing the sample size so as to change the sampling error and thus to compress or expand the curves, it is evident that if $c$ is moved in either direction, one type of error must decrease in probability while the other must increase in probability.

In the previous example, $\alpha$ and $n$ were chosen, leaving no control in the designation of $\beta$ and $c$. A more sophisticated approach, given $p_1$ and $p_2$, is to set $\alpha$ and $\beta$ and to solve for the necessary sample size and $c$.

Suppose that $p_1$, the break-even share of market, is 0.1 and that $p_2 = 0.20$ is a share of market that represents a substantial profit level. We desire the probability of rejecting the null hypothesis when the share of market is less than or equal to $p_1$ to be no greater than 5 per cent. We are also loath to give up substantial profits; hence we desire the

[6] Since we may read, from Figure 6-2, that the probability of rejection is 0.5, the probability of acceptance is $1.0 - 0.5 = 0.5$.

probability of accepting the null hypothesis when $p^*$ is greater than or equal to $p_2$ to be no greater than 10 per cent.[7]

We can now proceed to select a sample size and critical value $c$. The error probabilities $\alpha$ and $\beta$ are the greatest when $p^* = p_1$ and $p^* = p_2$ respectively. The associated standard errors are:

(*a*)
$$p^* = p_1 = 0.1$$
$$\sigma_{p_1} = \sqrt{\frac{0.1 \cdot (1 - 0.1)}{n}}$$
$$= \frac{0.3}{\sqrt{n}}$$

(*b*)
$$p^* = p_2 = 0.2$$
$$\sigma_{p_2} = \sqrt{\frac{0.2 \cdot (1 - 0.2)}{n}}$$
$$= \frac{0.4}{\sqrt{n}}$$

To have a probability of a type 1 error of 5 per cent on a one-tailed test, $c$ should be $1.65\sigma_{p_1}$ above $p_1$, according to a table of the normal distribution. Similarly, for a 10 per cent probability of a type 2 error, $c$ should be $1.28\sigma_{p_2}$ below $p_2$. From Figure 6-5 we can see that

$$1.65\sigma_{p_1} + 1.28\sigma_{p_2} = 0.2 - 0.1$$

or

$$1.65 \cdot \frac{0.3}{\sqrt{n}} + 1.28 \cdot \frac{0.4}{\sqrt{n}} = 0.1$$

[7] The levels of $\alpha$ and $\beta$ of 5 and 10 per cent respectively are very common. Nevertheless, the reader might well anticipate one thrust of the Bayesian attack by wondering why these two particular values should be selected.

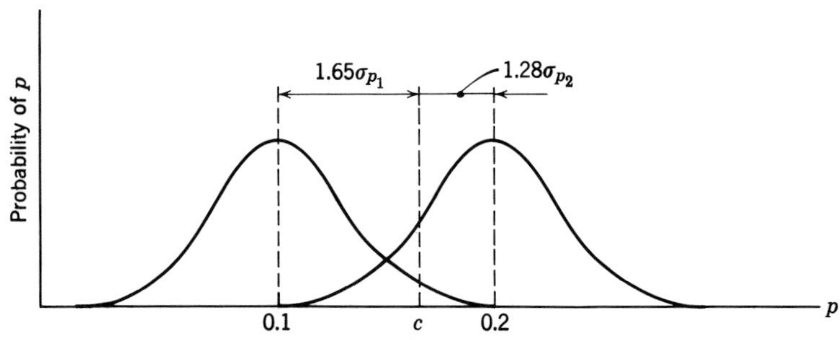


**Figure 6-5**

Solving, we obtain

$$\sqrt{n} = 9.87$$

or

$$n \doteq 100$$

Thus, in this case, a sample size of approximately 100 would actually be appropriate. We also have

$$\begin{aligned} c &= 0.1 + 1.65\sigma_{p_1} \\ &= 0.1 + \frac{1.65 \cdot 0.3}{10} \\ &= 0.15 \end{aligned}$$

The decision rule would then be to accept $p^* \leq 0.1$ if $p \leq 0.15$ and to reject $p^* \leq 0.1$ if $p > 0.15$. If $p_2$ were, say, 15 per cent and not 20 per cent, a larger sample size would be required for the same error probabilities.[8]

Suppose that it would be extremely difficult or too costly to actually obtain a sample size of 100; what could be done? The answer is obvious. We can either conduct the research on the basis of higher $\alpha$ or $\beta$ errors (or both) or not conduct the research at all.

## Risk

An *error characteristic* curve, that is, a curve that shows the error probability if $p^*$ is given, may be derived from the power curve shown in Figure 6-3. For market shares less than or equal to the break-even value $p = 0.1$, the probability of error is the same as the power. Both represent the probability of rejecting the null hypothesis. For market shares greater than 10 per cent, the probability of error is the probability of accepting the null hypothesis, which is unity minus the power. That is,

$$P\ (\text{error}|p > 0.1) = 1 - P\ (\text{rejecting } H_0|p > 0.1)$$

This curve is shown in Figure 6-6. In addition, the *conditional opportunity losses* (conditional on an error being made) are also shown in Figure 6-6. For $p^* \leq 0.1$, the opportunity loss would, in this problem, measure the losses incurred by accepting the new product; for $p^* > 0.1$ the opportunity loss measures the profits missed by not accepting the new product. The product of the two curves gives a quantity called the *risk* or *expected opportunity loss,* given the market share. Since

[8] The student should test his understanding thus far by seeing if he knows why a larger sample size would be required.

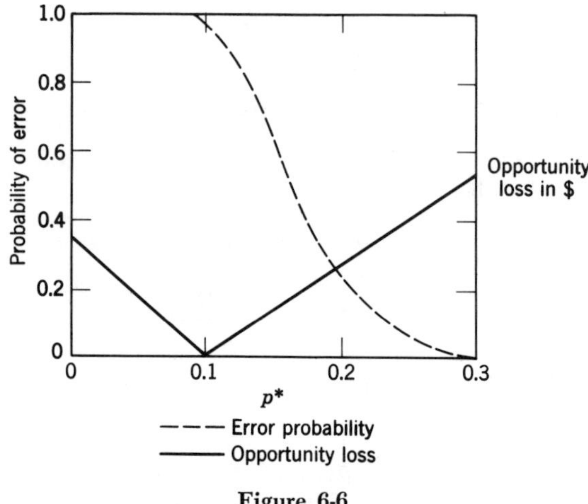


**Figure 6-6**

the risk is zero when either the probability of error or the opportunity loss is zero, the curve of risk typically takes on a shape similar to that shown in Figure 6-7 for a particular decision rule and sample size.

Let us look at an example. If $p^* = 0.08$, the correct action to take would be *not* to market the product. The product will be marketed, however, if we observe a value of $p$ greater than the critical value $c = 0.15$. This would constitute a type 1 error for which the probability of occurrence may be read off the curve in Figure 6-6 as approximately

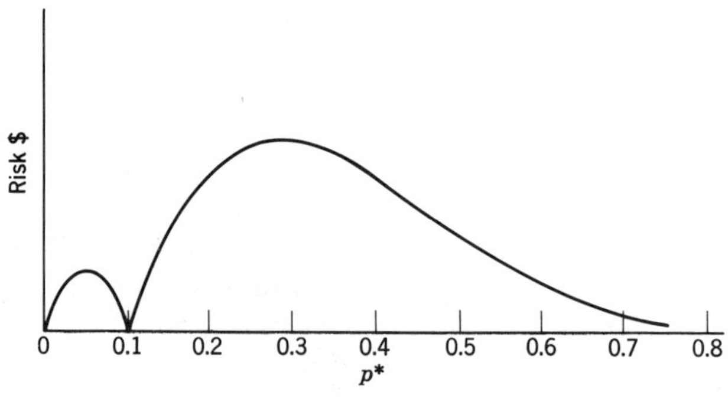


**Figure 6-7**

2 per cent. Suppose that the conditional opportunity loss when $p^* = 0.08$ is \$50,000. That is, if $p^* = 0.08$ and the product is marketed, the result is a \$50,000 loss. The expected opportunity loss or risk, given that $p^* = 0.08$, is the product of the probability of an error (0.02) and the opportunity loss if an error is made (\$50,000). This is seen to be \$1000.

Like the $\alpha$ and $\beta$ errors, one of the modes or peak values of the "butterfly" risk curve can be lowered only at the expense of raising the other, for a given sample size. Both modes can be lowered by increasing the sample size.

The reader, on reflection, should see some virtue in making a decision incorporating the risk function. One decision rule could be that the risk should be no greater than some specified value, no matter what the true market share.

With such a decision rule we would be looking at the whole possible range of market share values rather than just the two values $p_1$ and $p_2$. In fact, it may be argued that $p_1$, in particular, is not of importance since in the region of $p_1$ the opportunity loss is negligible. Thus it does not matter which hypothesis is accepted as long as the market share is close to the break-even value. This argument implies that the level of significance $\alpha$ overstates the probabilities of meaningful errors of the first kind, or at least the kind of errors that involve a significant loss of money.

Another advantage of the "maximum risk" decision rule is that the opportunity losses are incorporated directly into the decision. One can no longer claim that a decision is made without regard to the consequences of that decision.

Figure 6-8 illustrates the application of this decision rule. A value $b$ is selected as the upper limit of risk. Both modes of the risk function

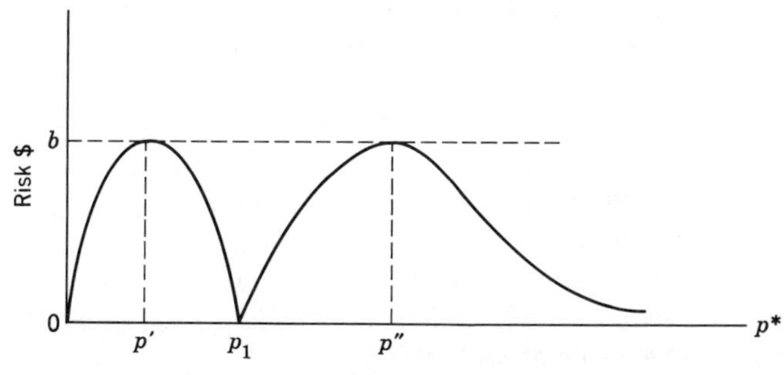


**Figure 6-8**

must reach the same level of risk $b$. If they did not, the sample size could be reduced after lowering the higher-risk made (at the expense of the lower-risk mode) by a change in the decision value $c$. The problem is to choose a sample size and decision value $c$ such that the risk is always less than or equal to $b$.

Suppose, however, that the greatest risks occur at market shares of $p'$ and $p''$. The lower value $p'$ may be considerably lower than $p_1$ and the higher value $p''$ considerably higher than $p_1$. In fact, we may be fairly certain in advance that we will experience neither a disaster equivalent to $p'$ if the product is marketed nor a success equivalent to $p''$. Why then worry about the risks associated with these market shares?

If the reader has not yet observed the fact that we have carefully abstained from attaching probabilities to the market shares themselves, he should now make that observation. All the probabilistic statements made have been in the form of a probability of observing a particular sample mean, *given* the market share. This is because most statistician define probability as a relative frequency. But, as in the case of a particular confidence interval, no long-run frequency interpretation of probability is possible for the market share.

Either the confidence interval $0 \leq p \leq 0.2$ includes the true mean or it does not; either the market share will be 0.2 or it will not. A probability of observing a particular sample $p$, given the true market share, is meaningful in the same sense as the probability of observing a head on the next toss of a coin is meaningful. We may toss the coin a number of times, if desired, and we may observe a number of samples. But we cannot take observations on the market share itself, except by a census, and then we would have this quantity with certainty.

This is a rather unfortunate state of events for we are not really interested in the sample statistic; we are interested in the population parameter. While we would like to know the probability of the population parameter being some quantity, given the fact that we have observed a particular sample, classical statistics gives us the probability of the sample, given the true parameter. Thus a gambler faced with a strange coin may toss it a number of times to test the hypothesis that it is fair. He may calculate the probability of observing a particular set of results, given the postulate that the coin is fair. But he cannot calculate the probability that the coin is fair, given the fact that he has observed a particular sample, *unless he is willing to sacrifice the relative frequency interpretation of probability*.

Bayesian statisticians do make this sacrifice, and in the next section we shall see how and why.

## BAYESIAN DECISION MAKING

The Bayesian concept of probability is best interpreted in the sense of what one would consider *fair betting odds*. One is willing to assign odds to the San Francisco Giants winning the pennant this year even though, in fact, they will either win or not win. But one cannot assign a probability to the Giants winning the pennant *this year* under a relative frequency interpretation of probability.

Thus the Bayesian notion of probability has a subjective cast. Two different baseball fans are very likely to have two different ideas as to the likelihood of the Giants being pennant winners, particularly if one is from San Francisco and the other from Los Angeles. If the task is to assign a specific probability[9] to the Giants winning the pennant, the probabilities will be different.

One may question the usefulness of an ephemeral probability that depends on the person who assigns it for its value and may even depend on exactly when the assigner was asked to assign the probability, as well as on such items as how his ulcer is behaving and whether or not he is on speaking terms with his wife. On the other hand, the assigner may be a baseball buff of long standing who has some genuine knowledge of the game or at least knows enough to realize that the Mets are out of contention on opening day. Should not his experience be used, particularly if he is about to make some small wager on the outcome of the race?

It should be clear that if subjective probabilities are to be used as if they were objective, the answer to the first problem is that assigned "betting odds" should obey the three axioms given in Appendix A of Chapter 4. That is, probabilities should be between zero and one; the probability of an event composed of two mutually exclusive events is the sum of the probabilities of the latter two events, and the sum of the probabilities assigned to a set of mutually exclusive events, one of which must happen, is unity.

In the baseball example, let $A$ signify the event that the Giants win the pennant this year; $B$ the event that the Dodgers win, and $C$ the event that any other team in the league wins.

If we felt that the Giants and Dodgers had equal chances at the pennant, while the rest of the league together had twice as good a chance as *either* the Dodgers or the Giants, we could use this information to assign subjective probabilities to the three events. From our feelings

[9] Again, the reader is reminded that it is subjective probability to which we refer. This distinction will not be made reference to again in this section.

about the race, we have

$$P(A) = P(B)$$

and
$$P(C) = 2P(A)$$

From the third axiom, $P(A) + P(B) + P(C) = 1$

This gives us three equations in three unknowns, which may be solved to yield

$$P(A) = 0.25$$

$$P(B) = 0.25$$

and
$$P(C) = 0.50$$

Note that the three probabilities lie between zero and one and thus satisfy the first axiom.

Suppose that we wanted to calculate the probability of event $D$, that either the Giants or the Dodgers win the pennant. Since $D$ is composed of the two mutually exclusive events $A$ and $B$, we have

$$P(D) = P(A) + P(B) = \tfrac{1}{4} + \tfrac{1}{4} = \tfrac{1}{2}$$

## Expected Risk

We are now ready to tackle the problem of the risk curve in Figure 6-8. Recall that this curve represents the expected opportunity loss or risk associated with each possible share of market for a particular sample size and decision rule. To evaluate the *strategy* of adopting this particular sample size and decision rule, the Bayesian would proceed to weight the risk for each possible market share by the prior probability of that market share occurring and so derive an overall *expected risk.*

We illustrate the procedure with the following example. Again, a 10 per cent market share is the break-even value for a new product. If a product is marketed and the market share is less than 10 per cent, we expect to lose $50,000 for each percentage point that the market share will be below the break-even value. If a product is marketed and gains a market share above the break-even value, we expect to gain $100,000 for each percentage point that the market share is above 10 per cent. Suppose, also, that only two values are considered possible for market share: 5 per cent and 20 per cent.[10] The product manager

[10] This simplification is introduced for ease of computation and so as not to obscure the underlying method.

assigns prior probabilities of 0.3 and 0.7 to the market shares of 5 per cent and 20 per cent respectively. A sample size of 100 is to be taken.

The conditional opportunity losses are derived from the following relationships:

$$\begin{aligned} \text{COL} &= \$50{,}000 \cdot (0.1 - p^*) \cdot 100 = 5 \cdot 10^6(0.1 - p) && p^* < 0.1 \\ &= 10 \cdot 10^6(p^* - 0.1) && p^* > 0.1 \\ &= 0 && p^* = 0.1 \end{aligned}$$

Thus for $p^* = 0.05$ the conditional opportunity loss is \$250,000 and for $p^* = 0.20$ the conditional opportunity loss is \$1,000,000.

We may now test a number of decision rules according to the sequence given in Figure 6-9. The calculation of conditional opportunity losses is given above. In order to derive the probabilities of incurring errors, given the actual market shares, it is first necessary to calculate the standard errors. For market shares of 5 per cent and 20 per cent and a sample size of 100, using the formula

$$\sigma_p = \sqrt{\frac{p^*(1 - p^*)}{n}}$$

the standard errors are seen to be 0.0218 and 0.04 respectively. The error probabilities are then calculated in exactly the same manner as for the $\alpha$ and $\beta$ errors derived earlier in the chapter.

Table 6-1 summarizes the calculations for a number of critical values $c$, and Figure 6-10 shows the resultant expected risks graphically.

It is evident that the minimum expected risk occurs when $c = 0.095$ and that the amount of this expected risk is \$3900. A natural question to ask now is whether or not the sample was worth the cost.

We should first calculate the risk incurred if no sample were taken. This quantity would be equal to the *expected value of perfect information,* since, if we had perfect information, we would be sure to take the right action and thus would not incur an opportunity loss (and would have zero risk).

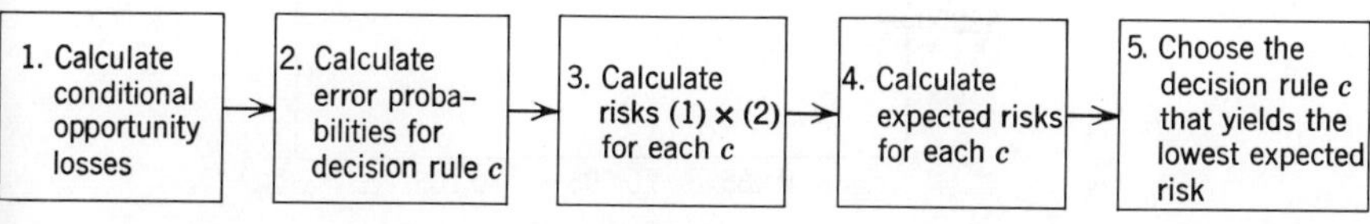


**Figure 6-9**

**Table 6-1**

| | $p^* = 0.05$ | | | $p^* = 0.20$ | | | |
|---|---|---|---|---|---|---|---|
| Decision Point $c$[a] | Probability of Error[b] | Conditional Opportunity Loss | Risk[c] | Probability of Error | Conditional Opportunity Loss | Risk | Expected Risk[d] |
| 0.055 | 0.4090 | $250,000 | $102,250 | 0.0001 | $1,000,000 | $ 100 | $ 30,700 |
| 0.085 | 0.0542 | 250,000 | 13,550 | 0.0020 | 1,000,000 | 2,000 | 5,500 |
| 0.095 | 0.0206 | 250,000 | 5,150 | 0.0034 | 1,000,000 | 3,400 | 3,900 |
| 0.105 | 0.0058 | 250,000 | 1,450 | 0.0088 | 1,000,000 | 8,800 | 6,600 |
| 0.115 | 0.0014 | 250,000 | 350 | 0.0168 | 1,000,000 | 16,800 | 11,900 |
| 0.125 | 0.0003 | 250,000 | 75 | 0.0306 | 1,000,000 | 30,600 | 21,400 |
| 0.155 | | 250,000 | | 0.1303 | 1,000,000 | 130,300 | 91,200 |
| 0.195 | | 250,000 | | 0.4507 | 1,000,000 | 450,700 | 315,500 |

[a] With $n = 100$, a decision value of $c = 0.05$ would represent exactly 5 successes. Since if we observe exactly $c$ successes, we assume that $p = 0.05$, a finite correction factor is added to make the normal approximation more accurate. That is, instead of $c = 0.05$, we have $c = 0.055$ or $5\frac{1}{2}$ successes. If we observe 5 successes, we assume that $p = 0.05$, but if we observe 6 successes, we assume that $p = 0.20$. Exact tables of the cumulative binomial distribution for $n = 100$ are also available.

[b] Since $np = 5$, the normal approximation is used. Actually, this represents an approximation, and an exact table for $n = 100$ is preferred. For larger samples, the approximation is very good.

[c] Risk = conditional opportunity loss × probability of error.

[d] Expected risk = 0.3 × risk (when $p^* = 0.05$) + 0.7 × risk (when $p^* = 0.20$).

If the product is marketed, the probability of error is 0.3 and the expected opportunity loss is

$$\text{EOL (marketing)} = 0.3 \cdot 250{,}000 = \$75{,}000$$

Similarly, the expected opportunity loss of not marketing the product

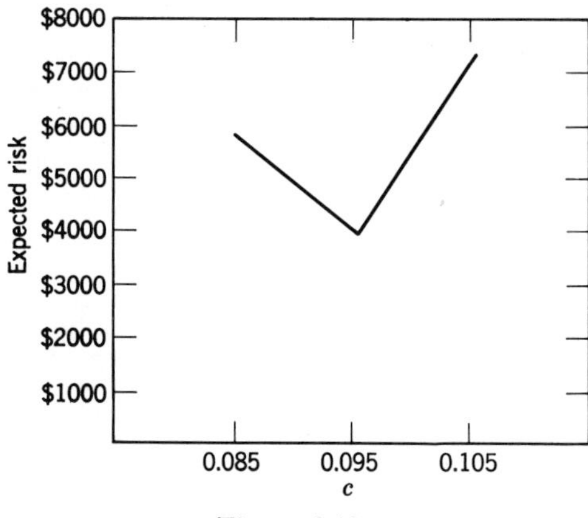


Figure 6-10

is

$$\text{EOL (not marketing)} = 0.7 \cdot 1{,}000{,}000 = \$700{,}000$$

It may be shown that taking the action that minimizes expected opportunity loss always leads to maximizing of expected profits. Thus, in this case, we would market the product, and the expected value of perfect information would be

$$\text{EVPI} = \$75{,}000$$

By taking the sample we have lowered the expected opportunity loss from $75,000 to $3900. Thus we should be willing to pay anything up to $71,100, the amount of the reduction, for the sample. Undoubtedly, a sample of size 100 would cost considerably less than this saving and would be economically justified.

It is not at all uncommon for a rather small sample size to remove most of the expected risk from the decision. In this example, the most we could expect in improvement would be $3900 over the sample size of 100 if we went to a larger sample. The actual calculations would be somewhat tedious, since we would have to repeat the present calculations for each projected sample size (actually, not a very formidable task for a computer). But we are certain that we have hit a region of severely diminishing marginal returns for larger samples and have therefore established an upper limit on possible improvement.

One might reasonably expect that the necessary calculations to this approach would get totally out of hand if our prior distribution were continuous rather than discrete. Fortunately, this is not necessarily the case. In fact, for a normally distributed prior distribution and linear opportunity losses, the risk is easily obtained.[11]

## Preposterior Analysis

The sequence of analysis described in the preceding section and shown schematically in Figure 6-9 is not the only possible approach yielding a solution under Bayesian analysis. The approach discussed below is commonly called *preposterior* analysis.[12] It is important to note that this approach *does not* yield a different solution to the approach of Figure 6-9, but it does provide the information in a somewhat different and more useful manner. In addition to providing the decision rule with

[11] See Schlaifer (1961, Chapter 20).

[12] The word "preposterior" literally means to decide beforehand what action will be taken for each possible sample result (posterior analysis) as well as to decide whether or not to take a sample in the first place.

the minimum expected risk, preposterior analysis also provides the decision maker with a revised prior or *posterior* probability of the true market share, given the sample. *The posterior probability distribution is the Bayesian estimator used instead of confidence intervals.*

A decision tree, shown in Figure 6-11, is commonly employed to analyze the decision in preposterior analysis. This tree portrays, chronologically, decisions and their consequences. Each branch indicates either a decision choice, a sample observation, or an outcome (the actual market share).

The first branch represents the choice of sampling or not sampling. Suppose that we choose not to sample, as represented by the lower path. The next decision to be made is whether or not to market the product. No matter which decision is made, the outcome will be a market share of either 5 per cent or 20 per cent.[13]

If we decide to sample, this decision is represented graphically by the selection of path $AD$. At $D$, we have a choice of a number of decision rules, in each case marketing the product ($O_1$) if $p > c$ and not marketing the product ($O_2$) if $p < c$. We then observe the sample results, that is, that $p$ which is the proportion of persons out of the total of 100 who indicate that they would purchase the product.[14] The decision whether to market the product is then made, followed by the actual market share indicating the correctness or error of the decision. Recall that a correct decision is one with zero opportunity loss.

The procedure of analysis is to start at the end of the decision tree and work back toward the beginning, attaching a value to each lettered node. The lower (no sample) branch will be analyzed first.

If we are at $C_1$, that is, if we have decided to market the product, we may experience an opportunity loss of \$250,000 with 30 per cent probability (shown in parentheses) or of \$0 with 70 per cent probability. Thus the expected opportunity loss associated with $C_1$ is $0.3 \times \$250{,}000 + 0.7 \times \$0$ or \$75,000. In a similar manner it is established that the expected opportunity loss associated with $C_2$ is \$700,000. Now, at node $B$ we have a choice of proceeding to $C_1$ by marketing the product or to $C_2$ by not marketing the product. Since the rule is to

[13] Should the decision be made not to market the product, the firm will not find out what the market share would be. Nevertheless, an opportunity loss of \$1,000,000 is presumed to have occurred if the market share would have been 20 per cent and if the product were marketed. An opportunity loss need not be out-of-pocket or even recognized to have taken place.

[14] We show only three values of $c$:0.085, 0.095, and 0.105. Actually, it is not necessary to look at all possible critical values. It is left as an excerise for the reader to show that no other value of $c$ less than 0.085 or greater than 0.105 can be better than $c = 0.095$.

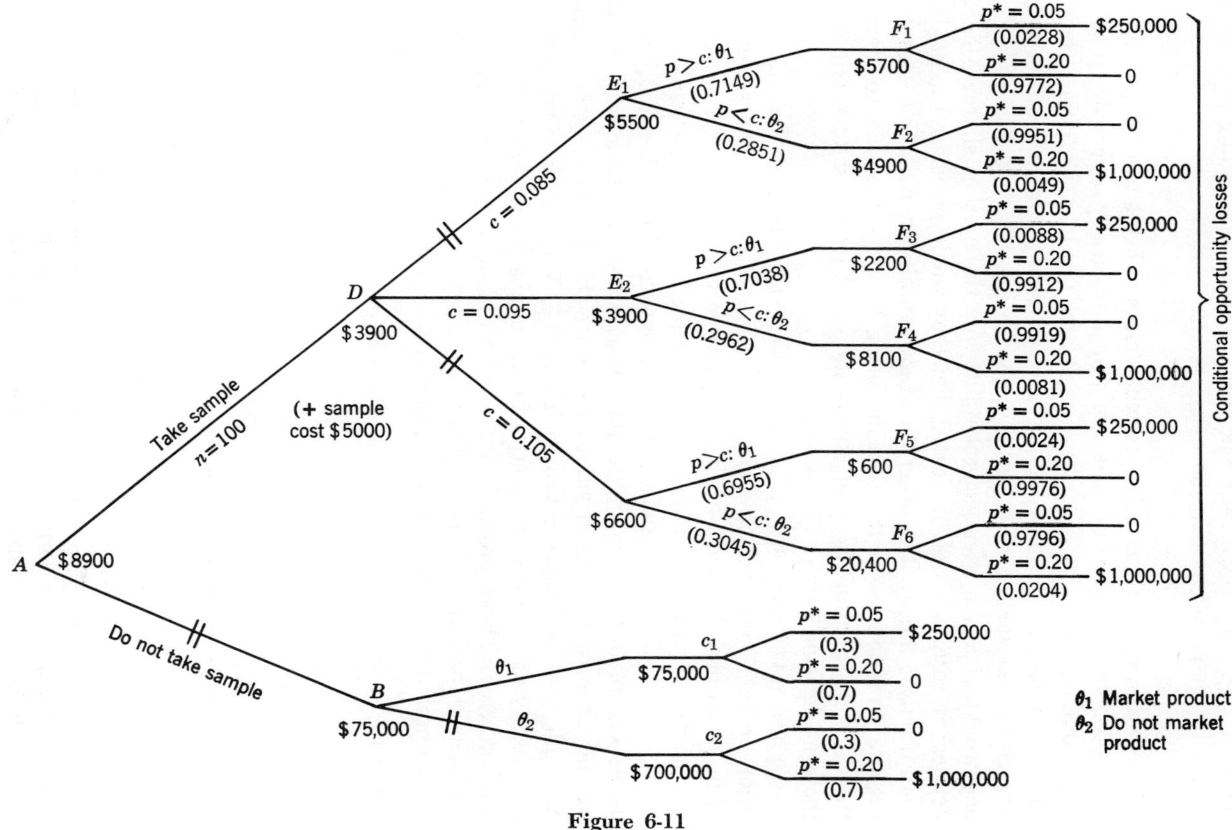

A
$8900
Take sample
n=100
(+ sample cost $5000)
D
$3900
c = 0.085
c = 0.095
c = 0.105
E1
$5500
E2
$3900
$6600
p > c: θ1
(0.7149)
p < c: θ2
(0.2851)
p > c: θ1
(0.7038)
p < c: θ2
(0.2962)
p > c: θ1
(0.6955)
p < c: θ2
(0.3045)
F1
$5700
F2
$4900
F3
$2200
F4
$8100
F5
$600
F6
$20,400
p* = 0.05
(0.0228)
$250,000
p* = 0.20
(0.9772)
0
p* = 0.05
(0.9951)
0
p* = 0.20
(0.0049)
$1,000,000
p* = 0.05
(0.0088)
$250,000
p* = 0.20
(0.9912)
0
p* = 0.05
(0.9919)
0
p* = 0.20
(0.0081)
$1,000,000
p* = 0.05
(0.0024)
$250,000
p* = 0.20
(0.9976)
0
p* = 0.05
(0.9796)
0
p* = 0.20
(0.0204)
$1,000,000
Conditional opportunity losses
Do not take sample
B
$75,000
θ1
θ2
c1
$75,000
c2
$700,000
p* = 0.05
(0.3)
$250,000
p* = 0.20
(0.7)
0
p* = 0.05
(0.3)
0
p* = 0.20
(0.7)
$1,000,000
θ1 Market product
θ2 Do not market product


Figure 6-11

select that action which yields the smallest expected opportunity loss, we choose to market the product, making the expected opportunity loss associated with node $B$ \$75,000. The fact that the path leading to $C_2$ is not selected is indicated by two short strokes: ⫽

The "take sample" path is somewhat more difficult to compute. There are two sets of branches that are probabilistically selected, from $F_n$ and from $E_i$, where $n = 1, 2, \ldots, 6$ and $i = 1, 2$, or 3. For the $F_n$ set, it is necessary to know the posterior probability of the market share $p^*$, given the fact that a certain observation has taken place. Thus one would attach a greater probability for the market share to be 20 per cent if, say, 25 people indicated that they would purchase the product than if only 5 did so. The other set of probabilities necessary to compute are the probabilities of the decision being to market or not to market, that is, that the proportion of buyers indicated by the sample is greater than the decision value $c$ or less than $c$.

We are given two sets of probabilities. The first is the subjective prior probability distribution of $p^*$, the market share. The second set of information is, for each of the two possible values of $p^*$, the probabilities of the proportion of buyers in the sample being any particular value $p$, as derived from the binominal distribution. From this distribution, as in Figure 6-9, we calculate the probabilities of error (and of not making an error) for each value of $c$. Since this has already been done, we shall use the values given in Table 6-1, keeping in mind that the probability of not making an error is one minus the probability of making an error. These probabilities, for values of $c$ of 0.085, 0.095, and 0.105, are repeated in Table 6-2.[15]

The probabilities that we would like to derive are those of the observa-

[15] We have chosen values of $c$ such that $P(p = c) = 0$.

TABLE 6-2

| | $p^* = 0.05$ | | $p^* = 0.20$ | |
|---|---|---|---|---|
| Rule $c$ | $P(p > c)$ | $P(p < c)$ | $P(p > c)$ | $P(p < c)$ |
| 0.085 | 0.0545 | 0.9458 | 0.9980 | 0.0020 |
| 0.095 | 0.0206 | 0.9794 | 0.9966 | 0.0034 |
| 0.105 | 0.0058 | 0.9942 | 0.9912 | 0.0088 |

tion exceeding or not exceeding $c$, that is,

$$P(p > c) \qquad \text{and} \qquad P(p < c)$$

as well as the posterior probabilities of the actual market shares, given the observation. If we denote the observation by $S$, where $S$ can be either $p > c$ or $p < c$, these posterior probabilities are

$$P(p^*|S)$$

where $p^* = 0.05$ or $0.20$.

The probability of the particular observation $S$ is the sum of the probabilities of all the mutually exclusive ways in which $S$ can occur. In our example, $S$ can occur either with $p^* = 0.05$ or with $p^* = 0.20$. Thus

$$P(S) = P(S \text{ and } p^* = 0.05 \text{ both hold}) + P(S \text{ and } p^* = 0.20 \text{ both hold})$$[16]

For example, the probability that we shall get an indication to market the product is given by

$$P(p > c) = P(p > c \text{ and } p^* = 0.05) + P(p > c \text{ and } p^* = 0.20)$$

Thus it is necessary to construct a joint probability table in order to calculate the complete set of probabilities of observations.

Posterior probabilities are derived from *Bayes theorem.* We have

$$P(p^*|S) = \frac{P(S \text{ and } p^* \text{ both hold})}{P(S)}$$

Again the table of joint probabilities, together with the derived probability $P(S)$, provides the solution. The joint probabilities are derived from the prior probability $P(p^*)$ and $P(S|p^*)$ as

$$P(S \text{ and } p^*) = P(p^*) \times P(S|p^*)$$

For example, if $c = 8.5$,

$$P(p > 0.085 \text{ and } p^* = 0.05) = 0.3 \cdot 0.0545 = 0.0163$$

$$P(p > 0.085 \text{ and } p^* = 0.20) = 0.7 \cdot 0.9980 = 0.6986$$

$$P(p > 0.085) = 0.0163 + 0.6986 = 0.7149$$

$$P(p^* = 0.05|p > 0.085) = \frac{0.0163}{0.7149} = 0.0228$$

These calculations are summarized in Table 6-3.

[16] For those familiar with set notation, $P(S) = \sum_{p^*} (S \cap p^*)$.

TABLE 6-3

| | Joint Probabilities $P(S \text{ and } p^*)$ | | Marginal | Posterior $P(p^*\|S)$ | |
|---|---|---|---|---|---|
| $S$ | $p^* = 0.05$ | $p^* = 0.20$ | $P(S)$ | $p^* = 0.05$ | $p^* = 0.20$ |
| $p > 0.085$ | 0.0163 | 0.6986 | 0.7149 | 0.0228 | 0.9772 |
| $p < 0.085$ | 0.2837 | 0.0014 | 0.2851 | 0.9951 | 0.0049 |
| | 0.3000 | 0.7000 | 1.0000 | | |
| $p > 0.095$ | 0.0062 | 0.6976 | 0.7038 | 0.0088 | 0.9912 |
| $p < 0.095$ | 0.2938 | 0.0024 | 0.2962 | 0.9919 | 0.0081 |
| | 0.3000 | 0.7000 | 1.0000 | | |
| $p > 0.105$ | 0.0017 | 0.6938 | 0.6955 | 0.0024 | 0.9976 |
| $p < 0.105$ | 0.2983 | 0.0062 | 0.3045 | 0.9796 | 0.0204 |
| | 0.3000 | 0.7000 | 1.0000 | | |

The "take sample" branch of the decision tree may now be analyzed. Again, we start at the end of the decision tree in Figure 9-11, working back toward the beginning. For example, if we are at $F_1$, this shows that a sample was taken, the decision value $c = 0.085$ was selected, and the sample proportion $p$ was greater than $c$, indicating the decision to market the product. Now, the market share may turn out to be 5 per cent with probability 0.0228 and a corresponding opportunity loss of \$250,000, or it may turn out to be 20 per cent with probability 0.9772 and zero opportunity loss. The expected opportunity loss associated with being at $F_1$ is then

$$0.0228 \cdot \$250{,}000 + 0.9772 \cdot \$0 = \$5700$$

If we are at point $D$, it is clear that the best decision rule is to adopt $c = 0.095$, since it has the lowest expected risk (\$3900). If the cost of the sample is \$5000, the total expected opportunity cost is \$8900. This is much less than the \$75,000 expected opportunity cost of not sampling. Thus we again decide to take a sample, using the decision rule to market the product if the sample proportion of buyers is greater than 0.095 and not to market if the converse is true.

It should be clear, without investigating other decision rules, that a value of $c$, less than 0.085 or greater than 0.105, better than $c = 0.095$ will not be found. If $c$ were chosen less than 0.085, the probability of marketing the product when it should not be will rise above that for $c = 0.085$

and so will the associated expected opportunity loss contributed by this error. But for $c = 0.085$, the component of expected opportunity loss from this kind of error is already $4100, as calculated from the probability of going from $E_1$ to $F_1$ and the associated expected opportunity loss of being at $F_1$. This is above the total expected risk associated with $c = 0.085$. Similarly, a value of $c$ greater than $c = 0.105$ must yield worse results than $c = 0.095$, because the probability of not marketing the product when it should be marketed becomes very large.

Table 6-3 illustrates dramatically the information contained in the sample. We start out believing that there is a 30 per cent probability that market share would be low and a 70 per cent probability that market share would be high if the product were marketed. This is certainly to be preferred to the situation where, whatever decision is made, we have a fifty-fifty chance of being wrong. Nevertheless, with the money involved, the amount of uncertainty is still too large to be borne comfortably.

The posterior probabilities for the optimum decision rule, however, are much more pleasing. If the sample results are favorable ($p > 0.095$), the probability of the market share being high goes up beyond 99 per cent, a rather nice figure on which to base a decision. If the sample indicates that sales will be low ($p < 0.095$), the probability associated with sales being indeed low is also over 99 per cent. One does not mind tossing in the towel on a product with these odds against success.

The reader should be wary of taking these probabilities literally, however. One must keep in mind that the techniques are designed for application to sampling from a population where the decision to be made by each person in the sample would be under exactly the same conditions as if we were actually marketing the product. Since this is almost never true, the results must be tempered to conform with the nature of the sample. For example, if the test market happened to be a supermarket, one would want to adjust for such factors as shelf space and unusual promotion by competitor at the time.

## SUMMARY

We have been concerned, in this chapter, with the problem of making a decision under uncertainty. If the consequences of all possible courses of action were known with certainty, there would be no excuse for a poor decision. But, as we have seen, there is no consensus as to the best strategies to employ when the consequences can only be anticipated with subjective likelihood of occurring.

Our decision sequence is:

1. A decision as to whether or not to gather sample information.
2. A decision as to the sample size.
3. A decision based on the results of the sample (if one is taken, otherwise on prior information alone) on a course of action.[17]

Traditional statistics, as outlined in the first part of this chapter, has had very little to contribute in assessing whether or not a sample should be taken or in selecting the size of the sample, particularly in business problems. The Bayesian approach is directly concerned with both problems. It dictates that a sample should be taken only if the expected value of the information obtained is greater than the expected cost of obtaining that information. Furthermore, the sample size is increased until a value is reached such that the marginal value of information equals the marginal cost.

If the expected cost of information is greater than the expected value of that information, the Bayesian approach is to take the course of action with highest expected value (or, equivalently, the smallest expected opportunity loss). Again, traditional statistics gives no guidance as to the proper course of action without sample information.

An additional controversy exists on the use of sample information, once obtained. We have seen that a variety of approaches are possible under traditional inferential statistics. We may make a decision on the basis of errors of the first and second kind or on the basis of risk (as defined statistically). In none of these approaches, however, do we make use of any prior knowledge or experience that might bear on the decision. The Bayesian decision rule, on the other hand, incorporates both prior knowledge and sample information.

The authors conclude that Bayesian statistics has greater applicability to marketing decisions than does inferential statistics. This statement probably does not hold for academic research because the economic consequences of making a wrong decision are almost impossible to evaluate. Thus academic research is commonly reported only when the probability of a result arising by chance is very small.

One final very important point concerning the Bayesian versus statistical inference approaches should be made. Where it is possible and economical to take very large samples, the two approaches will almost

[17] There are decision rules, the most well known being *minimax, minimax regret,* and the *Laplace criterion,* under which sample information has no value. An excellent treatment of these rules is found in (Luce and Raiffa 1957, Chapter 13). The minimax criterion is basic in game theory, but none of the criteria has wide use in practice.

always yield the same decision, since the prior probabilities become swamped by the sample information. It is in those cases where cost or practicality dictate small samples that prior knowledge is most useful and needed and the Bayesian approach is most advantageous.

## REFERENCES

A treatment of hypothesis testing may be found in any book on statistics. A clear description of power curves, error characteristics, and risk functions is much more difficult to discover. Good elementary expositions may be found in Bierman (1965) and Schlaifer, (1959, 1961). Decision rules under uncertainty are discussed in Bierman (1965) and Luce and Raiffa (1957). Bayesian statistics for business decisions are treated in Bierman (1965) and Schlaifer (1959, 1961), with the most sophisticated discussion found in Schlaifer (1959).

Bierman, H., Jr., and Others. *Quantitative Analysis for Business Decisions.* (Rev. Ed.) Homewood, Ill.: Richard D. Irwin, 1965.

Luce, R. D., & Raiffa, H. *Games and Decisions.* New York: Wiley, 1957.

Schlaifer, R. *Probability and Statistics for Business Decisions.* New York: McGraw-Hill, 1959.

Schlaifer, R. *Introduction to Statistics for Business Decisions.* New York: McGraw-Hill, 1961.

*Seven*

# Experimental Design

Decision making was discussed in Chapter 6 from the point of view of *observing* a random sample and deciding, on the basis of that sample, to accept or to reject a null hypothesis or to take some action. In Chapters 4 and 5 we discussed estimating population parameters in a similar fashion, by *observing* sample survey information. It should be noted that in these procedures the role of the researcher is passive; he does not manipulate the phenomena under study.

Frequently, however, it is of interest to subject a group of persons or a market to some *experimental treatment* so as to ascertain the effect of one or more dependent variables. This manipulation of the independent variables, and the ability to decide what *experimental unit* gets what treatment *rather than merely observing them,* marks the distinction between a true experiment and a sample survey.

In this chapter various forms of experimental designs are discussed. Then examples are given of the analysis of the data in simple cases from both the traditional and Bayesian points of view. More extensive treatments may be found in Campbell and Stanley (1963), Cox (1958), and Guenther (1964). An excellent treatise on experimentation in marketing has been provided by Banks (1965). The use of Bayesian approaches in experimentation, however, has not been extensively treated in the literature.

## Some Key Concepts

In this section we discuss four key concepts that are employed in the chapter. First we are concerned with *internal validity* and *external validity*. Next we examine the distinction between *field experimentation* and *laboratory experimentation,* and the relationship between these methods of experimentation and internal and external validity.

## External Validity

The reader will recall that validity is measured by bias. Perfect validity implies zero bias. Thus, even if an experiment were performed on the entire population of interest, the results could be invalid to some degree.

The external validity of an experiment refers to whether or not a bias is introduced that in some way makes the group under test *systematically different* (i.e., not the difference produced by chance) from the population of interest. In social research, the most common source of bias that reduces external validity in experimentation lies in the process by which the subjects are selected. It is frequently necessary to choose a group of subjects because of convenience rather than choosing them randomly from the population. University students, for example, are probably the most experimented upon population segment in the United States. Any inferences that may be made from such experiments then are difficult to generalize beyond the population of university students.

Other reasons for a lack of external validity will be discussed in the section on field versus laboratory experiments and in the discussion of design 8 in this chapter.

## Internal Validity

Even more important than external validity is internal validity. The question of internal validity is analogous to the question of response bias in survey. That is, internal validity refers to whether a bias exists with respect to the group under study, rather than the population as a whole. Such a bias is caused by variables other than the experimental treatment which *confound* (i.e., provide alternate explanations for) the results.

Unfortunately, as we shall see, attempts to improve internal validity often must take place at the expense of external validity, and vice versa.

## Field versus Laboratory Experiments

A field experiment is conducted in a natural setting, that is, the environment in which the experiment takes place corresponds to the natural environment of the behavior being studied. If one were interested in the behavior of supermarket shoppers, for example, the proper place for a field experiment would be a supermarket or supermarkets. Obviously, many things beyond the control of the experimenter may disturb such "natural" experiments.

A laboratory experiment takes place in an artificial environment where rigid control may be exercised by the researcher. For example, Pessemier (1963) performed an experiment in which shopping behavior was examined through purchases, in a laboratory setting, and photographs of the items were substituted for the items themselves.

It is evident that external validity is easiest to maintain in the field experiment. Since the experiment is performed in a natural setting, the problem of generalizing to the real world from the artificial environment of a laboratory experiment does not exist (although other factors reducing external validity are usually present). Thus the second major cause of a lack of external validity in an experiment relates to a lack of realism that may be present in an experimental setting when compared with the real-world behavior of interest. On the other hand, many of the variables beyond the control of the experimenter in a field experiment, which may affect the internal validity of the experiment, play no part in the laboratory experiment.[1]

In the section that follows we use the notation developed by Campbell and Stanley (1963) and later by Banks (1965) in classifying experiments. Campbell and Stanley's excellent categorization of the various causes of lack of internal and external validity is also presented.

## EXPERIMENTAL DESIGN AND VALIDITY

The basis of a true experiment is that (1) a comparison is available between a *test group* (or groups) that receives the experimental treatment and a *control group* that does not receive the treatment but otherwise goes through exactly the same procedures and (2) experimental units are assigned to the test or control group *by the experimenter* in such a manner that initial differences between the groups arise by chance alone.[2]

[1] A more complete coverage of the problems of field experimentation in marketing than is given here may be found in Uhl (1966).

[2] Contrary to popular opinion, it is not a requisite for a true experiment that all variables but one be kept constant. A true experiment may take place with more than one variable manipulated. Also, the control group may receive a treatment different from that given to the test group, in which case it is the *difference* in the treatment effects that is being investigated.

A preexperiment, according to Campbell and Stanley, is one in which (1) a control group either is not used or is self-selected (as opposed to being selected by the experimenter) and (2) measurement consists of only a single posttreatment measurement or a pretreatment and posttreatment measurement. Quasi experiments will be discussed later.

We shall adopt Campbell and Stanley's (1963) notation. The $O$ represents an observation, $X$ denotes an experimental treatment, $R$ represents random assignment to groups, a dashed line between comparison groups represents groups not equated randomly, and the time dimension of a listing of symbols in a line goes chronologically from left to right.

## Preexperiments

Preexperiments, or experiments where randomization of treatments to groups is not present, are discussed in this section.

### *The One-Shot Case Study*

The most misleading design is a simple

$$\text{design 1} \qquad X\ O$$

or what Campbell and Stanley (1963) term the "one-shot case study." Although examples of this design, as well as of other preexperimental designs, are abundant in the marketing literature, we shall confine our attention to hypothetical situations.

Suppose that a company introduces a sales contest among its salesmen ($X$) and then observes actual sales ($O$). Of course, an absolute level of sales contains no information as to the usefulness of the experimental treatment. This sales level must be compared, implicitly or explicitly, with the sales level expected without the experimental treatment. Design 1 provides no means of obtaining this comparison.

### *Premeasurement—Postmeasurement*

To make the comparison more explicit, a premeasurement-postmeasurement,

$$\text{design 2} \qquad O_1\ X\ O_2$$

is sometimes employed. The assumption is, of course, that the change $O_2 - O_1$ is caused by the experimental treatment $X$.

Neither in design 1 nor in design 2 is there any way to demonstrate what in fact would have taken place without the treatment. A host of outside variables, from the general level of prosperity to the state of the weather, may have contributed to the actual sales level. The motivation of winning the contest (if indeed there was any such motivation) is only one of the many variables that could have caused the observation $O$ in design 1 or the change $O_2 - O_1$ in design 2.

*Static Group Comparison*

A naïve method of overcoming the above objection[3] is formulated in design 3:

$$\text{design 3} \qquad \frac{X\ O_1}{\quad O_2}$$

There are two groups—a test group and a control group. The dashed line between the groups shows that the experimental units (salesmen, sales districts, or salesforces in the example) are *not* assigned randomly to the treatments. Observations $O_1$ and $O_2$ occur simultaneously. The experimental effect is taken to be $O_1 - O_2$.

An example of design 3 would be the hiring of a consultant to compare the sales results of companies that conduct sales contests among their salesmen with companies that do not. In this case the two groups of companies would likely have differed with respect to their promotional mix or in other ways, and these differences are more likely than the contest to be responsible for any experimental effect.

An example of the use of design 3 in the field of education takes place at many high school graduations when the principal speaker cites the economic advantages of a college education. It is pointed out that high school graduates average over $100,000 less in income over their working careers than do college graduates, the obvious point being that a college education is worth a great deal of money. A strong case can be made, however, for the two groups not being comparable. Since the group who did not finish college is probably less motivated and less capable on the whole, there are other explanations than a college education for the difference in the incomes of the two groups.

It is useful to consider the reasons for a lack of internal validity in the three preexperimental designs more carefully than we have so far. Seven of the eight classes of extraneous variables given by Campbell and Stanley that contribute to the problem are examined below.

## The Causes of Loss of Internal Validity

The seven variables causing a loss of internal validity that we examine are history, maturation, testing, instrumentation, statistical regression, mortality, and differential selection.

[3] The reader should note that the objections pertain to internal validity.

*History*

In design 2, a great deal can happen in the time between the first and second measurements. In fact, the longer the time interval, the more reasonable it is to assign the difference $O_2 - O_1$ to the effect of history rather than to the experimental treatment. In the example, if there is a six-month lag between the first sales measurement and the second sales measurement, it would be almost impossible to ascertain the effect of the contest. Similarly, in design 1, for the contest to be at all useful, it should last for some time (at least, say, for a full season in a fashion goods industry) and, again, numerous other things can happen in the interval.

Design 3 is superior to the other two designs with respect to history, since the extraneous confounding variables are assumed to affect both the test groups and the experimental groups equally. Of course, in a loosely controlled field experiment there are no guarantees that the two groups are affected equally or even that both are affected by the same variables. For example, if two "comparable" cities, one for test and the other for control, are chosen to test a promotional campaign, many things can happen in one city that do not happen in the other. The actions of competitors may differ between cities, the economy of one city may be buoyed or dampened by regional happenings, or one city may experience more unpleasant weather than the other during the experiment. Any of these extraneous effects could make it difficult to infer an experimental effect.

*Maturation*

Maturation is similar to history except that here we are concerned with changes in the experimental units themselves over time. This variable is of particular importance in the case of research on people who grow older, tire, get hungry, and so on. At the beginning of the contest, for example, a salesman may be highly motivated, but this level of motivation may change as he begins to be worn down during the selling season.

Since maturation is caused by the passage of time, the longer the duration of the experiment, the more disrupting this effect is likely to be. Design 3 is less likely to be seriously affected by maturation than designs 1 or 2, since the effect occurs to both groups.

*Testing*

If the premeasurement and postmeasurement of design 2 involve a test or a questionnaire, the subject may be conditioned to be more aware of the items on the test than he might otherwise be. For example, merely asking a housewife what brands of toothpaste she has on her shelf may cause her to reexamine her brand preference, or at least to become more self-conscious about her purchasing behavior. If the housewife knows that she will be asked the same question again at some future date, she may think in terms of buying those items that she thinks would be more acceptable. Thus she may substitute butter for margarine, premium brands for inexpensive brands, and the like.

Another difficulty with pretests involving tests of intelligence or achievement is that a marked learning effect is associated with most tests of these types. All university admissions offices, for example, take into account the fact that a student is likely to improve his score each time he takes the Graduate Record Examination.

In most cases, the researcher is well advised to consider whether a pretest is really necessary for his experiment. Often such tests are administered in marketing experiments more because of tradition than of real need.

### *Instrumentation*

Unfortunately, behavioral experiments employ cruder measuring instruments than do experiments in the physical sciences. One of the real difficulties is to keep these instruments, in a behavioral experiment, at least consistent, if not accurate.

Human observers measuring $O_1$ and $O_2$ may themselves change in their standards or methods, without realizing it, between observations. If different observers are involved, as may be the case where each subject is experimented upon separately, differences in measurement may be expected.

Similarly, the experimental treatment may not be administered uniformly if it is not administered to the whole test group simultaneously. A slightly different setting may be used, a different intonation of the voice may effect the subjects' attitudes, or a myriad of other seemingly minor or trivial details may confound the results.

### *Regression*

The effect of regression arise from selecting only subjects who maintain an extreme position in some pretest for the experiment. For example, suppose that only those salesmen who had sold poorly the previous year were enrolled in a sales contest. Of course, the purpose of the contest would be to encourage the salesmen to work harder.

The difficulty occurs because selling effort is not perfectly correlated with sales. Suppose that all salesmen in a company are equally capable,

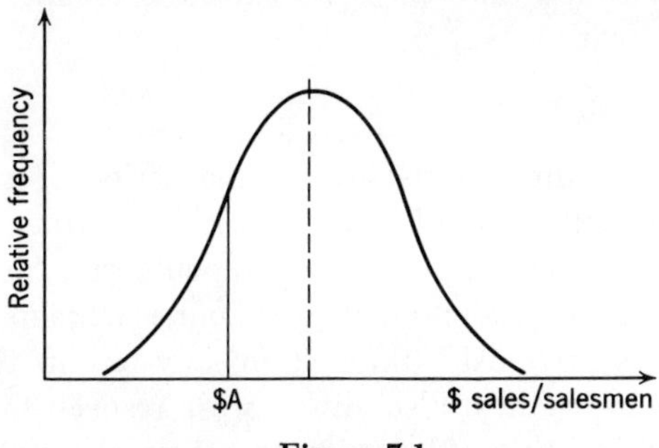


**Figure 7-1**

work equally hard, and have comparable territories. Nevertheless, because of random factors relating to their territories, customers, and luck, some salesmen will have had a good year and some a bad year. This is illustrated in Figure 7-1.

Suppose that those salesmen whose sales were below $A are selected to participate in the contest. Of course, by chance alone, most of the salesmen whose sales the previous year were below $A would do better the following year *without a contest.* Similarly, some of the salesmen who did better the previous year would do worse this year, again purely by chance.

Attributing the increase in sales of the "poor" salesmen to the contest would clearly be in error. Design 1 and design 2 provide no means of ascertaining whether or not the contest caused the change or whether a regression effect is present. Design 3 is somewhat better, since a comparison can be obtained between low producers who do receive the treatment (participating in the contest) and low producers who do not receive the treatment. Presumably, any regression effect would be operative on both groups, hence the difference would be attributable to the treatment.

*Differential Selection*

If the two groups of design 3 are self-selecting rather than assigned randomly, the results must inevitably remain suspect. Relaxing the assumption that all salesmen are cut from the same mold, those who choose to participate in the contest might be expected to be more highly motivated to better their performance than those who remain out of the contest. Thus any observed difference between the groups cannot be inferred to have resulted from the treatment.

In general, where chance does not play a role in the assignment of treatments to groups, one cannot apply statistical techniques to infer whether or not observed differences between the groups arise by chance or because of the treatments.

### *Mortality*

If a treatment is administered over some period of time, it is to be expected that some subjects will elect to withdraw from the experiment. The longer the time period, the more dropouts can be anticipated.

This is analogous to the problem of nonrespondents or refusals in a survey. Dropouts obviously differ from stay-ons in their willingness to participate, but do they also differ with respect to some variable being studied? It is impossible to answer this question satisfactorily.

Design 3 is particularly susceptible to problems of mortality. If the experimental treatment is tedious or unpleasant, dropouts are likely to occur primarily in the test group. If the control group feels left out or bored, dropouts might occur primarily in this group. For example, if salesmen were arbitrarily assigned to participate or not participate in the contest, some of those left out of the contest might feel discriminated against and resign or put in less effort than they might have done with no contest (in effect, a resignation).

### *Final Comments on Internal Validity in Preexperiments*

It should be apparent that the lack of internal validity in preexperiments makes any results obtained extremely suspect. Why then are preexperiments performed?

One reason, of course, is that an untrained or poorly trained researcher may not know better. It is our opinion, however, that few researchers do not realize that designs 1, 2, or 3 have severe deficiencies, even though they may not be able to adequately explain these deficiencies.

A second reason is that the "experiment" often arises as a by-product of something else and is not really an experiment. This is particularly true of designs 1 and 2. For example, if the goal of a company is to increase sales and if it is felt that a contest among the salesmen could accomplish this end, the sales manager might insist that all salesmen enter the contest, even though this might destroy any possibility of determining the effect of the contest. Sales managers are interested in sales, not hypothesis testing.

Unfortunately, much of the marketing experiment literature reports such "by-product" research. It is a requirement of the intelligent reader that he recognize such reporting and discount the findings.

A third explanation of the great number of preexperiments being performed lies in the frequent use of the *ex post facto* experiment. The ex post facto experiment is actually not an experiment at all, since the researcher does not administer the treatment, nor does he make the measurement. What he does is to compare a group that has been exposed to the treatment with a group that has not been exposed to the treatment, obtaining the data from secondary sources. This is essentially design 3. The appeal of ex post facto experimentation lies in the relatively small expense involved.

The external validity of preexperiments will be discussed later in the chapter.

### True Experiments

The essence of the true experiment is controlled assignment of subjects to conditions. It should now be evident that the advantage of this procedure is in the control of internal validity by ensuring that no systematic difference exists between the groups assigned to the various positions.

Three means of assigning subjects will be discussed: (1) simple randomization, (2) randomized matched subjects, and (3) single-group control.

In discussing these methods of randomization, it is useful to extend Campbell and Stanley's (1963) notation. In addition to $R$ representing random assignment of subjects to treatments, $P$ will represent randomized matched-pair subject assignment and $S$ will denote single-group control, that is, where each subject becomes his own control.

### Simple Randomization

Again, suppose that our company wishes to perform an experiment on the effect of a sales contest among salesmen on sales. For some of the reasons that we have already discussed, it would be unwise to discriminate individually between salesmen as to who would participate in the contest and who would not. It is, therefore, decided to run a contest in five of the company's ten sales districts.

To ensure that internal validity is not affected by the self-selection problem, the districts are assigned at random to the test (contest) group or the control (no contest) group. This design symbolically reads:

$$\text{design 4} \qquad \begin{matrix} R & X & O_1 \\ R & & O_2 \end{matrix}$$

The experimental effect is given by $O_2 - O_1$.

Differences will certainly exist between the two groups selected randomly, but these differences must arise by chance, hence the selection is unbiased. Unfortunately, this procedure still does not ensure that the two groups are equivalent, since the differences that may arise by chance may be substantial. One way to measure these differences is to pretest the groups on the dependent variable.

Unfortunately, researchers sometimes employ pretests to eliminate a few of the extreme subjects so as to make the groups more similar. Thus, although the two groups were randomly assigned to begin with, arbitrary discarding of some subjects negates this advantage and the selection can no longer be considered random. Furthermore, since one group is likely to have the high scorers eliminated and the other group the low scorers eliminated, the regression effects will be in different directions. This will either exaggerate or tend to cancel out any experimental effect, depending on which group receives the experimental treatment.

## Randomized Matched Subjects

One method of obtaining better matched groups is to select subjects in pairs matched in a pretest. Selection bias is avoided by assigning one member of each pair at random to the test or control group and then putting the remaining member in the other group, as shown in design 5:

$$\text{design 5} \quad \begin{matrix} O_1 \; P \; X \; O_2 \\ O_1 \; P \quad\;\; O_3 \end{matrix}$$

Pairing is achieved on the basis of $O_1$. The experimental effect is given by $O_3 - O_2$, which is equal to the sum of the intrapair deviations.

In this design, it is pair differences that are employed to test significance. If the experimental treatment has no effect, these pair differences should have an expected value equal to the original difference between the groups with small variance (due to the matching of pairs).

As an example, suppose that the ten sales districts in our continuing example were paired off on the basis of sales and that one of each pair were assigned to the contest or no contest group at random and the other district of the pair to the remaining group. The variability of pair differences can be expected to be smaller than the variability of subject scores; hence the ability to discriminate the experimental effect is increased over the method of simple randomization.

One note of caution is in order. Pairing reduces the degrees of freedom by a factor of 2, since it now requires two experimental units to generate a single observation. Provided that the pairs are relatively homogeneous and that the difference between pairs is great, this loss is more than overcome by the smaller resulting variance in pair differences. If the whole group of subjects under study is relatively homogeneous, however, pairing is less powerful than simple randomization.

### Single-Group Control

Even the matched-pair design does not ensure two equivalent groups. Ideally, each subject of the matched pair would be identical. If this were so, even the smallest experimental difference would be detectable.

If each subject would serve as his own control and be measured simultaneously under the two conditions as in design 6, two perfectly equivalent groups would result:

$$\text{design 6} \qquad \begin{matrix} S_1\, X_1\, O_1 \\ S_1\, X_2\, O_2 \end{matrix}$$

Note that there are not really two groups, but the subscript 1 under $S$ indicates that the same individuals are involved in both treatments.

Of course, this design is usually impossible. In many instances, exposing the subject to one treatment contaminates him for exposure to any other treatment (or no treatment). Furthermore, we know that even if it were possible to expose each subject to both treatments, this could usually not be done simultaneously, nor could measurement usually be obtained simultaneously.

Although simultaneous treatment and measurement can seldom be obtained, one can often administer the two treatments successively. The danger here is that the order of treatment is important. This can be guarded against by varying randomly the order in which the treatments are administered, as in design 7, a procedure known as counterbalancing. Design 7 is the most basic Latin square:

$$\text{design 7} \qquad \begin{matrix} R \left\{ \begin{matrix} S_1\, X_1 O_1 & \\ S_1 & X_2\, O_2 \end{matrix} \right. \\ \\ R \left\{ \begin{matrix} S_2\, X_2 O_3 & \\ S_2 & X_1\, O_4 \end{matrix} \right. \end{matrix}$$

In addition to being able to determine the treatment effect, counterbalancing also permits the order effect to be measured.

An interesting example of the use of single-group control and simultaneous treatment and measurement is provided by Stafford (1966) who investigated the effect of group pressures on brand loyalty. Ten housewives selected at random each were asked to name five other housewives with whom they enjoy shopping. The 50 housewives so selected were each offered, over a period of time, identical bread with no markings except for letter symbols. The outcome was that housewives tended to become brand-loyal and that they tended to become loyal to the same brands that were chosen by other members of the five-woman team.

In this experiment, the treatments were *not* the offerings of bread. The treatments were (1) being a member of a group and (2) not being a member of a group. The dependent variables were brand loyalty by group and brand loyalty across groups. Of course, the treatments occurred simultaneously, and so did measurement.

## Further Randomized Designs

In most instances, single-group control is impossible. Some of the advantages of the matched pair without actual matching may be obtained in design 8.

*Randomized Pretest–Postest*

The symbolical form of design 8 is:

$$\text{design 8} \quad \begin{matrix} R\ O_1\ X\ O_2 \\ R\ O_3\ \ \ \ \ O_4 \end{matrix}$$

Pretesting the two groups allow us to measure the difference between the two groups $(O_3 - O_1)$ before the experimental treatment is applied. Since both the experimental and the control groups receive the pretest, it is assumed that the effect of pretesting will occur equally in the groups. Thus the experimenter may protect himself against confounding produced by chance differences between the test and control groups, as well as against confounding due to pretesting. The experimental effect is given by $O_4 - O_2$. Note that although $O_2 - O_1$ gives a measure of the experimental effect, this measure is biased by any testing effect.

EFFECT OF PRETEST–EXPERIMENTAL TREATMENT INTERACTION ON EXTERNAL VALIDITY. Unfortunately, in addition to any testing effect, the pretest may interact with the experimental treatment to produce an effect that would not have occurred in the experimental treatment or pretest alone. The same effect can also result from the randomized matched-pair design 5. This is a question of *external validity,* the problem being that the experimental effect can be either amplified or reduced by the interaction of pretest and treatment. Thus one cannot generalize to a situation in which the same experimental treatment is involved, but no pretest is given.

The interaction effect is produced by the pretest sensitizing subjects to the dependent variable. For example, suppose that we want to know the effect of direct-mail promotion on toothpaste brand loyalty. We might ask housewives what brand of toothpaste they have on their shelves and then divide them randomly into one group that would receive mailed promotional material and another group that would not. After a suitable interval of time, the housewives could again be checked to see which brands they now had on their shelves.

It is obvious that the pretest could make the group receiving the flyer much more aware of the message contained than they might otherwise be. Thus extension of any results to conditions where no pretest was given would be dangerous.

If design 8 is to be used, interaction of treatment and measurement can best be guarded against by hiding the nature of the study and the items of interest from subjects. For example, in the toothpaste study designed to test the effect of mailings, it would be appropriate to ask housewives for information about many other shelf items other than toothpaste. It would also be necessary not to establish a connection in the mind of the housewife between the initial measurement and the receipt of mailed promotional literature.

*Solomon Four–Group Design*

Design 9, known as the Solomon four-group design, combines elements of designs 4 and 8:

$$\text{design 9} \quad \begin{array}{llll} R & O_1 & X & O_2 \\ R & O_3 & & O_4 \\ R & & X & O_5 \\ R & & & O_6 \end{array}$$

This design explicitly takes into consideration external validity factors. Measurements of possible causes of the observed effects are listed in Table 7-1.

Since the use of design 8 does not allow the researcher to estimate the effect of pretest nor does it provide any way to estimate the interaction of

**Table 7-1** Measurements in Solomon Four-Group Design

| Effect | Measurement |
|---|---|
| 1. Effect of pretest[a] | $\frac{O_6 + O_5}{2} - \frac{O_4 + O_2}{2}$ |
| 2. Effect of treatment[a] | $\frac{O_5 + O_2}{2} - \frac{O_6 + O_4}{2}$ |
| 3. Effect of pretest-treatment interaction | $(O_2 - O_4) - (O_5 - O_6)$ |

[a] Unadjusted for interaction.

pretest with experimentation, design 9 is clearly superior. Nevertheless, it is doubtful that this design is as useful as the simple two-group, no pretest, randomized design 4. The usefulness of a pretest is generally overvalued, unless one wishes to estimate the dependent variable before treatment for reasons independent of the experiment.

For example, if we wanted to estimate both the market share of our toothpaste among housewives and the effect of a promotional mailing, the pretest could provide useful information with respect to market share. Usually, however, the pretest will provide only redundant information about the population as a whole. In the example, the firm is likely to have independent knowledge of its market share.

Of course, this does not negate the need for a pretest in *paired* designs, such as design 5, where the pretest provides the necessary information for pairing.

## Expanded Designs

Our discussion so far has been confined to the effect of a single experimental treatment compared to no treatment (control) or to some other treatment. Thus we can say that the treatment does or does not appear to have some effect or that there is or is not a *difference* in the effect of two treatments. Often, however, this is insufficient.

### *Functional Relationships*

One reason for an expanded design is that the designs presented so far do not allow us to establish any functional relationship between an independent variable $X$ and some dependent variable $y$. Thus one might establish that advertising results in greater sales than no advertising by employing a design where a single level of advertising is the independent variable (with "no advertising" associated with a control group) and sales are the dependent variable. But no inference can be made beyond this. There would be no way in which one could predict sales for any level of advertising other than that employed in the experiment unless other information was consulted. One could not even infer that increased advertising would result in increased sales or that decreased advertising would result in decreased sales. *A functional relationship could only be established if several levels of advertising were employed, with each level regarded as another experimental treatment.*

### *More Than One Independent Variable*

Another reason for an expanded design is that we may wish to manipulate more than one independent variable in the experiment. For example, at the same time that the effect of advertising is investigated, the effect of shelf space may be investigated. If measurements are made over time, time itself becomes another experimental treatment.

*Extraneous Variables*

A third reason for expanding the design to accommodate more variables is control for the effects of extraneous variables. Thus if more than one experimenter were involved, if the order of treatments could be important, or if the treatments were to be administered in more than one location, these factors should be controlled in an expanded experiment.

## Randomized Blocks

The randomized matched-pair design 5 can be expanded if there are more than two treatments.[4] With two treatments, each block consists of a matched pair of subjects or other experimental units. If there are more than two treatments, each block consists of the same number of matched experimental units as there are treatments.

Consider the problem, previously discussed, of estimating the effect of mailed promotional material on sales of a product. Suppose that housewives are matched in blocks of three, either on purchasing behavior or other factors (such as socioeconomic classifications) related to behavior. Each housewife in a block is assigned one of three treatments at random so that every block receives all three treatments. The three treatments might be to receive zero, one, or two mailings in a certain period. As in the two-treatment case, it is the *differences* between purchases of housewives in a block that become the observations, not the individual purchases. Essentially, the approach is simply an extension of the paired random observations design. Like the latter design, the randomized block design is only efficient so long as there is homogeneity of subjects within blocks, but heterogeneity between blocks.

*Latin-Square Design*

Suppose that the effect of shelf space on sales of a particular brand is to be investigated. Three proportions of the total shelf space will be studied; one sixth, one third, and one half, denoted by treatments $X_1$, $X_2$, and $X_3$ respectively. It is decided to engage the cooperation of grocery stores in order to make the experiment as realistic as possible.

[4] Recall that a control group, which receives a level of zero of the experimental variable, is regarded as receiving one treatment.

One approach would be to engage a number of blocks of matched stores, three to a block, to participate in the experiment. Unfortunately, even if sufficient stores could be induced to cooperate, it is unlikely that they could be well matched. This difficulty can be overcome by an extension of design 7, the single-group control design in which experimental units act as their own control. Here each store would be subject to each treatment, with as many stores as there are treatments. The necessity to impose each treatment on each store also results in as many periods as there are treatments. This design is illustrated in Table 7-2.

The purpose of having as many stores as there are weeks (an extraneous variable) and treatments is to attempt to prevent order bias from affecting the results. If only one store were employed, one could not be certain that there were no carry-over effects from the previous week's treatment or that changing conditions from week to week, and not the shelf space, were responsible for the particular sales levels.

From Table 7-2, it may be noted that each treatment appears once in each time period and once in each store. Provided that there are no interaction effects between store and time period, the design eliminates the effects of these variables. But if something happened to store *A* in period 1 that did not happen to stores *B* or *C*, or that affected these stores differently, a bias could still be introduced into the results.

Extensions of the basic latin-square. The basic design can be extended for increased reliability as well as decreased bias. The basic design may be replicated by employing some multiple of the number of treatments as the number of test units. Instead of three stores, we could use six stores by employing a second replication of the original design, as in Table 7-3.

In addition to increasing reliability by the use of more experimental units, a second replication permits further balancing in the interest of reducing order bias. Thus while store *A* receives the treatment sequence

**Table 7-2** Latin-Square—Design 10

| | Store | | |
|---|---|---|---|
| Date | *A* | *B* | *C* |
| First week | $X_1$ | $X_2$ | $X_3$ |
| Second week | $X_2$ | $X_3$ | $X_1$ |
| Third week | $X_3$ | $X_1$ | $X_2$ |

TABLE 7-3

| | Store | | | | | |
|---|---|---|---|---|---|---|
| | Replication 1 | | | Replication 2 | | |
| Date | *A* | *B* | *C* | *D* | *E* | *F* |
| First week | $X_1$ | $X_2$ | $X_3$ | $X_1$ | $X_3$ | $X_2$ |
| Second week | $X_2$ | $X_3$ | $X_1$ | $X_3$ | $X_2$ | $X_1$ |
| Third week | $X_3$ | $X_1$ | $X_2$ | $X_2$ | $X_1$ | $X_3$ |

$X_1$ $X_2$ $X_3$, store *D*, which also receives $X_1$ first, receives the remaining two treatments in reverse order.

There are many further refinements of the Latin-square design. For example, the restriction of having, in each replication, as many rows and columns as there are experimental units is not always possible. If only two stores were willing to cooperate in our experiment or if we had only two weeks available, the simple symmetrical design would not be possible. Designs such as quasi-Latin-squares or lattice squares are aimed at fulfilling the same purpose as the Latin-square when the latter is impractical.[5]

### *Factorial Designs*

We may handle several experimental treatments in randomized block and Latin-square designs, but not simultaneously on each experimental unit. If the experimental treatments are additive, this is not serious. Unfortunately, if two or more factors are considered, they may react with one another so that, taken together, they may yield something greater or less than the sum of the individual values.

For example, in the hypothetical investigation into the effect of shelf space on sales, previously described, it must be assumed that the level of promotion was kept constant. Presumably, one could also investigate the effect of various levels of promotion while holding shelf space constant. One could then assume that *if* promotion and shelf space were both varied, the effects of the two factors would be additive, but one might well be wrong.

Assuming that price is kept constant, it is entirely conceivable that for a particular brand to make any kind of showing it either must

[5] A good elementary exposition of some of thesé designs is given by Cox (1958).

**Table 7-4** Factorial—Design 11

| | |
|---|---|
| Shelf space = 1/6, promotion = 0 | $X_1$ |
| Shelf space = 1/6, promotion = \$5000 | $X_2$ |
| Shelf space = 1/3, promotion = 0 | $X_3$ |
| Shelf space = 1/3, promotion = \$5000 | $X_4$ |

be well promoted *or* must receive good shelf space. On the other hand, both heavy promotion and good shelf space may yield high sales, but not so high as looking at the two factor levels individually might lead one to believe.

The only way to discover if two factors interact is to administer them simultaneously at various factor levels. Factorial designs do precisely this.

The simplest case is when each factor is shown at two levels. For example, we might consider shelf space to be one third or one sixth and promotion to be zero or $5000 in a particular market. There would then be four treatments, as shown in Table 7-4.

Of course, whatever results are obtained from such an experiment would be applicable also to one independent variable at a time. The effect of shelf space is measured by $X_3 - X_1$ and $X_4 - X_2$, while the effect of promotion is measured by $X_2 - X_1$ and $X_4 - X_3$.

Because of their complexity and cost, factorial designs are generally to be avoided in preliminary research. Single-factor preliminary studies are generally advisable to show promising avenues and to identify those factors that appear to be most important.

## QUASI-EXPERIMENTAL DESIGNS

It often happens, particularly in field research, that although the researcher has very little ability to control the "when" and "to whom" of the experimental treatment, he can control "when" and "to whom" of measurement. In many ways such studies are similar to the observational studies discussed in earlier chapters. The difference is that in a purely observational approach one samples from what is essentially a static situation. It is possible to employ an observational sample to estimate parameters or to look for variables that associate with one another. But it is only in an experimental setting that one may directly investigate causality.

Thus the distinction between an observational sample and a quasi-experimental sample is that in the latter an experimental treatment not under the control of the researcher is applied to the subjects and one is concerned with the effect of this treatment. We shall look at one such design in this chapter.[6]

## Time Series

A time series design, as shown in design 12, bears a superficial resemblance to design 2 about which we had very little of a complementary nature to say:

$$\text{design 12} \qquad O_1\, O_2 \cdot \cdot \cdot O_m\, X\, O_{m+1}\, O_{m+2} \cdot \cdot \cdot O_n$$

The design consists of a series of observations before and after the experimental treatment.

The advantage of this procedure lies in establishing a history of the dependent variable before and after the experimental treatment. One is then essentially looking to see if an established trend is disturbed at the time of the treatment.

Let us suppose that Figure 7-2 represents the rate of sales of beer over time. Observations of past week's sales are taken weekly at times $t_1$ through $t_6$ during the summer months. Suppose that temperatures are moderate over most of the period, but a heat wave occurs during the fourth week, as represented by the symbol $X$. Is it reasonable to conclude that the heat wave caused the abnormal consumption of beer?

Suppose that the fourth week, in addition to being abnormally warm, also happens to be the week of a large influx of tourists into the area to attend a music festival. It would then be dangerous to conclude that the heat wave caused all the extra guzzling. This suggests one criterion by which the cause of the experimental effect may be judged.

[6] Further designs are explored in Campbell and Stanley (1963).

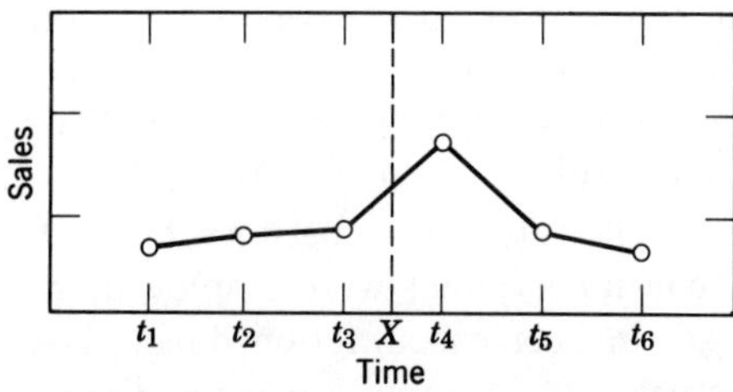


**Figure 7-2**

It seems clear that the fourth week of sales was quite different from previous and subsequent weeks, so that one feels safe in concluding that something different did indeed happen to sales that week. The explanation that it was weather that was responsible for increased beer consumption *must be considered against alternative reasonable explanations.*

In this instance, there are two competing explanations for the increased consumption of beer—weather and tourists. How may one decide between them? On the basis of this one quasi experiment alone there is no way to conclude whether one or the other or a combination of the two was responsible. The cause of this problem, with regard to the classification scheme previously outlined in the causes of failure of internal validity, is *history*. Other uncontrolled variables, besides the one of interest here (temperature), played a part.

If history was the confusing factor in this case, the way out of the box is to look at a number of histories so that the preponderance of evidence points to or away from temperature affecting beer consumption. There will be other weeks during which the temperature will be high and no music festival will be going on to confuse the issue.

Strictly speaking, one may seriously question our contention of establishing causality through a quasi experiment. Even in a perfectly controlled laboratory experiment, one never *proves* an hypothesis. One either decides to accept or reject on the basis of the evidence, although errors of the first or second kind may be associated with the decision. In a quasi experiment, the problem is compounded.

From the point of view of the marketing man, however, the philosophical problem is almost irrelevant. Unlike the academic researcher who is not inclined to publish his results unless the possibility of being wrong is remote, the marketer *must* make decisions. Although he would prefer his supporting evidence to be as good as possible—we are not making an apology for inferior or slipshod designs where better approaches are available—the marketer usually cannot wait for a preponderance of evidence on the basis of his experiment before making a decision.

The times series design, though superior to the simple pretest-postest design 2, clearly has many faults. Since this design is most suitable in the field, the absence of laboratory artificiality is favorable. But problems of external validity are acute. If testing cannot be done unobtrusively, there may be interaction between the testing and treatment. For example, if a consumer panel were employed, it could be loath to report large increases in beer consumption during hot weather or might be reluctant to increase its consumption beyond some "socially acceptable" level.

There may also be interaction between selection and treatment. Can we project our conclusions, perhaps based on a study in New York, to other areas of the country.

### The Value of Quasi Experiments

The time series design is illustrative of what can be done with quasi experiments. There are often cases, as in the example given with respect to the weather, where assigning the experimental treatment is out of the hands of the researcher. This does not mean that the researcher must then give up, but rather that he must make do with what is under his control.

Other quasi-experimental designs, as shown by Campbell and Stanley, have greater external validity than the design given here. This is accomplished through randomizing observation groups, even though the experimental treatments may not be randomized.

## A BAYESIAN VIEW OF EXPERIMENTAL DESIGN

The same argument that applied to Bayesian versus traditional statistics in sampling also apply to experimentation. We shall not repeat here the arguments in favor of either viewpoint, but shall concern ourselves with new issues raised in experimentation.

Very little has appeared in the literature about experimental design from a Bayesian point of view. In this regard, our remarks concerning probability and nonprobability designs in Chapter 5 still apply. The typical experimenter is concerned primarily with maintaining internal validity via randomization—he is less concerned with external validity. The conservative academic researcher seldom asserts that his results are applied to more than the set of subjects under the conditions described, and his conclusions are hedged liberally with *caveats*. This is as it should be. Until many different experiments and experimenters arrive at the same results from both replicating and different designs, a theory is unlikely to gain acceptance. It is in this manner that external validity is established.

This process is too slow and too costly for marketing decisions. Usually a single study must suffice before a decision is made. Under these circumstances, the Bayesian view is very appealing, since it provides a means of quantifying experience, past history, and judgment into the decision.

As in the sampling problem, the first step for the Bayesian is to specify a prior probability distribution on the states of nature. The second step

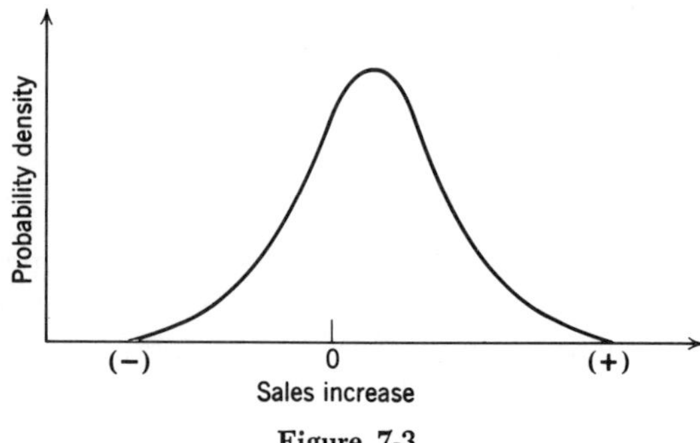


**Figure 7-3**

is to obtain the relevant payoffs or "loss functions" for each alternative course of action.

For example, the problem may be, as earlier in the chapter, whether or not to have a sales contest. We would begin by specifying a prior probability distribution over the possible states of nature. This could be a continuous distribution specifying the probability of sales increase (or decrease), as in Figure 7-3. It might simply be a two-state situation—sales will increase or will not increase—with two corresponding probabilities.

For each value of sales increase, a corresponding payoff must be established. If no further information were to be obtained, we could choose that action (the alternatives here being to establish a sales contest or not to establish a contest) which has the highest expected value. If further information is acquired, it must be such that the appropriate conditional probabilities can be established. Thus we must be able to specify, for example, the probability of an indicator that sales will increase, given that sales will actually increase, should a contest be undertaken.

The assessment of conditional probabilities may itself be personalistic. One must be prepared to choose a design that will sacrifice control on some potential confounding variable, if it is felt that the effect of this confounding variable is likely to be negligible, in order to gain greater control over a confounding variable that it *is* felt can be critical.

## ANALYSIS OF DATA

Of necessity, only a brief discussion of the analysis of data can be given here. The traditional approach, including *analysis of variance,* will be discussed first. Then a Bayesian approach to the same problem will be given.

## Application of the *t* Test

Consider design 4:

$$\text{design 4} \quad \begin{matrix} R & X & O_1 \\ R & & O_2 \end{matrix}$$

The experiment may be that we randomly assign salesmen to a test group, which will participate in a sales training seminar, or to a control group, which will not participate. Subsequently, the sales of both groups are observed. We are interested in testing the hypothesis that, except for *random* differences between the two groups, sales of the two groups will be the same after the test group receives the experimental treatment consisting of the seminar. This is stated as the null hypothesis

$$H_0: \mu_1 = \mu_2$$

There are three other simple hypotheses that may be stated as the alternative hypothesis.

(1) $$H_1: \mu_1 \neq \mu_2$$

(2) $$H_2: \mu_1 > \mu_2$$

(3) $$H_3: \mu_1 < \mu_2$$

In the first case, the alternative hypothesis is merely that the two means are different. In the second case, the alternative hypothesis is that the seminar has some positive effect on sales. In the third case, it is hypothesized that the seminar has a negative effect on sales.

The analyses of cases 2 and 3 are similar, but in the context of our problem, to determine whether or not a sales contest is worthwhile, case 2 seems more appropriate.

### *Cases 1 and 2*

As in tests of hypotheses in sampling (Chapter 6), we choose either to accept or to reject the null hypothesis at some level of significance. If the null hypothesis is rejected, the alternative hypothesis is accepted, as it were, by default. For a given level of significance $\alpha$, the sample size $n$ is chosen so that the probability of accepting the null hypothesis when it is "reasonably false"—that is, when $\mu_2$ differs enough from $\mu_1$, to matter—is less than some value $\beta$.

The experiment consists of sales measurements of subjects in each group. For convenience, we shall assume that the size ($n$) of each group is equal. The observed mean sales of the first group is $\bar{X}_1$ and that of the second group $\bar{X}_2$. If the null hypothesis holds, the distribution of the *difference* of the sample means, $\bar{X} = \bar{X}_1 - \bar{X}_2$, has mean zero and a pooled variance:

$$S^2 = \frac{S_1^2}{n-1} + \frac{S_2^2}{n-1}$$

where $S_1^2$ is the variance of sales *within* the test group and $S_2^2$ is the variance of sales *within* the control group.

The question arises, what is the appropriate probability distribution to apply to the distribution of $\bar{X}$?

The Random Sample. If the variance $\sigma^2$ of the population from which the groups are taken were known, if the groups were chosen at random from this population, if the sample size were large, and if the treatment were to have no effect, then $\bar{X}$ would be distributed normally with mean zero and variance $\sigma_{\bar{X}}^2 = 2(\sigma^2/n)$ (recalling that each of the two groups is of size $n$). In our example, the population of interest (the target population) is the population of sales of the salesmen. The variance of this population might very well be known and the other conditions fulfilled. In this case, we can apply the central limit theorem to the problem and use the distribution of $\bar{X}$ to test the hypothesis that $\mu_1 = \mu_2$. This hypothesis, may then be tested in exactly the same manner as we tested hypotheses, under similar conditions, in Chapter 6. For example, if the quantity

$$z = \frac{\bar{X}}{\sigma_{\bar{X}}} > 1.96$$

we would reject the null hypothesis at the 5 per cent level of significance.

Similarly, if the target population is normally distributed and the sample small, the $t$ distribution may be employed, as in Chapter 4,

If we assume case 2, a one-sided test is appropriate. That is, we reject the null hypothesis at the 5 per cent level only if $z$ is greater than $+1.65$, the value for which 5 per cent of the distribution occurs to the right of $z$, as in Figure 7-4. It should be noted that $z$ need not be as large for a one-sided test as for a two-sided test in order to be significant.

Groups randomly assigned, but not randomly selected from the target population. The usual case in experimentation is that the experimental units are *not* selected at random from the target population. University psychologists working with humans (as contrasted with those who work with rats, pigeons, or worms) typically use student volunteers

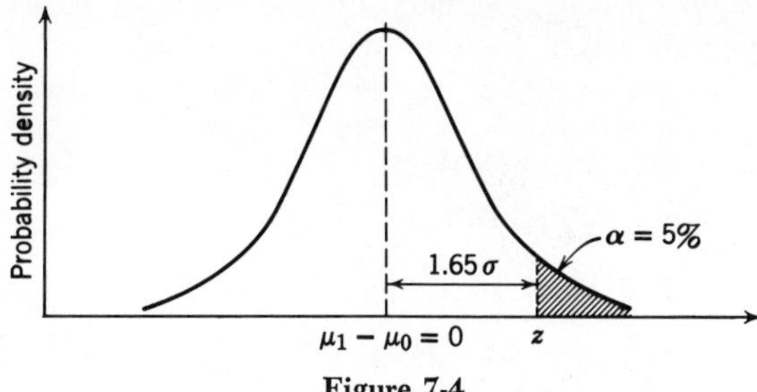


**Figure 7-4**

in experiments. Where the experimental units are stores, market researchers will work with those stores that cooperate, and typically the same stores will be used extensively. If the experimental units are test markets, these test markets are carefully *selected.*

It should be clear, under these conditions, that no non-Bayesian probability statements may be made concerning the target population, since the experimental units are not chosen probabilistically. The random phenomenon, *about which probabilistic statements may be made,* concerns the question to which group (test or control) a particular experimental unit will be assigned. It then becomes possible to assign a level of significance to any experimental result *with respect to the population consisting of the two groups taken together.*

For example, suppose that we wish to test the effect of a special diet as protection against the common cold. Forty students volunteer to take part in an experiment for a semester and are assigned randomly to the test and control groups in equal numbers. Suppose that it is found that the special diet group averages fewer days with colds.

The difference in health could have arisen by chance alone. Although the nature of the experiment does not allow the researcher to generalize beyond the 40 students in the experiment, the experimenter can make probabilistic statements about the effect of the diet on the student subjects and may assign probabilities to chance differences between the groups.

If we assume that the cold days are approximately normally distributed, the $t$ distribution may be used to test the null hypothesis that the special diet has no effect. Again, assuming that the two groups are of equal size $n$, the $t$ statistic is given by

$$t = \frac{\bar{X}}{\sqrt{\dfrac{S_1^2}{n-1} + \dfrac{S_2^2}{n-1}}}$$

with $2(n-1)$ degrees of freedom where $S_1^2$ and $S_2^2$ are the variances of the two respective samples.

For example, suppose that

$$\bar{X}_1 = 24.2 \text{ days}$$

$$\bar{X}_2 = 21.1 \text{ days}$$

$$S_1^2 = 10.2 \text{ days}$$

$$S_2^2 = 8.8 \text{ days}$$

$$\bar{X} = \bar{X}_1 - \bar{X}_2 = 3.1 \text{ days}$$

$$t = \frac{3.1}{\sqrt{\dfrac{10.2}{19} + \dfrac{8.8}{19}}} = 3.1, \text{ with } f = 38 \text{ degrees of freedom}$$

Consulting a table of $t$ values, we see that this is significant at the 5 per cent level for either a one-sided or a two-sided test.

## Analysis of Variance

It is possible to look at the same data a little differently. In particular, the analysis-of-variance approach allows us to extend our analysis to a number of different treatments and to test the null hypothesis,

$$H_0\colon \mu_1 = \mu_2 = \cdot\cdot\cdot = \mu_r$$

against the alternative,

$$H_1\colon \text{at least two means are unequal}$$

Table 7-5 presents a result of three treatments on sales within three stores as achieved in a Latin-square design.

**Table 7-5** (Sales in \$1000)

| | Treatment | | | |
|---|---|---|---|---|
| Store | 1 | 2 | 3 | Three Stores |
| *A* | 9 | 12 | 8 | |
| *B* | 7 | 10 | 4 | |
| *C* | 8 | 8 | 9 | |
| Total | 24 | 30 | 21 | 75 |
| Mean | 8 | 10 | 7 | 8⅓ |
| Variances $\sigma_i^2$ | 1 | 4 | 7 | |

**TABLE 7-6** Two Hypothetical Sets of Results

I

| | Treatment | |
|---|---|---|
| Store | 1 | 2 |
| *A* | 10 | 14 |
| *B* | 10.2 | 14.4 |
| Totals | 20.2 | 28.4 |
| Means | 10.1 | 14.2 |

II

| | Treatment | |
|---|---|---|
| Store | 1 | 2 |
| *A* | 4.0 | 10.4 |
| *B* | 16.2 | 18.0 |
| Totals | 20.2 | 28.4 |
| Means | 10.1 | 14.2 |

Before showing the calculations to be followed, we shall attempt to justify the procedure intuitively.[7] The wider the dispersion of values (and the consequently larger set of variances) *within* each treatment group, the harder it is to distinguish the significance of the differences between the group means. In Table 7-6, for example, we can compare two hypothetical results of a two-by-two Latin-square. Although in each case the mean values are the same for both case I and case II, most people would put very little faith in the differences between the groups in case II arising from the experimental treatments, because of the wide dispersion of values within each treatment group. The small within-group dispersion in case I seems superior evidence in favor of rejecting the null hypothesis.

Correspondingly, the greater the dispersion of the means themselves, the more likely it is that differences can be attributed to the experimental treatment and not to chance. Thus if we can find a ratio of the *between*-group variation (among the treatment means) to the *within*-group variation, it would seem reasonable to reject the null hypothesis when this ratio is high.

The so-called $F$ ratio is such a quantity. Furthermore, the $F$ ratio is a probability distribution, hence tests of significance may be performed.

The total sum of the squared deviations within treatments, denoted by $SS_w$, may be calculated from the individual variances.

[7] A more complete treatment may be found in any text on analysis of variance, for example Guenther (1964, Chapter 2).

We have

$$\hat{\sigma}_i^2 = \frac{n}{n-1} s_i^2 = \frac{n}{n-1} \cdot \frac{\sum_{j=1}^{n} (X_{ij} - \bar{X}_i)^2}{n} = \frac{\sum_{j=1}^{n} (X_{ij} - \bar{X}_i)^2}{n-1}$$

where $j$ represents the observation (store) and $i$ the treatment. Thus

$$SS_w = \sum_{i=1}^{r} \sum_{j=1}^{n} (X_{ij} - \bar{X}_i)^2 = \sum_{i=1}^{r} (n_i - 1)\sigma_i^2$$

where $r$ = the number of treatments. In our example in Table 7-5 all the $n_i = 3$ and

$$SS_w = 2 \cdot (1) + 2 \cdot (4) + 2 \cdot (7) = 24$$

The degrees of freedom associated with this quantity are the total of the degrees of freedom in the individual treatments:

$$f_w = 2 + 2 + 2 = 6$$
$$(\text{or } f_w = N - r = 9 - 3 = 6)$$

This takes care of the denominator of the $F$ ratio, a quantity that measures the internal dispersion of the experimental units within treatments.

The sum of squared deviations between the groups, denoted by $SS_A$, is given by

$$SS_A = \sum_{i=1}^{r} n_i(\bar{X}_i - \bar{X})^2$$

In this case,

$$SS_A = 3(8 - 8\tfrac{1}{3})^2 + 3(10 - 8\tfrac{1}{3})^2 + 3(7 - 8\tfrac{1}{3})^2 = 14$$

The degrees of freedom are one less than the number of treatments, 1 degree of freedom being lost in calculating the overall means, or

$$f_A = r - 1 = 3 - 1 = 2$$

The $F$ ratio is given by

$$F_{f_A, f_w} = \frac{SS_A/f_A}{SS_w/f_w} = \frac{14}{2} \div \frac{24}{6} = 1.75$$

Consulting tabled values of the $F$ distribution for $f_A = 2$ and $f_w = 6$, we see that our $F$ value would have to be 5.14 before we reject the null hypothesis. In this instance, the null hypothesis would *not* be rejected.

It may be shown that if $t$ has a distribution with $f$ degrees of freedom, then $t^2$ has an $F_{1,f}$ distribution (Mood and Graybill, 1963, p. 233). The upper one-tail $F$ test is thus exactly equivalent to a two-tailed $t$ test at the same significance level. Hence in a two-treatment case it would make no difference whether the $F$ or the $t$ test was used.

Finally, the computational procedure used in our $F$ test example may be simplified, but the simplified version fails to illustrate the reasoning behind the test.

## A BAYESIAN APPROACH

There are three elements in the Bayesian approach, whether in sampling or experimenting. First, a prior probability distribution on the actual states of nature must be specified. Second, the conditional probabilities of particular observations, given the possible states of nature, must be specified in order to incorporate the experimental or sampling results. Third, a loss function or payoff function is employed in decision making in order to take that action which has the highest expected value.

If analytical techniques are to be employed, the prior and conditional probabilities must be compatible. For example, in Chapter 6 we looked at the situation in sampling where only two possible states of nature (a Bernoulli situation) and binomial conditional probabilities existed and found it possible to establish a posterior distribution.

Suppose that we look at the problem of whether or not to hold sales seminars throughout the company. For convenience, we examine only two possible states of nature: $S_1$, the seminars increase sales 20 per cent (which would result in an increased discounted value of profits of $100,000 after subtracting the $30,000 cost of the seminars), and $S_2$, the seminars have no effect on sales. Our best judgement is that the probabilities of $S_1$ and $S_2$ are 0.3 and 0.7 respectively.

Suppose that an experiment of the design 4 type is considered,

$$\text{design 4} \quad \begin{array}{lll} R & X & O_1 \\ R & & O_2 \end{array}$$

which would cost $10,000.

Various decision rules, as in Chapter 6, must be considered. We shall consider only the decision rule to assume $S_1$ if sales of the test group average $1000 or more than the control group and to assume $S_2$ if they do not. Fifty salesmen are to be employed in the experiment, if it is undertaken.

On the basis of the sales of the 50 salesmen who will be subjects, it is possible to find an exact distribution of $\bar{X}_1 - \bar{X}_2$, the difference in the means of the two samples, assuming that the seminars have no effect. On the assumption that the seminars do have the effect of increasing *mean* sales 20 per cent, but do not affect the *variance*, another sampling distribution is established. From these two distributions we may calculate the conditional probabilities.[8]

Let $W_1$ be the event that

$$\bar{X}_1 - \bar{X}_2 \geq \$1000$$

and $W_2$ the event that

$$\bar{X}_1 - \bar{X}_2 < \$1000$$

Suppose that we establish the conditional probabilities to be

$$P(W_1|S_1) = 0.7 \qquad P(W_2|S_2) = 0.6$$
$$P(W_2|S_1) = 0.3 \qquad P(W_1|S_2) = 0.4$$

The appropriate decision tree is given in Figure 7-5.

From here on the problem is analyzed in exactly the same manner as in Chapter 6. Table 7-7 shows the calculation of the appropriate probabilities. The decision tree analysis indicates that the experiment, for this decision rule, is not worth the cost. It would be best just to go ahead and hold the seminars.

[8] It should be noted that *only* conditional probabilities are considered in traditional statistics. When objective data are unavailable, the Bayesian may assign subjective probabilities even here.

**Table 7-7** Joint Probability Table

| | $P(S_iW_j)$ | | | $P(S_i \mid W_j)$ | |
|---|---|---|---|---|---|
| Observation | $S_1$ | $S_2$ | $P(W_i)$ | $S_1$ | $S_2$ |
| $W_1$ | 0.21 | 0.28 | 0.49 | 0.43 | 0.57 |
| $W_2$ | 0.09 | 0.42 | 0.51 | 0.18 | 0.82 |
| | 0.30 | 0.70 | | | |

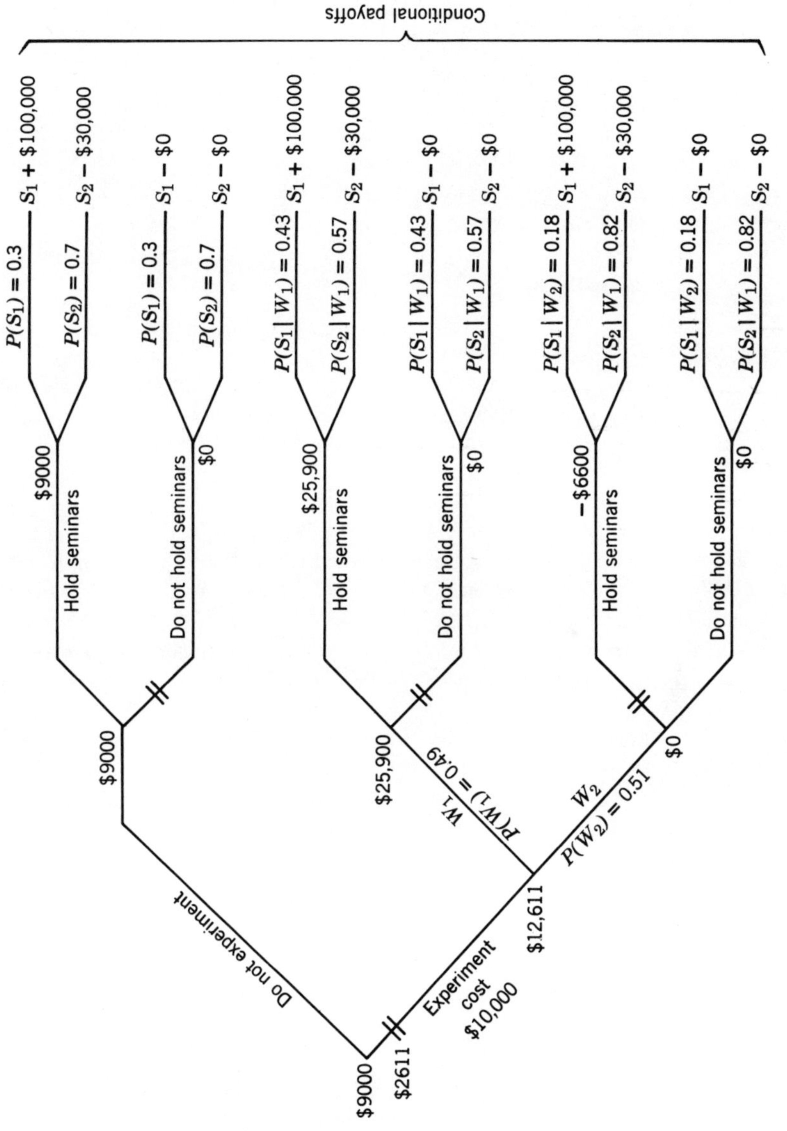

Conditional payoffs
$9000
$2611
Do not experiment
Experiment cost $10,000
$12,611
$9000
$25,900
$0
$W_1$
$P(W_1) = 0.49$
$W_2$
$P(W_2) = 0.51$
Hold seminars
Do not hold seminars
$9000
$0
$25,900
$0
−$6600
$0
$P(S_1) = 0.3$
$P(S_2) = 0.7$
$P(S_1 \mid W_1) = 0.43$
$P(S_2 \mid W_1) = 0.57$
$P(S_1 \mid W_2) = 0.18$
$P(S_2 \mid W_1) = 0.82$
$S_1$ + $100,000
$S_2$ − $30,000
$S_1$ − $0
$S_2$ − $0


**Figure 7-5**

## SUMMARY

We have looked at experimentation, in this chapter, from both a Bayesian and a traditional point of view. Although the authors lean toward the Bayesian approach, it must be admitted that traditional statistics has been developed much further with regard to experimentation than has Bayesian statistics.

Even though the complexities of real-world experimental situations are typically beyond the level of sophistication presented in this chapter, it is hoped that the reader has developed an appreciation for the role of experimentation in marketing.

## REFERENCES

Banks, S. *Experimentation in Marketing*. New York: McGraw-Hill, 1965.

Campbell, D. T., & Stanley, J. C. "Experimental and Quasi-Experimental Designs for Research on Teaching." In Gage, N.L. (Ed.), *Handbook of Research on Teaching*. Chicago, Ill.: Rand McNally, 1963.

Cox, D. R. *Planning of Experiments*. New York: Wiley, 1958.

Guenther, W. C. *Analysis of Variance*. Englewood Cliffs, N.J.: Prentice-Hall, 1964.

Mood, A. M., & Graybill, F. A. *Introduction to the Theory of Statistics*. (2nd ed.) New York: McGraw-Hill, 1963.

Pessemier, E. A. *Experimental Methods of Analyzing Demand for Branded Consumer Goods with Applications to Problems in Marketing Strategy*. Pullman, Wash.: Washington State University Press, 1963.

Stafford, J. A., "Effects of Group Influence on Consumer Brand Preferences," *Journal of Marketing Research,* February 1966, pp. 68–75.

Uhl, K. P. "Field Experimentation: Some Problems, Pitfalls and Perspective," *Proceedings of the Fall Conference of the American Marketing Association.* 1966.

PART II

# PROBLEMS AND CASES

Problems: Numbers 1–13

Cases:

1. Spiegel Pharmaceutical, Incorporated
2. Security Watch Company

## PROBLEMS

**No. 1. Purpose.** Estimation of a population mean from a random sample, size $n = 80$, and construction of upper and lower limits of the mean at various confidence levels.

---

Suppose that you, as a marketing research consultant, were hired by the Maxcase Distributing Company, Inc. to determine market data for a variety of industrial office supplies. Maxcase, Inc., has decided to extend its market area to encompass five Midwestern states and wants to know the current market demand for several of its offerings in the five-state area.

One of the items that you have been assigned to investigate is the current demand for IBM cards. Since external data on the demand for these cards is completely inadequate, you have decided to conduct your own survey. You have managed to obtain a list of all computer users over the new market area and have from this list derived a simple random sample of size $n = 80$. In gathering the necessary data, you interviewed each of the companies and obtained forecasts of their average monthly requirement for IBM cards over the next year. The results of this sample are shown in Figure 1.

1. Assuming that you know the population distribution to be approximately normal, that you have taken a completely random sample, and that each com-

| Company Number | Demand Cases/ Month | Company Number | Demand Cases/ Month | Company Number | Demand Cases/ Month | Company Number | Demand Cases/ Month |
|---|---|---|---|---|---|---|---|
| 1 | 3 | 21 | 6 | 41 | 4 | 61 | 8 |
| 2 | 1 | 22 | 2 | 42 | 8 | 62 | 1 |
| 3 | 6 | 23 | 4 | 43 | 5 | 63 | 9 |
| 4 | 2 | 24 | 8 | 44 | 1 | 64 | 3 |
| 5 | 9 | 25 | 6 | 45 | 9 | 65 | 7 |
| 6 | 5 | 26 | 3 | 46 | 3 | 66 | 12 |
| 7 | 7 | 27 | 8 | 47 | 9 | 67 | 5 |
| 8 | 0 | 28 | 5 | 48 | 6 | 68 | 4 |
| 9 | 3 | 29 | 7 | 49 | 8 | 69 | 2 |
| 10 | 5 | 30 | 3 | 50 | 4 | 70 | 9 |
| 11 | 1 | 31 | 4 | 51 | 5 | 71 | 7 |
| 12 | 7 | 32 | 11 | 52 | 11 | 72 | 5 |
| 13 | 4 | 33 | 6 | 53 | 5 | 73 | 10 |
| 14 | 7 | 34 | 2 | 54 | 4 | 74 | 0 |
| 15 | 2 | 35 | 4 | 55 | 10 | 75 | 4 |
| 16 | 8 | 36 | 7 | 56 | 6 | 76 | 7 |
| 17 | 5 | 37 | 6 | 57 | 1 | 77 | 5 |
| 18 | 7 | 38 | 10 | 58 | 8 | 78 | 6 |
| 19 | 10 | 39 | 3 | 59 | 5 | 79 | 4 |
| 20 | 2 | 40 | 6 | 60 | 3 | 80 | 9 |

**Figure 1**

pany's forecast is accurate, what is your best estimate of the average demand of potential customers in the five-state area?

2. What sampling distribution should be applied to this problem? Explain.

3. What would be the upper and lower limits if a 68.3 per cent confidence interval were required? A confidence interval of 90 per cent? Of 95 per cent? Of 99.7 per cent?

**No. 2. Purpose.** Construction of confidence intervals from small-sample estimates.

---

Bender Equipment, Inc. is a recently organized manufacturing company which is attempting to enter the market of heavy specialized construction and mining equipment. Because of the high degree of specialization and the size of capital investment required, Bender executives feel that virtually all of their projected business would be on a rental basis. There are currently two other manufacturers engaged in producing the type of equipment that Bender is contemplating—both of whom derive the major portion of their revenue from equipment rental.

Bender's engineering department has just completed development of a new crane which can be used for transporting loads that far exceed the capacity of conventional equipment. Bender's newly developed crane has several favorable characteristics, including simplicity of operation, minimum maintenance requirements, and better mobility than have the two types that currently hold the market. In light of this, Bender feels that their machine will compete quite well; however, there is no indication that it will completely capture the market.

Since Bender's product design features do not ensure a major portion of the market, the company executives have decided to compete on the basis of a lower daily rental price. A daily price of $250 appears to be sufficiently below the charges of the competing companies.

The company's sales department was called upon to compile a list of all potential equipment users throughout the country. In a few days' time the salesmen had completed a list of 5000 potential customers. From this list Bender has ascertained that it will be necessary to "sell" an average of 6 days' crane rental to each potential customer during the first business year in order to have a profitable operation.

In view of this, the sales department was asked to prepare an estimate (based on their list of 5000) of the average rental days during the first year. After much delay and protest over being required to make such a wild prediction, the sales department estimated that the average rental days for the first year would be 5.5 per potential customer.

Because of the highly uncertain nature of the salesmen's estimate, it was decided to take a sample of size $n = 20$ from the list of 5000 potential customers. The 20 customers selected to make up the random sample were to be flown to Bender headquarters from all parts of the country for a one-day demonstration of the model crane that had been developed. In addition to the demonstration, those making up the sample were to be given first-class treatment with respect to lodging, food, and entertainment. Immediately following the demonstration those present were asked if they would use the Bender crane and, approximately what number of days they would have use for it within the next year, in addition, each potential customer was asked for suggestions regarding possible improvements in the product.

The following results were obtained from the random sample:

$$\bar{X} = \text{arithmetic mean rental days (first year)} = 6.70 \text{ days}$$
$$S = \text{standard deviation (of the sample)} = 1.7 \text{ days}$$

Assume the population distribution to be approximately normal.

1. Compute the 50, 80, and 95 per cent confidence limits for mean rental days.
2. Are the results likely to be biased?

**No. 3. Purpose.** Construction of confidence intervals for nonnormal distributions—Tchebycheff's inequality.

---

If there were reason to believe that the distribution of the number of rental days per potential customer in Problem 2 was not a normal distribution, and if you had no idea how the population was distributed, what would the upper and lower limits of $\bar{X}$ be for a confidence interval of 90 per cent?

**No. 4. Purpose.** Determination of sample size.

---

Following the demonstration of the Bender crane (Problem 2) to the 20 potential customers, 15 of the sample of 20 indicated that they would use the Bender crane if it were available.

Bender, Inc. wants to know the proportion of the population that would use their crane when the need arose. For a 95 per cent confidence interval, which is no more than 5 percentage points wide, what size sample would have to be obtained?

Do this for two cases: (1) assuming the true proportion of the population to be not less than 65 per cent and (2) assuming that proportion which would require the largest possible sample size.

**No. 5.** What is the difference between sample bias and sampling error?

**No. 6.** Is it possible for sampling error to cause bias?

**No. 7.** What things can be done in order to ensure high returns from mail surveys?

**No. 8.** What techniques can be applied in order to minimize the various types of nonresponse errors in telephone and personal interviews?

**No. 9.** Suppose that you are investigating the smoking habits of undergraduate college students at Podunk University. Defining a heavy smoker as someone who smokes more than a half-pack of cigarettes a day on the average, you are interested in obtaining an estimate of the proportion of students who are heavy smokers. You suspect that this will vary with the student's sex and year in college.

You have available the following table, classifying the Podunk undergraduates:

| *Year* | *Number* |
|---|---|
| Freshman | 5000 |
| Sophomore | 4000 |
| Junior | 3000 |
| Senior | 2000 |

Design the appropriate stratified sample ($n = 300$). Give hypothetical results for your sample, calculate the overall estimated proportion of heavy smokers, and construct a 95 per cent confidence interval.

**No. 10.** Hypothesis testing—acceptance or rejection of a null hypothesis at a specified significance level.

---

A large supermarket chain has been approached by a trading stamp association on the subject of becoming one of their subscribers. The trading stamp association has offered terms that are substantially more attractive than those of competing organizations, but the president of the grocery chain is extremely hesitant about taking on the stamps. He feels that there are both advantages and disadvantages to such an arrangement. Because of widespread public controversy concerning higher retail prices precipitated by the cost of trading stamps, there is a question whether the offering of stamps would attract customers or would have the opposite effect of seriously hindering sales.

After much consideration, the supermaket chain decides that, unless evidence conclusively indicates that 50 per cent or more of those patronizing their stores approve of stamps, the association's offer should be turned down. A random sample of 200 customers reveals that 108 of them approve of the use of the trading stamps.

Should the company conclude that the percentage who like stamps is more than 50 per cent? Assume that the company is willing to reject the hypothesis that less than 50 per cent of its customers like stamps only if the probability of error is less than 5 per cent. Specify the decision rule.

**No. 11.** Determination of sample size—given $p_1^*$ and $p_2^*$ and setting singnificance levels $\alpha$ and $\beta$.

---

Lopar Industries, Inc. is a manufacturer of golfing equipment and sportswear. A major share of Lopar's sales are to small sporting goods stores and golf proshops throughout the country. In recent months, Lopar has experienced a sharp and significant increase in their accounts receivable balance. This increase in accounts receivable is partially due to a generally increasing sales level, but for the most part it appears to be a result of the addition of a large number of new accounts, which are taking the fullest advantage of Lopar's lax credit policy. Because of the large amount of funds tied up in their receivables, Lopar is finding it necessary to borrow sizable amounts of money (at relatively high interest rates) in order to finance expanding production.

To increase the receivables turnover, Lopar is considering the use of more rigid credit standards. Although on the surface this appears to be the obvious solution to the problem, the management of Lopar, Inc. has reason to believe that such a move would drive many of their customers to competitors who continue to offer easy credit terms. In comparing the costs of the alternative credit policies, it is determined that Lopar can lose as many as 5 per cent of its present customers because of the change, and still break even with respect to profit. There are, however, several members of the sales staff who violently oppose a change in the company's credit policy. These individuals point out that if Lopar were to lose 15 per cent of its customers, the company would find it necessary to pay less than the standard dividend to their stockholders—a situation that would cause extreme embarrassment to the Lopar management.

Before making a decision on a policy change, Lopar has decided to question a random sample of their customers as to their reaction to more rigid credit standards in the future. Based on the results of this study, on the assumption that customers will honestly report whether or not they would take their business elsewhere if credit were tightened, a decision will be made about credit policy.

Design a study such that the probability of tightening credit if more than 15 per cent of customers would switch is less than 5 per cent and the probability of not tightening credit if less than 5 per cent would switch is less than 10 per cent.

**No. 12.** Jones Candy Company: Calculation of expected risk.

---

The Jones Candy Company, one of the nation's leading manufacturers of confection products, has received a proposal from a Swedish candy manufacturer asking that the American firm import the Swedish candy and sell it under the Jones name. The Jones Company is currently marketing a large variety of candies, but does not produce the particular type of chocolate that the foreign candymaker proposes they add to their line.

The type of candy in question has only recently gained a significant amount of popularity in the United States. Within the past year Jones had considered producing the candy, but since its plants were already operating at capacity, and little capital was available for further investment, the idea of a possible expansion was abandoned.

After evaluating the market potential for this type of candy, and after forecasting the packaging, selling, and promotion costs, the Jones Company staff has announced that it will be necessary to gain a market share of 20 per cent in order to break even. It has also been determined that if Jones accepts the Swedish proposal, and the market share turns out to be less than 20 per cent, the company will lose $60,000 for each percentage point that they are under the break-even share of the market. In contrast, if the Jones Company decides not to accept the proposal, it is forecasted that they will sacrifice $25,000 for each percentage of the market share they could have gained above 20 per cent.

In order to evaluate its market share, the Jones Company has decided to take a random sample of size 100. It is estimated that this sample will cost approximately $5000 to complete.

Before taking the sample, the Jones Company President, who has had long years of experience and is noted for his expert opinion, estimated that there was a probability of 0.20 that the market share would be only 15 per cent and a 0.80 probability that it would be at 25 per cent once they had carried out adequate promotion to become established in the market.

1. Based on the President's probability assignments, calculate the expected risk for decision rules that set the critical value $c$ at the following values: $c =$ 0.155, 0.175, 0.195, 0.205, 0.225, 0.235, 0.245. Which of these appears to be the best critical value?

2. What is the expected value of perfect information? What is the expected value of the sample?

**No. 13.** Smart Publishing Company: A decisional problem.

---

The Smart Publishing Company is one of the nation's leading publishers of college and university textbooks. The Smart Company publishes books for student use in a wide variety of fields, but is especially noted for a complete line of texts on scientific and mathematical subjects.

A manuscript has just been submitted to the Smart Company for consideration by Dr. Hector Stardust, who is probably the world's foremost expert in the field of celestial mechanics. The manuscript, which is entitled *An Introduction to the Basics and Fundamentals of Celestial Mechanics,* contains the most recent developments and discoveries in the field and, according to those educators who have read it, appears to be one of the few books written on the subject that is really adequate for student use.

In considering the decision of "to publish or not to publish," the Smart Company is aware that despite the fact that this would be the most recent and complete textbook on the subject, several highly rated publications have recently been published and are available to the professional scientist and engineer. From this, the company has concluded that virtually all of their sales would take place on college and university campuses.

The Smart Company has managed to compile a list of all colleges offering courses for which Dr. Stardust's book would make a suitable text. From this list the company has ascertained that it will be necessary for the textbook to be used in 40 per cent of these courses in order to break even on the publishing venture.

In further analyzing its costs, the company determines that it will lose $40,000 for each 5 per cent under 40 per cent and profit by $30,000 for each 5 per cent of the schools above 40 per cent that would use the textbook.

In order to test the demand for the new book, the Smart Company has considered picking at random 60 colleges and universities from the list and sending to each a copy of the manuscript. After giving the professors sufficient time to study the manuscript, each would be asked if they would use it in their course if it were available in printed form. It has been estimated that a cost of $4000 will be incurred in typing the manuscript in readable form, reproducing it, and carrying out the sample.

Before proceeding with the sample, it has been estimated that there is a 0.4 probability that 25 per cent of the colleges will use the text and a 0.6 probability that 50 per cent will choose to use it.

1. Use a decision tree to analyze the decision in preposterior analysis. As alternative decision points, if the sample is taken, use $c = 0.30, 0.35, 0.40, 0.45,$

2. Should the Smart Company take the sample? If so, which of the values is the best one for the critical value $c$?

## SPIEGEL PHARMACEUTICALS, INCORPORATED*

Spiegel Pharmaceuticals is a major producer and seller of prescription and proprietary (nonprescription) drugs. Spiegel's headquarters and manufacturing facilities are located in a large Midwestern city. In addition, the company has branch marketing offices that are scattered throughout the country.

Early in 1967 Spiegel introduced a new first-aid dressing into the national market. This new dressing was made available to the public in either plastic tubes or aerosol cans for convenient application. During 1967 the new product, which was known as Pain-Stop, achieved only moderate consumer acceptance. To those who had originally "pushed" for the development and introduction of Pain-Stop, the first year's sales figures were a bitter disappointment. The initial studies made by Spiegel's marketing information staff had indicated that the product would meet with immediate and continued success.

Early in 1968 Spiegel executives began looking for ways to stimulate sales of Pain-Stop. At this time several of those on the marketing staff indicated the belief that the advertising budget and promotional effort were inadequate for a product of this type. While they readily admitted that as a percentage of its sales volume Pain-Stop was getting its "fair share" of the advertising budget, they claimed that the promotional effort for a new product should be three to five times greater than that for a product that has already been established in the market.

A proposal to increase the advertising outlay for Pain-Stop met considerable resistance from several Spiegel executives. For the past several years the company's selling expenses had averaged slightly over 40 per cent of the sales

* The name of the company and some of the figures are disguised.

dollar. Since this was somewhat above the industry average, a program had been initiated with the objective of reducing selling expenses where it appeared profitable to do so. In view of this, the Spiegel executive committee had flatly turned down the suggestion that a crash advertising program for Pain-Stop be instituted.

As a counterplan, Paul Burris, the company's director of marketing information, proposed that an experiment be performed to measure the effect of advertising expenditures on Pain-Spot sales. Mr. Burris proposed that the experiment be limited to a single metropolitan area and that the bulk of the expenditures be made for local spot television advertisement.

After much consideration, the executive committee of Spiegel Pharmaceuticals gave Mr. Burris and his staff the "go-ahead" on Mr. Burris' proposal. The major reason for their approval was that the experiment would not only give Spiegel information on the advertising effect for Pain-Stop, but would also give the company valuable data on the general effect of spot television advertisement.

## THE EXPERIMENT DESIGN

The metropolitan area of St. Louis, Missouri, was chosen as the object of the television spot campaign. It was decided that the advertising was to run for a period of eight weeks starting on March 7, 1968, and ending on May 7, 1968.

The effect of the advertising campaign was to be measured by auditing the inventories and shipments to 45 drugstores in the St. Louis area. From the inventory and shipment data, Pain-Stop sales volumes were to be projected for the various audit periods. The experiment was to consist of four audit periods of one month each. The drugstore audits were to begin on February 17, 1968, and the final period was scheduled to end on June 17, 1968.

The only numerical data to be collected were those for the 45 drugstores included in the audit. The reason for this was the easy accessibility of drugstores for audits. Up to the time that the experiment began, chain and independent drugstores represented 32 per cent of Pain-Stop shipments into the St. Louis area. Since the audit was not to include any significant figures for the rest of the market, it was decided to make telephone contact with rack jobbers and major chain supermarkets in order to get an idea in which direction sales were moving in the grocery outlets.

## DISCUSSION AND RESULTS OF THE EXPERIMENT

Spiegel's price to the retailer for both the tubes and the aerosol cans of Pain-Stop was 32.5 cents per unit. Since the average retail markup is about

**Exhibit 1** Pain-Stop Cost Per Unit

| Item | Tube | Aero-Can |
|---|---|---|
| Variable production costs | $0.102 | $0.110 |
| Allocation for fixed production costs | 0.031 | 0.025 |
| Sales and administration—variable* | 0.037 | 0.037 |
| Sales and administration—fixed* | 0.048 | 0.048 |
| Freight and transportation costs | 0.022 | 0.030 |
| Total cost | $0.240 | $0.250 |

* Includes normal advertising and promotional costs.

45 per cent, the usual retail price was 59 cents per can or tube. A breakdown of Spiegel's production and selling costs for Pain-Stop is shown in Exhibit 1.

The total cost for the eight weeks of spot television advertisements was $1250. Exhibits 3 and 4 show Spiegel factory shipments to drugstores and the *projected* sales volumes of Pain-Stop for the four audit periods. In addition, average inventory data are shown in Exhibit 2.

Telephone contact with rack jobbers and major grocery chains indicated a definite increase in Pain-Stop movement for the months of March and April, which corresponded to the advertising dates. A small minority of the chain supermarkets reported no change in Pain-Stop sales.

Also, while the overall average inventory for the St. Louis area was 9 units per store, the national average was only about 5.5 units.

## APPENDIX

## RESULTS OF DRUGSTORE AUDITS

**Exhibit 2** Inventory Data

| | Average Inventory | Month's Supply* |
|---|---|---|
| February 18–March 17 | 10.60 units/store | 4.5 |
| March 18–April 17 | 9.04 units/store | 2.8 |
| April 18–May 17 | 8.15 units/store | 2.6 |
| May 18–June 17 | 9.80 units/store | 2.9 |

* An indication of inventory turnover. Ratio of average inventory level to average monthly sales.

**Exhibit 3** Actual Shipments of Pain-Stop to Drugstores in the St. Louis Area (Spiegel Factory Shipments)

| | Units | Retail | Net Dollars | Units | Retail | Net Dollars |
|---|---|---|---|---|---|---|
| | | *February 1968* | | | *March 1968* | |
| Tubes | 1981 | $1169 | $643 | 2099 | $1238 | $681 |
| Aero-cans | 612 | 316 | 199 | 679 | 401 | 220 |
| Total | 2593 | $1530 | $814 | 2778 | $1639 | $901 |
| | | *April 1968* | | | *May 1968* | |
| Tubes | 3227 | $1904 | $1047 | 2886 | $1703 | $ 937 |
| Aero-cans | 1422 | 839 | 461 | 1034 | 610 | 336 |
| Total | 4649 | $2743 | $1509 | 3920 | $2313 | $1272 |

**Exhibit 4** Projected Unit Sales for Pain-Stop for the St. Louis Area from Audits of 45 Drugstores

| | Units | Retail | Net Dollars | Units | Retail | Net Dollars |
|---|---|---|---|---|---|---|
| | | *February 17–March 17, 1968* | | | *March 18–April 17, 1968* | |
| Tubes | 2165 | $1277 | $ 702 | 2750 | $1623 | $ 893 |
| Aero-cans | 991 | 585 | 322 | 1615 | 953 | 524 |
| Total | 3156 | $1862 | $1024 | 4366 | $2576 | $1417 |
| | | *April 18–May 17, 1968* | | | *May 18–June 17, 1968* | |
| Tubes | 2861 | $1688 | $ 928 | 2140 | $1263 | $ 695 |
| Aero-cans | 1286 | 760 | 418 | 1550 | 914 | 503 |
| Total | 4147 | $2447 | $1346 | 3690 | $2177 | $1192 |

* Projected sales figures are for all drugstores in the St. Louis area.

QUESTIONS

1. (*a*) Based on the classifications of experiments in the chapter, how would this experiment be classified?
   (*b*) What changes, if any, would you make in the experiment design?
2. What conclusions may be drawn from the experiment?
3. Based on this experiment, would you recommend an increase in advertising for new products?

## SECURITY WATCH COMPANY*

### INTRODUCTION

The Security Watch Company was founded in 1817. Because of great emphasis on quality of materials and fine craftsmanship, at the turn of the century the Security watch was considered the best American-made watch on the market. With capable management and continued attention to the finest quality, the company was a leader in the industry throughout the early 1900's.

In the 1930's, the Security Watch met its first crisis. The company had in the past concentrated on producing fine pocket watches. In the twenties and thirties, some of Security's competitors, as well as some new establishments, began promoting small compact wristwatches which became increasingly popular. Although slow to react to this trend, by 1940 the Security Watch Company was making what was considered the best wristwatches available and had once more taken its position among the leading watchmakers.

After World War II a major change took place in the market structure of wristwatches. In the past, when one purchased a personal timepiece he very often expected it to last for a lifetime. Wristwatches were a prestige item; and for those who could afford them jeweled watches with solid-gold cases were not uncommon. But in the 1940's and 1950's the demand for expensive jeweled watches abruptly decreased and yielded to a demand for functional, inexpensive watches.

The company was very slow to react to this change in the demand structure. There were two major reasons for this. First, the management was reluctant to produce a "cheap" timepiece for fear that it would destroy their fine reputation for the highest of quality and craftsmanship. Second, because their watches were almost completely handmade, Security lacked the technology, personnel, and equipment necessary to compete with mass-produced watches.

### THE LOW-PRICED WATCH

It was not until 1955 that the company finally introduced a line of wristwatches in the \$10–\$30 price range. Security's low-priced wristwatches did not meet with immediate market success, but by 1962 the company had gained a large share of the market and was among the leaders in the \$10–\$30 price range. The company felt that their eventual success in the lower price range was due to their reputation for high quality watches.

* The name of the company and the industry are disguised.

In 1967, the Security Watch Company again found its sales lagging significantly behind those of its major competitors in the low price range—Precision, Worthy, and Armor. The company estimated that very close to 50 per cent of the total retail sales for wristwatches was in the $10–$30 price range. For this reason, there was great incentive to capture a major share of the low-priced market.

In the forties and fifties there had also been a significant change in the channels of distribution. The leading producers of low-priced watches had a very broad distribution that not only included the traditional channels, but went into such retail outlets as drugstores and variety stores. Security had continued to follow its traditional pattern of selective distribution only to jewelry stores and the larger well-established department stores.

With respect to quality, all four brands (Security, Precision, Worthy, and Armor) were approximately equal. The primary variants among the four brands were promotional efforts and channels of distribution. It appeared that if Security were to increase its market share in the low-priced range, the optimum level and combination of promotional efforts, as well as the proper channels of distribution, would have to be ascertained. With this in mind, Security management decided in favor of experimental test-marketing. The objectives of the test-marketing program were:

1. To determine the effect on brand share of increased advertising and distribution efforts.
2. To determine the financial risks and requirements involved in greater promotional efforts and expanding channels of distribution.

## DESIGN OF THE EXPERIMENT

The test markets were selected in cooperation with Security's advertising agency, Selmore Advertising, Inc. of Chicago, Illinois. The population of subjects was defined as the entire adult population of the continental United States. It was hoped to draw a sample that would include all social classes, ranging from upper-upper to lower-lower, in cities with approximately equal demographic characteristics. The following criteria were applied in selecting the test markets that would be included:

1. Demographic characteristics that are approximately equal to those of the total United States population and approximately equal to each other.
2. Sufficient number of television sets in use.
3. Adequate television station coverage.

The criteria concerning television set use and station coverage were included because television was selected as the primary advertising medium. It was felt that recent data suggested that television provided the most efficient coverage per dollar spent. Also, advertising "impact" of television showed better results than that of any other medium for the type of product that Security Watch Company was marketing.

The test markets were selected in pairs:

1. Baton Rouge–Des Moines.
2. Flint–Austin.
3. Oklahoma City–Dayton.
4. Omaha–Spokane.
5. Gary–Wichita.

The purpose of the experiment was to test the following variables:

1. A special distribution effort in each of four sets of test markets.
2. The use of different levels of advertising in each of the different sets of test markets.

The sample was divided into the following pairs:

1. Baton Rouge–Des Moines–control market.
2. Flint–Austin—test market 1.
3. Oklahoma City–Dayton—test market 2.
4. Omaha–Spokane—test market 3.
5. Gary–Wichita—test market 4.

The dependent variables in the test market program were brand share and product volume exposure (PVE), which can be defined as per cent of total market sales represented by all stores displaying Security watches. For instance, PVE = 40 per cent meant that the Security watch was displayed by retail outlets making 40 per cent of the total wristwatch sales in the $10–$30 price range. Measuring the PVE provided a method of gauging the efficiency of distribution against competition.

The test-marketing program ran from August 1967 to August 1968. During the test period a commercial information organization, Research Data, Inc., was retained. Research Data, Inc. was to audit over-the-counter sales and obtain brand share figures together with PVE figures for the following brands:

Security
Precision
Worthy
Armor

The auditing firm presented in detail the method by which they selected the audit sample, but kept the actual store names strictly confidential.

The experimental variables in Security's test markets were advertising and personal selling. Measurement of advertising pressure was an essential part of the experiment. It was decided that "gross rating points" (GRP) would be an adequate method of measuring advertising pressure.

The GRP is a term that describes the number and frequency of television homes reached by an advertising message in a particular market. For example,

50% of all TV homes reached 1 time = GRP
100% of all TV homes reached 1½ times = 150 GRP

If a certain program had a GRP rating of 50, for instance, and Security wished to advertise at a rate of 150 GRP, three 1 minute ads could be scheduled in the test market for three succeeding program showings.

It was further agreed that "spot" television ads afforded the greatest degree of flexibility, particularly in view of the local nature of the test markets. One minute spot ads were produced and scheduled for the appropriate test markets. Time slots in each of the test markets were purchased. A predetermined GRP level was reached. The GRP levels of advertising for the various test markets were assigned as follows:

1. Baton Rouge–Des Moines—control markets (only normal national advertising).
2. Flint–Austin—test market 1 (special distribution).
3. Oklahoma City–Dayton—test market 2 (personal selling team + 50 GRP advertising).
4. Omaha–Spokane—test market 3 (personal selling team + 100 GRP).
5. Gary–Wichita—test market 4 (personal selling team + 150 GRP).

Teams of seven salesmen converged on each pair of test markets (but not the control market) periodically. Their duties and assignments are shown in Exhibit 1.

**Exhibit 1** Security Watch Market Test (Salesman Outline and Procedure)

*Purpose*

To prove out over-the-counter sales of Security low-priced wristwatches with advertising backing.

*Place*

Eight cities in four pairs:

Flint–Austin
Oklahoma City–Dayton
Omaha–Spokane
Gary–Wichita

*Primary Product Emphasis*

The $18.95 model wristwatches (men's and ladies').

*Secondary Product Emphasis*

All other wristwatches in the $10–$30 price range.

*Salesmen's Activity*

Salesmen and merchandising men should visit each city in their territories as soon as possible after being so instructed, to push programs to do the following:

1. Pay special attention to maintaining inventories of $18.95 and other wristwatches.
2. Outline low-priced wristwatch research for that particular area.
3. Take inventory of the $18.95 model watch and make four copies: for two merchandising men for that city, for the salesman himself, and for mailing to the marketing manager at company headquarters.
4. Solicit wholesalers' and chain headquarters' cooperation regarding research for that city:

(*a*) To obtain the distribution for Security watches that we know to be attainable, we shall grant immediately six-month terms on all wristwatches in the $10–$30 price range, provided that they will grant such terms to their retail dealers or, in the case of chain headquarters, to their branches. In all cases, terms must apply to retail dealers only in those cities. Our terms to direct accounts will apply to all their retailers in the $10–$30 price range if they cannot separate out that portion which is going into the cities named.

(*b*) We would like to have wholesaler's salesmen covering these cities to push wristwatch sales on six-month terms beginning at once.

(*c*) Salesmen and merchandising men should cover these cities thoroughly and take turnover orders for the low-priced watches for cooperating wholesalers and for chain branch orders if headquarters will pemit.

(*d*) Wholesalers and chain headquarters in these cities only should be asked to permit our salesmen and merchandising men to pick up any orders out of stock, on memo, so that they can deliver immediately when sales are made.

(*e*) If possible, our salesmen should arrange for sales meetings with wholesalers, but if this cannot be done within a day or two at most after the first call, the program should not be held up pending a meeting.

(*f*) Salesmen should assure the wholesalers that we shall guarantee them against any credit losses that may occur in low-priced wristwatch sales in cases where our salesmen and merchandising men may write up delivered orders for retailers to whom the wholesalers do not ordinarily want to sell.

*Salesmen Activity*

1. The men will be assigned to particular cities.
2. Each man will be assigned to certain wholesalers and chain headquarters for taking inventory and taking orders.
3. The men will present the $18.95 model first, with special emphasis on additional advertising where applicable and on six-month-guarantee sales terms.

4. Special emphasis is to be placed on getting our products and displays into any store that has Precision, Worthy, or Armor displays.

5. When an order is sold, the man will deliver it then and there and put it on display. He will write up a turnover delivered order on the particular wholesaler involved. The order must be signed by the retailer. The salesman must also rubber-stamp all copies of the order with the special "guaranteed sale" stamp that he will have for that purpose.

6. If immediate merchandise supplies are needed, the salesman should telephone his regional manager to make arrangement for transfer of such merchandise from other accounts in the territory or elsewhere in the region. When orders are written directly to the company, they are to be airmailed the same day to Security headquarters, where they will be processed for immediate filling.

7. When a salesman is certain that he has covered all possible retail outlets in his part of the city, he is to contact the other men working in the city and help them finish up. When a city is finished, salesmen should return any unsold merchandise they are carrying to the wholesalers from whom it was picked up, finish writing up all reports and mail them at once, and report to their regional managers by telephone for further assignment.

---

The market test began on August 1, 1967, and ended on August 1, 1968. A bimonthly system of manipulating the experimental variables was scheduled throughout the year. The timing was as follows:

*Step 1.* The first two weeks of the two-month period were devoted to distribution efforts. Seven salesmen were taken from their own territories and simultaneously assigned to each test market.

*Step 2.* The middle four weeks of the bimonthly period were devoted to spot television advertising at pressure levels prescribed by the GRP assignments for each test market.

*Step 3.* Auditing of the dependent variables (brand share and PVE) was done by Research Data, Inc. in the final two weeks of the bimonthly period.

This cycle was repeated in each market six times throughout the year.

A variety of personal selling and advertising tactics were employed in the test markets, which can be summarized as follows:

1. Advertising was concentrated on only one model (the $18.95 model) in the $10–$30 price range.

2. A regional sales manager supervised each test market distribution effort. Because two cities within test market 4 were to receive heavy advertising, the most competent regional sales managers were selected for this test market.

3. Route sheets were drawn up for each salesman, with each wholesaler or retail outlet listed on each route.

4. A "selling checklist" was provided for each salesman.

5. A daily sales quota was assigned each salesman.

6. A "breakfast" sales meeting was held three times each week to analyze distribution results and to give assistance.

7. Special sales report forms were designed.

8. Security Watch displays were placed with the retailer on "guaranteed sale" (consignment).

**Exhibit 2** Summary or Overall Experiment Results

| Market | Brand | Net PVE | ±Δ* | Share | ±%† |
|---|---|---|---|---|---|
| Control | Total | | | 100.0 | |
| | Security | 67 | +24.1 | 7.4 | +0.3 |
| | Precision | 79 | +11.3 | 16.2 | +1.1 |
| | Worthy | 90 | + 2.3 | 22.0 | −0.1 |
| | Armor | 82 | + 9.3 | 14.2 | −1.5 |
| Test 1 | Total | | | 100.0 | |
| | Security | 74 | +17.5 | 8.2 | +1.2 |
| | Precision | 80 | +15.9 | 16.0 | +1.4 |
| | Worthy | 84 | + 1.2 | 22.4 | −0.1 |
| | Armour | 76 | + 7.0 | 14.1 | −0.6 |
| Test 2 | Total | | | 100.0 | |
| | Security | 74 | +19.4 | 8.0 | +1.1 |
| | Precision | 69 | +15.0 | 17.0 | +1.9 |
| | Worthy | 89 | − 1.1 | 21.9 | −0.2 |
| | Armor | 73 | + 7.4 | 16.5 | −0.6 |
| Test 3 | Total | | | 100.0 | |
| | Security | 73 | +10.6 | 9.1 | +1.4 |
| | Precision | 69 | +19.6 | 15.6 | +0.8 |
| | Worthy | 94 | + 2.2 | 21.7 | +1.5 |
| | Armor | 79 | + 5.3 | 14.3 | −0.4 |
| Test 4 | Total | | | 100.0 | |
| | Security | 68 | + 9.7 | 10.5 | +3.6 |
| | Precision | 75 | + 1.4 | 17.0 | n.c.‡ |
| | Worthy | 90 | + 9.8 | 23.7 | +1.1 |
| | Armor | 78 | n.c.‡ | 16.2 | −1.2 |

* Per cent change in PVE from August 1967 to August 1968.

† Percentage points of change in brand share over the test period.

‡ No change.

Great care was taken to assure that the special distribution effort was kept as constant as possible in each of the test markets. Different combinations of sales manpower levels were not tested.

## RESULTS OF THE EXPERIMENT

Security PVE and brand share changes over the test period for each test market in Exhibits 3 and 4 are indicated. A complete summary for Security and its primary competitors is shown in Exhibit 2.

**Exhibit 3** Security Brand Share Change

| | 1967 | 1968 |
|---|---|---|
| 1. Baton Rouge–Des Moines—control markets | 7.1% | 7.4% |
| 2. Flint–Austin—distribution only | 6.9% | 8.2% |
| 3. Oklahoma City–Dayton—distribution + 50 GRP | 6.9% | 8.0% |
| 4. Omaha–Spokane—distribution + 100 GRP | 7.7% | 9.1% |
| 5. Gary–Wichita—distribution + 150 GRP | 6.9% | 10.5% |

**Exhibit 4** Security PVE Change

| | 1967 | 1968 |
|---|---|---|
| 1. Baton Rouge–Des Moines—control markets | 43% | 67% |
| 2. Flint–Austin—distribution only | 56% | 74% |
| 3. Oklahoma City–Dayton—distribution + 50 GRP | 55% | 74% |
| 4. Omaha–Spokane—distribution + 100 GRP | 62% | 73% |
| 5. Gary–Wichita—distribution + 150 GRP | 60% | 68% |

Security Watch brand share in the low price range made the percentage increases shown in Exhibit 5 during the test period that ended August 1, 1968.

**Exhibit 5**

| | Percentage Increase |
|---|---|
| 1. Baton Rouge–Des Moines—control markets | 4% |
| 2. Flint–Austin—distribution only | 17% |
| 3. Oklahoma City–Dayton—distribution + 50 GRP | 16% |
| 4. Omaha–Spokane—distribution + 100 GRP | 20% |
| 5. Gary–Wichita—distribution + 150 GRP | 52% |

There was no obvious explanation for the increase in PVE in the control markets (Baton Rouge–Des Moines).

## CONCLUSIONS DRAWN FROM THE EXPERIMENT

The management of the Security Watch Company realized that the experimental test-marketing program had some shortcomings, but felt that the following conclusions could be safely drawn:

1. Expansion of advertising for wristwatches in the low price range on a national basis (as projected from test market expenses) was financially unsound at all levels of advertising pressure. Brand share gain was not significant enough to justify such expenditures.
2. By concentrating on distribution (through better sales training and manpower reorganization), improvement in brand share was possible. Growth in brand share would be slow, but less risky than resorting to heavy advertising expenditures.
3. Low-priced wristwatches, as an advertised consumer product, are generally a "low-interest" item in the consumer's mind.

## QUESTIONS

1. Criticize the experimental design and suggest what you think would be a superior design.
2. What conclusions should the company have drawn from the experiment.

## PART III

# *Securing Marketing Information for Decision Making*

Part III contains six chapters, all of which are concerned with the securing of marketing information for decision making. Chapter 8 provides an overview or perspective of the various types of information discussed in Part III. It also provides an operational set of procedures for securing and using marketing information. Chapter 9 is concerned with programs designed to extract information on sales and costs from firms' experiences. Chapter 10 classifies the major types of information secured from respondents. It also discusses securing behavioral information. Chapter 11 evolves from Chapter 10 and goes on to discuss the techniques for securing psychological information. Chapter 12 is concerned with unanticipated information and commercial information. Chapter 13 provides a discussion on securing external secondary information.

After completing the six chapters in Part III, the reader should have a good notion of the types of marketing information needed by decision makers. Also, he should be familiar with the various major techniques for securing marketing information.

*Eight*

# Marketing Information for Decision Making: An Overview

The purpose of this chapter is to provide an overview or perspective of the marketing information needed for decision making within organizations. The chapter is divided into seven major sections, with the first one devoted to a brief review of the kinds of *problems* for which information is needed. The second section establishes two marketing information classification systems. The third and fourth sections discuss information found on the buyers' side and on the sellers' side of the market. The fifth section is concerned with on-line, real-time information, and the sixth section discusses future information. The final section examines a set of marketing research procedures designed to guide the collection and use of marketing information.

## PROBLEM AREAS FOR DECISION MAKING

Management, broadly speaking, faces four major and continuous decision-making tasks. These tasks dictate information needs. Basically, management must be able to (1) discern the *amount* of money needed for marketing activities. It must be able to (2) formulate adequate and appropriate *mixes* of the marketing ingredients, including prices and promotional and physical availability possibilites. It must (3) determine where the various marketing efforts[1] are to have impact (i.e., the geographical allocation of efforts). Finally, it must (4) determine

[1] Marketing efforts are defined here to mean the monetary value of all the company inputs into the marketing process.

*when* marketing efforts must be expended. These four problems are interrelated and dependent one upon the other, as are the accompanying information requirements.

These four problems are discussed only briefly to indicate the general nature of each problem and to suggest the resulting information needs. Additional discussion would be beyond the scope of this book. However, the reader is referred to various marketing management books such as Alderson and Green (1964), Howard (1963), and Kotler (1967).[2]

## Amount of Marketing Effort

The amount of money needed for marketing activities refers to the total quantity of marketing effort to be used by a firm within a specific time. This may be thought of as the total amount budgeted for all marketing activities.

It is not clear how various companies have made this decision. Some appear to have applied a historical per cent of sales; others have used about the same per cent as their competitors used. Also, it is likely that some companies have used their previous expenditures as a base, while other companies appear to have put all the funds they could spare into marketing activities.

Unfortunately, these intuitive approaches have produced less than satisfactory results. Instead, management has been substituting extensive consideration and analysis of information on sales volumes, market shares, costs, and potential. In turn, much more extensive information is being collected and used to help determine the appropriate amount of money to be spent for the marketing endeavor.

## Marketing Mix

The appropriate marketing mix refers to the composition of the marketing expenditures placed behind each product and service. This broad area includes planning and controlling both the amounts and the kinds of marketing activities that compose the mix. For example, at the top organization level, the main concern is with the best combinations of personal selling, advertising, price structures, physical availability of offerings, and other major marketing efforts. At other levels there is concern with such factors as the proper messages and appeals matched with the proper media for each product and service.

The problem of determining the marketing mix does not succumb

[2] Kotler's book (1967, Chapter 12) contains a particularly succinct and relevant discussion.

to easy solutions; in fact, even its dimensions appear difficult to determine. Clearly, though, marketing information dealing with potential, sales, and marketing costs is the bastion of the evolving marketing mix management.[3]

## Geographical Allocation

Geographical allocation of marketing dollars is concerned principally with *where* the various marketing activities impact for each of the firm's offerings. Just putting forth a quantity and quality of dollars does not produce optimum returns. Poor allocation has resulted from lack of attention as well as from a belief that efforts should be assigned according to potential (Howard, 1963, pp. 446–447).

Improvements are arising through the use of measures and estimates such as market opportunity, industry efforts, and industry sales. Semlow (1959) outlined a solution to allocate salesmen over a multiple market area. He indicated that decision makers must know potential, sales productivity of salesmen, sales, and variable marketing costs for each territory. In addition, decision makers should have an estimate of working capital and plant investment required at alternative sales volumes.[4]

## Allocation over Time

Virtually the same statements made about the geographical allocation of marketing dollars pertain to allocation of marketing dollars over time. That is, a firm can put forth appropriate quantities and qualities of effort, and in the right places, but still fall far below the company's objectives because of poor timing. There are at least four major time dimensions that management must consider: (1) time lags and carryovers, (2) seasonality, (3) cyclical variations, and (4) product life cycles. Once again, an understanding sufficient to permit control can be gained only through extensive marketing information.[5]

In summary, management must continually ask and answer questions about its marketing activities—how much, what mixes, where, and when?

[3] For a general discussion of the marketing information needed to manage the marketing mix problem, see Kotler (1967, pp. 274–281). Specific information needs can best be discerned through the construction and use of a realistic model of the firm and its environment. Models and model building were discussed in Chapter 3.

[4] See also Howard (1963, pp. 475–479).

[5] Readers seeking more information on this topic are advised to see Jastram (1955), Rogers (1962), and Tull (1965).

These, then, are the basic decision areas for which marketing information must be available. All four areas are closely interrelated in terms of both (1) their influence on each other, and (2) the marketing information required for meaningful management.

### Concluding Comments on Information Needs

Marketing information needs differ from one company to another. The content of any individual program is based largely on considerations of information benefits and the accompanying costs for the individual company. Obviously, both benefits and costs of information vary within as well as among industries. For example, manufacturers of home laundry equipment in the United States can secure (through their trade association) industry sales broken down by geographical areas and by products. Not all members pay the same price, nor do they gain identical benefits from this information. In contrast, manufacturers of furniture find information about their industry sales much more expensive but less useful. Yet some of the members apparently feel that the benefits exceed the costs.

These comments about the *use* of information have been made because information managers need to be familiar with their organizations' activities in order to discern and help fulfill information needs. Reading in the area of marketing management is recommended as a supplement to this brief section.

## INFORMATION FRAMEWORKS

The concern here is with helpful ways in which to view the many facets of marketing information. There are, of course, numerous ways to view both real objects and constructs. For example, a person watching a football game from high in a press-box overlooking the 50-yard line gets a far different view than does one watching the game from row 1 behind the goalposts. And each different position, or viewpoint, gives a somewhat different view of the proceedings. The same sort of situation exists relative to the view, or views, a person gets of marketing information. In this case, however, the different viewpoints are influenced principally by different classifications.

The most useful viewpoints or classifications are in terms of (1) the frequency of collection and use of the information (continually collected information versus special-problem information) and (2) the location of the information (buyers' side verus sellers' side and external versus internal). Information managers need and use both of these major viewpoints, as well as minor other ones, to help accumulate and catalog marketing information.

## Continually Collected Information versus Special Problem Information

Information collected and used primarily for planning and decision making in recurrent marketing operations is called *continually collected information or continuing data base.* It is *repeatedly or continually* collected, because it is needed in recurrent decision-making situations. The other distinguishing characteristic is that *it can be anticipated as to source, form, and availability,* because of prior use.

In contrast, there are special-problem situations that call for information in excess of, or different from, the normal range of recurrent planning and decision-making situations. In this book these are referred to as special-problem situations, and they give rise to the need for *special-problem information.* Such needs arise because management can neither anticipate the future in total nor afford all wanted information on a continuing basis.

In some respects a program of continually collected information is like a fire-prevention program and special-problem information is like a fire-fighting program in a modern fire department. A good prevention program can cut down both on the cost of fire protection and on fire losses. However, 100 per cent fire-prevention programs are not possible, because no one can either foresee enough of the future nor economically prevent all fires from arising. Of course, what may be *continually collected information* in one company may be *special-problem information* in another, and vice versa.

## Marketplace View: Buyers' versus Sellers' Side

The starting point is to gain an understanding of the term *marketplace.* Market has reference to both the demand for and the supply of a specified offering. For example, the digital computer market is composed of current and prospective *customers* and current and prospective *suppliers.* The commercial laundry equipment market is made up of current and prospective *customers* and *suppliers.* The customer side is referred to as the *buyers' side* of the market. The other side, the supplier side, is called the *sellers' side* of the market. Quite obviously, all markets have the two sides. *Information is available on the buyers' or sellers' side of the market.*

Normally, the dimension of the sellers' side of a market is determined by the buyers' side. For example, if buyers of upholstery material freely substituted leather for simulated-leather plastics, or vice versa, the sellers' side would include suppliers of both leather and simulated leather. In turn, the appropriate market measurements would include information about both supplying sources, not just about one of them. A market is determined, then, by the demands of buyers, *not* by the SIC (standard industrial classification) code or by traditional industry alignments. That is, the composition of the sellers' side of a market is dependent on the composition and behavior of the buyers' side. The upholsterers' willingness to use either leather or simulated leather prescribes the dimension of this segment of the upholstery market.

But why bother with such distinction? It helps clarify foggy and ambiguous thinking about markets, which in turn facilitates improved information use. For instance, a company such as General Motors operates on both buyers' and sellers' sides in a large number of *markets.* It is ridiculous for *marketing purposes* to say that G.M. is in the automotive industry market. Furthermore, any one of its divisions, such as Frigidaire, is a part of both sides of many markets. For marketing purposes it is virtually useless to say that the Frigidaire Division is a part of the home appliance market. Such a category title is too broad and ambiguous to be useful; on the other hand, it is not inclusive enough to include all of the Division's offerings.

Obviously, careful market segmentation (based on how buyers view the market) is a prerequisite to market measurement. Prior to segmentation, market boundaries are poorly defined and mass measurements and estimates are of little use. However, once a market is segmented with sufficient precision, one can examine it in considerable detail and provide useful information relative to market size, location, behavior, and so forth.

## Internal versus External Sources

Information may also be classified as *internal* or *external.* Internal information is that which is both generated and available within the using organization. In contrast, external information originates and is initially available only outside the using organization. Figure 8-1 presents some of the major types of internal and external information.

This view or classification is meaningful to information managers in that the problems of searching, securing, and supplying internal information are somewhat different from those of external information (Alexander and Berg, 1965, p. 516). External information, for example, normally involves (1) more extensive searching because of the multiplicity of

*Internal Information*
- Company sales (by various products, territories, and customers)
- Company costs (by various products, territories, and functions)

*External Information*
- Other companies' sales
- Other companies' costs
- Measures of potential
- Customer behavior:
  - Patterns
  - Explanations
- Other environmental conditions:
  - Economic conditions
  - Legal environment
  - Political environment

*Joint Internal/External Information*
- Market share
- Market position
- Effort share
- Effort rank

**Figure 8-1** Internal versus external information.

sources, (2) the securing of information from or through outside or independent information groups, (3) more explicit cost considerations because payments must be made to others, and (4) some measurement of other sellers' sales and marketing costs.

Internal information, by comparison, (1) requires less searching because of fewer possible sources, (2) normally must be secured from and through the using organization, (3) and involves information about the sales and marketing costs of the firm. Furthermore, the cost of the information is often less explicit because of the absence of price tags within the organization. There are other differences, but they will be observed later when the individual information facets are discussed.

## INFORMATION FROM THE SELLERS' SIDE

Figure 8-2 portrays the major types of marketing information (and their relationships) classified from the viewpoints of the buyers' and the sellers' sides of the market. A good place to start on this overview is on the left side of the figure—this is the sellers' side of the market.

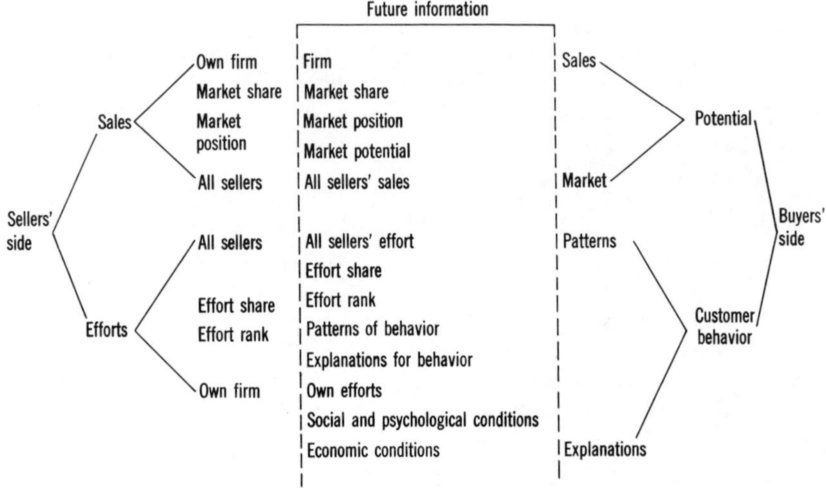


**Figure 8-2** Marketing information framework.

In other words, the left side represents suppliers with offerings that meet the needs of the buyers' side. The information on this side is concerned with the sellers' (1) *sales* and (2) marketing *efforts.*

## Sales Information

Sales information is divided into two distinct categories: (1) the firm's own sales and (2) all sellers' (industry) sales. Most of the information regarding the firm's *plant* sales (i.e., flows *into* channels) involves internal sources and collection. However, sales flowing out of the other end of the channel from final sellers to users normally must be gathered from the marketplace and are considered to be external.

A company *can* account for its sales into the channels (i.e., inflows) by products, packages, and customer locations, as well as by order size, customer type and size, and other segments. Internal sales analysis, as a rule, exceeds the traditional accounting needs of firms. Consequently, such programs arise only when marketing needs are sufficient to require their presence. Chapter 9 includes a discussion of sales analysis.

Information in regard to a firm's *outflows* from channels can be gained through returned warranty cards, tax or license reports, store audits, consumer panels, special marketing research activities, and middlemen reports. Obviously, company-owned outlets can permit direct access through the various units' sales records.

*Sellers'* (industry) sales figures are often available from public or commercial sources, including governmental sources, trade associations, and commercial trade sources. Both sales into and sales out of channels may be available, but these matters will be examined more fully in later chapters.

Finally, companies that know all sellers' (industry) sales along with their own sales can compute composite measurements such as *market share.*[6] With firm-by-firm sales data, they can determine *market positions.* (These information items are shown in Figure 8-2 between the entries of own firm sales and sellers' sales.)

Market share is the per cent of total sales (of all sellers) sold by an individual firm. For example, if the sellers' side sells 1000 units of an offering, a firm that sells 300 of these units would have a 30 per cent market share.

Market position, in contrast, is an ordinal ranking of sales of a firm in relation to the sales of each other seller. That is, it is a sales ranking of the individual offerings on the sellers' side of the market. For example, the market position of automobile *brands* for the year 1965 was (1) Chevrolet, (2) Ford, (3) Mustang, (4) Dodge, (5) Pontiac, and so on (*Des Moines Register,* 1966).

## Effort Information

Effort information refers to information concerning money used by the sellers' side of a market in promoting and distributing an offering. That is, the concern is with marketing activities such as personal selling, advertising, sales promotion, making a product physically available, price discounting, and securing and using marketing information. An individual firm needs information about (1) its own efforts and (2) the efforts of other sellers.

Most of the information regarding a firm's own marketing efforts is internal information. Unfortunately, these data do not normally arise through either the traditional accounting approaches or factory (production) cost accounting programs. Instead, they require the establishment and the use of marketing cost accounting programs. Such programs can be designed to gather specific and detailed information. These matters will be discussed in detail in Chapter 9.

Information regarding the marketing efforts applied to a firm's brands by independent members of a channel is largely external in nature. That is, it is generated outside the individual firm. However, when it is sought,

[6] An extensive discussion of market share measurements can be found in Oxenfeldt (1959).

it is normally compiled under the direction of the channel captain (Davidson, 1961). In such cases, the channel captain periodically "requires" certain information from the various channel members.

### *Sellers' Marketing Efforts*

Information about marketing efforts expended by a sellers' side of a market presents problems quite different from those just examined. This information usually comes from external sources. For example, a firm may consider such sources as Dun and Bradstreet, broadcasters' logs, trade associations, other voluntary "conferences," governmental sources such as the Departments of Commerce, Defense, and Agriculture, public news releases, and purchased intelligence reports—just to mention a few.

The major problems associated with securing external information are locating and evaluating the reliability of the available information. These topics are discussed in Chapters 12 and 13.

### *Composite Effort Measurements*

A number of useful composite measurements can be computed when marketing effort information is available. A firm that has information about both its own and all other sellers' (industry) efforts can compute *effort share.* Effort share is the per cent of total efforts (of all sellers) put forth by an individual firm. When detailed information by type of effort is available, measurements such as advertising effort shares can be computed. And when a firm possesses measures of efforts by individual firms, it can rank the various companies' efforts. The nature of these composite measurements should be sufficiently clear from the prior discussions of market share, market position, and effort share.

These comments, of course, are not meant to suggest that all firms (or even most firms) will find all or even any of these measures sufficiently beneficial to offset their costs. This will depend both on the costs and on the benefits. What this does suggest is the many information alternatives, and their relationships, that are to be found on the sellers' side of the market.

## INFORMATION FROM THE BUYERS' SIDE

The buyers' side of a market, as previously indicated, is composed of all present and prospective customers for an offering. For example, the buyers' side of the market for various brands of household dishwasher detergents would be composed of all households that use automatic dishwashers. The buyers' side for an offering such as coin-operated, commercial dry-cleaning equipment would be composed of people who presently are customers or who might seriously contemplate ownership of such equipment. The buyers' side of a market is *not* always easy to identify, but, then, that is one of the problems to be examined in this section of the book. For now suffice it to say that customers and prospective customers need to be identified and, oftentimes, grouped by segments.

Information from and about the buyers' side of a market can be divided into two separate parts: (1) potential and (2) customer behavior. These information facets are shown on the right side of Figure 8-2.

## Potential

Potential refers to the *capacity* of markets to purchase and/or consume the offerings of the sellers. Another term occasionally used in place of potential is opportunity. Potential or opportunity is basically a quantitative measure or estimate either of the absolute or of the relative number of units that a market segment has capacity to buy or use in a specified period.

Some persons divide measures of potential into *market* potential and *sales* potential. *Market* potential refers to the *capacity* of the various segments of the market to buy or use the offerings from *all* of the sellers. In other words, it is an all-sellers' (industry) measure relating to a specific offering, a specified geographical market, and a peroid of time. Sales potential is described as a measurement that indicates the share of market potential for an individual seller.

This brief discussion has only attempted to define and describe the term *potential,* so as to enable the reader to see its fit relative to other facets of *continually collected information.* Potential, including various ways to measure it, is discussed in Chapter 14.

## Customer Behavior Information

Customer behavior information is concerned with (1) *behavior* of customers and (2) *explanations* for their behavior. There is much concern with identifying the various groups or segments of customers that populate the buyers' side of a market, how these segments behave relative to an offering, and why they behave as they do. In Figure 8-2 these aspects of customer behavior are divided into *patterns* (how customers behave) and *explanations* (why they behave so).

Information on customer behavior is different from measures of potential. Potentials are used to measure *consumption capacity.* Behavior information, on the other hand, delves into the customers' actual actions, responses, and associated explanations. Measures of potential and customer behavior information complement, not duplicate, each other, and knowledge of one aids in securing and understanding the other. They aid management in predicting both the aggregate magnitude of responses and the form of responses that will arise from markets.

### *Patterns of Behavior*

Patterns of behavior are concerned with the offerings that buyers have considered or bought, and when, where, and how they considered or bought them. The focal point is what has happened on the buyers' side of a market relative to the offerings, efforts, and environments. That is, the concern is with customer behavior and not with explanations for behavior. Studies of customer behavior provide information on (1) brand loyalty, (2) reactions to advertising and other elements of an offering, (3) prepurchase considerations and behavior, and (4) specifics of buying behavior—places, frequencies, times, and numerous other details not available through sales analysis.

Brand loyalty. Brand loyalty (or brand switching) information is concerned with patterns of repeat purchases for specific brands.[7] For example, purchasers of toilet tissue, dinner napkins, and facial tissues exhibit little brand loyalty. They tend to switch among various available brands. However, some brands, even among these products, tend to receive considerable repeat-purchase loyalty. Kleenex brand facial tissues and Crown Zellerbach dinner napkins are two such brands. Some customers appear to be continual switchers in numerous product categories, while others remain uniformly loyal (Tucker, 1964). Information on patterns of loyalties (Farley, 1964) and lack of loyalties can be very useful to management.

Reactions to company offerings. The buyers' side of a market reacts to sellers' efforts in numerous ways in addition to making purchases. Some of this information is needed anew by management on a frequent if not continuous basis. For example, numerous companies buy Starch, Nielsen, and other evaluations of their own and other companys' advertising campaigns. These evaluations report on such things as the incidence and extent of seeing, hearing, and/or remembering various advertisements.

Also, information about buyers' *knowledge* of such things as products, prices, and product use is useful. Pharmaceutical companies, for example, are very sensitive to physicians' awareness of their brand names, as well as to attitudes about the efficacy of their products.

[7] For two early studies of brand loyalty, see Banks (1950) and Cunningham (1956).

Specifics of buying behavior. To make decisions, management must know such things as *who* purchased the product, *when, where,* and the *frequency of purchase.* However, typical *sales* data available through firms' records are too aggregate to disclose purchase clusterings, frequencies, or other specifics of buying behavior.

An important task is identification of *users*—more specifically, the heavy users. It is believed that about 70 per cent of the aspirin purchased in the United States is accounted for by less than 30 per cent of the purchasers. Somewhat similar statistics are believed to prevail for numerous other consumer as well as industrial offerings. The same pertains to when, where, and how customers buy. Aggregate sales data available in a firm may indicate sales by types of outlet and by time periods. However, more detailed behavior information is needed to make decisions about in-store display locations, specifics of advertisement timing, and so forth.

Prepurchase considerations and behavior. Prepurchase considerations and behavior information are concerned with who decides what products and brands are to be purchased, how various offerings are compared, and the numerous other decision-making activities leading up to the actual decisions. Housewives, for example, *purchase* a major share of such products as breakfast foods and beer. But *how* are various brands selected and by *whom?* Purchasing agents frequently only place purchase orders that have been instigated by other members of the organization. Obviously, aggregate sales data do not disclose this information—and it is needed.

### *Collecting Information on Patterns of Behavior*

Information about patterns of customer behavior is collected in many ways. Commercial research firms, which search, secure, and transmit information on a weekly or monthly subscription basis, may be used. Company salesmen and detail men may be employed, and some firms find consumer panels and diary reports very informative. The basic problem is to tap the source of behavior—the customers. And customers must be observed in sufficient quantity to enable sellers to detect existing patterns of behavior.

The *frequency* of collection of information on behavior is largely dependent on the stability of customers' behavior and the various stimuli. For example, the type of advertising evaluation information collected by Starch and Nielsen is needed frequently because advertising campaigns and buyers' responses change frequently. In contrast, consumer behavior relative to packaged table salt remains relatively stable and, consequently, information as to when, where, and how it is purchased can be collected infrequently.

Customer behavior information that is collected frequently is treated in this book as *continually collected information.* The searching-securing, transmitting, analyzing, and handling of such information encourage planned, routinized information programs. In contrast, infrequently collected behavioral type of information is treated as *special-problem information.*

### *Explanative Information*

Explanations basically attempt to answer *why* various groups of customers show certain patterns of behavior. For example, why do certain segments of buyers demonstrate high loyalty for brands of automatic dishwasher detergent, but at the same time switch brands of detergent and soap used in washing machines? Why do certain groups of people use aspirin? Why do some people prefer cigars to cigarettes or pipes and other people use no tobacco products? Explanations for these and numerous other behavior patterns of buyers are sought as an aid in predicting future behavior. Coupled with patterns of behavior they can be quite helpful.

Explanatory information, as a rule, is more difficult to secure, to analyze, and to use than is information on behavior patterns. The information tends to be more difficult to search and secure because customers have both less knowledge of why they have behaved in certain ways and more difficulty in communicating the "why" explanations. Also, they appear to be more secretive and less willing to expose their reasons for behavior. For example, there is evidence that men who will not travel by aircraft carrier, when asked why, give answers that are not equivalent to admitting fear. However, when the question is rephrased and they are asked if they have friends who do not travel by airplane and, if so, why not, fear does appear in their answers as a major consideration—for their friends only, of course (Ferber and Wales, 1958).

Also, analysis has been complicated by answers' being sought where none are available. For instance, if people are asked why they like ice cream—aside from its sweet flavor and coolness—or why they prefer a specific color, number, or size, once the surface-level answers are exhausted, there is little need for further probing, because there are no further answers. Yet explanatory answers are wanted and questions are asked, and confused analysts have tried to replace the poor and cursory answer information with depth analysis. All of this has added to the confusion surrounding the searching and securing, transmitting, analyzing, and using of explanatory information.[8]

[8] Not all writers would agree with this statement; for example, see Packard (1957).

When explanative information is collected and used as a continuous part of routine decision-making situations, it fits into the category of *continually collected information.* An appropriate illustration is the information provided by "warranty return card" questionnaires, which ask such questions as the following:

Why did you purchase this product?

1. For a gift?
2. For your own use?
3. As a replacement for a worn-out unit?

Considerable explanatory information is *not* collected on a continuing basis. Then it is *special-problem information.*

## ON-LINE, REAL-TIME SYSTEMS

*Continually collected information* can be collected, analyzed, and transmitted periodically in batches; or, at the other extreme, individual transactions can be noted and immediately transmitted and used without any batching activity. The latter, live-operation information is often referred to as on-line, real-time (OLRT) information.[9] The OLRT *systems* are those in which numerous inflows of OLRT information are considered together to arrive at various decisions.

The SABRE program (Parker, 1965) used by American Airlines is a OLRT passenger reservation system. Each reservation request is transmitted directly to a computer and, based on information already stored in the computer, is either confirmed or rejected, with the remaining space-available figure in the storage unit modified accordingly. A computer has been programmed to make the routine decisions. The benefits from a closed SABRE-type reservation system are obvious. Decisions are made in light of knowledge of current conditions, and the company can give immediate reservation responses. Other OLRT systems have been established to control machine tools in manufacturing operations, to control chemical process operations, and to control some other manufacturing processes and reservation systems.

The present-day practicality of OLRT handling of masses of marketing information is questionable. There is, on the one hand, the technological state of the art in terms of both hardware and software. A company must have available a computer with a large storage capacity and with

[9] On-line means compiling information instantaneously as events occur. Real-time means supplying the information to managers so that they can control the operation within the short or instantaneous period.

random access capabilities. Problems of use are also complex in that a company must be able to adequately program all inputs and outputs of information so that data can be found, used, and updated on command. Both adequate computer and adequate programming capabilities are expensive.

OLRT systems, to be practical, must provide sufficient benefits in the form of better decisions and faster responses to justify the added cost as compared to batch-processing information systems. Currently three major factors limit the benefits to be obtained through the use of OLRT information. First, in most open marketing system situations, only incomplete parts of the total necessary decision information can be available on a real-time basis. In such situations most of the real-time advantages are lost as decision makers wait for batched information. A second major difficulty associated with OLRT systems is the inability of real-time users to react on an individual activity basis. Most marketing operations are set up on a batch basis. The final customer may buy individual units, but channel orders, shipments, inventories, payments, and most other marketing operations are more economically handled on a batch basis. Finally, there is little need to be able to make decisions much faster than an organization can respond. If coats, for example, can be shipped to Chicago only once a day, there is little point in making numerous decisions throughout the day. Instead, information should be batched until the one time at which the best decisions can be made.

It should be clear that *continually collected information* can be either batched (over various time periods) or treated on a OLRT basis. The length of the batch period (if any) is dependent principally on managements' use of the information. Finally, batching systems under today's technology are much less costly than are OLRT systems.[10]

## FUTURE INFORMATION

Future information is merely information about the future, that is, about future events and experiences. Up to this point the discussion has focused on information about past events and experiences, including OLRT information. With past information, the central focus is on accurately observing, recording, and analyzing situations either when they occur or after they occur. Clearly, the distinguishing characteristic of

[10] The reader seeking more information as well as other points of view concerning on-line and real-time information is referred to Blumenthal (1965), Dearden (1966), Hartmann (1965), Parker (1965), and Ream (1964).

information about the future is that it is about situations that have not yet occurred. In turn, some additional techniques and tools are necessary that are not needed in connection with past information.

Future information is a necessary ingredient of *planning*. Basically, an organization wants to *foresee* (1) the environment in which it must operate, (2) the alternative lines of action that will be available, and (3) the ways in which the environment (including other firms in a market) will react to various actions. Then the firm can make plans, or, in other words, select objectives and prescribe what appears to be the most advantageous course of action, so that its resources can be marshalled in anticipation of the activities.

In that much of the total marketing effort must be launched some time in advance of its scheduled impact, there is no need to argue the merits of planning, as contrasted with no planning. Such an argument and listing of advantages would be akin to listing the merits of a person breathing or not breathing. The meaningful questions about planning are basically the following. (1) When should it be done (relative to when the events are scheduled to occur)? (2) What information should be used? (3) How should the information be used and the planning accomplished? Question 2 pertains most directly to the material in this book, while questions 1 and 3 pertain more directly to discussions of planning and managing per se.

The *controlling* of activities also partakes of both past and future information. That is, plans serve as guidelines to be used in controlling operations. Controlling involves frequent if not continuous checking of outcomes against anticipated events. Replanning and redirecting come about through comparison of past events. In other words, and this is the main point, planning and controlling (decision-making)[11] activities all require information about the future as well as about the past.

Management wants future information about each major piece of past information. These major types of future information are depicted on Figure 8-2. Such information includes (1) all sellers and own firm sales, (2) market shares and ranks, (3) effort expenditures, (4) effort shares and ranks, (5) market potential, and (6) customer behavior patterns. Management also wants to foresee economic, social, and psychological conditions.

Obviously, some of the information pertains to environmental variables that are totally beyond the control of the predicting organizations. In other cases, the individual firm can exercise some degree of control over variables. For example, market potential cannot be influenced by the

[11] Decision making is defined as choosing among alternative courses of action.

individual firm. In contrast, the firm can control, within some limits, the amount to be spent on marketing efforts. In general, the more control a firm has over a variable (or set of variables), the more accurately the outcome can be predicted.

The methods, tools, and techniques employed in estimating future events and experiences are discussed in Chapter 15.

## MARKETING RESEARCH PROCEDURES[12]

One last topic that is concerned with providing a perspective on marketing information remains to be discussed in this chapter: *marketing research procedures.*

Before any information is collected in any study, researchers must first establish their objectives. It is essential that researchers ascertain exactly what information is to be obtained and in what manner this information is to be used. It is for this reason that the last section of this perspective chapter is devoted to a discussion of a set of marketing research procedures that are designed to guide the collection and use of information.

The reader is reminded of an earlier discussion (Chapter 3) that contained comments on problem-solving models. Those earlier comments certainly should not be forgotten. In fact, the procedures outlined in this section are designed to make the earlier comments more operational for all information situations.

Research studies differ considerably, but virtually all marketing research is approachable through more or less common procedures. These procedures, which are outlined below, provide operational guidelines, whether research involves experimental designs, makes use of survey designs, or deals with continually collected or special-problem information.

1. Identify and define the problems.
2. Formulate the problems into hypotheses.
3. Plan a research design to test the hypotheses.
4. Collect and tabulate the data.
5. Analyze and interpret the information.
6. Present the findings to prospective users.

### Identify and Define the Problems

An investigator, upon arriving on a scene, is *not* usually confronted with a clear-cut identification and definition of the problems at hand.

[12] These procedures provide a framework from the long-standing, often-used book, *Marketing and Distribution Research,* by Lyndon O. Brown (1955).

Instead, like a physician, he is confronted with conflicting bits and particles of symptoms and other information. The initial situation must be carefully observed, so that the problems can be identified and defined and made less general. The marketing researcher, like the physician, cannot succeed by treating either symptoms or general problems. He must be able to make sufficient observations and gain sufficient knowledge of the situation to be able to identify and define specific and basic problems. In other words, either implicitly or explicitly, he must abstract the crucial considerations from the real world and construct a model or models.

The physician, for example, may know that the general problem is that his patient is sick. Similarly, the marketing investigator may know that some segment of a business is sick. In both situations the general problems must be identified and defined into specific problems. General problems do not afford solutions.

Often an investigator starts by discerning the seriousness of the illness. He does this by relating present measurements to past, predicted present, and competitive measurements. Then he attempts to identify specific problems that contribute to the illness. For example, many a researcher has sought answers to the following types of questions:

1. How does the promotional program compare with past and competitive programs?
2. How does the product line compare with past and competitive offerings?

In general, the researcher must ask specific questions about both the company's operations and the various aspects of the environment in which it operates. He must move from the general and ambiguously defined problems to a series of more specific problems whose dimensions can be carefully defined.

He moves from the general to the specific by first acquainting himself with the general situation. He, so to speak, learns the language of the problem situation by examining both the secondary and the internal information that is available. As he learns more about the situation, he begins to tentatively identify the problems, and he ranges further afield, asking more questions and seeking more information to further identify and define the problems and opportunities.

Obviously there are no set amounts of time, money, and contacts required. Some situations move rapidly from the starting point to problem identification and definition; other situations virtually defy diagnosis. In any event, the investigator cannot move on to the formulation of operating hypotheses until he has tentatively identified and defined the specific problems. That is, as a first stage he must abstract the too complex and general world into models he can think about and work with.

### Formulate the Problems into Hypotheses

The second stage of the research procedure involves transforming the specific problems into hypotheses that can be tested. Basically, hypotheses are tentative explanations about some specific events. In Chapter 6 we viewed briefly the use of hypotheses (and null hypotheses) in statistical decision-making settings. We hypothesized that the market share of a new product, if it were introduced, would be above 10 per cent. As a null hypothesis, we stated that the market share for the new product, if the firm introduced it, would be below 10 per cent.

Hypotheses are used to direct research investigations and in so doing to limit the scope of investigations. The market share hypothesis mentioned above directs the study so that the researcher will *not* investigate market potential, market rank, or other aspects of the problem that do not bear directly on the decision to introduce or not introduce the product. Furthermore, it focuses attention on the crucial interval immediately around 10 per cent market share.

Hypotheses, to be of maximum use in marketing, must be *testable*. We could state, for example, that a current advertising campaign had increased company *profits* by, say, at least 40 per cent. Or, as a null hypothesis, we could state that a current advertising campaign had *not* increased company profits by 40 per cent. Unfortunately, regardless of which form it takes, this hypothesis virtually defies testing. It is almost impossible to bring evidence to bear on the hypothesis. A hypothesis more subject to testing would be that, say, 45 per cent or more of the market is aware of our product. This hypothesis, however, would be useful only insofar as it gave proper direction to the study.

How do testable hypotheses arise? Basically they come about from the information and intuition that the researcher can bring to bear on a specific problem. In Chapter 6 we suggested that they might arise from analogies, implicit theories, historical data, experiments, and/or surveys. A person, for example, observes that his automobile does not start. He turns on the car radio to assess the condition of the car battery, he tries the starter, he switches on the ignition and views the gas gauge, he raises the hood of the car and searches for loose wires or other unusual conditions. These observations are his search for alternating explanations for the condition that he has noticed. He may hypothesize that replacement of the old battery with a new one will allow the car to start.

How could a company arrive at a hypothesis that stated that the company could attain at least a 10 per cent market share if it introduced a new product? Such a hypothesis could be based on demand and cost estimates and analysis, brought together through a model. In turn, the model might indicate that a market share of 10 per cent or more would produce sufficient profit for the company and one below 10 per cent would not.

## Planning the Research Design

Stated very simply, planning the research design involves finding the most appropriate way(s) to test the hypotheses. That is, the focal points of this stage are the hypotheses, and the major activity is planning the remainder of the research investigation. To accomplish this stage, the investigator must discern the types and sources of information that are needed for testing the hypotheses. He must discern the type of design (e.g., survey or experiment) that is most appropriate in testing the hypotheses. Units to be observed must be selected, and appropriate data collection instruments must be drawn up and tested. The investigator must ascertain, with some degree of confidence, that the called-for information, if collected, will actually test the hypotheses. Finally, he must estimate the costs of testing.

## Collecting and Tabulating Data

Once plans are completed, an investigator must proceed to collect and tabulate information. Many a researcher has complained about the messiness of empirical data; this stage is the first stage where he will be wallowing in data, unless adequate advance precautions have been taken. More specifically, the investigator should have a perspective rendering model in mind. Also, he must be certain that the data collection is appropriate, uniform, and on schedule in all markets. Consistent measuring instruments and methods must be used among the various units to be observed so as to make findings comparable.

Precoding of data collection forms can provide meaningful time savings when data flow back to the investigator. Precoding is merely on-data collection form coding, which tells the persons tabulating the incoming responses how to transform the information onto punch cards or other data-handling devices. A precoded page from a questionnaire is illustrated in Figure 8-3.

Editing of data-collection instruments at several points is desirable. The field observer should examine each form to make certain that it is readable and free of omissions. Also, an editor at the central collection

Part A—Page 3

3. C. Parking:

1. Is parking space: (check *one* in each column)

| *Near motel office:* | *Near motel units:* | *Parking area surface:* |
|---|---|---|
| ___Spacious | ___Spacious (one per unit) | ___Paved |
| ___Adequate | ___Adequate | ___Gravel |
| ___Limited | ___Limited | ___Dirt |
| ___None | ___None | |

2. Garages or carports:
*Provided for each unit:* Adjacent to unit___ In common cluster___ *None:*___

D. Landscaping: (check X appropriate spaces)

| | *Appearance* Good | *Fair* | *Poor* | *None* |
|---|---|---|---|---|
| Lawns | ___ | ___ | ___ | ___ |
| Trees | ___ | ___ | ___ | ___ |
| Shrubs | ___ | ___ | ___ | ___ |
| Fencing | ___ | ___ | ___ | ___ |
| Other: ________ | | | | |

E. Auxiliary Features (Outside)
(check if present and advertised)
*Check X if*

| *Present* | *Advert.* | |
|---|---|---|
| ___ | ___ | Swimming pool |
| ___ | ___ | Children's playground |
| ___ | ___ | Night flood lights |
| ___ | ___ | Trailer park |

(Number of spaces________)

4. ADVERTISING:

A. Which of the following features are advertised?
Note: Part B provides a section for you to ask management if these features are present in the motel and management's opinion of the value of such features. All we want here is to know if these are advertised and how.

| *Check X if advertised* *In front* | *Elsewhere* | |
|---|---|---|
| ___ | ___ | Restaurant |
| ___ | ___ | Cocktail lounge |
| ___ | ___ | Gift shop |
| ___ | ___ | Ice maker |
| ___ | ___ | Soft-drink dispenser |
| ___ | ___ | Television |
| ___ | ___ | Room phones |
| ___ | ___ | Refrig. Air Cond. |
| ___ | ___ | Air cooled |
| ___ | ___ | Meeting rooms |
| ___ | ___ | Local service clubs |

Which one(s)?________

| *Check X if advertised* *In front* | *Elsewhere* | |
|---|---|---|
| ___ | ___ | Kitchenettes |
| ___ | ___ | Pets allowed (or not?) |
| ___ | ___ | Room service |
| ___ | ___ | Valet service |
| ___ | ___ | Coffee served free |
| ___ | ___ | Rental rates |
| ___ | ___ | Credit cards accepted |

Which one(s)?________

| ___ | ___ | Referral Assn. |
|---|---|---|

Which one(s)?________

| ___ | ___ | State Assn. |
|---|---|---|

Which one?________

B. What types, sizes and heights of signs are used in front?

| *Type* | *Check if present* | *Size (ft. × ft.)* | *Height (feet)* | *Visibility from road* Good | *Fair* | *Poor* | *Physical Appearance* Good | *Fair* | *Poor* |
|---|---|---|---|---|---|---|---|---|---|
| Neon | | | | | | | | | |
| Marquee | | | | | | | | | |
| Animated | | | | | | | | | |
| Painted | | | | | | | | | |
| Billboard: | | | | | | | | | |
| Lighted | | | | | | | | | |
| Unlighted | | | | | | | | | |
| Other: ________ | | | | | | | | | |

C. How does sample motel's advertising compare with nearest competitors? (if any)
Better___ Same___ Worse___ Comment:________

D. Is the motel office clearly marked? Yes___ Fair___ No___

*CONTROL:* Date:________, 1960
Interviewer: ________
Photo: Roll___ Exposure___
*or* Post card attached___

OFFICE: Edited by:________
Reviewed by:________
Punched by:________
Verified by:________

*Card 1*
51___ 52___ 53___ 54___ 55___ 56___ 57___ 58___ 59___ 60___ 61___ 62___ 63___ 64___ 65___ 66___ 67___ 68___ 69___ 70___ 71___ 72___ 73___ 74___ 75___ 76___ 77___ 78___ 79___ 80___

*Card 2*
11___ 12___ 13___ 14___ 15–16 ___ 17___ 18–19 ___ 20___ 21___ 22___ 23___ 24___ 25___ 26___ 27___ 28___ 29___ 30___ 31___ 32___ 33___ 34___ 35___ 36–39 ___ 40–43 ___ 44___

**Figure 8-3** Precoded questionnaire.

point must ascertain that the responses are internally consistent on individual collection instruments and among all forms handled by each field source. The editor can identify obvious errors and omissions and make corrections that otherwise might eliminate information. At other times the best that he can do is to block the entrance and use of doubtful data.

Tabulation alternatives are often available. They are dependent on such considerations as the amount of information to be recorded, the form in which it appears (e.g., open-end questions, projective techniques[13]), the number of cross tabulations that will be needed, and investigators' personal preferences. Ferber and Verdoorn (1962) have suggested that hand tabulation is appropriate for small-scale studies (300 or fewer observational units). Also, hand tabulation may be preferable when depth interviews, projective techniques, or numerous open-end questions are employed and are complimented by need for few tabulations and a plentiful supply of clerical labor. Mechanical tabulations are preferred under more or less opposite conditions. Quite clearly, cost is the major consideration on jobs that can be handled in a number of different ways.

## Analyzing and Interpreting Information

The investigator must once again come face to face with the "messiness" of empirical data. Data do not neatly fit preenvisaged explanation patterns. Instead, as initially received and simply tabulated, data often display masses of nothingness. At other times as patterns emerge from early tabulations and simple analyses, disruptive and deviant forces may be observed in the findings. Clear-cut, black-and-white findings do not often emerge of their own accord from empirical data. Investigators must be equipped to analyze and interpret their information relative to their models.

Analysis takes many forms and shapes. It ranges all the way from simple cross tabulations to very complex statistical analysis designed to help display various features of the data. Some of the analytical techniques have already been discussed, particularly in Chapters 4 through 6. The key consideration in this chapter, however, is simply what is best called the *analytical ability* of the investigator. This, basically, is his ability to view a total problem (through the use of either an implicit or an explicit model), collected data, the already proposed hypotheses—and their tests—and to be able to conceive other plausible relationships and explanations in the information. Then he must be able to test for these relationships.

[13] These techniques are discussed in Chapters 10 and 11.

The analytical aspects of a study depend largely on the nature of the specific problems and the directing hypotheses. If only one hypothesis is being tested—for example, "new product, $x$, will be able to gain at least 10 per cent market share"—the analysis is limited to the statement set forth in the hypothesis. Such an analysis and interpretation employing both a classical and a Bayesian approach are presented in Chapter 6.

Intermediate interpretation is part and parcel of analysis. An investigator is continually looking at his information and asking what it means. In doing this he is interpreting the information. Such intermediate interpretation moves an investigator into further analysis. In addition, though, when the findings are all in and the analyses and intermediate interpretations are complete, an investigator must conclude by relating the findings to the problem. That is, he must make his final interpretation.

A word of warning is appropriate because of man's love to make sweeping and dramatic interpretations. An investigator's findings are most relevant to a specific problem, in a specific location, and under specific conditions at some point in time. These interpretations should be presented first with the specific conditions in view. Then, but only then, should the investigator interpret his findings more generally—expanding beyond the initial confines, but, of course, with far less confidence. This is done separately, after the principal interpretations have been established.

## Communication of Findings to Prospective Users

Communication of findings to prospective users is the final stage of the set of research procedures. Just like each of the other stages, it is crucial to the successful completion of a study. It is a truism, but yet in need of saying that *unused findings are useless findings.*

The findings can be presented in a number of alternative ways. In some situations the new findings are used to update the older information within the system. When more unique, special-problem information has been secured and warrants decision makers' immediate and direct attention, two or more different reports typically are used. A technical report explaining the research design and presenting detailed supporting findings is prepared for critical evaluation. A so-called "popular report," with major emphasis on producing sufficient impact to gain adoption of the major recommendations, is prepared for those who are interested principally in the findings. Of course, it is not unusual for individuals to be interested in both the popular and the technical reports.

*The Technical Report*[14]

This report emphasizes research design, important assumptions, detailed findings, and major limitations and supporting data. Although it is a technical report, it should be as readable as possible.

The following outline is suggested:

1. Summary of the findings—a brief review of the major findings.
2. Nature of the investigation—the general objectives of the investigation, the hypotheses, the general types and sources of data and analysis, and so forth.
3. Methods employed—both the specific methods (e.g., sample design, selection of test units) and explanations of modifications and compromises that were made.
4. The data—their sources, characteristics, limitations, difficulties of collection, and so forth. Data-collection forms normally are referred to here, but become a physical part of the technical appendix.
5. Analysis of the data and detailed findings—all of the findings, with supporting data in tables and charts. This is the main body of the report.
6. Conclusion—a *detailed* summary of the findings and their limitations and implications relative to the focal problem of the investigation.
7. Bibliography.
8. Technical appendixes—explanations of specific statistical techniques and/or measurement devices used in the investigation.
9. Supplemental tables—general background material that is not considered to be sufficiently relevant to appear in the body of the report.

*The Popular Report*

This report focuses on *communication* of the major findings and recommendations. In turn, it must talk the receivers' language and be in a form that they can readily comprehend. However, it *cannot* be permitted to distort the findings through incomplete reporting or "artsy" emphasis.

The following outline is suggested:

1. Findings and implications—with a strong emphasis on the findings of the most practical interest and on their operational implications.
2. Recommendations for action—this part, which may be a part of item 1, makes positive recommendations for action.
3. Objectives of the study—a brief review of how the study arose and the resulting objectives.

[14] These guidelines are drawn from Ferber and Verdoorn (1962).

4. Methods employed—a brief nontechnical (to the audience) description of the method used.

5. Results—the body of the report, presenting the results in clear, nontechnical terms.

6. Technical appendixes—more detailed information on the methods employed and on the results.

7. Supplementary tables—tables pertinent to the study, but too detailed to appear earlier.

The popular report can be written, oral, or, as is typically best, presented in an oral-graphic manner together with a written popular report which can stand alone for later review.

## SUMMARY

The central purpose of this chapter has been to provide a useful *perspective* or *overview* of marketing information for decision making. There are many ways in which such information can be viewed or classified. To properly accumulate, order, and show relationships, the various information particles have been discussed in terms of their frequency of collection and use and in terms of their source locations relative to the (1) market and (2) using organization. According to the first view, information arises from the buyers' or sellers' side of the market or some combination thereof. According to the last view, information is internal or external to the using organization.

Information arising from the sellers' side of a market can be divided into the categories of (1) sales and (2) efforts. Major *sales* information includes own-firm and other sellers' sales, as well as market share and market position. Major marketing *effort* information includes own-firm efforts, other sellers' efforts, and effort share and effort rank.

Information arising from the buyers' side of the market has been divided into measures of potential and customer behavior. Potential can be further divided into *market* and *sales* potential. Customer behavior has been separated into patterns of *behavior* and *explanations* for behavior. Other measurements of marketing activities and market reactions can be gained, but the ones mentioned here are generally considered to be the most useful.

Future information, or, in other words, information about future events, has received separate treatment. Basically—in addition to information on past events—management wants estimates or predictions relative to the outcome of virtually all of these events in a certain future period. Such future information is largely dependent on the availability of adequate past information coupled with appropriate forecasting procedures.

All of the information facets discussed in this perspective chapter that need further explanation will be discussed in the chapters that follow. The next chapter is devoted to a discussion of collection of internal sales and marketing cost information.

## REFERENCES

Alderson, W., & Green, P. *Planning and Problem Solving in Marketing,* Homewood, Ill.: Richard D. Irwin, 1964.

Alexander, R., & Berg, T. *Dynamic Management in Marketing,* Homewood, Ill.: Richard D. Irwin, 1965.

Banks, S. "The Relationships Between Preference and Purchase of Brands," *Journal of Marketing,* October 1950, pp. 145–157.

Blumenthal, S. C. "Management in Real Time," *Data Processing Magazine,* August 1965, pp. 18–23.

Brown, L. *Marketing and Distribution Research,* (3rd ed.) New York: Ronald Press, 1955.

Cunningham, R. "Brand Loyalty—What, Where, How Much?" *Harvard Business Review,* January-February 1956, pp. 116–128.

Davidson, W. "Channels of Distribution—One Aspect of Marketing Strategy," *Business Horizons,* Special Issue, 1961, pp. 84–90.

Dearden, J. "Myth of Real-Time Management Information," *Harvard Business Review,* May-June 1966, pp. 123–132.

*Des Moines Register*. Des Moines, Ia.: Des Moines Register and Tribune, January 4, 1966.

Farley, J. "Why Does Brand Loyalty Vary Over Products," *Journal of Marketing Research,* **I,** November 1964, pp. 9–14.

Ferber, R., & Verdoorn, P., *Research Methods in Economics and Business,* New York: Macmillan, 1962.

Ferber, R., & Wales, H. (Eds.) *Motivation and Market Behavior,* Homewood, Ill.: Richard D. Irwin, 1958.

Hartmann, H. C. "Management Control in Real Time is the Objective," *Systems,* September 1965, pp. 26–28.

Howard, J. *Marketing Management: Analysis and Planning,* (Rev. ed.) Homewood, Ill.: Richard D. Irwin, 1963.

Jastram, R. N. "A Treatment of Distributed Lags in the Theory of Advertising Expenditure," *Journal of Marketing,* July 1955, pp. 36–46.

Kotler, P. *Marketing Management: Analysis, Planning, and Control,* Englewood Cliffs, N. J.: Prentice-Hall, 1967.

Oxenfeldt, A. "How to Use Market-Share Measurement," *Harvard Business Review,* January-February 1959, pp. 86–95.

Packard, V. *The Hidden Persuaders,* New York: David McKay, 1957.

Parker, R. W. "The SABRE System," *Datamation,* September 1965, pp. 49–52.

Ream, N. J. "On-Line Management Information: Part One—Planning a System," *Datamation,* March 1964, pp. 27–30; "Part Two—Installation and Implementation," April 1964, pp. 39–50.

Rogers, E. M. *Diffusion of Innovation.* New York: Free Press of Glencoe, 1962.

Semlow, W. "How Many Salesmen Do You Need?" *Harvard Business Review,* May-June 1959, pp. 126–132.

Tucker, W. "The Development of Loyalty," *Journal of Marketing Research,* August 1964, pp. 32–35.

Tull, D. "The Carry-over Effect of Advertising," *Journal of Marketing,* April 1965, pp. 46–53.

*Nine*

# Securing Internal Sales and Cost Information

Business organizations spend large amounts of money on many marketing activities. In a recent year the Proctor and Gamble Company spent more than $466 million for selling and administration expenses out of total expenditures of $605 million. Ford Motor Company, for selling and administrative expenses, spent more than $640 million out of total expenses of $1512 million. Anheuser-Busch Brewing Company spent $64 million for selling and administrative expenses out of total expenses of about $86 million. These figures are typical of large manufacturers selling consumer products.[1] Marketing costs are greater than manufacturing costs in many industries, such as the tobacco, soap, toiletry, patent medicine, and some food product industries.

Furthermore, most manufacturers' sales are generated from a variety of products sold to many customers in numerous geographical markets. Manufacturers' marketing *costs* and *sales* are dynamic and complex and arise out of numerous activities and locations.

Securing adequate internal information for decision making has been difficult. Horngren (1967, p. 299) has written:

> One of the roughest duties of the accountant is to devise a convincing scheme for assigning costs to the various parts of an organization for appraisal of performance, product costing, and special decisions.

It has been common for some business organizations to simply ignore all *but* their aggregate net sales figures and to classify their marketing costs only by the objective of the expenditure.

[1] For more information on companies in these various industries, see St. Clair (1966).

The purpose of this chapter is to view the problems and the ways of providing decision makers with relevant internal *sales* and marketing *cost* information. The chapter is divided into four sections. The first one is concerned with traditional accounting information. The second section examines the topic of information segments. The third section looks at sales analyses, and the final section discusses measuring marketing costs.

## TRADITIONAL ACCOUNTING INFORMATION

The traditional accounting approach has kept track of costs by object of expenditure such as payroll, payroll tax, taxes, heat and power, telephone, and materials. Table 9-1, an income statement is illustrative of the summary type of information output. (Supporting statements would provide somewhat more detailed information.)

This approach and the resulting information are of more than historical interest because virtually every business firm, for internal and external reporting, possesses such information. Information about marketing activities exists as a by-product. Consequently, decision makers should ask (1) what information is available and (2) how it can be used.

### Available Information

Sales information tends to be joint for several products, if not product lines. Indeed, decision makers are fortunate when there are detailed underlying accounting structures that disclose sales by various brands, packages, package sizes, and so forth. Also, it is unusual to find accounting reports that detail sales information as to the types or locations of various customers.

The same general statements also hold true relative to costs. The various accounts (by object of expenditure) have been established and allocations made to them, in order to *account* for costs. These accounts have *not* been established to provide information about marketing. Such output is incidental. Admittedly, statements for external reporting (such as Table 9-1) do not disclose all of the detailed underlying accounting information. However, the fact still remains that little internal reporting has been available for use in making marketing decisions.[2]

[2] Some companies with distinct product lines and with separate sales forces and separate advertising programs prepare detailed operating statements by product lines. Also, some companies with distinct territory divisions prepare detailed operating statements by major divisions (Horngren, 1967, p. 305).

**Table 9-1** Income Statement for Year Ended December 31, 1967; Zebra Manufacturing Corporation

| | | | |
|---|---|---|---|
| Gross sales | | | $5,742,000 |
| Less: return sales and allowances | | | 78,000 |
| Net sales | | | $5,664,000 |
| Cost of goods sold | | | |
| Finished goods inventory, January 1, 1967 | | $ 313,500 | |
| Cost of Production for Year | | 2,757,270 | |
| Finished goods available for sale | | $3,070,770 | |
| Finished goods inventory, December 31, 1967 | | 186,000 | |
| Cost of goods sold | | | $2,884,770 |
| Gross profit | | | 2,779,230 |
| Selling expenses | | | |
| Advertising and sales promotion | $ 478,627 | | |
| Sales salaries | 1,153,058 | | |
| Sales travel expense | 195,802 | | |
| Sales office expense | 348,093 | | |
| | | $2,175,580 | |
| Administrative expense | | | |
| Office and officers' salaries | $ 302,800 | | |
| Stationery and supplies | 35,230 | | |
| Office taxes | 15,836 | | |
| General office operating expense | 65,434 | | |
| Bad debt expense | 23,500 | | |
| Depreciation | 2,500 | | |
| | | $ 445,300 | |
| Other expenses | | | |
| Federal income taxes | $ 24,250 | | |
| Interest expenses | 36,550 | $ 60,800 | $2,681,680 |
| Net income for year ended December 31, 1967 | | | $ 97,550 |

*Source:* Hypothetical.

Before internal accounting information can be used in marketing, the account inputs must be known. Cost categories with functional titles, such as *advertising* and *sales promotion,* frequently may *not* include all of the advertising and promotion costs, but may include foreign costs such as contributions and entertainment. The foreign costs creep in because the account seems to be as good a cost depository as is available. On the other hand, advertising costs such as advertising payroll and advertising payroll taxes too often are allocated to general accounts such as payroll and payroll taxes.

### Use of Available Information

The second question that arises is: "How can available information be used?" The answer depends on the quality and quantity of information that is available. Under the worst conditions (accounts with numerous foreign entries and absences of necessary information), even ratio analysis (advertising to sales, travel expenses to sales, etc.) is hopeless. However, as individual accounts serve as meaningful cost depositories for such activities as advertising, personal selling, and salesmens' traveling expenses, the information can be used to partially analyze and manage these activities. Cost standards and controls, of sorts, can be established for the individual activities as well as for ratios of the activities one to another and to net sales.

When standards are prepared for nondetailed accounts, their main contribution is that they help raise questions. For example, the income statement shown in Table 9-1 indicates a ratio of *advertising* and *sales promotion* to *net sales* of about 1 to 12. If this ratio is substantially different from previous periods or from a projected ratio (or from comparable sellers), the question is raised: "Is the expenditure out-of-line?" In short, ratios help raise questions, but they provide very few answers.

## WHY HAS MARKETING COST ANALYSIS LAGGED?

Traditionally, accountants have not been primarily concerned with information for marketing decision making. Instead, their internal reporting has dealt mainly with financial and production matters. J. Howard (1963, pp. 170–171) in commenting on this matter has said:

> Some of the most frustrating problems that a marketing manager faces in his need for cost data arise because, historically, accountants have not been concerned with decision making outside the realm of finance.

There is evidence that distribution cost analysis has been slow in developing because of inherent difficulties not found, for example, in analysis of production costs. Herring (1966), Heckert and Miner (1953, pp. 14–16), Horngren (1967, p. 336), and Crisp (1961, pp. 8–12) have listed major difficulties:

1. Distribution agencies are numerous and varied.
2. Distribution activities vacillate more than do production methods.
3. The human element is a source of greater variation in distribution than in production.
4. Distribution activities are difficult to standardize (because of the difficulties listed above).
5. Basic information is difficult to obtain.
6. Distribution costs are difficult to interpret because more of them are indirect (joint).

Regardless of the reasons for the slow development of management accounting in marketing, Horngren (1967, p. 366) has written:

> Marketing managers are increasingly discovering that traditional guesses, hunches, and reliance on general rules of thumb are no longer enough. Detailed data accumulation and analyses, including budgets and standards, point toward the products, territories, distribution channels, order sizes divisions, departments, and employees that most sorely need attention. The use of management accounting in marketing is bound to increase because it can yield fruitful insights at little cost.

## INFORMATION SEGMENTS

Decision makers need more information than they get from traditional accounting records. Sevin has pinpointed the need:

> In most businesses a small proportion of the territories, customers, orders or products are responsible for the overwhelming bulk of the sales volume. For example, one manufacturer found that 78 per cent of his customers produced slightly more than two per cent of the sales volume; another found 46 per cent of the number of products manufactured accounted for only three per cent of sales volume (Sevin, 1958, p. 12).

Marketing managers must be familiar with the sales and cost relationships. With multiple products and territories, managers have many alternatives and must be able to shift or concentrate efforts and resources toward the most profitable courses of action. Sales and cost analyses are the principal avenues through which relevant internal information can be obtained.

Sales and cost analyses are the assembling of the various items of sales and costs into meaningful classifications and their comparison in these forms with alternative sales and costs. More specifically, they are techniques used by individual business firms for the determination of specific sales and cost patterns for various *segments* of the business.

Decision makers seek information on the cost and sales of various *things:* a territory, a product line, a sales group, a process, or a type of customer. These *things* are defined as *segments.* A *segment* is any line of activity or part of an organization for which a separate computation of costs or sales is sought (Horngren, 1967, p. 299). For example, all customers who order more than $40 worth of merchandise at one time are a segment; so are those who are credit customers, and conceivably each customer could be regarded as a segment.

Some commonly used segments for sales and cost analysis are:[3]

1. Products and package variations.
2. Territories (i.e., information control units).
3. Channels of distribution.
4. Order sizes.
5. Types of customers.
6. Method of sale.

These segments are sometimes discussed in terms of *cost centers, sales centers,* or *profit centers,* depending on what information is assembled. A *cost center* is the smallest segment or area of responsibility for which *costs* are accumulated (Horngren, 1967, p. 69). A *sales center* is the smallest segment or area of responsibility for which sales are accumulated. To complete the picture, a *profit center* is a segment of a business that is responsible for both revenues and expenses (Horngren, 1967, p. 338).

Profit has reference to contribution to profit and unallocated (joint) costs, not net profit. The contribution approach to the analysis of marketing performance is far superior to the full costing approach, which fails to distinguish between vital influences of various sales and cost behavior patterns. Under the contribution approach, only *separable costs* (those directly identifiable with a particular segment) are assigned to each segment. The *joint costs* (those common to all the segments in question and not clearly or practically allocable except on some questionable basis) are not allocated.[4]

## Which Segments Should Be Analyzed?

Few companies would want to continuously analyze numerous segments, because it would be too costly. Which segments should a firm

[3] For a more complete listing, see Heckert and Miner (1953, p. 24). Attention in this chapter will be focused principally on product and territory analyses. For discussion of analyses of other segments, see Crisp (1961), Heckert and Miner (1953), and Longman and Schiff (1955).

[4] For illustrations of separable and joint costs, see Horngren (1967, p. 303).

consider for sales, cost, or "profit" analyses? The general answer is: those segments (and subsegments) that are (1) subject to current control and (2) likely to contain relevant information.[5]

Control is a matter of degree. In the long run, virtually all segments are subject to some degree of managerial control from some managerial area of responsibility. Segments (and subsegments) to be analyzed should be subject to current influence from currently controllable marketing efforts. For example, a manufacturer may receive many unprofitable *small orders* (the segment in question is order size), but be able to change the situation by installing a minimum order size or a small-order charge or by selling to the small-order customers through wholesalers. In contrast, a retailer may have a similar small-order problem, but not be able to bring current marketing efforts to bear to change the current situation. He would not have current control.

To be *relevant,* information about the segment must (*a*) provide insight into the future and (*b*) be different under available alternatives. Horngren (1967, pp. 406–407) uses an illustration of a person attempting to make a decision which of two theaters to attend. The person knows that both theaters are showing identical programs. The seats and the viewing and sound facilities of each are near-equal and the theaters are an equal distance from the person. From past experience the person knows that the admission price at one of them is 50 cents and at the other 90 cents. He assumes that this admission price has not changed. The *relevant costs* are the 90 cents and the 50 cents, the *future costs* that will be different under the available alternatives. Past experience is used as the predictor of relevant costs. The important costs are not what were paid in the past, but what the person expects to pay today.

To continue the illustration, the person usually purchases popcorn at the theater. He expects the cost for comparable popcorn at either theater to be 25 cents. This is also an expected future cost, but it is *not* relevant because it will be the same under both alternatives—it does not involve a difference.

As the specific segments are selected for analyses, the subsegments must be specified. It does not suffice, for example, to say that product analyses will be done. Specifically, what products or product line segments will be appropriate? An illustration may provide some insight.

### *A Product Illustration*

A large brewing company in recent years has brewed and sold four different brands (Brewing, 1963). In virtually all of its markets, it has sold an ale and a popular-priced beer. In the Midwest it has also mar-

[5] The likely benefits from the information must exceed the costs of securing it.

keted a second brand of beer, and in the Pacific Northwest it has sold yet another brand. Its sales analyses problems might appear quite simple—let each brand be a subsegment for analyses. This, however, would not provide sufficient relevant information for decision making. Instead, the analyses should be by brands, by types of containers, and maybe even by packages.

Looking only at packaged sales, such analyses would be concerned with different sizes and types of containers in which each brand appears. This would include two-way 12-ounce brown bottles, one-way brown bottles (stub neck and regular), 11-ounce bottles, 12-ounce regular cans, soft-top and tab-open cans, 11-ounce cans, glass quarts, and so forth. In addition, analyses by *package* could include 6 packs, 8 packs, 12-unit "party" packs, case sales, and so forth.[6]

Analyses can be extended too far as well as not far enough. For example, if ale were offered in both brown and green bottles, but the color of the bottle made no sales difference, no analysis would be appropriate.

## A Look at One Segment—The Territory

Sales and cost analyses by territory are concerned with *where* sales and costs have occurred. Instead of using the ambiguous term "territory," the discussion from this point on will be in terms of *information control units*. An information control unit (ICU) is defined as the smallest geographic unit for which company sales, costs, and related information are accumulated.[7] The ICU, in other words, is the geographical basis for cost, sales, and profit centers.

The ICU can be compared with a playing card. So long as the basic units are each maintained intact, they may be assembled, aggregated, reshuffled, reaggregated, and, in general, used in many different activities. However, once a playing card is cut up or in some way mutilated, its usefulness is severely limited. So it is with ICU's. The specific ICU should be selected so that it can be kept intact over many years for continuing comparisons of data as well as to minimize setup costs.[8] The ramification of this requirement will be seen as ICU's are examined more closely.

[6] When the container is an important aspect of an offering, sales analysis by type of container is appropriate.

[7] See Crisp (1961, Chapter 8) for a somewhat different discussion of information control units.

[8] A more extensive discussion can be found in Still and Cundiff (1958, pp. 593–599).

*Selection Criteria*

The basic criteria for use in selection of ICU's are the same as for any other segment or subsegment: the ICU's must provide *relevant information* and be *subject to control.*

Relevant information along specific product lines is most likely to be available when the selected ICU's are:

1. Small enough to be sufficiently homogeneous.
2. Large enough to be self-contained.
3. Sufficient sources of environmental information.

Basically, each ICU should be sufficiently homogeneous (internally common) to make the activities within units alike, the major differences occurring among the various ICU's. For example, a manufacturer of bathing suits would *not* want to use *states* as his ICU. Swimsuit sales and accompanying marketing costs would be vastly different among the various Arizona counties of Pima (Tucson), Maricopa (Phoenix), and Cochise County (Tombstone). A state aggregation would hide the differences, yet sales and cost analyses should expose differences.

ICU's should be large enough to envelop the marketing activities attributed to them (essentially self-contained). That is, products that have been listed as being sold to resellers in an area, should be resold in that ICU. For the swimsuit seller, for example, counties would be self-contained if most sales made to retail outlets in each county were in turn purchases by residents of those counties.[9] If, however, sales were made to a wholesaler in one county who resold all over the state, counties would not be self-contained. As a generalization, the larger the ICU, the more likely it will be self-contained. This obviously leads to some conflict with the selection of homogeneous ICU's.

ICU's should contain sufficient sources of environmental information. Such information is necessary to help explain sales and cost patterns. In addition, the ICU's serve as base units for measurement of potential, for quota setting, and for forecasting. External information normally includes measures of market size, wealth, and willingness to buy.

## Alternative ICU's

The considerations of homogeneity, self-containment, and availability of sufficient environmental information are in terms of the specific products offered for sale and the types of markets within which they are

[9] For other illustrations, see Crisp (1961).

sold. For example, a seller of computer-automated switching equipment (e.g., Collins Radio Company) could seriously consider the individual customer as its ICU. This unit might also be appropriate for its aircraft ground-approach control equipment. Such an ICU would be out of place for its offering of "ham" radio equipment. An organization canvassing door to door may find the city block or census tract most useful, whereas a seller of commercial farm feed may select the township or county as the most appropriate ICU.

Also, a seller does *not* need to employ the same ICU throughout his entire market. A seller may select the county as his ICU for use in most of the United States, but employ a smaller unit in the large metropolitan areas. In turn, in Europe and other places where he uses market-skimming practices, individual nations may be appropriate ICU's.

Some commonly used ICU's are:[10]

1. Individual customers.
2. City blocks.
3. Census tracts.
4. Townships.
5. Incorporated towns and cities.
6. Trading areas.
7. Counties.
8. Standard metropolitan statistical areas.
9. Media-coverage areas.
10. Salesmens' territories.
11. ZIP code areas.
12. States.
13. Census regions.
14. Nations.

Individual customer sites. This refers to the specific locations of individual customers and prospective customers and is most meaningful to sellers of high-priced industrial offerings with a limited number of buyers. External information usually relates to the specific prospect and is collected directly from them.

City blocks. The most serious limitation is that very limited external information is available indexed by city block. Also, city blocks are so numerous that in large markets the immense number of ICU's presents difficult control and information-handling problems.

Census tracts. These are areas that have been so designated to achieve some uniformity among population characteristics, economic

[10] Additional comments relative to the various alternatives can be found in Baier (1967, pp. 136–190), Stanton and Buskirk (1959), and Still and Cundiff (1958).

status, and living conditions (U.S. Bureau, 1960). The average tract contains about 4000 residents, and there were 23,000 of them listed in 1960. More published information is available for this unit than for the two previously mentioned. The Census of Population (U.S. Bureau, 1960) contained data on census tracts for some 15 different population characteristics and 20 housing characteristics.

Because of the great number of census tracts, difficulties in keeping both internal and environmental information current are encountered. Also, problems of self-containment frequently occur, but they can be handled by aggregating census tracts.

TOWNSHIPS. Townships are geographical divisions of counties. They are found in only 21 states. Very little local government follows township boundaries, but considerable county information is recorded by townships. However, most of this information is not published. Some sellers (particularly sellers of agricultural offerings) sample from the township unit, but such data are too expensive for extensive use. These units normally are small enough to be sufficiently homogeneous, but they must be aggregated to be self-contained.

INCORPORATED TOWNS AND CITIES. Much market information is collected and published for this unit. For example, the census of population, census of business, and survey of buying power, as well as others, publish numerous statistics about towns and cities with over 2500 population. This unit can be very small (e.g., throughout North and South Dakota, in Montana), and it can also be very large (St. Louis, Chicago, New York, and so forth). In both cases it is a relatively poor ICU, because it is not self-contained.

TRADING AREA. A trading area is defined as the geographical region including and surrounding a central city whose trade normally flows into the hub city.[11] A trading area is based on normal trading patterns and virtually discounts political boundaries such as cities and counties. By definition such units are basically self-contained.

This unit is impractical to use because different products normally have different trading areas. Also, an even more serious drawback is that very little published environmental information is available. An information unit lacking readily available and cheap external information is about as useful as a flat bathtub.

COUNTIES. Counties are the most frequently used ICU's in the United States. This popularity occurs because virtually all information available in the larger ICU's is available at the county level. In addition, counties appear to be sufficiently homogeneous for numerous types of products.

[11] Huff (1964), Stanton and Buskirk (1959), and Still and Cundiff (1958) indicate how trading areas can be calculated.

Some people have argued that counties are too numerous (just over 3000 in the United States) and too small to justify collection of environmental information. Business organizations have apparently felt otherwise. This is partially explained by the fact that some companies use less than all of the counties. Also, improved data processing, as well as the ready availability of current county data on tape and card decks, has facilitated use of this unit.

The county is *not* a very adequate unit for densely populated areas in that it is too large to provide detailed information. Data for such counties as Cook, Los Angeles, Wayne, King, and Philadelphia do not facilitate control *within* each of these units. Frequently when the county serves as the common ICU control unit, a smaller unit must be used in the larger metropolitan market areas. Clearly, self-containment becomes a problem.

STANDARD METROPOLITAN STATISTICAL AREA (SMSA). This unit is defined as a *county* or group of contiguous counties that contain at least one city of 50,000 inhabitants or more or "twin cities" with a combined population of at least 50,000 (U.S. Bureau, 1960). Counties are considered contiguous when they are essentially metropolitan and are socially and economically integrated with the central city.

The advantages offered by this ICU are that (1) it tends to be more self-contained than the individual county, (2) SMSA's are only about one-tenth as numerous as counties (yet account for about 70 per cent of consumer good sales), and (3) much external SMSA data are readily available on tape and card decks. The major limitation of this unit is that in large metropolitan areas the information is too aggregative to facilitate control *within* each of the units. Once again, as with counties, smaller-scale units must be used in the large metropolitan markets.

MEDIA-COVERAGE AREAS. This unit refers to the area covered and exposed to market media. For example, television broadcasting stations may offer meaningful coverage within a 30-mile radius from their transmitting towers. Newspapers may offer similar geographical coverage. Sellers that view such media as their major means of promotion may align both their information and their marketing operations with these boundaries rather than divide massive media expenditures along other lines. As a result, these units do tend to be self-contained.

Unless the media boundaries coincide with county or SMSA boundaries, environmental information tends to be very limited. Finally, in large metropolitan markets, detailed information is not available because the unit is too large.

SALESMENS' TERRITORIES. Salesmens' territories in most companies change too frequently to serve as permanent ICU's. Such changes disrupt data continuity. Also territories tend to cut across both political and trade boundaries, so that there is a general lack of environmental data as well as lack of self-contained units. However, the sales territory is excellent in that the information and the decision-making boundaries coincide. Normally, to achieve this advantage, territories are aligned along boundaries of ICU's rather than vice versa.

ZIP CODE AREAS. The Post Office Department ZIP Code Sectional Center System has divided the country into 552 areas with about 314 multicoded cities. The Post Office Department has described each area as follows:

1. A hub city that is the natural center for local transportation.
2. About 40 to 75 post offices in the area.
3. The most remote post office to be no more than two to three hours away by normal driving time.

The one convenient feature that the ZIP units offer is that they are readily identifiable for mail selling, sampling, and interviewing. This one factor may make this unit applicable as an ICU for companies that sell principally by mail. Even here it has serious shortcomings, the worst of which is that the ZIP boundaries do *not* coincide with counties or other units, hence environmental information on people, incomes, and willingness to buy is not readily available. Additional discussion on the advantages and disadvantages of the use of ZIP areas as ICU's can be found in Baier (1967, pp. 136–140).

STATES. States provide a wealth of environmental market data. However, they tend not to be self-contained (except for state-stamped goods such as liquor and tobacco products), because large cities often are on state boundaries and commerce flows quite freely among the states. Second, states are too large to be homogeneous. New York City is far different from upstate New York, Cook County with over half the population of Illinois is quite different from downstate Illinois. These are the kinds of heterogeneities that make the states difficult to use for most products.

CENSUS REGIONS. The census region, like states, are normally too large to provide sufficiently detailed information.[12] For all practical purposes, the comments made about states pertain to census regions.

NATIONS. Sometimes firms that market their products in numerous countries use individual nations as their ICU's. This unit can be applicable when (1) trade restrictions lead to self-contained markets, (2) the national markets are relatively small (so that the data are sufficiently

[12] Census regions in the United States are: (1) Pacific, (2) Mountain, (3) West North Central, (4) West South Central, (5) East North Central, (6) East South Central, (7) Middle Atlantic, (8) South Atlantic, and (9) New England.

DATE 9-30-67 — AMANA REFRIGERATION DEALERS

DIST. 1120 Triple-A Dist.
Notown, U.S.A.

| --------- DEALER --------- NUMBER | NAME / CITY / STATE | O T | | AMANA FREEZER | DEEP FREEZER | REFRIG. FREEZER |
|---|---|---|---|---|---|---|
| ******** | *************** | * | | ******* | ******* | ******* |
| 00010 00 | Jones Wholesale | M | 65 TOTAL | | | |
| | Notown, U.S.A. | | 66 TOTAL | 2 | 3 | 2 |
| | | | SEPT. 66 TOTAL | 2 | 2 | 1 |
| | | | SEPT. 67 TOTAL | 10 | 12 | |
| | | | CUMULATIVE 66 Y-T-D | 2 | 2 | 1 |
| | | | CUMULATIVE 67 Y-T-D | 50 | 73 | |

| --------- DEALER --------- NUMBER | NAME / CITY / STATE | O T | | AMANA FREEZER | DEEP FREEZER | REFRIG. FREEZER |
|---|---|---|---|---|---|---|
| ******* | *************** | * | | ******* | ******* | ******* |
| 00020 00 | Conner Appl. | P | 65 TOTAL | 15 | 12 | 32 |
| | Anytown, U.S.A. | | 66 TOTAL | 9 | 13 | 5 |
| | | | SEPT. 66 TOTAL | | | |
| | | | SEPT. 67 TOTAL | | | |
| | | | CUMULATIVE 66 Y-T-D | 6 | 10 | 5 |
| | | | CUMULATIVE 67 Y-T-D | 3 | 11 | 1 |

| --------- DEALER --------- NUMBER | NAME / CITY / STATE | O T | | AMANA FREEZER | DEEP FREEZER | REFRIG. FREEZER |
|---|---|---|---|---|---|---|
| ******** | *************** | * | | ******* | ******* | ******* |
| 00040 00 | Smith's Elec. | A | 65 TOTAL | 5 | 6 | 5 |
| | Anytown, U.S.A. | | 66 TOTAL | 4 | 1 | 2 |
| | | | SEPT. 66 TOTAL | | | |
| | | | SEPT. 67 TOTAL | | | |
| | | | CUMULATIVE 66 Y-T-D | 4 | 1 | 2 |
| | | | CUMULATIVE 67 Y-T-D | | | |

| --------- DEALER --------- NUMBER | NAME / CITY / STATE | O T | | AMANA FREEZER | DEEP FREEZER | REFRIG. FREEZER |
|---|---|---|---|---|---|---|
| ******** | *************** | * | | ******* | ******* | ******* |
| 00060 00 | Hamilton Appl. | A | 65 TOTAL | 18 | | 35 |
| | Notown, U.S.A. | | 66 TOTAL | 7 | 2 | 3 |
| | | | SEPT. 66 TOTAL | | | |
| | | | SEPT. 67 TOTAL | | | |
| | | | CUMULATIVE 66 Y-T-D | 5 | 2 | 3 |
| | | | CUMULATIVE 67 Y-T-D | 5 | | |

**Figure 9-1** Sales analysis sheet. (*Source:* Amana Refrigeration, Inc.)

detailed), or (3) market-skimming programs are used, resulting in less extensive data needs.

## SALES ANALYSIS

How do companies actually go about analyzing their sales by segments of their business? Sales analyses are relatively simple, once the specific

PURCHASE RECORD

| TOP MOUNTS | R. AIR COND. | C. AIR COND. | DE-HUMID. | SIDE BY SIDE | | | | TOTAL PROD. |
|---|---|---|---|---|---|---|---|---|
| ******* | ******* | ******* | ******* | ******* | ******* | ******* | ******* | ******* |
| 7 | | | | 24 | | | | 38 |
| 6 | | | | 15 | | | | 26 |
| 8 | | | | 5 | | | | 35 |
| 6 | | | | 15 | | | | 26 |
| 58 | 176 | | 61 | 34 | | | | 452 |

| TOP MOUNTS | R. AIR COND. | C. AIR COND. | DE-HUMID. | SIDE BY SIDE | | | | TOTAL PROD. |
|---|---|---|---|---|---|---|---|---|
| ******* | ******* | ******* | ******* | ******* | ****** | ******* | ******** | ******* |
| 30 | 19 | | | 2 | | | | 110 |
| 14 | 11 | | | 13 | | | | 65 |
| 2 | | | | 1 | | | | 3 |
| 1 | | | | 1 | | | | 2 |
| 14 | 2 | | | 11 | | | | 48 |
| 10 | 33 | | | 3 | | | | 61 |

| TOP MOUNTS | R. AIR COND. | C. AIR COND. | DE-HUMID. | SIDE BY SIDE | | | | TOTAL PROD. |
|---|---|---|---|---|---|---|---|---|
| ******* | ******* | ******* | ******* | ******* | ******* | ******* | ******* | ******* |
| 9 | 12 | | | 4 | | | | 41 |
| 11 | 38 | | 12 | 5 | | | | 73 |
| | | | | | | | | |
| 9 | 18 | | 12 | 5 | | | | 51 |
| 9 | 7 | | | 6 | | | | 22 |

| TOP MOUNTS | R. AIR COND. | C. AIR COND. | DE-HUMID. | SIDE BY SIDE | | | | TOTAL PROD. |
|---|---|---|---|---|---|---|---|---|
| ******* | ******* | ******* | ******* | ******* | ******* | ******* | ******* | ******* |
| 19 | 26 | | | 10 | | | | 108 |
| 9 | 28 | | | 25 | | | | 74 |
| | | | | | | | | |
| 9 | 28 | | | 19 | | | | 66 |
| 13 | | | | 29 | | | | 47 |

**Figure 9-1** (Continued)

subsegments to be analyzed have been selected. Basically, a procedure must be established so that, as shipments are made (or orders are received, or customers are billed), information is recorded regarding such things as the number of each type of product (by package size, etc.) shipped to each type of customer and location. The specific information that is recorded is dependent on the sales segments that a company wants to analyze.

Once such data are available on punched cards or other computer-input devices, they can be tabulated by products, by ICU's, by customer types, and by other segments as needed. Sales reports can be prepared on various subsegments (such as individual products or ICU's) for use by individual product or sales managers. Also, composite reports covering all products and all ICU's can be prepared for use by others. And, of course, current data can be compared in cross-sectional analysis as well as over time, using past sales and projected sales. A sales analysis output sheet used by Amana Refrigeration, Inc. is shown in Figure 9-1.

## MEASURING MARKETING COSTS

Marketing *cost* analyses are not so simple, easy, and inexpensive as are sales analyses. As a consequence, many firms that do analyze their sales do *not* analyze their costs. Whereas sales can be readily classified by types of products, customers, ICU's, and other segments of the business, many marketing costs *cannot.* Take, for example, the *costs* of advertising a multiple line of products. How should the salaries paid to advertising personnel be divided among the various products, among the various ICU's, and among other segments?

### Functional Analysis

The common *starting point* of a cost analysis is to set up a procedure to classify marketing costs and to assign them to major marketing functions. These functions (activities) often include personal selling, advertising, sales promotion, transportation (outbound), credits and collections, warehousing and handling, and information services (Heckert and Miner, 1953, p. 18).

The basic criteria for the selection of functions, and their subfunctions (functional operations), are the same as for other segments. Selected functions, as discussed earlier, should provide *relevant information* and be *subject to control.*

In general, the functions (and functional operations) that will provide relevant information are those for which

(*a*) relatively large costs are incurred, and
(*b*) a majority of the costs are direct or separable.

A firm, such as The Maytag Company, which extends no credit to its dealer organization, has no need for a functional account termed *credits* and *collections.* In contrast, the company's costs for personal

**TABLE 9-2** Functional Cost Analysis; Zebra Manufacturing Corporation

| | | |
|---|---|---|
| Personal selling | | $1,642,556 |
| Supervision | $497,995 | |
| Field selling | 824,197 | |
| Telephone and mail orders | 102,477 | |
| Commission calculation | 13,200 | |
| Pricing and extensions | 69,936 | |
| Invoice typing | 112,366 | |
| Miscellaneous | 22,385 | |
| Advertising and sales promotion | | $ 692,972 |
| Physical production | $271,583 | |
| Copy and artwork | 222,625 | |
| Catalogs | 27,104 | |
| Direct mail | 37,515 | |
| Conventions and exhibitions | 36,255 | |
| Point of purchase displays | 94,208 | |
| Miscellaneous | 3,682 | |
| Transportation and warehousing | | $ 121,863 |
| Storing | $ 40,882 | |
| Shipping | $ 68,627 | |
| Routing | 12,350 | |
| Credit and collection | | $ 44,215 |
| Posting | $ 23,500 | |
| Credit authorization | 12,315 | |
| Inside collection | 6,108 | |
| Outside collection | 2,292 | |
| Information services | | $ 33,466 |
| Sales and cost analysis | $ 7,674 | |
| Market analysis | 12,345 | |
| Forecasting | 9,342 | |
| Statistical analysis | 4,105 | |
| Miscellaneous and joint costs (not allocated to functions) | | $ 146,612 |
| Total costs | | $2,681,680 |

*Source:* Table 9-1.

selling and advertising are relatively large, and separate functional accounts (and functional operations) would be appropriate.

The costs of some major marketing functions are predominately joint (common to multiple functions and not clearly or practically allocable except on some questionable basis) and are not separable for analyses. The merchandising and planning function in many companies, for example, is scattered among numerous departments and accomplished by persons who are primarily engaged in other activities. In contrast, functions such as personal selling and advertising are normally found under individual managers and contain a high proportion of costs separable by activities. Table 9-2 is illustrative of the kinds of functions and functional operations to which costs are allocated.

The *second step* in accumulating marketing costs by functions is to establish the formulas for the allocation of the separable costs among the functional activities. For example, a drug-house detail man may divide his time between making calls on dentists and druggists and building displays in drugstores. The expenditures for his service may include such payments as salary, commissions, travel expenses, and payroll taxes. How should these expenses be allocated among the two major functions, *personal selling* and *sales promotion?*

Ideally, the basis of allocation should reflect the cause of cost changes within each function. In addition, accounting literature recommends that the basis be understandable, be independent, and offer adequate control (Bierman, 1959; Horngren, 1967; Kennedy and Kurtz, 1960).

The *third step* is to allocate the various costs to the functions and functional operations. The direct costs, by their nature, need not be divided and are assigned straight to the appropriate functions and functional operations. Next, the separable costs are allocated to the appro-

| Treatment / Type of Cost | Total Cost Allocated to One Segment | Select Basis for Allocation among Segments and Allocate | No Reasonable Basis for Allocation |
|---|---|---|---|
| Direct | X | | |
| Separable | | X | |
| Joint | | | X |

**Figure 9-2** Treatment of various types of costs.

priate functions and subfunctions (Bierman, 1959, p. 257). The joint costs normally should *not* be allocated. The treatments applied to these various kinds of costs are shown in Figure 9-2.

This order of cost allocation is followed because the direct costs are clearly and solely related to the individual functions. The separable costs are second in order of assignment because they are second in order of certainty of assignment.

Companies that have very few product lines or sell in very few territories may find that functional cost analyses provide sufficient internal information for decision making. However, companies with numerous products or many territories need further allocation of the aggregated functional costs into additional segments (ICU's, products, etc.) in order to reveal the manner in which the marketing efforts are being applied.

## Analyses by Other Segments of the Business

The steps in the analyses by other segments of the business have been listed by Heckert and Miner (1953, p. 24) as follows:

1. Determine which segments will be analyzed.
2. Classify the functionally categorized costs as to whether they are direct, separable, or joint for each segment to be analyzed.
3. Select appropriate bases of allocation to be applied to the separable costs.
4. Allocate the costs to the segments to be analyzed.
5. Prepare the final analyses and their interpretations for use by decision makers.

### *Segments to Be Analyzed*

The first step is to select the segments and subsegments for analyses. The basic criteria for segment selections have been discussed previously. The reader should recall that the basic criteria are that segments must be *subject to control* and must *provide relevant information.* In general, the segments and subsegments that will provide relevant information are those for which

(*a*) relatively large costs are incurred, and
(*b*) a majority of the costs are separable.

Marketing cost analyses normally will not penetrate to as many subsegments as will accompanying *sales* analyses. A company, for example, may find *sales* analyses of each container and each package variation of each brand appropriate, but not trace marketing costs for each of these offering variations.

There are two major explanations for the difference. First, sales information is relatively easy to secure in that most orders and invoices list sales by products, package variations, and customers and their locations. In contrast, related cost information is not readily available. It appears here and there and often is of a joint nature, particularly when further subsegmenting is desired. For example, advertising costs, personal selling costs, and other costs often relate to numerous products, packages, and ICU's.

Second, marketing cost differences may *not* be present even when there are sales differences. A company may use different containers and packages, for example, but not promote these differences or incur other marketing cost differences. And part of our earlier definition of *relevant information* was that it made a difference between alternatives.

### *Classify the Functional Costs*

The second step is to classify the functionally categorized costs as to whether they are direct, separable, or joint for each segment to be analyzed. An analysis of advertising costs by *car body style* (convertible, station wagon, two-door sedan, etc.), for example, would result in the costs of advertising pertaining only to station wagons being classified as direct costs. Costs of advertisements pertaining to two or more body styles would be classified as separable costs, if they could be identified with particular body styles. Finally, costs such as the salary of the advertising director and office overhead costs would be classified as joint costs.

The costs in each of the functional classifications must be reclassified for each segment of the business that is to be analyzed. For example, those costs pertaining only to station wagon advertisements which would be direct for an analysis by body style would *not* be direct costs for an analysis by ICU's. In turn, cooperative advertising costs incurred in individual ICU's (with ads featuring one or several body styles) would be classified as direct costs for analysis by ICU's.

### *Selection of Bases for Allocation*

The third step is concerned with the selection of the bases for the allocation of the various separable costs. Obviously, the direct costs need no allocation. They pertain directly and solely to the individual segments. Separable costs (such as those mentioned earlier that pertained to both station wagons and convertibles) need to be allocated.

The same considerations that were discussed earlier under functional cost analyses are germane. The reader should recall that *causes* of cost changes are preferred as bases, so long as they are understandable, independent, and offer adequate control.

The selection of bases for the allocation of cost has received considerable attention in the accounting literature. Horngren's discussion (Horngren, 1967, pp. 365–380) is particularly relevant, because he distinguishes between *order-filling* and *order-getting* activities. He indicates the order-filling functions (warehousing, handling, packaging, shipping, billing, credit, and collection) are subject to work-measurement techniques. These measurement techniques can provide standard units of measure (control factor units) to be used as bases for allocation of costs. For example, the costs of billing may be related to various segments by *lines per hour;* warehouse labor costs may be related by *pounds or cases handled per day;* costs of posting accounts may be related to *postings per hour;* and so forth.

Finding appropriate allocation bases for *order-getting* costs (costs incurred to obtain sales rather than as a result of sales) is not so simple. Some order-getting costs are subject to specific measurement of efforts and results. Examples would be the "selling" of drug wholesale salesmen and other *order-taking* salesmen. Other order-getting activities that do not show direct relationships between efforts and results present more difficulties.

Heckert and Miner (1953) discuss some of the more traditional ways of selecting bases. The newer statistical and mathematical approaches that show signs of help are described in such books as *Executive Decisions and Operations Research* by Miller and Starr (1960).

### *Allocation of Costs to Segments*

The fourth step is the allocation of the major individual costs to specific segments. To use the body style segment illustration, the costs of the advertisements that pertain *only* to station wagons, being direct costs, would be charged against the station wagon category. Next, the costs of the advertisements featuring the two body styles (separable costs) would be allocated between the two styles, based (perhaps) on time or space. This procedure would be followed for each other major direct and separable cost item until they were allocated to the appropriate segments.

### *Analyses of Accumulated Costs*

The final major step is to analyze the cost data output, engage in necessary subanalyses, combine the costs with appropriate information from the sales analysis program, and summarize and communicate the information to decision makers in the organization.

The cost information by various segments is meant to provide only good estimates of the ways in which the marketing dollars have been spent. The purpose is *not* to account for *all* of the expenditures by each segment nor, even if possible, to be absolutely accurate. The purpose is to provide marketing cost information to aid in decision making.

## Illustration: Marketing Cost Analyses

Analysis of marketing costs by product segments has been selected as an illustration because it (1) does exemplify the general procedures used with each of the major segments and (2) is more commonly used than are other dimensions.

Not every business organization has need for continuing analyses of costs by products. Our illustration has assumed that this organization does have such a need. Such a need is likely to arise when a company has a multiple number of offerings *and* the associated marketing costs vary from offering to offering and over time.

### *Define the Product Dimensions*

A manufacturer of home laundry equipment is used for illustrative purposes. A number of simplifying assumptions are made to keep the discussion brief. The company, in 1967, manufactured and marketed three major and distinct product lines for the consumer household market.

1. Conventional (wringer type) washing machines.
2. Automatic washing machines.
3. Automatic clothes dryers.

The conventional washer line was composed of three basic models, the major distinctions being the shape and the metal content of the washing tub. In addition, these models were available with liquid-fuel engines.

The automatic washer line was composed of three major lines, and each line contained numerous variations in optional equipment. In all, more than 20 different units were available. The dryer line was also composed of three major lines, and each line contained numerous options. Some of these options were very basic and were featured in promotional efforts. For example, the offering included both gas and electric dryers. In addition, the top-price line included both vented and nonvented dryers, as well as an automatic moisture-sensing control and other features.

There were more than 20 different dryer offerings. Although not all products have been listed, it should be clear that this one company manufactured and marketed more than 50 different products.

Should the company estimate the marketing costs associated with each individual product? Certainly not, and for a variety of reasons. Some of the individual products, for example, were sold in such limited quantity that, even though unique marketing expenditures were present, the cost of information would *far* exceed possible benefits.[13] The marketing costs for some of the lines were so homogenized that they could *not* be economically separated. The three conventional washer models, for example, were marketed largely without distinction among the models. Therefore, these models could be categorized together and costed as one. These, then, are the sorts of considerations that would dictate the actual product categories for which marketing costs would be traced.

For the ensuing discussion, the more than 50 individual products have been collapsed into six main product categories—(1) conventional washers, (2) low-priced automatic washers, (3) medium-priced automatic washers, (4) top-line automatic washers, (5) automatic gas dryers, and (6) automatic electric dryers. Subanalyses within each of the six categories (although not shown) would be appropriate from time to time because of the relatively broad product groupings.

### *Classify the Costs*

The first step would be to complete a functional cost analysis such as was described earlier in this chapter. Then these individual functional entries would be classified as direct, separable, or joint costs.

Table 9-3 presents a cursory view of the various costs. Note that the table is arrayed first on a *functional* basis and then by the directness of each cost item. The first entry, for example, is the functional activity designated as advertising and sales promotion expenses (line 1). Within this category the direct cost items appear first, the separable cost items next, and then the joint cost category. The first direct cost category is media costs for individual product line advertisements (line 3). Other direct costs are: (1) copywriting, artwork, and music, (2) cost of physical production, and (3) dealer point-of-purchase promotion. Each of these relate only to individual product lines. These direct costs are charged directly to each product category.

The separable cost categories (lines 9–13) include physical production,

[13] Liquid-fueled conventional washers, for example, were sold to foreign missionaries and similarly isolated persons, but this was hardly a line that would encourage cost analysis.

**TABLE 9-3** Multidimensional Cost Analysis

| Line | (1) Description of the Cost | (2) Total Cost | (3) Basis for Allocation | (4) Costs Charged to Conventional Washers | (5) Costs Charged to Low-Priced Automatic | (6) Costs Charged to Medium-Priced Automatic | (7) Costs Charged to Top-Line Automatic | (8) Costs Charged to Gas Dryers | (9) Costs Charged to Electric Dryers |
|---|---|---|---|---|---|---|---|---|---|
| 1 | ADVERTISING AND SALES PROMOTION EXPENSES | | | | | | | | |
| 2 | *Direct Costs* | | | | | | | | |
| 3 | Media costs for individual product line advertisements | $ 500,000 | These costs relate to individual product lines and are charged directly to the appropriate categories | $250,000 | — | — | $ 50,000 | $100,000 | $100,000 |
| 4 | Copywriting, artwork, music, etc., for individual product line advertisements | $ 90,000 | | $ 40,000 | — | — | $ 8,000 | $ 20,000 | $ 22,000 |
| 5 | Costs of physical production for individual product line advertisements | $ 150,000 | | $ 70,000 | — | — | $ 10,000 | $ 30,000 | $ 40,000 |
| 6 | Dealer point of purchase program | $ 20,000 | | $ 6,000 | — | — | — | $ 8,000 | $ 6,000 |
| 7 | Total direct advertising and sales promotion costs | $ 760,000 | | $366,000 | — | — | $ 68,000 | $158,000 | $168,000 |
| 8 | *Separable Costs* | | | | | | | | |
| 9 | Costs of physical production for joint line advertising | $ 450,000 | Accumulated by advertising job number and allocated in the same proportion as media | $ 59,850 | $ 37,800 | $ 104,850 | $ 120,150 | $ 59,850 | $ 67,500 |
| 10 | Costs of copywriting, artwork, etc., for joint line advertisements | $ 600,000 | Same | $ 79,800 | $ 50,400 | $ 139,800 | $ 160,200 | $ 79,800 | $ 90,000 |
| 11 | Media costs for joint line advertisements | $3,000,000 | Distributed to product lines according to space and/or time | $400,000 | $250,000 | $ 700,000 | $ 800,000 | $400,000 | $450,000 |
| 12 | Point of purchase display | $ 150,000 | Distributed to product lines on basis of space used | $ 30,000 | $ 15,000 | $ 35,000 | $ 35,000 | $ 20,000 | $ 15,000 |
| 13 | Demonstrations | $ 130,000 | Distributed to product lines on basis of time used | $ 5,000 | $ 15,000 | $ 30,000 | $ 30,000 | $ 25,000 | $ 25,000 |
| 14 | Total separable costs | $4,330,000 | | $574,650 | $368,200 | $1,009,650 | $1,145,350 | $584,650 | $647,500 |
| 15 | *Joint Costs* | | | | | | | | |
| 16 | Advertising administration and overhead; e.g., executive salaries, travel, and entertainment | $ 350,000 | Not allocated | — | — | — | — | — | — |
| 17 | Cost of institutional advertisements | $ 120,000 | | — | — | — | — | — | — |
| 18 | Promotional public relations | $ 135,000 | | — | — | — | — | — | — |
| 19 | Miscellaneous expenses | $ 150,000 | | — | — | — | — | — | — |
| 20 | Total joint costs | $ 755,000 | | — | — | — | — | — | — |
| 21 | Total allocated advertising and sales promotion expense | $5,845,000 | | $940,650 | $368,200 | $1,009,650 | $1,213,350 | $742,650 | $815,500 |

| | | | | | | | | | |
|---|---|---|---|---|---|---|---|---|---|
| 22 | SELLING EXPENSES | | | | | | | | |
| 23 | *Direct Costs* | | | | | | | | |
| 24 | Salaries and expenses of salesmen and managers of individual product lines | $ 140,000 | These costs relate to individual product lines and are charged directly to each line | $ 20,000 | — | $ 8,000 | $ 30,000 | $ 42,000 | $ 40,000 |
| 25 | Payroll tax, insurance and retirement benefits related to individual product line personnel | $ 19,000 | | $ 2,800 | — | $ 1,600 | $ 3,600 | $ 6,000 | $ 5,000 |
| 26 | Communications, office and miscellaneous expense related to individual product line personnel | $ 22,000 | | $ 3,600 | — | $ 2,600 | $ 5,500 | $ 5,400 | $ 4,900 |
| 27 | Total direct selling cost | $ 181,000 | | $ 26,400 | — | $ 12,200 | $ 39,100 | $ 53,400 | $ 49,900 |
| 28 | *Separable Costs* | | | | | | | | |
| 29 | Salaries and expenses of general line salesmen | $1,500,000 | Time studies average by time devoted to each product line | $285,000 | $195,000 | $ 345,000 | $ 430,000 | $125,000 | $120,000 |
| 30 | Payroll tax, insurance and retirement related to general line salesmen | $ 225,000 | Same as general line salaries and expenses | $ 42,750 | $ 29,250 | $ 51,750 | $ 64,125 | $ 19,125 | $ 18,000 |
| 31 | Order writing | $ 17,000 | Number of orders | $ 4,400 | $ 3,500 | $ 4,000 | $ 3,000 | $ 1,100 | $ 1,000 |
| 32 | Billing | $ 7,000 | Number of billing line | $ 1,200 | $ 2,000 | $ 1,500 | $ 1,000 | $ 700 | $ 600 |
| 33 | Space occupancy and related space | $ 151,000 | Time study of salesmen's activities | $ 28,690 | $ 19,630 | $ 34,730 | $ 43,035 | $ 12,835 | $ 12,080 |
| 34 | Total separable selling costs | $1,900,000 | | $362,040 | $249,380 | $ 436,980 | $ 541,160 | $158,760 | $151,680 |
| 35 | *Joint Costs* | | | | | | | | |
| 36 | Salaries and expenses of general sales managers and sales administrators | $ 200,000 | | — | — | — | — | — | — |
| 37 | Payroll tax, insurance and retirement related to sales executives | $ 30,000 | Not allocated | — | — | — | — | — | — |
| 38 | Entertainment | $ 250,000 | | — | — | — | — | — | — |
| 39 | Training | $ 90,000 | | — | — | — | — | — | — |
| 40 | Communication, supplies, occupancy, and miscellaneous expenses | $ 200,000 | | — | — | — | — | — | — |
| 41 | Total joint selling costs | $ 770,000 | | — | — | — | — | — | — |
| 42 | Total allocated selling expense | $2,851,000 | | $388,440 | $249,380 | $ 449,180 | $ 580,260 | $212,160 | $201,580 |

*Source:* Hypothetical.

copywriting, artwork, music, media, point-of-purchase displays, and demonstrations. In each case they pertain only to advertisements that promote two or more different product categories.

The first joint cost category is the administrative and overhead cost associated with the advertising function (line 16). Other joint cost categories are institutional advertising, promotional public relations, and miscellaneous expenses (lines 17–19). These have been classified as joint costs because there appears to be no logical, measurable (empirical) relationship among these expenses and the six individual product categories.

The left-hand column of the selling expense function (starting on line 22) should be examined to see how other major costs might be classified.

### *Select Bases for Cost Allocation*

Next, bases must be found to allocate the separable costs to the six product accounts. Column 3 in Table 9-3 indicates the bases selected for the allocation. For example, media costs of advertisements featuring two or more of the product categories are allocated based on the proportion of total advertisement space and/or time devoted to each product category (line 11). Salaries and expenses of the general line salesmen (under the selling function) have been allocated on the basis of time studies that measured the proportion of time, on the average, devoted to each of the products (line 29). Such an allocation basis is appropriate to the extent that it reflects the relative efforts and time devoted to each specific category. Bases for allocating other separable costs can be observed in Table 9-3 (column 3). These bases are meant to be illustrative rather than authoritative.

Joint expenses have *not* been allocated in this illustration. Some accountants recommend that joint distribution costs be allocated on an arbitrary basis (Rayburn, 1967). This does *not* mean that the costs would be allocated haphazardly. Instead, it indicates the allocations should appear reasonable (not necessarily defendable) to the person making the allocation. We believe that the allocation of joint costs provides no additional useful information for decision makers.

### *Allocate Costs to Product Categories*

The next step is merely a clerical or mechanical operation. The allocation formulas (column 3) are applied to the various cost items (column 2), and the allocated amounts are charged against each of the six appropriate product categories. These allocated amounts are shown in columns 4 through 9 of Table 9-3.

### *Comments about the Preceding Steps*

Two comments about the prior steps are needed. First, the three prior steps are accomplished when the program is established. They are *not* redone with each new batch of data. They are reexamined and evaluated, and corrections and changes are made as needed.

Second, the first three steps require extensive participation from decision makers familiar with the organization's marketing information needs and marketing costs. Once the first three steps have been completed, the actual allocation and computational procedures can be programmed for computer runs. Prior to actual programming, decision makers must anticipate (1) the various product categories (columns 4–9), (2) the various cost *items* (not the amounts) that will be present (column 1), (3) the classification of each cost item (column 1), and (4) the bases for allocating each of the cost items to the major product categories (column 3).

### *Analyze and Report Cost Information*

The direct costs for each product category and then joint costs are accumulated in that order. The direct costs are subtracted first from the dollar gross margins. This leaves *contribution to separable and joint costs and profit.* Next, the separable costs are subtracted, leaving *contributions to joint costs and profits.*

Decisions need to be made as to (1) the cost comparisons that will be made among the various cost categories and with past data, (2) the manner in which product cost data should be combined with comparable sales data, and (3) the marketing costs that will be selected for viewing (and by whom).

This step, like the first three, is accomplished when the program is first established. From that point on it is examined and evaluated—with corrections and changes made from time to time—to bring the program more in line with decision makers' changing needs.

A careful examination of Table 9-3 should serve to reinforce the numerous comments pointed out in the text. Obviously, this product illustration has not been exhaustive. It has been presented to point out the general procedures and concepts involved in a program of marketing cost analysis.[14]

[14] For illustrations of how sales and cost information can be used in decision making, see Barry (1967) as well as earlier chapters in this book.

## SUMMARY

This chapter has been concerned principally with the problems and ways of providing individual business organizations with detailed internal information about their own sales and marketing costs. Traditionally, companies have collected little internal information for decision making in marketing per se. The traditional accounting approach, by object of expenditure, has *not* provided sufficient marketing information. However, marketing information programs are being expanded. This is occurring both because decision makers perceive greater need for such information and because technological advances, particularly in data processing, permit development.

*Sales* analysis is relatively easy and inexpensive to develop, and its information outputs are quite useful to multiproduct, multimarket companies. Through sales analysis a company can trace its sales by products and by various ICU's. In addition, analyses of other segments can be run as subanalyses or when special problems arise.

Marketing *cost* analysis is more difficult and expensive than sales analysis. The major explanation is simply that the cost input data are splintered in numerous pieces and in many locations, and their assembly into meaningful segments is more difficult.

Marketing cost analysis is typically concerned with tracing costs associated with various product lines and territories. However, there are numerous other segments that can be analyzed. Only direct and separable costs are allocated and analyzed. The joint costs are left unallocated because by definition there is no logical basis for distributing them. After all, the purpose of cost analysis is to provide information to decision makers, *not* to account for all costs.

## REFERENCES

Baier, M. "Zip Code—New Tool for Marketers," *Harvard Business Review,* January-February 1967, pp. 136–140.

Barry, J. W. "Accounting's Role in Marketing," *Management Services,* January-February 1967, pp. 43–50.

Bierman, H. *Managerial Accounting: An Introduction.* New York: Macmillan, 1959.

The Brewing and Allied Industries. *The Brewing World.* Boulder, Colo.: May 1963.

Crisp, R. D. *Sales Planning and Control.* New York: McGraw-Hill, 1961.

Heckert, J. H., & Miner, R., *Distribution Costs.* New York: The Ronald Press, 1953.

Herring, D. "Distribution Cost Analysis," *Management Services,* September-October 1966, pp. 52–59.

Horngren, C. T. *Cost Accounting: A Managerial Emphasis.* (2nd ed.) Englewood Cliffs, N.J.: Prentice-Hall, 1967.

Howard, J. *Marketing Management: Analysis and Planning.* (2nd ed.) Homewood, Ill.: Richard A. Irwin, 1963.

Huff, D. L. "Defining and Estimating a Trading Area," *Journal of Marketing,* July 1964, pp. 34–38.

Kennedy, R., & Kurtz, R. *Introductory Accounting.* Scranton, Pa.: International, 1960.

Longman, D., & Schiff, M. *Practical Distribution Cost Analysis.* Homewood, Ill.: Richard D. Irwin, 1955.

Miller, D. W., & Starr, M. K. *Executive Decisions and Operations Research.* Englewood Cliffs, N.J.: Prentice-Hall, 1960.

Rayburn, L. G. "Setting Standards for Distribution Costs," *Management Services,* March-April 1967, pp. 42–52.

St. Clair, F. J. (Ed.) *Moody's Industrial Manual: American and Foreign.* New York: Moody's Investors Service, 1966.

Sevin, C. H. "Cost Control in Selling by Manufacturers," *Distribution Costs: A Key to Profits.* Chicago: American Marketing Association, 1958, pp. 12–15.

Stanton, W., & Buskirk, R. *Management of the Sales Force,* Homewood, Ill.: Richard D. Irwin, 1959.

Still, R., & Cundiff, E., *Sales Management,* Englewood Cliffs, N.J.: Prentice-Hall, 1958.

U.S. Bureau of the Census, *Census of the United States, 1960.* Washington, D.C.: Government Printing Office.

*Ten*

# Securing Information from Respondents

This chapter and the next one focus on the important topic of securing information from and about respondents by the use of questionnaires, scaling devices, and other data-collection instruments.[1] Information requirements and collection environments vary immensely. Information, for example, is collected from experiments as well as from nonexperimental or survey research studies. Sometimes respondents are asked questions. At times respondents or the results of their behavior are simply observed, sometimes with their permission, at other times without. Consequently, many different types of studies employing a wide variety of information-collection instruments must be viewed.

## TYPES OF INFORMATION

The types of information sought from respondents constitute a major influence on how the information is collected. Consequently, a principal division of the material between this and the following chapter is by type of information. The major types are information about the following characteristics of respondents:

1. Behavior.
2. Intentions.
3. Knowledge.
4. Socioeconomic traits.
5. Attitudes-opinions.
6. Motivations.
7. Psychological traits.

[1] Some aspects of this topic, of course, have been considered in preceding chapters.

Some of the seven information categories are almost self-descriptive, but a brief view of the content and use of each type of information may be helpful.

## Behavior

Behavior information has reference to what respondents have done or, in some cases, are doing. It has reference to respondents' physical actions and as such is only incidentally concerned with the other types of information. Respondents can be queried as to the nature of their past behavior, they can be asked to keep records of their behavior, *results* of their behavior (instead of the actual behavior) can be observed, and, finally, their behavior can be observed as it is occurring.

Behavior information permits a wider range of collection techniques than does any one of the other types of information. It can be collected through the many communication as well as observation techniques. In contrast, respondents' intentions, knowledge, attitudes, motivation, and psychological traits must be gathered through communication (except for what researchers can infer from observed behavior).

A major reason for seeking information from respondents is to make useful predictions about the future. What respondents have done in the past appears to influence what they will do in the future. Admittedly, it is difficult to discern respondents' past experiences and their future environments, but, nonetheless, past and present behavior must be examined to obtain a more positive predictive base.

Composite behavior information offers a better predictive base than do scattered isolated parts. The seeker of information, early in the design of his studies, should carefully consider all that needs to be known

| | Purchase Behavior | Use Behavior |
|---|---|---|
| Who | ____________ | ____________ |
| When | ____________ | ____________ |
| Where | ____________ | ____________ |
| How | ____________ | ____________ |
| What quantities | ____________ | ____________ |
| With what | ____________ | ____________ |

**Figure 10-1** Behavior checklist.

about respondents' behavior toward a specific phenomenon. A checklist, such as that shown in Figure 10-1, can help to accomplish this.[2] This chart should suggest consideration of such topics as who purchases the offering, who uses it, when it is purchased and when it is used, and how it is purchased and used. Quite clearly each of these questions contains many dimensions. For example, how is the offering purchased—cash or credit, through catalog or in person, on a convenience or shopping basis?

## Intentions[3]

Intentions have reference to respondents' anticipated or planned future behavior. A respondent, for example, may indicate plans to buy a new car and/or intentions to quit smoking within the next year.

Intention information may provide a very useful predictive base, but only if the respondents are in a better position to predict their particular behavior than are the information gatherers. Intention information receives relatively limited use in marketing, because most respondents fail to perceive and/or express the numerous contingencies that separate their intentions from their behavior. The respondents who intend to quit buying cigarettes may mean that they intend to stop buying *if* they can stop smoking. The if's are likely to be conditioned by uncalculables such as resulting weight change, nervous conditions, or environmental changes. When there are few contingencies and/or the respondent can and will consider the influence of the contingencies, intention information can provide a useful predictive base.

Other considerations influence the usefulness of intention information. When the lapse of time between expressed intention and actual behavior is brief, intentions, in general, come closer to reflecting behavior. The respondents who indicate intentions to purchase new cars (and plan to do it within the week) are more likely to purchase new cars than those who plan on making their purchases at a later date. "Strength" or intensity of intentions also has a bearing on resulting behavior. Respondents who feel very certain that they will buy new cars are more likely to do so than are those who are only somewhat certain that they will make the purchase. Finally, intention information relative to habitual behavior generally provides better predictions than do intentions about nonhabitual behavior. Cigarette-smoking respondents, for example,

[2] The suggestion for this checklist matrix came from a book by Fred T. Schreier (1963, p. 251).

[3] An excellent discussion of the use and gathering of intention information can be found in Lorie & Roberts (1951, Chapter 14).

are better able to predict how many packages of cigarettes they will purchase than to predict how "loyal" they will be to a newly introduced brand.[4] For good reason, intention information is known as "iffy" information. The respondent means *yes* or *no if, if, if!*

## Knowledge

Information on knowledge has reference to what respondents do and do *not* know about specific offerings and their uses. There is frequently at least some relationship between knowledge of an offering and related behavior. Starch Readership Service indicates, for example, that respondents who know of an advertisement (and the more they remember) are more likely to be influenced by it than others with less or no knowledge. Physicians, we hope, prescribe medicines whose efficacy they are knowledgeable about.

High-priced, infrequently purchased products (e.g., houses, cars, color television sets, guns) and/or products whose use is associated with high risk (e.g., power saws, self-medications) encourage many people to seek information prior to purchase. Extensive knowledge, however, is not needed prior to the purchase of some offerings (e.g., convenience goods such as candy, gum, and pencils). In other cases, sufficient knowledge to activate purchases is secured just before the behavior (e.g., wheelchairs, specific books, eyeglasses). In the last two situations, measurement of respondents' knowledge does not provide a very adequate predictive base. Finally, the extent of knowledge possessed by individual respondents may simply fail to relate to future behavior.

## Socioeconomic and Psychological Traits

Socioeconomic characteristics or traits have reference to such information as respondents' ages, incomes, formal education, gender, occupations, housing, and other related variables commonly referred to as classification data. Psychological traits have reference to respondents' states of mind such as rigidity, neuroticism, extroversion, and other personality characteristics. These traits, to be useful, must be measurable and must make a difference in future behavior.

Socioeconomic and psychological traits are frequently helpful in forecasting future events. Green and Tull (1966) report that the Radio Corporation of America found that the first color television set purchasers had relatively higher incomes and more formal education and

[4] For empirical data relative to relationships between intentions and behavior, see Hastay (1954) and Federal Reserve (1962).

were older on the average than the purchasers of black-and-white sets. Such socioeconomic information can be very useful in preparing marketing plans and strategies. The W. A. Sheaffer Pen Company, on the other hand, has found traditional socioeconomic variables virtually useless in that they do not appear to correlate with pen purchases or pen ownership (Riley, 1966). They, in turn, have experimented with the measurement and use of psychological variables such as romance, provincialism, sophistication, and transience.[5] The measurement and use of psychological traits have received far less attention and use than socioeconomic variables. However, as marketing managers focus more attention on consumer behavior, the psychological variables are receiving more attention. Psychological traits and their measurement are discussed in the next chapter.

## Attitudes-Opinions

Attitudes have reference to respondents' views or feelings toward some phenomenon. Opinions may be differentiated from attitudes as being verbal expressions of attitudes. However, present measurement instruments and needs in the field of marketing lead us to treat them as one throughout this book.

Attitude-opinion information has been collected by marketing people, psychologists, sociologists, and others to serve as predictive bases. Gallup and others are famous for their opinion polls and the resulting ability (and inability) to foresee future behavior.

The relationship of attitude-opinion information to future respondent behavior may appear to be quite simple and direct. Seemingly, the more favorable the attitude-opinion for one alternative, the more favorable the behavior toward it compared to other alternatives. That is, if measurements indicate that respondents view Camaros more favorably than Mustangs, would we not expect them to purchase more of the former?

Unfortunately, attitude measurement, though endowed with considerable promise, has been far less than a predictive paragon. Some of the difficulties have appeared to be due to poor measurement instruments, too great a lapse of time between attitude expression and behavior, inadequate consideration of alternative attitudes, and inference beyond the limits of the attitudes.

Attitudes-opinions and their measurement and use are discussed in the next chapter. In numerous respects, attitude measurement instru-

[5] For other findings relative to the usefulness of socioeconomic and psychological traits, see Newman (1966).

ments are both more complex and different from those of information collection discussed in this chapter.

**Motivation**

Motivation information has reference to *why* respondents have behaved in various ways. For example, an investigator may want to know why certain respondents smoke cigars while others smoke pipes. Motivation is used in this context in a far broader (i.e., less precise) manner than in psychology, where it usually has reference to the *interforce* or *drive* that propels, but does not direct, persons. Here, when we talk about motivation, our concern combines both drive and direction.

Motivation information can be very useful to decision makers, for it can give indications as to which offering features have had appeal, which have been neutral, and which have been negative. Pity the automobile salesman who promotes transportation to the prospect who is seeking romance, or, for that matter, vice versa. As with other types of information, decision makers attempt to use past information on motivation as a predicting base of how people will behave in the future. And, whether true or not, there is some belief that motivations tend to be more stable than behavior and, consequently, to offer better information for predictions.

The collection of the first four types of information mentioned above—behavior, intention, knowledge, and socioeconomic traits—is discussed in the remainder of this chapter. Attention is first focused on *criteria* for information from and about respondents. Then the *communication* method of securing information is viewed in terms of (1) the general forms that data-collection instruments can take, (2) the question sequences of instruments, and (3) the content of questions that make up instruments. The last section of this chapter discusses the *observational* method of securing information.

## INFORMATION CRITERIA

In attempting to collect information from respondents, investigators must strive to acquire sufficiently *accurate* and *unambiguous* information at appropriate *costs* and within specified *time* limits. At all stages in designing information collection studies, investigators ask and attempt to answer the question: "Will use of this design, this collection medium, this questionnaire form, this flow of questions, this wording, this supervision, and so forth, achieve the information with sufficient accuracy and freedom from ambiguity in time and at an appropriate cost?" Sometimes to meet one criterion, ground must be given on some other criterion. For example, a manager may want information from a study immediately, but in order to obtain more accurate information, it may be necessary to relax the time restriction.[6]

The term *accuracy* is used here in the same context as it has been used throughout the book. That is, it means the extent to which the collected information reflects the true situation. When, for example, respondents misstate their ages, obviously inaccurate information is reported. Of course, there are numerous sources of inaccuracy, but these will be discussed later.

*Ambiguity* is different from accuracy. For example, two 51-year-old women, when asked to report their ages, may answer "At my last birthday I was 51 years old" and "I am between 40 and 52." Both answers are accurate. The first response is quite free of ambiguity, whereas the second one is relatively ambiguous. Complete freedom from ambiguity is *not* a practical possibility. The key question, instead, is—what degree of ambiguity is permissible?

## COMMUNICATION METHOD

There are basically two methods for seeking information from and/or about respondents. Respondents can be *communicated* with (vocally or in writing) and they can be *observed* (Lorie and Roberts, 1951). The communication method can be used to seek all types of information. The observational method, however, by its very nature, is limited to the collection of behavior information, since direct observation of attitudes, intentions, motivations, knowledge, and psychological traits is normally not feasible. The communication method is examined first.

Ferber and Hauck (1964) outline three necessary conditions for a true response to a question:

1. The respondent must understand the question.
2. The respondent must be able to provide the information.
3. The respondent must be willing to provide the information.

The relevant point is "How are these three problems handled?" Certainly it *cannot* be said that complete answers to these problems are available. Securing information from respondents is far from being a science. Like portrait painting, there are some general guidelines to assist beginners along the way, but artistic (creative) talent is an additional requisite

[6] For further discussion of these, see Lorie and Roberts (1951).

for success. The general guidelines are considered in the pages that follow.

## Response Bias

A requisite for obtaining valid replies to questions of a confidential nature in interviews is that the interviewer provide a prejudice-free, nonjudgmental atmosphere during the interview (Pomeroy, 1963). Since most interviewers are incapable of this, it is incumbent on the research organization to carefully screen and train interviewers. Interviewers should also be sensitive to such telltale signs of falsity as hesitations, blushing, uneasiness, and attempts to evade the question.

Although some questions pertaining to very confidential matters are best asked in a personal interview, there are a class of other questions that are more likely to be answered validly either on the telephone or by mail. These are questions in which the respondent's answer may (as he sees it) either elevate or lower him in the eyes of the interviewer or in which the respondent may wish to give the interviewer answers that he thinks the interviewer would want to hear. Thus one study of a group of borrowers indicated that borrowing was more likely to be admitted in a mailed response than in an interview (Lansing, Ginsburg, and Braaten, 1961). In the study by Nuckols (1964) previously discussed, it was found that a mail sample of insurance holders yielded less biased results than did interviews. Nuckols also concluded that mailed questionnaires could be longer than is generally believed.

There is also evidence that telephone interviews are likely to yield more candid answers than personal interviews (Hochstum, 1962). The general conclusion seems to be that a respondent is most likely to be candid when the interview is impersonal, and certainly mailed questionnaires and telephone interviews are more impersonal than are personal interviews.

## The Choice—Personal Interview, Telephone, or Mail

This section summarizes the merits and demerits of the three principal forms of surveys.[7]

### *Cost*

By far the most costly technique is the personal interview. The cost per response in mailed questionnaires is generally low, but can increase

[7] An excellent summary of the findings up to 1961 concerning mail surveys may be found in Scott (1961).

if the initial nonresponse rate is high. Telephone interviewing varies in cost, depending on whether long-distance calls are involved and on the average length of each call, but it is generally far cheaper than personal interviews.

*Nonresponse Bias*

Both personal interviewing and telephone interviewing usually have low nonresponse rates, although in the former case this is accomplished at considerable expense by way of call-backs. The response rate in a mail survey can be as little as 15 per cent or as much as 95 per cent, depending both on the skill of the researcher and on the circumstances beyond his control. Although it is difficult to generalize, a response rate of 40 to 50 per cent is a typical range in marketing surveys.

*Response Bias*

The danger of what we have called response bias is probably greatest in the personal interview, where bias may emerge from the interviewer-respondent relationship. In mail surveys, a similar but lesser bias is introduced by the fact that it is not always certain who has replied and by the danger that respondents will read a section of the questionnaire rather than answering question-by-question. The response bias in telephone interviewing has not been well studied, but the evidence that exists indicates that this bias is low.

*Flexibility*

The most flexible survey method is the personal interview. Interviews, once initiated, are seldom terminated because of the length of the interview. All of the senses may be used, whereas the telephone interview is confined to the sense of hearing and the mail survey is confined to the sense of sight. On the other hand, both mail and telephone surveys reach a wider and more diversified audience.

*Conclusion*

The survey method chosen must depend on a number of factors, including cost, reliability, and the peculiar advantages or disadvantages of each method. If little funds are available, personal interviewing is out of the question. On the other hand, if the respondent must be probed at some length in order to obtain psychological data not readily available from a questionnaire, personal interviews are mandatory. If visual material must be presented, telephone interviewing is out of the question, unless combined with a mailing of the material. But if a quick response is desired to a question that need not be answered at great length, telephone interviews are ideal. Where the response rate is of great concern, a mail survey is hazardous. But where a wide and numerous sample must be reached, mail surveys are to be preferred.

A final note of caution must be inserted here. Just as amateur surgery can be disastrous, so can an amateur survey. This chapter was designed to provide an introduction into a fascinating and highly complex field, but an expert knowledge requires broader training and practical experience. The field of marketing research is not for the do-it-yourselfer.

## THE COLLECTION INSTRUMENT

Ferber and Verdoorn (1962) have suggested that the paramount considerations in the construction of information-collection instruments are the following:

1. The general form of the instrument.
2. The question sequence of the instrument.
3. The questions that make up the instrument.

## GENERAL FORM

General form has reference principally to the extent to which an instrument is *structured* and/or *disguised.* A structured instrument is one in which the questions and/or observations *and* the alternative responses or behavior are largely present prior to field collection of data. A series of specific questions are asked and normally the respondent is restricted to such answers as "yes," "no," "O.K." or to placing a check mark in an appropriate box. Mail questionnaires, for example, must be highly structured, since mail respondents simply do not take well to answering a series of open-end questions. They tend to ignore such questions or, at best, to insert simple answers, whether they are accurate or not. Also, recipients who feel overwhelmed with such open-response questions have a tendency to be nonrespondents (Ferber, 1949, p. 246).

In contrast, a relatively nonstructured instrument would involve a topic "to be discussed" with respondents. Each succeeding question would be based largely on the respondents' prior answers. An investigator, for example, might seek to discover by way of an unstructured study how respondents proceeded to buy a series of different products. Such studies call for somewhat lengthy personal interviews. The inter-

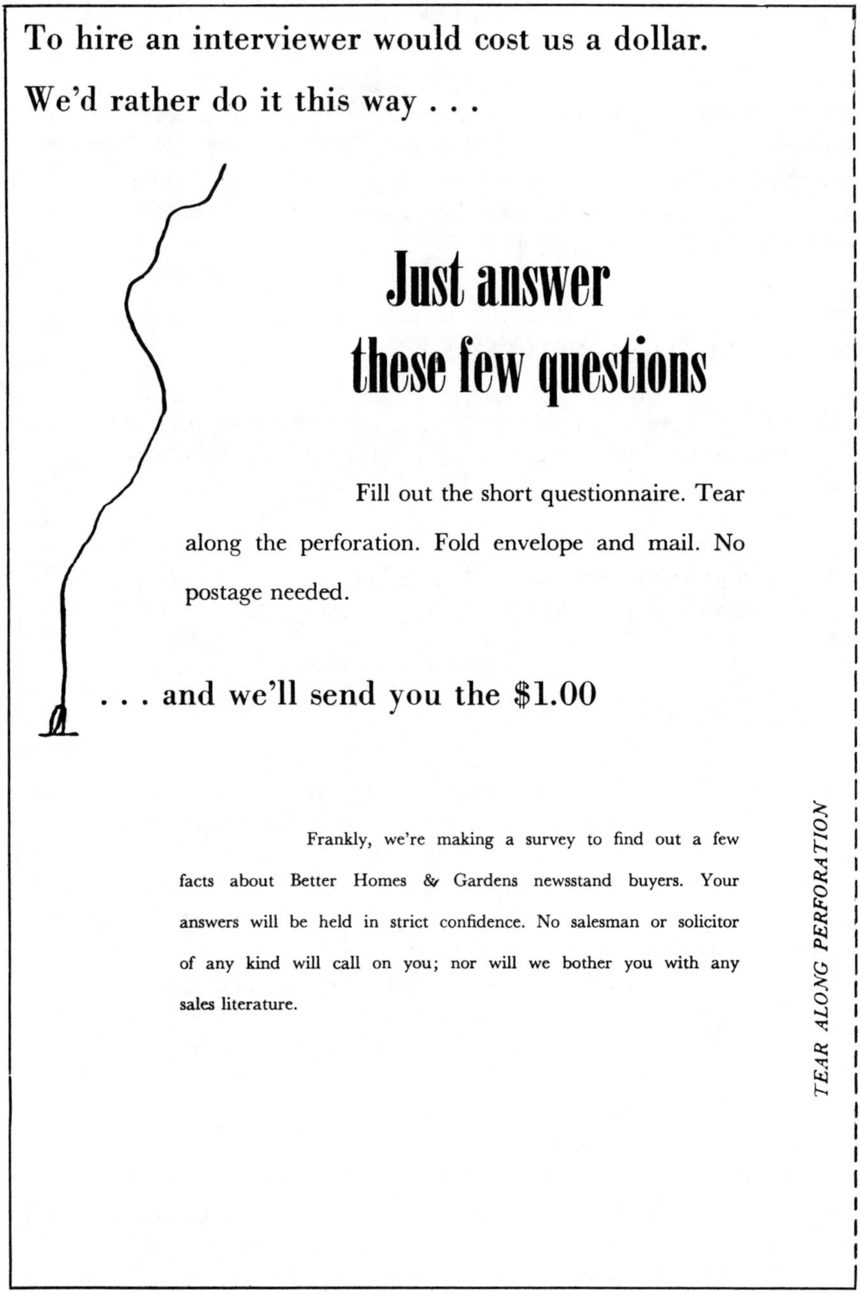

To hire an interviewer would cost us a dollar.

We'd rather do it this way . . .

**Just answer these few questions**

Fill out the short questionnaire. Tear along the perforation. Fold envelope and mail. No postage needed.

. . . and we'll send you the $1.00

Frankly, we're making a survey to find out a few facts about Better Homes & Gardens newsstand buyers. Your answers will be held in strict confidence. No salesman or solicitor of any kind will call on you; nor will we bother you with any sales literature.

*TEAR ALONG PERFORATION*

**Figure 10-2** A structured—nondisguised mail questionnaire. *Source:* Meredith Publishing Company.

## RUSH! *This offer expires October 31, 1956*

1. In the past 12 months, how often have you or any member of your family bought copies of *Better Homes & Gardens?*

   ☐ This issue is the first in past 12 months ☐ Almost regularly (from 7 to 11 issues)
   ☐ Once in a while (from 2 to 6 issues) ☐ Regularly (every month)

2. What is the last previous issue you bought?______________ month __________ year

3. From what type of store did you buy this October issue?

   ☐ Drugstore ☐ Newsstand ☐ Hotel
   ☐ Confectionery ☐ Cigar store ☐ Other
   ☐ Supermarket food store ☐ Department store
   ☐ Other grocery store ☐ Terminal (air, bus, R.R.)

4. Please check any of the following which influenced your purchase of this issue.

   U ☐ You regularly purchase Better Homes & Gardens.
   L ☐ You heard a radio commercial about this issue.
   O ☐ You were sent to buy this issue by someone else.
   P ☐ You heard about a particular article and wanted to read it.
   M ☐ You saw a newspaper ad about this issue.
   Z ☐ The titles listed on the cover drew your attention to articles inside.
   X ☐ You scanned the table of contents and found something interesting.
   T ☐ You looked through the magazine and found it interesting.
   F ☐ You were attracted by the cover illustration.
   H ☐ Other influence (what?) ______________________________

5. Which one of these would you say was <u>most important</u> in leading you to buy this issue?

   Please write in code letter found at left of the ☐__________.

6. Do you remember seeing a newspaper ad about this issue?

   ☐ Definitely remember an ad ☐ Don't remember ☐ Not sure

7. If you saw or think you saw an ad, in what newspaper?____________________
   City Name of paper

8. About how large was this ad? (Please check below.)

   ☐ One column 12 in. to 16 in. long ☐ Two columns 12 in. to 16 in. long
   ☐ One column 6 in. to 8 in. long ☐ Two columns 6 in. to 8 in. long
   ☐ One column 2 in. to 4 in. long ☐ Two columns 2 in. to 4 in. long

9. Do you remember hearing a radio commercial about this issue?

   ☐ Definitely remember a commercial ☐ Don't remember ☐ Not sure

10. If you heard a commercial, from what radio station?____________________

11. Which member of the family are you?

    ☐ Man of the house ☐ Homemaker ☐ Other (explain)__________

Be sure to give name and address on other side so we can send you $1.00.

Figure 10-2 (Continued)

viewer normally directs the interview and is responsible for recording the responses.[8]

## Disguised-Nondisguised

Disguised-nondisguised has reference to the extent of information identifying the sponsor and the purpose of the study and, in general, of any other information that is made known to the respondents. On some occasions it is appropriate to identify to respondents both the sponsor and the purpose of the study. In other instances greater effort is taken to disguise such information. Figures 10-2 and 10-3 illustrate two data-collection instruments used in connection with structured-nondisguised studies. A structured-disguised information-collection instrument is illustrated in Figure 10-4.

The extent to which a study should be structured and/or disguised

[8] For a discussion of the advantages of structured and unstructured questionnaires, see Walters (1961).

**FIRST A WORD ABOUT YOUR USE OF CHEESE**

**1. Can you remember how you first became acquainted with Maytag Blue Cheese?**

**____ heard about it from a friend**

**____ received some as a gift**

**____ read about it in a food column in a paper or magazine**

**____ from an advertisement—and can you remember where?____________**

**____ some other way (in a few words please tell me how)____________**

**2. In about what year did you first order Maytag Blue Cheese—**

**____ for yourself or family? ____ for others?**

**3. Have you given our cheese as a gift—**

**____ Yes ____ No**

**____ to members of the immediate family including married sons or daughters?**

**____ to relatives outside the immediate family?**

**____ to other family friends?**

**____ to persons you employ?**

**____ to business or professional friends or customers?**

**____ to others (and please specify the relationship)____________**

**4. Please try to recall for me how it was you started giving Maytag Blue Cheese as a gift—instead of something else?**

**Figure 10-3** A structured—nondisguised mail questionnaire. Maytag Dairy Farms, Inc., Newton, Iowa. *Source:* Uhl & Associates.

5. Is there a flavor besides our BLUE, SWISS, CHEDDAR, and EDAM Cheeses you might like to have available in our mailer packages?

____ Yes And what flavors?________________

____ No

6. Please check the following items you would like to be able to order along with your cheese—

____ cheese knife or slicer
____ cheese serving trays or dishes
____ fancy cheese container or preserver
____ something else (please specify)________________
____ nothing else—just cheese

7. Does our current assortment of package sizes (1 lb. to 5 lbs.) and prices ($2.50-$12.25) meet your gift giving needs?

____ would like a larger, more expensive cheese package available
____ would like a somewhat more expensive combination package (i.e.,
____ cheese/gift)
____ the current assortment is adequate for my gift giving needs
____ would like some other size or price assortment (please specify)
________________

NOW JUST TWO QUESTIONS ABOUT YOUR PROFESSION OR BUSINESS

8. What line of business or profession are you in?________________

9. And what is your title or position? For example, advertising director, president, head cashier, sales manager? Please be specific.

________________

FOUR FINAL QUESTIONS

10. Do you eat Maytag Blue Cheese? ____ Yes ____ No

11. What about other members of your family? –

____ all like it ____ most like it ____ some like it ____ none like it

12. Please list your family's 3 favorite magazines or papers other than your own local paper. ________________

________________ ________________

13. We try to please, but we know there is room for improvement. What could we do to serve you better? (Your brief comments would be helpful.)

________________

________________

Thank you so very much.

Please mail your answer in the stamped and addressed envelope.

**Figure 10-3** (Continued)

Interviewer's Name ____________
Date ____________

*MILK SURVEY*

Phone number called ________
Address listed ______________

******************************************************************

INTERVIEW FEMALE HEAD OF HOUSEHOLD ONLY:

Hello, we are making a study of family milk use in this area. I would like to ask you a few questions such as:

1. About how many ½ gallons of milk did your family use this last week? (Probe) Less than 1, 1–4, 5–10, over 10?

| | *Check One* |
|---|---|
| Less than 1 | ________ |
| 1–4 | ________ |
| 5–10 | ________ |
| Over 10 | ________ |
| Don't know | ________ |

(IF NO MILK IS USED CHECK "LESS THAN 1" AND SKIP TO QUESTION #18)

2. About how much of that milk was low fat or skim milk? (Probe) None of it, less than ½, about ½ of it, most of it?

| | *Check One* |
|---|---|
| None of it | ________ |
| Less than ½ | ________ |
| About ½ | ________ |
| Most of it (or all) | ________ |
| Don't know | ________ |

(IF SHE DOES *NOT* USE LOW FAT OR SKIM MILK, SKIP TO QUESTION #5.)

3. In your opinion which milk tastes best—low fat (skim), regular, or extra rich milk?

| | *Check One* |
|---|---|
| Skim | ________ |
| Regular | ________ |
| Extra Rich | ________ |
| No difference | ________ |
| Don't know | ________ |

4. In the last year or two has your family been using—*less* low fat or skim milk, or *more* low fat milk, or about the same as in the past?

| | *Check One* | |
|---|---|---|
| Less skim | ________ | |
| More skim | ________ | (If "more skim", see 4a.) |
| No or little change | ________ | |
| Don't know | ________ | |

**Figure 10-4** A Structure-Disguised Telephone Questionnaire. *Source:* Uhl & Associates.

4a. *Why* have you been using more low fat or skim milk?
(Probe) Weight consciousness, other health concern, more economical, or why?

Weight ________
Other health concern ________
More economical ________

5. Next we want to ask you:
Where did you get your milk this last week—mostly at the store, mostly by home delivery, about half and half?

Mostly at the store ________
Mostly at home ________
About ½ and ½ ________
Other (specify) ________
Don't know ________

6. Has this changed much in the past year or two?
Yes ________ No ________ Don't know ________

6a. More from the store ________
More at home ________

7. And can you tell us why you prefer to get your milk (the one they say in #5)?
________________________________________

8. Now we want to ask you about the milk container:
What *size* milk container do you prefer?
(Probe) Quart, ½ gallon, gallon, or what size?

*Check One*
Quart ________
½ gallon ________
Gallon ________
Other size ________
No difference ________

9. And what *kind* of container do you prefer?
(Probe) Glass, waxed paperboard, plastic, or doesn't make much difference?

*Check One*
Glass ________
Waxed paperboard ________
Plastic ________
No difference ________
Others (specify) ________________

10. Next, I want to read several phrases to you—on each of them just tell me the *first* two or three things you think of:
(IF SHE ONLY NAMES A DAIRY, WRITE IT DOWN BUT PROBE: And what else?

Iowawampum? ________________________________
________________________________________

Golden Guernsey? ________________________________
________________________________________

Quality Chekd? (DO NOT RECORD)

**Figure 10-4** (Continued)

11. Now, please name the dairies that serve your town.
(DO *NOT* READ THE LIST; AND NOTE CAREFULLY IF THEY SAY BAKER'S OR BAKER'S GOLDEN GUERNSEY)
(PROBE)—And can you think of any others?

| | |
|---|---|
| Baker's | ________ |
| Baker's Golden Guernsey | ________ |
| Borden's | ________ |
| Iowawana | ________ |
| Sanitary | ________ |
| Others (Don't specify) | ________ |
| Don't know | ________ |

12. Can you recall which dairy talks about:
(DO *NOT* READ THE DAIRY NAMES)

| | Baker's | Borden's | Iowawama | Sanitary | Other | Don't know |
|---|---|---|---|---|---|---|
| (1) Elsie the cow.................... | | | | | | |
| (2) Golden Guernsey Milk........... | | | | | | |
| (3) Happy Holstein Milk............ | | | | | | |
| (4) For the Active Family........... | | | | | | |
| (5) Quality Chekd.................. | | | | | | |
| (6) Very Big on Flavor............. | | | | | | |
| (7) Iowawampum.................. | | | | | | |

13. What brand of milk did you use the most of last week? (DO NOT READ THE LIST; WRITE A *1* IN THE SPACE SHE NAMES, NOTING IF SHE SAYS BAKER'S OR BAKER'S GOLDEN GUERNSEY).

| | |
|---|---|
| Baker's | ________ |
| Baker's Golden Guernsey | ________ |
| Borden's | ________ |
| Iowawama | ________ |
| Sanitary | ________ |
| Other (Don't specify) | ________ |
| Don't know | ________ |

14. Did you use any other brands of milk last week? (CHECK ON #13 ANY DAIRIES NAMED)
15. Have you switched brands of milk in the last year or two?
Yes ________ No ________ Don't know ________

(If yes, see 15a.)

**Figure 10-4** (Continued)

15a. What brand(s) have you switched away from?

Baker's ________

Borden's ________

Iowawama ________

Sanitary ________

Others (specify) ______________________

Don't know ________

15b. Can you tell us the most important reason for switching to another brand?

________________________________________________

16. Why do you use a certain brand of milk?
(PROBE)—richer, better tasting, more economical, more satisfying, or is there some other reason?

Richer ________

Taste ________

Economical ________

More satisfying ________

Other reason ________

Don't know ________

17. What price did you pay for last ½ gallon of

| 1) Low fat or skim milk | | | 2) Regular milk | | |
|---|---|---|---|---|---|
| Definite reply | _____ | cents | Definite reply | _____ | cents |
| Seemed to guess | _____ | cents | Seemed to guess | _____ | cents |
| Don't know | _____ | | Don't know | _____ | |

And finally, we want to ask you a few questions about your home and family.

18. How many years have you lived at your present address?
(PROBE)—less than 1 year, 1–3 years, or over 3 years?

Less than 1 year ________

1–3 years ________

Over 3 years ________

19. And do you own or rent?

Own ________

Rent ________

D. K. ________

20. How many children are there *at home* under 5 years old? ________
21. How many children between the ages of 5 and 15 *at home?* ________
22. And how many persons, including yourself, over 15 years? ________

22a. And how many of those over 15 drink milk regularly? ________

23. Approximately what age group does your husband fit in—under 30, 30–40, 41–50, over 50? (IF SHE HAS NO HUSBAND, ASK FOR HER AGE AND ALSO MARK THE LAST LINE.)

Under 30 ________

30–40 ________

41–50 ________

Over 50 ________

No husband ________

**Figure 10-4** (Continued)

24. And last year—which general grouping would include your *family* income —under \$3000, \$3000–\$5000, \$5001–\$8000, Over \$8000?

| | |
|---|---|
| Under \$3000 | ________ |
| \$3000–\$5000 | ________ |
| \$5001–\$8000 | ________ |
| Over \$8000 | ________ |
| Don't know | ________ |

25. Which grouping includes the last school grade *you* completed—grade school (1–8), high school, college, graduate college?

| | |
|---|---|
| Grades (1–8) | ________ |
| High school (9–12) | ________ |
| College | ________ |
| Graduate College | ________ |

**Figure 10-4** (Continued)

is largely dependent on the specific information being sought, how it is sought, the respondents, and the environment in which the information is sought. Of course, the underlying concern is to obtain information sufficiently accurate and free from ambiguity within required time and cost limits. These matters will be discussed in more useful detail in the following pages.

## QUESTION SEQUENCE

Question sequence, like general form, makes a difference in recipients' understanding of what is being sought, in their willingness to be respondents, and even in their ability to respond. Numerous prospective respondents feel that they have inadequate time for pleasurable activities, and answering questions of a personal nature for unknown strangers provides little pleasure. To say the least, prospects are less than eager. When a question-asking session starts by requesting a woman respondent to indicate her exact age, family income, and formal education and then proceeds to ask her to indicate the most important reasons for marrying the father of her children, the chances of securing a repertoire of accurate answers are greatly diminished.

### Instrument Introduction

The three major instrument vehicles (i.e., telephone, mail, face-to-face) require different introductions to the respondents. The telephone typically is used for short-duration, highly structured questioning. The interviewer needs to establish rapport immediately in order to retain the listener as a respondent. A very brief message of what is being sought is all that should normally precede the first question. The listener should be given little opportunity to withdraw from the conversation.

Each of the statements below has been successfully used as an introductory statement on telephone interviews:

Hello, we are making a study of family milk use in this area. I would like to ask you a few questions such as . . . .

Hello, I am ________ of ________. We are doing a research study about beverages. I am going to read off a list of beverages. Would you please tell me . . . .

Hello, I am making a survey of precooked prepared foods, I need your answers to just a few important questions.

Both mail and face-to-face media permit and encourage the use of somewhat more lengthy introductions. It is not uncommon, for example, prior to actual information collection, to call and/or write prospective respondents and tell them a little bit about the study and who is conducting it. Figure 10-5 shows such a letter. Such action helps to secure cooperation.

Sometimes introductions must be delayed until the actual time of questioning. The introduction seeks to establish sufficient rapport to see the respondent through the series of questions. The most difficult task is to get the recipients started, but a start does not assure a successful completion. This is why the entire instrument must present a continuous, smooth flow.

The introduction to mail questionnaires may appear as separate covering letters. Such a letter is illustrated in Figure 10-6. Very short mail questionnaires, however, may introduce themselves. The more successful introductions seem to center in "You, as a respondent, are of vital importance to our study and here is why!" "We need *your* help, please." Very subtle obligating techniques increase responses. As was indicated in Chapter 6, recipients of mail questionnaires feel more obligated to respond when preaddressed, prestamped envelopes are used (Gullahorn, 1959). The presence of "tokens of appreciation" (money, stamps, gifts, etc.) is often worth the cost. Other obligating appeal ploys are also used effectively (Kephart and Bressler, 1958; Levine and Gordon, 1958).

Similar sorts of considerations pertain to face-to-face interview situations. The interviewer greets the prospective respondent and must quickly establish rapport. Obviously, what the interviewer says is important. The introduction should be only as long as is needed to gain access

A MEMO TO MOTEL MANAGEMENT:

Cooperating Associations and Individuals

H. H. (Joe) Mobley
Executive Vice-Pres.
American Motor Hotel Assn.
Kansas City, Missouri

W. L. Edmundson, Jr.
Motel Consultant
Houston, Texas

Elmer Jenkins and
H. D. Cochran
National Touring Bureau
American Automobile Assn.
Washington, D. C.

Dr. Joseph W. Thompson
Director
Tourist & Resort Program
Michigan State University
East Lansing, Michigan

Will you help us to help you? We do not want your money - we do not want your business. We do want information and your opinions on how to run a motel. If you will give us this, we will return the favor by giving you a report which will tell you how others run their motels.

The University of Arizona has been awarded a research grant to do a nation-wide study of motel operation this year. Cooperating in this research are the individuals and groups listed at the left, state motel associations, endorsing associations, and the leading motel trade publications. The project is one of the most comprehensive studies of motel operation ever to be attempted. The findings will be of wide interest to you and every other motel operator.

Your motel has been scientifically selected as one of 2,000 motels chosen throughout the United States to represent the total of around 50,000 motels in operation in the nation. An interviewer will visit you at some time during the next few weeks requesting a bit of your time in obtaining information and your opinions about motel operation. May we "count you in" as one of the 2,000 motels representing the entire nation?

Our interviewers are largely faculty in Business Administration at The University of Arizona. They are responsible persons trained for this job. You may be assured that utmost care will be used to insure that your answers are handled in confidence and will be used in statistical tabulations only.

You will receive a letter from our interviewer a few days prior to his expected arrival date. He will tell you about the project and ask a few questions after he has arrived in your area and identified himself to you. If you wish a free copy of our final report, please tell him this at the completion of the interview.

May we look forward to your cooperation which will help you and the entire motel industry?

Cordially,

Lauren W. Casaday
Project Director

L-1 Source: University of Arizona

**Figure 10-5** Letter preceding personal interview. *Source:* University of Arizona.

to the appropriate respondent and to assist in reaching the first question and to help assure the completion of the interview.

## *Early Questions*

To respondents the first few questions are much like the first few steps on questionable ice. Respondents who feel they are on thin ice are likely to stop or turn back. When they feel firm footing, respondents are more likely to proceed. Some general comments can be given on what does and does not provide firm footing.

In all surveys some questions are less intimate, less difficult to raise, and less boring to answer than others. Some of these kinds of questions

**BETTER HOMES & GARDENS**

MEREDITH PUBLISHING COMPANY • DES MOINES 3, IOWA

Dear Reader:

I need your help - the answers to the questions in the enclosed "Confidential report to the editors of Better Homes & Gardens."

In editing Better Homes & Gardens and to answer questions frequently asked of us, we need a variety of background information about our readers. Your answers to the questions, along with those of other readers, will provide much needed information. They will help us to better serve you and our other readers.

This study is mostly about home furnishings, repairs, remodeling, and building. Whether you have done a little or a lot, whether your answer is yes or no, it is important to us. Please read each question carefully and give us your answers.

Since this study is going only to a small group, you represent several thousand readers. So you see it is very important that we have your answers. They will be used only in tabulating totals.

Won't you please answer the questions and return the booklet to me within the next few days in the stamped envelope provided.

We are counting on your help, and as a small token of our appreciation we are sending you a crisp new dollar bill.

Thank you very much,

Hugh Curtis

HC:cn

Editor

NEW YORK CHICAGO PHILADELPHIA CLEVELAND DETROIT ATLANTA LOS ANGELES SAN FRANCISCO

**Figure 10-6** Introduction to a mail questionnaire. *Source:* Meredith Publishing Company.

should normally provide a start. And if none of the questions qualify as a starting point, a contrived question(s) may be used. Two points should be kept in mind for the early questions. These questions should *not* probe into intimate, personal affairs *nor* be difficult to answer.

In a sense, people are very strange. Many are easily embarrassed and wish not to talk about the use of such products as toilet tissue, undergarments, and body deodorants and about their incomes and ages.[9]

The best way to discover what topics affront, embarrass, and/or are not subject to discussion by a respondent group, is to talk with the respondents and get to know them prior to the preparation of the data-collection instrument. Housewives who are college graduates may not be embarrassed or offended by questions about their formal education, but they may be very embarrassed about discussing their brassiere brand preferences. In contrast, "topless" waitresses may be very embarrassed by questions about their formal education, but be willing respondents in regard to brassiere brands. Consequently, these kinds of questions should not be asked early. Such questions may be asked later.

Easy-to-answer questions encourage response and should be used at the start. Questions can be difficult to answer because of respondents' poor memory, of the necessity of computations, of a necessity to search for records, of lack of knowledge, and/or because much thinking and/or writing is required. Such difficulties present impasses unless respondents are permitted honorable D.K.'s (don't know's).

Easy-to-answer questions are those which, for the most part, (1) call for short "yes" or "no" or check mark answers, (2) do not call for much thinking and recall, and (3) do *not* pose the respondents as either right or wrong. The opening questions on several of the illustrated data-collection instruments provide just these kinds of easy-to-answer questions that most persons are willing to answer.

## Instrument Flow

Once the flow of accurate information has started, the sequence of questions (and the other controllable variables) must be such that accurate and unambiguous information continues to flow. Remember that answering someone else's series of questions about someone else's products and problems can hardly be considered by respondents as an enjoyable task. Yet, on the other hand, bear in mind that successful face-to-face interviews of one and two hours, mail questionnaires of seventy or more questions, and telephone interviews of twenty-five minutes are not unheard of. However, the construction of such lengthy instruments calls for considerable creative skill.

[9] For a study reporting on this topic, see Sjorberg (1954).

Topics that are of interest to respondents normally make a data-collection job easier. Sometimes, however, a researcher must quiz men about the purchase and use of baby clothes or quiz women about wrench sets and about other "dull" topics.

Flows of questions that are logical to respondents aid recall, thinking, and, in general, help to retain respondents' cooperation. An investigator seeking to know the sequence and the time over which respondents have owned various makes of cars should *not* start by asking first, "Have you ever owned a Ford? If so, when?" and so on for each car brand. He would get more accurate answers faster by working back on a time path from present to past and also from the general to the more specific. For example, respondents might be asked:

What make(s) of car(s) do you presently own? In what year and what month did you buy it? What make did you own prior to the one you own now? In what *year* did you buy that car? And can you recall the month?

Related topics are best grouped together so that respondents do not need to refocus their thinking from, say, their house to food purchases, to intentions toward savings, toward the best location for a new grocery store, and so forth. A data-collection instrument can range over many topics, but the movement among topics (as within topics) should appear smooth to the respondents.

When numerous hard-to-answer, embarrassing, or offensive questions must be asked, it is best, on most instruments, to intersperse them with easy-to-answer, nonembarrassing, and nonoffensive questions. Quite simply, pleasant-to-answer questions following painful questions are less likely to terminate a flow of responses than one painful questions heaped on another.

A few final comments about the flow of questions may be helpful. Respondents should not be conditioned to give inaccurate answers because of sequences of question rewards and punishments. For example, when "no" or "D.K." answers permit respondents to go immediately to the next question, but "yes" answers call for more elaboration, respondents are likely to provide more "no" or "D.K." answers.

Finally, the best way to determine whether or not a sequence of questions is appropriate, once general rules and intuition have been exhausted, is to simply test instruments under realistic conditions.[10] Such tests may point out structural, sequential, and other unnoticed flaws.

[10] One survey study that asked questions about family life, work experiences, social participation, and three other related topics indicated that the six *blocks* of questions could appear in any sequence without influence on the findings (Bradburn and Mason, 1964).

## QUESTION FORMULATION[11]

Simple subjects, such as models of cars owned and books read, might appear to pose little problem in gaining accurate responses. Yet a study by Cantril (1947, pp. 102–103) indicated that respondents interviewed and reinterviewed in a three-week period gave consistent answers on car ownership only 86 per cent of the time. Lorie and Roberts (1951) relate a story about measuring readership of *Gone With the Wind.* When respondents were asked. "Have you read this book?" more "yes" replies were received than were known to be possible. When the question was rephrased to "Do you intend to read *Gone With the Wind?*" only those who had read it indicated so, and the affirmative response was much lower. These two illustrations should make clear that man does not hold "truth" above all else, but instead must be "encouraged" to provide accurate responses.

Berelson and Steiner (1964, Chapter 17) have said so well what men have known so long about themselves.

> He (man) is a creature who adapts reality to his own ends, who transforms reality into a congenial form, who makes his own reality. . . . In his quest for satisfaction, man is not just a seeker of truth, but of deception, of himself as well as others.

Those who prepare studies to collect information from men must continually be aware of the need to provide the proper environment and encouragement to respondents to obtain accurate information sufficiently free of ambiguities. Wording of questions, the persons who ask them, and how they are asked can all lead to accuracy distortions and ambiguities.

An appropriate starting place is to see why inaccuracies and ambiguities arise from improper question formulation. The major sources are respondents who (1) simply do not understand questions (ambiguous communication), (2) are not *able* to provide the answers, and (3) are not *willing* to provide the answers.

### Do Not Understand Questions

Why do respondents not understand questions? The two major faults are poor question construction and use of words not familiar to respondents.

[11] More extensive information on question formulation can be found in Parten (1950, Chapters 5 and 6) and Payne (1951).

Poor question construction normally is due to (1) ambiguity, (2) lack of mutual exclusiveness, and (3) lack of meaningfulness. For example, ambiguity is present in a question like "What *kind* of T.V. set do you own?" Does the question refer to color as contrasted with black-and-white, console or table model, brand, or just what? The question does not specify the dimension that is sought.

A question that inquires "Did you buy yellow, white or buttered popcorn?" is not *mutually exclusive,* but instead asks two questions. Responses in all probability would be confusing, and certainly better responses would be gained through the use of two separate questions.

A *meaningless* sort of question would be "How are you doing these days?" It is useless. What do answers such as "fine," "O.K.," or "terrible" mean? Also, when questions are too long, they lose clarity and meaningfulness. For example, the overuse of words in the following question make it confusing: "The last time you or your spouse purchased a tin of smoked oysters from a store in a town, did you consider several different brands or did you consider just two brands or did you consider only one brand?" An easier-to-understand phrasing would be: "When you last purchased a can of smoked oysters, how many brands did you consider?" In general, questions should be limited to no more than 20 words. If more than 20 words seem necessary, perhaps two questions are called for.[12]

### *Unfamiliar Words*

It is very easy for a question to be misunderstood. The same word or combination of words may have different meanings to different people. Studies have shown that even nominal changes in verbal measurement devices can lead to significant changes in responses (Rugg, 1941, 1942).

An excellent example of both the vagueness and richness of words is provided by the perennial debate topic, "Resolved that the Pen is Mightier than the Sword." Taken literally, the proposition is ridiculous. As almost every schoolboy who takes the negative side of the debate is quick to point out, if attacked by a thug, a sword provides somewhat greater protection than the pen.[13] If the topic of the debate is interpreted as, "Resolved that the Writings of Man have had a Greater Impact on the World than have the Armies of Man," the question takes on a totally different cast.

Words and phrases like *dentifrice, interstate, intrastate, atypical, medium whole grain cereal, silicon-based,* and *polyunsaturated* are fre-

[12] Additional illustrations of poor question construction can be found in Ferber and Verdoorn (1962, p. 224).

[13] An exception might be made for the tear-gas variety of pen.

quently not understood by consumers, and their use should be avoided. Information-collection instruments are not places appropriate for researchers to display their vocabularies. Words that have multiple meanings, such as *grip, junket, muffler, mule,* and *shrimp,* must be clear in the context in which they are used, or else not be used at all. A question asking, *How is your grip?* would be quite meaningless unless respondents knew what *grip* was being discussed.

Unanchored adjectives or adverbs like *expensive, cheap, costly, high, deep, long, short, normally, frequently, seldom, high, low, big,* and *small* should be avoided unless researchers know the respondents' frames of reference. Persons who spend $37 per pair for shoes may refer to $25 shoes as being cheap, while the wearer of $14 shoes may consider them expensive.

Such inclusive words as *never, ever,* and *always* should generally be avoided unless the investigator truly means "have you ever," that is, ever at any time (Payne, 1951).

Laudatory, derogatory, and other biasing words and phrases should not be used. Investigators should not incorporate words that are a part of a firm's advertising campaigns into data-collection instruments, unless a test of those specific words is planned. "When was the last time you bought *mountain-grown* Hills Brothers' Coffee?" "Have you flown *the friendly skies* with United?" "Are you for or against urban renewal for this *beautiful, tax-producing,* two block area?" Use of such words tends to lead suggestive respondents to invalid answers.

The major preventive step is to ascertain whether or not each question means the same to respondents as it does to the originator of the questions. Thus if a study included a question asking, "Do you use a *granulated* detergent?" the researcher would be well advised to investigate the meaning of the words *granulated* and *detergent* to respondents.

## Ability to Provide Answers

Whether it is because people like to be helpful or because they do not want to appear unknowledgeable, people will often answer questions about which they know nothing. A famous example of this was provided by a study in which respondents were asked their opinion of the Metallic Metals Act (Gill, 1947). Some 70 percent of those interviewed had an opinion, in spite of the fact that no such piece of legislation exists.

Almost every survey includes questions on demographic characteristics and income. Many respondents may yield inaccurate answers unintentionally. Ferber and Hauck (1964) have shown that information is more accurate when the respondent has consulted records before replying. Unfortunately, asking people to consult records may result in a lack of cooperation and even in a lower response rate. One may generalize that if the accuracy of the question is important, it may be necessary to persuade respondents to consult records.

Ambiguous answers frequently arise when respondents are permitted to frame their own responses. Individuals asked to indicate the number of cigarettes they have smoked in the past year, for example, may respond with answers such as "over 2000," "about the same number as last year," or "between 1000 to 20,000."

When respondents cannot provide accurate, unambiguous answers, they must be encouraged to reply that they do not know the answer. Finally, questions that are unanswerable to most respondents should not be asked.

### *Remembering and Forgetting*

Inaccuracies and excessive ambiguities may be avoided by helping respondents to remember. The question arises, "What factors affect memory?" The major factors are (1) the events to be recalled, (2) the persons who are attempting recall, (3) length of time elapsed since the events, (4) the experiences of the respondents since the events, and (5) the recall aids provided to the respondents (Lorie and Roberts, 1951, Chapter 5).

Investigators have very little control over factors 1, 2, and 4. However, they can exercise considerable control over the time lapse (3) and aids to recall (5).

Respondents, in general, can remember for a longer time those events that are *habitual* to them. For example, a person who has two eggs, toast, and coffee every morning for breakfast can likely recall what he had to eat for his breakfast two weeks ago as well as when and what he ate the last time he did not consume his normal breakfast.

Important events are also subject to recall for a longer time. Not all events are equally important to all persons. Important events generally include those that seem to cause considerable change in a person's financial status, take a considerable amount of time, and/or have considerable emotional impact—whether it be happy or sad. Finally, events that deviate considerably from the commonplace (for the individual) are more subject to recall. For example, a man is more likely to recall the last time he saw a woman smoking a cigar or pipe than smoking a cigarette. He is more likely to recall each previous new car purchase than he is each oil change, and so forth.

### *Aids to Memory*

Investigators are able to both aid and hinder recall, as well as have little influence on recall. We have already talked about starting respondents at the right point and flowing question in a direction to aid recall.

In addition, recall aid on individual questions can be provided. Such aid can vary among use of what is called "recognition methods" to "aided recall" to "unaided recall."

Basically, "recognition method" has reference to helping people recall by showing them the actual alternatives or facsimiles thereof. An interviewer asking the brand of toothpaste that respondents use would display the actual products or pictures of them.

When "aided recall" is used, verbal symbols are employed instead of the actual product or picture. In this situation the respondent would be asked a question such as:

Which one of the following brand(s) of toothpaste did you last use?

Colgate
Gleem
Crest
Pepsodent
Stripe

The "unaided recall" title is a misnomer. It really only means that the actual alternatives, facsimiles, or word symbols are not displayed. Instead, the respondents would be asked a question such as: "What brand of toothpaste did you last use?"

### *Recall Biases*

The various recall aids must be carefully applied, so that systematic biases are not introduced into the responses. Both the "recognition" and "aided recall" methods may introduce positional biases, order biases and affirmative biases and may also contribute to familiarity biases.

*Positional* and *other biases* have reference to respondents' tendency to select response alternatives that appear in favorable locations or places. The first and second words, pictures, packages, and other items in an array, for example, are more likely to be noted and selected than are the eighth or ninth items in an array of twelve or thirteen items (Payne, 1951, p. 84). Also, English-reading respondents have a tendency to note and select items appearing in the upper left hand corner of a page rather than in other locations (Becker, 1954).

These *positional* and *order biases* can be controlled by rotating the order or the position of the alternative answers so that the alternative answers appear in each location an equal number of times. That way different respondents see the alternative answers in different locations (Kinard, 1955).

An *affirmative bias,* in general, has reference to a tendency of respondents to either respond with a *yes* answer or to select from only the shown alternatives, even when the instrument permits them to name some other alternative.[14] For example, respondents, when presented cards picturing the ten best-selling brands of toothpaste and a blank card saying "Some Other Brand?," have a tendency to pick from among the ten named brands even though the accurate answer is some other brand.

One way to prevent this bias is to present all of the alternative answers, but this is not always possible. A second solution is to place somewhat more attention on the open-response alternative and make it very easy to use. Finally, this bias can be avoided by using the "unaided recall" method.

A *familiarity bias* is a tendency for some respondents to select the alternative answers that seem most familiar. Respondents questioned about their last purchase of flashlight batteries, brand of beer, scotch whiskey, and numerous other extensively advertised products, have a tendency (above what is accurate) to report brands that are familiar to them. Some of these people simply do not recall that they purchased "Long Glow Batteries," "Mother Pearl Beer," or Peter Dawson Scotch Whiskey.[15]

## UNWILLING TO RESPOND

Respondents may understand the questions and have sufficient information to be able to respond, but be unwilling to respond with sufficient accuracy and freedom from ambiguity. A host of reasons lead to such situations. Respondents may feel that accurate, precise answers would (1) cause them some loss of prestige, (2) conflict with views they attribute to the instrument, (3) take too much time and/or effort, and/or (4) invade their privacy.

Typically, research directed by universities is fortunate in that respondents will reply to questions they normally would refuse to reply to. Other organizations may develop excellent reputations over the years. For example, the Institute for Sex Research, Inc. claims not to have violated a confidence in more than twenty years, and this reputation (particularly among prison and underworld groups) is apparently widespread (Walters, 1961).

Market research companies and industrial firms usually do not have the opportunity to establish a widespread reputation in the community for confidentiality. This illustrates one virtue of a consumer panel—an

[14] For more detailed discussion of the problem, see Wells (1961).

[15] Additional illustrations and discussions of the various biases can be found in Lorie and Roberts (1951).

ongoing relationship and trust is built up over time between the research organization and members of the panel.

When respondents are unwilling to be truthful, the kindest "respondents" are those who simply will not respond. Unfortunately, through conditioning and for other reasons, many respondents provide inaccurate and/or ambiguous responses.

### *Loss of Prestige*

It is not uncommon for respondents to seek greater prestige through the use of inaccurate as well as ambiguous responses. For example, surveys of magazine readership turn up far more readers of *Harpers* and *Saturday Review* and far fewer readers of pulp paper romance and detective magazines than are known to exist (American Marketing, 1937, p. 66). Many respondents report that they have brushed their teeth, used underarm deodorant, bought premium-priced beer, and other such activities that they have not really done in order to appear more "respectable" or proper. Man is quite vain and given the opportunity will often toot his tune as Mr. Alright Guy.

### *Conflict with Instrument Views*

Numerous respondents seek to provide answers that they think investigators want, regardless of the truth. In turn, inaccurate and ambiguous information arises. A WCTU member, who looks like Carrie Nation, asking fellow Methodist members in rural America if they have abstained from alcoholic beverages gains a far higher affirmative response than behavior suggests does actually exists. And such inaccurate responses are not limited to questions about alcoholic beverages (Smith and Hyman, 1950; Wyath and Campbell, 1950). Green and Tull (1966, p. 133) report that when the Carnation Company was "identified" in an interview situation, more respondents were found to use their evaporated milk than when they were not identified. No doubt this "pleasing nature" is present in many people and extends over numerous products. Of course, even when only a small proportion of the persons interviewed given inaccurate or ambiguous responses, poor information will result.

### *Time and Effort Restraints*

Respondents may give inaccurate and/or ambiguous responses in order to save time and effort. They may not want to think through to a correct and/or specific answer. A person asked to indicate the brands of cars he has owned in the past 20 years, for example, may indicate that he has owned all Fords.[16] Such a response is far faster, and more

[16] Ambiguities would arise if, instead of an inaccurate answer, he indicated he had owned "about all Fords."

likely to forestall the question of when each was owned, than if he had truthfully described when and why he owned a Hudson Hornet, a Frazier, and a Corvair. Respondents try to save time and effort when they are indifferent to a line of questioning.

*Protect Privacy*

Finally, inaccurate and ambiguous answers are used by respondents to protect their privacy. Often such answer alternatives are easier to use than no responses at all. Some respondents, for example, feel that the subject of family income is a private matter. Occasionally, respondents in answering mail questionnaires will join two separate income ranges together to make their information more ambiguous.

| | | |
|---|---|---|
| | ________ | 2,000–4,999 |
| X { | ________ | 5,000–7,999 |
| | ________ | 8,000–10,000 |
| | ________ | 11,000–12,999 |

Some high-income respondents, to protect their privacy, will report incomes lower than are actually the case.[17]

## Detection of Inaccuracies and Ambiguities

The final question is, "When *prevention* of inaccuracies is not feasible, how can they be detected and kept from disrupting research studies?" One solution is to ask for essentially similar information at two widely separated points in the collection instrument. For example, to discern persons' ages, respondents can be asked the year in which they were born. Later they can be asked how old they are. If greater disguise is needed, a reasonably safe approach is to ask respondents what year they graduated from high school. Unfortunately, the investigator may not be able to identify which of the responses are correct. Also, if a flow of answers to a series of questions seem inconsistent, interviewers and/or editors should suspect inaccurate responses.

A second check on the accuracy of some responses is immediate verification of some or all of the responses. Respondents, for example, who have indicated use of, say, Eveready flashlight batteries, can be asked to trade their old batteries to the interviewer for new long-life ones. Respondents' pantries, closets, magazine racks, bathrooms, and so forth can often be audited (on one pretense or another) after they have indicated the brand and product possessed (American Marketing, 1937,

[17] These two practices have been observed on several survey research projects conducted by one of the authors.

p. 66). In this verification check, there is opportunity to obtain correct answers.

A third check involves comparing findings from the study with what was previously known (Hyman, 1944). For example, in a market where premium-priced beers hold a 25 per cent market share, a market-wide study indicating 65 per cent would be suspect. Respondents' ages clustering around final digits of 0's and 5's are suspect in that one would expect equal distribution on last digits reported from 0 through 9.[18]

### Interviewer Cheating

Inaccuracies can also be attributed to interviewer cheating. The most obvious source of such inaccurate responses is in the interviewers' attempts to provide answers unaided by respondents. On occasion they will simply proceed to provide answers all by themselves. At other times they will seek the help of other, still inappropriate persons.

Several checking practices are possible. To discourage such deception, interviewers can be told that interviews will be subject to actual verification call-backs. This can actually be accomplished, but its threat alone may be a sufficient deterent.

Cheat answers frequently are self-disclosurers. That is, when compared with legitimate answers the cheat answers often stand out as unusual responses. The difficult-to-detect cheat answers occur when interviewers hurry interviewees along by skipping over and providing their own answers for only some of the questions.

The best protections against interviewer cheating are to hire experienced interviewers, see that they are adequately trained and instructed, and pay them in accordance with the demands placed on them. Interviewers who are puzzled, frustrated, underpaid, and faced with what appear to them as unreasonable expectations are the ones most likely to cheat (Bennett, 1948).

## INFORMATION VIA OBSERVATION

Observation *can be* substantially superior to communication when behavior information is to be collected. It generally is more accurate and less ambiguous. Observers, however, can miscount, mistally, and simply fail to see relevant happenings. Different observers may not see events the same way. For example, an observer watching people attracted by

[18] A good illustration of this tendency can be found in U.S. Census (1940).

| Time: start | Time: minutes elapsed | Set. No. ______________ Description of activity | Activity code symbol |
|---|---|---|---|
| 0900 | 05 | Reported for work, man came in, wanted service shop, directed him there | 0 |
| 0905 | 10 | On floor, waiting for sales meeting to start, no activity | 0 |
| 0915 | 25 | Sales manager conducts sales meeting: (1) showed and explained 2 new wall charts highlighting product differences between Chevrolet and Ford: the "Ford-Chevrolet Comparison by Series" and "Engine Comparison" charts. (2) Showed slide film on product comparison of Ford vs. Chevrolet: "Hidden Values." (3) Gave out booklets containing recap of film. (4) Went over day schedule of activity with salesmen. Subject salesman merely directed to work outside dealership in A.M., on floor P.M. Had not seen film previously. | 0 |
| 0940 | 12 | Make ready to leave for outside calls: fueling car, assembling sales literature, reviewing prospect list. | 0 |
| 0952 | 6 | Telephoned bird dog service station manager. No prospects reported. | 0 |
| 0958 | 12 | Driving to first prospect. | 0 |
| 1010 | 05 | Called at home for woman on suggestion of her son who had his car serviced and remarked to salesman that his mother wanted . . . | 0 |

*Activity code*

F—Fact to face contacts with prospects and customers
W—Waiting time while on floor duty (not otherwise occupied)
T—Telephone contacts with prospects and customers
M—Mail contacting of prospects and customers
O—Other work (specify)

*Be sure to specify, wherever applicable:*

(1) Just *what* is salesman doing?
(2) Exactly *where* is he?
(3) What is his *intention?*
(4) *Outcome* of prospect contacts
(5) Just *who* is involved?
(6) Is *supervision* present?
(7) *Origin* of prospects
(8) Prospect's *present car?*
(9) Salesman acting on *own initiative?*

*Source:* Ford Motor Company

**Figure 10-7** Observation form.

a new package may only report those who pick up the package. Another observer may report all persons who seem to at least see the package.

Typically, ambiguity arises when investigators attempt to infer beyond what they have actually observed. The presence of a copy of *Playboy Magazine* in the living room of a Sig Ep housemother does not necessarily mean that she has purchased it or even read it. Cans in a cupboard may merely point out what is *not* being used. On the other hand, tire brands on cars are a good indication of brand use and ownership.

Thus much of the ambiguity arising from observations can be controlled simply by not making unwarranted assumptions. Instead of making such assumptions, observation can often be followed up by communication. The Sig Ep housemother can be queried, "Have you read this magazine?" "Did you buy it?" Observations are often a helpful adjunct to communications, and vice versa.

Cost and time requirements of the observational method generally are higher when "respondent" cooperation must be gained. When they participate as unknowing subjects, both time and cost considerations may make observation more appropriate than communication.

Observation takes numerous forms. The pantry, magazine rack, bathroom, garage inventories, each have reference to the general types of products that the interviewers hope to observe. Store audits are used to discern quantities of sales at the retail level. A garbage inventory reportedly has been used to observe discarded containers and products in order to discern what products selected households have used. Observation is used to discern traffic patterns both in stores and in other locations. Buying behavior has been observed to see "how" people select various products. The Ford Motor Company used a "time and motion" study in an attempt to discern why some salesmen sold many cars and some sold few cars. (See Figure 10-7.) Several additional techniques are described in Chapter 12 under the heading of Commercial Information.

## SUMMARY

This chapter has focused attention on the topic of securing information from and about respondents, through the use of various data-collection forms. Problems associated with the collection of information on respondents' behavior, intentions, knowledge, and socioeconomic traits have for the most part, been grouped together. This has been possible because the collection problems are similar. On the other hand, the collection of information about respondents' motivations, attitudes, and psychological traits presents different problems. Accordingly, these topics are treated separately, in the following chapter.

Information about respondents can be collected through both verbal communication and observation. Verbal communication permits a wider range of information collection than does observation. In turn, though, observation techniques tend to provide more accurate and less ambiguous answers. Their dual use is common.

The basic problems of the communication approach are to phrase questions so that respondents will (1) understand the questions being asked, (2) have the ability to answer the questions, and (3) be willing to answer the questions. The paramount considerations in constructing adequate collection instruments are determining (1) the general form of the instrument, (2) the question sequence of the instrument, and (3) the make-up of the individual questions. These three considerations, along with a host of nondata-collection form factors, must be handled in order to communicate with respondents.

The observation approach can take on a variety of forms. Audits of various inventories as well as observation of events as they are occurring are commonplace. Observation can result in quite accurate and unambiguous findings, so long as observers do not attempt to infer beyond their observations.

The following chapters delve into other ways of collecting various types of information.

## REFERENCES

American Marketing Association, *The Technique of Marketing Research.* New York: McGraw-Hill, 1937.

Becker, S. L. "Why an Order Effect?" *Public Opinion Quarterly.* Fall 1954, pp. 271–278.

Bennett, A. S. "Observations on the So-Called Cheater Problem Among Field Interviewers," *International Journal of Opinion and Attitude Research,* Spring 1948, p. 89.

Berelson, B., & Steiner, G. A. *Human Behavior: An Inventory of Scientific Findings.* New York: Harcourt, Brace & World, 1964.

Bradburn, N. M., & Mason, W. M. "The Effect of Question Order on Response," *Journal of Marketing Research,* November 1964, pp. 57–61.

Brown, L. O. *Marketing and Distribution Research.* (3rd ed.) New York: The Ronald Press, 1955.

Cantril, H. *Gauging Public Opinion.* Princeton, N.J.: Princeton University Press, 1947.

"Quarterly Survey of Buying Intentions," *Federal Reserve Bulletin,* November 1962.

Ferber, R. *Statistical Techniques in Market Research.* New York: McGraw-Hill, 1949.

Ferber, R., & Hauck, M. "A Framework for Dealing with Response Errors in Consumer Surveys," *Proceedings of the 1964 Fall Conference,* American Marketing Association, pp. 533–540.

Ferber, R., & Verdoorn, P. J. *Research Methods in Economics and Business.* New York: Macmillan, 1962.

Gill, S. "How Do You Stand On Sin?" *Tide,* March 1947, p. 72.

Green, P. E., & Tull, D. S., *Research for Marketing Decisions,* Englewood Cliffs, N.J.: Prentice-Hall, 1966, p. 124.

Gullahorn, J. T., & Gullahorn, J. E. "Increasing Returns from Nonrespondents," *Public Opinion Quarterly,* Spring 1959, pp. 119–121.

Hastay, M. "The Dunn & Bradstreet Survey of Business Expectations," *Proceedings of the Business & Economic Section,* American Statistical Association, September 1954, pp 93–123.

Hochstum, J. "Comparison of Three Information Gathering Strategies in a Population Study of Sociomedical Variables," *Proceedings of the Social Statistics Section,* American Statistical Association, 1962, pp. 154–159.

Hyman, H. "Do They Tell the Truth?" *Public Opinion Quarterly,* Winter 1944, pp. 557–559.

Kephart, W. M., & Bressler, M. "Increasing the Response to Mail Questionnaires: A Research Study," *Public Opinion Quarterly,* Summer 1958, pp. 123–132.

Kinard, A. J. "Randomizing Error in Multiple Choice Questions," *Journal of Marketing,* January 1955, pp. 260–262.

Lansing, J. B., Ginsburg, G. P., & Braaten, K. *An Investigation of Response Error.* Urbana, Ill.: Bureau of Economic and Business Research, University of Illinois, 1961.

Levine, S., & Gordon, G., "Maximizing Returns on Mail Questionnaires," *Public Opinion Quarterly,* Winter 1958–59, pp. 568–575.

Lorie, J. H. & Roberts, H. V., *Basic Methods of Marketing Research,* New York: McGraw-Hill, 1951.

Newman, J. *On Knowing the Consumer,* New York: Wiley, 1966.

Nuckols, R. C. "The Validity and Comparability of Mail and Personal Interview Surveys," *Journal of Marketing Research,* February 1964, pp. 11–16.

Parten, M., *Surveys, Polls, and Samples,* New York: Harper & Brothers, 1950.

Payne, S. L. *The Art of Asking Questions,* Princeton, N.J.: Princeton University Press, 1951.

Pomeroy, W. B. "The Reluctant Respondent," *Public Opinion Quarterly,* Summer 1963, pp. 287–293.

Riley, R. T. "Use of Psychographic Variables," Sheaffer Pen Company Report. Fort Madison, Ia.: 1966.

Rugg, D. "Experiments in Wording Questions: II," *Public Opinion Quarterly,* March 1941, pp. 91–92.

Rugg, D., & Cantril, H. "The Wording of Questions in Public Opinion Polls," *Journal of Abnormal and Social Psychology,* 1942, pp. 469–495.

Schreier, F. T. *Modern Marketing Research—A Behavioral Science Approach.* Belmont, Calif.: Wadsworth Publishing, 1963.

Scott, C. "Research on Mail Surveys," *Journal of the Royal Statistical Society,* Ser. A, **124,** 1961, pp. 143–205.

Sjoberg, G. "A Questionnaire on Questionnaires," *Public Opinion Quarterly,* Fall 1954, pp. 423–427.

Smith, H. L., & Hyman, H. "The Biasing Effect of Interviewer Expectations on Survey Results," *Public Opinion Quarterly,* Fall 1950, pp. 491–506.

U.S. Census, 1940. *Population,* Vol. 4, Part 1, p. 9.

Walters, J. H., Jr. "Structured or Unstructured Techniques?" *Journal of Marketing,* April 1961, pp. 58–62.

Wells, W. D. "The Influence of Yeasaying Response Style," *Journal of Advertising Research,* June 1961, pp. 1–12.

Wyath, D. F., & Campbell, D. T. "A Study of Interviewer Bias as Related to Interviewers' Expectations and Own Opinions," *International Journal of Opinion and Attitude Research,* Spring 1950, pp. 77–83.

*Eleven*

# Securing and Using Psychological Information

In this chapter we discuss how to obtain and use psychological information. Our concern is primarily with attitudes, psychological traits, motivations, and their relationship to marketing. The first section of the chapter is confined to a discussion of the uses of attitude, trait, and motivation information in making marketing decisions. The second section of the chapter deals with categories of measurement scales. Finally, the third section deals with measuring attitudes, traits, and motivation.

## MARKETING USE OF ATTITUDE, TRAIT, AND MOTIVATION INFORMATION

The marketing man, unlike the political scientist, psychologist, or sociologist, is interested in attitudinal, trait, or motivation information about consumers only inasmuch as such information relates to sales through the analysis of consumer behavior. An excellent monograph detailing the state of the art with respect to the analysis of consumer decision making has been recently provided by Nicosia (1966). We shall briefly sketch the framework from which most behavioral theories and virtually all of the modern theories of consumer behavior have evolved. In the words of Nicosia (1966, p. 76):

> Two main classes of variables make up the [decision] process' morphology: (i) those that describe the individual or unit of behavior denoted as (I); and (ii) those that describe the individual's environment denoted as (E). With respect to the functional relations describing the mechanisms of the process, it is assumed that behavior (B) results from the interaction between the subject and his environment—that is, between the two sets of variables I and E.

The individual, I, is the subject of this chapter. We are concerned mainly with his attitude toward products, brands, vendors, and himself; his economic and sociopsychological traits;[1] and, to a lesser degree, his motivations or reasons why he makes certain decisions.

Our general understanding of consumer behavior is dependent on the development of behavioral models in the sense described in Chapter 3—that is, on models employing numerous variables and a set of equations to represent the relationships between these variables. Marketing knowledge has not yet reached this stage. Nevertheless, numerous special-problem situations arise where cost and time factors require a model with a minimum of independent variables or where simple models represent all that can be done under the current state of the art. The success of an advertising campaign or the perceived advantages of a new product are examples of special-problem situations where decisions are made with attitudinal information used in naïve models.

## Attitudes

There are two categories of interest in attitude measurement. The first category, which we shall term "people-ranking," represents measurement to rank individuals on an attitudinal dimension. For example, users of a certain product may be ranked according to satisfaction with the product. The second category, which we shall call "alternative-ranking," consists of ranking alternatives with respect to an attitudinal dimension. An example of the second category is the ranking of various brands of a product on some like-dislike scale.

### *People-Ranking Attitudes*

There is one fundamental reason for measuring people-ranking attitudes in marketing, that is, the use of such rankings for useful market segmentation. Attitudes ranked for this purpose may have no connection to the product and still prove useful. For example, if it were established that people who tended to be in favor of extending the National Park system also tended to drink Pepsi-Cola, such knowledge would be invaluable to the Pepsi-Cola Company.

The key to market segmentation is differential response. That is, we seek to segment the market so as to make the individual segments as homogeneous as possible and the difference between segments as great as possible with respect to buying behavior. There is no point, for example, in segmenting a market according to age, income, sex, personality,

[1] Only psychological traits are discussed in this chapter.

or any other variable unless each segment demonstrates different buying behavior.

The people-ranked attribute may be employed as either a dependent or an independent variable in segmentation. For example, we may suppose that people who possess a favorable image of our product are more prone to buy it than people who look upon the product unfavorably.[2] Since attitudinal information may be easier to measure in an experiment than is actual buying behavior, the individual's attitude toward the product may be employed, with some trepidation, as a surrogate of buying behavior.

Another example may be taken from the area of the diffusion of innovation—the study of the manner in which innovations move from the producer to consumers. It should be evident that it is of considerable importance to identify key population segments (if they exist) who are the early users of an innovation. Should there be some segment of the population, *distinguishable from the population at large,* who influence the majority of buyers in their buying decisions, the identification of this segment is of considerable importance.

Consider the following description of the early users of an innovation:

> The first group to adopt an innovation are called innovators. This is the group that is most apt to make risky decisions. They are typically the youngest group in age and the highest in social status and wealth. Innovators rely heavily on impersonal and scientific information sources and communication with other innovators. In their social relationships innovators are often opinion leaders as well . . . they have professional, business, or social contacts outside of their immediate social circle. . . . It is estimated that innovators constitute 3 to 5 per cent of many groups or communities (Zaltman, 1965, p. 45).

It would appear that the innovator is more likely to read the *New Yorker* than *The Reader's Digest.* Their adoption decisions tend to be rational, and they rely on information from other innovators and "scientific" sources before making a decision to adopt an innovation. At an early stage, mass media are thus best used to make the innovator aware of the innovation and to tell him something about it.

The preceding paragraphs illustrate the value of identifying innovators so as to know how and where to reach them and on what basis to communicate. By definition, innovators respond very differently from late adoptors of an innovation, but this information is of no value unless

[2] Of course, this is only true other things being equal. Palda (1966), in fact, concludes that there is little evidence to support the inference that attitude change precedes purchase behavior, a natural inference if one is to assume that positive changes induce a greater probability of purchasing. This has obvious importance for promotion.

we can differentiate between innovators and late adoptors on some other basis than the dependent variable—the tendency to adopt innovations. This differentiation is attempted on the basis of traits and people-ranking attitudes, while appeals to innovators are based on attitudes, motivations, and, to a lesser degree, traits.

### *Alternative-Ranked Attitudes*

Whereas with people-ranked attitudes the goal is to rank individuals on some scale with respect to the degree to which they possess certain attitudes, with alternative-ranked attitudes the goal is to register the judgment of individuals with respect to competing alternatives. In marketing these alternatives could be such things as brands, advertisements, radio or television commercials, stores, or firms. To be most useful, such attitudes should be more specific than a general "liking" for the alternative and should be expressed in terms of specific attributes. A constellation of such attributes constitutes the image of the alternative in the eyes of the individual.

For example, suppose that a large number of people rate a particular automobile high on workmanship and conservative design (thus low on "raciness") as compared to other automobiles. If this image corresponds to the self-image of the buyer, the automobile would be more likely to be purchased than some other automobile with an image of raciness and power.

Unfortunately, it is usually difficult to obtain specific attitudes toward an alternative because of the so-called "halo effect." Respondents who are in favor of the alternative have a tendency to rate the alternative highly on all dimensions, while respondents who dislike the alternative tend to rate it as poor on all dimensions.

The halo effect is a phenomenon familiar to any college professor who has tried to learn something about his course through a questionnaire. Those who like the course tend to find the presentations excellent, the reading material well selected, the instructor possessing the wisdom of Socrates and the humor of Bob Hope, and the course high on every dimension. Those who dislike the course tend to find the presentations poor, the reading material chosen without reason, the instructor dull and humorless, and the course poor on every dimension measured. It is an understatement that such responses are difficult to interpret.

The major implications of alternative-ranked attitudinal studies for marketing are (1) to predict buying behavior and (2) to indicate correct promotional appeals and product changes. Buying behavior, as has already been stated, is difficult to predict because other factors in addition to attitudes play a role in the buying decision.

When attitudinal differences reflect real rather than imaginary brand differences, attitudinal information can be of great importance in product design. On the other hand, when such perceived differences are imaginary, the implications for management are with respect to promotional appeals and not product design.

For example, if a particular brand of beer appears to have low consumer acceptance because it is regarded as leaving a bitter aftertaste, blind taste tests should be undertaken to determine whether or not the beer really does leave a more bitter aftertaste than do other beers. If it is found that it does not, management may either drop the brand or attempt, through advertising, to change the attitude of consumers toward the brand with respect to aftertaste. If it is found that the brand does indeed leave a bitter aftertaste, the appropriate correctional measure would be a change in the product itself.

## Psychological Traits

*A Dictionary of Psychology* defines a trait as "an individual characteristic in thought, feeling, or act, inherited or acquired." To be classified as a psychological trait, a characteristic must be stable and manifest itself in a wide variety of situations.[3] The existence of psychological traits must be determined empirically. A number of traits have been so identified.

A short quotation from Eysenck, in which he is discussing the trait "persistence," should clarify what is meant by a trait:

> What do we mean when we say that a given person is persistent? We mean, surely, that he tends to carry on activities in the face of boredom, or pain, or exhaustion, long after other people less persistent than himself might have stopped. Implied in the notion of this trait of persistence is the assumption that persistence will be shown by a given person, not only in one particular situation, but in a wide range of situations. . . . Thus, the notion of generality is quite essential to our concept of a trait (Eysenck, 1958, pp. 207–208).

One way of looking at the concept of "personality" is that an individual's personality consists of the constellation of psychological traits he possesses. Thus personality, along with income, age, and other factors, contributes to the "set" that an individual brings to a buying situation. As such, trait information may become important to the marketing manager. We say "may become important" rather than "have become impor-

[3] Attitudes, although we discuss them separately, are also traits.

tant," since attempts to relate psychological traits to buying behavior have not had great success thus far.[4]

The usefulness of market segmentation by psychological traits, if it can be done, is obvious. Such information would permit more intelligent design of products and more effective promotional appeals. The lack of success so far may be indicative that psychological market segmentation does not, in general, exist. This conclusion, however, is not yet warranted on the basis of the sketchy research done to date. Advancements in the science of constructing personality tests and careful selection of the appropriate test for the particular investigation hold promise for better future results. Most personality tests currently employed were developed and validated by clinical psychologists on abnormal patients. Using such tests for the very different population of interest to marketers is of doubtful value.

## Motivation

In the preceding chapter it was stated that motivation information is "why" information. Such information is obviously very difficult to obtain, if indeed it exists. Neither observation nor experimentation studies can tell us exactly why an individual does what he does, although the latter comes closer to establishing causality.

There is much ambiguity related to what we mean by "why." One may hypothesize that a bonus plan will cause salesmen to work harder and, perhaps, conduct an experiment that lends support to the hypothesis. But two difficulties are apparent if we try to infer that the efforts of salesmen under the bonus plan are due to the plan itself. First, the plan is only one variable influencing effort. It may contribute to effort

[4] There are examples of limited success. Tucker and Painter (1961), in a small-scale experiment, found some relationships such as a positive correlation between *ascendency* (a tendency to dominate in relations with others) and *sociability* (enjoyment of and tendency to seek the company of others) and the acceptance of new fashions. The arbitrary grouping of categories (after viewing the data) in order to achieve significant results, and intercorrelations of the traits, however, make the conclusions suspect. There have also been attempts by Massy, Frank, and Lodahl to find relationships between psychological traits (measured by the Edwards Personal Preference Schedule) and brand loyalty, store loyalty, and consumption of beer, coffee, and tea using panel data (personal communication, Ronald Frank). Only negligible correlations were found. Evans (1959) used the Edwards Personal Preference Schedule to try to establish discrimination between Ford and Chevrolet owners. The results showed that the psychological traits measured had little discriminating power.

and thus establish a difference between salesmen under the plan and those not under the plan *other things being equal,* but this difference may be small compared to the total amount of effort. Other variables, such as debt, the sales manager, ambition, and so on, may play a much more important role in influencing the amount of effort expended by a salesman.

The second reason accounting for the ambiguity in answering any motivation question relates to the depth with which one is attempting to establish causality. If we say that one group of salesmen work harder than another group because the first group has a bonus plan, this raises the question of why the bonus plan works. Answering this question, if it could be answered, would in turn raise other questions in a never-ending chain of causality.

Measurement of motivation will be briefly discussed later in the chapter, but a few comments will be made here. Most purchases are made through a combination of reasons, some of which the buyer is aware of and some of which the buyer is unaware of. We may decide to buy a pair of gloves for a particular rational reason—to keep our hands warm. Almost any reasonably made pair of gloves, however, will accomplish this. The decision to buy a particular pair of gloves over all the other available gloves may be tied to a number of motivations, some of which the buyer can articulate and will, some of which the buyer can articulate but will not, and some of which may be unknown to the buyer on a conscious level. Thus merely asking the buyer why he bought the gloves he did may yield misleading or only partially valid answers. There is some question, however, whether the techniques associated with "motivational" research accomplish much more, since the validity and reliability of the techniques employed are generally poor in those cases where attempts to obtain validity and reliability data have been made.[5]

This is not meant to be an overall indictment of the area of motivational research, but rather an attempt to place it in perspective. Highly skilled and highly trained interviewers are a necessity in such research, backed up by even more highly skilled and paid experts (generally psychologists) to interpret the findings. The time required in obtaining data and analyzing them, per subject, must be measured in hours. Inevitably, then, such studies tend to be of small scale in terms of the numbers of subjects. If the findings are regarded as hypotheses to be further tested on a larger scale using more conventional techniques, motivational

[5] The reader who is skeptical on this point is invited to read the rather scathing indictment by Eysenck (1958, Chapter 5). A number of articles by proponents of motivational research are to be found in Ferber and Wales (1958).

research can be an invaluable tool. In the opinion of the authors, however, attempts to employ such findings without corroboration are generally to be avoided.

### Conclusion with Regard to the Marketing Use of Psychological Information

Up to the present, socioeconomic and demographic information has justifiably played a larger part in marketing decisions than has psychological information. It seems clear, however, that advances in the behavioral sciences, coupled with refinements in measurement techniques, will result in a greater and more significant role for psychological information in the future than in the past.

Webster has stated the present role of behavior science as follows:

> First, behavioral science can help . . . to make specific predictions about the behavior of customers, distributors and competitors. Unfortunately, there are not many areas where behavioral science permits such precise prediction in marketing. Second, concepts from the behavioral science can help the marketing manager to narrow the range of alternative actions being considered by helping him assess those outcomes that are most likely to follow a given course of action. . . . The third application is in providing insights into WHY people behave as they do in certain marketing situations. . . . His [the marketing manager's] objective may be to identify new advertising appeals or to determine ways for increasing the rate of product usage. (Webster, 1966).

It is important to note the limitations that Webster attaches to the usefulness of behavioral science in his statement, as well as the implications for legitimate and useful applications. Unfortunately, considering the current state of the art, the phrases "can help" and "providing insights" are the strongest statements that can be made. Twenty years from now a totally new and more vital role may be in store for the behavioral sciences, just as the present role is much greater than it was twenty years ago.

## MEASUREMENT

Although everyone uses measurement every day of his life, few people stop to think about the basic differences in the various measurements taken. Measurements of the number of people in a room, the temperature of the house, the ranking of breakfast cereals in order of preference, and the weight of a bag of potatoes do not differ only because the units of measurement (number, degrees, rank, and pounds) differ; the difference is more fundamental.

The most commonly employed classifications of measurement (originally proposed by Stevens, 1951) in increasing order of measurability are nominal, ordinal, interval, and ratio. The last two both come under the heading of cardinal measurement.[6]

## Nominal Scale

We are all familiar with one of the less attractive elements of modern life—the fact that although one's parents give one a name, we also are identified by a multiplicity of numbers. We have social security numbers, credit card numbers, and membership numbers granted by every organization to which we belong.

The normal arithmetic operations of adding, subtracting, multiplying, or dividing are meaningless with respect to such identification numbers. Generally, the fact that one person has a higher or lower number than another also carries no information.[7] The one useful measurement that can be obtained is to find the total number of identification numbers in order to find the total number of members of the organization.

Assigning numbers so as to identify is termed using a *nominal* scale of measurement. Since the only permissible operation on such a scale is counting, theoretically any unique symbol (e.g., a letter of the alphabet) would serve equally well as a number.

## Ordinal Scale

Whenever a number reflects a rank with respect to some attribute, measurement conforms to an *ordinal* scale. For example, consider rank in a graduating class. The number "two" assigned to a graduate identifies him in a particular way—as having the second highest grade point in his class.

Such numbers carry more information than numbers on a nominal scale, but still do not allow meaningful use of arithmetic operations. For example, the difference in the ranking between the first and fifth ranked graduates is the same as the difference in ranking between the fifth and ninth ranked graduates. But this in no way implies that the

[6] Ackoff (1953, p. 178) restricts the use of the term "measurement" to cardinal measurement.

[7] The identification number itself may yield such information as geographical location or date of joining the organization, to cite two examples, but these numbers are themselves not meaningfully amenable to the usual arithmetic operations.

differences in academic achievement between the first and fifth ranked and the fifth and ninth ranked are the same.

In the case of ordinal scales, symbols can serve as well as numbers for identification only if the symbols themselves have a natural and well-understood ranking. Thus a grade of A in a course signifies a higher ranking than a grade of B.

### Interval Scale

Although it is meaningful to say that the temperature rose 20 degrees yesterday from 20° Fahrenheit to 40° Fahrenheit, it is meaningless to say that 40° Fahrenheit is twice as hot, or contains twice as much temperature, as 20° Fahrenheit. This is because the zero point on the Fahrenheit scale was originally arbitrarily set at the temperature produced by mixing equal quantities (by weight) of snow and salt. If the zero point had been chosen in some other arbitrary manner, the ratio between any two temperatures would change.

Any scale in which the zero point is arbitrary, but in which all the normal arithmetic operations may be performed meaningfully with respect to *intervals,* is known as an *interval* scale. Thus we may say that the interval from 20° Fahrenheit to 40° Fahrenheit is twice as large as the interval from 10° Fahrenheit to 20° Fahrenheit.

It was seen in the chapter on hypothesis testing and can be seen from elementary statistics that statistical tests on a null hypothesis usually depend on the probability of observing a sample statistic within a certain *interval* around the population parameter or (in a one-sided test) to one side of the population parameter. Statistical tests, such as the $t$ test or tests relying on the central limit theorem, apply to measurements on an interval scale.

In addition, the mean or average of something measured on an interval scale carries meaning. The average temperature during a week, for example, carries information; the average social security number (on a nominal scale) does not.

### Ratio Scale

A ratio scale differs from an interval scale in that the ratio scale has a natural zero. Thus weight in pounds and length in inches are examples of ratio scales. All arithmetic operations may be performed on measurements employing a ratio scale. Any value may be considered a multiple of some other value. For example, one is permitted to say that 2 pounds is twice as heavy as 1 pound.

### Summary on Measurement

An excellent summary of the concepts involved in measurement may be found in Ackoff (1953). There currently exists a controversy regarding measurement scales and procedures. For our purposes, however, the fourfold classification of nominal, ordinal, interval, and ratio scales is sufficient.

It should be evident that the necessary assumptions behind each scale—nominal, ordinal, interval, and ratio—become more restrictive in the order of scales given. Nevertheless, in some sense, the information contained by a measurement increases in the same order. For example, we must assume a natural zero for a ratio scale but not for an interval scale. Ratio scales, however, allow comparisons of both absolute magnitudes and differences, whereas interval scales permit only the latter.

As we shall see, this creates a problem in psychological measurement. Most psychological scales fall naturally into the category of ordinal scales, with further assumptions usually added to convert them to interval or ratio scales so that the resulting measurements may carry more information.

## MEASURING PSYCHOLOGICAL INFORMATION

In this section we describe the major measurement techniques that have proved popular in actual usage in marketing or that seem to have particular promise. The treatment must necessarily be brief. More extensive treatments of attitude measurement may be found in Edwards (1957). The *Annual Review of Psychology* publishes an article every second year on recent advances in attitude scaling. An excellent treatment of objective personality measurement devices may be found in Cattell and Warburton (1963). *The Mental Measurements Yearbook* (Buros) and *Tests in Print* (Buros, 1961) provide extensive lists and critiques of psychological tests. Frederick (1957) and Smith (1954) have written basic works on motivation research. In addition, a number of books, such as Ferber and Wales (1958) and Britt (1966), have readings that provide at least superficial treatments of motivational research techniques.

### Attitude Measurement

Six attitude measurement techniques are discussed here: the *method of paired comparisons,* the *method of equal-appearing intervals,* the *method of summated ratings, the semantic differential,* the *scalogram approach,* and the *Sherif approach.* Other scales are briefly mentioned.

*Paired Comparisons*

Suppose that one wanted to rank four brands of cereal on the basis of how wholesome they are considered to be *relative to one another.* Notice that this implies measurement on an interval scale; that is, there is no absolute point of zero wholesomeness, but there is some continuum whereby one can compare *differences* of wholesomeness.

The method of paired comparisons, developed by Thurstone (1959), may be employed to obtain rankings on such a scale. There are a number of steps required in the analysis:

1. Obtain a judgment group that will perform the necessary comparisons.
2. Obtain judgments, from each member of the group on which cereal is considered more wholesome when comparing the four cereals in pairs, such that each cereal is paired with every other cereal. This involves $n(n-1)/2$ comparisons by each judge—six comparisons in this case.
3. Construct a matrix that represents the frequency with which brand $i$ is rated more wholesome than brand $j$ for all brands. Transform this matrix from frequencies to proportions.
4. Using Thurstone's law of comparative judgment, obtain scale values for each brand.

Suppose that 100 housewives are obtained to form a judgment group. Table 11-1 represents a hypothetical frequency of responses for the group.

**Table 11-1** Frequency of Considering Brand $i$ More Wholesome Than Brand $j$

| $j$ \ $i$ | $A$ | $B$ | $C$ | $D$ |
|---|---|---|---|---|
| $A$ | — | 75 | 60 | 30 |
| $B$ | 25 | — | 35 | 10 |
| $C$ | 40 | 65 | — | 20 |
| $D$ | 70 | 90 | 80 | — |

We see, for example (by looking above the diagonal) that 75 judges rated brand $B$ more wholesome than brand $A$. Twenty-five judges (looking below the diagonal) rated brand $A$ more wholesome than brand $B$. No ties are allowed in the judging, hence the total must sum to 100.

Table 11-2 shows Table 11-1 translated into proportions, with one modification. Although no brand is rated against itself, it is assumed that such a rating would yield proportions of 0.50.

**TABLE 11-2** Proportions Considering Brand $i$ More Wholesome Than Brand $j$

| $j$ \ $i$ | $A$ | $B$ | $C$ | $D$ |
|---|---|---|---|---|
| $A$ | 0.50 | 0.75 | 0.60 | 0.30 |
| $B$ | 0.25 | 0.50 | 0.35 | 0.10 |
| $C$ | 0.40 | 0.65 | 0.50 | 0.20 |
| $D$ | 0.70 | 0.90 | 0.80 | 0.50 |
| Sums | 1.85 | 2.80 | 2.25 | 1.10 |

THE LAW OF COMPARATIVE JUDGMENT. So far, all the evidence indicates an ordinal ranking, with brand $B$ regarded as most wholesome, brand $C$ next, brand $A$ next, and brand $D$ last. Before an interval scale can be constructed, further assumptions are required. Thurstone's law of comparative judgment provides such a step. Furthermore, the use of this law since its first publication in 1927 gives some evidence of its lasting value.[8] We shall briefly sketch the essence of this law and its implications in this problem.

Thurstone assumes that each stimulus gives rise to a *discriminal process,* that is, to a reaction by an individual when asked to judge an attribute. The reaction or discriminal process is not constant, but it is assumed that the distribution of discriminal processes is normal, as in Figure 11-1.

Figure 11-1 shows the distribution of the discriminal processes for two stimuli, $A$ and $B$, on a psychological continuum. Suppose that $A$ and $B$ are two brands of cereal and the continuum represents the attitude of wholesomeness. It is evident that the mode of $B$ is higher than the mode of $A$, and more often than not $B$ would be preferred to $A$. If the dispersions of the discriminal process are the same for all stimuli (i.e., $\sigma_i = \sigma_j = \sigma$) and if the intercorrelations $r_{ij}$ are the same (i.e., $r_{ij} = r$), we have case V

[8] Thurstone's major papers are reprinted in Thurstone (1959).

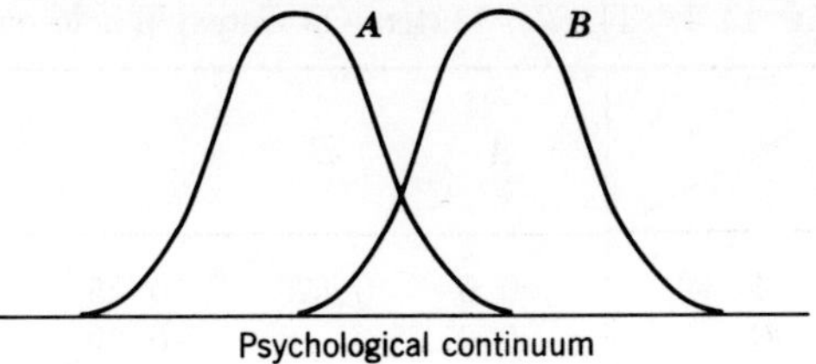


**Figure 11-1** Discriminal processes *A* and *B*.

of the law of comparative judgment.[9] If $\bar{S}_i$ and $\bar{S}_j$ are the model discriminal processes for $i$ and $j$, the normal deviate measuring their separation is easily shown to be

$$Z_{ij} = \frac{\bar{S}_i - \bar{S}_j}{\sqrt{2\sigma^2 \cdot (1 - r)}}$$

for case V. The denominator $\sqrt{2\sigma^2 \cdot (1 - r)}$ is a constant. Since measurement is on an interval scale, we are justified in changing the scale by multiplying all values by this constant,[10] yielding

$$Z_{ij} = \bar{S}_i - \bar{S}_j$$

Since this separation is assumed to be normally distributed with unit variance and mean $\bar{S}_i - \bar{S}_j$, if we knew the value of $\bar{S}_i - \bar{S}_j$, we could calculate the proportion of times that $S_i - S_j$—the difference of the actual discriminal values observed in a given trial—would be positive and the proportion of times that it would be negative. Whenever this value is positive, $i$ is rated higher than $j$, and vice versa. For example, if $Z_{ij} = 1.65$, $i$ would rate higher than $j$ 95 per cent of the time and $j$ higher than $i$ 5 per cent of the time.

We do not know the value of $Z_{ij}$, but we do know the proportion of times that $i$ is preferred to $j$ and vice versa. In fact, $Z_{ij}$ is what we are trying to derive, since it measures the separation between the stimuli on the attitude scale. Fortunately, just as we can derive the proportions from $Z_{ij}$, we can estimate $Z_{ij}$ (notationally, $\hat{Z}_{ij}$) from the proportions by entering a normal distribution table. Table 11-3 shows values of $\hat{Z}_{ij}$ obtained in this manner for our cereal example. Thus Table 11-3 is derived from the proportion shown in Table 11-2.

[9] Thurstone originally considered the correlations to be zero in case V, but this is not necessary.

[10] This is essentially what we do in changing measurement from feet to yards, although this measurement is on a ratio scale.

**TABLE 11-3** The $\hat{Z}_{ij}$ Matrix On Cereal Wholesomeness*

| $j$ \ $i$ | $A$ | $B$ | $C$ | $D$ |
|---|---|---|---|---|
| $A$ | 0.0 | 0.67 | 0.25 | −0.52 |
| $B$ | −0.67 | 0 | −0.39 | −1.28 |
| $C$ | −0.25 | 0.39 | 0 | −0.84 |
| $D$ | 0.52 | 1.28 | 0.84 | 0 |
| Sums | −0.40 | 2.34 | 0.70 | −2.64 |
| Means | −0.10 | 0.585 | 0.175 | −0.66 |
| Means + 0.66 | 0.56 | 1.245 | 0.835 | 0 |

* $\hat{Z}_{ij}$ to two significant decimal places.

To find the best estimate of a scale value for $\bar{S}_i$, the following procedure is used, which shall illustrate for cereal $A$. We note that

$$\begin{aligned} Z_{AA} &= \bar{S}_A - \bar{S}_A \\ Z_{AB} &= \bar{S}_A - \bar{S}_B \\ Z_{AC} &= \bar{S}_A - \bar{S}_C \\ Z_{AD} &= \bar{S}_A - \bar{S}_D \end{aligned}$$

Thus $Z_{AA} + Z_{AB} + Z_{AC} + Z_{AD} = \bar{S}_A - (\bar{S}_A + \bar{S}_B + \bar{S}_C + \bar{S}_D)$

or $\bar{S}_A = \frac{1}{4}(Z_{AA} + Z_{AB} + Z_{AC} + Z_{AD}) + \frac{1}{4}(\bar{S}_A + \bar{S}_B + \bar{S}_C + \bar{S}_D)$

In general

$$\bar{S}_i = \frac{1}{n}\sum_{j=1}^{n} Z_{ij} + \frac{1}{n}\sum_{j=1}^{n} \bar{S}_j$$

where there are $n$ stimuli. Since the origin on an interval scale is arbitrary, and since all $\bar{S}_i$ terms contain the same quantity $1/n \sum_{j=1}^{n} \bar{S}_j$, we may drop this term, yielding:

$$\bar{S}_i = \frac{1}{n}\sum_{j=1}^{n} Z_{ij}$$

These calculations in the cereal example yield values of −0.10, 0.585, 0.175, and −0.66 for $\bar{S}_A$, $\bar{S}_B$, $\bar{S}_C$, and $\bar{S}_D$ respectively.

Finally, we again find it convenient to move the origin to the lowest value on the attitude scale so that all resulting values are positive. This results in values of 0.56, 1.245, 0.835, and 0 for the four modal discriminal estimates.

Conclusions: Paired Comparison Scale Analysis. It should be recalled, from the discussion of interval scales, that the fact that $\bar{S}_B$ has a value of 1.245 and $\bar{S}_A$ a value of 0.56 does *not* permit us to say that the former is twice as large as the latter. Any ratio statements must be confined to *differences* between discriminal values, and not to the discriminal values themselves. We are entitled to say, for example, that the difference between the wholesomeness attributed to cereal $B$ and the wholesomeness attributed to $D$ is more than twice as great as the difference between the wholesomeness attributed to $A$ and the wholesomeness attributed to $D$. This is like saying that a rise in temperature of 20 degrees is twice as large as a rise of 10 degrees, although we cannot say that a temperature of 20 degrees is twice as much as a temperature of 10 degrees.

It should also be noted that the assumptions that are employed in case V of the law of comparative judgment are quite restrictive. Techniques have been developed for testing these assumptions and for proceeding where they do not hold. The reader is advised to read Edwards (1957) or some other text on attitude measurement for a discussion of such techniques, but we shall point out what we believe to be a serious weakness of such tests.

In employing tests of significance, it is very important to note the statement of the null hypothesis. As mentioned in Chapter 6, the null hypothesis in scientific work is generally formulated to play "devil's advocate," that is, it makes the statement that the results arise by chance and not because of the experimental treatment. A level of significance of 5 per cent implies that this null hypothesis is rejected only if the probability of the results arising by chance alone is less than 5 per cent. In other words, the researcher constructs the null hypothesis to play the role of critic, not of advocate, for his discovery.

The null hypotheses formed in testing the assumptions behind the law of comparative judgment, on the other hand, tend to be exactly opposite in philosophy to those described above. The researcher formulates the null hypothesis to state that the assumptions are true and thus will reject such assumptions only if the probability of the observed results is very small, given that the assumptions is true.[11] The type 2 error of accepting the assumptions when they are false may be very large, but this error is typically ignored.

Paired comparisons of statements. It should be noted that the stimuli need not be brands or products, but could also be statements. For example, the method of paired comparisons could be employed to scale statements relating to the image of a firm. Anderson (1966) used

[11] For example, the chi-square goodness of fit test is usually employed to test case V assumptions.

this method to develop an attitude scale on which nine statements (taken from a much larger set of statements, most of which were rejected as being ambiguous or factual) were recorded. They were such statements as:

1. General Electric benefits everyone.
2. General Electric has more good points than any other company.
3. General Electric serves society well.

.
.
.

9. General Electric is too selfish to benefit society.

A judging group was employed which judged paired statements as to which was more favorable to General Electric. This resulted in placing these statements along a continuum.

An unresolved controversy still is present concerning whether or not the attitudes held by members of the judging group affect the resulting scale. This criticism applies to any scale constructed by a judging panel. Summaries of the controversy may be found in Edwards (1957) and Sellitz, Jahoda, Deutsch, and Cook (1959).

Once the scale has been obtained, its use is essentially the same as that of scales derived via the method of equal-appearing intervals. For this reason, a discussion of applications of the scale is deferred until after the treatment of the latter method.

### *The Method of Equal-Appearing Intervals*

A major drawback to the method of paired comparisons is that the number of pairs to be compared can be very large. For example, with $n \cdot (n - 1)/2$ preferences to be stated, 20 stimuli require 190 comparisons. Thurstone's method of equal-appearing intervals has been widely used where a large number of statements are to be employed in an attitudinal scale. It cannot be used, however, in comparing products directly (as in the wholesomeness of cereal example).

As with paired comparisons, a list of statements is given to a judging panel. Usually, at least 200 statements are necessary. Each statement is usually typed separately on a plain card.

Each judge is required to assign the statements to one of 11 piles. The first pile contains statements considered to be at the negative end of the attitudinal continuum and the eleventh pile of statements at the positive end of the continuum. For example, if a set of statements relating to cereal wholesomeness contained the statement, "The cardboard package is more wholesome than the cereal," we could expect that this statement might be placed in pile 1 by many judges. The statement, "It is better for you than any food I could name," might well find itself placed in pile 11 by many judges.

The judges are told that the median pile, pile 6, should contain statements judged neutral, that is, neither positive nor negative. The 11 piles are placed equidistant from one another, which encourages the judges to consider the psychological distances between adjacent piles as a constant.

Those statements that show a high variability with regard to where they are placed or that do not correlate highly with individual scores obtained on the remaining statements are discarded. Techniques have also been developed to eliminate judges who give inconsistent replies or place a high proportion of the total number of replies in one pile. Values from 1 to 11 are assigned the respective piles, and each statement is assigned either its mean or median scale value.

There is one significant difference between scales developed by the method of equal-appearing intervals and scales developed by paired comparisons. Since the sixth pile in the method of equal intervals contains statements judged neutral, this implies a natural origin at the value of six. Thus if one accepts the assumptions of the method, measurement is on a ratio scale rather than an interval scale.

### *Application of Thurstone Scales*

There are various ways to apply a set of scaled statements, once they have been obtained. The most common is to have respondents check those statements with which they agree. Usually, a score representing the mean of the agreed values is assigned for that attitude, although some researchers (who are hedging that only ordinal measurement is attained) will assign the median value. Another approach that is sometimes used is to ask the respondent to check only the one or two statements that most closely approximate his feelings.

One difficulty in application arises because of the failure to include the dispersion in the statements checked in the analysis. If one person checks only one statement with value 5 and another checks three statements with values, 3, 5, and 7, both individuals are assigned the same score. But do they both really have the same attitude? No agreement on this point has yet been reached by researchers in the area.

A second difficulty arises because the scales do not measure the intensity with which a person possesses a certain attitude. For example, one person may think that our cereal is not very wholesome, but wholesomeness may not be very important to him. He may be more concerned with taste and texture or he may not eat cereals at all. Another person may consider wholesomeness as the most important quality of a cereal and rate our cereal low. Stressing wholesomeness in promotion would be of little use to the first person, but of paramount importance to the second. Sellitz et al. (1959, p. 309) suggest that scattered responses on statements may imply that an individual has no attitude on the subject, but this point has not been well researched. The interpretation may well depend on whether or not the statements are mutually exclusive. For example, consider the pair of statements:

1. One cannot be healthy without including at least one bowl of cereal a day in one's diet.
2. Cereal is moderately good for you.

Most people would consider that one can be healthy without eating foods that are "moderately good for you." Thus it would be difficult to assess the attitude of someone who checked both statements. On the other hand, if the qualifier "moderately" were omitted from the second statement, to most people the first statement would imply the second. Thus it might be difficult to interpret the attitude of someone who checked the first and *did not* check the second.

### *The Method of Summated Ratings*

The method of summated ratings (although by a different name) was first proposed by Likert (1932). The principal advantage of the method consists in doing away with the need for a judging group.

As in the case of the previous methods, the first step in applying this method is to derive a list of statements concerning a particular attitude. The subject is then asked to express his degree of agreement or disagreement, typically on a 5-point scale.[12] Thus he may check one of the following: strongly agree, agree, uncertain, disagree, or strongly disagree. Weights of 2, 1, 0, —1, and —2, respectively, are generally assigned to the 5 points if the statement expresses a favorable attitude, with these weights reversed if the statement expresses an unfavorable attitude.

Assigning scores. The assigned score to an individual is achieved in three stages. At the first stage, his score is merely the sum of the individual scores on the statements. For example, if an individual checked "agree" on $n$ favorable statements, his score would be $n \cdot 1$ or $n$. The next step is to perform an item analysis on the statements.[13] Although various forms of item analysis may be employed, the goal

[12] Scales containing more or less points are sometimes used.

[13] An item analysis is an analysis undertaken to find which items prove to be good differentiators between high and low scorers.

is to find a set of 20 to 25 statements that correlate highly with the overall score.

Finally, each individual is assigned a score based on the statements retained. A ranking of subjects is thus obtained.

CONCLUSIONS. One might expect the method of summated ratings to result in quite different rankings of individuals with respect to some attitude than would be obtained using Thurstone's methods. In fact, however, Edwards and Kenney (1946) found extremely high correlations between rankings by both methods.

The principal advantage of the Likert technique is that a judging group is no longer required. Edwards (1957, p. 169), however, concludes that advances in techniques have lowered the time and effort required in judging statements to the point where the two methods are comparable.

Another advantage of the Likert method is that subjects, in being permitted to express degrees of agreement or disagreement with respect to statements, find it relatively easy to respond. Inevitably, methods that require a simple dichotomous agreement or disagreement to statements result in problems for subjects who find themselves in partial but not complete agreement.

A disadvantage of the Likert scale is that a single subject's score, except if extreme, is meaningless except in relation to scores of other subjects. That is, there is no natural origin in the scale. This is not serious if the attitude of two groups are to be compared or if *changes* in attitude after some experimental treatment are of interest.

Although Likert scales are employed to compare mean attitudes between groups, it is not clear that this procedure is justified. The mean is meaningless as a statistic unless we have cardinal measurement. This objection can be overcome, however, by using the median rather than the mean in any comparison of groups.

### *Scalogram Analysis*

A scale quite different from other scales discussed in this chapter has been developed by Guttman (1944; 1947). An ordered set of statements constitute a Guttman or unidimensional scale if agreement with one statement implies agreement with all statements that are less positive (but not negative.) For example, if the statements indicate the degree of liking vanilla ice cream, on a Guttman scale we could expect anyone who agrees with a statement implying a great liking to agree with all statements that imply lesser liking. For example, we might expect anyone who agrees with the statement "Vanilla ice cream has a marvelous flavor" to also agree that "I enjoy vanilla ice cream."

Statements are ranked as follows.[14] The set of statements (derived by intuition, as Guttman suggests, or by item analysis) are administered to a group. If a subject agrees with a statement, he is given a score of unity on that statement and if he disagrees with the statement he is given a score of zero. The answer sheets are then arranged in order of total score. If the scale is perfectly unidimensional, each subject would agree with all statements agreed to by subjects having a lesser total score. This is illustrated in Table 11-4 for three questions (fewer than would be used in practice) and eight subjects. Furthermore, so long as we know that the scale is perfect, we can reproduce any person's response from his score. The proportion of times we would be correct gives what Guttman calls the *coefficient of reproducibility.* A coefficient of reproducibility of 0.90 or more is considered a necessary condition for the scalability of the statements. But Edwards and Kilpatrick (1948) point out conditions for which this coefficient would have to be considerably higher before being accepted as evidence of scalability.

If the coefficient of reproduciability is low, this indicates either that no attitude along this dimension really exists or that the scale is not unidimensional, that is, there is more than one variable operative. In the example given previously, it is possible that reproducibility could be low because we are attempting to develop a single scale of taste for both ice cream and vanilla. If reproducibility were low, the suggested

[14] The technique to be described here has been called the Cornell technique by Guttman (1947). Equivalent techniques are available.

**Table 11-4** Perfect Scoring on a Guttman Scale

| Subject | Statement | | | | | | Score |
|---|---|---|---|---|---|---|---|
| | 1 | | 2 | | 3 | | |
| | Yes | No | Yes | No | Yes | No | |
| 1 | 1 | | 1 | | 1 | | 3 |
| 2 | 1 | | 1 | | 1 | | 3 |
| 3 | | 0 | 1 | | 1 | | 2 |
| 4 | | 0 | 1 | | 1 | | 2 |
| 5 | | 0 | | 0 | 1 | | 1 |
| 6 | | 0 | | 0 | 1 | | 1 |
| 7 | | 0 | | 0 | | 0 | 0 |
| 8 | | 0 | | 0 | | 0 | 0 |

approach would be to develop individual scales for both vanilla and ice cream and then investigate the correlation between the scales.

BETWEEN-GROUP COMPARISONS. Although the Guttman technique, as described so far, permits a ranking of individuals, it does not permit one to distinguish individuals with a favorable attitude from individuals with an unfavorable attitude. By assuming that those who are neutral with respect to an attitude will tend not to feel intensely about it, Guttman has derived a procedure for determining a breakpoint between favorable and unfavorable groups. The procedure is summarized below.

In addition to being asked whether or not he agrees with a particular statement, each subject is also asked to check how strongly he feels about his response (if he agrees) along a 5-point scale from "Don't feel strongly at all" at the lower end to "Feel very strongly" at the upper end. The median intensity for each respondent class is then plotted against the cumulative per cent of respondents, as in Figure 11-2. If, for example, 20 per cent of the group had the most favorable score and also had a median intensity score of 5, this would be plotted as shown in the figure. In this hypothetical case 60 per cent of the group would be considered generally favorable and 40 per cent unfavorable. Guttman claims the V or U shape curve is typical, thus making it relatively easy to separate the unfavorable group from the favorable group.

This set of subjects could be compared with other sets of subjects to determine (by the percentage who hold favorable attitudes) which set holds a generally more favorable attitude. The same group could also be assigned the same scale with different stimuli in order to derive

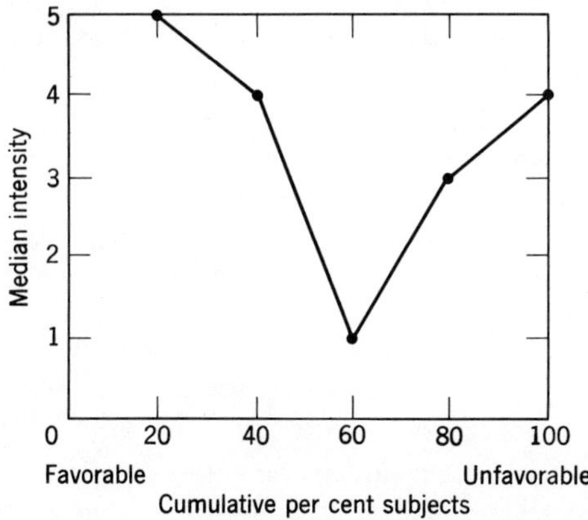


**Figure 11-2** Guttman intensity graph.

relative attitudes to the two stimuli. Richards (1957), for example, used a variation of the Guttman technique to compare three types of ball-point pens.

Conclusions. The Guttman scale has not been widely employed in marketing problems, although it has its advocates in psychology. Perhaps the reasons for its lack of popularity lie in the fact that (*a*) measurement is on an ordinal scale, (*b*) the derivation of the list of statements for a unidimensional scale is apparently something of an art requiring considerable insight and practice, and (*c*) it is difficult to combine scales for an overall attitude.

### *The Semantic Differential*

Although the semantic differential, derived by Osgood, Suci, and Tannenbaum (1957), is a newer technique than the preceding methods, it has had wide popularity. As originally conceived, the semantic differential was thought of as a means of measuring the meaning of an object to an individual. In marketing terms, the object may be a firm and the meaning is the company's image. The technique, however, is applicable to other attitudes and attitude changes.

The subject rates a stimulus, such as the General Electric Company or Oreo cookies, on a series of 7-point scales. The scales are bipolar, that is, the end points represent extreme opposite opinions, for example, good-bad or fast-slow. Using factor analysis, Osgood, Suci, Tannenbaum, and their associates have isolated three dimensions (factors) that have emerged in most applications:

A. Evaluation—scales measuring favorable versus unfavorable attitudes. The scales that generally load best on this factor are nice-awful, beautiful-ugly, clean-dirty, pleasant-unpleasant, fair-unfair, and fragrant-foul. This is the most important factor as measured by factor loading.

B. Potency—scales measuring strong-weak, thick-thin, rugged-delicate, large-small, wide-narrow, and loud-soft.

C. Activity—scales measuring fast-slow, angular-rounded, sharp-dull, active-passive, and ferocious-peaceful. The interpretation of this factor is not clear.

The purpose of a factor analysis in problems such as these is to permit the selection of a minimum number of scales that, together, would completely specify the image or meaning of the object. Ideally, one scale would represent each factor and each scale would be independent. This ideal is never met in practice, but a few scales do adequately represent

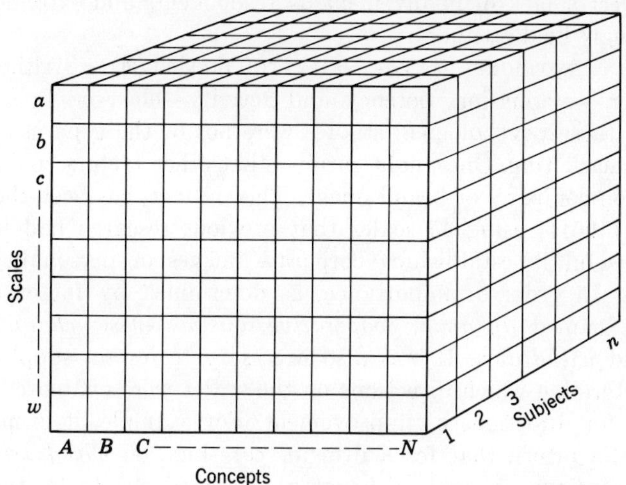


**Figure 11-3** *n* subjects rate *n* concepts on *w* semantic differential scales.

each factor and the factors have very small intercorrelations in most applications.

Figure 11-3 illustrates what happens when *n* subjects rate *n* concepts on *w* scales. Each cell in the cube represents a specific rating (1 to 7) by a subject of a particular concept on a particular scale. A vertical slice in the cube would give an overall rating for a single subject. A generalized attitude toward a specific concept or image could be obtained by slicing the cube along the subject dimension, with the mean of all subjects representing the attitude on a particular scale.

The evaluative and potency factors have been widely used in subsequent work, particularly the former. Although Osgood and his associates have attempted to find scales applicable to any concept, much of the research in the past ten years has been performed using scales developed specifically for the particular concept. For example, if one were scaling attitudes toward a soft drink, it might be appropriate to create a bipolar scale for carbonation. One end of the scale could be called "far too bubbly" and the other end "flat." A factor analysis designed for this particular study would then be necessary if one tried to relate this scale to other scales.

The semantic differential does *not* provide a method of evaluating how strongly an attitude is held without making a further assumption. This assumption, similar to Guttman's for his scales, is that neutral ratings reflect a lack of involvement by respondents and extreme ratings reflect strongly held attitudes.

MARKETING VERSIONS OF THE SEMANTIC DIFFERENTIAL. Although the three factors—evaluation, potency and activity—emerged in a number of studies, these psychological studies were not of the type usually performed in marketing. One might surmise that other factors could emerge in studies on company or brand image. This, in fact, has been the case.

Spector (1961), using 45 scales that previous research had indicated as being useful in establishing corporate images or personality, found six factors. In order of importance, as determined by factor analysis, these were named *dynamic, cooperative, business-wise, character, successful,* and *withdrawn.* It was also necessary to obtain supplementary data to determine which directions on the scales were evaluated as good by asking for directions of improvement. For example, it is not necessarily true, a priori, that for a firm to score high on *withdrawn* (aloof, secretive, cautious) is bad, although this turned out to be the case.

Mindak (1961) has modified the semantic differential to measure specific attitudes relating to beer. The original one-word polarized scales were replaced by phrases tailor-made for each product. Figure 11-4 shows Mindak's scale for three beer brands. Unfortunately, the lack of a factor-analytic design does not permit one to know if the scales are independent or even important.

CONCLUSIONS. The original work of Osgood and others in isolating general factors and scales has tended to be supplanted, at least in marketing applications, by either new factor-analytic approaches or by

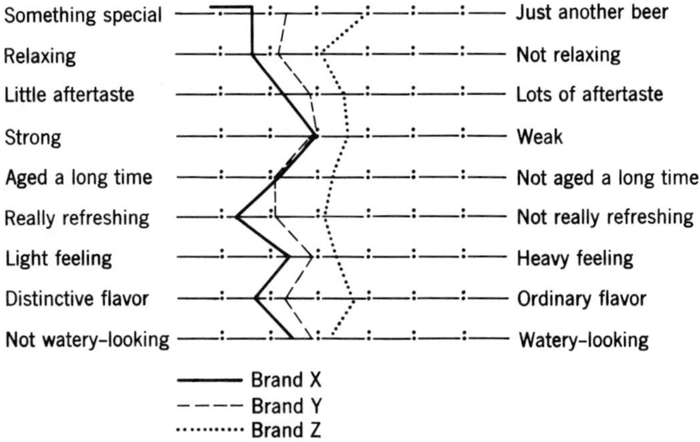


**Figure 11-4** Specific product image.

tailor-made *ad hoc* scales. This trend is due to the fact that the original factors are sometimes difficult to interpret in the marketing context (it is of little practical interest to know that your firm gets high ratings on goodness but low ratings on ruggedness) and that different factors seem to apply to marketing images. Nevertheless, it would seem to the authors that, unless meaningful semantic differential scales can be found that are general to most marketing applications, the other scales discussed in this chapter are to be preferred for marketing.[15]

### *Sherif Method*

One of the newer approaches to attitude measurement is that advocated by Sherif, Sherif, and Nebergall (1965) and their associates. Both the content and intensity of attitudes are measured using three concepts called the *latitude of acceptance,* the *latitude of rejection,* and the *latitude of noncommitment.* Since a concise name for this method has not been given, we shall call it the Sherif method.

The developers of the method define the respective latitudes as follows (p. 24):

> *Latitude of acceptance* is the position on an issue (or toward an object) that is most acceptable, plus other acceptable positions.
>
> *Latitude of rejection* is the most objectionable position on the same issue, plus other objectionable positions.
>
> *Latitude of noncommitment* [is] defined as those positions not categorized as either acceptable or objectionable in some degree.

The findings of a number of studies indicate that these three measures say a great deal about a person's attitude, on a number of dimensions. The latitude of rejection is greatest for subjects who take an extreme position, and for these subjects the latitude of rejection is greater than the latitude of acceptance. That is, people who take an extreme position tend to have fewer statements they can accept than statements they find objectionable. They also tend to find neutral statements objectionable.

Persons who take moderate positions, on the other hand, generally reject positions at either the positive or the negative extreme in about the same proportion. They accept about the same number of positions as they reject and thus will also tend to have the highest latitude of noncommitment.

[15] Note that a recent study (Hughes, 1967) concludes that the semantic differential is more sensitive than the Thurstone techniques. However, the brevity of the report, with little information on how the scales were chosen or even if an item analysis was used, and the low reliability reported in a control group make the results suspect.

The studies involving the Sherif method have not found, however, that adopting a moderate position necessarily involves a lack of intensity of attitude. When a subject feels intensely about his moderate position, his latitude of rejection tends to be as high as that of subjects holding extreme positions. In fact, there are some subjects holding an extreme position who have a low latitude of rejection and a low involvement or intensity.

The latitude of acceptance tends to be fairly stable, usually including the most acceptable position and the positions immediately adjacent. It thus serves to identify the stand a subject takes. The latitude of rejection is the best indicator of the level of involvement of an individual. Across issues, the latitude of noncommitment tends to identify the general relative involvement in an inverse relationship.

METHODOLOGY—AN HYPOTHETICAL EXAMPLE. Suppose that one were investigating a firm's image with respect to "modernness." Two basic methods may be employed. The first is to take a list of statements (usually nine) that through content analysis and pretesting are ranked in order from one extreme to the other, with the midstatement considered neutral. The subject chooses which statement is most acceptable to him, which least acceptable, and which other statements are acceptable or objectionable.

The other procedure, called the own-categories procedure, requires a large number of statements which the subject proceeds to place in piles according to whether or not he judges them to belong together on a ranking of favorableness or unfavorableness toward the object. As in the case of nine statements, the subject is then asked which pile is most acceptable to him, which most objectionable, and which other piles are acceptable or objectionable. The proportion of items in the piles then determines the respective latitudes.

Suppose that we had a list of nine statements on modernness that had been pretested:

A. This company is the most modern in this or any industry.
B. This is an extremely modern company.
C. This is a modern company.
D. I guess you might call the company modern.
E. It is hard to place this company as modern or antiquated.
F. I guess you might call the company antiquated.
G. This company is antiquated.
H. This company is extremely antiquated.
I. This company is the most antiquated in this or any other industry.

An individual's response might be to consider statement C the most acceptable and statements B and D also acceptable. Statement I might be considered the most objectionable and statements H and A also objectionable. We could identify this individual as considering the company moderately modern with latitudes of acceptance, rejection, and noncommitment all equal to 3. Another individual might consider statement A the most acceptable, statements B and C also acceptable, and statements E through I objectionable. This individual could be identified as being committed to the strongest position possible in favor of the company's modern image, having a latitude of acceptance of 3, a latitude of rejection of 5, and a latitude of noncommitment of 1. The second individual, in addition to possessing a more extreme attitude than the first, also is much more strongly committed to his attitude.

Conclusions. What kind of aggregate information could we obtain from a study using the Sherif method? We could identify the proportion of people who agree with each statement as well as the intensity of agreement. We could group statements and thus form the percentage in favor and the percentage against the overall object measured. We could quite accurately measure *changes* in the percentages holding various positions and changes in intensity.

This is quite a lot, but the method does not allow measurement of the overall group attitude on an interval scale. Of course, a great deal of doubt still exists whether any attitude-measuring device really measures on an interval scale.

### *Other Scales and Concluding Comments*

A number of other attitude scales have been devised—far too many to cover here.[16] However, we shall briefly mention a few that have been used in marketing or show particular promise. Crespi (1961) has employed a scaling device, the Stapel scale, somewhat similar to the semantic differential. Abrams (1966) compared four scaling devices, somewhat similar to Likert scales, in which only the proportions of extreme responses were looked at. Applying these scales to products, one scale in particular seemed to correlate closely with actual shelf inventories. Reynolds (1966) employed a 10-point, poor-to-excellent scale to find product preferences via the standard deviation of responses. The *Q* sort (Stephenson, 1953) employs techniques similar to the method of equal-appearing intervals to group individuals with respect to attitudes.

There is no one attitude-scaling device that is superior to all others in all circumstances. The various scales, when compared with one another, appear to be at least monotonic (i.e., an increase in one scale

[16] Shaw and Wright (1967) have compiled a book on generalized attitude scales that covers most of the standard scales.

always corresponds to an increase in the other). If, however, two scales could be found measurable on an interval scale, they would necessarily be related linearly to one another. No two scales have yet demonstrated this relationship.

All of the scales discussed in this chapter have been proved useful in practice. At this time, the best advice to the researcher is probably to use the scale with which he has the greatest familiarity, particularly if the scale has been used in similar problems.

## Measurement of Psychological Traits

There are essentially four means of measuring psychological traits: by the judgment of a trained psychiatrist or psychologist, by personality inventories, by projective techniques and by actual behavior. Each of these will be discussed briefly.

### *Interview*

The interview by a clinical psychologist or psychiatrist is perhaps the most common means of identifying psychological disorders. With the faith of the layman, we shall conclude that such identifications are generally carried out quite well, particularly with respect to patients exhibiting marked disorders. For the purposes of obtaining marketing information, however, such interviews are not very practical or useful.

The marketing practitioner would find market segmentation on the basis of psychological traits a worthwhile promotional tool, if such segmentation could be achieved. He is interested, however, not in the classification of a particular disturbed individual seeking psychiatric help, but in the classification of a mass of *normal* individuals for the identification of traits that correlate with their behavior as buyers. Thus individual ratings are not of great use to marketing.

### *Personality Inventories*[17]

The personality inventory is the principal source of information on psychological traits. Originally, such inventories were designed by reviewing the literature on a particular trait and noting all the symptoms associated with that trait. For example, the first such inventory, designed for the American Army in World War I by Woodworth, was intended

[17] An excellent brief description of personality inventories and their origin is given by Eysenck (1958). It is obviously important for marketing researchers who might use such inventories to have some understanding of their history and construction, but anyone who has to construct a questionnaire can also benefit from what psychologists have learned in inventory design.

to spot potential neurotics. Woodworth proceeded to comb textbooks on psychiatry for symptoms such as headaches and nightmares that were associated with neurosis. This led to a list of questions corresponding to another list of symptoms.

It was eventually discovered that the validity of such tests is negligible. Different inventories designed to measure the same thing generally turned out to have insignificant correlations and to be relatively unrelated to individual ratings by psychiatrists.

The difficulty in these inventories, as in many marketing research questionnaires, was that it was assumed that people knew the answers to the questions and that they would answer objectively if they knew the answers. Most questionnaires were loaded with adverbs like "frequently" or "often" that are subject to various interpretations. Leaving such adverbs out of the questions generally does not improve them. For example, a question like "Do you daydream a lot?" in the Maudsley Medical questionnaire, which must be answered yes or no, depends on how a person interprets "a lot." Asking merely "Do you daydream?" does not improve the question, since everyone daydreams at some time or other.

The solution to the problem is to recognize that the interpretation of the question or its answer is not important. What is important is the fact that a person answers yes or no to the question.

If, on some independent basis, subjects can be divided into a group who possesses a psychological trait and another group who do not (or if the extent to which the trait is held can be established for each subject) and then the questionnaire subjected to an item analysis, one can obtain questions that have been empirically validated as discriminating between those who possess the trait and those who do not.[18] A "lie-scale," consisting of questions that everyone must truthfully answer yes, but that seemingly reflect badly on the person who does answer yes, is generally also added to identify those persons who give the socially acceptable answer.

The great difficulty with this approach is that outside criteria to measure psychological traits are generally not available. Thus the factor-analytic approach has been extensively used.

The use of factor analysis in personality inventories is similar to their use in attitude studies, as previously discussed. A long list of items is reduced to a much smaller list of factors. These factors are not necessarily related to a trait found by some independent criteria, however, which makes their interpretation difficult. Until a factor that has been

[18] The daydreaming question from the Maudsley Medical questionnaire has actually been empirically validated.

identified on some personality inventory is also found to be reflected in some form of behavior, the factor remains of theoretical interest only.

### *Actual Behavior*

It will be recalled that one identifies a person as having a particular trait only if the person demonstrates that trait in a variety of situations. This suggests another way in which traits may be measured. Test situations are constructed in which the behavior of subjects is examined to see if it is consistent in the different kinds of conditions created to show the behavioral implications of the trait.

In a marketing context, for example, if we were looking for a truly "brand-loyal" person, he could be identified by loyalty to one particular brand in each of a variety of product categories and buying situations. He would generally buy the same make of car after each trade-in, the same breakfast food, the same brand of gasoline, the same brand of cigarettes, and so on. If we could not find people who behave in this manner, we would have to conclude that a general trait of brand loyalty does not exist, even though individuals could be brand-loyal in specific product categories.

### *Projective Tests*

A large variety of tests, grouped under the heading of projective tests, have become popular with some psychologists.[19] These tests have as their basis a device that presumably allows the subject to express his subconscious feelings without being subject to the normal defenses of the conscious. Particular personality types are expected to make particular kinds of responses, thus allowing the investigator to infer the personality type from the response. The techniques employed include word association tests, incomplete-sentence tests, the well known Thematic apperception test, the Rorschach test, and other related techniques.

The following generalizations are true of most projective techniques. First, users of such techniques hide the purpose of the study from the subject in order not to inhibit the conscious behavior of interest. Second, reflecting the origins of the techniques in clinical psychology, the goal is not so much to group people together in group norms but to identify the manner in which a particular subject differs from such norms. Third, unlike personality inventories, which try to measure specific traits, the projective techniques emphasize the total personality in the environment of the test.

The following are brief descriptions of the methodology of a few pro-

[19] See Bell (1948) for an extensive and sympathetic review of such tests.

jective techniques. In the Thematic apperception test (TAT), the subject is given a series of pictures and is asked to say what he thinks is the situation in the picture, the events that led up to it, the likely outcome, and the feelings of the characters. The pictures range from the relatively innocuous (a young woman looking into space) to the dramatic (a boy, huddled on the floor, with a revolver beside him).

The Rorschach technique requires the subject to report what he sees in a series of inkblots. The incomplete-sentence test requires the subject to complete such sentences as "I am a man (woman) because . . . ." These examples should suffice to outline the nature of the techniques.

Although the tests are fairly standardized, the interpretation is not. Furthermore, the subject's behavior, hesitations, time to respond, and so on, are often of more interest than the content of the response. Thus it is not surprising to find that the validity of the tests is generally low and that a considerable controversy exists with respect to their use.

What makes these devices of particular interest to marketing is the fact that they have become part of the arsenal used by motivation researchers. Their use in that context is fully as controversial as their use as personality measures.

### *Conclusions*

The field of personality testing has developed considerably in the past decade, particularly with respect to objective devices. Hundleby, Pawlick, and Cattell (1965) have recently published an invaluable book describing 21 personality traits that have emerged from a number of factor-analytic studies and the tests that may be employed to measure them. This book should prove invaluable in consumer studies.

## Motivation Research

It will be recalled that motivation research in marketing deals with questions of the *why* of consumer behavior. Practitioners of motivation research have tended to come from the tradition of clinical psychology. They have employed modifications of projective techniques together with a technique called the *depth interview* to a great extent.

### *Projective Techniques in Motivation Research*

Philosophically, projective techniques in personality measurement do not have the same goals as in motivation research. Whereas they are used to differentiate individuals in clinical work, they are used to find group generalizations in motivation research. In addition, such techniques in motivation research *do not* really establish motivations, they establish attitudes (Eysenck, 1960). For example, a study of coffee concluded that coffee is generally regarded as "sinful" (Newman, 1959). A study of prunes indicated that 70 per cent of nonusers did not think that prunes are glamorous, concluding that the image should be changed to a more glamorous one (Schrier, 1958). Obviously, such studies infer motivation from attitude, raising the question of whether the more usual devices of attitude research would not serve as well or better.

### *Depth Interviews*

The so-called depth interview, as a technique, differs from projective techniques in two respects. First, the area of interest in the study is generally revealed to the subject, since it is to be extensively probed. Second, the interview is relatively unstructured, requiring the interviewer to ask questions that lead the subject to talk freely and under relatively little guidance about the topic under study.

### *Conclusions*

Motivational research can be useful in precisely those situations where projective techniques are useful in clinical psychology—where there are inhibitions that tend to prevent the conscious from recognizing true underlying attitudes. The results of such studies, depending as they do a great deal on the subjective interpretations of the interviewers and on small, convenience samples, should be treated as hypotheses for further study rather than as demonstrated facts.

## FINAL COMMENTS

The use of behavior information by most firms is probably the least efficient and most misunderstood of the many kinds of marketing information collected. Advances in personality and attitude measurement, however, will inevitably lead to a much more general and useful implementation of behavioral information than at present. The future student of marketing may well find it necessary to minor in psychology, if that time has not already arrived.

## REFERENCES

Abrams, J. "An Evaluation of Alternative Rating Devices for Consumer Research," *Journal of Marketing Research,* May 1966, pp. 189–193.

Ackoff, R. L. *The Design of Social Research,* Chicago: University of Chicago Press, 1953.

Anderson, R. D. "A Comparison of Four Attitude Scaling Technique," Unpublished Master's Thesis, University of Iowa, 1966.

Bell, J. E. *Projective Techniques.* New York: Longman's Green, 1948.

Britt, S. H. *Consumer Behavior and the Behavioral Sciences.* New York: Wiley, 1966.

Buros, O. K. (Ed.) *Tests in Print.* Highland Park, N.J.: The Gryphon Press, 1961.

Buros, O. K. (Ed.) *The Mental Measurements Yearbook.* New Brunswick, N.J.: Rutgers University.

Cattell, R. B., & Warburton, F. W. *Principles of Personality Measurement and a Compendium of Objective Tests.* Urbana, Ill.: University of Illinois Press, 1963.

Crespi, I. "Using a Scaling Technique in Surveys," *Journal of Marketing,* July 1961, pp. 69–72.

Edwards, A. L., & Kenney, K. C. "A Comparison of the Thrustone and Likert Techniques of Attitude Scale Construction," *Journal of Applied Psychology,* 1946, pp. 72–83.

Edwards, A. L., & Kilpatrick, F. P. "Scale Analysis and the Measurement of Social Attitudes," *Psychometrica,* 1948, pp. 99–114.

Evans, F. B. "Psychological and Objective Factors in the Prediction of Brand Choice, Ford versus Chevrolet," *Journal of Business,* October 1959, pp. 340–369.

Eysenck, H. J. *Sense and Nonsense in Psychology.* (Rev. ed.) Baltimore: Penguin Books, 1958.

Eysenck, H. J. "Organization, Nature and Measurement of Attitudes." In *Attitude Scaling.* London: The Market Research Society, 1960.

Ferber, R., & Wales, H. G. (Ed.) *Motivation and Market Behavior.* Homewood, Ill.: Richard D. Irwin, 1958.

Frederick, J. G. *Introduction to Motivation Research.* New York: Business Bourse, 1957.

Guttman, L. A. "The Cornell Technique for Scale and Intensity Analysis," *Educational Psychological Measurement,* 1947, pp. 247–280.

Guttman, L. A. "A Basis for Scaling Qualitative Data," *American Sociological Review,* 1944, pp. 179–190.

Hughes ,G. D. "Selecting Scales to Measure Attitude Changes," *Journal of Marketing Research,* February 1967, pp. 85–87.

Hundleby, J. D., Pawlick, K., & Cattell, R. B. *Personality Factors in Objective Test Devices.* San Diego: Robert R. Knapp, 1965.

Likert, R. "A Technique for the Measurement of Attitudes," *Archives of Psychology,* 1932, p. 14.

Mindak, W. A. "Fitting the Semantic Differential to the Marketing Problem," *Journal of Marketing,* April 1961, pp. 28–33.

Newman, J. W. "Pan-American Coffee Bureau (A)." In Borden, N. H., & Marshall, M. V. (Eds.), *Advertising Management, Text and Cases.* Homewood, Ill.: Richard D. Irwin, 1959.

Nicosea, F. *Consumer Decision Processes.* Englewood Cliffs, N.J.: Prentice-Hall, 1966.

Osgood, C. E., Suci, G. J., & Tannenbaum, P. H. *The Measurement of Meaning.* Urbana, Ill.: University of Illinois Press, 1957.

Palda, K. S. "The Hypothesis of a Hierarchy of Effects: A Partial Evaluation," *Journal of Marketing Research,* November 1966, pp. 388–391.

Richards, E. A. "A Commercial Application of Guttman Scaling Techniques," *Journal of Marketing,* October 1957, pp. 166–173.

Schrier, F. T. "Reason Analysis versus Motivation Research," Cited by Robbins, W. D. (Ed.), *Marketing Association Proceedings of the 1958 National Conference,* American Marketing Association.

Sellitz, C. Jahoda, M., Deutsch, M., & Cook, S. W. *Research Methods in Social Relations* (Rev. ed.) New York[3]: Holt, Rinehart and Winston, 1959.

Shaw, M. E., & Wright, M. M. *Scales for the Measurement of Attitudes.* New York: McGraw-Hill, 1967.

Sherif, C. W., Sherif, M., & Nebergall, R. E. *Attitude and Attitude Change.* Philadelphia: W. B. Saunders, 1965.

Smith, G. H. *Motivation Research in Advertising and Marketing,* New York: McGraw-Hill, 1954.

Spector, A. J. "Basic Dimensions of the Corporate Image," *Journal of Marketing,* October 1961, pp. 47–51.

Stevens, S. S. "On the Theory of Scales of Measurement," *Science,* **103,** 1946, pp. 677–680.

Stevens, S. S. (Ed.) "Mathematics and Psychophysics." In *Handbook of Experimental Psychology.* New York: Wiley, 1951.

Stephenson, W. *The Study of Behavior: Q-technique and its Methodology.* Chicago: University of Chicago Press, 1953.

Thurstone, L. L. *The Measurement of Values.* Chicago: The University of Chicago Press, 1959.

Tucker, W. T., & Painter, J. J. "Personality and Product Use," *Journal of Applied Psychology,* 1961, pp. 45, 325–329.

Webster, F. E., Jr. "The Behavioral Sciences and the Marketing Manager," *Business Review,* October 1966, pp. 25–35.

Zaltman, G. *Marketing Contributions from the Behavioral Sciences.* New York: Harcourt, Brace & World, 1965.

*Twelve*

# Securing Unanticipated and Commercial Information

Men see and judge the affairs of other men better than their own.
*Terrance*

Nobody can give you wiser advise than yourself.
*Cicero*

This chapter is about two different kinds of information used in marketing: (1) unanticipated information and (2) commercial information. The purpose of this chapter is to provide broad perspectives of both types of information. More specifically, the reader should strive to discern what is included in each of the two information categories, how each type of information is searched and secured and, in general, managed, and how these two types of information fit into marketing information programs.

The first section provides a discussion of unanticipated information. The starting point is definition and description of the concept so that the reader can relate its usefulness to an organization. Then the information-handling and managing problems are presented.

Commercial information is discussed in the second section. Numerous commercial sources and services are classified and categorized in an attempt to provide analytical perspective of this unwieldy area. The thought, of course, is to make various alternatives, and their uses, more visible for use by decision makers.

## UNANTICIPATED INFORMATION[1]

*Unanticipated or incidental information is useful information that cannot be* anticipated as to (1) availability, (2) sources, and (3) forms. Most of these information particles, standing alone, are so small and seemingly insignificant to a company's needs that they are termed incidental.

Availability simply means that a researcher does not even know if specific information relative to a certain topic exists. That is, *unlike* for secondary information, an investigator can, at best, only speculate that there might be specific information on a given topic available to him at some place and point in time. Under these conditions he can hardly anticipate the sources and forms. Even when he can begin to anticipate that such information should be available, the researcher can hardly anticipate where to find the information. That is, he may sense that such information should be in existence, but the locations remain sufficiently nebulous that searchers cannot be meaningfully sent to sources for specific pieces of information. Finally, such information is initially so hazy that researchers cannot anticipate if it will appear verbally or in writing and whether it will be in cursory perspective, incidental detail, or some other form. That is, in keeping with the prior description, the forms or shapes in which such information may appear cannot be anticipated.

### Illustration: Unanticipated Information

An illustration should help to clarify and define the nature of unanticipated information. In this case a series of seemingly unrelated incidents proved to provide the unanticipated information. A draftsman for a writing-instrument manufacturer received a complimentary sample of a Japanese-built sign pen from a West Coast importer. He used it, told a few close associates about it, and ordered a half dozen of each of five colors. Later he reordered three dozen of each color. Almost simultaneously, two representatives of the same writing-instrument company noted a Japanese-built sign pen in a few artist supply stores on the West Coast. One of them purchased a dozen for use around his home. Also, his secretary asked him where he purchased the pens. About two months prior to all of these events a buyer in the purchasing department of the writing-instrument company had heard about some new materials

[1] For more information and some different views on unanticipated information, see Albaum (1963 and 1964). His research has been particularly useful to this section.

being used in construction of writing instruments. He had no need for them and was not interested in them.

Less than one year after these seemingly unrelated events had occurred, the Japanese sign pen came to the unmistakable attention of the executives of the writing-instrument company. Some of their pen lines were down in sales by as much as 12 per cent—because of a broad market acceptance of the Japanese sign pen. The incidents that were experienced by a company draftsman, two salesmen, and a buyer provided a nucleus of incidental or unanticipated information. Unfortunately, these particles of unanticipated, incidental information were not treated as useful marketing information. In fact, their importance was not realized until later—when the company's profits were already damaged.

## Managing Unanticipated Information

The searching, securing, analyzing, and managing of unanticipated information is quite different in many respects from those for other types of information. More specifically, the fitting of unanticipated information into marketing information systems tends to require somewhat different information management than has been described in preceding chapters.

Common information and environmental *problems* confront companies and provide considerable insight into the requisites for management of unanticipated information. Specifically, employees are exposed to considerable useful information, but typically fail to recognize much of it as valuable and fail to collect and transmit such useful information to appropriate analyzing and using places in their organizations.

### *First Problem Area*

The reader should consider first the matters of selective exposure, selective perception, and selective retention. People, in part, can control their exposure to various events and circumstances. For example, just as many persons do not like to view an injured puppy, many a research engineer, finance man, and personnel man keep themselves from being exposed to what they consider the marketing "folderol." That is, they may withdraw from actual exposure (i.e., the sensing) of what may be valuable information.

Selective perception suggests that persons do not sense all of what they are exposed to. For example, a salesman may perceive competitive product prices that are *lower* than his, but not those that are *higher* than his. An advertising man may be very aware of competitive mass media advertisement, but be virtually unaware of competitive point-of-purchase material.

Finally, there is the matter of selective retention. A person may be exposed to and perceive an event or situation, but not recall it after a short period of time. Recall ability may be lost because an event was deemed unimportant or too common or for numerous other reasons. For example, a salesman may recall that a competitive product was priced lower than his product, but he may not recall how much lower. An advertising copy man may be able to recall competitive copy but not the media in which it appeared.

The ramifications of selective exposure, perception, and retention suggest a major problem that must be faced by information managers who want to manage incidental information. Key persons within an organization must have broad exposure horizons. That alone, however, is not enough. They must realize that what may appear to them to be incidental information may be very useful information. They must perceive and retain relevant information.[2]

### *Second Problem Area*

Another major consideration that, in turn, provides insight into the management of unanticipated information is that persons who do possess relevant information often *do not know they have anything of value.* Furthermore, they do not know who, if anyone, needs the information. They must know where to transmit it and how to transmit it. Also, persons who need information often do not know if it is available, let alone where the needed information is to be found. Although these problems are common to all information situations, they are particularly oppressive in the area of unanticipated information because of its incidental (i.e., inconsequential-appearing) nature. These, then, are the two major concerns or problems that provide insights into requisites for management of unanticipated information.

Successful management of unanticipated information evolves around what can best be called (1) the human element and (2) the organizational aspects. These facets, of course, must be meshed together in order to make unanticipated information available to decision makers.

### *The Human Element*

The first requirement is the identification of key information persons. These are persons who are likely to have considerable contact with relevant information sources. For example, salesmen have exposure to the marketplace, including both buyers and other salesmen who sell to com-

[2] A more extensive discussion can be found in Berelson and Steiner (1964).

petitors. Such key persons, both within and outside the organization, must be identified so that they can be made more information-sensitive and, in general, useful. Also, this is saying that the key persons must be identified so that funds can be used in the "training" of a limited number of persons, rather than all persons.

Once key persons are identified, they must be trained in the searching and handling of information. First, they must be *aware* of the need for broad exposure, critical perception, and information retention. On the first point, persons cannot view "their" specialty areas as their only areas of concern. For example, a salesman should not avoid or dismiss information about customers served by other salesmen in his company. A purchasing agent *should* be interested in why a competitor is using a new material, and so forth.

Second, key people must be trained to be sensitive to various information facets. It is meaningless to merely tell people to be receptive and perceptive to information. Instead, searchers must have knowledge as to what they should look for, where they should look, and how they should look.

In part, this means that they must not be overly sensitive to the value of isolated information facets nor be asked to evaluate the value of each particle of information. Much of this task can only be performed at a central point. An excellent encouragement to increase information sensitivity is to reward it. Such rewards are praise and encouragement. These coupled with immediate monetary reward are particularly effective in creating climates of information sensitivity.

Finally, along the human element line, key people must be encouraged to *transmit* their information discoveries. Unanticipated information flows best when individuals have incentives and encouragements to pass it. When transmitters are subject to ridicule or when they find personal gains from holding back information, little unanticipated information will flow.

### *Organizational Aspects*

Some special organizational framework is required for unanticipated information programs. Basically, such organizational frameworks should strive to (1) maximize securers' knowledge as to what to do with secured information; (2) maximize the knowledge of prospective users of the existence of information; (3) reduce the probability of information biases and distortions; (4) provide means whereby incidental information particles can be evaluated and related to company needs; (5) reduce to a minimum the time between which information is initially secured, transmitted, analyzed, and available for use.

An information system with a centralized control office is virtually mandatory to accomplish these tasks.[3] It directly facilitates each of the tasks. With one office as the receiver of information, securers know *where* to send information. At least they know that there is only one receiver. Users also know the *one* source to turn to for incidental (unanticipated) information. They need not search among numerous units. As a consequence of securers' knowing where to send information and prospective users' knowing where to find information, the time waste between securing and using information is reduced. Such direct handling also reduces distortions due to multiple transmitting, analysis, condensation, and so forth. Finally, the only way to know which information is of value and to fit jigsaw puzzle parts together, and to know what parts are missing, is to have a central staging and assembling location.

Two other organizational aspects are in particular need of emphasis. First, direct transmission lines must be open from securers to an information office and directly from central storage units to possible users. And key people, both suppliers and users, must not be inhibited from using the information channels. Finally, the unanticipated information—in various stages of completeness—must be stored and readily available.

### Summary on Unanticipated Information

In many companies unanticipated information has gone virtually unrecognized and unmanaged. That is, its management has occurred more by chance than by design. This has *not* been because of explicit considerations of the possible benefits and associated costs. Instead, it has been due largely to failure to recognize that there is such a thing as unanticipated information. In turn, too few companies have attempted to manage this type of information.

## COMMERCIAL INFORMATION

The term "commercial information" really has reference to the information and services that are available from commercial sources or suppliers. Companies find that they can buy numerous types of information and related services from a host of different sellers. *Commercial information is defined as information that is available for purchase through outside sources.* Closely aligned, but not synonomous, are commercial information *services.* These are information-related services that are available for purchase from outside sources. They include such activities

[3] Albaum (1963) has suggested that several offices are superior to one office.

as data processing, field interviewing, and statistical analysis. Some commercial sources offer both information and related services, others offer only services.

In the discussion that follows, the concern is with both commercial information and the related services that are available to managers of marketing information. However, the focus is on primary information in contrast to secondary information. Secondary information is discussed in the next chapter.

Some using companies buy virtually all of their information needs from commercial sources. At the other extreme of the continuum, there are, no doubt, some information-using companies that are yet to buy their first piece of commercial information. This situation, though, is quite uncommon, and the reasons will become obvious as we view commercial information and services and their sources.

## Purchase or Provide Own Information?

Cost is one criterion used to decide whether information and related services should be provided by the using company or purchased from a specific outside commercial source. Admittedly, this criterion is not easy to apply, nor is it the sole consideration. Cost considerations would be simple to apply if all other things were equal, but they never seem to be. There are situations where alternative types of information can be used to fulfill a common need. For example, store audit information gives an indication of sales at the retail level, as does consumer panel data and some other types of data. However, each such alternative offers some unique features that make them difficult to compare on a straight price basis.

A company needing specific information on its image among consumers in specific markets may elect to garner this information on its own or it may ask one or more commercial groups to make proposals. When seeking bids on such a specific need, cost (i.e., price) considerations alone are not enough. The prospective buyers must also consider the likely reliability, accuracy, and timeliness of the information that each supplier proposes to provide. Answers in these areas are largely based on the capacities and previous experiences of the various alternative sources.

### *Consideration Criteria*

For now, let us return more specifically to the question of buying information and services outside, as contrasted with providing them from within. Generalizations are somewhat difficult, if for no other reason than because personal preferences vary. Also, tradition, on the one hand, and continual searching and exploring of alternatives, on the other hand, cause cross-currents of behavior.

Ferber, Blankertz, and Hollander (1964) and Quittmeyer (1961) have indicated some situations that tend to suggest one alternative as against the other. First, sales and cost analyses, such as those described in Chapter 9, are normally conducted by the users. This situation prevails because company personnel are simply more familiar with the flow, the handling, and the storage of information within their own company. Furthermore, detailed records do not need to be exposed to numerous outside clerical people, and, finally this type of work does not require the intellectual detachment often available only through outside sources.

Second, special-problem-solving research is the most likely type to be contracted out to outside groups—particularly when (1) specific problem areas can be envisaged as researchable entities, (2) there is need for specialized know-how and/or equipment, and (3) intellectual detachment is necessary. For example, a company wishing to evaluate the acceptance of a new package design would find it convenient to contract with a commercial organization that has numerous cooperating store units in which to place the old and the new designs and that, in general, is very familiar with various field designs and related statistical techniques. Furthermore, such an outside organization does not need to "prove" that the new package is superior, as might an inside marketing man who has authorized and perhaps even initiated sizable expenditures for its development. In such a situation, intellectual detachment can be very meaningful. On the other hand, use of a commercial source does not guarantee such detachment. Many a commercial source has been more parrot than investigator.[4]

Finally, many specialized information activities are purchased from outside organizations because continued full-time use by only one supplier-user is not feasible. Very few users, for example, maintain their own field-interviewing staffs; many users cannot use full-time psychologists or sociologists, and so forth. These are services that few companies could utilize full-time. Therefore, they buy from commercial sources only the help they need.

These, then, are the major reasons that have fostered and given support to the development and availability of numerous types of commercial information and related services.

[4] Such an arrangement may be just that which is desired by the hiring company. See "What Management Consultants Can Do" (1965).

### Finding Commercial Sources

There is no directory or index that *describes* the available commercial information, services, and their sources. There are, however, directories that *list* organizations that engage in marketing research and information activities.[5] These directories do *not* describe the complement of information and services that are available, because this field is very dynamic. Detailed descriptive directories would be outdated even before they could be published.

A manager, in searching for detailed and specific description is advised to pursue the advertisements in various professional journals and to examine the indexes listing marketing research and information organizations. He can follow up with direct inquiries to the specific supplying sources. Some evaluation of various commercial offerings can be obtained through previous users (although supplier-provided lists of previous clients are likely to be biased). Also, various facets of some of the more widely used information services have received attention in professional journals and various books (Buzzell, 1964; Cordell, 1962; Fothergill and Ehrenberg, 1965; Gruber, 1966; Rotzall, 1964; Sobel, 1958). Some of these examinations tend to be very penetrating.

### Syndicated versus Custom Information

Commercial marketing information consists of two main types: it may be either of a syndicated or of a custom nature. Syndicated reports are normally designed to fit the needs of many users. Duplicate reports are available to all who wish to purchase them. In contrast, custom information presumes a confidential relationship between the commercial supplier and the user, and, of course, the information is secured and supplied explicitly and solely to the one user. These two types of information will be discussed in more detail as commercial information is examined. Many commercial sources offer both custom and syndicated information services. Of course, commercial information may be either continually collected or special-problem information.

### Types of Commercial Information

Commercial information arises principally in four major ways: through (1) panels, (2) store audits, (3) field enumerations, and (4)

[5] Such as American Marketing Association (1966) and the Department of Commerce.

independent sample surveys. These four are not mutually exclusive, but they do provide reasonable perspective for viewing the major types of commercial information.

## Panel Information

Panels are basically ongoing groups of persons who periodically report on various facets of their buying behavior, attitudes, intentions, and/or motivations. There are a number of different types of panels that may be used in different ways. Some panels, for example, simply report on their activities as consumers. That is, they do *not* serve as recipients of new products, or test new copy material, or receive other special treatment apart from that given other persons in the market. They simply are the preselected units to be repeatedly observed. Such a panel can often provide accurate information on industry sales.

Some panels report on or are observed relative to only a small facet of their consumer activities. For example, the A. C. Nielsen Company maintains panels of cooperating television homes in which Audimeters and Audilogs have been placed to monitor the stations tuned in and to discern who is watching the programs. These particular panels are concerned only with television viewership.

Another use of panels is as early tryer-user groups. In such cases, panel members are the first to receive and try new products, new packages, new advertising messages, and so forth. One supplier of this kind of service is National Family Opinion, Inc., which is described later.

A third type of panel is that which is composed of a group of dealers or some other special marketing group. Such panels may be used to report on inventory levels and on sales variations and, in general, to serve as a more direct link to the market. Store *panels* are frequently maintained for purposes of store *audits*. As such, they would fit into the panel category as well as in the store audit category that is discussed in the next section. Two cases in point are the Ehrhart-Babic Store Audits and the Burgoyne Retail Sales Studies. Both of these organizations provide custom information that comes about from auditing store panels.

Sometimes panel members are assembled in theaters and other meeting halls to observe and be observed as they react to proposed advertising materials. They may be assembled to view, taste, and/or test new products. Sometimes as a group they are called on to discuss various offerings. Hopefully, as groups they are more candid and more talkative and informative than as individuals.

When information from panels is available to all who wish to pay the price, it is considered syndicated information. Panel information available from a commercial source, but only to one client, is custom information. Of course, some individual using companies (e.g., Sheaffer Pen Company) maintain their own panels to produce information only for their own use. Such a panel does not result in commercial information, but in many respects is similar to the commercial panels.

### *Advantage of Panel Use*

Probably the greatest advantage derived from panel information, and not available through other approaches, is a continuing picture or pattern of the activities of the panel members. Such continuing observations can provide accurate information on industry sales and product and brand loyalties without resorting to extensive respondent recall. Additionally, panel data provide more composite cross-sectional and over-time information in general.

A second advantage of the panel approach is that new sample designs do not need to be constructed each time more information is needed. The panel, once it is set up, tends to remain more or less intact, and newly needed information is drawn from the established panel. This also results in a closer rapport with panel members (than with one-time interviewees) who, accordingly, are likely to provide more candid responses. Also, classification data need not be collected anew each time, and yet, over a period of time, panel members may become extensively classified. In turn, use of panels permits more attention to be focused on specific information needs.

### *Disadvantages of Panel Use*

These favorable statements have not been meant to suggest that panel techniques are free of difficulties. There are also accompanying problems. Typically, the most severe problems occur in establishing and keeping panels intact so that inference can be made from the panel responses to the universes. This normally means that probability sample designs should be used to select panel members from the universes. Selecting the members is easy—getting them to be ongoing, cooperative members is difficult. It is common for as much as 50 per cent of the selected members to either not join initially or to drop out after a very short period of time (Cordell, 1962, and Sobel, 1959). Unfortunately, the non-cooperating units do not appear to be typical of those who participate as panel members. Specifically, there is evidence that the dropouts have less interest in the topics to be considered (Hazard, 1961). Consequently, most panels appear to present some bias in their information.

A second major difficulty is that panels tend to age. New panel members must be added to take the place of aging panel members. This involves major problems in maintaining a randomly selected representative panel.

Another source of bias may arise if panel members react differently than they normally would, because of their participation on the panels. For example, if a family in the Nielsen television viewership panel quits changing channels as commercials appear—because of the presence of an Audimeter—the family is not behaving normally. They have been conditioned. Members of the MRCA panel *may* buy fewer "cheap" brands upon becoming reporting members of the panel; others may become more aware of their buying activities and behave differently.

Finally, to the extent to which members of panels fail to record their activities, the reported information is biased. Most panels try to encourage their members to write down their purchases daily, but it appears that many persons fail to do this and instead record the information they can remember when it is time to submit the diary.[6]

### *Market Research Corporation of America (MRCA) Panel*

The MRCA maintains a national consumer panel of more than 10,000 families. These families are classified by such characteristics as occupation of family head, age of housewife, number of children and their ages, education of family head, total family income, and location by region and city size. Weekly these families mail in "diaries" in which they have recorded specific food, drug, and household item purchase details such as brands purchased, weight or quantities in units, number of units, kinds of containers or packages, prices per unit, any special promotion such as coupons or deals, and store name and type in which each item was purchased. The households are awarded points that vary in magnitude with the completeness of their reports. These points are accumulated and exchanged for prizes—ones that, hopefully, do not alter the families purchasing behavior relative to panel items.

The MRCA reports monthly to its clients on brand loyalty in terms of the number and characteristics of brand-loyal households. It can contrast them with brand-switching households. Also, some insight can be gained into the effect of special promotion, price discounts, and other factors.

### *A. C. Nielsen Radio-Television Indexes*

The Nielsen Radio-Television Indexes, which have been controversial in recent years, are designed to determine the size and the makeup of the radio and television audiences for specific programs. A device

[6] For further discussion of panels, see Boyd and Westfall (1960).

called an Audimeter is connected to television and radio sets in panel homes. This device indicates when the sets are on and the stations to which they are tuned. In addition, Nielsen has available Audilogs—devices on which household members can record the stations being received and the number of men, women, teenagers, and children observing the program. Participants are requested to record this information for each quarter hour of viewing. The number of households containing Audimeters is quite small: about 1200 homes in 1965 and probably no more that 2000 homes today (Facing Schedule, 1965).

These national Nielsen TV Ratings are issued to clients each two weeks. These reports include estimates of the total, average, and share of audience of each of numerous programs.

*National Family Opinion, Inc.*

A somewhat different kind of panel than those previously described is maintained by National Family Opinion, Inc. This organization maintains a mail panel of about 30,000 United States families. Clients can have their questions asked of all of the panel on an exclusive questionnaire or they can have their questions go to the panel along with those of other clients. In addition, clients can screen the total panel to select specific members whom they may want to question or expose to new products, advertising, packaging, or something else. For example, a seller wishing to get dog owners' views of a new flea collar could screen the panel for dog owners and then proceed to contact this specific group.

Other panels providing somewhat similar information services are available. For example, Market Facts, Inc. maintains Consumer Mail Panels, Inc. A client can use it much as he would use the National Family Opinion panel.

## Store Audits

Store audits, like panels, may be the source of either syndicated or custom commercial information, as well as private information. Commercial syndicated store audits, however, are the most common because of the cost advantages associated with auditing numerous products and brands at one time. Additionally, few using companies are interested in establishing their own store audit operations.

The store audit is really a periodic check to discern the sales of certain products and brands in specific outlets during specified time periods. Most store audits reflect previous inventory *plus* dealer purchases (minus returns) = stock available for sales *minus* present inventory = consumer sales. Additionally, during store audits, investigators may describe various deals, couponing, price discounting, special promotions, and other factors that may have influenced sale of various brands. Basically, this is all there is to the actual audit itself. Of course, the task of securing cooperation from a sample of retail stores so that projections can be made to a larger group can be quite difficult. Also, the physical job of counting stock and checking invoices is enough to drive a man to drink.

The next concern is with the use of store audit information. For the most part, it is used to provide estimates of sales (both by individual brands and total industry) at the retail level for specific time periods. Factory sales merely indicate sales *into* channels, but a channel is like a pipeline that may be anywhere from full to empty. Many manufacturers want to know what is selling at the retail level at various times and how it relates to current marketing activities. Store audit information can help provide much of this information—as, of course, can consumer panel information.

A somewhat special, but important, use of store audits is the monitoring of the introduction of new products. Manufacturers cannot be satisfied by measures of sales to empty channels. A critical dimension is sales by the channel to users.

### *A. C. Nielsen Company*

The largest and probably best known commercial organization that engages in store audit activities and provides syndicated information is the A. C. Nielsen Company. Its Food-Drug Index service, which is only one of several of their services, collects data on a continuing basis for about 3000 items that are sold principally through drug and grocery stores. At last count, some 1600 cooperating food stores and 750 drug stores were audited. These cooperating stores receive marketing information and cash payment for their cooperation. Unfortunately, not all stores cooperate with the Nielsen Company, nor are all types of grocery and drug stores audited. Companies using the audit data to project sales by various market segments must proceed with considerable caution.

A client buying the Food-Drug Index receives information on total sales of the product class, sales of their own brand, and sales of each major competing brand. As a result, the client can compute both market share and market position. The Nielsen reports also cover retailer purchases of the product for each time period, retailer inventory and stockturn, per cent of audited stores stocking each item, and, finally, retail and wholesale prices and information on special sales and retailer advertising. This information is provided by various market segments, including regions, cities by size categories, and the United States, and by segments such as store ownership type (chain versus independent) and store sales volume categories.

*Custom Store Audits*

Ehrhart-Babic Associates and Burgoyne Indexes, Incorporated are illustrative of commercial information organizations that use store audits to provide custom information services. Both of these organizations offer complete handling of store audits for clients who wish to test market new products, new packages, new displays, deals, cents off, and a host of other marketing variations. In these store audits, the commercial organizations are prepared to handle all activities including selling to the channel, distributing, warehousing, merchandising and billing, as well as auditing. Control of these activities helps to ensure control of relevant variables, and such control is particularly relevant when matched panels, side-by-side tests, and various intricate field designs are required. In these situations, the audit organizations report only to their clients. Other firms, of course, can audit their competitor's activities, or try to confound them, but first they must find them.

## Field Enumerations

A number of commercial organizations collect information from virtually all sources of specific types that will cooperate with them. The F. W. Dodge Corporation, which makes monthly reports on many facets of building construction projects, claims to collect information from ". . . the 165,000 architects, engineers, contractors, owners, public officials, and others directly responsible for construction projects. The data is collected by 1400 news gathers in 106 Dodge offices—controls include 1,600,000 telephone calls and 2,000,000 personal calls each year" (Dodge Company).

This company provides over 20,000 building-project reports a month, county by county, on some 267 different types of construction activities. It provides clients with such information as the kinds of buildings (i.e., hotels, schools) that are to be undertaken or are under way in each market, the types of structures, number of stories, floor space, and valuation in dollars. The information can be ordered in many different forms and via many different vehicles. The type of information that is available is shown in Figure 12-1. A client buying the full complement of information for the entire national market would spend about $22,000.

There are other types of information that are obtained from what are basically field enumerations. Dun and Bradstreet through a 2000-man field force and 138 offices collects current information on over 300,000

```
JAN 11 1966-                                              LA 2 No. 006 444E
                                                          1ST REPT 2-10-65

(A)  SMITH ELEMENTARY SCHOOL (ALTS AND ADDN) AND (B) BALDER JUNIOR HIGH SCHOOL
     (ALTS AND ADDN) $360,000 (TOTAL)
PRESKO BLANCO CALIF (ORANGE CO) (A) 103 MARKET ST
     (B) ADAMS AVE S W CORNER COSTA DR
OWNER TAKING BIDS ON GC (A AND B) DUE FEB 16 AT 2 PM (PST)
OWNER - PRESKO BLANCO SCHOOL DIST JOHN T JONES (SECY) 421 DAY ST PRESKO BLANCO
     CALIF (432-1237)
ARCHT - ADAMS AND CASEY ASSOC 363 HULBERT ST LOS ANGELES CALIF (432-1234)
ENGR (STRUCL) - VERNON L THOMPSON 14 MAIN AVE ARCADIA CALIF (444-6262)
ENGR (PLBG-HTG-VENTG AND ELEC) - JACK SMITH 38 ELM DR
     AMES CALIF (468-3471)
     BRK AND STUCCO EXT WALL FACING - C B BACKUP - ALUM EXT
     TRIM - 1 STY-NO BASMT- (A) $200,000- 12,000 SQ FT-
     (B) $160,000- 9,500 SQ FT- (A) and (B) WALL BEARING
     CONST-CONC SLAB FLR CONST-WD JOIST RF CONST-WD
     RF DK-INCLS (A) 12 CLASSRMS- LIB AND READING RM-
     ADMIN OFF- (B) 8 CLASSROOMS-STORAGE RM-ADMIN OFF-
     (A AND B) PRD CONC FDNS- GAS FIRED W A HTG-HDWD
     TERR VINYL ASB TILE AND CARPETING FIN FLRG-ALUM
     SASH-WD AND ALUM DRS-PLASTG-ACOUST CEILINGS-FIRE
     AND LAWN APKRS-NO DEMOL OR AIR CONDTG INVL
GC INCLS ALL TRADES
PLANS AND SPECS OBT FROM ARCHT - $50 DEP REQ - REF TO ACTUAL BIDDERS-
     ½ REF TO NON BIDDERS
5% BID BOND AND 100% PERF BOND REQ
COMPLETE PLANS AND SPECS ON FILE IN OUR L A PLAN ROOM
```

**Figure 12-1** A Dodge report. Used by permission of F. W. Dodge Division, McGraw-Hill Information Systems Company.

manufacturing firms in the United States. For approximately $20,000 per year, clients can get 20 items of information on each of the firms on printed forms, punched cards, or magnetic tape. The information includes basic identification data, activity information (such as line of business, size information in terms of employees, sales volume, and net worth), and further evaluation data.

R. L. Polk and Company, through field-enumeration work, prepares city directories on more than 5500 United States cities. Their directories list for most households the names of all adults, their marital status, job titles and places of employment, telephone numbers, and whether the residence is owned or rented. Somewhat similar information is secured for each business firm in each town surveyed.

The same company's Motor Statistical Division and Motor List Division enumerate county car-registration records to determine who buys what cars. This information is available in a variety of forms ranging from the vehicles' serial numbers (to account for all vehicles sold) to the number of various brands sold in specific markets.

Companies interested in the amount of advertising that is being used by competitors may turn to several sources that, basically, employ the field-enumeration approach. The Publishers Information Bureau (P.I.B.) supplies comprehensive monthly reports on national magazine and network television advertising. They indicate month-by-month expenditure data and a cumulative total to date within the report year. All data are listed by seven basic industry classifications and then into further subgroupings that include individual companies. These data all arise from monitoring of the appropriate media.

Media Records, Inc. provides a somewhat similar type of information—but about advertising expenditures in newspapers. In this case, the company has selected about 400 major newspapers and monitors ads of certain advertisers. They do not use a formal sample design.

Rorabaugh Reports cover spot television advertising activities in the major television markets of the country. All television stations are asked to report each national and regional spot advertisement (by brand and company) active on their stations during each quarter. Information includes the number of spots, the time period, and the type of activity. Rates are applied to these figures to gain a rough estimate of expenditures. In a recent year, 300 of the 486 television stations in the United States provided information.

There are obviously other types of information arising from field enumerations, but the range of this type of data has been indicated.

## Independent Sample Surveys

The fourth technique commonly used by commercial organizations to secure information for clients is the independent sample survey. In contrast to the panel technique, a new, or independent, sample is drawn for each new major study. This technique is used by sellers of both syndicated and custom information.

The technical aspects of this technique are the same whether the research is accomplished by a commercial information supplier or by the using company. Therefore, the reader is referred to earlier parts of this book for a review of the technical aspects of this method.

Perhaps an examination of a few of the different types of information services that use this technique will be useful to the reader.

### *Starch Readership Service*

The Starch Magazine Advertisement Research Service estimates the extent of readership of advertisements in consumer, farm, and business magazines, as well as in a handful of newspapers. The number of observations included in their samples varies by publication, but, as a rule, is no less than 100 males and 100 females and no larger than 200 of

SATURDAY EVENING POST FEBRUARY 24 1968 26 ADS

MEN

| PERCENTAGES | | | READERS PER DOLLAR | | | COST RATIOS AND RANKS | | | | | | Starch Advertisemen[t] | |
|---|---|---|---|---|---|---|---|---|---|---|---|---|---|
| NOTED % | SEEN-ASSO. % | READ MOST % | NOTED # | SEEN-ASSO. # | READ MOST # | NOTED Ratio | NOTED Rank | SEEN ASSO. Ratio | SEEN ASSO. Rank | READ MOST Ratio | READ MOST Rank | PAGE | SIZE & COLOR |
| | | | | | | | | | | | | Alcoholic Beverages | |
| 23 | 16 | 6□ | 56 | 39 | 15 | 119 | 8 | 98 | 14 | 250 | 2 | 65 | 1PBW JR. |
| 57 | 51 | 8 | 42 | 37 | 6 | 89 | 17 | 93 | 15 | 100 | 10 | 72 | 2P4CB JR. |
| | | | | | | | | | | | | Auto. Cars | |
| 52 | 45 | 8 | 56 | 49 | 9 | 119 | 8 | 123 | 8 | 150 | 5 | 21 | 1P4CB |
| 59 | 51 | 9 | 33 | 29 | 5 | 70 | 20 | 73 | 20 | 83 | 14 | 40 | 2P4CB S |
| 69 | 68 | 13 | 44 | 44 | 8 | 94 | 15 | 110 | 9 | 133 | 8 | 54 | 2P4C |
| 44 | 40 | 12 | 82 | 75 | 22 | 174 | 3 | 188 | 3 | 367 | 1 | 61 | 1PBW |
| 61 | 56 | 7 | 76 | 70 | 9 | 162 | 4 | 175 | 4 | 150 | 5 | 69 | 1P4C |
| 68 | 61 | 9 | 85 | 76 | 11 | 181 | 2 | 190 | 2 | 183 | 3 | 3C | 1P4C |
| | | | | | | | | | | | | Auto. Trucks | |
| 47 | 45 | 5 | 59 | 56 | 6 | 126 | 6 | 140 | 5 | 100 | 10 | 2 | 1P4C |
| | | | | | | | | | | | | Clothing Accessories | |
| 15 | 5 | * | 19 | 6 | | 40 | 26 | 15 | 26 | | | 45 | 1P4C |
| | | | | | | | | | | | | Drugs/Remedies | |
| 27 | 24 | 2 | 95 | 84 | 7 | 202 | 1 | 210 | 1 | 117 | 9 | 16 | 1/2VPBW |
| 26 | 23 | 5 | 49 | 43 | 9 | 104 | 12 | 108 | 10 | 150 | 5 | 79 | 1PBW |
| | | | | | | | | | | | | Food | |
| 32 | 26 | * | 40 | 33 | | 85 | 18 | 83 | 18 | | | 39 | 1P4C |
| 24 | 21 | 1 | 26 | 23 | 1 | 55 | 24 | 58 | 22 | 17 | 21 | 53 | 1P4CB |
| | | | | | | | | | | | | Hhld. Appliances | |
| 15 | 12 | 1 | 28 | 22 | 2 | 60 | 23 | 55 | 23 | 33 | 19 | 19 | 1PBW |
| | | | | | | | | | | | | Insurance/Finance | |
| 47 | 36 | 1 | 45 | 35 | 1 | 96 | 14 | 88 | 16 | 17 | 21 | 10 | 2PBW |
| 28 | 22 | 3 | 52 | 41 | 6 | 111 | 11 | 103 | 12 | 100 | 10 | 17 | 1PBW |
| | | | | | | | | | | | | Medical Equip. | |
| 12 | 8 | 1 | 74 | 50 | 6 | 157 | 5 | 125 | 7 | 100 | 10 | 4 | Digest BW |
| 36 | 26 | 6 | 59 | 42 | 10 | 126 | 6 | 105 | 11 | 167 | 4 | 5 | 1PBWB |
| | | | | | | | | | | | | Photography | |
| 52 | 48 | 3 | 56 | 52 | 3 | 119 | 8 | 130 | 6 | 50 | 18 | 22 | 1P4CB |
| | | | | | | | | | | | | Publications | |
| 9 | 8 | * | 33 | 29 | | 70 | 20 | 73 | 20 | | | 42 | 1/2PBW JR |
| | | | | | | | | | | | | Radio/TV/Phono Equ[ip.] | |
| 23 | 14 | 3 | 29 | 18 | 4 | 62 | 22 | 45 | 24 | 67 | 17 | 15 | 1P4C |
| 35 | 28 | 4 | 44 | 35 | 5 | 94 | 15 | 88 | 16 | 83 | 14 | 75 | 1P4C |
| | | | | | | | | | | | | Tobacco Cigarettes | |
| 35 | 30 | 5□ | 38 | 32 | 5 | 81 | 19 | 80 | 19 | 83 | 14 | 71 | 1P4CB |
| 50 | 42 | 2□ | 48 | 40 | 2 | 102 | 13 | 100 | 13 | 33 | 19 | 4C | 1P4C |
| | | | | | | | | | | | | Toilet Goods Women | |
| 43 | 18 | * | 24 | 10 | | 51 | 25 | 25 | 25 | | | 2C | 2P4CB |

*SYMBOLS USED WITH PERCENTAGES:*

* Less than one half of one per cent.
□ Read most for Ads with fewer than 50 words.
** Read most or Seen-Asso. not applicable to this Ad.

*SYMBOLS USED WITH SIZE/COLOR:*

‡ Size Approximate
V Vertical Fraction
H Horizontal Fraction
G Gatefold
JR. Junior
DIG Digest Size
ISL. Island
# Insert
S Spec. Position Ch[arge]

Full run Ads are reported here. Cost ratios are ranked when 10 or more Ads are reported.

**Figure 12-2**

WOMEN

| adership Report | PERCENTAGES | | | READERS PER DOLLAR | | | COST RATIOS AND RANKS | | | | | |
|---|---|---|---|---|---|---|---|---|---|---|---|---|
| ADVERTISER | NOTED % | SEEN-ASSO. % | READ MOST % | NOTED # | SEEN-ASSO. # | READ MOST # | NOTED Ratio | NOTED Rank | SEEN ASSO. Ratio | SEEN ASSO. Rank | READ MOST Ratio | READ MOST Rank |
| lfschmidt Vodka | 18 | 13 | 5□ | 51 | 37 | 14 | 96 | 15 | 88 | 15 | 233 | 3 |
| dweiser | 49 | 41 | 4 | 41 | 34 | 3 | 77 | 18 | 81 | 17 | 50 | 19 |
| mouth | 29 | 26 | 2 | 36 | 32 | 2 | 68 | 21 | 76 | 18 | 33 | 21 |
| eral Motors | 29 | 20 | 1 | 19 | 13 | 1 | 36 | 26 | 31 | 26 | 17 | 24 |
| vrolet | 39 | 31 | 3 | 29 | 23 | 2 | 55 | 23 | 55 | 22 | 33 | 21 |
| erican Motors | 11 | 9 | 2 | 24 | 19 | 4 | 45 | 25 | 45 | 24 | 67 | 17 |
| smobile | 28 | 18 | 4 | 40 | 26 | 6 | 75 | 19 | 62 | 21 | 100 | 11 |
| tiac | 32 | 25 | 4 | 46 | 36 | 6 | 87 | 16 | 86 | 16 | 100 | 11 |
| lge Trucks | 20 | 13 | 1 | 29 | 19 | 1 | 55 | 23 | 45 | 24 | 17 | 24 |
| Beers Cons Mines | 42 | 31 | 5 | 60 | 44 | 7 | 113 | 10 | 105 | 13 | 117 | 9 |
| tac | 32 | 26 | 3 | 129 | 105 | 12 | 243 | 1 | 250 | 1 | 200 | 4 |
| ctin | 32 | 28 | 3 | 69 | 60 | 6 | 130 | 7 | 143 | 8 | 100 | 11 |
| pbells Soup | 66 | 63 | 6 | 94 | 90 | 9 | 177 | 4 | 214 | 2 | 150 | 7 |
| ecal Prods | 56 | 54 | 13 | 69 | 67 | 16 | 130 | 7 | 160 | 6 | 267 | 2 |
| ver Vacuum | 47 | 40 | 8 | 101 | 86 | 17 | 191 | 2 | 205 | 3 | 283 | 1 |
| Mutual Life | 36 | 19 | 1 | 40 | 21 | 1 | 75 | 19 | 50 | 23 | 17 | 24 |
| ual of New York | 20 | 13 | 1 | 43 | 28 | 2 | 81 | 17 | 67 | 20 | 33 | 21 |
| h Hearing Aid | 14 | 10 | 1 | 99 | 71 | 7 | 187 | 3 | 169 | 5 | 117 | 9 |
| Sunlamp | 50 | 39 | 6 | 94 | 73 | 11 | 177 | 4 | 174 | 4 | 183 | 5 |
| k Camera | 43 | 39 | 4 | 53 | 48 | 5 | 100 | 13 | 114 | 10 | 83 | 16 |
| ebster Dict | 17 | 12 | 2 | 72 | 51 | 8 | 136 | 6 | 121 | 9 | 133 | 8 |
| ne Symph Swps | 39 | 28 | 7 | 56 | 40 | 10 | 106 | 11 | 95 | 14 | 167 | 6 |
| TV | 46 | 44 | 4 | 66 | 63 | 6 | 125 | 9 | 150 | 7 | 100 | 11 |
| erfield | 28 | 24 | 5□ | 35 | 30 | 6 | 66 | 22 | 71 | 19 | 100 | 11 |
| F Tareyton | 50 | 43 | 3□ | 55 | 47 | 3 | 104 | 12 | 112 | 11 | 50 | 19 |
| l Loving Care | 83 | 72 | 7 | 53 | 46 | 4 | 100 | 13 | 110 | 12 | 67 | 17 |



**Figure 12-2** (Continued)

each for each publication. The units to be observed for each publication are selected by interviewers on a quota basis, which parallels each publication's circulation pattern. Starch describes this as a national sample.

The field procedure used by Starch is to first approach respondents to determine whether they qualify as readers of the issue by virtue of having noted any part of the specific issue. Those who qualify are questioned on their observations and readings of specific ads. Basically, readers are led through each magazine, ad by ad and by each major part of each ad, and are quizzed as to what they can recall.

Results available to clients indicate the per cent of respondents who qualified as readers who "noted," "seen-associated" (i.e., identified the offering or advertiser), and "read most" (i.e., read 50 per cent or more of the written material) of each ad. Information is also provided on the observation and reading of component parts of each advertisement. In addition, Starch provides measures of what they call (1) "readers per dollar" (number of readers times per cent "noted," "seen-associated," or "read most" divided by space costs), (2) "cost ratios" (reader/$ *divided* by the median "readers/$ for all half or larger ads in the same issue), and (3) rankings of "readers/$ for all ads in each publication. Figure 12-2 displays the types of information provided.[7]

*Other Users of Independent Sample Designs*

Numerous commercial suppliers of custom information make extensive use of independent sample surveys. Some of the samples are designed for the sole use of one client, while others serve as information-securing vehicles for numerous clients.

The Gallup Organization, for example, conducts a new survey at least once every three weeks. For each survey an independent national probability sample of 1500 people (21 years of age or over) is selected for personal interviews. An individual client may have only one question asked or as many as twenty. Classification data covering some twelve characteristics are collected. In addition, Gallup conducts surveys of special publics such as business leaders, financial analysts, and purchasing agents. In its special surveying Gallup employs telephone and mail survey techniques as well as personal interviews.

Centelibus employs only telephone interviewing in contrast to the Gallup Organization's personal interview survey. Once again, clients can specify the number of questions they want asked, and the commercial

[7] The price of this information for consumer magazines in 1966 was scaled from $50/report (i.e., coverage on one issue) to $30/report when two or more reports were purchased per month for four or more consecutive months. Reports on business publications and newspapers were somewhat costly.

organization provides demographic classification questions. Centelibus uses a national probability sample of 3000 adults over 18 years of age and equally divided between males and females. Their current schedule calls for four surveys a year. Information from the clients' questions are provided in tabulated form and only to the client. Although prices do not stay constant for long, some idea about them can be gained from a 1966 price schedule. The first question was priced at $650, the second at $550, and each succeeding one at $500. Each free-response question was priced at an additional $200, and each cross tabulation was priced at $20. Various discounts altered this price schedule somewhat.

More common than the multiple-client sample survey is the survey conducted for only one client. Many of the suppliers of commercial information that were mentioned earlier provide this type of service. The service can vary all the way from a situation where the commercial organization merely conducts the field survey to ones where it defines problems to be investigated, sets up the research design, designs the data-collection forms, determines the appropriate sample design, and carries the research all the way through to its completion.

A somewhat different kind of sample than those previously mentioned is illustrated by one maintained by the Des Moines Register and Tribune for testing newspaper advertising copy. They have drawn three "matched" samples, each consisting of 2000 subscribers, from the Des Moines metropolitan area. The samples are matched at a very small scale, in that single newspaper routes are selected at random from each census tract and designated as an "A" route. Then "B" and "C" (matched route samples) are systematically selected from routes adjacent to the initially selected route. The only difference in the papers delivered to the different routes is the client's ad. The client is provided with the names, addresses, and telephone numbers of each household included in the sample. In turn, the client can conduct the follow-up research it deems appropriate to estimate the influence of the various advertisements and to relate it to readers' characteristics. These routes are not used like panels, but instead, once they have been used, new routes are selected to replace them.

## Commercial "Spies"

The commercial "spy" may provide an avenue for securing marketing information. A commercial "spy" is basically a person who secures and knowingly releases confidential company information to persons not authorized to receive it. Such an individual may work for love, money, spite, or some combination of the three. He may be an authorized handler of the information or he may secure it through devious methods. In any event, the concern here is with securing marketing information about competitive products through such a person. The main question is, How important (or how good) an alternative is the commercial spy as an avenue for marketing information?

There have been numerous popular articles about industrial espionage. *Business Week* published an article, "Industrial Spying Goes Big League" (1962), *Harvard Business Review* contributed "Industrial Espionage" (Furash, 1959), the *Wall Street Journal,* "Business Spy" (Guilfoyle, 1959) and "Savings from Spying" (Schorr, 1961), and *Fortune* magazine discoursed at length under the "Business Espionage" title (Smith, 1956). Others have preached the defensive side. *Management Methods* published "How to Protect Yourself Against Business Spies" (1960) and *Duns Review and Modern Industry* asked, "Your Company Secrets: Are they Safe?" (Lorke, 1958).

The current conclusion must be that *use* of commercial spies as an avenue for competitive *marketing* information is relatively minor. Marketing information, generally, is more readily and cheaply available through cooperative arrangements, published material, the marketplace itself, and legitimate commercial collection sources.

Securing information through commercial spies is relatively expensive. There are many reasons—the nature of the activity, the economic risk to the individual, and so on. Furthermore, the greater the variety of products sold and the less centralized the information programs, the more contacts are needed to secure such information. In addition, many companies simply do not possess detailed marketing information even for their own use. Finally, and probably even more important, most business managers simply do not feel that the "rules of the game" permit commercial spying for marketing information (Hazard, 1961). These "rules" come back to a basic business belief that any tactic that is employed can be used in retaliation. Business espionage is not "worth the candle."

## Other Commercial Services

Not explicitly mentioned up to this point are several other types of commercial offerings available to users of marketing information. A number of commercial organizations, for example, maintain facilities and programs for exposing consumers and measuring their reactions to new products, new advertisements, new packages, and so forth. Typically, these organizations *select* a group of people, *gather* them together in a meeting room, *expose* them to the new offering, and by various means attempt to *gain* their responses to the new offering. One of these organizations is the Schwerin Research Corporation, which offers its theater system for pretesting proposed television commercials. Another is Burke Marketing Research, Inc. Its program involves getting an audience into its "Television Laboratory," exposing them to the television commercials, and gaining viewers' responses through both electronic attitude indicators and self-administered questionnaires. The Gallup Organization maintains a center (Mirror of America) where consumers can be exposed to and questioned about new products, packages, advertisements, and so forth.

A second type of service that has not been explicitly mentioned is field-interviewing facilities. There are organizations that offer complete conduct of field-interviewing work. That is, they take the questionnaire, secure answers from specified sources, and then turn the completed questionnaires back to the clients. In addition, many of these organizations offer services on the design of questionnaries and stand ready to tabulate and report the information.

A third type of service is specialized consulting help in technical areas such as the design of samples and the design and conducting of motivational research designs. Finally, there are services such as John Felix Associates, Inc. that are principally concerned with data-processing problems. This organization, for example, does *not* write questionnaires or do field research, analysis, or report writing. It operates an IBM System 360 computer, along with other data-processing equipment, and provides data-consulting services, computer programming, systems analysis, keypunching, computer time rental, and related services.

## Commercial Information Summary

In summary, this section has attempted to provide a view of the extent of commercial information and services that are available to users of marketing information. Clearly, there is a great variety—almost any information service package is available, from the performance of a simple task to the complete handling of a whole research project. Both syndicated information and custom information can be purchased.

No attempt has been made to list all of the organizations that offer commercial information and services. Instead, attention has been devoted to the *types* of information and services that are available and to how the information arises. Most commercial information arises through panels, store audits, field enumerations, or independent sample surveys. Some suppliers of commercial information and services offer information that employs two or more of the techniques. But enough for now on primary commercial information and sources. The reader should know the general types of commercial information and services that are available and how to search for and evaluate them.

## REFERENCES

Albaum, G. "The Hidden Crisis in Information Transmission," *Pittsburg Business Review,* July 1963, pp. 1–4.

Albaum, G. "Horizontal Information Flow: An Exploratory Study," *Journal of Academy of Management,* March 1964, pp. 21–33.

American Marketing Association. *A Geographical Listing of Marketing Consultants and Research Agencies,* 1966.

Berelson, B., & Steiner, G. A. *Human Behavior: An Inventory of Scientific Findings.* New York: Harcourt, Brace and World, 1964.

Boyd, H., Jr., & Westfall, R. *An Evaluation of Continuous Consumer Panels as a Source of Marketing Information.* Chicago: American Marketing Association, 1960.

Buzzell, R. D. "Predicting Short-Term Changes in Market Share as a Function of Advertising Strategy," *Journal of Marketing Research,* August 1964, pp. 27–31.

Cordell, W. N., & Rahmel, H. A. "Are Nielsen Ratings Affected by Noncooperation, Conditioning or Response Error?" *Journal of Advertising Research,* September 1962, pp. 45–49.

Department of Commerce. *Directory of Foreign Advertising Agencies and Marketing Research Organizations.* Washington, D.C.: Government Printing Office, 1966.

F. W. Dodge Company. *Planning For Improved Distribution.* New York: F. W. Dodge Company, A Division of McGraw-Hill, Inc.

"Facing Schedule of Inept Collapse," *Des Moines Sunday Register,* October 31, 1965, p. 3-T.V.

Ferber, R. Blankertz, D. F., & Hollander, S., Jr. *Marketing Research.* New York: The Ronald Press, 1964, p. 31.

Fothergill, J. E., & Ehrenberg, A. S. C. "The Schwerin Analyses of Advertising Effectiveness," *Journal of Advertising Research,* August 1965, pp. 298–306.

Furash, E. "Industrial Espionage," *Harvard Business Review,* **38,** November-December 1959, pp. 6–8.

Gruber, A. "Position Effects and the Starch Viewer Impression Studies," *Journal of Advertising Research,* September 1966, p. 14.

Guilfoyle, J. "Business Spy," *Wall Street Journal,* March 3, 1959.

Hazard, L. "Are Big Businessmen Crooks," *Atlantic Monthly,* November 1961.

"How to Protect Yourself Against Business Spies," *Management Methods,* July 1960.

"Industrial Spying Goes Big League," *Business Week,* October 6, 1962, pp. 65–66.

Lorke, A. "Your Company Secrets: Are They Safe?" *Dun's Review and Modern Industry,* **72,** August 1958, p. 44.

Quittmeyer, C. L. "Management Looks at Consultants," *Management Review,* March 1961, pp. 4–10.

Rotzall, K. "The Starch and Ted Bates Correlative Measures of Advertising Effectiveness," *Journal of Advertising Research,* March 1964, pp. 22–24.

Schorr, B. "Savings from Spying," *Wall Street Journal,* August 15, 1961.

Smith, R. "Business Espionage," *Fortune,* **53,** May 1956, pp. 118–121.

Sobel, M. G. "Panel Mortality and Panel Bias," *Journal of The American Statistical Association,* March 1959.

"What Management Consultants Can Do," *Business Week,* January 1965, pp. 88, 104.

*Thirteen*

# Securing External Secondary Information

External secondary information is one of the mainstays in virtually every marketing information system and research program. It may not appear as exciting and glamorous as other types of information, but nonetheless external secondary information is of fundamental importance to successful marketing. It serves as the base and the starting point for the solution of nearly all marketing problems. It provides background and serves to indicate what is already known.

An information manager *must* have more than cursory insight into the availability of external secondary information. In fact, only after the external secondary information has been inventoried should primary information be searched and secured. Quite obviously, external secondary information is of great importance to decision makers.

This is an appropriate place to examine the dimensions of this external secondary information category. First, it is *external* to the information-seeking firm. That is, this type of information is generated and initially, at least, is searched, secured, analyzed, transmitted, and put into storable forms outside the seeking firm. It is in this sense that it is external.

Second, it is *secondary* information. Secondary information can be contrasted with primary information. The distinction is not always clear. However, in general, primary information is that which is *originated* by a researcher in view of specific needs. In contrast, secondary information is that which is already in existence, having been searched-secured, analyzed, and stored by other persons. For instance, if the publisher of Life magazine collected information about the characteristics of his subscribers, in order to better orient the magazine to the audience, the survey would provide primary information to the publisher of *Life*. This very information provided by *Life* to other users, however, would be secondary information to these other users. Now, if the user ran his own field survey to discern the *Life* audience characteristics, he would be collecting primary data.

### *Secondary Sources of Secondary Information*

One other somewhat similar-sounding phrase should be introduced at this time. Secondary information can be obtained directly from the originating sources or from secondary *sources.* For example, a Census of Population report for Los Angeles County would be an originating source. In contrast, a *Business Week* report or a Chamber of Commerce bulletin reporting on the information in the Census publication would be a secondary source.

As a generalization, the originating source is the preferred source from which to secure external secondary information. There are several reasons for such a preference. Originating sources are more likely to explain how and why the information was collected. Also, the originating source is more likely to present all of the information, whereas a secondary source is more likely to report only that which it deems appropriate. Finally, each additional repeating source presents another possible source of error. These, then, are the major reasons for securing external secondary information from the originating sources.

On the other hand, there may be very good reason to use some secondary sources of secondary information. Such sources may simply be more convenient to secure and use—and yet be sufficiently reliable. For example, a publication such as the *Survey of Buying Power,* which relies primarily on Census reports, is extremely convenient because it contains information on numerous markets and in many dimensions. To get similar information, a researcher would need to turn to several different originating publications, search through numerous pages, and extrapolate several series of data.

Another factor favoring the use of secondary information from secondary sources may be its availability on punched cards or magnetic tape in form for computer input.[1] The point is that users of secondary information should not always turn to the originating sources. There are occasions when secondary sources of secondary data should be used.

[1] This is *not* meant to imply that originating sources do not employ punch cards or magnetic computer tape records. The Bureau of the Census is making much of its information available via both of these methods of output. For example, the 0.1 per cent sample of the 18th Decennial Census is available on tape or cards in alphanumeric form (for $1500) and the 0.01 per cent sample is available on punched cards (for $500).

## USE OF EXTERNAL SECONDARY INFORMATION

An immense amount of secondary information is available. Some decision makers make good use of it; others seem to pretend that all of their information-requiring problems are original. The simple fact is that with all that is occurring in the environment of virtually all firms, no firm can afford to ignore external secondary information. In fact, it would be the most unusual firm that would ignore such information.

External secondary information is useful in many different ways. First, such information can serve as *general references* to help firms to be in contact with their environments. For example, a company may want to know about population trends, changes in disposable personal income, retail sales activities, legal developments, proposed packaging requirements, and consumer sentiments. Furthermore, a company may want to know such specifics as industry inventory levels, price policies of competitors, and industry sales—to mention only a few. Such reference information often is available from governmental sources, universities and colleges, trade associations, and numerous different commercial publishers that put out such periodicals as *Business Week, Duns Review,* and *Iron Age.* Such alternative information sources will be described later.

External secondary information is useful in the *solution of specific problems.* In fact, secondary information is examined in the early stages of most research and information problems. The findings serve as background, provide approaches to investigations, and even supply specific solutions. In other words, secondary information may provide techniques for solving problems, it may provide useful data, and, of course, it may even provide complete solutions.

For example, a large dairy was prepared to survey a market in order to ascertain the proportion of households that regularly purchased a majority of their milk needs from retail stores. However, a search of external sources indicated that such information was available from a local newspaper. No new data collection was needed. In another situation a research director wanted to use a mail survey, but did not know how to handle the nonresponse units. A search of several professional journals provided answers to all of his questions and, additionally, raised (and answered) other questions that he would not have anticipated on his own.

Finally, in many situations the only alternative to the use of secondary information is no information. Much secondary information is such that no one company could or would want to marshal the resources to gather the information. Most of the federal Census material as well as much state and local government information would fit into this category. Needless to say, such secondary information can be very valuable in providing part of a firm's continuing data base.

## MANAGING SECONDARY INFORMATION

External secondary information frequently presents unique searching, securing, analyzing, storing, and managing situations. That is, such information is frequently handled differently than internal and primary information. This is a major reason for discussing external secondary information as a separate entity.

The basic and unique characteristic of such information is that it has already been searched, secured, analyzed, and placed in some storable form somewhere. Normally, these components have been performed in view of the primary user's needs—or at least they have not been performed in view of secondary users' needs and do not readily fit the needs of the secondary users.

In this sense, secondary information is somewhat like a secondhand suit of tailor-made clothes. Such used suits can be found in many places in addition to tailors' shops. Therefore, the first problem for a buyer is finding a used suit. Once it is found, a prospective user examines the suit and, if it passes his cursory inspection, he tries it on for fit. In some cases it may fit rather exactly and even justify a relatively high purchase price. On the other hand, the fit may be such that considerable alterations are needed to make the suit wearable. Then a prospective user must trade off the alteration costs against the estimated value of the tailored suit. And finally, in some cases, the suit is such a poor fit that no reasonable amount of retailoring will make it fit a prospective user. Then a prospective user must search on for other secondhand suits or consider having one tailor-made.

### Searching-Securing

The *search* for and the *securing* of external secondary data are somewhat unique. By definition the information has been secured and stored somewhere by others. The *search* problem centers in *finding* the information—with little emphasis on techniques for securing it. That is, research designs, data-collection forms, and so forth are of very minor consequence. The major search-secure concern is with sorting through the mass of possible sources and information, not knowing for a fact that the sought-after information is actually available.

Sound search programs are virtually mandatory, but, unfortunately, there is not much comment that can be made about general search procedures. In some situations a researcher, through experience, knows just where to find needed information. However, in numerous situations he only believes that certain information is available—with little more than a guess as to where it might be found.

Quite obviously a researcher cannot know in detail all sources of all information. On the other hand, the more information sources he is familiar with, the easier is his search task. Practically speaking, research people are most familiar with those sources that they have used most frequently. An experienced researcher may index as many as 100 different information sources for almost instant recall.

A very important thing to remember is that just because a familiar source of needed information cannot be recalled, it does *not* mean that a source does not exist. That is, a researcher must not limit himself to the alternatives he can recall—he must continually be able to expand his search to unfamiliar sources. Major sources of marketing information are discussed later in this chapter.

### *Search by Subject*

For the more obscure secondary information searching situations, the researcher, with subject in mind, can turn for help to (1) other persons who are likely to have faced a need for similar information or to (2) various information indexes. The first alternative needs little amplification. The key question is—can past users be readily located?

The researcher first tries to identify users who might know of the availability of needed information. If such information would be used only by similar sellers, the inquiry would be limited to these sellers. If, on the other hand, past users cannot be readily identified, the researcher may wish to direct his search to a professional association with a multiplicity of contacts. For example, the American Management Association or the American Marketing Association might know of the availability of obscure information. Another approach is to turn the task over to a commercial consulting organization such as Search and Summary,[2] which specializes in finding and transmitting external secondary information.

The second general type of search path is through information indexes.

[2] Search and Summary, P. O. Box 4271, Western Station, Milwaukee, Wisconsin.

Even along this path an inexperienced searcher can become bogged down in a maze of indexes. Hundreds of indexes are available. They seemingly index and categorize everything from authors to zithers. Fortunately, a researcher's problem is not as difficult as it might at first appear. There are a few indexes of indexes for researchers who know not where to start. For example:

1. *Guide to Reference Books, and Supplements,* by C. M. Winchell (Chicago: American Library Association, 1951—supplements through 1962). This index to indexes is organized by subject and indicates for each subject the available references. Some 6000 reference sources are described in some detail.
2. *How and Where to Look It Up,* by R. W. Murphy (New York: McGraw-Hill, 1958). A part of this book discusses the major indexes of periodicals, directories, and commercial and governmental sources of information. Another part of this book discusses specific sources and indicates how to find information on people, places, and things.

Some of the major information guides are listed and described in the Appendix to this chapter. They are listed there because secondary information is so important and information guides play such a focal role in securing secondary information. In turn, the reader is advised to examine personally each of the guides.

## Storage

The information used most frequently can often be placed within a firm's storage facilities. Bound and indexed publications permit typical library-type storage by type and name of publication. However, nonindexed general-subject publications are best clipped and the clippings filed by major subject. In other words, an indexed publication such as *The Wall Street Journal* could be left intact and filed under its title, because the researcher could move from the index to the appropriate issue. In contrast, nonindexed publications, such as the *Chicago Tribune,* should be examined upon receipt, the relevant articles clipped, summarized, or copied, and filed by subject.

The actual physical storage may vary all the way from traditional library rack-and-file storage to the use of Videofile and Photochromic Micro Image, coupled with computerized search-and-retrieval facilities. Obviously, microfilming, card storage, and tape storage offer practical alternative that help reduce storage space and speed retrieval. The places and types of storage (and related retrieval programs) depend on such considerations as the nature of the information, the amount of information retained, available storage and retrieval facilities, and the importance of such information to the business organization.[3]

Sources of information that are infrequently used and unimportant should not be brought into the confines of the individual firm. Instead, the researcher should turn to libraries and other private and public sources for this information. Basically, the question of ownership and place of storage of information comes down to the consideration of the various alternatives, their likely benefits, and associated costs.

## Analysis and Evaluation

Once information is uncovered, the emphasis changes to analysis and evaluation of both the source per se and the information. Such dual evaluation and examination must proceed largely in view of the use planned for the information. The overall key considerations are: (1) is the information such that it fits or can be adjusted to fit the needs? and (2) is the source sufficiently dependable? These are dual considerations, and one without the promise of the other is quite meaningless.

Relative to the usefulness of the information, a researcher must ask: "Relative to our needs, is this information for the correct time periods, does it appear in the correct units of measurement, and does it provide sufficient breath, depth, and detail?" And to the extent that it does *not* meet the needs, he must ask, "Can the weaknesses be remedied?"

Source evaluation is another matter. The researcher basically seeks to discern the *accuracy* of the reported information. Ideally such an evaluation involves consideration of both (1) the research procedures that gave birth to the information and (2) *why* the research was accomplished.

Both built-in biases and faulty research procedures can result in inaccurate findings—and the two combined can produce wild distortions. Faulty research procedures are difficult to discern unless flagrant violations occur. Research flaws, even major ones, may be glossed over, if discussed at all. The careful inspector of another man's work must anticipate the types of defects that are most likely to be present—and look for them. Cursory inspections offer little more insight than an original researcher wishes to provide.

The biases of the original information sources are obvious at times. For example, the Montgomery Ward Company would no doubt depict its product line offering quite differently than would a competitive analy-

[3] For a more complete description of the various storage devices, retrieval systems, and related decision criteria, see "Information Retrieval" (1965).

sis by Sears, Roebuck, and Company. Such biases are relatively easy to detect and work with.

The most difficult sorts of biases to detect and adjust for are those originating (perhaps unconsciously) in investigators. For example, virtually every business, government, and university researcher wishes to discover relationships, concepts, and, in general, "things" previously undiscovered by other men. Consequently, over the years reports of new findings have been far more numerous than actual new findings. The spectacular has a tendency to displace the mundane.

There are numerous other sources of bias. Many an advertising agency research man, for example, would like to show favorable findings relative to clients' advertising campaigns. Media researchers like to work for aggressive, dynamic organizations whose publications appeal to the avant-garde. Captive research departments often believe that their products and packages are superior to all competitive offerings. These kinds of feelings often slip into what are meant to be objective findings. Hopefully, blatant biases will be detected by watchful users of secondary information and minor biases will be of minor consequence. However, the basic warning must be that *users* of secondary data must continually be sensitive to both blatant and accidental biases.

Almost no secondary information should be accepted without being questioned—merely because it is in print and published, and perhaps by the "right" people. That is, researchers should not mistake form for substance. Virtually all secondary information should be evaluated as to likely accuracy. Some information and information sources must be held under a strong light before being accepted—others can be examined in a rather cursory manner. A tap that has dispensed only clean water in the past needs only slight inspection. On the other hand, water from unfamiliar taps must be tested so that the user does not pollute his system with poison.

### *Specific Guidelines*

Although general comments can be useful in gaining perspective, more detailed guidelines are a necessity. Specifically, the evaluator of secondary information would do well to seek answers to the following questions.[4]

1. In what environment was the study conducted?
   *a.* Is there a full statement of the problems to be resolved by the investigation?

[4] The general guideline for this discussion was borrowed from Criteria for Marketing and Advertising Research (The Advertising Research, 1953).

*b.* Who financed the study?

*c.* What organization participated in the study—what were their interests, qualifications, and findings?

*d.* When was the information collected and how representative was that period relative to prior and following periods?

*e.* What is the date of the published report?

*f.* Are the uncommon terms adequately defined?

*g.* Are copies of the data-collection forms and related materials available for examination?

*h.* Is the methodology adequately described?

2. Was the research design appropriate?

*a.* What type of research design was used—was it an observational or an experimental design?

*b.* Was the general research design appropriate in view of the problem?

*c.* Was appropriate information collected? This includes consideration of the ability and willingness of respondents to give valid responses.

*d.* Was sufficient information collected? Were enough test units observed in the experiment? Relative to a survey, one must determine the adequacy of the sample size.

*e.* Does the research design support the information secured? Does the secured information support the stated conclusions of the study? This raises two questions: Do the findings support the statements made about the units actually observed (i.e., does the study have internal validity)? If so, what about the inference made beyond the observed units—is it warranted? In other words, does the study have external validity?

3. Was the research design properly carried out (i.e., implemented)?

*a.* Was the information-collection process satisfactory?

*b.* Was the raw information properly edited, tabulated, and analyzed?

*c.* Is the raw information available for examination?

*d.* What nonsampling biases appear to be present? Specifically, it often is worthwhile to see if the target population and the sampled population are the same. Also, nonresponse bias may be present in information resulting from surveys. Finally, the users of secondary information should be aware of the many sources of biases that have already been discussed in earlier chapters.

4. Have correct statistical tools been properly applied?

*a.* An altogether too common a flaw is the application of standard error formulas to data that arose through nonprobability designs. For example, confidence intervals cannot be meaningfully applied to quota sample findings.

*b.* Have parametric procedures been applied to nonparametric data?

*c.* Have sample findings been properly reported as sample statistics or in probability terms? Or, have they been distorted as population certainties?

*d.* Have uncommon mathematical and statistical manipulations been explained (at least in footnotes)?

*e.* Do charts and tables give accurate portrayals or do they distort or exaggerate the findings. There are numerous ways in which to distort both numerical and graphic findings.

These criteria do not present a complete checklist for all types of secondary information. They place the greatest emphasis on secondary information that is based on sample findings. However, most findings are sample findings—not complete enumerations—hence the emphasis is applicable.

Also, the criteria are particularly useful to researchers with limited research experience. In the process of doing research and reporting findings, researchers learn, so to speak, "the tricks of the trade." That is, through their own research activities they gain insight into and appreciation of how biases and distortions can arise. In turn, they know what to look for when shaking down the "findings" of others. Nonetheless, the criteria can serve even experienced investigators as a reminder of possible problems among secondary information.

Finally, one additional comment about these criteria is appropriate. The criteria are useful for two purposes. Their initial intended purpose is to aid in the appraisal and evaluation of secondary information. But the other very useful purpose is to help the primary researcher both plan the various stages of his research project and—prior to its final-form release—to provide an internal self-appraisal.

## SOURCES OF EXTERNAL SECONDARY INFORMATION

External secondary information is typically searched for by subject matter. That is, situations and problems give rise to need for specific information—and that information is sought. But where is it sought? This section focuses attention on major *sources* of marketing information.

Knowledge of the major sources can help searchers move more directly to needed information. The types of sources discussed include (1) federal, state, and local government, (2) trade, professional, and technical associations, (3) industrial organizations, (4) financial data sources, (5) commercial, trade, and other publication sources, and (6) general library sources.

## Federal, State, and Local Government Sources

Governments collect and disseminate more information than any other type of source. To the uninitiated, the various types of information that are available can be almost unbelievable. It ranges, for example, from estimates of the number of wild horses (or, if you prefer, whooping cranes) in the United States to the number of retail food stores in each county to the number, breeds, and even names of dogs registered in various counties.

The typical pressing problem faced by both the experienced and the inexperienced researcher is *locating* the necessary information and *securing* it in a readily usable form. Governmental units collect masses of public information useful in marketing. Admittedly, nondisclosure requirements call for some combining of data before they can be made public (e.g., individuals' income tax returns, individual stores' tax returns) and some information is confidential, but most data are open to the public.

Data from governmental sources, as from other sources, may be published—and by either governmental units or private publishers. For example, the major findings from the Census of Business are originally published by the federal government. On the other hand, F. W. Dodge Reports, which are described in the chapter on commercial information, arise from unpublished but public government records.

### *Unpublished Information*

Unpublished public information abounds, but is relatively difficult to both secure and use. Also, it seems to be somewhat less reliable than published information. County courthouses provide a bastion of public, unpublished information. Births, deaths, marriages, divorces, and other so-called vital statistics are publically available. Additionally, real estate valuations, personal property ownership records, dog and other pet ownership information (by owners' names), and related sorts of information are available. In numerous counties, individual ownership of tractors, manure spreaders, and other major pieces of farm machinery (by model and year) are recorded. Also, livestock is frequently listed, as is ownership of miscellaneous other items.

The uniformity of recordings, the quality of the information, and the completeness of the records vary extensively even within any one state. Some county office holders exhibit great fastidiousness in recording promptly, clearly, and completely the events occurring in their counties. Others apparently run for election—and reelection—on the promises that they will not record any information in an understandable manner. Generally, the greatest laxities occur where there is no requirement to report or publish the information.

County recorded information typifies the realm of public-unpublished information. At best, such information is costly to secure and difficult to evaluate. Yet there are times when such sources are the best sources.[5]

### *Published Information*

The federal government is the largest single source of marketing information. In fact, it is so large that one should be familiar with the various governmental agencies and offices and the types of information they possess.[6]

THE BUREAU OF THE CENSUS. The Bureau of the Census (within the Department of Commerce) collects and publishes more information useful to marketing managers than does any other agency or office of the federal government. The statistical heart of marketing research information is supplied by the seven major censuses compiled by the Bureau at regular intervals. Their publications are (1) Census of Governments, (2) Population and Housing Censuses, (3) Census of Mineral Industries, (4) Census of Manufacturers, (5) Census of Business (which includes retail trade, service establishments, and wholesale trade), (6) Census of Agriculture, and (7) Census of Transportation. Each of these are issued as major reports, as well as in supplemental issues. In addition to these specific publications, the Bureau publishes numerous other studies. Users are advised to check the Bureau's *Catalog of Publications* and its *Monthly Supplement* for a more complete listing.

Finally, the Bureau will run special tabulations of data when their resources permit. For example, they have special runs that indicate the number of retail outlets within various sales volume groups for selected markets. Basically, the Bureau can and will make such special tabulation runs, for which they have data available, so long as disclosure restrictions are not violated and the runs can be fit into their work schedule. Special charges are made for these services.[7]

[5] For example, in numerous counties, local new-car dealers jointly support the collection and weekly dissemination of new-car sales information from county records to the various dealers.

[6] For a more extensive discussion, see Frank (1964).

[7] For a specific illustration see Crisp (1957 pp. 166–167).

DEPARTMENT OF COMMERCE. The United States Department of Commerce, by statute, is responsible for the development of foreign and domestic commerce and the industries and transportation facilities of the United States. To facilitate such activities, the Department maintains a series of field offices which can be most useful in describing and making Commerce information available.

Some of the major Commerce publications are *Survey of Current Business, Business Statistics,* and *County Business Patterns.* There are numerous other specific as well as general publications.

DEPARTMENT OF AGRICULTURE. The United States Department of Agriculture provides an immense amount of information useful to marketing. Agriculture studies include information on various ways of packaging and marketing numerous agricultural products and even studies relative to such things as store layout and supermarket locations. It makes studies of potential, consumer preferences, merchandising methods, buying practices, wholesaling, and numerous other topics. These studies are easily located through the agency's catalog of publications.

Finally, the Department has been a leader in developing and refining experimental and observational research study designs. Many a researcher, although not specifically interested in the packaging of oranges (or potatoes), would be well advised to emulate some of the research designs employed to study these problems.[8]

OTHER FEDERAL SOURCES. In this brief space even an introductory listing of federal sources of information is impossible. Additional major sources include the (1) Executive Office of the President, (2) Congress, (3) Department of Health, Education, and Welfare, (4) Department of the Interior, (5) Department of Labor, and (6) Department of the Treasury. It should be remembered that the federal government supplies more information useful in marketing than any other one source. Also, its output appears to be increasing in both quantity and quality. Because of the maze of supplying agencies, offices, and information, researchers who are uncertain about sources of federal information should turn first to a publication such as *Government Statistics for Business Use* (Hauser and Leonard, 1956) or *Market Analysis: A Handbook of Current Data Sources* (Frank, pp. 32–92, 1964).

STATE AND LOCAL GOVERNMENT. The type and quality of information available from state and local government is largely dependent on the accompanying administrative, regulatory, and planning activities of the various governmental units.

Quantitative facts arise through the presence of fees, permits, licenses,

[8] For example, see U.S. Department of Agriculture (1961).

registrations, and various taxes. Also, vital statistics and various industry data are frequently collected locally for transmittal to other agencies. Finally, various planning and development and commerce commissions both collect data for their own use and for distribution to other users.

Each state as well as many of the provinces of Canada and states of Mexico issue various periodic publications. The various types of publications can be viewed by general types or groups of publications. For example, many states have provided periodic *directories* of manufacturers, new plants, products, and assortments of basic industrial data.

Numerous states publish statistical summaries of both current and past business and industry activities. Frequently, these appear as annual reviews. State economic activity reports are rather commonly published by both state agencies and university bureaus of business and economic research. Periodic statistical reports often are heavy in agriculture, labor, and retail and wholesale activity information. Labor series include reports on the level of employment, hours and wages, and cost of living. Agricultural reports abound in quantity and market price information. The wholesale/retail data largely reflect the level of retail activity by areas and wholesale price levels.

The basic point is that there are numerous sources and types of information available from local sources. The person seeking local and state government information often needs to turn to basic reference works. In this field one of the best is *The Book of States* (The Council), which is a biennial report. The various university and college bureaus of business and economic research are listed in the *Directory of University Research Bureaus and Institutes* (Gale Research, 1960). These research groups are in a good position to know both what information is available and where it can be acquired. The annual *Municipal Year Book* (International City Managers' Association) is full of text and tables that summarize city trends and statistics compiled by numerous different sources. Finally, specific mention should be made of quasi-governmental port authorities. They not only report on their own activities, but also on the activities within the region they serve.

## Trade, Professional, and Technical Associations

Trade, professional, and technical associations exist in many fields of business, science, and technology. Many of these associations are interested in securing and disseminating information. In the area of marketing, the major professional associations that disseminate much information include the American Marketing Association, the Chemical Market Research Association, American Economics Association, American Psychological Association, and Operations Research Society of America.

Trade associations, as a rule, are established and maintained by business competitors within an industry. Two of their main objectives are to (1) research common problems and to (2) assist members with information about the industry and its environment. Some of their information is available for public consumption. The American Home Laundry Manufacturers Association information and the Aerospace Industry Association information discussed in an earlier chapter are illustrative of the available information.

A researcher not sufficiently familiar with the various associations would be wise to start with the *Encyclopedia of Associations* (Gale Research Co., 1964).

### Industrial and Business Organizations

Industrial and business organizations may both have and be willing to release needed information. A researcher normally should not turn directly to his competitors for information. The Justice Department may frown upon the implications of such an interchange of information. However, noncompetitive companies may exchange very useful information. For example, an Eastern restaurant chain may provide very useful operating information to a similar but noncompeting Western chain. Pillsbury, General Foods, or General Mills may provide useful information to a Midwestern cookie manufacturer who uses their flour.

The most difficult problems in securing information from industrial and business organizations are knowing (1) which firms are likely to possess the necessary information and (2) whom to contact within the organization. There is no good substitute for firsthand knowledge, but, lacking this, a researcher may turn to *Thomas Register of American Manufacturers* (Thomas Publishing Company), which is a directory of manufacturers classified by products. Once likely source companies have been selected, he may turn to *Poor's Register of Corporation Directors and Executives, United States and Canada* (Standard and Poor's Corp.) to determine the names of the persons to contact.

### Financial-Data Sources

There are quite a large number of financial-data sources that possess very useful marketing information. Large publicly owned companies, as a rule, must make regular reports to the Securities Exchange Commission as well as to their shareowners. Such information is openly available.

The typical report includes information on revenues major expenses, profits, types of products produced or sold, number of employees, number and location of plants, number of retail outlets, new acquisitions and sales, and sometimes even major internal changes.

Firms attempt to submerge both their revenue and their expense information in iceburglike accounts. However, limited-line firms such as Schlitz Brewing Company, The Maytag Company, and American Motors Company cannot "hide" information nearly as well as can General Electric, General Motors, and other full-line companies.[9]

Financial information about many of the larger firms is available from *Moody's Investors Services, Inc., Standard Corporation Records* published by Standard and Poor's Corporation (New York), and other financial reporting sources.

### Commercial and Trade Publication Sources

There are a fairly large number of firms that are in the business of publishing commercial and trade information. For example, R. L. Polk and Company and Ward's Reports, Incorporated both publish information on the automotive field. *Doane Agricultural Digest* is a publication on farm management, and F. W. Dodge Corporation specializes in the collection and publication of data for the building products and construction industry. The major sources and type of such information were examined in detail in the chapter concerning commercial information.

Trade publications provide valuable sources of information within many trades and industries. Their titles typically are a tip-off to the trade areas covered. For example, *Food Topics, Electrical Merchandising Weekly, Chemical Week,* and *Heating and Ventilating* all provide a wealth of information about the named industries. Such publications, while often free to the trade, must carry worthwhile industry information in order to gain readership.

Some trade publications cut across product lines and follow more functional lines. Typical of these are *Industrial Marketing, Sales Management,* and *Purchasing.* These publications offer considerable information about the topics listed in their titles.

A researcher who wishes to explore trade publications should turn to an index called *Business Publication Rates and Data* (Standard Rate and Data Service, Inc.) for a listing of the various trade publication sources.

[9] For a firsthand view of this see *Moody's Industrial Manual: American and Foreign* (1967).

### Library Sources

Many public, university, and college libraries maintain extensive collections of business information. Virtually all of the publications listed in this book, for example, are available in at least one library in almost every state. In fact, even some of the published commercial services are available. State universities and the larger private universities and colleges normally contain the larger collections, but municipal libraries should not be ignored.

Special libraries containing business information should also be searched. These libraries are often supported by various private business organizations such as trade associations, chambers of commerce, and commercial firms. Normally their collections cover the organization's subject area in considerable depth and with a variety of documents ranging from published books to unpublished papers. Some special libraries are open to the public, but many are private and require specific permission for their use.

There is no list of market research libraries per se. However, the *Directory of Special Libraries and Information Centers* (Gale Research Co., 1963) includes some 10,000 entries and indicates the subject and compositions of each collection. Another general publication that lists special libraries, subject collections of general libraries, and federal document depositories is the *American Library Directory* (R. R. Bowker Company).

As a final comment, a researcher attempting to discern the body of knowledge regarding a specific subject should not overlook general and special library sources. After all—libraries are information depositories.

## SUMMARY

Secondary information serves as the base and the starting point for the solution of nearly all marketing problems. It serves to describe the general environment, to prescribe possible methodologies, to provide facets of information, and, on occasion, even to provide complete solutions. Basically, secondary information must be investigated first in order to determine what is already known.

External secondary information presents relatively unique information-handling problems. Most of these arise because such information has previously been searched, secured, analyzed, and placed in storable form—all in view of the primary users' needs. As has been noted, routine search patterns are not the rule of order. Information sources that have been used frequently in the past may be readily recalled from memory. However, when memory fails, the researchers must undertake search either through the use of various indexes or through more knowledgeable persons. Haphazard search is almost never feasible. There simply is too much information in too many sources.

Once information is found, emphasis changes to analysis and evaluation of both the information and its sources. Basically, one must make certain that (1) the information fits the needs and that (2) the sources are trustworthy. Both of these matters have been discussed in general terms, and, additionally, a specific list of guideline questions has been provided.

Secured external secondary information can be stored in many different forms. Of course, the first question is simply, "Should it be retained?" The places and types of storage depend on such considerations as the nature of the information, the frequency and manner of use, the amount of retained information, available storage and retrieval facilities, and the importance of the information to the organization. Many different storage and retrieval systems are available.

The last section of the chapter explores various major sources of external secondary information. The types of sources discussed include: (1) federal, state, and local governments, (2) trade, professional, and technical associations, (3) industrial organizations, (4) financial-data sources, (5) commercial, trade, and other publication sources, and (6) general library sources. Although not every source can be described, or even listed, the major indexes and reference books are listed in an appendix to enable the reader to move from this chapter to the next step in the search for secondary information.

APPENDIX

## SOURCES OF EXTERNAL SECONDARY INFORMATION

### *A. General Information Guides*

1. Arthur H. Cole, *Measures of Business Change* (Homewood, Ill.: Richard D. Irwin, Inc., 1952). This index classifies several hundred national, regional, and local business indexes. It gives particular emphasis to private series. The various indexes are listed by subject, with each described and identified as to compiler, frequency of current publications, and period covered. Unfortunately, this publication does not cover additions made since 1952.
2. Philip M. Hauser and William R. Leonard, *Government Statistics for Busi-*

*ness Use,* 2nd ed. (New York: Wiley, 1956). This book provides a guide to federal government statistics. However, it does not cover all the statistical series compiled by the government and of interest to business. The various statistical series are described in some detail.

3. Edwin T. Coman, Jr., *Sources of Business Information,* 2nd ed. (Berkeley: University of California Press, 1964). This book, organized by subject areas, is designed to identify and to describe major sources of business information. It also contains a brief guide to business indexes.
4. Nathalie D. Frank, *Market Analysis: A Handbook of Current Data Sources* (New York: Scarecrow Press, 1964). This book lists virtually all of the major sources of external secondary marketing information. In addition, it contains an index that permits a researcher to trace subjects to various sources. Each of the hundreds of sources are described as to their nature and content.
5. Paul Wasserman et al. (Eds.), *Statistics Sources* (Detroit: Gale Research Co., 1962). This is a specialized bibliography devoted to all kinds of publications that include statistics. It lists over 6000 subject classifications and over 9000 sources.
6. Edgar Gunther and Frederick A. Goldstein, *Current Sources of Marketing Information* (Chicago: American Marketing Association, 1960). This annotated bibliography of primary sources of data covers items published from 1954 through 1959. National, regional, state, and industry data are indexed along with more general information.
7. *Statistical Services of the United States Government* (Washington, D.C.: Bureau of the Budget, 1963). This publication discusses the statistical system of the federal government and describes each of the major federal economic and social statistical series.
8. *Monthly Catalog of United States Government Publications* (Washington, D.C.: Superintendent of Documents). This catalog indexes all publications of the federal government issuing agency. Annual and decennial indexes by subject are also compiled.
9. *Monthly Checklist of State Publications* (Library of Congress). State documents *received* by the Library of Congress are indexed by state and by department or issuing agency. Also, an annual index compiled by subject is published. Unfortunately, not all state documents find their way to the Library of Congress.
10. *Marketing Information Guide* (Washington, D.C.: U.S. Department of Commerce). This index, which is published monthly by the Department of Commerce, provides an annotated list of *selected* current materials of interest to marketing people. Items are classified by source: federal government, state government, international organization, business, professional, and insti-

tutional. Unfortunately, the selected list is far from comprehensive. A semi-annual subject index is published each January and July.

Entries 3 and 4 are particularly useful in that they provide more complete enumerations and descriptions of available sources of information. The following three sections present selected lists of guides to (1) books, monographs, and bulletin, (2) periodicals, and (3) summary volumes of statistics.

*B. Guides to Books, Monographs, and Bulletins*

1. *Card Catalog.* A listing of special libraries is included in *Market Analysis,* by Frank. In every library the card catalog is the basic index to books and other independent publications held in the library. This catalog is organized by subject and author.
2. *Cumulative Book Index.* This volume indexes by subject all English-language books published throughout the world.
3. *Book Review Index* (Detroit: Gale Research Co.). This monthly publication provides an index of book reviews appearing in several hundred periodicals. Each year about 8000 titles and 15,000 reviews are listed.
4. *Public Affairs Information Service* (New York: Public Affairs Information Service). This index, organized by subject, covers selected ". . . books, pamphlets, periodical articles, government documents, and any other useful library material in the field of economics and public affairs." It includes items from all English-speaking countries and emphasizes factual and statistical information.
5. *Index of Publications of Bureaus of Business and Economic Research.* This guide is classified by institution and subject and covers all publications by bureaus of the association.
6. *Index to American Doctoral Dissertations* (Ann Arbor, Mich.: University Microfilms, Inc.). This annual volume lists, by subject field and author, lists all doctoral disserations accepted by American and Canadin institutions of higher learning.

*C. Guides to Periodicals*

1. *Ulrich's Periodical Directory* (New York: R. R. Bowker Co., 1963). This publication is a guide to periodicals. It lists approximately 20,000 current foreign and domestic periodicals. They are grouped by general subject. The index indicates for each periodical the details of publication, typical, items appearing in it, and where it is indexed.
2. *Applied Science and Technology Index* (New York: The H. W. Wilson Company). This is a cumulative index listing articles appearing in about 200 periodicals in engineering, applied, science, and industry.

3. *Business Periodicals Index* (New York: The H. W. Wilson Company). This publication indexes (by subject) all the articles appearing in approximately 120 periodicals covering all aspects of business.
4. *International Index to Periodicals* (New York: The H. W. Wilson Company). This publication indexes (by subject) all articles appearing in about 150 learned journals.
5. *Readers Guide to Periodical Literature* (New York: The H. W. Wilson Company). This publication indexes (by subject) over 100 periodicals. These periodicals are of the more popular variety and, accordingly, the information sources tend to be less useful.
6. *New York Times Index* (New York: The New York Times Company). This publication indexes (by subject) all articles appearing in the *New York Times*. This index, along with the following one, is particularly useful in locating information associated with known years.
7. *The Wall Street Journal Index* (New York: Dow Jones and Company, Inc.). This publication, arranged in two sections (corporate news and general news), indexes corporate news alphabetically by firm and general news by subject.

*D. Summary Volumes of Socioeconomic Statistics*

Indexes aid in the pursuit of needed information, but, of course, do not provide the information per se. Obviously, indexes are fundamentally important because of mans' inability to know and remember the thousands of sources of available information. However, there are one to two dozen general *summary volumes* of statistics that many information managers keep in mind—if not readily available in their libraries. Some of the more prominently used general summary volumes are listed and described below. Of course, other summary volumes that relate to specific products, topics, and areas are also available.

1. *Statistical Abstract of the United States*. Published annually by the U.S. Bureau of Census. This abstract carries data on industrial, social, political, and economic organization of the United States Information is taken from ". . . most of the important statistical publications, both governmental and private."
2. *Survey of Current Business and supplements* (Washington, D.C.: Government Printing Office). This is a comprehensive source of over 2000 statistical series covering economic and industrial activities. Weekly supplements carry current data on a number of series. Special supplements are issued irregularly on such subjects as national income, income distribution, and foreign investments.
3. *Historical Statistics of the United States, Colonial Times to 1957* (Washington, D. C.: Bureau of the Census, 1959). This volume includes about 6000 statistical series extending back to the earliest years for which data were

recorded. A useful part of the volume is the description of each series and definitions of terms.

4. *Monthly Labor Review* with annual supplements (Washington, D.C.: Government Printing Office). It includes a variety of information on employment, wages, labor turnover, and price indexes.
5. *Federal Reserve Bulletin* and *Banking and Monetary Statistics* (Washington, D.C.: Board of Governors of the Federal Reserve System). The *Bulletin* is issued monthly. It includes statistics on retailing, consumer and wholesale prices, consumer credit, national income, and crop reports, as well as much data on banking and monetary activities. *Banking and Monetary Statistics* provides historical data (primarily from 1914 to 1941).
6. *Minerals Yearbook* (Washington, D.C.: Government Printing Office). It provides a comprehensive summary of mineral activity in the United States. It appears in three volumes: *Metals and Minerals, Fuels,* and *Area Reports.*
7. *Economic Almanac.* Published in New York biennially by the National Industrial Conference Board. This is a statistical compendium presenting statistical series on business, labor, government, and related topics.
8. *Commodity Yearbook.* Published annually. Imports and exports, production, consumption, and price statistics for the United States, major foreign countries, and the world are reported for numerous agricultural products minerals, petroleum, and some selected products such as alcohol, fur, and rayon.
9. *Agricultural Statistics* (Washington, D.C.: Government Printing Office). Published annually. This is a compendium of the more important statistical series developed by the Department of Agriculture as well as some data from other government agencies.
10. *Foreign Commerce Yearbook* (Washington, D.C.: Government Printing Office). This volume includes selected basic economic statistics for 87 foreign countries.
11. *Quarterly Summary of Foreign Commerce of the United States* (Washington, D.C.: Government Printing Office). Published quarterly. Indicates exports and imports by commodity for the United States and for foreign countries in total.
12. *Standard and Poor's Trade and Securities Statistics.* Published monthly by Standard and Poor's Corporation (New York). Contains statistics on banking, production, labor, commodity prices, income, trade, building materials, railroads, utilities fuels, metals automobiles, rubber, textiles chemicals, paper, agriculture, leather, tobacco, and securities.
13. *Statistics of Income* (Washington, D.C.: Government Printing Office). This annual publication is divided into three reports and provides statistical data on (1) tax returns on individuals, (2) tax returns on corporations, and (3) United States business tax returns (sole proprietorships and partnerships.)

14. *Survey of Buying Power.* Published annually by Sales Management, Inc. (New York). This publication provides information, both absolute and relative, on population, income, and retail sales (by a number of categories) for each county and city over 10,000 population in the United States, Canada, and Mexico. This information is also available on punch card and magnetic tape.

## REFERENCES

The Advertising Research Foundation, Inc. *Criteria for Marketing and Advertising Research.* New York: 1953.

The Council of State Governments. *The Book of the States.* Chicago.

Crisp, R. *Marketing Research.* New York: McGraw-Hill, 1957.

Frank, N. D. *Market Analysis: A Handbook of Current Data Sources.* New York: The Scarecrow Press, 1964.

Gale Research Company. *Directory of University Research Bureaus and Institutes.* (1st ed.) Detroit: 1960.

Gale Research Co. *Encyclopedia of Associations.* Detroit: 1964.

Hauser, P., & Leonard W. *Government Statistics for Business Use.* (2nd ed.) New York: Wiley, 1956.

"Information Retrieval," *Business Management,* **28,** June 1965, pp. 36–40, 62.

International City Manager's Association, *Municipal Year Book.* New York.

St. Clair, F. J. (Ed.) *Moody's Industrial Manual: American and Foreign.* New York: Moody's Investors Service, 1967.

Standard and Poor's Corporation. *Poor's Register of Corporation Directors and Executives, United States and Canada.* New York.

Standard Rate and Data Service, Inc. *Business Publication Rates and Data.* Skokie, Ill.

U.S. Department of Agriculture. "Frozen Concentrated Orange Juice," *Marketing Research Report,* No. 457, March 1961.

Thomas Publishing Company. *Thomas Register of American Manufacturers.* New York.

# CASES

# PART III



## JANITORIAL SERVICES, INC.*

Janitorial Services, Inc. is a distributor of janitorial supplies to a variety of customers including hospitals, schools, and office buildings. The company sells such supplies as uniforms, chemicals, paper products, and electrical cleaning appliances to institutions throughout a three-state area. Janitorial Service's sales were approximately $4.5 million in 1968, and their gross profit margin was about 30 per cent.

Fortunately, the company is able to hold routine selling costs at a minimum by using telephone and mail solicitation of their older, established customers. The sales staff consists of a sales manager, six field sales representatives, and four telephone and mail solicitors, who operate from Janitorial Service's business office. The field sales representatives spend about 70 per cent of their time seeking new customers and demonstrating the company's products to those not familiar with them. The remainder of the sales representatives' time is spent on making calls and routing sales to old customers.

You, as the firm's market and sales analyst, have been instructed by Robert Bell, the company's president, to perform a cost analysis on the basis of customer size.

* The name of the company and some of the figures are disguised.

**Exhibit 1** Detailed Income Statement

| | | | |
|---|---|---|---|
| Gross sales | | | $4,435,000 |
| Less: Returns and allowances | | | 35,000 |
| Net sales | | | $4,400,000 |
| Cost of goods sold | | | $3,100,000 |
| Gross profit | | | $1,300,000 |
| Wages and salaries | | | |
| Administrative salaries | | | |
| Officers' salaries | $175,000 | | |
| Staff salaries | 50,000 | | |
| | | $225,000 | |
| Sales salaries | | | |
| Sales manager | $ 12,000 | | |
| Field salesmen | 48,000 | | |
| Mail and phone solicitors | 18,000 | | |
| | | $ 78,000 | |
| Accounting salaries | | | |
| Head accountant | $ 9,000 | | |
| Secretarial and clerical | 20,000 | | |
| | | $ 29,000 | |
| Warehouse, receiving, and handling wages | | | |
| Supervisor | $ 8,500 | | |
| Clerical | 12,500 | | |
| Labor | 25,000 | | |
| | | $ 46,000 | |
| Credit and collection salaries | | | |
| Supervisor | $ 10,000 | | |
| Secretarial | 8,000 | | |
| | | $ 18,000 | |
| Total wages | | $396,000 | |
| Overhead and operating charges | | | |
| Salesmen travel | $ 45,000 | | |
| Collection agency | 3,000 | | |
| Telephone | 8,400 | | |
| Shipping | 252,000 | | |
| Utilities | 7,500 | | |
| Mailing | 3,100 | | |
| Advertising | 35,000 | | |
| Equipment depreciation | 15,000 | | |

**Exhibit 1** (Continued)

| | | | |
|---|---|---|---|
| Entertainment | 2,000 | | |
| Auditing services | 500 | | |
| Materials and supplies | 20,000 | | |
| Rent | 5,000 | | |
| Inventory taxes | 12,000 | | |
| Inventory insurance | 3,500 | | |
| Interest on inventory | 64,500 | | |
| Total overhead and operating | | $496,500 | |
| Other expenses | | | |
| Interest on debt | $ 52,000 | | |
| Federal income taxes | 150,000 | | |
| Total other expenses | | $202,000 | |
| Total expenses | | | $1,074,500 |
| Net income | | | $ 225,500 |

**Exhibit 2** Customer Groups by Purchase Size

| 1968 Total Purchases | Number of Customers | Number of Separate Orders | Dollars Sales | Number of Salesman Calls | Number of Invoices or Collection Notices |
|---|---|---|---|---|---|
| 0–$50 | 5,500 | 4,800 | 210,000 | 1,000 | 9,800 |
| $50–$100 | 3,900 | 4,100 | 300,000 | 1,100 | 7,500 |
| $100–$200 | 1,500 | 5,100 | 180,000 | 1,700 | 8,200 |
| $200–$500 | 2,400 | 6,400 | 740,000 | 2,100 | 7,500 |
| $500–$1000 | 900 | 6,100 | 620,000 | 3,100 | 11,200 |
| $1000–$2000 | 850 | 9,800 | 1,250,000 | 7,500 | 12,100 |
| $2000–$5000 | 300 | 7,300 | 800,000 | 4,300 | 9,400 |
| $5000 and up | 50 | 6,400 | 515,000 | 2,200 | 8,300 |
| | 15,400 | 50,000 | $4,435,000 | 23,000 | 74,000 |

You are able to obtain a breakdown of the company's operating expenses for 1968 from the accounting office. (These expenses are reproduced in Exhibit 1.) The accounting department also has records of 1968 sales to each of the firm's customers. Your first task is to arrange these purchase records in usable form. After classifying each of the company's customers according to the size

**Exhibit 3** Functional Cost Assignments

I. Personal selling
  Mail and telephone solicitor's salaries
  Telephone
  Mailing
II. Advertising and sales promotion
  Advertising
  Entertainment
III. Transportation and warehousing
  Warehouse receiving and handling wages
  Shipping
IV. Credit and collection
  Collection agency
  Credit and collection salaries
  Auditing services
V. Carrying costs
  Inventory taxes
  Inventory depreciation
  Interest on inventory

of their annual purchases, you are able to supplement these data with information given you by the sales maneger and the credit department. This information includes (1) total number of calls made by a salesman to each customer and (2) total number of invoices and collection notes sent to each customer in 1968. (The results of distributing these data among the various customer classes are shown in Exhibit 2.)

You have decided to group the firm's expenses into five functional costs. These functional classifications are personal selling, advertising and sales promotion, transportation and warehousing, credit and collection, and carrying costs (see Exhibit 3).

1. Allocate expenses from the Income Statement to the five functional classifications.

2. Suggest a basis of allocation (e.g., sales dollars, number of salesman calls, total number of orders, number of customers, or number of invoices and collection notices sent) of the expenses in the functional classifications to each customer class.

3. From the data given, calculate the cost of selling to the various sizes of customers. Does it appear to be profitable to serve each of the customer classes?

## ASTRO FEEDS, INC.*

Astro Feeds, Inc. is a producer and seller of various animal feeds, supplements, and trace minerals. Its headquarters are located in No Cheer, Iowa.

On September 30, 1953, Channel 8, Cedar Rapids, Iowa, first went on the air, and Astro Feeds, Inc. began its present-day sponsorship of the Ole Olreg Show. The program has been broadcast each Friday evening from 6:30 to 6:45 P.M. and has featured country and Western music. Each program has carried two Astro Feed commercials. The Ole Olreg Band, in the past, has been named the number 1 Western band by Downbeat Magazine.

From 1953 to 1965 the number of farms in Iowa declined from 196,251 to 153,669, a decrease of 22 per cent. The average size of farms increased from 177 to 223 acres, an increase of 26 per cent. Total land in farms declined 1.4 per cent during the period. Changes in livestock farming have taken place as the number of farms has declined and average size per farm has increased. The average size of feeding operation has increased while the number of farms raising hogs, feeding cattle, keeping laying hens, and milking cows has declined.

Several areas of concern stemmed directly from these farm changes. First, Astro Feeds, as a supplier to the farm market and as an advertiser on television, became concerned that perhaps television was no longer an appropriate, practical, and economical medium for reaching the farm market. Along with the decline in the number of farms and farm viewers, the number of urban viewers had increased. Therefore, the cost per farm viewer prospect was believed to have increased, perhaps to a point where it was unreasonable.

Second, farming had changed from a small-farm family-centered way of life to large-scale commercial operations and had become more like other business enterprises that rely heavily on purchased inputs. Astro Feeds wondered if farmers' purchasing habits had changed and become more like those of a business purchasing agent. There was some reason to believe that operators of large farms tended to be influenced more by price and specifications.

Third, Astro Feeds thought that country and Western music might be declining in popularity. If this was happening, sponsorship of a program of country and Western music could leave the sponsor in a doubtful position. This raised a question of whether the percentage of farmers viewing the Ole Olreg Show was declining.

Fourth, Astro Feeds was concerned with determining the cost of the Ole Olreg Show per prospective livestock feed user in the Channel 8 area. This would include, if possible, a determination of the cost per viewer.

Fifth, a general evaluation of the use of television as a medium for reaching the farm market in terms of consumer behavior was needed.

* The name of the company and some of the figures are disguised.

## OBJECTIVES

With this background information, the following general research objectives were proposed:

1. Determine the cost per prospect to reach livestock farms via television in the Channel 8 area.
2. Determine the cost per livestock farm viewer.
3. Determine the broadcast sources that farm people rely on for information at different times of the day.
4. Determine whether the size of farm operations of the viewers of the Ole Olreg Show is below average.
5. Measure rural liking for country and Western music.
6. Evaluate television as a medium for advertising to the farm market.

## VIEWING AREA

From the Iowa Assessors Annual Farm Census 1965, compiled by Iowa Crop and Livestock Reporting Service, the number of farms within a 60-mile radius of the Channel 8 tower was determined to be 28,750. The tower is located northwest of Cedar Rapids near Iowa Highway 150 North of Urbana and in the northeast corner of Benton County. Signals of sufficient strength reach out 60 miles. It is quite possible that the television waves would be strong enough to reach out 80 or 90 miles or more. However, considering the location of other television stations at Davenport, Rock Island, Moline, Ames, and Des Moines, a 60-mile radius would seem to be the maximum practical limit. There is another television station at Cedar Rapids and one at Waterloo.

According to the United States Census of Agriculture, 1964, the percentage of Iowa farms with television was 94. According to another Iowa Crop and Livestock publication ("Number and Size of Farms, Geographic Patterns in Iowa, State Farm Census, Supplement Number Three, Farm Counts"), 81 per cent of the farms in the northeast district were livestock farms, while the east central district had 78 per cent and the state average was 76 per cent. From this information it would seem fair to assume that 78 per cent of the farms within a 60-mile radius of the Channel 8 tower were livestock farms and that 94 per cent of the livestock farms had television. The number of livestock farms with television within a 60-mile radius of the tower would have been 21,080.

| | |
|---|---|
| Total in 60-mile radius | 28,750 farms |
| 78 per cent livestock | 22,425 farms |
| 94 per cent with television | 21,080 farms |

## THE SURVEY SAMPLE

A mail survey was selected to reach the study objectives. The questionnaire, consisting of three pages, was believed to be too long for a telephone survey, and a personal interview survey would have been too costly.

Since names of all farmers within a 60-mile radius of the Channel 8 tower were not readily available, a nonprobability sample design was selected. Two sample areas were chosen: Stanwood, Iowa, and Newhall, Iowa. Stanwood, which is located in the northern part of Cedar County, is 49 miles from the Channel 8 tower on a straight-line basis. It was estimated that there were 176 farms in the Stanwood trade Area. Newhall, Iowa, which is located in the eastern part of Benton County, is about 15 miles west of Cedar Rapids and 24 miles from the tower. There were an estimated 174 farms in the Newhall 60-square-mile trade area. Astro Feeds had dealers at both of these locations.

Stanwood was selected because it had a dealer direct-mail list of only 79 names. Most dealer direct-mail lists have considerably more than 100 names. It was recognized that there might be large bias in using the Astro dealer direct-mail list because it included selected names of Astro customers and prospects. Nevertheless, the list of 79 farm accounts was selected as the sample.

In the Newhall area a boxholder mailing was used. There was only one rural route out of Newhall. It consisted of 92 rural boxes. All 92 boxes served as the sample. As it turned out, this was the smallest rural route, in terms of number of patrons, found within a 60-mile radius of the Channel 8 tower. Most rural routes had well in excess of 150 boxes.

The size of the two samples was in keeping with the size of the rural trade area for livestock feed for each of these locations. Both trade areas, in terms of livestock feed, were quite small in comparison with most towns.

Structured-disguised questionnaires were mailed from Rock Island, Illinois, on Thursday, January 5, 1967. The Stanwood area questionnaires were sent to the 79 names obtained from the direct-mail list, while the 92 questionnaires to Newhall went to rural boxholders. One dime was included with each questionnaire as an incentive.

The research director thought a source of possible bias was the 10-cent postage that was required to mail out the three-page questionnaire and cover letter. He thought that the 10-cent stamp could result in the questionnaire receiving more than normal attention, especially in the case of a boxholder.

Questionnaires were returned to a post office box at Rock Island in postage-paid business-reply envelopes. Questionnaires were picked up on January 19 at Rock Island, two weeks after mailing. No follow-up mailing was made.

## THE QUESTIONNAIRE

The three-page questionnaire and cover letter are reproduced below.

M. L. WHITE RESEARCH ASSOCIATES
P. O. Box 86, Rock Island, Illinois 61201

Dear Mr. Farmer:

Perhaps you have been asked to fill out questionnaires about your farm operations before. Maybe you answered them or maybe you threw them in the wastebasket because you didn't think your answer mattered.

Let me assure you that your answers are important. Our client is one of the companies serving farmers who feel that by getting first-hand information from farmers themselves they can more readily gear their operations to meet the needs of farmers like you.

Please note that in no way can you be identified with this questionnaire. Your answers will be completely anonymous. The answers you give will be used only in combination with all the others we receive to give my client a composite picture of the farming operation in your area.

The coin attached to the top of this letter is not to be considered as payment for your information or for your time in filling out the questionnaire. It is, however, our way of saying thanks for your cooperation. Perhaps there is a favorite boy or girl you would like to give it to—or have a cup of coffee on us.

Please return the questionnaire in the enclosed postage-paid envelope. We would appreciate receiving your questionnaire no later than the week of January 15, 1967.

Many thanks for your help.

Sincerely,

Fred H. Holscher
Vice President

FHH:sk

*THIS QUESTIONNAIRE TO BE COMPLETED BY THE MALE HEAD OF THE FAMILY*

1. Where do you live? (check one)
   ( ) On a farm
   ( ) On a farm, not engaged in farming
   ( ) In town, not on a farm
   ( ) On an acreage outside of town
2. If you live on a farm or on an acreage, how many acres do you have? (Include acres under cultivation and in pasture)
   ________________ Acres

*IF YOU ARE NOT ENGAGED IN FARMING SKIP TO QUESTION NO.* 8

3. Do you own the farm or acreage on which you live?
   ( ) Own all of it
   ( ) Own part, rent part
   ( ) Rent all of farm
   ( ) Manage farm for someone else
   ( ) Farm laborer
4. Are you currently raising hogs? Yes ________ No ________

4a. If yes, how many hogs did you market in 1966? ________

4b. If you feed your hogs a commercial feed, what brand or brands do you feed?

________________________

Brand of commercial hog feed

________________________

5. Did you feed any cattle for market in 1966? Yes ________ No ________

5a. If yes, how many beef cattle did you market in 1966? ________

5b. Do you feed commercial feed to the cattle fed for market?
Yes ________ No ________

5c. If you feed commercial feed to your beef cattle, what brand or brands of commercial feed do you use?

________________________

Brand of commercial cattle feed

________________________

6. Are you currently milking dairy cattle? Yes ________ No ________

6a. If yes, how many dairy cows are in your herd? ________

6b. If you feed commercial feed to your dairy cows, what brand or brands do you feed?

________________________

Brand of commercial dairy feed

________________________

7. Did you have a laying flock of chickens in 1966?
Yes ________ No ________

7a. If yes, how many birds did you have? ________

7b. If you feed a commercial feed to your laying flock, what brand or brands do you feed?

________________________

Brand of commercial poultry feed

________________________

8. What broadcast source do you rely on for information on the following? (Please check)

| | *Radio* | *Television* |
|---|---|---|
| Morning News | ________ | ________ |
| Morning Markets | ________ | ________ |
| Morning Weather | ________ | ________ |
| Noon News | ________ | ________ |
| Noon Markets | ________ | ________ |
| Noon Weather | ________ | ________ |
| Evening News | ________ | ________ |
| Evening Markets | ________ | ________ |
| Evening Weather | ________ | ________ |

9. Do you enjoy Country and Western music? Yes ________ No ________
10. How often do you watch the following TV programs? If you don't watch any one or all of them please be sure to mark "Never watch it."
    a. Swingin' Country, Channel 7, *11:30 AM Daily* (Check one)
       At least 3 times a week ________
       At least once a week ________
       Maybe once a month ________
       Never watch it ________
    b. Ole Olreg, Channel 8, *6:30 PM Fridays* (Check one)
       Nearly every week ________
       At least once a month ________
       Less than once a month ________
       Never watch it ________
    c. Ernest Tubb, Channel 9, *6:00 PM Saturdays* (Check one)
       Nearly every week ________
       At least once a month ________
       Less than once a month ________
       Never watch it ________
11. Now, so that we will be able to combine your answers with others we receive, will you please answer the following:
    a. What is your age? ________
    b. How many years of high school did you attend? ________ (years)
       Years of college attended? ________ (years)
    c. Not including yourself, how many persons are now living in your home and what are their ages?

| *Males* | *Ages* | *Females* | *Ages* |
|---|---|---|---|
| ________ | ________ | ________ | ________ |
| | ________ | | ________ |
| | ________ | | ________ |
| | ________ | | ________ |

QUESTIONS

1. Criticize all aspects of this special marketing research study.
2. Is the sample design appropriate?
3. Will the questionnaire provide information to meet the objectives?
4. What response biases could be anticipated?
5. What nonresponse bias could be anticipated?
6. Indicate the ways in which the study could be improved.

## ELLIS PRODUCTS, INC.*

Mr. Robert Ellis, President of Ellis Products, Inc., a producer and seller of household chemicals, was considering the manufacture and sale of a "high-expansion" chemical foam to be used in firefighting. The new high-expansion foam was discovered quite by accident by the two research chemists employed by Mr. Ellis. The two chemists had been attempting to develop a powerful household cleanser that could be produced more economically than the conventional brands on the market when they discovered that one of the compounds that they had synthesized would expand by several hundred times in the form of foam when it was properly mixed with water.

Upon ascertaining that a possible use of their new development might be as a chemical foam for firefighting, Mr. Ellis immediately demanded that a thorough search be made of the patents granted and applied for.

### HISTORY

Chemical firefighting foam is an aggregate of tiny gas-filled bubbles, which have the property of forming a fluid blanket over combustible materials, thus smothering a fire by excluding the air. Foam also has the property of adhering to surfaces, so that it does not dissipate readily, and since it contains water that is dispersed in very tiny films, it has cooling properties that prevent reignition. Because of these properties and their low density, chemical foams have been extremely effective in extinguishing fires in flammable liquids.

Chemical foams have been on the market for a number of years. The first such foam to be used was what is known as sodium bicarbonate foam. This foam is formed by a chemical reaction from the combination of bicarbonate of soda, a foam-stabilizing agent, aluminum sulphate, and water. The resulting product is a mass of tiny long-lasting bubbles of carbon dioxide gas, which are not easily broken down by either agitation or heat. Sodium bicarbonate

* The name of the company and some of the figures are disguised.

foam has an expansion ratio in the neighborhood of 20 to 1. The two most efficient of the materials presently being sold are potassium oxalate monohydrate and potassium iodide. These newer foams are from two to four times as effective as the conventional sodium bicarbonate type and have expansion ratios up to several hundred to one.

In recent years several advances have been made in the development of "high-expansion" mechanical foams. These high-expansion foams are dry powders that are mixed with water and air in a vessel, called a solution foam generator, before being directed toward a fire. The high-expansion foams have expansion ratios near 1000 to 1, but have the major disadvantage of requiring expensive and bulky equipment for their use.

## THE INITIAL INVESTIGATION

Mr. Ellis felt that the first step in determining the feasibility of their new product would be to compare it to the brands presently on the market. In addition to laboratory tests, some actual firefighting tests were carried out by the Ellis Products engineering staff. The results of these experiments showed Ellis' new product to be clearly superior to any foam available. In addition to the comparison tests, the Ellis Foam was tried in all major foam-generating equipment and it seemed to be compatible.

At this point Mr. Ellis began an investigation of the available market for the company's new product. It appeared that the market opportunities were nearly unlimited. Chemical foams had long been available in almost all oil refineries and chemical plants where the processing and handling of flammable liquids present a fire hazard. Also, with the development of better foams, their use had been extended to extinguishing fires in combustibles such as wood and fabrics. Because of their effectiveness in ordinary applications, foam units were finding their way into municipal fire departments. In addition, automatic fixed foam-generating equipment was being designed and installed in buildings, and small foam extinguishers were being manufactured that could be privately purchased. Other applications were in cargo holds and boiler rooms of ships transporting flammable materials or using oil for fuel, and at airports.

Ellis Products had been able to produce their new foam powder in quantities adequate for testing purposes by employing a small pilot plant which they had constructed from idle equipment. Mr. Ellis estimated that the construction of a new foam powder plant capable of making commercial quantities would require an investment of about $350,000. The firm had already set aside about $200,000 for new plant investment, and several banks had indicated to Mr. Ellis that they were willing to loan several hundred thousand to Ellis Products, Inc. whenever they needed it.

The raw materials for the Ellis foam were substantially cheaper than those used in producing competitor's brands, but the Ellis process seemed to be no more complex than existing processes for the manufacture of chemical foams. For this reason, Mr. Ellis felt that they could sell their product for 20 to 25 per cent less than competing brands—provided they were able to gain a significánt market share. By pricing their new product at 20 per cent less than competitors, it was estimated that it would be necessary to sell an average of 875,000 pounds per year of the new product over the next three years in order to insure a 10 per cent return on investment.

Despite the fact that the Ellis firm had a superior product available for what appeared to be an unlimited market, there were several things that bothered Mr. Ellis. First, the company's present product line consisted solely of consumer goods that were sold throughout Eastern and Midwestern states. Ellis Products, Inc. had a limited sales staff which sold only to large wholesalers in the Eastern half of the country. If Mr. Ellis were to decide to market the new development, it was obvious that the product could not be distributed solely through present channels and substantial additions would have to be made to his present sales staff—especially if the company were to attempt national distribution.

Another element of great concern was the fact that although the new development was clearly superior to any chemical foams presently available, there was no guarantee that this condition would continue indefinitely. In recent years other firms had rapidly been making new developments in this field, and Mr. Ellis realized that he had neither the financial resources nor a research staff comparable to those of some chemical foam manufacturers.

To further compound his anxieties, Mr. Ellis had recently read that it was estimated that from 50 to 98 per cent of new products are not successful.[1] Another estimate placed the failure rate at 80 per cent.[2]

Mr. Ellis was aware that rights to their discovery could probably be sold for a considerable profit to any of the firms manufacturing firefighting foams, but he was even more aware of the potentially higher profit if he were to successfully market the high-expansion foam himself. For this reason, he decided to postpone a decision on what to do with the new development until substantially more information concerning the product's potential sales volume could be gathered.

## PLANNING FOR A DETAILED INVESTIGATION

In early May of 1967 Mr. Ellis commissioned the company's director of marketing information to compile a list of all known and all prospective users of fire-extinguishing foams. Cal Miller, the director of marketing information,

[1] Samuel C. Johnson and Conrad Jones, "How to Organize for New Products," *Harvard Business Review,* **35,** No. 3 May-June 1957, p. 50.

[2] New Porduct Introduction for Small Business Owners (Small Business Management Series No. 17, Small Business Administration, Washington, D.C., 1955).

was instructed to have this information plus a suggested survey design and any other pertinent information available for an Ellis staff meeting in early June of 1968.

Cal Miller had spent nearly 25 years as a sales representative for Ellis Products, Inc. During this period he had accumulated a knowledge of Ellis products and customers unmatched by anyone in the organization. When his age and his health made it increasingly difficult to do the amount of traveling that the sales position demanded, Mr. Miller was assigned the staff job of director of marketing information. Mr. Miller had been able to make many valuable contributions to the firm in his new position. Most of his success, he reasoned, was attributable to his knowledge of the existing product line and his ability to understand Ellis customers.

Mr. Miller managed to obtain a list of nearly 14,000 users and prospective users of chemical foams. For the most part, this list was compiled as a result of contact with major industrial suppliers throughout the country. The list included a variety of organizations that manufactured and stored chemical and petroleum products, municipal fire departments, airports, building contractors, and a number of shipping companies.

Upon finishing what he thought to be a fairly complete list of the industrial users, Mr. Miller began the task of designing a survey that would aid Mr. Ellis in the decision of whether or not to market the new product. It was Mr. Miller's opinion that the survey should uncover the following information:

1. From what supplier the foam is usually purchased.
2. The average annual use of foaming materials.
3. The users' average inventory of foam powders.
4. Both the nature and the amount of technical services and information that the users expect from foam manufacturers and suppliers.
5. The types of foam-generating equipment that the user has available.
6. The brand(s) of foam presently in stock.
7. The brand of foaming material last purchased.
8. The number of brands that have been tried.
9. Any additional data that would be relevant in the estimation of Ellis' potential market share.

Mr. Miller decided that no matter what method was used to contact those included in the survey, a complete census would involve costs far in excess of what he believed to be the value of the information. He also believed that because of the geographical dispersion and the many different types of prospective customers, a relatively large proportion of his list should be included in the survey in order to get an accurate picture of the situation. For these reasons, he concluded that a mail survey would be the best way of securing the information that Ellis Products needed.

One week before the proposed staff meeting, Mr. Ellis called in Mr. Miller and the executive vice-president, Gil Hollis, to make the final plans for the approaching meeting. At this time Mr. Miller expressed the fear that his lack of experience in designing and conducting surveys was seriously hampering his progress. After being assured by Mr. Ellis that he understood his situation and that the marketing information group would be given all the help available, the conversation drifted to the problem at hand.

Mr. Miller As I said before, because there are so many types of customers and because they're scattered in all parts of the country, I think the only way to reach enough of them at a reasonable cost is through a mail questionnaire. As you can see, I've already put together a questionnaire which I think should satisfy our needs. (See Exhibit 1.)

V-P: I don't see how we can get much out of a questionnaire. Most of these people aren't going to be convinced that we could have the best product on the market simply because we tell them so. What I think we should do is pick a reasonable size for a sample; then put on a demonstration for them proving that we have a superior foam. After such a demonstration we could then test their reactions.

Mr. Ellis That's not really getting to our problem though, Gil. Even if we do enter the chemical foam market, we aren't going to be able to afford to actually demonstrate our foam to more than a small proportion of the prospective customers. I do have some ideas along these lines though. If we can justify entering the market, it would be possible to make films of actual fire-fighting demonstrations which our sales representatives could show to interested customers. As far as a mail survey is concerned, we could easily present some convincing test data which would show just how we compare with the rest of the foams being sold.

Go ahead, Cal. What else have you come up with on a possible mail questionnaire?

Mr. Miller Well, as you've noticed, I've made a list of almost 14,000 organizations who are either now using chemical foams or probably will be in the near future. As near as I can tell about 45% of the present foam sales are to those who process and store chemicals and petroleum products, about 30% to municipal fire departments, 10% to airports, and the remainder to shipping companies and automatic installations in buildings.

What I think we should do in choosing our sample for the survey is divide the list into these separate customer classes and select from each class that number which corresponds to their proportion of the market. For instance, since about 30% of the total sales are to municipal fire departments, if 1000 were included in our survey we should include 300 fire departments.

V-P: What you're talking about is a stratified sample and I don't think it's a very good idea. Such a sample is biased. It doesn't necessarily give all of the prospective customers an equal chance of being included in our survey. Besides that, just because the industry's sales dollars are distributed in certain proportions today doesn't mean that they'll continue to be. For instance, the increased use of chemical foams for ordinary firefighting applications is certainly going to push up the proportion of sales to municipal fire departments and new building installations in the future.

Mr. Miller What do you suggest then? Just throwing all the customer classes together and taking our chances on the number of each type that we get?

V-P: Yes. I think that those included in the survey should be randomly selected. If you are able to devise a truly random method of selection then I'm willing to bet that the proportion of a certain customer class that ends up in the sample will be very close to the proportion of that class contained in your list.

Mr. Miller What's wrong with taking a stratified sample and insuring ourselves that the sample will contain the correct proportion of each group?

V-P: I guess there's nothing terribly wrong with taking a stratified sample if those in each of the groups are randomly selected. I just don't think it's necessary. The main point that I was trying to make before was that I don't believe the current distribution of chemical foam sales is the proper basis for our sample design.

Mr. Ellis Let me interrupt here. What worries me most about a mail survey is that we may not get enough returned questionnaires to do us any good. As I recall several years ago we sent out free samples of a new window cleaner with a prepaid postcard attached. The postcards simply asked whether or not the person liked the product and whether they would buy it again. Less than 30% of the postcards were returned. It didn't take us long to find out that those 30% were either lying or weren't at all like the population in general. We went ahead and planned our production from the sample information, and we ended up making enough of that stuff in three month's time to last nearly two years.

V-P: If we were able to manage only 30% returns from a survey connected with a product which we're known for, what can we expect in a field where we're not known at all?

Mr. Miller I don't think it's as bad as all that. In the first place, we're looking at what would have to be classified an industrial market, and I can think of a lot of reasons why such customers would be more willing to cooperate than the average consumer. For one thing, these people are in the business of protecting human lives and valuable property. Because of this, they should continually be looking for ways of more efficiently doing their jobs.

Mr. Ellis I've been thinking. Don't you think it's highly possible that we're totally ignoring what could someday be a major outlet for chemical foams? I'm talking about a consumer market. From all I've been able to learn, an ever-increasing number of small foam extinguishers for home and private use are being manufactured today. I'm sure that this does not presently represent a major segment of the market, but consumer sales would certainly fit much better into our present channels of distribution.

Mr. Miller I guess the best way to get information on the consumer market would be to contact as many local fire equipment suppliers as possible.

Mr. Ellis I've considered hiring a market research consultant to help us design a survey and forecast our sales in the chemical foam market. It'll cost us some money, but in the long-run it's probably the best thing to do.

## QUESTIONS

1. What are your reactions to the executive vice-president's comments on how those included in a sample or survey should be selected?
2. Devise a method of selecting a group to be included in a survey from the list of 14,000.
3. If Ellis Products, Inc. were to use a mail survey, how could they ensure a good return rate?
4. Will Mr. Miller's questionnaire adequately provide the information that Ellis Products needs?

**Exhibit 1** Ellis Products, Inc.—Mail Questionnaire

1. (*a*) Do you presently use chemical or mechanical foams as part of your fire prevention protection program?

Yes ________

No ________

(*b*) If yes, what brand name?

American La France Foamite ________
Purple-K ________
Fyr-Fyter ________
National Foam ________
Pyrene ________
Other, Specify ________

**Exhibit 1** (Continued)

2. (*a*) Approximately how many pounds of foam did you use *last* year?

0–100 lb. __________
101–200 lb. __________
201–400 lb. __________
401–600 lb. __________
601–1000 lb. __________
Over 1000 lb. __________

(*b*) When did you last purchase an order of foam?

(month and year) __________

(*c*) What brand name did you purchase? __________

3. Generally speaking, what *average* inventory (stock on hand) do you carry of chemical foam?

0–100 lb. __________
101–200 lb. __________
201–400 lb. __________
401–600 lb. __________
601–1000 lb. __________
Over 1000 lb. __________

4. What type of supplier presently fills your order?

Industrial Supplier __________
Manufacturer __________
Local Fire Equipment Distributor __________
Other, Specify__________

5. (*a*) Does your present supplier of chemical or mechanical form answer your questions concerning its use?

Yes __________
No __________

(*b*) Have you ever asked your supplier for information concerning the use of foams?

Yes __________
No __________

(*c*) Would you enjoy such information?

Yes __________
No __________

(*d*) What kinds of information do you feel are most useful?

Technical Performance Data__________
Applications __________
Shipping Information __________
Storage and Handling Instructions __________
Personnel Training __________
Other, Specify__________

6. What kinds of foam generation equipment do you presently have available for use?

**Exhibit 1** (Continued)

| | | *Year Purchased* |
|---|---|---|
| Portable Chemical Generator | ________ | ________________ |
| Fixed Chemical Generator | ________ | ________________ |
| Portable Mechanical Generator | ________ | ________________ |
| Fixed Mechanical Generator | ________ | ________________ |
| Hand Chemical Extinguisher | ________ | ________________ |
| Other | ________ | ________________ |

7. How many brands of foaming material has your firm tried?

   Specify Number ________________

8. What factors caused you to try other brands?

   Lower Price________________

   Fast Delivery________________

   Terms of Payment________________

   Superior Performance________________

   Other, Specify________________________

9. Who usually purchases the firefighting foam in your organization?

   ________________________________________________

   (Purchasing Agent, Building Supervisor, Production Manager, Safety Director, etc.)

PART IV

# *Potentials and Forecasts: Two Important Market Measurements*

Part IV explores two important market measurements that are constructed by many marketing information managers. The measurement and use of potential are discussed in Chapter 14. Chapter 15 is concerned with techniques for forecasting various items of marketing information.

*Fourteen*

# Measuring and Using Potential

Information on potential is often vital to the marketing decision maker. He finds it useful in making decisions about advertising, personal selling, and, in general, whenever he has problems dealing with the geographic allocation of marketing dollars. In addition, information on potential can be helpful in estimating the size of a total market as well as in many other ways.

Potential has been defined, measured, and used for at least the past four decades. D. R. G. Cowan's book (1938) provides an indication of the work accomplished by 1938. Hummel's book (1961) gives evidence of the continuing concern.

The purpose of this chapter is to discuss the measurement and use of potential. The starting point is a definition of potential. Then, various macro and micro measurement methods are considered.

## Definition of Potential

*Potential is the absolute or relative maximum capacity of segments of a buyers' side of a market to purchase a specific type of offering in a specified time.*[1] What does this definition mean? This concept of potential can be likened to the capacity of various amounts of water at various temperatures, with different amounts of sugar already present and with dissimilar mineral content, to dissolve and hold sugar in sus-

[1] Various writers have used the terms *sales* potential and *market* potential, and not always in agreement (Crisp, 1961, pp. 52–53; Hummel, 1961, pp. 6–8). We believe that there are better measures available than *sales* potential (the shares of market potential an individual firm expects to receive). Consequently we discuss only one type of potential and need no designation of *market* or *sales*.

pension. The maximum amount of additional sugar that can be dissolved and held in suspension is the potential.

Therefore, potential refers to the maximum additional capacity of various market segments to purchase an offering.[2] The assumption is made that purchasers in each market have adequate opportunity to know about and purchase the offering. Consequently, potential (unlike sales) is not influenced by the variations in sellers' activities in the market *during the time period.* It represents a maximum that could be sold under ideal selling conditions (Still and Cundiff, 1958, p. 605).

Potential does have reference to a specific time period and to specified geographical markets. Furthermore, it has reference to an assortment of offerings that the buyers perceive as having a very high cross-elasticity of demand. Finally, potential is influenced by prior purchases of the offering. Durable goods, for example, can partially saturate individual markets.

The reader should be able to distinguish potential from sales forecasts. For example, an industry forecast is concerned with an estimate of dollar or unit sales of a product that is *likely to be sold* in a specific time period under a given marketing plan.[3] Such a forecast takes into account the actual selling efforts that are expected to be active in each market during the period and it is concerned with anticipated sales.

## Potential: Some Measurement Considerations

Estimates of potential are computed for each essentially *dissimilar* product or product line. That is, dissimilar products, *as viewed by the buyers' side of the market, cannot* be grouped together. For example, potential should *not* be computed jointly for clothes washers and dishwashers, nor for contact lenses and conventional framed eyeglasses. On the other hand, some grouping of somewhat different offerings is virtually mandatory. Automatic clothes washers with somewhat different prices and features are likely to be grouped together, as are different types of contact lenses.

The potential for one type of product sold to two or more very different types of customer groups is computed separately for each, because the decision maker needs separate measurements. A furniture manufacturer, for example, who sells an identical line of chairs to both a commercial

[2] Offering includes more than the physical product. It is the total offer. See Otteson, Panscher and Patterson (1964, p. 218).

[3] Stanton and Buskirk (1959, p. 511) define a sales forecast as "an estimate of dollar or unit sales for a specified future period under a proposed marketing plan or program."

and a household market should compute potential separately for each different customer group.

The same information control units that a firm uses in its sales and cost analysis programs should serve as the geographical basis for the computation of potential. If the county ICU has been used for sales and cost analysis, for example, it should also be used to compute potential.

Potential can be measured as an *absolute* dollar or unit amount or as a *relative* per cent of the total market. For example, the potential for replacement convertible car tops in the United States could be expressed as 540,000, in Texas as 54,000, and in Alaska as 5400. Expressed in relative terms, the United States market might be 100 per cent of potential, Texas 10 per cent, and Alaska 1 per cent.

### Potential: Some Uses

Some decision makers want absolute measures of potential for each market segment, so that they can compare them with industry sales. The concern is *not* with attaining 100 per cent of potential, but rather with the detection of "undersold" or "oversold" market segments. For example, detection of low sales attainment (relative to potential) in a market segment may indicate previously unknown allocation opportunities.[4]

Absolute estimates of potential may be used to derive relative measures (this was done in the convertible top illustration). In such situations, the absolute value for each market segment is divided by the total potential for all the markets, and each market segment is designated as containing some part of 100 per cent. Although the techniques may *not* be readily apparent at this point, relative measures of potential can also be prepared without absolute measures of potential.

Relative measures of potential are used in many decision-making activities. One common analysis involves comparison, market by market, of relative potential with companion relative *company* selling efforts and sales. For example, a company may note that only 2 per cent of *its* sales occurred in a market with 11 per cent of potential.[5] There are other uses for relative measures of potential. A few of these will be examined as the various methods of estimating potential are explored.

Finally, it is worth noting that profit-oriented decision makers should *not* use measures of potential as sales goals. Tapping a market to its

[4] For an illustration, see Crisp (1961, pp. 55–56).

[5] An illustration of this appears in Telfer (1962).

full capacity to buy (i.e., to potential) is not likely to produce maximum profits. Maximum profits arise through direction of marketing expenditures so that marginal net revenues are everywhere equal.

## MACRO METHODS OF ESTIMATING POTENTIAL

Many companies that have good estimates of industry sales in each market use the sales index values as indexes of potential. Table 14-1 portrays such a situation for a seller of commercial hog feed. His market consists of five counties. Estimated total sales of all sellers in the market were 40,000 tons, with the absolute sales by counties as indicated in column 2. Column 3 indicates sales in each county as a per cent of total sales in the five-county market.

This technique provides many companies with very appropriate estimates of potential. Replacement convertible car top *sales,* for example, reflect relative potential even better than the presence of convertible cars. Sales of commercial neon signs by counties also give a good indication of the relative potential for commercial neon signs in the near future.

In these examples the commonsense reasoning is that opportunity for future sales is likely to appear in about the same places and the same relative magnitudes as in the past. Although shifts in consumption occur, many are sufficiently gradual to make immediate past sales indicative of future potential. Hog feed sales are likely to remain high in hog-producing counties where very recent sales have been high. Little hog feed is likely to be sold in Cook County (Chicago) or Cochise County (Ari-

**TABLE 14-1** Sales Index as a Potential Index

| (1)<br>Market Segment | (2)<br>Hog Feed<br>Total Sales (Tons) | (3)<br>Sales<br>Index | (4)<br>Potential |
|---|---|---|---|
| Linn County | 3,000 | 7.5% | 7.5% |
| Johnson County | 6,000 | 15.0 | 15.0 |
| Washington County | 11,000 | 27.5 | 27.5 |
| Marengo County | 13,000 | 32.5 | 32.5 |
| Iowa County | 7,000 | 17.5 | 17.5 |
| | 40,000 | 100.0% | 100.0% |

*Source:* Hypothetical.

zona). The one has too many people and related activities, and the other is too hot, dry, and remote from consumption centers.

A somewhat different problem is present when a product is *not* currently static in its life cycle. Then supplemental data are needed to measure potential (Massy, 1962).

A more analytical examination will better indicate the conditions that permit or prohibit use of a sales index as an index of potential. *First, the buyers' side of the market in all segments must have been aware of the general offering (but not necessarily of all brands) and the offering must have been available to the buyers.* In other words, industry sales can be used when they are indicative of the buyers' reactions to the offering and when the offering has been essentially similar among the market segments (as perceived by the possible buyers).

Such situations are *not* unusual for offerings that have been on the market for several years. For example, such conditions should prevail for various body styles of automobiles, for automobile accessory equipment, for types and flavors of established cake mixes, and for outdoor commercial signs. Numerous other offerings could be listed.

The first criterion is not met if the market segments have not been exposed or have been only sporadically exposed to an offering or if extensive new uses for the offering have been developed.

*Second, to use an index of sellers' sales, an adequate index must be available.* There are three major facets to this problem:

1. Industry sales for the offering category must be available. In our illustration, hog feed sales—not feed *supplement,* trace mineral, or the more inclusive livestock feed sales—must be known. Sellers' sales do not necessarily mean 100 per cent of all sellers, but that enough sales are known for the sales index to be representative of total sales.[6]

2. The available sales index must correspond to the information control units used by the company. In our illustration, this would be by counties.

In some situations where the sales index values are not initially available by correct ICU, the data can be adjusted. However, to do this, absolute industry sales figures must be available. A short illustration will suffice to suggest how this can be accomplished.

Assume that hog feed sales are available only by blocks of nine counties, but are needed by individual counties. Through use of regression

[6] Trade associations can be excellent sources for information on industry sales. Trade associations that report industry sales require each member to submit his own sales data. In turn, these are usually compiled by types of products and by ICU's (but not identified by company) and distributed to the members.

analysis, the relationship between hog feed sales in each of the nine-county blocks can be related to independent variables that are identifiable in both the nine-county blocks and the individual counties. Once these statistical relationships are established, the magnitude of each of the individual variables in each county can be identified and the sales data by nine-county blocks can be allocated to the individual counties. So, even where the industry ICU's are too large, it may be possible to scale them down to the needed size. Of course, when sales data are available for units smaller than needed, the data can be aggregated.[7]

3. The time period for which the sales data are available must fit the potential requirements. For example, a sales index for the past year may provide a sufficiently current potential index for the ensuing year if sales patterns are not expected to change. Under more dynamic conditions, however, the application of moving averages or some other extrapolating technique may give a better approximation. The important consideration is that a potential index reflect potential for the right time period, not for some prior period.[8]

In conclusion, although the sales index is extensively used, there are four major situations in which it *cannot* serve as an adequate estimate of a potential index:

1. It *cannot* be used when the offering is relatively new to or being used in new ways on the buyers' side of the market.
2. It *cannot* be used unless adequate sellers' sales data are available.
3. It *cannot* be used when the dynamics of the situation are changing.
4. It *cannot* be used when an absolute measure of potential is needed.

Consequently, where any one or more of the four situations prevail, some alternative method of estimating potential must be used. Single and multiple variable indexes may provide suitable alternatives.

## Single- and Multiple-Variable Indexes[9]

The relative potential for table salt in each market could probably be determined through the use of data on human population. Unfortunately, few other estimates of potential can be derived through the use

[7] For a discussion of getting a better information fit for both products and ICU's for industrial products, see Henderson (1963).

[8] This comment also holds true for every other method of measuring potential. Forecasting methods are discussed in another chapter.

[9] These are commonly referred to as single- and multiple-*factor* indexes. We use the term *variable* in order to avoid conflict with the term *factor analysis,* which is used later.

of a single variable. More frequently, several variables are needed to gain an adequate estimate. Relative potential for an offering, such as household snowblowers, could probably be estimated through a number of variables, such as average annual snowfall, number of households, and discretionary income.

*Specific or General Index?*

Not only may indexes be single- or multiple-variable, but they may be *general* or *specific*. A specific index is one that is specifically constructed to estimate potential for an offering. The multiple-variable index for household snowblowers (see Table 14-3) was designed specifically to measure potential for that one offering and, accordingly, is a specific index.

A general index is one that is designed to be used for a number of different offerings. "The Buying Power Index," which appears annually in the *Survey of Buying Power Guide,* provides both a good illustration of a general, multiple-variable index and insight into why numerous companies use such a ready-made index. Three variables—population, effective buying income, and retail sales—have been weighted 2, 5, and 3, respectively, and combined to provide an estimate of potential for consumer-type shopping goods. A copy of a page from the 1966 *Buying Power Guide* is shown as Table 14-2.[10]

The purchase and use of such an index can be compared with the purchase of a suit of clothes. A tailor-made suit normally fits a person (particularly one of unique build) better than does a mass-produced suit off the rack. However, the tailor-made suits, like specific indexes, normally carry much higher price tags. The key questions to ask and answer are:

1. Is there a general index available that is sufficiently good for the offering?[11]
2. Is its price sufficiently low (relative to the fit) to justify use of the index?

Admittedly, these considerations appear to be on the vague side—just as the selection of a suit would appear to a person never having experienced the alternatives. However, in actual practice an information director could evaluate the two information alternatives.

Single- and multiple-variable indexes of potential normally are used when sufficiently current or complete industry sales data are *not* avail-

[10] The weighting procedures and construction techniques can be found in any of the recent annual issues of the publication.

[11] For additional comments on this topic, see American Marketing (1957, p. 10).

**Table 14-2** Survey of Buying Power

| COLORADO | | SM POPULATION ESTIMATES, 12/31/65 | | | | RETAIL SALES—SM ESTIMATES, 1965 | | | | | | | | | | | SALES—ADVG. INDEXES | | |
|---|---|---|---|---|---|---|---|---|---|---|---|---|---|---|---|---|---|---|---|
| Counties Cities (continued) | Met. Area Code | Total (thousands) | % of U.S.A. | Households (thousands) | Urban Pop. (thousands) | Total Retail Sales ($000) | % of U.S.A. | Food ($000) | Eating Drink. Places ($000) | General Mdse. ($000) | Apparel ($000) | Furn.-House-Appl. ($000) | Automotive ($000) | Gas Station ($000) | Lumb. Bldg. Hdwre. ($000) | Drug ($000) | Sis. Activity | Buying Power | Quality |
| Crowley | | 3.6 | .0018 | 1.0 | — | 2,304 | .0000 | 392 | 159 | 95 | — | 20 | 1,070 | 271 | 248 | 29 | 50 | .0012 | 67 |
| Custer | | 1.2 | .0006 | .4 | — | 351 | .0003 | 275 | 66 | — | 24 | — | — | 223 | 165 | 40 | 50 | .0004 | 67 |
| Delta | | 15.3 | .0079 | 5.0 | 3.7 | 18,412 | .0065 | 4,622 | 926 | 1,867 | 619 | 474 | 3,534 | 2,088 | 1,826 | 849 | 82 | .0060 | 76 |
| Denver | 73 | 529.0 | .2710 | 182.4 | 529.0 | 970,177 | .3443 | 166,741 | 86,891 | 214,060 | 51,204 | 54,142 | 185,638 | 56,145 | 42,924 | 40,502 | 127 | .3252 | 120 |
| △Denver | | 529.0 | .2710 | 182.4 | — | 970,177 | .3443 | 166,741 | 86,891 | 214,000 | 51,204 | 54,142 | 185,638 | 56,145 | 42,924 | 40,502 | 127 | .3252 | 120 |
| Dolores | | 2.0 | .0010 | .5 | — | 2,392 | .0009 | 536 | 109 | 291 | — | — | — | 372 | 690 | 204 | 90 | .0008 | 80 |
| Douglas | | 5.8 | .0030 | 1.7 | — | 7,961 | .0028 | 1,431 | 7.7 | 225 | 276 | 39 | 2,659 | 833 | 963 | 88 | 93 | .0026 | 87 |
| Eagle | | 4.9 | .0025 | 1.4 | — | 4,327 | .0016 | 987 | 256 | 392 | 101 | 164 | 849 | 769 | 207 | 94 | 64 | .0016 | 64 |
| Elbert | | 3.4 | .0017 | 1.1 | — | 2,352 | .0008 | 693 | 280 | 166 | — | — | 196 | 188 | 327 | — | 47 | .0012 | 71 |
| El Paso | 60 | 184.9 | .0947 | 55.8 | 140.0 | 270,919 | .0961 | 52,661 | 20,966 | 37,497 | 15,978 | 16,413 | 54,000 | 24,727 | 18,666 | 9,651 | 101 | .0924 | 98 |
| △Colorado Springs | | 89.1 | .0457 | 30.3 | — | 208,811 | .0741 | 42,412 | 14,752 | 22,787 | 14,032 | 15,405 | 46,939 | 17,244 | 13,989 | 5,580 | 162 | .0550 | 120 |
| Fremont | | 21.1 | .0109 | 6.5 | 12.4 | 23,875 | .0085 | 6,131 | 2,054 | 2,860 | 725 | 1,363 | 4,583 | 2,610 | 1,531 | 1,067 | 78 | .0089 | 82 |
| Garfield | | 12.6 | .0064 | 4.1 | 3.8 | 27,373 | .0097 | 6,284 | 3,092 | 1,265 | 1,536 | 982 | 5,276 | 3,896 | 1,994 | 1,185 | 152 | .0069 | 108 |
| Gilpin | | .7 | .0004 | .4 | — | 1,547 | .0006 | 189 | 701 | — | — | — | — | 99 | 51 | 100 | 150 | .0005 | 125 |
| Grand | | 3.5 | .0018 | 1.1 | — | 8,268 | .0029 | 1,574 | 1,335 | 274 | 84 | 100 | 1,337 | 1,362 | 991 | 495 | 161 | .0019 | 106 |
| Gunnison | | 6.2 | .0031 | 1.7 | 3.9 | 11,919 | .0043 | 2,727 | 1,482 | 909 | 259 | 627 | 1,571 | 1,676 | 1,385 | 298 | 139 | .0034 | 110 |
| Hinsdale | | .2 | .0001 | .2 | — | 353 | .0001 | — | 87 | — | — | — | — | 177 | — | — | 100 | .0003 | 300 |
| Huerfano | | 7.4 | .0038 | 2.2 | 4.8 | 7,826 | .0028 | 2,115 | 796 | 338 | 321 | 233 | 1,295 | 1,424 | 303 | 348 | 74 | .0026 | 68 |
| Jackson | | 1.7 | .0009 | .5 | — | 2,410 | .0008 | 438 | 276 | 100 | 38 | 27 | 568 | 523 | 215 | 21 | 89 | .0008 | 89 |
| Jefferson | 73 | 188.7 | .0967 | 56.0 | 159.7 | 287,637 | .1021 | 61,810 | 19,573 | 58,927 | 7,938 | 10,937 | 65,336 | 22,454 | 11,834 | 13,771 | 106 | .1059 | 110 |
| Kiowa | | 2.2 | .0011 | .7 | — | 4,037 | .0014 | 504 | 260 | 362 | 161 | — | 309 | 1,046 | 581 | 80 | 127 | .0011 | 100 |
| Kit Carson | | 6.9 | .0035 | 2.1 | — | 13,070 | .0047 | 1,930 | 430 | 938 | 317 | 261 | 2,273 | 1,997 | 3,061 | 483 | 134 | .0035 | 100 |
| Lake | | 7.7 | .0040 | 2.1 | 4.5 | 12,493 | .0044 | 3,184 | 985 | 661 | 589 | 491 | 1,923 | 1,276 | 644 | 2,043 | 110 | .0037 | 93 |

| | | | | | | | | | | | | | | | | | | |
|---|---|---|---|---|---|---|---|---|---|---|---|---|---|---|---|---|---|---|
| La Plata | 20.0 | .0102 | 5.8 | 11.2 | 28,873 | .0103 | 6,390 | 1,944 | 5,543 | 1,256 | 1,105 | 5,014 | 2,102 | 1,957 | 810 | 101 | .0095 | 93 |
| Larimer | 64.6 | .0331 | 20.4 | 44.6 | 109,483 | .0388 | 21,585 | 7,531 | 10,352 | 4,464 | 6,385 | 23,929 | 8,461 | 12,565 | 4,625 | 117 | .0329 | 99 |
| Fort Collins | 32.3 | .0166 | 9.9 | — | 66,060 | .0234 | 12,788 | 3,764 | 7,686 | 2,804 | 4,666 | 15,499 | 4,622 | 6,806 | 2,388 | 141 | .0185 | 111 |
| Las Animas | 17.5 | .0090 | 5.2 | 10.6 | 19,880 | .0071 | 4,748 | 1,476 | 2,649 | 668 | 619 | 4,204 | 2,079 | 1,138 | 636 | 79 | .0066 | 73 |
| | | | | | | | | | | | | | | | | | | |
| Lincoln | 5.0 | .0026 | 1.6 | — | 8,876 | .0031 | 1,168 | 834 | 377 | 445 | 33 | 1,867 | 2,157 | 1,070 | 188 | 119 | .0026 | 100 |
| Logan | 20.5 | .0105 | 6.0 | 11.5 | 33,207 | .0118 | 6,259 | 2,293 | 2,335 | 2,119 | 1,097 | 9,411 | 2,518 | 3,151 | 880 | 112 | .0102 | 97 |
| Sterling | 11.5 | .0059 | 3.7 | — | 28,794 | .0102 | 5,691 | 2,044 | 2,209 | 2,119 | 1,097 | 7,183 | 2,312 | 2,402 | 880 | 173 | .0072 | 122 |
| Mesa | 54.6 | .0279 | 16.8 | 25.8 | 107,853 | .0383 | 24,416 | 5,774 | 13,849 | 3,888 | 4,316 | 26,402 | 8,942 | 7,458 | 4,247 | 137 | .0297 | 106 |
| Grand Junction | 22.4 | .0115 | 7.5 | — | 91,060 | .0323 | 19,087 | 4,839 | 13,003 | 3,724 | 4,258 | 22,019 | 6,499 | 6,136 | 3,975 | 281 | .0181 | 157 |
| Mineral | .4 | .0002 | .2 | — | 745 | .0003 | 173 | 70 | — | — | — | — | 148 | 211 | — | 150 | .0002 | 100 |
| Moffat | 7.5 | .0039 | 2.4 | 4.3 | 14,498 | .0051 | 3,278 | 1,040 | 1,211 | 406 | 535 | 3,985 | 1,498 | 1,485 | 208 | 131 | .0043 | 110 |
| Montezuma | 14.0 | .0071 | 4.0 | 7.0 | 23,659 | .0084 | 5,287 | 1,317 | 2,536 | 557 | 839 | 5,784 | 2,914 | 2,028 | 599 | 118 | .0066 | 93 |
| | | | | | | | | | | | | | | | | | | |
| Montrose | 19.4 | .0100 | 5.7 | 5.3 | 23,277 | .0083 | 5,780 | 1,497 | 1,989 | 1,490 | 806 | 3,354 | 2,392 | 2,399 | 887 | 83 | .0076 | 76 |
| Morgan | 21.1 | .0108 | 6.2 | 11.4 | 33,912 | .0120 | 6,967 | 1,829 | 2,380 | 1,625 | 1,357 | 5,030 | 3,072 | 5,442 | 1,123 | 111 | .0099 | 92 |
| Otero | 24.1 | .0123 | 7.2 | 13.5 | 34,743 | .0123 | 8,321 | 2,179 | 3,961 | 1,202 | 1,752 | 7,466 | 2,395 | 3,343 | 1,201 | 100 | .0104 | 85 |
| Ouray | 1.8 | .0010 | .6 | — | 1,136 | .0004 | 134 | 309 | 278 | — | — | — | 243 | 50 | 85 | 40 | .0007 | 70 |
| Park | 1.6 | .0008 | .5 | — | 2,266 | .0008 | 254 | 447 | 577 | — | — | 145 | 400 | 150 | 110 | 100 | .0008 | 100 |
| Phillips | 4.0 | .0023 | 1.0 | — | 7,325 | .0026 | 1,112 | 282 | 241 | 169 | 150 | 1,564 | 782 | 1,739 | 293 | 113 | .0023 | 100 |
| | | | | | | | | | | | | | | | | | | |
| Pitkin | 3.2 | .0017 | 1.0 | — | 10,815 | .0039 | 1,845 | 3,480 | 265 | 612 | 94 | — | 737 | 1,651 | 231 | 229 | .0026 | 153 |
| Prowers | 13.4 | .0068 | 4.0 | 7.9 | 27,271 | .0097 | 5,599 | 1,928 | 2,739 | 922 | 816 | 4,646 | 2,717 | 4,380 | 695 | 143 | .0066 | 97 |
| Pueblo 214 | 129.3 | .0663 | 35.2 | 111.7 | 196,302 | .0696 | 49,246 | 14,272 | 27,492 | 9,756 | 10,623 | 42,499 | 14,694 | 9,387 | 8,539 | 105 | .0613 | 92 |
| △Pueblo | 97.8 | .0501 | 27.8 | — | 175,917 | .0624 | 43,693 | 10,526 | 25,618 | 9,480 | 10,349 | 42,248 | 11,950 | 4,816 | 8,283 | 125 | .0518 | 103 |
| Rio Blanco | 5.2 | .0027 | 1.5 | — | 6,729 | .0024 | 1,467 | 445 | 304 | 283 | 103 | 1,490 | 1,237 | 787 | 323 | 89 | .0023 | 85 |
| Rio Grande | 11.4 | .0058 | 3.1 | 3.4 | 18,202 | .0065 | 4,238 | 541 | 914 | 1,115 | 982 | 3,676 | 2,019 | 2,366 | 687 | 112 | .0050 | 86 |
| Routt | 5.6 | .0029 | 1.8 | — | 7,984 | .0028 | 1,563 | 641 | 1,051 | 325 | 38 | 1,312 | 1,662 | 680 | 439 | 97 | .0024 | 83 |

See Section C for Metropolitan Area data.



Triangles indicate central cities of Standard (△) and Potential (△) Metropolitan Areas.

able. The conceptual basis for this index is very similar to the sales index estimate of potential. Therefore, no further comment about the foundation of this estimating procedure appears necessary. However, it is still necessary to discern how such an index of potential can be constructed.

*Arbitrary-Variables Method*

There are several different ways to construct indexes of potential. Or, it should be said, there are a number of ways in which the index variables can be selected and weighted. A person who has been involved in the marketing of a particular product for numerous years, may, from his own experience, be able to deduce both a usable set of index variables and their weights. This informal consideration of experience is frequently referred to as the arbitrary-"factors" method (Stanton and Buskirk, 1959 p. 494). As the title implies, personal judgment is relied on for both the selection and the weighting of the variables.

For example, a person contemplating the potential for household snowblowers would first attempt to pinpoint the variables believed either to influence need for the product or to be associated with its purchase. Accordingly, appropriate variables might seem to include some measures of snow, people, discretionary income, and acceptance of product innovations. On the other hand, another estimator might build an index by using data about associated products such as sale of snow tires, tire chains, snow shovels, and ice-melting salt.

The second step would be to weight the selected variables. If snow, people, income, and innovation acceptance were considered about equal, they each would receive equal weight. If these variables were considered to be of different importance in the sale of the product, different weights in accordance to each variable's importance would be assigned. These weights would be products of the estimator's judgment.

The arbitrary method results in measures of relative potential only as good as the estimator's experience. Furthermore, the estimator in justifying the selected index variables and their weights can only say that "they're based on experience"—his own experience informally selected and considered. Such "justification" is best accepted in a type of organization or position where experience is not questioned. In other situations a method requiring *less* intimate market experience and more reliance on data examination is required.

*Multivariate Regression Method*

Limited experience can be aided considerably through the use of various quantitative techniques, such as factor analysis and regression analysis. Specifically, these techniques are used to both help select and weight the variables to be used in an index. Regression analysis is used to identify the *extent* of covariations of one or more random "independent variables" with one "dependent" variable and to determine the functional relationships among the independent and dependent variables.

In the multivariate regression analysis, the analyst ideally uses some measure of industry sales (by ICU's) as his dependent variable. Then—aided by simple correlation analysis or factor analysis—he selects variables that appear to explain (statistically) the industry sales. This is only a preliminary screening or selecting procedure. The further selection occurs as each "promising" variable is tried and examined in a regression formula. The analyst attempts to find a group of independent variables that jointly will explain most of the variance in the dependent variable (industry sales).

Once a sufficiently high explanation is achieved, the analyst will examine each of the selected independent variables as to their net relative contribution to the explanation. In the snowblower illustration, for instance, the analyst might find the regression line represented as

$$X_1 = 20.9 + 0.2125X_2 + 3.2443X_3 + 0.1112X_4$$

In this equation, $X_1$ represents the dependent variable, sales of household snowblowers. The regression coefficients refer to sales of snowblowers per 0.2125 snow shovels, 3.2443 inches of snow, and 0.1112 people. These coefficients indicate the relative influence of each of the variables on the dependent variable and can be assigned as factor weightings. More detailed explanation of the statistical construction techniques and the associated problems can be found in numerous statistical textbooks (Ferber, 1949; Roccaferreca, 1964; Yamane, 1964).

There is one point unique to the marketing problem that is in need of additional explanation. At several points in the discussion it has been said that the multivariate regression method was used when industry sales were *not* available. However, in the immediate preceding discussion, industry sales were specified as the ideal dependent variable. How can this method be used when industry sales are *not* available and yet are needed as the dependent variable?

There is no complete solution. However, if industry sales are available (1) for part of the market or (2) for some past period, a partial solution is present.[12] The available industry sales are used as the dependent vari-

[12] However, sales of an individual firm cannot be used. They only tell the company's success relative to how it allocated its past selling efforts. This, clearly is *not* an indication of market opportunity.

able and the analyst infers from his findings to the other markets or to the current time period.

*Multiple-Variable Method Illustration*

So far the discussion has centered on methods of (1) *selecting* and (2) *weighting* variables to be used in estimating relative potential. Once these two tasks have been accomplished, whether by judgment or by multivariate regression methods, the data regarding each variable in each information control unit must be brought together as an estimate of potential. This is shown in Table 14-3. The relevant information about each variable is listed (columns 2, 4, and 6). Then each variable in each information control unit is weighted. The weighted variables are shown in columns 3, 5, and 7. Next the sum of the variables for each information control unit is computed and shown in column 8. Finally, each control unit total is divided by the weighted sum of all

**TABLE 14-3** Multiple-Variable Index—Household Snowblowers (Montana)

| | Snowfall | | Households | | Income | | | |
|---|---|---|---|---|---|---|---|---|
| County | Per Cent of Montana Total | Weighted Per Cent:5 | Per Cent of Montana Total | Weighted Per Cent:3 | Per Cent of Montana Total | Weighted Per Cent:2 | Weighted Sum of the Three Factors | Relative Potential |
| (1) | (2) | (3) | (4) | (5) | (6) | (7) | (8) | (9) |
| 1. Beaverhead | 1.02 | 5.10 | 1.12 | 3.36 | 1.06 | 2.12 | 10.58 | 1.06 |
| 2. Big Horn | 0.98 | 4.90 | 1.21 | 3.63 | 1.06 | 2.12 | 10.65 | 1.07 |
| 3. Blaine | 0.82 | 4.10 | 1.09 | 3.27 | 0.97 | 1.92 | 9.29 | 0.93 |
| 4. Broadwater | 1.92 | 9.60 | 0.40 | 1.20 | 0.35 | 0.70 | 11.50 | 1.15 |
| 5. Carbon | 1.21 | 6.05 | 1.30 | 3.90 | 0.97 | 1.92 | 11.87 | 1.19 |
| 6. Carter | 1.36 | 6.80 | 0.36 | 1.08 | 0.35 | .70 | 8.58 | 0.86 |
| 7. Cascade | 2.75 | 13.75 | 10.53 | 31.59 | 12.53 | 25.06 | 70.40 | 7.04 |
| 8. Chauteau | 1.11 | 5.55 | 1.04 | 3.12 | 1.24 | 2.48 | 11.15 | 1.12 |
| 9. Custer | 1.82 | 9.10 | 1.95 | 5.88 | 1.94 | 3.88 | 18.86 | 1.89 |
| 10. Daniels | 1.37 | 6.85 | 0.55 | 1.65 | 0.44 | 0.88 | 9.38 | 0.94 |
| 11. Dawson | 1.25 | 6.25 | 1.65 | 4.95 | 1.68 | 3.36 | 14.56 | 1.45 |
| 12. Deer Lodge | 1.69 | 8.45 | 2.38 | 7.14 | 2.29 | 4.58 | 20.17 | 2.02 |
| 13. Fallon | 1.97 | 9.85 | 0.56 | 1.68 | 0.44 | 0.88 | 12.41 | 1.24 |
| . | . | . | . | . | . | . | . | . |
| . | . | . | . | . | . | . | . | . |
| . | . | . | . | . | . | . | . | . |
| 52. Treasure | 2.12 | 10.60 | 0.17 | 0.51 | 0.18 | 0.36 | 11.47 | 1.15 |
| 53. Valley | 0.82 | 4.10 | 2.20 | 6.60 | 2.47 | 4.94 | 15.64 | 1.56 |
| 54. Wheatland | 1.75 | 8.75 | 0.44 | 1.32 | 0.44 | 0.88 | 10.95 | 1.10 |
| 55. Wilaux | 2.11 | 10.55 | 0.23 | 0.69 | 0.18 | 0.36 | 11.60 | 1.16 |
| 56. Yellowstone | 7.54 | 37.70 | 11.33 | 33.99 | 13.89 | 27.78 | 99.47 | 9.95 |
| Total | 100.00 | 500.00 | 100.00 | 300.00 | 100.00 | 200.00 | 1000.00 | 100.00 |

*Sources:* Census of Population, 1960, various other publications, and experts' estimates.

the variables in the information control units to produce the individual estimates of potential shown in column 9.[13]

*The Method of Factor Analysis*

It is conceivable that a very large number of variables may initially be thought to correlate with the independent variable measuring potential. Without a great deal of difficulty, for example, one could derive more than 50 variables that could be useful in a regression on the potential for snowblowers.

The method of *factor analysis* has long been used in psychology for problems in which it is desired to reduce a large number of variables to a smaller number of factors.[14] The underlying postulate is that variables that "move together" (i.e., are highly correlated) can be "explained" by a single variable, called a factor. A small number of factors may then replace a large number of variables.

If one wishes to predict some variable on the basis of a number of independent variables (which are not statistically independent of one another), the factor-analytic approach may be used to obtain a smaller number of factors than independent variables. The variables that "load" (i.e., correlate) most highly with the factors may then be employed in the regression. For example, this technique was employed by Twedt (1962) in reducing 34 predictive variables for advertising readership to 6 factors.

In some instances, the coefficients of the independent variables in the regression equation may themselves be of interest. This is particularly true when the value of the independent variable is controllable. In the Twedt study, for example, one of the predictive variables was the size of the illustration in square inches. An advertiser could use this variable to determine the effect on readership of changes in illustration size. But in order to accomplish this, he would need a good estimate of the coefficient associated with illustration size. For example, if this coefficient had a value of unity, it could be inferred that the per cent readership would increase approximately 1 per cent for each square inch of added illustration space.

Unfortunately, the estimates of the coefficients of the independent variables tend to be less reliable the greater the intercorrelation between independent variables. This is known as the problem of *multicollinearity*.

[13] The reader who wishes to view another illustration should see Still and Cundiff (1958, pp. 609–611).

[14] Actually, there are a number of methods employed under the common heading of factor analysis. Coverage of these methods may be found in Harmon (1960) or Lawley and Maxwell (1963).

In a recent paper Scott (1966) has shown that the method of factor analysis can be extended to obtain relatively reliable estimates of the coefficients of the original variables where multicollinearity is a problem.

Thus in finding measures of potential by regression analysis, factor analysis has two applications. The first use is in reducing the number of independent variables to a smaller and more manageable number of factors. The second use is in obtaining reliable estimates of the coefficients in the original regression equation when the problem of multicollinearity is acute.

## MICRO METHODS OF ESTIMATING POTENTIAL

Another general approach to estimate potential is by micro methods. The methods previously examined start with *aggregate* industry sales or aggregate variable data and then segment data by information control units. They are known as *macro* approaches. The *micro* methods, in contrast, start with individual buyer purchases of the product and aggregate forward to estimates of potential by information control units.

A number of different micro methods are available. The two basic methods are commonly known as (1) the census method and (2) the market survey method. The first one is generally applicable only in determining potential for industrial offerings. However, the survey method can be used in estimating potential in consumer and institutional markets as well.

### Census Method[15]

The census method involves querying or estimating the number of units that will be purchased by *each* (and every) user (and prospective user) on the buyers' side of the market. In other words, first the analyst must determine who the users and prospective users are (all of them) and then he must be able to discern the quantity of the offering each of them anticipates buying from the sellers. The total amount to be used by *each* individual buyer, divided by the total amount to be purchased by *all* buyers, gives the relative potential for each account or buyer.

Obviously, this method works best when (1) there are few users and they are known and (2) the users are able to estimate their purchases in advance. Such requirements pretty well limit use of the method to industrial offerings. In fact, there are few industrial offerings that en-

[15] A more extensive discussion of this method can be found in Hummel (1961, pp. 137–151).

counter such a market. Consequently, there is little occasion to use this method.

### Market Survey Method[16]

The market survey method, in contrast to the census method, is based on a *survey* of a sample group of users and prospective users selected from the total market.[17] The respondents selected in the sample are surveyed relative to their anticipated purchases or relative to their past purchases. Also, such surveys inquire about related customer characteristics that can be identified in the market and, in turn, can be used to infer to the total market. For example, to determine potential for an industrial product, an analyst must discern from respondents (1) the number of units to be purchased, (2) how (in what activity) they are to be used, and (3) the relationship between the number of employees in the plant (or value added by manufacturing) and the rate of use of the product. The survey questions normally are of the following type:

Does your plant use (name of the product)? If yes—
How many (name of the product) were used in your plant last year?
How were they used, that is, what were the applications?
Next year do you intend using—(1) about the same?
(2) more?
(3) fewer?

Respondents are also asked related classification data such as number of production employees and value added by manufacturing. With this kind of information, an analyst, by the use of secondary information, can identify the customers and prospective customers throughout the market, estimate the quantity of units that customers in each information control unit are likely to use and, in turn, prepare estimates of relative potential.

The market survey methods also can be used to determine the potential for consumer offerings. The application is about the same as for an industrial offering except that individual consumers must be surveyed. The basic pattern is to (1) select a sample group of consumers from the total market, (2) identify the extensiveness of their use of the offering, and (3) identify variables that appear to influence or to be associated with their use of the product, as well as the relative influence (weight) that each variable has on the purchase of the offering. Then the sample survey findings are projected to the company's information

[16] A more extensive discussion of this method may be found in Hummel (1961, pp. 103–123).

[17] Sample designs and survey techniques were discussed in earlier chapters.

control units according to the relative presence of the independent variables in each unit. The relative potential present in any one information control unit is determined by dividing the weighted value in that control unit by the sum of all of the weighted values for all of the control units. In other words, the arithmetic is identical to that shown in Table 14-3 for the multiple-variable index.

This market survey method is different from the multiple-variable index only in that a market survey of individual customers' intended uses serves as the information base. That is, individual customer use (instead of aggregates of industry sales) serves as the dependent variable, and the independent variables are selected and weighted on the basis of primary information from the survey (instead of secondary sources).

## The S.I.C. Modification

At first glance there might appear to be numerous other methods of estimating potential; however, most of the other titles only present modifications of the methods already discussed. For example, one S.I.C. code (Standard Industrial Classification) approach that is widely used in industrial marketing is a modification of the market survey method. Perhaps a discussion of this approach will both illustrate the basic aspects of the S.I.C. approach and give some indication of the various modifications that are possible.

An analyst must first determine the types of industries that would logically be users of the offering. A careful study of his company's sales invoices, plus prospect information from the sales group, plus information from other sellers (as it is available) will give sufficient insight into the types of manufacturing plants that use the product. Then, user plants are identified by the Standard Industrial Classification (S.I.C.) system code that embraces them (Henderson, 1963). For example, the analyst may discover some dozen different major industries that use rubber wringer rollers. The 12 might include metal-cutting machine tools (S.I.C. 3541), construction machinery (S.I.C. 3531), and mining machinery equipment (S.I.C. 3532). Once the analyst has ascertained that he has adequately identified the buyers' side of the market for the offering, the universe has been identified.

Next a sampling design is constructed, a sample is drawn, and the selected plant managers, or other able spokesmen, are asked to answer the types of questions presented earlier in the market survey method discussion. This time each plant is identified by an S.I.C. number.

From the survey information, the rate of use of rubber wringer rollers per production employee or per dollar of value added, or some other combination of factors, is discerned for each of the different S.I.C. industry groups. For example, the metal-cutting machine industry may use an average of one unit of the product for each 10 production employees or for each $5000 of value added. In contrast, the construction machinery industry may average only one unit of product per 30 production workers or for each $15,000 of value added, and so forth for the other industries that use the product.

Knowing (1) which industries use the product and (2) having related the degree of use to one or more influencing or associated variables (which must also be reported in secondary sources), the analyst can proceed to compute potential. Using the secondary sources of information (*Census of Manufacturing, Iron Age,* and other such applicable publications), the analyst geographically locates each plant in each industry category. Then he ascertains the magnitude of the variable that indicates rate of product use (e.g., number of production employees or dollar value added) for each plant. For example, the metal-cutting machine tool industry in Illinois in 1958 had about 4000 production employees. A 1 to 10 use rate would indicate a potential of 400 units. The construction machinery industry in Illinois had about 27,000 production workers. This coupled with a use rate of 1 to 30 would give an estimate of 900 units. The same procedure would be followed for each of the other using industries located in Illinois, and a total absolute potential could be computed for the Illinois market. The same would be done for each other information control unit. Finally, the relative potential in each of the ICU's could be computed by dividing the potential in each ICU by the sum of the potential in all of the ICU's.[18]

## ESTIMATING POTENTIAL: NEW PRODUCTS[19]

Estimating potential for new products is particularly difficult, because both buyers and sellers lack experience with the new product. By definition, there are no past industry sales to use either in building a market potential index or as a dependent variable in the multivariate regression method. Furthermore, it is rather meaningless to ask prospective customers how many units they can use unless they have enough product experience to know what the new offering will substitute for or what undone task it will do. In such situations, both buyers and sellers can propose estimates of potential, but such estimates (free of experience) are likely to be little better than guesswork.

[18] Another illustration employing an S.I.C. approach may be found in Hummel (1961).

[19] The term "new product" has reference to offerings that are new to the market and are not considered to be close substitutes for existing products.

As a rule, good estimates of potential *cannot* be obtained until at least a segment of the market has been thoroughly exposed to the new offering and has had sufficient opportunity to react to it. For new products, test market experience (or other early market experience) is a prime requisite for the computation of potential.[20] Depending on the nature and the extent of the test market experience, the previously described micro and macro methods may be used in conjunction with the test market experience to compute estimates of potential. However, the reader must keep in mind that as the product moves through its life cycle, a dynamic, demand situation is present. This is likely to call for data to supplement the sales data.

## SUMMARY

This chapter has been concerned with the measurement and use of potential. Potential, in this book, has been defined as the absolute or relative maximum capacity of segments of a buyers' side of a market to purchase a specific type of offering in a specified time. Before measures of potential can be computed, one must (1) identify the *product* or offering group under study, (2) determine the applicable information control units to be used, and (3) ascertain that the information and method to be used will result in a *timely* measure of potential.

Measures of potential can be computed by either macro or micro methods. The two commonly used aggregate or macro estimating methods involve use of (1) the industry sales index and (2) single- and multiple-variable indexes. The industry sales index method provides a superior estimate of relative potential when adequate industry sales are available and when the product is established in all market segments.

Micro methods (census methods and market survey methods) are used either when industry sales are not available (i.e., not even partially available) or when *absolute* measures of potential are needed. In general, the micro methods are more costly, because they require collection of primary, external data through market surveys. Furthermore, there is nothing inherently more accurate about the micro methods than about the macro methods. Consequently, the micro methods are used principally in situations in which *insufficient* industry sales data are available to permit use of either a sales index approach or a multivariant regression analysis for selecting and weighting variables in a multiple-variable index.

[20] Readers interested in test markets and experimental designs should see Chapter 7 and Berdy (1965), Gold (1964), and Hardin (1966).

## REFERENCES

American Marketing Association. *Market Potentials and Use of Census Data.* Proceedings of the Seminar on Market Potentials and the Use of Census Data, 1957.

Berdy, E. M. "Testing Test Market Predictions: Comments," *Journal of Marketing Research,* May 1965, pp. 196–200.

Cowan, D. R. G. *Sales Analysis from the Management Standpoint.* Chicago: University of Chicago Press, 1938.

Crisp, R. *Sales Planning and Control.* New York: McGraw-Hill, 1961.

Ferber, R. *Statistical Techniques in Market Research.* New York: McGraw-Hill, 1949.

Gold, J. A. "Testing Test Market Predictions," *Journal of Marketing Research,* August 1964, pp. 8–16.

Hardin, D. H. "A New Approach to Test Marketing," *Journal of Marketing,* October 1966, pp. 28–31.

Harmon, H. H. *Modern Factor Analysis.* Chicago: University of Chicago Press, 1960.

Henderson, H. R. "Relating Company Markets to SIC," *Journal of Marketing,* April 1963, pp. 42–45.

Hummel, F. *Market and Sales Potentials.* New York: Ronald Press, 1961.

Lawley, D. N., & Maxwell, A. E. *Factor Analysis as a Statistical Method.* London: Butterworths, 1963.

Massy, W. F. "Television Ownership in 1950: Results of a Factor Analytic Study." In *Quantitative Techniques in Marketing Analysis.* Homewood, Ill.: Richard D. Irwin, 1962. Pp. 440–441.

Otteson, S. F., Panscher, W. G., & Patterson, J. M. *Marketing: The Firm's Viewpoint.* New York: Macmillan, 1964.

Roccaferreca, G. *Operations Research Models for Business and Industry.* Chicago: Southwestern Publishing Company, 1964.

Scott, J. T., Jr. "Factor Analysis and Regression," *Econometrica,* July 1966, pp. 552–562.

Stanton, W., & Buskirk, R. *Management of the Sales Force,* Homewood, Ill.: Richard D. Irwin, 1959.

Still, R., & Cundiff, E. *Sales Management.* Englewood Cliffs, N.J. Prentice-Hall, 1958.

Telfer, R. "How to Measure Sales Against Market Potential in the Construction Industry," *Journal of Marketing,* **26**, January 1962, p. 35.

Twedt, D. W. "A Multiple Factor Analysis of Advertising Readership," *Journal of Applied Psychology,* June 1952, pp. 207–215. Reprinted in R. E. Frank, A. A. Kuehn, W. F. Massy, *Quantitative Techniques in Marketing Analysis,* Homewood, Ill.: Richard D. Irwin, 1962.

Yamane, T. *Statistics: An Introductory Analysis.* New York: Harper and Row, 1964.

*Fifteen*

# Forecasting Marketing Information

Forecasting is an activity that has challenged men for thousands of years. Joseph's Old Testament prophecy about the seven good years and seven lean years was reportedly perfect.[1]

The needs for forecasts have changed little over the years; men alone and in organizations have planning problems for which forecasting is an essential element in decision making.[2] The objective of forecasting, now as in the past, is to accurately foresee the future.

The dreams and hunches that served Joseph so well still see some service, but far more forecasting work is based on various fundamental approaches. Business forecasters today are equipped with numerous techniques, many data, and data-handling equipment that has not been available before. Forecasters are coming to rely more on statistics and econometrics and are now able to consider and use much more data than ever before because of the availability of electronic computers.

The purpose of this chapter is to introduce the subject of forecasting as it applies to marketing information. At best this chapter can provide the reader with an overview of the available forecasting procedures, suggest when and why various procedures seem most suitable, point out some of the problems that are likely to be encountered, and provide a link to additional sources of information on forecasting.

[1] Thanks are due to Butler and Kavesh (1966, p. 1) for reminding us of this early forecaster.

[2] The use of forecasts in management decisions is discussed in Ulin (1966, pp. 515–516).

## FORECASTING STAGES

The discussion in this chapter is organized by *stages* in the forecasting activity. The five stages considered important are:

1. Selection of a forecasting procedure.
2. Determination of the data that are required and available for the forecast.
3. Computation of the forecast.
4. Appraisal of the forecasted values.
5. Ex post evaluation of the forecasted values and the forecasting methods.

Stage 1 and to a lesser degree stages 4 and 5 will be examined in some detail. Stages 2 and 3 receive little elaboration.

### Stage 1: Selection of a Forecasting Procedure

Selection of a forecasting procedure is dependent on knowledge of the following:

1. Events that are to be forecasted.
2. Decision-making activities that need forecasts.
3. Alternative procedures for constructing forecasts.
4. General availability of data relating to the situation.

#### *Events to Be Forecast*

The starting point in the entire forecasting procedure is formulation of a precise statement about the events to be forecast. This statement must prescribe the product(s), the market areas, the future time period, and the market measurement to be forecast. There are numerous possible product ambiguities. A forecast, for example, could pertain to an individual product, to several product lines, to a company's entire output, or to an industry's offerings.

A similar range of ambiguity pertains to the market area designation. Are values to be forecast for individual information control units, for some larger market segments, or for the total market? Furthermore, what time periods are the forecasts to cover? Periods are best stated in specific calendar dates. Finally, what market measurement is to be forecast—sales, market share, potential, brand loyalty, or what?[3]

[3] For additional discussion about specifying the events to be forecast, see Ulin (1966, pp. 515–516).

### *Decision-Making Activities That Need Forecasts*

The activities that are to make use of forecasts influence the selection of forecasting procedures. Some sales forecasts, for example, serve as irrevocable foundations for the assumption of millions of dollars of sunk costs. Such uses call for accurate forecasts and, fortunately, can afford costly forecasting procedures. Other forecasts are needed only to give hints of market demand for products that might receive further consideration for joining a company's line. Then low-cost, less accurate forecasts can be used.

### *Alternative Procedures for Constructing Forecasts*

Numerous forecasting procedures are available. They should *not* be considered as being directly competitive one with another, but rather, as available procedures to fit various needs. Frequently they supplement one another.

Each of the numerous forecasting techniques will not be treated individually, because there are simply too many. However, the many variants are often considered to reside in four distinct categories of procedures (Ferber and Verdoorn, 1962, p. 442):[4]

1. Judgment procedures.
2. Surveys of expectations or polling procedures.
3. Mechanical extrapolation procedures.
4. Analytical or econometric procedures.

### *Judgment Forecasts*

This title *is* descriptive of the procedure whose main ingredient or focal point is *judgment*. This is sometimes referred to as the seat-of-the-pants method (Ferber and Verdoorn, 1962, p. 461). This method is relatively *free* of data, there is little need for ranking and weighting of variables, and computer time is no problem. Virtually all that is required is a lifetime of relevant experience along with clear insight and sound judgment. And, of course, a little omniscience is not inappropriate. Basically, the forecaster draws upon his experiences, as best he can remember them—recalling the general environment and the relevant variables and how they are likely to influence the outcome—and then someway hooks everything together to arrive at a forecast. In some situations two or more "forecasters" will work independently of

[4] Some writers divide forecasting procedures into the categories: (1) judgmental polling procedures, (2) extrapolation procedures, (3) correlation and leading indicator procedures, and (4) econometric model procedures (Cunningham, 1966).

each other to forecast a value. Then, forecast values and considerations are compared and the differences resolved.

USE OF THE JUDGMENT PROCEDURES. This method of forecasting may have a place in three different kinds of situations. One situation may be where there are so many influencing variables and unknown and complex forecasting climates that no more formal method can be applied. In such a situation, where quantitative treatment of the variables is truly out of the question, the choice is often between a judgment-based forecast and *no* forecast. If ex post evaluations of previous judgment-based forecasts have been favorable, further use seems appropriate.

A second type of situation that encourages consideration of the judgment procedure is one that is sufficiently simple to enable brief experience and insight to permit accurate forecasts. Such situations may be found occasionally where forecast values are not changing or continue to change in the same way over long periods of time. Thus conceivably the Maytag Company could adequately forecast market share for conventional washing machines through use of the judgment procedure. A second example would be a situation in which a company knew that it could sell all it could produce and knew its production capacity.

Finally, there are situations that simply cannot afford the use of a more costly forecasting procedure. In such a situation ex post evaluation must be employed to discern when the judgment procedure has been more helpful than no forecast.

CONCLUDING COMMENTS ON JUDGMENTS PROCEDURES. The judgment procedures are too ambiguous and loose to permit the pinpointing of faulty activity within the forecasting process. Even through ex post (after the forecast event is history) evaluation, about all that can be examined is the degree to which the forecast values are accurate. The process cannot be dissected to determine what did and did not work. Consequently, judgment procedures are not subject to much improvement through appraisals and evaluations. Obviously this is a serious weakness.

Perhaps the final comment could be left unsaid. The judgment method is probably still the most frequently used one in general business operations (Ferber and Verdoorn, 1962, p. 361). This may come as a disquieting conflict in view of the prior discussion. However, there is evidence that other procedures are growing in relative importance and especially in critical use situations. In general, the more rigorous analytical approaches that are subject to appraisals and evaluation and consequent improvements should be used.

### *Surveys of Expectations or Polling Procedures*

The forecasting techniques grouped under this title all involve asking (i.e., surveying) knowledgeable persons about specific future events. Accordingly, use of this method presumes the presence of businessmen or consumers who jointly have better future insight than does the forecaster.[5] Some evidence indicates that the closer the knowledgeable persons are to the consumer market, the more able they are to predict the near future. A European group, the IFO—Institut für Wirtschaftsforschung—has discovered that

> the forecasts of shoe retailers have generally been more accurate than the forecasts of shoe wholesalers, and in turn have usually been more accurate than the forecasts of shoe manufacturers, which in their turn have generally been more accurate than the forecasts of leather traders, tanneries, and traders of hides (Ferber and Verdoorn, 1962, p. 455).

Survey procedures have been used for both consumer and industrial offerings. Some of the better known survey-based forecasts in the industrial field are the National Industrial Conference Board surveys of capital appropriations, McGraw-Hill survey of order expectations by machinery producers, and their surveys of annual sales expectations, Fortune's "Business Mood" survey, and the Commerce Department-SEC and McGraw-Hill capital budget surveys. Frequently mentioned consumer surveys used in forecasting are those of the Census Bureau, the University of Michigan Survey Research Center, and the Sindlinger-NICB.

Cohen (1966) has said that the value of surveys transcend the supplying of numbers for the forecast:

> Perhaps the greatest use that surveys can perform for the skilled practitioner is to bring him to the market place. Too often, the forecaster can become enamored of his own point of view, his own techniques, his own biases, and consequently his vision of what is happening all around him may dim.

When businessmen are surveyed, the normal procedure is to ask how many units they anticipate using during the period of the forecast. Additionally, they may be asked if such an amount represents a change from the present period, and, if so, why they anticipate a change. For example, a forecaster may ask:

How many (factional horsepower motors) will your company purchase next year?

Does this quantity, relative to the present year, represent (1) an increase, (2) a decrease, (3) about the same number?

What are the major factors you believe will influence your company's purchase of (motors)?

[5] Businessmen and customers who have made plans may, for example, know more (in a given environment) than does a forecaster.

In addition, similar questions about specific brands can be asked.

Consumer surveys frequently collect two kinds of information. The first is information about buying intentions in the context of buying plans. The second is information about consumers' psychological attitudes.

Surveys of businessmen have been taken much more seriously than those of consumers (Cohen, 1966, p. 75). Part of the explanation must be that businessmen do more planning and, accordingly, are in better positions to report on their expectations. Furthermore, businessmen's discrepancies between their behavior and their plans appear due largely to their inability to take into account the impact of governmental policy and other environmental changes. Consumers, on the other hand, tend to plan less, have less knowledge of their environment, and have less stable anticipations. Information on consumer buying plans has been more accepted and used than information on their psychological attitudes (Tobin, 1959).

CONCLUDING COMMENTS ON POLLING PROCEDURES. The various *survey* methods involve considerable judgment. First, the forecaster needs judgment to discern who the knowledgeable persons are and how their opinions should be integrated into a forecast. Second, this method is expensive because of the recurring need to design surveys and collect and analyze information. Third, this method can be used only in situations where there are knowledgeable persons whose attitudes and intentions can be accurately portrayed through a survey. Fourth, "knowledgeable persons" are most likely to be present when inquiry is made about established products that buyers normally (1) advance-*plan*-purchase (e.g., houses, cars, new plant, EDP systems) or (2) purchase rather habitually (e.g., haircuts, beer, sweeping compound, typewriter ribbons). New products and unplanned, infrequently purchased offerings do *not* fit well with the survey method. Finally, this forecasting method provides its best predictions for the immediate short-run, unaffected by disruptive influences.[6]

### *Mechanical Extrapolation Procedures*

The forecasting techniques grouped under the title of mechanical extrapolation procedures attempt to identify movements or trends that existed in past time periods. The dependent variable is the event to be predicted, such as market share or company sales. Determinant variables are not considered individually, but, instead, appear collectively under the heading of *time*. Extrapolation assumes that the variable will

[6] For some excellent references on the Survey of Expectations Forecasting Procedure, see Keezer, Ulin, Greenwald and Matulis (1960), Mueller (1963), and Hastay (1960).

follow its previously established pattern, and the problem is to determine a curve that fits the data.

This forecasting method is appropriate when patterns of past movements have been relatively constant and when abrupt distortions are not likely.[7] Also it provides a possible approach when individual demand determinants *cannot* be identified and related to the event to be forecast. Finally, Adams and DeJanosi (1966) consider this method appropriate for use when "better" methods are not justified.

Common and crucial to all mechanical extrapolation methods are considerations about (1) which data are relevant and (2) how best to fit an "explanatory" curve to the selected data.[8] Table 15-1 and Figure 15-1 present the rudiments of these problems. A forecast employing *all* of the data and a least-squares straight-line fit would result in a forecast for 1968 of over 17,000 units. In contrast, using the same procedure but only the data from 1961 through 1967, the forecast would be about 10,500 units. Clearly, the straight-line least-squares fit should *not* be applied to the whole range of data. However, for the 1961 data and on, it may provide an adequate prediction. Obviously, other predictions could have been gained through use of other years and other curves. A business forecaster's safeguard is knowledge of the past data and the environment from which they have arisen. Then he can better select

[7] For an illustration suggesting use of very limited past data to predict retail sales, see Kelly (1967).

[8] Brown, Buck, and Pyatt (1965) suggest a need for disaggregating data on durable goods as an early step in forecasting.

**TABLE 15-1** Zebra Company Sales: 1954 to 1967.

| (1) Year | (2) Sales | (1) Year | (2) Sales |
|---|---|---|---|
| 1954 | 1000 | 1961 | 16000 |
| 1955 | 4500 | 1962 | 15000 |
| 1956 | 6000 | 1963 | 13500 |
| 1957 | 7000 | 1964 | 13750 |
| 1958 | 9000 | 1965 | 13000 |
| 1959 | 10500 | 1966 | 11000 |
| 1960 | 10750 | 1967 | 12000 |

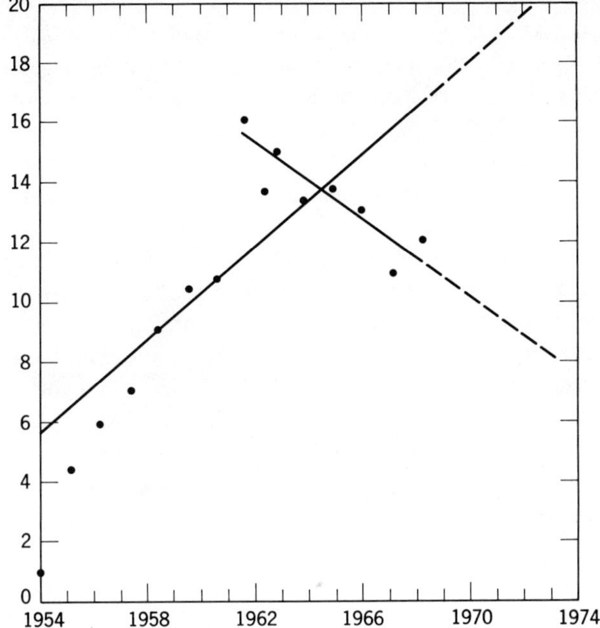


**Figure 15-1** Zebra Company sales: 1954 to 1967. *Source:* Table 15-1.

his data, "explain" deviations in the data, and proceed to fit an appropriate curve to the adjusted data.[9]

What mechanical extrapolation methods are available? A wide range exists, but they can be categorized as naïve "models," moving averages, or mathematical trends. Each of these will be examined.

NAÏVE MODELS. Naïve models range all the way from no-change models ($X_{t+1}$ will be the same as was $X_t$) to *equal* per cent change models ($X_{t+1}$ will be changed by the same amount as $X_t - X_{t-1}$)[10] to models that predict the change to be some proportion of the past change (change in $X_{t+1}$ is equal to some proportion of the change that occurred in $X_t$). Further refinements can be worked into these models to adjust for seasonal and other variations.

[9] For a discussion of improving forecasts through the use of newly available data, see Whiteman (1966).

[10] The equal per cent change model, as it commonly appears, is expressed as

$$\text{next year's sales} = \text{this year's sales} \times \frac{\text{this year's sales}}{\text{last year's sales}}$$

The "rationale" underlying the naïve models is that what has happened in the immediate past will continue to happen in the future. These models have appeal because, in general, they appear sufficiently simple to understand, they require little data and little statistical manipulation, and they can produce fast predictions. Cunnyngham (1966, p. 140) has pointed out that a naïve projection model is not necessarily foolishly simple or unsophisticated. It is basically a way of forecasting a time series by itself.

The more complex models, which include a number of adjustment factors, can produce useful checks on other forecasting methods. Additionally, there is evidence that where conditions are somewhat stable or are changing in a relatively uniform manner, the naïve models may provide accurate short-range forecasts. Thus despite some analytical weaknesses, forecasters should be familiar with naïve models.[11]

Moving averages. Moving averages are series of averages that serve to approximate the trend of a series of data by canceling out the high and low values. Each average is an arithmetic mean of several values

[11] For an illustration of a naïve model, see Vreeland (1963).

**Table 15-2** Moving Averages, Zebra Company Sales: 1954 to 1967

| (1) Year | (2) Sales | (3) Sales for Three-Year Period | (4) Three-Year Moving Average |
|---|---|---|---|
| 1954 | 1000 | | |
| 1955 | 4500 | 11500 | 3833 |
| 1956 | 6000 | 17500 | 5833 |
| 1957 | 7000 | 22000 | 7333 |
| 1958 | 9000 | 26500 | 8833 |
| 1959 | 10500 | 30250 | 10833 |
| 1960 | 10750 | 37250 | 12417 |
| 1961 | 16000 | 41750 | 13917 |
| 1962 | 15000 | 44500 | 14833 |
| 1963 | 13500 | 42250 | 14083 |
| 1964 | 13750 | 40250 | 13417 |
| 1965 | 13000 | 37750 | 12583 |
| 1966 | 11000 | 36000 | 12000 |
| 1967 | 12000 | | |

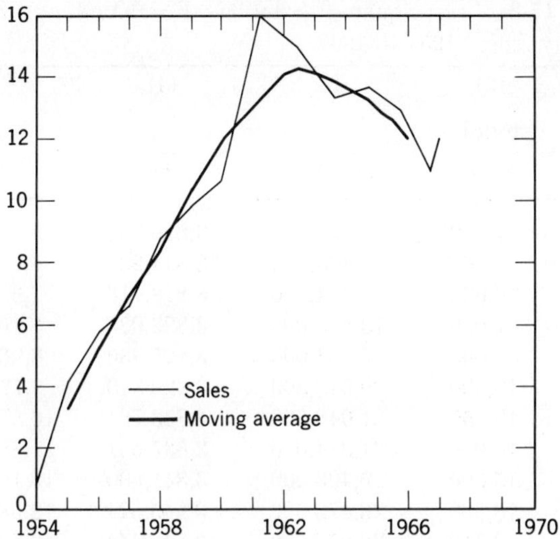


**Figure 15-2** Zebra Company sales: three-year moving average (1954 to 1967). *Source:* Table 15-2.

plotted at the center date. The period represented by each moving average ideally should approximately equal the length of the major cycles in the data.

Table 15-2 and Figure 15-2 help illustrate two relevant points about the use of moving averages. First, moving averages follow major changes in the dependent variable and consequently stay within the range of the historical data. This is meaningful for predicting short-run changes. However, moving averages do not provide a good base for long-run forecasting because they do not demonstrate trend relations.[12] Second, values at the end of the series (e.g., 1967) cannot be computed, but, like the period being forecast, must be estimated. Thus the most recent figure from which the extrapolation must proceed is older than the most recent recorded experience.

Mathematical trends. Mathematical trends involve methods by which mathematical relations are derived to represent or fit the data to be projected. A very simple illustration that used a least-squares straight-line criterion was shown in Figure 15-1. The computations for each of the two curves are shown in Tables 15-3 and 15-4.

[12] For a discussion of moving averages and their computation, see Yamane (1964, pp. 337–339) and Neiswanger (1965, p. 505).

**Table 15-3** Least-Squares Solution—$\bar{Y} = b\bar{X}_1 + a$; Zebra Company Sales: 1954 to 1967

| (1) Year ($\bar{X}_1$) | (2) Sales ($\bar{X}_0$) | (3) $\bar{X}_0\bar{X}_1$ | (4) $\bar{X}_{12}$ | (5) $\bar{Y}$ |
|---|---|---|---|---|
| 1954 | 1,000 | 1,952,000 | 3,810,304 | 5,749.56 |
| 1955 | 4,500 | 878,850 | 3,814,209 | 6,553.95 |
| 1956 | 6,000 | 11,724,000 | 3,818,116 | 7,358.34 |
| 1957 | 7,000 | 13,685,000 | 3,822,025 | 8,162.73 |
| 1958 | 9,000 | 17,604,000 | 3,825,936 | 8,967.12 |
| 1959 | 10,500 | 20,548,500 | 3,829,849 | 9,771.51 |
| 1960 | 10,750 | 21,048,500 | 3,833,764 | 10,575.90 |
| 1961 | 16,000 | 31,344,000 | 3,837,681 | 11,380.29 |
| 1962 | 15,000 | 29,400,000 | 3,841,600 | 12,184.64 |
| 1963 | 13,500 | 26,473,500 | 3,845,521 | 12,989.07 |
| 1964 | 13,750 | 26,977,500 | 3,849,444 | 13,793.46 |
| 1965 | 13,000 | 25,519,000 | 3,853,369 | 14,597.85 |
| 1966 | 11,000 | 21,604,000 | 3,857,296 | 15,402.24 |
| 1967 | 12,000 | 23,580,000 | 3,861,225 | 16,206.63 |
| 27419 | 143,000 | 280,248,500 | 53,700,339 | |

$\bar{X}_1 = 1{,}958.5 \qquad \bar{X}_0 = 10{,}214.28$

$$b = \frac{N\Sigma\bar{X}_0\bar{X}_1 - (\Sigma\bar{X}_0)(\Sigma\bar{X}_1)}{N\Sigma\bar{X}_1{}^2 - (\Sigma\bar{X}_1)^2}$$

$$= \frac{(14)(280{,}248{,}500) - (143{,}000)(27{,}419)}{(14)(53{,}700{,}339) - (27{,}419)^2} = 804.39$$

$$a = \bar{X}_0 - b\bar{X}_1 = 10{,}214.28 - 804.39(1{,}958.5) = -1{,}564{,}419.72$$

$$\bar{Y} = 804.39\bar{X}_1 + (-1{,}564{,}419.72)$$

*Sales Prediction for 1968:* 17,011.02

Some of the more frequently used curves are:

1. An arithmetic trend, which is a straight line and assumes that the growth will be by a constant absolute amount each period.
2. A semilog trend, which assumes a constant percentage change each year.
3. A modified exponential, which gradually approaches but never reaches a constant asymptote, assumes that each increment of change will be a constant percentage of the previous ones.

**TABLE 15-4** Least-Squares Solution—$\bar{Y} = b\bar{X}_1 + a$; Zebra Company Sales: 1961 to 1967

| Year ($\bar{X}_1$) | Sales ($\bar{X}_0$) | $\bar{X}_0\bar{X}_1$ | $\bar{X}_1^2$ | $\bar{Y}$ |
|---|---|---|---|---|
| 1961 | 16,000 | 31,344,000 | 3,837,681 | 15,660.70 |
| 1962 | 15,000 | 29,400,000 | 3,841,600 | 14,928.56 |
| 1963 | 13,500 | 26,473,500 | 3,845,521 | 14,916.42 |
| 1964 | 13,750 | 26,977,500 | 3,849,444 | 13,464.28 |
| 1965 | 13,000 | 25,519,000 | 3,853,369 | 12,732.14 |
| 1966 | 11,000 | 21,604,000 | 3,857,296 | 12,000.00 |
| 1967 | 12,000 | 23,580,000 | 2,861,225 | 11,267.86 |
| 13734 | 94,250 | 184,898,000 | 26,946,136 | |

$\bar{X}_1 = 1962\bar{X}_0 = 13{,}464.28$

$\bar{Y} = 732.14\bar{X}_1 + 1{,}449{,}922.96$

*Sales Prediction for 1968:* 10,535.72

4. A logistic curve, which has the shape of an elongated S, assumes a growth involving increasing increments from an initial low value and then a gradual slowing down as "maturity" is approached.[13]

Mathematical trend techniques are superior to other mechanical extrapolation techniques for long-term estimates. However, they tend to be inferior for short-term forecasts because long-run curves are sought and short-run changes are largely ignored.

In summary, the naïve models, moving averages, and mathematical trends assume that the future will mirror the past. Individual influencing variables are not sought. Instead, forecasts are based on the information derived from the past history of the variable being projected.[14]

### *Analytical Forecasts*

Analytical forecasting procedures differ from the extrapolation procedures in that they forecast on the basis of information obtained from other economic variables rather than from past history of the variable being projected (Cunnyngham, 1966, p. 146). In other words, the indi-

[13] See a standard statistical textbook, such as Croxton and Cowden (1955) or Neiswanger (1965), for more detailed information.

[14] A time series analysis is illustrated in considerable detail in McLaughlin (1963). Crawford (1966) discusses how mechanical extrapolation procedures can be adapted to early assessment of new product success.

vidual variables thought to influence the events to be forecast are sought out, and their relationship both to the dependent and other independent variables are determined and stated mathematically.[15]

SINGLE-EQUATION APPROACHES. Analytical forecasting methods include a wide range of forecasting approaches that can be described as (1) single-equation approaches or as (2) more complete model systems. The single-equation forecast attempts, through one equation, to provide a close relationship between the variable being forecast and other predicting (independent) variables.[16]

Single-equation forecasts can include only one explaining variable, but such simple relationships are not often found. A number of variables are normally needed, and even then the functional relationships rarely offer complete explanations. Forecasters attempt to include major influencing variables and avoid those that contain no statistical projection information, but merely correlate with the variable being forecast.[17]

The forecaster, at times, can find explanatory variables that precede or lead the dependent variable. For example, construction contracts lead or precede construction expenditures, sale of Barbie Dolls precede sale of Barbie Doll wigs, and dishwasher sales precede sales of dishwasher detergents. Obviously, however, the discovery of one lead factor is not tantamount to accurate forecasting.[18]

Forecasters also search for explanatory variables whose values can be predicted (anticipated) with greater accuracy and ease than the value of the variable to be forecast. In turn, these anticipated values are used in predicting equations in place of the variables' current values. For example, a forecaster may discover that gasoline sales in a market are adequately explained by a combination of the (1) number of cars registered, (2) number of gasoline stations, and (3) price of gasoline in the market (relative to surrounding markets). The identification of these three explaining variables is useful only to the extent to which their values can be accurately predicted for use in the forecasting equation.

Single-equation forecasts are sometimes used when the independent (explaining) variables are not sufficiently independent of the dependent variable. For example, a prediction of Thunderbird car sales based on a single-equation forecast that used the "independent" variables (1)

[15] For an illustration of a search for predictive variables, see Martin (1967).

[16] For an example, see Crampen (1966).

[17] Kuehn and Rohloff (1967) warn of the perils of using information that is too aggregated.

[18] A discussion of the nature and use of leading indicators for forecasting movements of the economy can be found in Lempert (1966).

dollars of Thunderbird advertising, (2) price of Thunderbirds relative to past selling season, and (3) number of competitive units sold, would snare the forecaster in this very problem. One or more of these so-called "independent" variables are influenced in the period of the forecast by the dependent variable. Advertising expenditures in the market are influenced by the number of Thunderbirds sold, current Thunderbird prices are likely to be influenced by the number sold during the current period, and the same thing is likely to be true about the sale of competitive brands. In this sort of situation the independent variables feed on or interact with the dependent variables, and, accordingly, the "independent" variables are not likely to offer a very satisfactory explanation through a single equation.[19]

Nevertheless, the single-equation forecast can be very useful when the dependent variable does not importantly interact or affect the magnitude of the "independent" variables during the forecasting period. If it does interact, but not instantaneously (i.e., its influence is only felt in succeeding periods), the single-equation approach is satisfactory. Therefore, when the forecasting situation permits use of general independent variables (e.g., the presence of people who have money and are willing to buy), a single equation forecasting approach may suffice.

Complete model systems. Complete model systems attempt to portray real-world situations in simplified yet useful predictive forms, but, *unlike* the single-equation models, contain two or more equations. Generally, the more complete model systems come closer to describing the real-world situation than do the single-equation models. However, there are simply too many influencing variables interacting in too many ways to expect complete statistical explanation.[20]

In the formulation and use of predicting models, three aspects, in particular, must receive consideration. These aspects evolve around the (1) use and designation of various types of variables, (2) types of equations employed, and (3) use of dynamic versus static models. Only cursory definitional comment about each of these aspects is within the scope of this chapter; however, more detailed discussion can be found in Ferber and Verdoorn (1962), Johnston (1962), and Klein (1962).

*Variables.* Relative to variables to be used in a model, the forecaster must consider (1) the use of random or stochastic variables, (2) lagged versus current variables, (3) interdependence of the variables, and (4) the extent to which each variable is controllable. Let it suffice to say that a random variable is frequently introduced into models with each

[19] A multiple-equation, dynamic model, however, could provide a good predictor.

[20] For additional discussion on complete model systems, see Ferber and Verdoorn (1962, pp. 459–461).

functional relationship to represent sources of error that cannot be individually identified, measured, and entered into the model. A stochastic variable, designated by $U$, is shown in a behavioral type equation later in the chapter.

*Lagged* versus *current* variables and the problem of interdependence of variables were discussed in connection with the single-equation forecast models. Interdependent variables present relatively few problems in the more complete model systems, because their interdependent relationships can be fit back into the forecasting model.

Finally, the forecaster should classify the model variables by the degree to which his company can control each of them. Such identification permits consideration of alternative intensities and resulting outcomes.

*Equations.* Types of equations used in models include three—those that prescribe (1) definitions, (2) technical relations, and (3) behavior relations. The behavioral-relations equation provides the core of most models. These equations are supported and clarified through definitional and technical-relations equations. For example, a base forecast of national income ($Y$) in terms of private sector ($X_p$) and government sector ($X_g$) expenditures and tax receipts ($T$) is[21]

$$Y = X_p + X_g$$

This is a definitional equation—it defines national income.

$$X_p = X_0 + (Y - T) + U$$

is a behavioral equation, indicating how the variables are related.

$$T = T_0 + tY$$

is a technical equation, clarifying or explaining how tax receipts vary with $Y$. The $U$ in the behavior equation is a random variable, mentioned earlier, which is used to represent sources of error. The $X_0$ and $T_0$ are constants.

*Types of models.* Static or dynamic models can be used. Basically, dynamic models have action and reaction chains that are *not* completed within the same time period. In contrast, in a static model the action and reaction are completed and a state of no change is reached during the period. For example, a model indicating a change in price and an instantaneous adjustment in the quantity that can be sold at that price is a static model. In contrast, if the model reflected that the price change resulted in competitive price changes and repeated price changes and changing demand over time, the model would be said to be dynamic.

[21] This illustration was borrowed from Ferber and Verdoorn (1962, pp. 405–406).

CONCLUDING COMMENTS ON ANALYTICAL FORECASTING PROCEDURES. These brief comments about the analytical forecasting method can provide little more than general description and categorization of analytical forecasting methods and the associated problems. Analytical methods, in general, are more demanding than the other forecasting methods in terms of information requirements, time, and technical competence of forecasters. The more complex approaches virtually require use of a computer, and, in fact, simulation models require considerable computer time for development, actual run-time, and continual updating.

The analytical forecasting procedures have rendered substantial benefits. These approaches inquire into the principal variables believed to influence the variables to be predicted. They provide users with explicit systems in which information can be assembled and weighed. Furthermore, they are concrete and subject to both careful appraisal and evaluation—and this applies to both the forecasts and the procedures. Consequently, many companies have developed and do use analytical forecasting procedures.

## Stages 2 and 3: Assemble Data and Compute Forecast

The *second stage* consists of assembling the data to be used in the forecasting activity. Then, once the information is in correct form, the *third stage,* computation of the forecast can be completed. Stages 2 and 3 are not considered further in this chapter. Information on these topics can be found elsewhere in this book, as well as in books on forecasting.

## Stage 4: Appraisal of the Forecast

The *fourth stage* is *appraisal* of the forecast. Appraisals are conducted after the forecasted values are derived but before they are used. Appraisals are examinations of the forecasted values. They can partake of both statistical reliability checks and plausibility checks (Ferber and Verdoorn, 1962, pp. 470–473).

Only those forecasts that are derived from a mathematical trend or from an analytical equation are subject to statistical reliability checks. The general procedure is to compute the standard error of the forecast, so that the forecaster can estimate the range of sampling error. Admittedly, the more complete, multiequation predicting models do not lend themselves to the simple standard error considerations but, because of their complexities, call for more elaborate checks.

All four forecasting procedures result in estimates that are subject to plausibility checks. The plausibility (i.e., the adequacy) of forecast values can be considered through (1) use of alternative forecasting approaches, (2) comparison with past values, and (3) evaluation with commonsense values. Each check involves considerable judgment.

## Stage 5: Evaluation of the Forecast

The *fifth* and final forecasting stage is *evaluation* of the forecast *values* and the forecasting techniques.[22] This stage is clearly an ex post examination—that is, this evaluation of the forecast proceeds only after the events are a matter of history. The evaluation of the forecast values should proceed on two bases—accuracy on an *absolute* basis and accuracy on a *relative* basis.

### *Accuracy on an Absolute Basis*

Accuracy on an *absolute basis* involves comparison of forecast values with the actual outcomes. Such comparisons should be made both over time (i.e., for each time period the method has been used) and over space (e.g., for each of the markets). Such a double evaluation serves to put a solitary bit of either good or bad "luck" in proper perspective.

### *Accuracy on a Relative Basis*

Relative accuracy has reference to the degree of accuracy (over time and space) obtained by the forecasting method *relative* to simpler, less expensive methods. A forecast that is quite accurate on an absolute basis may receive a relatively low rating if a simpler, less expensive alternative forecasting method would have done about as well. A particular critical concern is the relative ability of a chosen method to anticipate turning points.

Clearly these ex post evaluations should not be overlooked.[23] They provide the best insight into past biases and weaknesses. Knowing what has been right and wrong in past forecasting situations, the forecaster should be able to improve his forecasting ability.

## SUMMARY

The discussion in this chapter was organized by stages in the forecasting activity. In the first stage the forecaster must select a forecasting

[22] For more information about evaluation of forecasts, see Chartener (1966) and Ferber and Verdoorn (1962, pp. 476–480).

[23] Adams and DeJanosi (1966) decry and partially explain why many business forecasters fail to evaluate their past forecasts.

procedure. This involves consideration of (1) the events to be forecast, (2) the decision-making activity that needs the forecast, (3) the alternative procedures for constructing forecasts, and (4) the availability of data.

The many available forecasting techniques were considered to reside in four distinct categories of procedures: judgment procedures, surveys of expectations or polling procedures, mechanical extrapolation procedures, and analytical or econometric procedures. Each of these procedures was discussed.

The second stage of forecasting is determination of the data that are required and available. Stage 3 is computation of the forecast. The fourth stage is the appraisal of the forecasted values, and the fifth and final stages is concerned with ex post evaluation of both forecasting methods and forecast values.

## REFERENCES

Adams, F. G., & DeJanosi, P. E. "Statistics and Econometrics of Forecasting." In Butler, W. F., & Kavesh, R. A. (Eds.), *How Business Economists Forecast.* Englewood Cliffs, N.J., Prentice-Hall, 1966. Pp. 3–30.

Bratt, E. *Business Forecasting,* New York: McGraw-Hill, 1958.

Brown, D. A., Buck, S. F., & Pyatt, F. G. "Improving the Sales Forecast for Consumer Durables," *Journal of Marketing Research,* August 1965, pp. 229–234.

Butler, W. F., & Kavesh, R. A. (Eds.) *How Business Economists Forecast.* Englewood Cliffs, N.J.: Prentice-Hall, 1966.

Chartener, W. H. "Evaluating Forecasts." In Butler, W. F., & Kavesh, R. A. (Eds.), *How Business Economists Forecast.* Englewood Cliffs, N.J.: Prentice-Hall, 1966. Pp. 519–530.

Cohen, M. "Surveys and Forecasting." In Butler, W. F., & Kavesh, R. A. (Eds.), *How Business Economists Forecast.* Englewood Cliffs, N.J.: Prentice-Hall, 1966. Pp. 55–87.

Crampen, L. J. "A New Technique to Analyze Tourist Markets," *Journal of Marketing,* January 1966, pp. 27–31.

Crawford, C. M. "The Trajectory Theory of Goal Setting for New Products," *Journal of Marketing Research,* May 1966, pp. 117–125.

Croxton, F. E., & Cowden, D. J. *Applied General Statistics* (2nd ed.) Englewood Cliffs, N.J.: Prentice-Hall, 1955.

Cunnyngham, J. "Analyzing Econometric Predictions and Projections," *Science Technology and Marketing,* The American Marketing Association, 1966.

Ferber, R., & Verdoorn, P. *Research Methods in Economics and Business.* New York: Macmillan, 1962.

Hastay, M. "The Formation of Business Expectations about Operating Variables."

In *The Quality and Economic Significance of Anticipations Data*. Princeton, N.J.: Princeton University Press, 1960.

Johnston, J. *Econometric Methods*. New York: McGraw-Hill, 1962.

Keezer, D. M., Ulin, R. P., Greenwald, D., & Matulis, M. "Observations on the Predictive Quality of McGraw-Hill Surveys of Business' Plans for New Plants and Equipment." In *The Quality and Economic Significance*. Princeton, N.J.: Princeton University Press, 1960. Pp. 369–385.

Kelly, R. F. "Estimating Ultimate Performance Levels of New Retail Outlets," *Journal of Marketing Research,* February 1967, pp. 12–19.

Klein, L. R. *An Introduction to Econometrics*. Englewood Cliffs, N.J.: Prentice-Hall, 1962.

Kuehn, A. A., & Rohloff, A. C. "Fitting Models to Aggregate Data," *Journal of Advertising Research,* March 1967, pp. 43–47.

Lempert, L. H. "Leading Indicators." In Butler, W. F., & Kavesh, R. A. (Eds.), *How Business Economists Forecast*. Englewood Cliffs, N.J.: Prentice-Hall, 1966. Pp. 31–41.

Martin, P. "Savings and Loans in New Submarkets: Search for Predictive Factors," *Journal of Marketing Research,* May 1967, pp. 163–166.

McLaughlin, R. L. "The Breakthrough in Sales Forecasting," *Journal of Marketing,* April 1963, pp. 46–54.

Mueller, E. "Ten Years of Consumer Attitude Surveys: Their Forecasting Record," *Journal of the American Statistical Association,* December 1963, pp. 899–917.

Neiswanger, W. *Elementary Statistical Methods*. New York: Macmillan, 1965.

Tobin, J. "On the Predictive Value of Consumer Intentions and Attitudes," *Review of Economics and Statistics,* February 1959, pp. 1–11.

Ulin, R. P. "The Use of Economic Forecasts in Management Decisions." In Butler, W. F., & Kavesh, R. A. (Eds.), *How Business Economists Forecast*. Englewood Cliffs, N.J.: Prentice-Hall, 1966.

Vreeland, C. "The Jentzen Method of Short-Range Forecasting," *Journal of Marketing,* April 1963, pp. 66–70.

Whiteman, I. R. "Improved Forecasting Through Feedback," *Journal of Marketing,* January 1966, pp. 45–51.

Yamane, T. *Statistics: An Introductory Analysis*. New York: Harper and Row, 1964.

PART IV

# CASES

1. Telematic Company
2. Empire Publishing Company
3. Mustang Aviation Corporation

## TELEMATIC COMPANY*

The Telematic Company was established in 1939 for the purpose of manufacturing household vacuum cleaners and related accessories. In the years prior to World War II Telematic was able to establish national distribution of their products by concentrating on new and changing machine design and a wider assortment of accessories than offered by the majority of their competitors.

The household vacuum cleaner business has been a highly competitive one almost from the time Hoover introduced the first one, an upright model, in 1908. Since that time there have been a large number of brands on the market; many of which have been available for only a short time because of business failures. In 1958 there were 50 manufacturers of household vacuum cleaners with 20 or more employees, and by 1963 this figure had fallen to 34. In 1963 the manufacturing firms producing household vacuum cleaners were located as shown in Figure 1.

Sales of household vacuum cleaners have been generally increasing since the early 1900's when practically no one owned such a machine. In 1967, 53,300,000 households, or 90.67 per cent of the total United States households, had vacuum cleaners. The data in Figure 2 illustrate the growth in vacuum cleaner sales.

In early 1968, Mr. Hodges, president of the Telematic Company, asked James Mason, the company's marketing director, to make a detailed study of the

* The name of the company and some of the figures are disguised.

**Figure 1** Geographic Distribution of Household Vacuum Cleaner Production

| State | Ohio | New York | California | Illinois | Oklahoma | All Others |
|---|---|---|---|---|---|---|
| Number of firms | 10 | 6 | 4 | 3 | 2 | 9 |

*Source:* U.S. Department of Commerce, Bureau of the Census, Washington, D.C.

potential for Telematic vacuum cleaners. It was the president's opinion that an adjustment in the firm's selling effort may be required to compensate for shifts in the United States population and for possible shifts in the disposable income of American consumers. He pointed out that since the early forties, when the company achieved national distribution, Telematic had maintained the same number of salesmen covering the same geographic areas. Mr. Hodges was especially concerned about the West Coast area. In the state of California alone the population had grown from 5,677,000 in 1940 to 19,225,700 in 1966. This represented far more than the national average—California was ranked only fifth in population by states in 1940, but was first before 1965.

Mr. Hodges gave his marketing director the responsibility of evaluating the effectiveness of Telematic's present selling efforts, and in addition assigned him the task of developing a measure that could be used on a continual basis in allocating the firm's selling efforts.

Telematic's headquarters and the single manufacturing plant were located in a large Midwestern city. The company's annual sales of vacuum cleaners and accessories increased from a meager $160,000 in 1940 to more than $20

**Figure 2** Manufacturer's Sales and Retail Value of Household Vacuum Cleaners

| Year | Sales (1000 units) | Retail Value—Approximate |
|---|---|---|
| 1950 | 3529 | $280,000,000 |
| 1955 | 3270 | 286,000,000 |
| 1960 | 3313 | 311,000,000 |
| 1964 | 4507 | 329,000,000 |
| 1965 | 5107 | 398,000,000 |
| 1966 | 5525 | 425,000,000 |

*Source:* U.S. Department of Commerce, Bureau of the Census, *Statistical Abstract of the United States*, Washington, D.C.

**Figure 3** Telematic Sales Volume to Appliance Wholesalers in Selected States—1967

| State | Per Cent of Company Sales to Wholesalers |
|---|---|
| Alabama | 1.2 |
| California | 9.2 |
| Illinois | 15.1 |
| Iowa | 3.1 |
| Kansas | 2.0 |
| Massachusetts | 1.3 |
| Minnesota | 2.3 |
| Missouri | 6.1 |
| New York | 6.7 |
| Ohio | 16.2 |
| Oregon | 0.5 |
| Texas | 6.7 |
| Wisconsin | 9.3 |
| Others | 20.3 |
| United States totals | 100.0 |

*Source:* Telematic Company records.

**Figure 4** Telematic Sales Volume to Franchise Dealers in Selected States—1967

| State | Per Cent of Company Sales to Franchise Dealers |
|---|---|
| Alabama | 3.2 |
| California | 5.1 |
| Illinois | 11.2 |
| Iowa | 5.8 |
| Kansas | 3.7 |
| Massachusetts | 2.2 |
| Minnesota | 5.3 |
| Missouri | 7.1 |
| New York | 8.1 |
| Ohio | 12.3 |
| Oregon | 1.6 |
| Texas | 4.9 |
| Wisconsin | 7.4 |
| Others | 22.1 |
| United States totals | 100.0 |

*Source:* Telematic Company records.

**Figure 5** Sales Management's Survey of Buying Power Data for Selected States

| State | Per Cent of United States Population | Per Cent of United States Total Households | Per Cent of United States Retail Sales | Per Cent of United States Effective Buying Income | Per Cent of United States Buying Power |
|---|---|---|---|---|---|
| Alabama | 1.78 | 1.64 | 1.34 | 1.26 | 1.39 |
| Arizona | 0.84 | 0.80 | 0.80 | 0.77 | 0.71 |
| California | 9.75 | 10.45 | 11.02 | 11.12 | 10.86 |
| Illinois | 5.46 | 5.63 | 6.38 | 6.59 | 6.30 |
| Iowa | 1.43 | 1.47 | 1.52 | 1.45 | 1.47 |
| Kansas | 1.15 | 1.21 | 1.13 | 1.06 | 1.13 |
| Maine | 0.50 | 0.49 | 0.49 | 0.42 | 0.46 |
| Massachusetts | 2.75 | 2.77 | 2.92 | 3.02 | 2.94 |
| Minnesota | 1.83 | 1.79 | 1.90 | 1.80 | 1.84 |
| Missouri | 2.29 | 2.43 | 2.51 | 2.28 | 2.35 |
| Nevada | 0.24 | 0.25 | 0.27 | 0.27 | 0.26 |
| New Hampshire | 0.34 | 0.34 | 0.36 | 0.33 | 0.34 |
| New York | 9.18 | 9.66 | 9.40 | 10.59 | 9.95 |
| Ohio | 5.34 | 5.31 | 5.30 | 5.44 | 5.38 |
| Oregon | 0.99 | 1.06 | 1.10 | 1.02 | 1.04 |
| Texas | 5.53 | 5.42 | 5.21 | 4.72 | 5.03 |
| Washington | 1.56 | 1.65 | 1.63 | 1.67 | 1.64 |
| Wisconsin | 2.15 | 2.11 | 2.11 | 2.08 | 2.11 |
| Others | 46.89 | 45.52 | 44.61 | 44.11 | 44.80 |
| United States totals | 100.00 | 100.00 | 100.00 | 100.00 | 100.00 |

*Source: Sales Management's Survey of Buying Power*, June 10, 1967. Copyright 1967; further reproduction is forbidden.

million in 1966. About 75 per cent of Telematic's sales were made to their franchise dealers, the remainder going to appliance wholesalers. Retail prices of Telematic vacuum cleaners varied from $79.95 to $139.95 for a deluxe model with all attachments included. The usual gross margin to the retailer was 20 to 25 per cent depending on the model. Because of Telematic's excellent reputation for good machines with a complete assortment of accessories, the company's marketing department usually had little difficulty in establishing a franchise in any area.

James Mason felt that the first step in carrying out this assignment would be to set up a good index of potential for Telematic's products. Mr. Mason was aware of the index published annually by the *Sales Management* magazine in *Sales Management's Survey of Buying Power*. This annual publication includes what is known as the "buying power index." This general index employs three factors—population, effective buying income, and retail sales, with the factors assigned weights of 2, 5, and 3 respectively.

The marketing director felt that he needed a very similar index set up on a geographic basis, yet he was reluctant to simply use the general published index of potential. Mr. Mason was not sure that the weights assigned to the three factors used by *Sales Management's Survey of Buying Power* fit Telematic's situation in the national market. In addition, he was sure that other factors had a substantial affect on Telematic's position in the household vacuum cleaner market. Supplemental information is shown in Figures 3, 4, and 5.

QUESTIONS

1. Develop a weighted multiple factor index that Telematic could use in determining the relative potential in any market.
2. State your reasoning in assigning weights to the various factors that are selected.
3. Calculate relative potentials for at least three of the states included in Figure 4.

## THE EMPIRE PUBLISHING COMPANY*

The Empire Company is a well-known publisher of periodicals, paperbacks, and hardbound books, and in addition does a considerable amount of contract printing. For the last two decades the Empire Publishing Company has printed and sold the Empire Almanac, which gives long-range weather forecasts, information about heavenly bodies and ocean tides, and a variety of of miscellaneous facts.

In May of 1966 the vice-president of marketing for Empire was planning production of 1967 Almanacs. Because of the time required for distribution of the Almanacs and the full production schedule for the last part of 1966, it would be necessary to complete the printing of the Almanacs by the end of July.

The Almanacs were sold to wholesalers at a price of 40 cents per copy. Any of the printed Almanacs that were not sold by the end of 1967 would have to be destroyed at a loss to the Empire Company.

The task of forecasting the demand for the Empire Almanac had been handled over the years by the assistant sales manager, who has recently reached the

* The name of the company and some of the figures are disguised.

age of 65 and retired. You, as a marketing research analyst, have been asked by the vice-president of marketing to analyze sales data for the past ten years and from this data to project sales of the 1967 Almanacs.

Upon exploring the files for Almanac sales data, the only historical information that you are able to come up with are the number of Almanacs produced in each of the past ten years and the total demand for Almanacs in each of these years. You have also discovered that the number of Almanacs produced annually for the past ten years represented the assistant sales manager's forecasted demand. Unfortunately, the assistant sales manager left behind no information on his method of forecasting. Apparently his highly accurate forecasts were a result of a great ability for forecasting and his experience in selling Almanacs.

The table below summarizes the demand for Empire Almanacs for the past ten years.

| *Year* | *Actual Demand* (100,000 copies) |
|---|---|
| 1957 | 1.80 |
| 1958 | 2.12 |
| 1959 | 2.45 |
| 1960 | 2.80 |
| 1961 | 3.06 |
| 1962 | 3.80 |
| 1963 | 4.60 |
| 1964 | 5.51 |
| 1965 | 6.62 |
| 1966 | 7.45 |

QUESTIONS

1. Since no one expert enough to make a forecast on the basis of judgment alone is available, what forecasting methods could be applied?
2. Which forecasting method do you feel would give the best results?
3. Estimate the 1967 demand for Empire's Almanacs. How many Almanacs should Empire produce?

## MUSTANG AVIATION CORPORATION*

A long-range planning meeting has been called by the Board of Directors of the Mustang Aviation Corporation. The purpose of the meeting is to discuss

* The name of the company and some of the figures are disguised.

the future of the utility aircraft business and to outline the various plans and objectives that the Mustang Corporation should implement in order to ensure itself a strong position in the industry's future.

As marketing information director for the Mustang Corporation, Mr. Richard T. Lange has been asked to accumulate as many data as possible and from these data to make sales forecasts both for Mustang Aircraft and for the Civil Aircraft Industry as a whole. Mustang's president has asked the marketing information director to prepare three-year, five-year and ten-year forecasts for single-engine aircraft of the type produced by the Mustang Corporation.

Mustang Aviation was originally founded on the West Coast in early 1946 by two World War II veterans—James Haste and Paul Early. Both Mr. Haste and Mr. Early had been air force pilots during the war and prior to the war had received degrees in aeronautical engineering. Although the company was originally set up as a partnership, the capital requirements of meeting postwar demand for single-engine aircraft had forced the partners to incorporate their business in 1947. The new corporation was called The Mustang Aviation Corporation.

Immediately after the war there was a fantastic boom in civil aircraft demand. Not only was there general economic prosperity, but substantial amounts of money were available to war veterans who wished to continue their flying careers outside the military. Unfortunately, Mustang Aviation, like most light-aircraft manufacturers, had neither the production facilities nor the financial resources to meet the great demand for private and business aircraft. As a result of this shortage, the greater part of the postwar aircraft demand was filled by military surplus craft. In 1946 and 1947 alone nearly 50,000 aircraft were sold from military surplus stockpiles.

In the few years following the fantastic postwar demand for light aircraft there was a serious recession in the demand for these airplanes. This recession left the Mustang Corporation in a particularly difficult situation. The company had made major capital investments in order to "beef up" their production facilities, which had consistently operated at capacity during 1946 and 1947. During 1948, 1949, and 1950 the Mustang Aviation Corporation was able to avoid financial disaster only by laying off the bulk of their employees and by accepting whatever contract work they could muster from larger aircraft manufacturers. This contract work for the most part consisted of precision machining and assembly of parts for commercial and military aircraft.

The major stockholders had blamed the losses incurred in these three years on poor management planning. As a result of this, there had been some drastic changes in management personnel in the early fifties. Mr. Lange had come to Mustang in 1953 and since that time had found the corporate owners very unreceptive to proposed changes. This overconservaticism, he felt, was a direct result of the company's financial crisis in the late forties.

Since 1951 there has been a relatively slow but consistent increase in the dollar volume of new aircraft sales. At the same time, there has also been a slower, but general, increase in the total number of new aircraft sold. It is significant to note a trend in the average cost of new aircraft. In 1954 the average price of the 3089 new units sold in the general aviation class was $13,000. The average price of the 9459 units sold in 1964 was in excess of $28,000. In addition, the total number of active civil aircraft has increased from 60,921 in 1950 to 97,743 in 1965.

The Mustang Aviation Corporation manufactured only single-engine aircraft for either private or business use. The company manufactured six basic models: the Mustang 10, 15, 20, 25, 30, and the Mustang 40. The Mustang 10 was a small, economical two-passenger plane, which was used principally as a training

**Exhibit 1** Summary of Civil Flying

| Item | 1940 | 1950 | 1960 | 1962 | 1963 | 1964 | 1965 |
|---|---|---|---|---|---|---|---|
| Airports in operation | 2,331 | 6,403 | 6,881 | 8,084 | 8,814 | 9,490 | 9,566 |
| Public | 1,031 | 2,272 | 2,780 | 3,178 | 3,451 | 3,644 | 3,570 |
| Private | 1,300 | 4,131 | 4,101 | 4,906 | 5,363 | 5,846 | 5,996 |
| Total civil aircraft | 17,928 | 92,809 | 111,580 | 124,273 | 129,975 | 137,189 | 142,083 |
| Active aircraft | N.A.* | 60,921 | 78,760 | 86,287 | 87,267 | 90,935 | 97,743 |
| Total pilots | N.A. | N.A. | 348,062 | 365,971 | 378,700 | 431,041 | 479,770 |
| Airline transport | 1,431 | N.A. | 18,279 | 20,032 | 20,269 | 21,572 | 22,440 |
| Commercial | 18,791 | N.A. | 89,904 | 96,047 | 96,341 | 108,428 | 116,665 |
| Private | 49,607 | N.A. | 138,869 | 149,405 | 152,209 | 175,574 | 196,393 |
| Student | 110,938 | 44,591 | 99,182 | 95,870 | 105,298 | 120,743 | 139,172 |
| Other | N.A. | N.A. | 1,828 | 4,617 | 4,583 | 4,724 | 5,100 |
| Flight instructors | N.A. | N.A. | 31,459 | 28,873 | 29,618 | 32,158 | 34,904 |
| Hours flown (1000's) | | | | | | | |
| General aviation | 3,200 | 9,650 | 13,121 | 14,500 | 15,106 | 15,738 | 16,733 |
| Business | 314 | 2,750 | 5,699 | 5,431 | 5,740 | 5,823 | 5,857 |
| Commercial | 387 | 1,500 | 2,365 | 3,051 | 3,172 | 3,305 | 3,348 |
| Instructional | 1,529 | 3,000 | 1,828 | 2,385 | 2,417 | 2,675 | 3,346 |
| Personal | 970 | 2,300 | 3,172 | 3,489 | 3,626 | 3,777 | 4,016 |
| Other | — | 100 | 57 | 144 | 151 | 158 | 166 |

*Source:* U.S. Department of Commerce, Bureau of the Census, *Statistical Abstract of the United States—1966*, Washington, D.C.
* N.A.: information not available.

aircraft. In contrast, the Mustang 40 was a powerful single-engine plane, which was sold either for business use or as a luxury private plane. Additional data on the various Mustang models are shown in Exhibit 5.

Mr. Lange has been able to accumulate the data displayed in Exhibits 1 to 12 in order to assist him in his analysis and forecasts.

**Exhibit 2** Civil Aircraft Shipments,* 1950 to 1965

| Type | 1950 | 1955 | 1959 | 1960 | 1962 | 1963 | 1964 | 1965 |
|---|---|---|---|---|---|---|---|---|
| General aviation | 3391 | 4563 | 7802 | 7726 | 6797 | 7629 | 9459 | 12,053 |
| Single-Engine | N.A.† | 3755 | 6785 | 6438 | 5765 | 6317 | 7812 | 10,023 |
| 1–3 Pass. | N.A. | 786 | 1649 | 1366 | 1247 | 1404 | 2187 | 3,545 |
| 4 Pass. + | N.A. | 2969 | 5136 | 5072 | 4518 | 4913 | 5625 | 6,478 |
| Multiple-engine | N.A. | 808 | 1017 | 1288 | 1036 | 1311 | 1647 | 2,030 |
| Commercial transports | 129 | 113 | 262 | 238 | 146 | 80 | 158 | 221 |
| Rotorcraft | N.A. | 144 | 178 | 217 | 306 | 413 | 450 | 372 |

*Source:* U.S. Department of Commerce, Bureau of the Census, *Statistical Abstract of the United States—1966,* Washington, D.C.
* Shipments of complete aircraft.
† N.A.: information not available.

**Exhibit 3** Value of Aircraft Shipments—1947 to 1963—for Commercial and Personal Aircraft (In Thousands of Dollars)

| Year | Value of Shipments (Personal Only) | Value of Shipments (Commercial and Personal Combined) |
|---|---|---|
| 1947 | $ 57,020 | 179,093 |
| 1954 | N.A.* | 291,705 |
| 1958 | N.A. | 988,237 |
| 1959 | N.A. | 1,229,087 |
| 1960 | N.A. | 1,269,678 |
| 1961 | 291,982 | 1,261,213 |
| 1962 | 267,556 | 1,054,028 |
| 1963 | 157,797 | 718,921 |

*Source:* U.S. Department of Commerce, *Census of Industry, 1963,* Washington, D.C.
* N.A.: Information not available.

**Exhibit 4** Selected Financial Items for the Aircraft Industry, 1964 (Includes Aircraft Parts)

| Assets per Employee | Sales per Employee | Sales per $ Capital Investment | Return on Capital Investment | Return on Sales |
|---|---|---|---|---|
| $9,430 | $19,465 | 3.29 | 11.0% | 3.7% |

*Source:* U.S. Department of Commerce, Bureau of the Census, *Statistical Abstract of the United States—1966*, Washington, D.C.

**Exhibit 5** General Aviation Classes

| Class | Some Representatives | Characteristics | Price Range |
|---|---|---|---|
| I | Cessna 150<br>Piper Cub 150<br>Champion<br>Mustang 10<br>Mustang 15 | 2-passenger, light, economical, good training craft, good for private owners | $ 7,000–9,400 |
| II | Beechcraft Musketeer<br>Piper Cherokee 160<br>Mooney Master 20D<br>Mustang 20<br>Mustang 25 | 1 to 3-passenger, greater speed than class I, only light baggage capacity | $12,000–16,000 |
| III | Cessna 180<br>Piper Cherokee 235<br>Mooney Mark 21<br>Mustang 30 | 4-passenger, increased speed and load capacity, used for personal transportation and limited freight hauling | $16,000–20,000 |
| IV | Beechcraft Bonanza<br>Cessna 210<br>Piper Commanche 260<br>Mustang 40 | 4-passenger, largest single-engine craft, used as a small business craft or as luxury transportation for private owners | $25,000–45,000 |

**EXHIBIT 6** All Aircraft—Value of Backlog Orders, Net New Orders, and Sales (Value in Millions of Dollars)

| Year | Backlog January 1 | Net New Orders | Net Sales | Backlog December 1 |
|---|---|---|---|---|
| 1951 | 5,039 | 11,100 | 3,473 | 12,666 |
| 1955 | 14,852 | 9,323 | 8,470 | 15,705 |
| 1960 | 12,120 | 11,373 | 10,999 | 15,452 |
| 1961 | 15,452 | 13,418 | 14,948 | 14,147 |
| 1962 | 14,147 | 14,963 | 15,972 | 13,137 |
| 1963 | 12,647 | 17,637 | 16,407 | 13,904 |
| 1964 | 13,904 | 17,970 | 16,686 | 15,188 |

*Source:* U.S. Department of Commerce, Bureau of the Census, *Statistical Abstract of the United States—1966,* Washington, D.C.

**EXHIBIT 7** United States Registered Civil Aircraft by Engine Power and Number of Seats—1965

| Engine Power | Total | Active | Inactive |
|---|---|---|---|
| *By total rated takeoff* | | | |
| 1-engine | 117,188 | 76,170 | 41,108 |
| 100 hp and less | 40,127 | 20,838 | 19,289 |
| 101–200 hp | 43,873 | 31,379 | 12,494 |
| 201–350 hp | 28,268 | 21,739 | 6,529 |
| 351–500 hp | 3,464 | 1,545 | 1,919 |
| 501–700 hp | 869 | 430 | 439 |
| Over 700 hp | 587 | 239 | 348 |
| *By number of seats* | | | |
| 1-engine | 117,188 | 76,170 | 41,108 |
| 1–3 seats | 59,545 | 30,367 | 28,778 |
| 4–5 seats | 54,747 | 43,123 | 11,624 |
| 6–20 seats | 3,296 | 2,680 | 616 |

*Source:* FAA—Office of Management Services, *Census of U.S. Civil Aircraft,* May 1965.

**EXHIBIT 8** Active Civil Aircraft in Relation to Population and Area by FAA Region—1965

| FAA Region | Active Civil Aircraft Per 1000 Square Miles | Per 1000 Population | Population Per Square Mile | Number of Aircraft | Per Cent of Total |
|---|---|---|---|---|---|
| Eastern | 57.6 | 2.7 | 216.9 | 18,275 | 20.6 |
| Southern* | 29.9 | 3.5 | 85.3 | 10,032 | 11.3 |
| Central | 28.8 | 5.7 | 50.5 | 24,464 | 27.6 |
| Southwest | 23.4 | 6.8 | 34.4 | 12,985 | 14.6 |
| Western | 23.5 | 7.5 | 31.5 | 21,304 | 24.0 |
| Alaskan | 2.7 | 62.9 | .4 | 1,476 | 1.7 |
| Pacific | 25.7 | 2.4 | 109.1 | 140 | 0.1 |
| Total | 25.1 | 4.7 | — | 88,742 | 100 0 |

*Source:* FAA—Office of Management Services, *Census of U.S. Civil Aircraft*, May 1965.

* Includes Puerto Rico and the Virgin Islands.

**EXHIBIT 9** General Aviation Aircraft by Type of Flying—1965

| Type | Number of Aircraft | Per Cent of Total |
|---|---|---|
| Personal | 46,721 | 53 |
| Business | 21,127 | 24 |
| Instructional | 6,855 | 8 |
| Commercial | 11,797 | 13 |
| Air taxi | 5,267 | 6 |
| Aerial application | 4,901 | 5 |
| Industrial special | 1,811 | 2 |
| Other | 2,060 | 2 |
| Total | 88,742 | 100 |

*Source:* FAA—*Statistical Handbook of Aviation*, September 1965. Washington, D.C.

**Exhibit 10** Population (in Millions), Income, and Savings (Current Prices, Billions)

| Year | Population | National Income | Personal Income | Disposable Personal Income | Personal Savings |
|---|---|---|---|---|---|
| 1945 | 139,928 | 181.5 | 171.1 | 150.2 | 29.6 |
| 1950 | 152,271 | 241.1 | 227.6 | 206.9 | 13.1 |
| 1955 | 165,931 | 331.0 | 310.9 | 275.3 | 15.8 |
| 1956 | 168,903 | 350.8 | 333.0 | 293.2 | 20.6 |
| 1957 | 171,984 | 366.1 | 351.1 | 308.5 | 20.7 |
| 1958 | 174,882 | 367.8 | 361.2 | 318.8 | 22.3 |
| 1959 | 177,830 | 400.0 | 383.5 | 337.3 | 19.1 |
| 1960 | 180,684 | 414.5 | 401.0 | 350.0 | 17.0 |
| 1961 | 183,756 | 427.3 | 416.8 | 364.4 | 21.2 |
| 1962 | 186,656 | 457.7 | 442.8 | 385.3 | 21.6 |
| 1963 | 189,417 | 481.9 | 465.5 | 404.6 | 19.9 |
| 1964 | 192,120 | 517.3 | 496.0 | 436.6 | 24.5 |
| 1965 | 194,583 | 559.0 | 535.1 | 469.1 | 25.7 |
| 1966 | 196,842 | 609.7 | 580.4 | 505.3 | 26.9 |
| 1970* | 208,615 | 621.0 | 595.0 | 514.0 | 42.0 |
| 1975* | 227,929 | 759.0 | 729.0 | 626.0 | 56.0 |
| 1980* | 250,489 | 897.0 | 863.0 | 738.0 | 70.0 |

*Source: Economic Report of the President,* U.S. Government Printing Office, Washington, D.C., January 1967.
* Estimated.

**Exhibit 11** Annual Sales of Mustang Aircraft Units

| Class | Model | 1947 | 1950 | 1955 | 1960 | 1961 | 1962 | 1963 | 1964 | 1965 | 1966 |
|---|---|---|---|---|---|---|---|---|---|---|---|
| I | 10 | 48 | 11 | 51 | 137 | 178 | 193 | 221 | 287 | 313 | 318 |
| | 15 | 36 | 3 | 62 | 152 | 177 | 192 | 232 | 278 | 247 | 292 |
| II | 20 | 15 | 5 | 23 | 98 | 203 | 157 | 278 | 362 | 453 | 471 |
| | 25 | 13 | 6 | 31 | 84 | 148 | 140 | 193 | 218 | 271 | 318 |
| III | 30 | 7 | 2 | 34 | 127 | 131 | 227 | 317 | 323 | 397 | 403 |
| IV | 40 | 0 | 0 | 5 | 138 | 195 | 251 | 262 | 306 | 303 | 459 |
| Total | | 119 | 27 | 203 | 736 | 1032 | 1160 | 1503 | 1774 | 1984 | 2261 |

*Source:* Mustang Aircraft Corporation records.

**Exhibit 12** A Comparison of Total Active Civil Aircraft and Active General Aviation Aircraft by Type of Aircraft; December 31, 1958–1964 (1958 = 100)

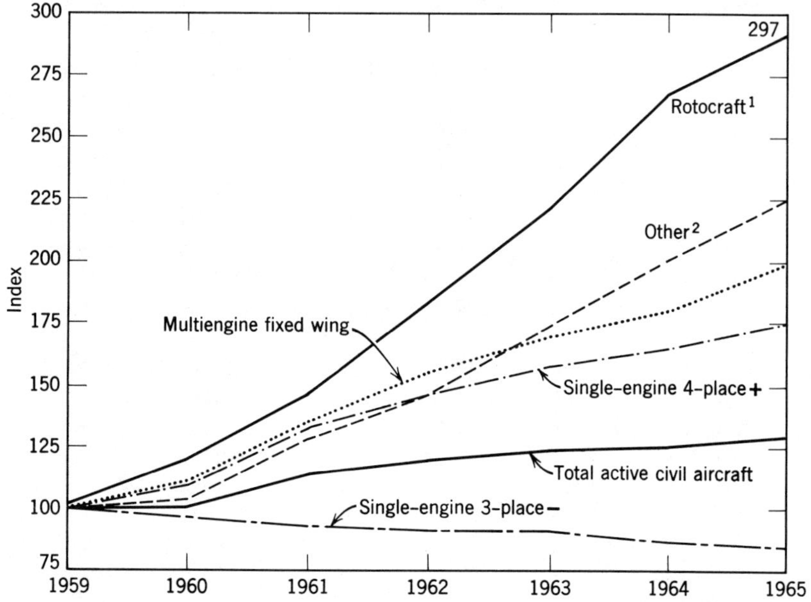


*Source:* FAA—Statistical Handbook of Aviation, September 1965, Washington, D.C.

[1] Includes gliders, dirigibles, and balloons.

[2] Includes autogiros, excludes air-carrier helicopters.

QUESTIONS

1. Estimate the demand for all single-engine civil aircraft for 1970, 1972, and 1977.
2. Estimate the sales volume for the Mustang Aviation Corporation for 1970. 1972, and 1977.
3. What qualifications would you make concerning your forecasts?
4. What other data do you think would be helpful?

PART V

# *Organizing for Marketing Information*

Part V is the final part of the book and contains only one chapter. This final chapter discusses considerations and alternatives for organizing the marketing information functions, including marketing information systems. The material is largely exploratory in nature.

Hopefully, this chapter will help readers to understand the major organizational problems as well as present some alternative responses. Readers who are particularly interested in organizational problems may wish to review Chapter 2, marketing information systems, in conjunction with Chapter 16.

*Sixteen*

# Organizing for Marketing Information

Whenever a group of people work together to achieve a common set of goals, problems of organization are present. Organizations arise to provide working arrangements. There are obviously alternative ways to do this.

This chapter is concerned with marketing research and information organization to help firms meet their marketing needs. In Chapter 2, there was a brief discussion on the organization for the successful *installation* of a marketing information system. The concern in this chapter is with the organization of *ongoing* systems.

In the first section we consider several concepts that are universally important to organization design. In the second section we examine four differently oriented marketing and marketing information organizations: function, product, customer, and region. We discuss existing organizations and, when applicable, also explore the dimensions that future marketing information systems may take. The emphasis is on analysis, not on prediction.

Before discussing some of the alternative organizations, we should briefly review two concepts of organization design—specialization and coordination. Specialization brings substantial gains in productivity. As Adam Smith (1909, pp. 9–18) pointed out long ago, this is due to increases of dexterity, saving of time by not passing from one type of work to another, and development of machines to abridge labor. Later writers have added that differences in peoples' natural abilities and reduction of wasteful duplication of tools and facilities are also important.

The gains to be achieved through specialization are conditioned by the task of *coordinating* the outputs of specialized activities into usable forms. One may assert that the principal purpose of formal organizations, such as those described in this chapter, is to facilitate the achievement of organizational goals by providing structures that do not create artificial barriers to the interaction between people.

There are numerous concepts of organizational design where the best principle is far from clear (centralization versus decentralization).[1] Also, students of organization must remember that every formal organization is intertwined with many informal relationships and groups that influence organizational performance. Throughout this chapter the intent is to suggest skeletons of information organizations. The discussion must, of necessity, all but omit the complexities of the informal group communications and interactions vital to the success of any organization.

### *Informal Relationships*

Marketing information flows both vertically (formally) and horizontally (informally) within marketing organizations. Andersen and Cundiff (1965) report that in four Texas-based companies informal information flows were the most important. This informal communication took place in four ways. First, there was the voluntary exchange of information through information copies of correspondence. Second, special-purpose committees such as new product committees facilitated horizontal flows. A third type of information flow took place during staff meetings. Finally, the most frequent was the informal, nonperiodic exchange of information when executives met to discuss matters in general.

Andersen and Cundiff also indicated that there was little *requirement* to exchange marketing information. Most of it flowed at the discretion of the individual managers. Furthermore, specialized information was sought from the managers, who served as the centers of communication for the specialized areas. This left the attainment of coordinated decision making up to the individual managers.

Our concern is to apply the major concepts or principles of organization to the problem of designing effective marketing research and information organizations. We need to examine the ways in which the advantages of specialization may be achieved.

## Marketing Pressures[2]

Marketing organizations must accommodate four basic sources of marketing pressures: various functions, products, regions, and customers.

[1] Much has been written on this topic. For a brief essay an selected references on the topic, see Albers (1965, Chapter 8). The topic also receives some attention later in this chapter.

[2] For additional discussion of this topic, see Kotler (1967, Chapter 6) and Lazo and Corbin (1961, Chapter 3).

These four pressures get accommodated in various ways in different industries and even by different firms within industries.

The resulting marketing organizations often are unique. Rarely are all four pressures accommodated equally. Instead, the one or ones believed to be the most important receive major attention in the organization and the others receive limited attention or are completely ignored. When companies sell numerous and varied products to relatively homogeneous markets, the organizations are likely to orient around the products. When regional differences in marketing are considered the most important, regionally oriented organizations are likely to develop. Customer-oriented organizations may arise when different customers must be treated in vastly different ways. Finally, a functional framework may develop when the other three pressures are not particularly demanding. In each situation, the other pressures may be built in on a subsidiary basis.

These four pressures influence the organization of marketing research and information activities as well as the overall marketing organization.

## FUNCTION-ORIENTED MARKETING ORGANIZATION

Function-oriented organization has been popular with many firms that have recognized marketing as an important problem and decision-making area. Typical of this organization framework is the one shown in Figure 16-1 of The Maytag Company.[3]

Under this arrangement marketing specialists have taken on responsibilities for marketing research, advertising, sales promotion, sales, and other functional specialties. Normally, no one of these specialists has been specifically responsible for a given product or market. Instead, the top marketing manager (Vice-President of Marketing) has been ultimately responsible for the integration and coordination of the individual efforts into sound marketing programs. Consequently, he has held ultimate responsibility and, for practical purposes, sole responsibility for the success or failure of his firm's products in each geographical area.[4]

In this type of organization, managers of the functionally specialized units are often responsible for the determination and assembly of much of the marketing information they need (Anderson and Cundiff, 1965).

[3] The nonmarketing parts of the organization are illustrated to show the formal relationship with marketing.

[4] For an extensive discussion of organizations used in marketing, see Lazo and Corbin (1961, particularly Chapter 3).

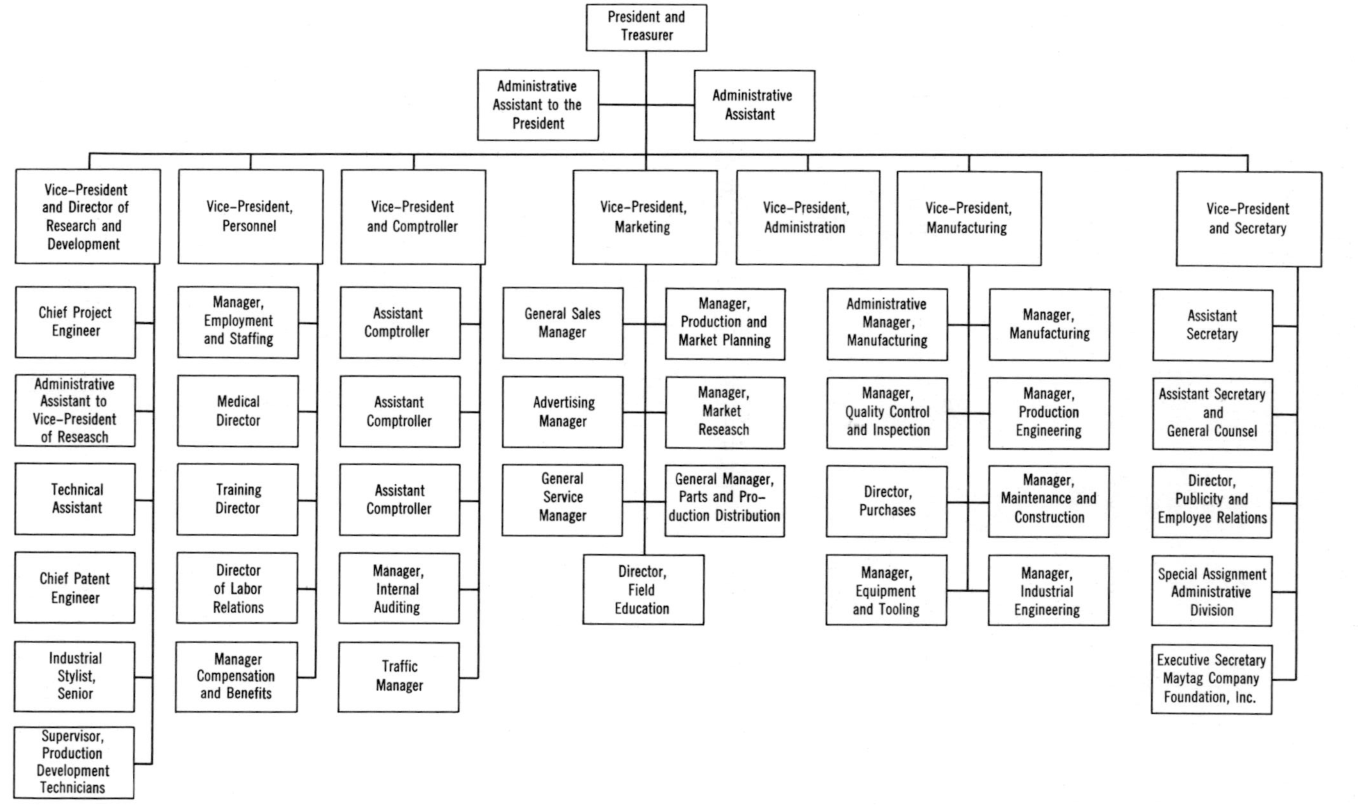


**Figure 16-1** The Maytag Company. *Source:* The Maytag Company, 1967.

Starch reports (see Chapter 12), for example, are usually bought by advertising managers or their advertising agencies. Sales managers usually require direct reports from their salesmen, and so forth.

In many firms the marketing research specialty is not even formally recognized. The most recent American Marketing Association report of marketing research activities in the United States indicated that 45 per cent of the responding companies did not have a formal marketing research department (Twedt, 1963, p. 11).[5]

## Function-Oriented Marketing Research Departments

The quality of marketing research departments within different companies varies immensely. Usually they are shown on organization charts on a common plane with the advertising and sales departments. In practice, however, some are shrouded in their organizations with few people, little budget, and little influence. To quote William R. Davidson (1964, p. 10), a recent past president of the American Marketing Association, ". . . the typical corporation's investment in marketing research is minimal . . . and it indicates a reluctance within industry to invest in research dealing with people, markets and marketing . . . ."

In such situations the departments are concerned with a small part of the total marketing information needs of their firms. Lee Adler has provided a particularly lucid portrayal of the plight of such marketing research departments:

> The research director inherits a legacy of practical difficulties. Gaps exist between marketing research needs and fulfillment—and there is one major explanation. Marketing management problems are broad-scale and complex. However, researchers define such delimited problems for investigation that the findings either deal with too small a part of the total problem or cannot be related to the total problem. As a result, researchers have little link with reality as far as marketing executives are concerned (Adler, 1960, pp. 113–114).

Other persons, including Oxenfeldt (1964, pp. 78–79) and Kotler (1967, p. 194) have made similar observations.

On the other hand, many marketing research departments regularly provide continuing data bases, as well as large quantities of special-problem information for their decision makers. The American Marketing Association study cited earlier (Twedt, 1963, p. 41) listed 34 types of marketing research activities. The eight most common (in order of im-

[5] An earlier study (Crisp, 1958, p. 13) reported that 37 per cent of all responding companies did *not* have formal marketing research departments.

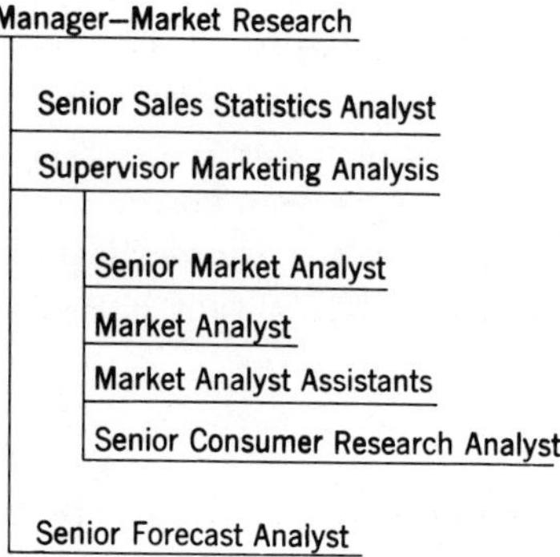


**Figure 16-2** Market Research Department, The Maytag Company. *Source:* The Maytag Company, 1967.

portance) were development of market potential, market share analysis, determination of market characteristics, sales analysis, competitive product studies, new product acceptance and potential studies, short-range forecasting, and long-range forecasting.[6]

How do function-oriented marketing research departments organize to provide such activities?[7] The organization of the Market Research Department of The Maytag Company (Figure 16-2) provides one case in point. This department provides three major types of activities. It analyzes, compares, and reports on company sales by product and by market; it engages in nonroutine, special-problem research; and it prepares sales forecasts.

## Function-Oriented Information System

The Maytag Company illustration pertained only to what that company has termed "market research." What about a more complete mar-

[6] The Crisp (1958) study was much more explicit. It listed the most popular and regularly performed research activities as well as those infrequently performed. Sales forecasting was performed regularly by over 70 per cent of the reporting companies, as was analysis of competitive position. Analysis of market size was done by 67 per cent of the companies. Other activities that were reportedly performed regularly by over 50 per cent of the companies were market size study, analysis of potential, setting sales quotas, and determining market characteristics.

[7] Readers are warned of overreliance on the use of organization charts; they show only the formal structure of who reports to whom. They do not show, except in the most cursory manner, who really affects what decisions, who influences whom, or the channels of information and communication flow. For a more extensive argument on this point, see Randall (1960).

keting information system that could handle many of the activities, such as those discussed in Chapter 2? What might it look like and how could it function? Once again, there are organization alternatives. When certain pressures are particularly demanding or critical, they may be separated out for special attention. A firm, for example, may include a new product information group in an otherwise function-oriented structure, as in Figure 16-3. In turn, Figure 16-3 should not be perceived

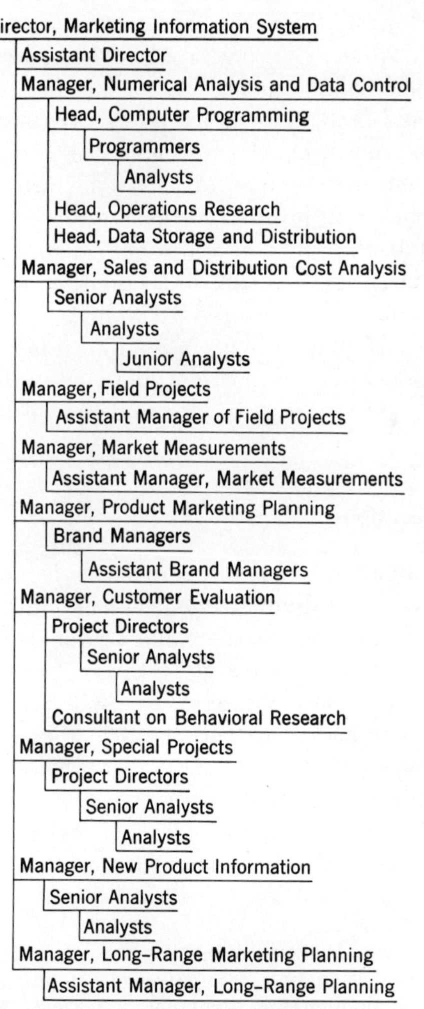


**Figure 16-3** Function orientation.

as an ideal structure. Instead, it suggests one form for a function-oriented marketing information system.[8]

A look at one of the groups within the office suggests the degree of specialization that is possible. The Field Projects group would be responsible for all field studies, that is, for studies taking place in the marketplace. When outside field forces are needed, the Field Project group would be responsible for their retention and supervision. The Field Project group would also provide special training and other help in the design and implementation of field studies to inside groups (e.g., the sales force) and they may conduct field work themselves. In each instance the Field Project group is the field work specialist.

Lest this organization be misperceived, a few observations are needed regarding the relationships among the various functional groups. Some of the groups would tend to be more information-using and condensing than generating or consulting. For example, the Numerical Analysis and Data Control group, for the most part, would provide services for the other groups. In contrast, information generation as well as considerable condensation would take place in Sales and Distribution Cost Analysis, Market Measurement, and Customer Evaluation groups. Further information condensation and use would occur in the Long-Range Planning and the Product Planning groups as well as in the director's office. Finally, the director's office would coordinate activities, assign priorities, arbitrate disputes, and, in general, plan and control the marketing information office.

## Selection Considerations

When would a function-oriented organization be used? It appears most advantageous for short-to-limited-line firms selling their various offerings through essentially similar channels. That is, this structure is appropriate for firms like The Maytag Company, Anheuser-Busch, and the numerous other firms that have (1) relatively few products or product lines and (2) relatively similar and related marketing problems even among their somewhat varied product lines. In these cases this orientation is particularly effective, because it permits a maximum of information specialization and, therefore, the advantages of specialization. In addition it affords extensive perspective throughout the marketing information function.

[8] Far too little experience has been accumulated to date to permit comprehensive and conclusive recommendations for organizing total marketing information systems. Instead, we hypothesize some organizations that appear to merit consideration.

This structure does not provide the most effective orientation for the multiproduct firms or firms facing heterogeneous marketing problems. It simply cannot provide sufficient attention to individual product lines, individual customers, or regional differences without overwhelming problems of coordination.

## PRODUCT-ORIENTED MARKETING ORGANIZATION

Product-oriented marketing organizations can be built in a number of different ways. Large companies that are highly diversified, such as General Electric, General Motors, DuPont, and Ford Motor Company, are divided (decentralized) into major product divisions. General Motors, for example, has nine car, truck, and body divisions, sixteen automotive component divisions, one household appliance division (Frigidaire), four engine divisions, and two defense divisions (St. Clair, 1967, p. 3093).[9] General Electric is divided into six product groups or divisions: Consumer Products, Aerospace and Defense, Components and Construction Materials, Electric Utility, Industrial, and Information and International (St. Clair, 1967, p. 2891).

Figure 16-4 shows a general product division model. While this model

[9] Organization charts of the world's largest company, the General Motors Corporation, can be seen in Albers (1965, pp. 113, 168–170).

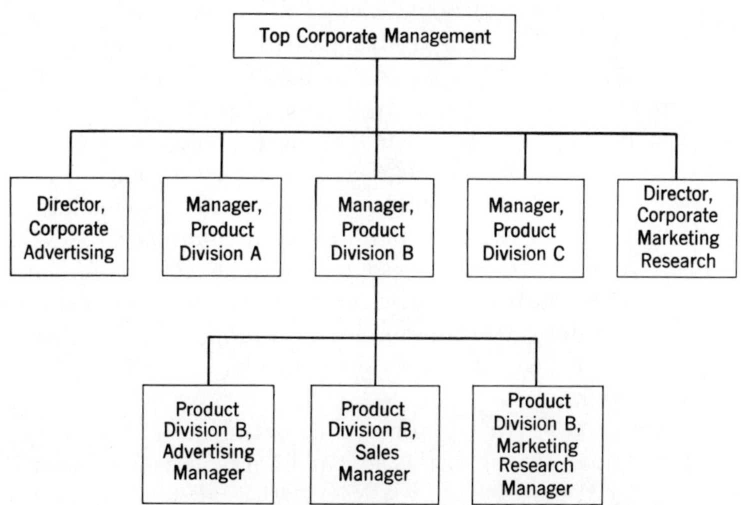


**Figure 16-4** Product Division model.

shows marketing research and advertising activities at both corporate and product division levels, not all firms are organized in this manner. Some place one or both functions at only one of the levels.

When marketing research appears at both levels, the relationships between the two levels as well as the division of duties varies among companies. Some divisional research offices report to the corporate research offices. In other cases the relationships between the two offices are on a voluntary basis.[10]

Kotler (1967, pp. 143–144) has indicated the major factors that influence location of the marketing research activities. Some economies may be gained by placing marketing research at the corporate level if it (1) minimizes the duplication of personnel, space, and equipment, (2) permits the hiring of a few extremely competent persons, or (3) facilitates better coordination of separate product programs. On the other hand, if marketing research problems of individual product divisions are radically different, or if the corporate staff lacks adequate acquaintance with individual products, divisional operations are advantageous. Of course, to get adequate product attention, the corporate marketing research office could be oriented by products.

Figure 16-5, which shows the Mennen Company organization, indicates another way to gain product attention. This type of organization makes major use of product managers. All of the products are distributed through one sales force, advertising is handled by one advertising manager, and there is one manager of marketing research. (Numerous variants of product manager organization have been used.)

Under this type of organization, each of the many products in a firm's line has a manager-guardian, and supposedly there are no orphans to be lost or trampled in the mass of products and functions. Individual product managers are usually charged with preparing appropriate merchandising plans and proposals, but they usually receive very little line authority. To accomplish planning needs, product managers scramble among their organizations persuading, seeking, and assembling advice and information. In brief, they pull scattered information together in behalf of their products. They need to determine *what* information is needed, *where* it is located, and *how* can it be secured. They then secure, analyze, and transform this information into proposed marketing plans. Thus product managers are very much involved in the management of marketing information.

The marketing research office is usually retained in the product-oriented organization. However, the advent of product managers has re-

[10] For a description of the division of duties between the divisional and the corporate level at the General Electric Company, see G-E (1958).

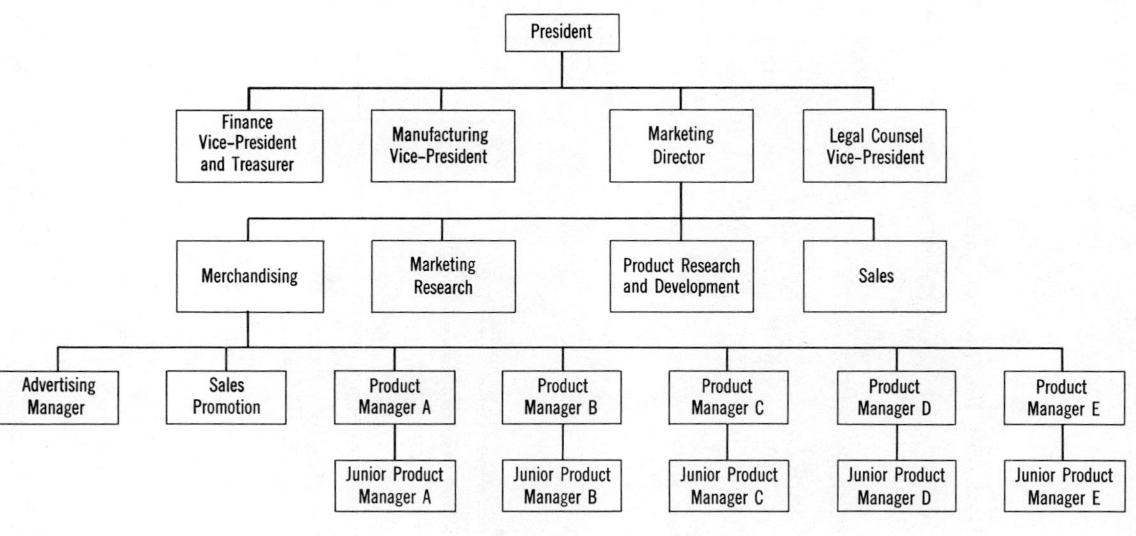


**Figure 16-5** Mennen Company. *Source:* The Mennen Company.

sulted in some changes. Marketing research activities have become more operationally oriented and less planning-oriented (product managers, e.g., have typically prepared their own sales forecasts). The marketing research units have become more technique-, method-, and "doing"-oriented. They serve more as operational arms by helping in research design, information collection, purchase, and analysis.[11]

## Product-Oriented Marketing Research Departments

Some marketing research departments, such as that of the Pillsbury Company (Figure 16-6), have been product-line-oriented. New product research is assigned to a new product research manager. The three product research managers use the specialized research activities of the behavioral research manager, econometrician, field administrator, and librarian. For example, the grocery products market research manager may turn to the librarian for sources of published relevant information or other information stored on magnetic tape or disk files. If such information proves inadequate, the product research manager may decide

[11] For more extensive views of product manager activities, see Ames (1963), Evans (1964), Sekiguchi (1964), and Uhl (1966).

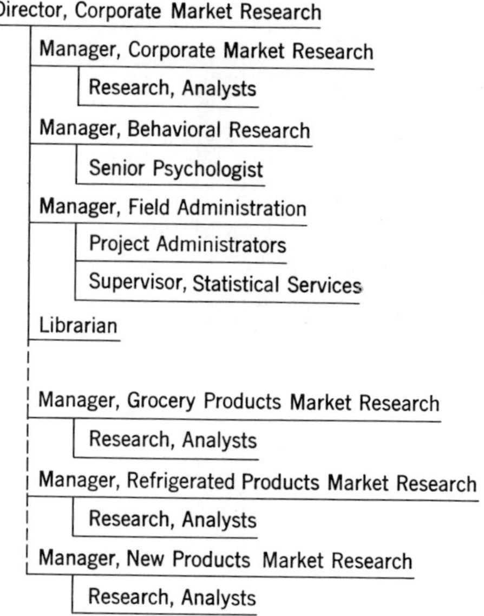


**Figure 16-6** Market Research Department, The Pillsbury Company, 1967. *Source:* The Pillsbury Company, 1967.

to design a research study that will provide the needed information. The various information specialists would likely be involved in various phases of the study design, implementation, and analysis, both individually and in team efforts.

## Product-Oriented Marketing Information System

At this point it is appropriate to consider a product-oriented system. Basically, as a research office is broadened, each additional information activity might be placed either under individual product information managers or separately as a specialized composite whole (like the econometrician) available jointly to the managers.

For example, where might a marketing sales and cost analysis section be added to a product-oriented information system? Conceivably, such a section could be added to each product line area. However, sales and cost analysis is quite specialized (as was noted in Chapter 9), and both machine and men utilization advantages accrue to a consolidation. In addition, no special advantages are likely to result from physically locating this information activity in each of the several product areas. Regardless of where it is located, one segment of analysis (see Chapter 9) must be by products. Consequently, it appears that this activity can be best managed as a specialized whole rather than as a part of each of several product areas.

As a second example, where might a brand or product manager activity be added? Conceivably, this activity could be consolidated in one specialized merchandising office or it could be added as a part of each product information section. Because of the prior concentration of information activities by products, it appears that this planning activity could best be managed as a part of each product section.

The specialized nature of the sales and cost analysis activity and the product manager function makes their placement within an information system relatively clear. Not all information activities fit so positively. Figure 16-7 shows a possible skeleton structure for a product-oriented marketing information organization.

In this structure there has been centralization of (1) numerical analysis and data storage, (2) sales and cost analysis, (3) management of incidental and secondary data, (4) specialized consultation on behavioral research and operations research, and (5) administration of field projects. Most of the other information activities have been assigned by product lines.

The typical product group contains (1) a section manager, (2) an information coordinator, assisted by product planning managers, (3)

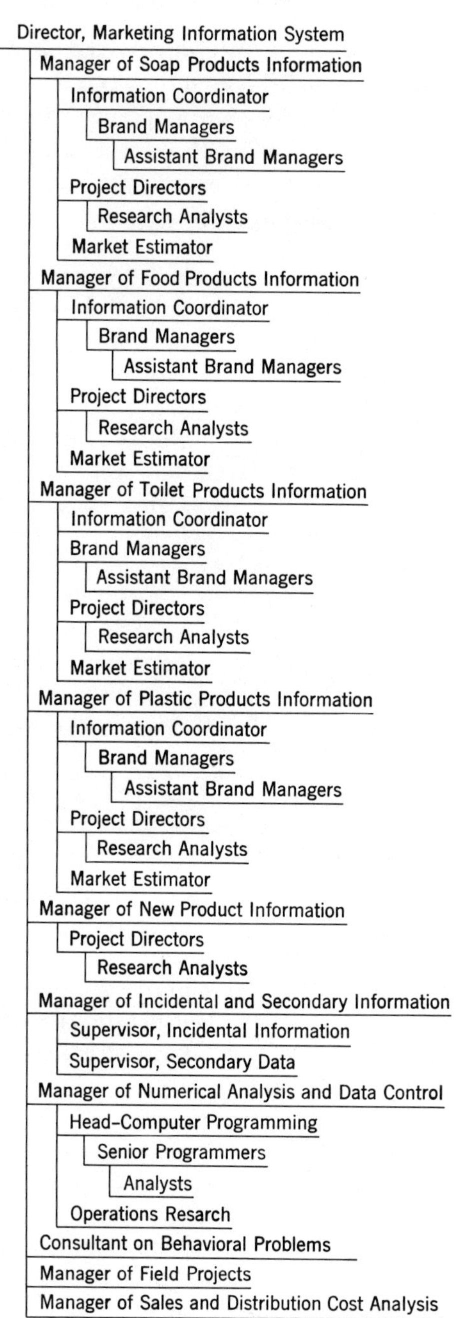


**Figure 16-7** Product orientation.

project directors (to initiate and carry through special-problem-focused research), assisted by research analysts, and (4) market estimators (to provide market measurements). The various product information managers would be charged with fulfilling the corporation-wide marketing information needs for their assigned products. However, the actual information may be stored, analyzed, and so forth in several locations. Finally, various product group managers would use the specialized services of the nonproduct-oriented information managers (e.g., the behavioral and the operation research consultants) in their activities.

### Selection Considerations

The product-oriented marketing information organization may be an appropriate alternative for firms with many products whether they use product divisions or one centralized organization. Companies organized by product divisions that want a centralized information system (or part of it) at their corporate level are likely to use a product orientation. Also, other multiple-product companies (without product divisions) that face unique markets and marketing techniques, because of their different products, are likely candidates. The product orientation is appropriate in both of these situations, because it focuses attention on individual products (or product lines). When product marketing problems give the most pressure, product orientation is appropriate.

Small, short-line firms, or company divisions with few products, do not need a product orientation. They are likely to have sufficient attention already focused on individual products because of their few numbers.

## REGIONALLY ORIENTED MARKETING ORGANIZATION

Companies selling over a wide geographical area will usually have regional specialization of at least their field sales. In some situations entire marketing organizations may be structured predominately along regional lines. This is most likely to occur when regional problems dominate and customers and products are relatively homogeneous. A regional orientation, for example, has been used by at least one large brewer who thought that regional brewers provided the major competition.

Figure 16-8 shows a regionally oriented organization (both production and marketing). In this model, four regional vice-presidents report to the executive vice president. Reporting to each regional vice-president is a regional marketing director, who in turn has reporting to him an advertising manager, market research and planning manager, service manager, and field sales manager.

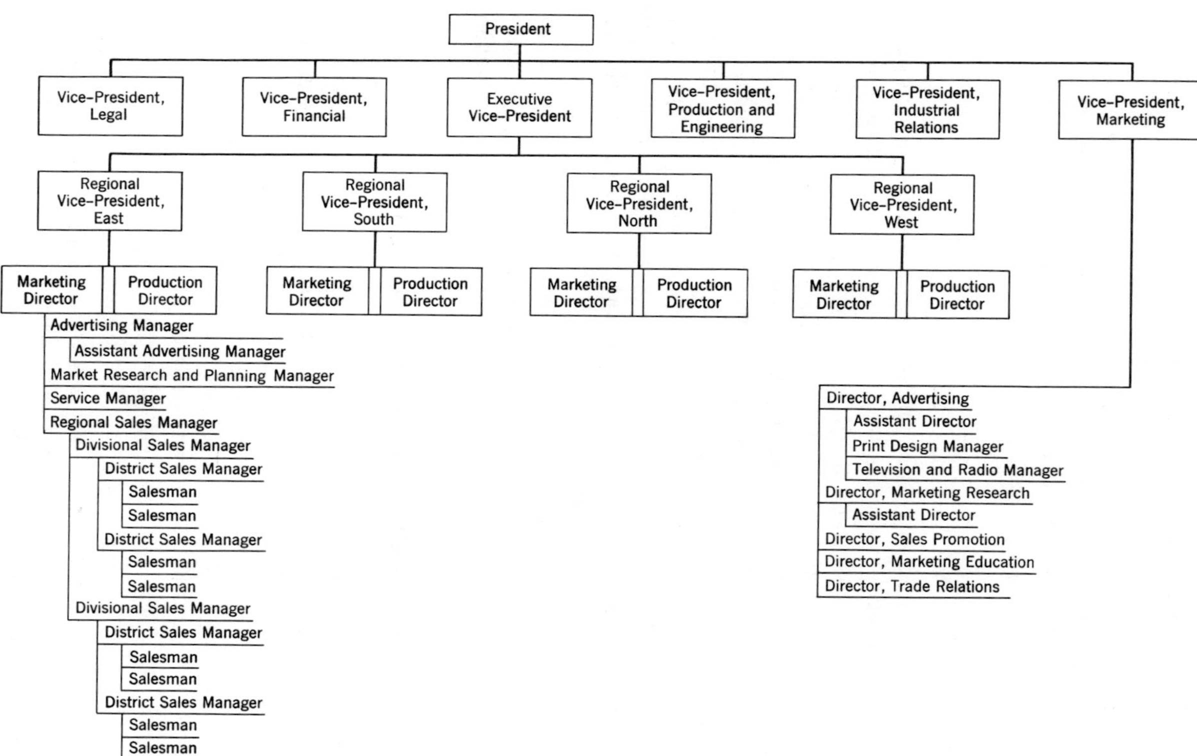


**Figure 16-8** Regionally oriented organization. *Source:* Hypothetical.

At the corporate level there is a vice-president of marketing. He has a staff that includes directors of advertising, marketing research, sales promotion, marketing education, trade relations, and market administration.[12]

When marketing research appears at both levels, the relationship between the levels as well as the division of activities varies among companies. Basically, the same issues that were discussed in connection with the multiproduct division firms are involved here.

### Regionally Oriented Marketing Research Departments

The regional marketing research offices shown in Figure 16-8 are regionally oriented in the sense that they are principally concerned with the information activities within their regions. However, to the best of our knowledge, centralized, regionally oriented, company-wide information systems would not be appropriate. Instead, the offices would be organized by functions, products, or customers.

## CUSTOMER-ORIENTED MARKETING ORGANIZATION

A customer-oriented framework may be particularly appropriate for firms that market to various customer groups who are distinctly different in their buying behavior or product needs (Kotler, 1967, p. 145). The Scott Paper Company (Figure 16-9), for example, has divided its marketing into two distinct customer groups at the top level—retail and industrial. It has further divided the industrial customers group by three customer types—government sales, national accounts, and other industrial customers.

Some of its customers are in separate categories, because their product needs are distinct and selling to them requires specialized product information. Other customers (government) are in separate categories, not necessarily because they buy different products, but because their buying behavior is such that different marketing activities are required.

The Scott Paper Company organization shows a corporation-wide location of marketing research and several other marketing activities under a corporate director of marketing services. Some firms using a customer orientation place marketing research within each individual customer group, as illustrated in Figure 16-10.

[12] For additional information on regionally oriented marketing organizations, see Lazo and Corbin (1961, Chapter 3).

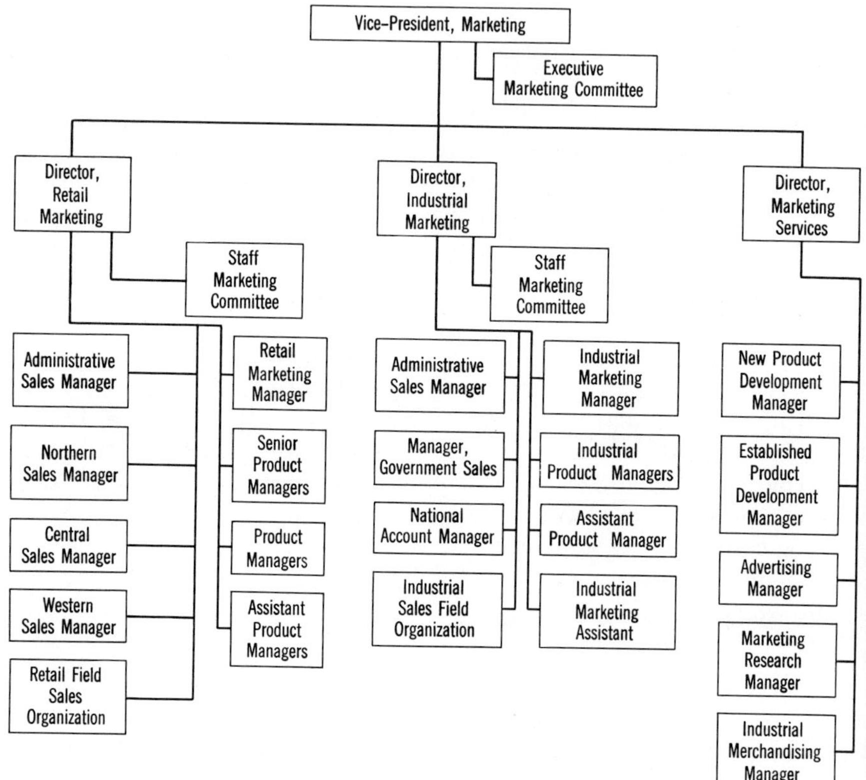


**Figure 16-9** Scott Paper Company. *Source:* Sekiguchi (1964).

## Customer-Oriented Information System

With a customer orientation, the marketing information organization focuses principally on the various customer groups rather than on functions or products. Figure 16-11 shows one possible framework that could be used to manage information activities such as those discussed in Chapter 2.[13]

In this hypothetical organization, three of the four managers are charged with the information activities for individual customer groups (government, industrial, and consumer). The fourth manager (numerical

[13] As an alternating framework, each of the three customer information groups could be placed under the jurisdiction of the appropriate customer group marketing directors.

analysis and data control) provides his specialty to the three other groups.

The three different customer groups contain somewhat different activities. The government group, for example, is the only one with a Washington, D.C., office and the consumer group is the only one with a behavioral study unit.

Sales and distribution cost analyses units have been appended individually to the industrial and to the consumer groups. Such an arrangement is likely to arise only when sales and cost analyses problems are vastly different from one customer group to another. Normally, as observed earlier, this activity would be consolidated in one specialized department.

## Selection Considerations

The customer-oriented information system is a very appropriate alternative for firms that have oriented their other major marketing activities along customer lines. It continues the alignment.

In addition, firms that feel pressure for more customer orientation, but cannot achieve it in terms of field sales or other activities, may use it with respect to the organization for obtaining information. Such situations may arise when distinct customer groups are present but are

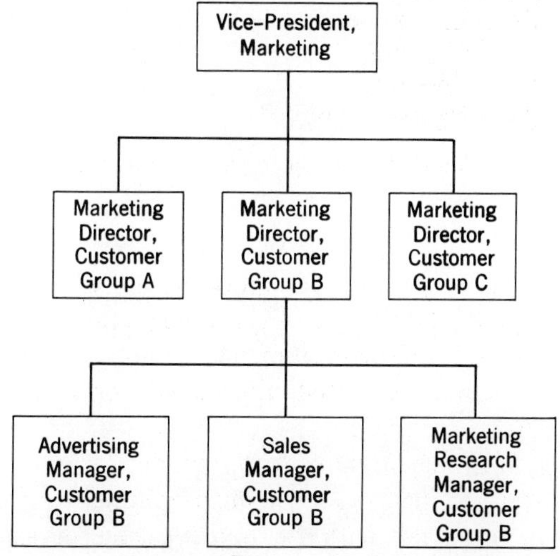


**Figure 16-10** Customer group model. *Source:* Hypothetical.

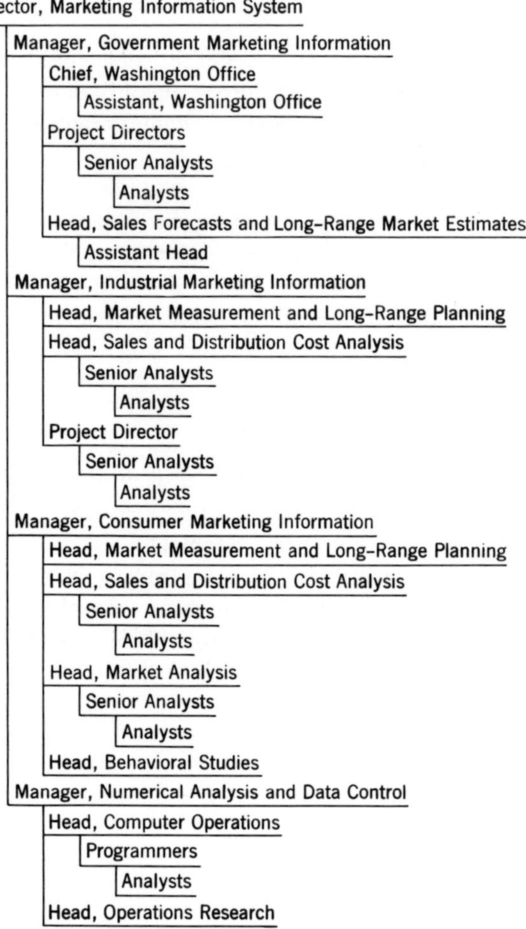


**Figure 16-11** Customer orientation.

too small and widely dispersed to support specialization in selling activities. Also, customers may fit in several customer categories and not want several different salesmen from one company calling on them. In these situations, customer-oriented information organizations may provide just the necessary attention.

Finally, some customer-oriented firms divide the information activity between the corporate level and customer groups. Basically, the same issues that were discussed with the multiproduct division firm earlier in the chapter are involved here.

## LOCATION WITHIN THE ORGANIZATION

To quote Lazo and Corbin (1961, p. 150):

> There is a considerable diversity of informed opinion and business practice with respect to answers to the question: "Where does marketing research best fit into the company's organizational structure?"

Some consideration was given to this subject earlier in the chapter when the delegation of marketing activities between the corporate and divisional levels was discussed.[14] The remaining major question is: Should the marketing information system be under the jurisdiction of marketing people or under that of others (whether centralized or decentralized)?

A number of studies have indicated the most frequent arrangements for marketing research offices (Breen, 1959; Crisp, 1958; Twedt, 1963). They agree that approximately 50 to 55 per cent of all marketing research managers report to sales or marketing managers. One of the studies (Breen, 1959, p. 22) indicates that about 37 per cent of the managers report to top corporate, nonmarketing management, while the other studies reported lower figures.

Prescriptive advice about where marketing research offices should report has been given by Lazo and Corbin (1961, pp. 153–159) and the National Industrial Conference Board (Marketing, 1955). Both sources have drawn extensively on empirical evidence.

They appear to agree that if the research activities are confined to those associated with sales or marketing, the department should report to a sales or marketing executive.[15] The major reason has been that such a marketing information department works primarily with and for persons in the marketing division. The work of the department, as a member of the marketing division, may be enhanced if it is viewed and treated as one of the family. Furthermore, being a member of the family, an information department may better understand the marketing division's information problems and needs.

When the activities of the research department are more inclusive and the department serves other parts of the company, it is likely to report to a top-level, nonmarketing executive. To paraphrase a comment from the Conference Board Study (1955, p. 7), a marketing research department that has expanded its activities so that it serves the financial, production, and administrative parts of the company as well as market-

[14] For a more extensive discussion on this matter of centralization versus decentralization, see Marketing (1955, pp. 10–12.)

[15] Bund and Carroll (1957, pp. 276–277) make the same observation.

ing is often placed directly under a top (nonmarketing) corporate executive.

The Conference Board Study (1955, p. 7) proposed several criteria to determine the placement of a marketing research department within a company. The location should provide: (1) freedom from the influence of those whom its work affects, (2) maximum efficiency of operations; and (3) the cooperation and support of the manager to whom it reports.

Based on the criteria, findings, and comments of Lazo and Corbin and the Conference Board Study, we expect, in general, that the more broadly based, multiple-activity research and information systems will report to top corporate management and, as more departments undertake more information activities, more of them will report to top corporate management.[16]

The organization and location of integrated marketing information systems certainly need more real-world trial and error before much can be said. Cox and Good (1967), who have screened more than 50 companies and have reviewed over 100 articles on information systems, have commented:

> Many companies we have observed have not really come to grips with the difficult problem of providing the organizational arrangements and leadership necessary for successful MIS development.

However, they have recommended that the head of the MIS represent the area that uses and pays for the information services. And, finally, an observation by a leading authority in accounting provides some thought for the future (Horngren, p. 736):

> Advanced business systems tend to break down traditional department walls and tend to redefine managers' duties—freeing them for more attention directing and problem solving.

## SUMMARY

Organizations arise to provide arrangements under which groups of people can work together to achieve common sets of goals. Effective organization must achieve a proper mixture of specialization and coordination.

Marketing organizations are shaped by the pressures of products, customers, regions, and functions in combination with tradition, current personnel, management philosophy, and a host of other considerations

[16] There certainly is conflicting opinion on this matter. For example, see Cox and Good (1967).

too elusive to pinpoint. The results are a multiplicity of frameworks for organizing marketing activities.

The many pressures carry throughout organizations to shape the internal structures of marketing research and information departments. These departments rarely align in response to a single pressure but, instead, reflect many.

The location of marketing research departments has largely reflected the activities they have performed and the information they have provided. The broadly based groups that have provided information for both marketing and nonmarketing decision makers tend to report to top, nonmarketing managers. It seems likely that marketing information systems will follow this pattern.

## REFERENCES


Adler, L. "Phasing Research into the Marketing Plan," *Harvard Business Review,* May-June 1960, pp. 113–114.

Albers, H. H. *Principles of Organization and Management,* (2nd ed.) New York: Wiley, 1965.

Ames, B. C. "Payoff from Product Management," *Harvard Business Review,* November-December 1963, p. 142.

Andersen, R. C., & Cundiff, E. W. "Patterns of Communications in Marketing Organizations," *Journal of Marketing,* July 1965, pp. 30–34.

Breen, G. E. *A Survey of Marketing Research.* Chicago: American Marketing Association, 1959.

Bund, H., & Carroll, J. "The Changing Role of the Marketing Function," *Journal of Marketing,* January 1957, pp. 275–277.

Cox, D. F., & Good, R. E. "How to Build a Marketing Information System," *Harvard Business Review,* May-June 1967, pp. 145–154.

Crisp, R. D. "Marketing Research Organization and Operation: A Survey of Company Practice," *Research Study, 35.* New York: American Management Association, 1958.

Davidson, W. R. "Marketing Renaissance." In Greyser, S. A. (Ed.), *Toward Scientific Marketing.* Chicago: American Marketing Association, 1964.

Evans, G. H. *"The Product Manager's Job, Study 69.* New York: American Management Association, 1964.

"G-E Under Decentralization Reaps Record Sales and Profits," *Sales Management,* March 7, 1958.

Horngren, C. T. *Cost Accounting: A Managerial Emphasis.* (2nd ed.) Englewood Cliffs, N.J.: Prentice-Hall, 1967.

Kotler, P. *Marketing Management: Analysis, Planning and Control.* Englewood Cliffs, N.J.: Prentice-Hall, 1967.

Lazo, H., & Corbin A. *Management in Marketing.* New York: McGraw-Hill, 1961. 1961.

"Marketing Business and Commercial Research in Industry," *Studies in Business Policy 72.* New York: National Industrial Conference Board, 1955.

Oxenfeldt, A. *Marketing Practices in the T.V. Set Industry.* New York: Columbia University Press, 1964.

Randall, C. B. "The Myth of the Organization Chart," *Dun's Review and Modern Industry,* February 1960, p. 38.

St. Clair, F. J. *Moody's Industrial Manual: American and Foreign* (1967 ed.) New York: Moody's Investors Service, 1967.

Sekiguchi, H. "The Product Manager Concept and Its Role in Product Administration," unpublished Ph.D. dissertation, University Library, University of Iowa, 1964. (Available through University Micro Films, Ann Arbor, Mich.)

Smith, A. *An Inquiry into the Nature and Causes of the Wealth of Nations* (1776). New York: P. F. Collier, 1909.

Twedt, D. W. (Ed.) *A Survey of Marketing Research: Organization, Functions, Budget, Compensation.* Chicago: American Marketing Association, 1963.

Uhl, K. P. "Better Management of Market Information," *Business* Horizons, Spring 1966, pp. 75–82.

PART V

# CASE

Dura-Lex Chemicals, Incorporated

## DURA-LEX CHEMICALS, INCORPORATED: Consultant's Attempt to Reorganize Marketing Research Department

In the United States Dura-Lex Incorporated is one of the major chemical manufacturers. The company has manufacturing plants in 25 states and sales offices in 43 of the 50 states. It's main products include animal feed supplements, agricultural chemicals (principally fertilizers), plastics, and a wide variety of industrial chemicals.

The company's products were sold in all 48 continental states as well as overseas, and 17 manufacturing plants that were wholly owned had been established.

In the fall of 1967 the Vice-President of Marketing for Dura-Lex hired a consultant and assigned him the task of reorganizing the firm's Marketing Research Department (see Exhibit 2).

Dura-Lex was divided into five geographical divisions: New England, Southern, Midwestern, Southwestern, and Northwestern. Each of these geographically decentralized divisions had charge of carrying out the manufacturing, promotional, and sales functions within its area.

In addition to the five geographical divisions, several staff functions were performed from Dura-Lex Headquarters Division in New York City. These included Marketing Services, Production and Engineering, and the Corporate Controller. The Marketing Research Department was the responsibility of Dura-Lex National's Vice-President of Marketing and was considered a staff function (see Exhibit 1).

The basic responsibility of the Marketing Division was to develop short-range and long-range marketing programs and strategies. As part of this, criteria

**Exhibit 1** Dura-Lex Chemicals

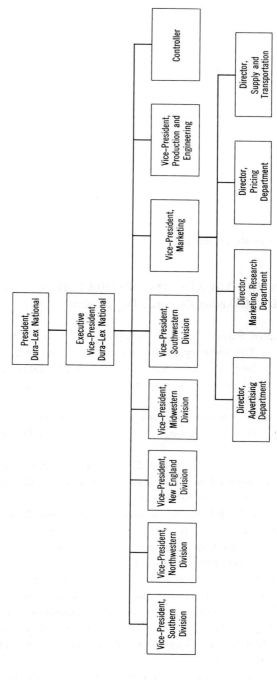

- President, Dura-Lex National
  - Executive Vice-President, Dura-Lex National
    - Vice-President, Southern Division
    - Vice-President, Northwestern Division
    - Vice-President, New England Division
    - Vice-President, Midwestern Division
    - Vice-President, Southwestern Division
    - Vice-President, Marketing
      - Director, Advertising Department
      - Director, Marketing Research Department
      - Director, Pricing Department
      - Director, Supply and Transportation
    - Vice-President, Production and Engineering
    - Controller

**Exhibit 2** Organization of Market Research Department

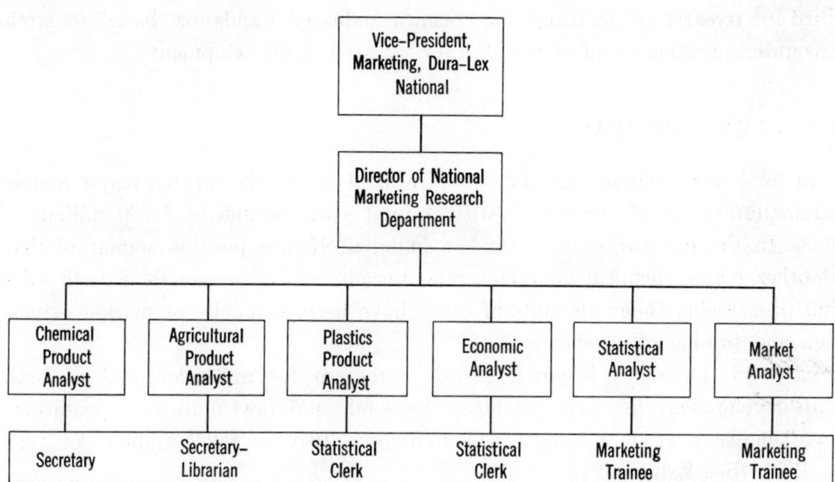


had to be set in order to decide which products should be marketed and which markets should be concentrated on. The basic function of the Marketing Research Department was to aid in the development of these criteria and to collect the market data necessary to make marketing decisions.

## THE CHEMICAL INDUSTRY

The Chemical Industry has achieved better than average growth in the last decade. From 1958 to 1963, sales of the chemical industry averaged a 6.5 per cent growth per year (as compared to 4.9 per cent for all industries). In 1964, 1965, and (the first half of) 1966, these sales grew at the rate of 11.2 per cent, 10.4 per cent, and 11.8 per cent respectively. (*Source: Standard and Poor's Industry Surveys,* Chemicals-Basic Analysis, November 3, 1966.) Sales and profits for twenty companies, each with sales of $150 million or more in 1957, are shown in Exhibit 7. Because adequate capital has been available, the industry has had no real difficulty in purchasing for itself sufficient plant and equipment.

Materials supply, however, is a very difficult problem for the chemical industry. This problem is very serious for the heavy chemical industry and for some types of organic chemicals. Because material shortages exist, it is necessary to find new methods of producing satisfactory substitutes for critical materials. The search for new and better substitutes and for more efficiency in existing processes is largely supported by industrial investment in research and development. In a survey sponsored by the National Science Foundation, the chemicals industry reported an expenditure of $595 million in 1957. Two thirds of this went for support of research in industrial chemicals and the remaining one third for research in the drugs and chemical industry. Funds for "basic" research accounted for 20 per cent of the total for research and development.

## DURA-LEX CHEMICALS

In total sales volume Dura-Lex easily ranked among the top ten major chemical manufactures of the world, with a total sales volume of $1290 million in 1966. In the postwar years Dura-Lex found itself in a position similar to that of other major chemical manufacturers. Because of stable growth in both sales and profitability, huge amounts of funds have been available for market expansion and product diversification.

In 1948, Dura-Lex began a "crash" program for expansion and research and development for new products. Research and development expenditures have increased from a meager $4.2 million in 1946 to $62.2 million per year in 1966. (See Exhibit 6.)

## STATUS OF THE MARKETING RESEARCH DEPARTMENT

The need for the reorganization of the market research function of Dura-Lex's Marketing Division became apparent from a variety of complaints by the geographical Vice-Presidents of Operations—especially the Vice-President of Southern Operations.

About the middle of 1965 the Vice-President of Southern Operations sent a report to national headquarters in New York expressing a desire to enter the Southern market with an improved type of molded plastic pipe. The particular type of pipe had been developed in the Midwestern Division of Dura-Lex in 1964 and had had almost immediate market success. The Southern Vice-President suggested that plans immediately be made for production of the pipe in their Southern Division plastics plant, so that sales in the Southern region could be developed as quickly as possible. This plant was producing the same type of resin used in molding the pipe, hence the only added investment required was that for the necessary molding equipment. An estimate of capital investment for this equipment had been attached to the original proposal.

After receiving the report, the National Executive Vice-President referred it to the Vice-President of Marketing and asked that both the Southern industrial and consumer markets for the pipe be investigated. The project was assigned to the Marketing Research Department, but because the marketing research personnel were busy investigating the need for a new fertilizer plant in Oregon and were just completing other projects, no more than minor attention could be devoted to the Southern assignment until mid-1966.

In the meantime, one of Dura-Lex's chief competitors had introduced a similar type of plastic pipe into Southern markets and, according to the Vice-President of Southern Operations, was rapidly capturing the available market.

When the Marketing Research Department found itself able to devote full attention to the project, a great amount of difficulty was encountered in gathering the necessary information. The Marketing Research Department had long since discovered that market information was not so reliable or plentiful in Southern states. In most situations they had been able to gain a large amount of information from their marketing and sales personnel, but because the Southern Vice-President had developed a certain amount of hostility toward the national office, less than the usual amount of cooperation was received from the Southern division.

The Marketing Research Department was originally organized in 1955 and at that time consisted of only three people. Currently the department is made up of an agricultural product analyst, a chemical product analyst, a plastic products analyst, an economic analyst, a statistical analyst, and a market analyst. In addition the department had a secretary, a secretary-librarian, two statistical clerks, and two marketing trainees. (See Exhibit 2.)

During his initial investigation of the problems concerning the Marketing Research Department the consultant concluded that although there were some able and experienced people in the department, there was a definite lack of the type of leadership required to carry out the responsibilities assigned to the marketing research function. He also felt that the department had made no provision for the continuous flow of routine information, that it had no definite research procedure, and that research reports were both poorly written and incomplete.

The consultant stated that the principal task of the National Marketing Department is to perceive the real needs of the customers and organize both marketing and production functions so as to meet these needs as closely as possible. It was the consultant's idea that a well-organized and competent market research staff could do more in this area to aid top management than any other department.

The consultant went on to observe that the Marketing Research Department was making poor use of the information sources that were available. Much information was not gathered at all, and large amounts of information were gathered but were not analyzed and remained in unusable form.

## THE CONSULTANT'S INVESTIGATION

After an initial study and observation of the Marketing Research Department's work and personnel, the consultant decided to arrange a trip for an interview with the Vice-President of Southern Division in order to get an idea of the information needs of his geographic area and at the same time to consider any suggestions that the Vice-President might have on how to obtain the required information most efficiently.

The consultant found the Vice-President of Southern Division more than willing to cooperate in providing suggestions for the reorganization of Dura-Lex's national marketing research function. The Southern Vice-President advocated reorganization on a completely decentralized basis. He stated that the company's production and sales functions were completely decentralized and that it follows that market information activities should be carried out on a similar basis.

Part of the consultant's meeting with the Southern Vice-President follows:

Consultant: Mr. Hanley, do you believe the National Marketing Research Department is doing an adequate job of filling your marketing information needs?

Vice-President: Definitely not. The only information that we ever receive from the Marketing Research Department is their project reports and memorandums.

Consultant: What do these project reports and memorandums consist of?

Vice-President: Well, the project reports are formal reports containing the results of their research studies. For instance, the investigation of market potential for a new product, or sales forecasts of old products which are marketed in our division. More often than not these reports are requested by us, and the time lag between the request and the final report is fantastically long. A good example of this is their study of the market potential for plastic pipes in the South. That delay cost this company more money than I care to mention. Our own sales men had gathered enough information for us to safely enter the market, but . . . .

Consultant: And what do the memorandums consist of?

Vice-President: Mostly a bunch of blow. They contain a lot of high-sounding theoretical stuff that those guys have probably copied out of a marketing journal or book somewhere. I seriously doubt if those things have contributed a single dollar to our annual sales. What we need is a continuous flow of organized information which will help us sell our products on a day to day basis. We also need more information on what new products are available from research. Every year this company spends millions of dollars on R and D, and it's years before we get any benefit from it at all. Everything that is developed is introduced first in the New England Division, and only after it has been completely proven do we get a shot at it.

Consultant: It's my understanding that your sales staff is to provide you with this continuous day-to-day information, and that you are to rely on the international staff for investigations of market potential, sales forecasts and any special projects which you feel you cannot adequately handle.

Vice-President: Our salesmen are busy people. Most of them are technical people. They are not the average run of the mill salesmen. In addition to selling our products, they give field trials of our agricultural and chemical products. As far as I'm concerned we're putting an undue burden on them by asking them to collect the amount of market data which they are presently gathering. What we need is a well-staffed Marketing Research Department right here in the Southern office.

Consultant: Who processes and organizes the data which your salesmen gather?

Vice-President: Our sales manager supervises the processing of data. In addition to our salesmen he has a secretary and two clerks under him, and believe me, they're swamped.

Consultant: I've given some thought to a decentralized marketing research function. How large a staff do you think would be required in order to fill your needs without the existence of a national staff?

Vice-President: It appears to me that we need a staff just about the size of the Marketing Research Department in New York.

Consultant: That would probably mean about five times the present expense for economic and marketing research. Don't you think that would be prohibitive?

Vice-President: No. Five times the over-all expense would probably yield us ten times the present amount of usable information. In addition, our own staff could recognize and attack problems long before the New York office would even know about them. In my opinion it wouldn't take long to off-set the increased salaries with higher sales volumes and added profits.

Consultant: Don't you think it would be possible to fill your needs with only a director of marketing research and say an economic analyst, a statistical analyst, and enough clerks, secretaries, and field interviewers to handle their work?

Vice-President: You're forgetting that we produce and sell a wide variety of products to many different types of customers. We need people in such a department that know our products. It is doubtful that any one person could have adequate knowledge of say both our agricultural market and industrial chemical market.

The Vice-President then presented some ideas on what he felt should be some of the responsibilities of a Southern Marketing Research Department:

1. Set up interviews and questionnaires.
2. Contact government and private agencies personally.
3. Set up wholesale and retail audits of consumer goods.
4. Report effectiveness of theme or promotional theme.
5. Prepare sales forecasts.
6. Investigate potential for new products.
7. Assist in formulating sales and general marketing strategies.

On his return to the New York office the consultant presented some of the ideas of the Southern Vice President to Dura-Lex National's Vice-President of Marketing. This marketing executive was opposed to decentralizing the economic and market research activities. Part of a meeting between the consultant and Vice-President of Marketing follows:

Vice-President: I'm sure Mr. Hanley would like to have his own marketing research staff in the Southern office. As far as that goes, it would be nice to have a complete staff in every division. The problem is, we're in this business to make a profit and therefore must balance our expenses with the incremental profit which we derive from these expenses.

Consultant: Do you believe that the opening of four separate marketing research departments would cause expenses in excess of the added profits which they could contribute to the National Division as a whole?

Vice-President: I don't believe we could begin to justify five geographically decentralized departments. The waste and duplication among the four separate staffs would be too much to take. We would not only have to stand the expense for the wages of several people nearly duplicating each other's work, but would also have to stand overhead and other expenses at nearly five times what they should be. For instance, our New York office subscribes to a variety of journals, periodicals, and surveys which would be helpful to almost any economic and market research department. Filling these subscriptions for a total of five departments would amount to thousands of dollars of added annual expense.

Consultant: Then do you believe that the present economic and marketing research organization can fill future requirements?

Vice-President: I think the idea of a central staff is basically sound, but we do need improvements. First, there are a few weak lines in our present staff so some personnel changes are in order. The only reason for this condition is the low salaries that we've paid our marketing people in the past. In order to get competent personnel we're going to have to pay for them.

Beyond this, I think our major problem is one of communication. Getting information from our regional sales departments is often like extracting teeth. Granted, our salesmen are very busy, but we are performing services for them which will hopefully help them sell more of our products. What we need is some of our own people in those offices.

Consultant: How many people do you think you need?

**Exhibit 3** 1967 Annual Budget: Dura-Lex National Marketing Research Department

| | |
|---|---|
| Salaries and wages (Director \$12,000, Product Analysts 3 × \$9,000, Economic Analyst \$10,000, Market Analyst \$8,000, Statistical Analyst \$8,000, Marketing Trainee 2 × \$6,000, Statistical Clerk 2 × \$5,500, Secretary \$4,500, Secretary-Librarian \$4,500) | \$ 97,000 |
| Special studies | 25,000 |
| Travel | 25,000 |
| Subscriptions to journals, periodicals, and surveys | 20,000 |
| Overhead and miscellaneous charges | 18,000 |
| Total | \$185,000 |

**Exhibit 4** Estimated Annual Expenses If Marketing Research Is Decentrallized: Dura-Lex—Decentralized Marketing Research Departments (Five)

| | |
|---|---|
| Salaries (includes staff personnel in regional offices only) | \$260,000 |
| Wages (includes field representatives and interviewers) | 60,000 |
| Travel expenses | 60,000 |
| Subscriptions to journals, periodicals, and surveys | 65,000 |
| Overhead and miscellaneous charges | 45,000 |
| Total | \$490,000 |

**Exhibit 5** 1967 Estimated Annual Expenses: Dura-Lex—Centralized Market Research Department with Divisional Representatives

| | |
|---|---|
| Salaries (includes staff personnel in New York Office only) | \$125,000 |
| Wages (field representatives and interviewers) | 85,000 |
| Special studies | 20,000 |
| Travel expenses | 25,000 |
| Subscriptions to journals, periodicals, and surveys | 20,000 |
| Overhead and miscellaneous charges | 18,000 |
| Total | \$293,000 |

Vice-President: Well, definitely one in each of our five regional division offices plus enough people to handle the leg work which our regional salesmen don't have time for. The exact number would vary from division to division. We may need as many as six or seven in the New England Division and as few as two or three in the Southern Division. Under such a system the man placed in a division headquarters would be our liaison with divisional operations and would relay all information in both directions.

Following his interview with the Marketing Vice-President the consultant sat down to the task of recommending an efficient and workable organization scheme for the market research activities of Dura-Lex National. He realized that in order to do this he would have to separate the prejudices and generalities of those with whom he had talked and get down to the hard facts of the situation at hand. One of his first steps was to estimate annual expenditures that would be required for the proposals that had been suggested to him. (See Exhibits 3, 4, and 5.) Exhibit 6 gives the Dura-Lex income statement for

**Exhibit 6** Dura-Lex Chemicals, Incorporated: 1966 Consolidated Earnings Statement

| | 1966 | 1965 |
|---|---|---|
| Net sales | $1,290,000,000 | $974,000,000 |
| Cost of goods sold | 629,100,000 | 468,100,000 |
| Selling and administrative expense | 298,200,000 | 229,500,000 |
| Depreciation, amortization | 64,100,000 | 48,800,000 |
| Research and development expense | 62,200,000 | 46,400,000 |
| Patents and miscellaneous write-offs | 300,000 | 1,000,000 |
| Employee pension funds | 20,100,000 | 17,600,000 |
| Operating profit | $ 216,000,000 | $172,600,000 |
| Royalties and service charges | 11,500,000 | 9,300,000 |
| Income from corporate investments | 9,900,000 | 7,900,000 |
| Interest income | 6,600,000 | 6,500,000 |
| Total income | $ 244,000,000 | $196,300,000 |
| Interest expense | 6,900,000 | 5,300,000 |
| Before-tax income | $ 237,100,000 | $191,000,000 |
| United States & Foreign | 105,300,000 | 77,400,000 |
| Net income | $ 131,800,000 | $113,600,000 |

**Exhibit 7** Sales and Profits, Twenty Large Chemical Firms (in Millions of Dollars)

| | 1948 | 1950 | 1955 | 1960 | 1963 | 1964 | 1965 | (Preliminary) 1966 |
|---|---|---|---|---|---|---|---|---|
| Sales | 5,200 | 6,057 | 9,325 | 12,205 | 14,623 | 16,469 | 17,938 | 19,920 |
| Profits after taxes | 525 | 724 | 930 | 1,058 | 1,182 | 1,400 | 1,627 | 1,736 |

*Source: Statistical Abstract of the United States,* 1967.

1966, and Exhibit 7 shows sales and profits over time for 20 large chemical producers.

QUESTIONS

1. What other information should the consultant seek before reaching a decisions?
2. With the given information, which form of organization (centralized or decentralized) do you think more closely fits the needs of Dura-Lex?
3. Can you suggest an alternative and possibly more efficient organizational structure?

# Name Index

# Subject Index